PRAISE FOR PRIOR EDITIONS

"Comprehensive, objective, insightful . . . quite simply, the definitive book on the subject—an absolute must-read for applicants."

Don Martin, Associate Dean for Admissions and Financial Aid, University of Chicago Graduate School of Business

"Richard Montauk has written an invaluable guide on how best to apply to business schools. His is the most thoughtful, most comprehensive reference I know. Follow his advice, think through the issues he presents, and your applications will all but write themselves."

Fran Hill, Director of Admissions, Haas School of Business (University of California, Berkeley)

"In an increasingly competitive world an MBA degree is ever more important. . . . Montauk's book is a great read and an exceptional resource for preparing yourself for admission to a top MBA program."

Linda Baldwin, Director of Admissions, Anderson School (UCLA)

"Getting into a top MBA program is not as difficult as most people think—all you need is *How to Get Into the Top MBA Programs*. By providing the strategies and advice you need, Montauk's book is an essential road map to success. Everything from detailed advice on writing your essays to interviewing strategies is laid out in simple, easy terms. Unless your mother plans to donate a library, or your uncle is on *Forbes*'s list of the world's richest people, I'd recommend that you buy this book."

Tom Fischgrund, editor of *The Insider's Guide to the Top 10 Business Schools*

"I definitely recommend *How to Get Into the Top MBA Programs*. It is comprehensive, covering in detail every aspect of the admissions process—and does so in a well-organized and user-friendly fashion."

Myriam J. Perignon, Director of the MBA Programme, INSEAD (France)

continued . . .

"This comprehensive book provides an A-to-Z guide of how to maximize your chances of getting into one of the world's top business schools. It is a small investment that should pay big dividends."

Julia Tyler, Director, MBA Programme, London Business School

"What sets *How to Get Into the Top MBA Programs* apart from other guides are its comprehensiveness and scope. Montauk is extraordinarily thorough in his treatment and provides an international perspective, which is refreshing and valuable."

Jon Megibow, Director of Admissions, Darden Graduate School of Business Administration

"This is a comprehensive, well-presented guide that will be a valuable resource for MBA applicants. It is thorough, relevant, and user-friendly."

Judith Goodman, Assistant Dean, Admissions and Student Services, University of Michigan Business School

"A well-organized, accessible and informative guide to successful applications. Not only is *How to Get Into the Top MBA Programs* a user-friendly source of 'everything you need to know,' it is a model for effectively presenting this information."

Meg Manderson, Associate Director of Admissions, MIT Sloan School of Management

"Attending a full-time MBA program requires an investment of two years and, typically, more than $100,000 in tuition and forgone earnings. Richard Montauk provides expert advice on how to maximize your return on this investment by giving you an insider's view on how to successfully navigate the tricky process of applying to the best business schools. The secrets of doing well in the applications process—particularly with the written essay questions and the personal interviews with admissions personnel—are exceptionally valuable. If you are serious about applying to one of the top schools, buy this book first."

Ronald N. Yeaple, Ph.D., author of *The MBA Advantage: Why It Pays to Get an MBA*

"Richard Montauk has produced the most comprehensive and insightful review of how to approach selection of and entry to a good business school. The book is of enormous value to those approaching this critical two-way selection process."

Professor Leo Murray, Dean, Cranfield School of Management (UK)

"Packed with wonderful tips guaranteed to improve your chances of being accepted to a top MBA programme. All aspiring MBAs should get a copy."

Carol Giraud, Director of Marketing and Admissions, INSEAD (France)

"Current and comprehensive . . . Montauk has covered every aspect of the application process. This is a valuable resource for every MBA applicant."

Fran Forbes, Director of Admissions, Graduate School of Business, The University of Texas (Austin)

"Drawing on extensive research and experience in counseling MBA candidates, Richard has written a comprehensive, well-balanced book that will be invaluable for anyone considering an MBA."

Connie Tai, Director of Admissions, Rotterdam School of Management

"This book serves as an intelligent guide to help you find your way through the maze of an MBA application."

Kal Denzel, Director of MBA Admissions, IMD (Switzerland)

"The subtitle of this book could be 'How to Get Into Your Favorite Business School in Ten Easy Lessons.' Maybe it cannot improve your product, but it can surely help you to improve your marketing, your advertising, and your packaging (of yourself). . . . This book is both amusing and amazing: It is an amusing read that gives you an amazing mass of tips on how to get into your favorite business school."

Gabriella Aliatis, Director of Admissions, SDA Bocconi School of Management (Milan)

"*How to Get Into the Top MBA Programs* provides an excellent description of the intricacies involved in the admissions process of top American and European business schools in a straightforward and easy-to-read format."

Mary Clark, Assistant Director of Admissions, IESE (Barcelona)

"*How to Get Into the Top MBA Programs*. . . is unquestionably the best book on the subject."

Marjorie DeGraca, Director of Admissions, Haas School of Business (University of California, Berkeley)

How to
Get Into
the
TOP MBA
PROGRAMS

4th Edition

RICHARD MONTAUK

Prentice
Hall Press

PRENTICE HALL PRESS
Published by the Penguin Group
Penguin Group (USA) Inc.
375 Hudson Street, New York, New York 10014, USA
Penguin Group (Canada), 90 Eglinton Avenue East, Suite 700, Toronto, Ontario M4P 2Y3, Canada
(a division of Pearson Penguin Canada Inc.)
Penguin Books Ltd., 80 Strand, London WC2R 0RL, England
Penguin Group Ireland, 25 St. Stephen's Green, Dublin 2, Ireland (a division of Penguin Books Ltd.)
Penguin Group (Australia), 250 Camberwell Road, Camberwell, Victoria 3124, Australia
(a division of Pearson Australia Group Pty. Ltd.)
Penguin Books India Pvt. Ltd., 11 Community Centre, Panchsheel Park, New Delhi—110 017, India
Penguin Group (NZ), 67 Apollo Drive, Rosedale, North Shore 0745, Auckland, New Zealand
(a division of Pearson New Zealand Ltd.)
Penguin Books (South Africa) (Pty.) Ltd., 24 Sturdee Avenue, Rosebank, Johannesburg 2196,
South Africa

Penguin Books Ltd., Registered Offices: 80 Strand, London WC2R 0RL, England

While the author has made every effort to provide accurate telephone numbers and Internet addresses at the time of publication, neither the publisher nor the author assumes any responsibility for errors, or for changes that occur after publication. Further, the publisher does not have any control over and does not assume any responsibility for author or third-party websites or their content.

PRINTING HISTORY
Prentice Hall trade paperback 2nd edition / July 2002
Prentice Hall trade paperback 3rd edition / July 2005
Prentice Hall trade paperback 4th edition / August 2007

Prentice Hall 4th edition ISBN: 978-0-7352-0423-2

The Library of Congress has cataloged the 2nd edition as follows:

Montauk, Richard.
How to get into the top MBA programs / Richard Montauk.
p.   cm.
Includes index.
ISBN-10: 0-7352-0319-9   ISBN-13: 978-0-7352-0319-8
1. Master of business administration degree.   2. Master of business administration degree—Europe—Handbooks, manuals, etc.   3. Master of business administration degree—United States—Handbooks, manuals, etc.   4. Business schools—Handbooks, manuals, etc.   I. Title.

HF1111.M66 2002
658'.0071'1—dc21   200203151

PRINTED IN THE UNITED STATES OF AMERICA

10 9 8 7 6 5 4 3 2 1

Most Prentice Hall books are available at special quantity discounts for bulk purchases for sales promotions, premiums, fund-raising, or educational use. Special books, or book excerpts, can also be created to fit specific needs. For details, write: Special Markets, Penguin Group (USA) Inc., 375 Hudson Street, New York, New York 10014.

Dedicated to the memory of my father

Howard S. Montauk
1927–1988

And my mother
Shirley M. Montauk
1925–2000

ACKNOWLEDGMENTS

I wish to thank those people who have been so helpful to the development and writing of *How to Get Into the Top MBA Programs*:

First, the *admissions directors* and program directors at leading business schools around the world who have been so generous with their time and knowledge in discussing how decisions are made at their schools. In particular, I would like to thank those I interviewed for this book and who have allowed themselves to be quoted at length throughout the text:

Katherine Lilygren and Linda Baldwin (Anderson/UCLA); Rose Martinelli, Patty Keegan, and Don Martin (Chicago); Linda Meehan (Columbia); Sara E. Neher, Barbara Millar, and Jon Megibow (Darden/Virginia); Kelli Kilpatrick (Fuqua/Duke); Peter Johnson, Marjorie DeGraca, and Fran Hill (Haas/UC Berkeley); Brit Dewey and James Miller (Harvard); Tom Hambury and Ann W. Richards (Johnson/Cornell); Michele Rogers and Brian Sorge (Kellogg); James Hayes, David Ardis, and Judith Goodman (Ross/Michigan); Rod Garcia and Meg Manderson (Sloan/MIT); Sharon J. Hoffman (Stanford); Isser Gallogly, Jaki Sitterle, and Mary Miller (Stern/NYU); Fran Forbes (Texas); Sally Jaeger, Dawna Clarke, and Henry Malin (Tuck/Dartmouth); Thomas Caleel, Professor Howard Kaufold, and Suzanne Cordatos (Wharton); Anne Coyle (Yale); Rossana Camera and Gabriella Aliatis (Bocconi, Italy); Dr. John Mapes and Professor Leo Murray (Cranfield, UK); Christy Moody (ENPC, France); Mary Granger (ESADE, Spain); Isabelle Cota, Pantea de Noyelle, Jean Loup Ardoin, and Jason Sedine (HEC, France); Ling Tee, Genevieve Slonim, and Mary Clark (IESE, Spain); Katty Ooms Suter and Kal Denzel (IMD, Switzerland); Janine Serieys, Joelle du Lac, Carol Giraud, Helen Henderson, and Professor Ludo van der Heyden (INSEAD, France); David Bach and Gamaliel Martinez (Instituto de Empresa, Spain); Dr. Simon Learmount (Judge/Cambridge, UK); Julia Tyler, Lyn Hoffman, and Claire Harniman (London); Andrew Dyson and Helen Ward (Manchester, UK); Kirt Wood, Connie Tai, and Gea Tromp (Rotterdam, Netherlands); Alison Owen and Maxine Hewitt (Saïd/Oxford, UK); and Erin O'Brien (TRIUM program—HEC/Paris, LSE, Stern/NYU).

Second, the *career services directors* at leading business schools: Glenn Sykes (Chicago); Regina Resnick (Columbia); Everette Fortner and John Worth (Darden/Virginia); Roxanne Hori (Kellogg); Andy Chan (Stanford); Pamela Mittman (Stern/NYU); Peter Degnan (Wharton); Katty Ooms Suter

(IMD, Switzerland); Mary Boss (INSEAD, France); and Graham Hastie and Chris Bristow (London).

Third, the *financial aid directors*: Marta Klock (Anderson/UCLA); Priscilla Parker (Chicago); Kathleen Swan (Columbia); Larry Mueller (Darden/Virginia); Paul West (Fuqua/Duke); Debi Fidler (Haas/UC Berkeley); James Millar (Harvard); Ann W. Richards (Johnson/Cornell); Charles Munro (Kellogg); Pamela Fowler and Michael White (Ross/Michigan); Colleen MacDonald (Stanford); Julia Min (Stern/NYU); Sharon Brooks (Wharton); and Karen Wellman (Yale).

Fourth, *our clients*, from whom we have learned a great deal, and particularly those who have allowed their work to be reproduced in Part IV and elsewhere in the book.

Fifth, *my colleagues* in the United States and Europe (particularly Krista Klein and Christa Weil Menegas), who have been instrumental to the development of my thinking about the applications "game" and to the development of this book as well.

—*Richard Montauk*

PREFACE

Approximately one million people seriously consider applying to MBA programs each year. Some hundreds of thousands actually do apply. Not all of them are aiming for the world's best programs, but most of them do want to get into the best program they can manage. They are your competition, the people who can stand in the way of your getting into the school that you want. Maximizing your chances of getting into a top program by outshining this competition is where my company comes in.

Degree of Difference has been helping people get into top MBA programs for years—better programs than they ever realistically expected to attend. This book can do the same for you. *How to Get Into the Top MBA Programs* was written to give you the kind of information and advice that is simply not available from any other source:

- An inside view of what leading business schools are looking for in applicants (based upon interviews with over four dozen admissions directors and our own extensive experience)

- Solid, detailed advice to help you assess and upgrade your own credentials

- A step-by-step guide to take you through the whole application process, showing you:

  —How to choose the right school

  —How to determine your optimal marketing strategy

  —How to write high-quality essays for maximum impact

  —How to choose and then manage your recommenders

  —What to expect in your interviews and how to persuade your interviewers that you have what it takes

- And once you are admitted, you'll learn how best to prepare for business school and to get the most out of your MBA program.

If you would like my help on an individualized basis, please contact:

Degree of Difference
Telephone: **(415) 273-1078**   *or*
www.degreeofdifference.com

126 Aldersgate Street
Barbican, London EC1A 4JQ
Telephone: +44 (207) 608-1811

How to Benefit Most From This Book

Admissions directors at the world's top business schools admit that the hardest aspect of getting an MBA from their schools is getting in. Getting through a top program may be demanding, but let's face it—almost 99 percent of the people who enroll get their degrees. At a school like Stanford, however, only 8 to 10 percent of the people who apply are admitted. Numerous other top schools accept only one in seven or eight applicants.

The reason it is so difficult to get into these schools is clear. The value of an MBA from a top school is immense. As later chapters discuss, graduates of the top schools earn salaries that are, on average, double or more what graduates from lesser schools make. There is even a pronounced difference in the earnings of graduates from the top-ranked and tenth-ranked schools in the United States (as well as in Europe, Asia, and Latin America). Increased salaries are not the end of the story. Greater career choice, increased job security, faster promotions, more interesting work, higher status, and numerous other benefits also result from a top MBA, so it is no wonder that so many people want to get into the best school they can manage.

DEGREE OF DIFFERENCE'S TRACK RECORD

My company, Degree of Difference, has been helping thousands of business school applicants get into the world's top schools for years. We have been hired by individuals, colleges, and even associations of business executives to help them market themselves or their members. They have often come to us either after failing to get into their desired schools or after recognizing that they did not understand the whole application process well enough to do a good job on their applications. With our help, many of them have gotten into various of the world's finest MBA programs. In fact, it is their view as well as our own that we have generally helped them get into a program one to two "tiers" above what they had or could have managed by themselves.

How to Get Into the Top MBA Programs continues the work we have done with our clients. This book provides the necessary strategic understanding and detailed guide to the admissions process so necessary for top results. Although it is designed for the individual working on his or her own to get into the best MBA program possible, it also provides a foundation for those of our clients wanting to enhance their experience with Degree of Difference.

GETTING INTO A BETTER SCHOOL

The purpose of this book is to help applicants get into the best business school possible. Schools want candidates who will be successful corporate (and non-profit) executives, civic leaders, and entrepreneurs. They assess a great deal of information to find them. Some of this is objective and quantifiable, such as a candidate's Graduate Management Admission Test (GMAT) score, whereas much of it is not, such as what a candidate intends to do in the future. The objective elements of an application, which can be termed a candidate's credentials, are obviously important. The subjective elements, however, are ultimately much more important.

Stanford could fill its class with candidates from the world's top universities—people who graduated in the top 10 percent of their class; scored 700 or better on the GMAT; and have worked for the world's preeminent technology companies, consulting firms, and investment banks. Of course it accepts some people who fit this profile, but it actually rejects more of them than it accepts. The point is that schools are looking for more from its candidates than fancy résumés.

Schools admit people rather than résumés. Harvard, for example, wants people who have "demonstrated senior management potential," which is not the same thing as getting a high GMAT score. Schools look for leaders—people who work well as part of teams, who are determined to make an impact, and who have thought carefully about how they want their careers to progress. Given a certain baseline of achievement, they will look at far more than someone's grade point average or GMAT score because those are simply inadequate predictors of leadership, teamwork, and other critical skills.

Schools do consider objective credentials, but only as part of the total picture of the person. They use all of the information they get, including the essays candidates write, the recommendations submitted on their behalf, and the results of application interviews, to determine whether someone will be a successful business leader, entrepreneur, or whatever.

Darden's long-time admissions director, Jon Megibow, put it succinctly: "We are convinced that the 'who' is even more important than the 'what.' We look for people who are more than a set of credentials, more than a set of technical or professional skills. The only way to get a handle on the who is by interviewing applicants, by reading their essays to see whether they are multifaceted human beings, and by examining the recommendations. A one-dimensional person, no matter what his numbers—his credentials—will not be successful as a general manager."

In fact, the essays, recommendations, and interviews are doubly useful for schools. They not only show these leadership and other qualities but also suggest how schools should interpret the so-called objective data. A grade point average of 3.5 on a 4.0 scale means different things in different contexts. If a student had to work 30 hours per week at a demanding job, that performance looks better. Similarly, if the person is a gifted mathematician but chose to take a lot of writing courses to improve a weakness, that performance again looks better. The only way that schools know how to interpret a grade point average, let alone someone's work experience or aspirations, is by hearing what the applicant (and the applicant's recommenders) say about it. In other words, the essays, recommendations, and interviews not only present new information but also "frame" the objective data.

How to Get Into the Top MBA Programs shows you how to maximize the value of your credentials by presenting them in the best way. It does this in several ways:

- It shows what leading business schools are looking for in their applicants and exactly how they interpret the different parts of the applicant's folder.

- It explains the nature of the admissions process, including showing who evaluates your application and how the final decisions are reached.

- It explains and illustrates how you can (and should) improve your own marketing efforts—via your application essays, recommendations, and interviews—to increase your chances of admission at the schools you most want to attend.

The key is to develop your own personal marketing strategy. This must be comprehensive because a disjointed set of essays, or a recommendation that is at odds with what you say about yourself, is the kiss of death for your application. To maximize your chances, you must take advantage of every opportunity to show how professional you are, and why you should be admitted.

This book will show you how to prepare applications that distinguish you from the rest of the applicant pool and show you in your best light. It will show you the mistakes applicants typically make, and how (and why) to avoid them.

Admissions directors routinely note that only 5 to 10 percent of applicants market themselves really well. This gives you a great opportunity to improve your chances by learning how to create a professional-quality application.

WHO SHOULD READ THIS BOOK?

This book is geared toward people who want to get into the best business school they can. It analyzes and discusses each step of the process in a thorough, detailed fashion. Although the text is weighted in terms of getting into the top schools, frankly anyone who wants to improve his or her candidacy to any school, in the top 20 or not, would benefit from an understanding of application strategy.

The book does not assume that you are an American applying to an American business school, although that is the most common applicant profile. The examples used include many Americans but also a number of European, Asian, and Latin American candidates. Similarly, the business schools considered include the top American and European schools.

USING THIS BOOK

UNIQUE FEATURES

How to Get Into the Top MBA Programs provides a thorough explanation of how you can get into the best schools possible. It guides you through each step of the process, showing you at each point how to develop your own marketing strategy. The unique features include:

- Advice from over thirty admissions directors on every aspect of the application process
- 111 actual applicant essays, including:
  - —Successful applications to 19 of the world's top schools
  - —Submissions by applicants from all walks of life, from accounting to the arts, banking to marketing, consulting to engineering, and so on
- Detailed advice on how to write persuasive essays for maximum impact
- In-depth advice regarding how to get the best possible recommendations
- Solid advice on:
  - —How to choose and finance the right program for you
  - —How to prepare for business school and how to get the most out of the program once you go
- A detailed timetable so that you'll know what to do and when

▪ A complete explanation of what top schools look for in applicants, and how you can meet their needs

HOW TO PROFIT MOST FROM THIS BOOK

The key to maximizing the value of this book is to start the whole admissions process early—earlier than you might believe necessary. As Chapter 6, "Application Timetable," shows, it is ideal to begin the process a year or more before you expect to begin classes. Starting early, and using this book throughout the process, will allow you to complete strong, persuasive applications in the most efficient manner possible.

This book is designed to be used efficiently by people with radically different needs. Some will want to read it cover to cover, but many will want to dip into it for help on specific problems they face. Here are some suggestions for how to get the most out of the book, depending upon your own situation.

YOU ARE IN THE MIDST OF YOUR APPLICATIONS NOW

If you have applications due in just a few weeks, you must read several core chapters of the book immediately to avoid making terrible mistakes. Chapter 7 shows you how business schools will evaluate your applications, Chapter 8 shows you the basics of how to market yourself, and the introduction to Chapter 9 shows you how to think about your essays. You will also want to read the analyses of specific essay questions that you are going to answer. In addition, if you have yet to choose your recommenders, or if they have not yet sent in your recommendations, read Chapter 11 to see how you can improve what they say. Before your interviews, you will certainly want to read Chapter 12 on interviewing. When you have time, read the other chapters, or the executive summaries of them, to understand the application process more fully. Part III, which covers the post-application period, is important reading for you after you have finished your applications.

WHAT IF ONE OF YOUR APPLICATIONS IS DUE IN A WEEK?

Do not panic! This book can get you up to speed fast. Before going any further in your applications, be sure to read the executive summaries of each chapter and read Chapter 8 thoroughly. Then consult the relevant essay topics (the ones you are working on at the moment) in Chapter 9 and look through the discussion in Chapter 10 of how to write a strong and persuasive essay. Also be sure to read Chapter 11 on recommendations before giving the "go-ahead" to your recommenders.

YOU ARE GOING TO APPLY TO SCHOOLS IN THE NEAR FUTURE

If you intend to apply to schools in the next several months, you will probably want to get an overview of the application process by reading the executive summaries of each chapter now, plus Chapters 7 and 8, which will explain the fundamentals of what you want to demonstrate in your applications. Read Chapter 6 to be sure you do not miss the starting dates for important activities. Then read each chapter as it becomes relevant to your effort, starting with Chapters 9 and 10, which will show you how to prepare your essays.

YOU WILL NOT APPLY UNTIL SEVERAL YEARS FROM NOW

If you are not going to apply to schools for another two or three years, read Chapters 7 and 8 now. These will show you how best to ready yourself for admission while you still have the opportunity to improve your credentials dramatically. Then read Chapter 6 to determine when to start the process for keeps. Later on you can read the executive summaries of each chapter (about 15 to 18 months before you intend to go) to prepare for the application process itself.

In general, some chapters will not be relevant to everybody. For example, people who have already done their research and determined which schools to apply to can happily skip Chapter 3, "How to Choose the Right School for *You.*"

A FINAL NOTE: THE APPLICATION PROCESS MAY PROVE HELPFUL (AS WELL AS PAINFUL)

Many applicants look upon the task of producing hundreds of details about their pasts, writing dozens of essays about intimate or obscure topics, securing recommendations from old professors and current bosses, and enduring interviews as a modern form of "death by a thousand cuts." They feel that it is trial enough simply to research the schools and figure out which ones would be appropriate for them, let alone to have to manage the data-, paper-, writing-, and time-intensive application process.

If that is your view, keep in mind that the application process, however imperfect it may be, forces applicants to think seriously about where they want to go in their careers and in their lives, and how they are going to get there. Too few people do this career planning at any point, let alone at this most appropriate of times. Applicants to business schools, whether they are in their mid-twenties or mid-thirties, are highly likely to be right at the point where sensible decisions about these matters can yield a lifetime of benefits, and a failure to consider their options carefully can result in opportunities missed—opportunities that will not be offered again. Confronting such important career decisions might open doors you never even realized existed.

CONTENTS

Part III   ON THE ROAD TO BUSINESS SCHOOL

Part IV   APPLICATION ESSAY EXAMPLES

Part I

THE
CONTEXT

1

WHY GET AN MBA?

— EXECUTIVE SUMMARY —

■

There are numerous, good reasons to get an MBA.

■

Not all MBAs are of equal value; graduates of the top schools command
a premium in the marketplace.

■

There are many different types of MBA programs:
—One-year (European model) as well as two-year (American model).
—Part-time (and executive) as well as full-time.
—Programs vary in length, focus, philosophy,
and structure.

■

To understand what to expect at business school,
consult the Appendix to Chapter 2.

*O*nce upon a time, a high school diploma was a sufficient credential to get a good executive job. Then, as more and more people went to college, a high school diploma was no longer enough to land an executive position. A college degree sufficed for a time, but as more and more people got MBAs, even a college degree was no longer enough. That was the case in the 1970s. Since then, the number of people getting an MBA has increased to the point that simply having a degree is insufficient to get plum jobs; the *quality* of the MBA program has become determinative.

This "degree creep" has been matched by the recognition that managers now have far more demands placed upon them than in the past. It is no longer enough just to master a narrow function. In addition to developing strong technical skills, managers must possess a range of such softer skills as the ability to influence people, manage interfaces with other departments, negotiate with individuals from all walks of life, manage their own career in the newly complicated job environment, and more. Managers must also know how each part of the company fits with the other parts, how the company competes, and how it should compete. The disappearance of much of middle management means that even at what were once junior positions in a company, this sort of knowledge is becoming more and more critical. It is all the more important in smaller organizations, start-ups, and entrepreneurial ventures, which are responsible for more and more employment. This increased complexity has made advanced managerial education much more necessary than it was in the past.

Thus, the educational key to managerial success is getting an MBA that both trains you well in your chosen field and is of the highest possible reputation. This does not mean that everyone needs an MBA, but there are a host of people who sensibly view it as a major stepping stone to career success.

SOME COMMON REASONS FOR GETTING AN MBA

The MBA is a very flexible degree, which can serve either to broaden your knowledge of business or to develop your knowledge of a particular function, such as finance. Therefore, it is often viewed as having something for everyone. Although this is obviously an overstatement, there are certainly many valid reasons to get an MBA. Some of those most commonly expressed by prospective MBA students are that they:

- Want to change careers
- Want to advance in their current fields
- Want to shift from individual contribution to managing others
- Want to learn to manage a technical or artistic field they are currently in
- Are between jobs and want to use the time well
- Seek an intellectually challenging and interesting experience
- Need an advanced degree to obtain a useful job in their country or field
- Want to upgrade weak (undergraduate) academic credentials
- Want sufficient skills to start and run a business
- Want to grow their small or start-up business, but need more skill and credibility (for dealing with lenders, investors, or customers) to do so
- Want to improve their pay
- Want to develop their network of contacts
- Want to work in a different country or region

All of these are sensible reasons for getting an MBA. There are others, of course, but it is possible to go into too much detail in enumerating them. London Business School, for example, uses a much simpler classification; it separates people into "vertical" and "transitional." In other words, those wishing to climb the career ladder in their current field are classified as "verticals," whereas those wishing to change fields are classified as "transitionals."

WHAT DOES AN MBA PROGRAM DO?

A good business program will teach things that cannot ordinarily be mastered on the job, such as finance, statistics, and managerial economics. It can also compress the time necessary to learn things that can be learned on the job, but only over a long period and with great effort and luck. In addition, it shows how different functions work, how they are related, how companies in different industries compete, and how they manage in different environments. The best programs also prepare their students to manage in the new global, information-driven environment.

It does all of this by being, in part, a boot camp for managers. Students are drilled in the basics and forced to crunch through a massive amount of material; cooperate and compete with colleagues very different from themselves; and, in general, live life at a speeded-up pace. The net result is a graduate with broadly recognizable skills and attributes.

---

*The **positive attributes** associated with MBAs from top schools include:*

➤ Superior intelligence, as demonstrated by the admissions hurdles they needed to clear

➤ Willingness to invest in themselves, as shown by their pursuit of a graduate degree

➤ Willingness to work long and hard, again as shown by their pursuing an MBA

➤ High motivation: self-starting and self-confident

➤ Desirable blend of theoretical knowledge and practical experience (especially now that the top schools are making sure that their programs are a blend of the two)

➤ Strong analytical skills and a wide perspective, including an understanding of how the whole of the business functions and fits together

➤ Strong communication and interpersonal skills

➤ Ability to work well in teams, with a wide range of people

➤ Willingness and ability to work under great time and performance pressures

---

*The **negative attributes** are:*

➤ Expectations of large salaries and rapid promotions

➤ Lack of loyalty to a company, being devoted instead to their own careers

➤ In sum, being a prima donna

Of course, a graduate gains more than just a set of skills and attitudes. The reputation and connections of the school, along with a hardworking career services department, will help you to gain an appropriate job. The alumni network of the school, plus the contacts you develop during the course, will be assets forever. Indeed, on your résumé the degree itself will have long-term value.

A WORD OF WARNING FOR CAREER CHANGERS

Many people get an MBA to facilitate a career change, but a word of warning is in order. Those who intend to make a dramatic change must plan carefully. It should not be difficult for a medical doctor to become a hospital manager, given her substantial experience in hospital operations. The same is not likely to be true for a commercial photographer who wishes to become an investment banker. This switch will probably only be possible if she has strong quantitative skills and does a great deal during business school to work on projects concerning investment banking, including part-time work of a related nature.

Your prior experience will be important in determining the potential employers that will be interested in you. To overcome a lack of relevant experience, take full advantage of the time that you are in business school. Go beyond just taking relevant courses. For example, do an independent study with a professor who is well-known in this field. Even better, demonstrate a mini "track record" in your new field. Get an academic internship at a relevant company or, if need be, do something on a volunteer basis to get your foot in the door of such a firm. Get active in relevant student clubs or groups. Join the local and national or international branches of the industry association most closely tied to your target field. Those in two-year programs can go further, by working in this field or a related one during the summer between academic years and on a part-time basis during the second year. And if you can spare the time before school starts, do a preprogram internship in your target field.

Even with these ideas in mind, however, do not blithely assume that you can make the career change you desire. Be sure to discuss your proposed change with the career services officers at the relevant schools to determine whether and how you should go about it.

THE VALUE OF GOING TO A TOP SCHOOL

As the number of MBA holders in the world increases, so does the importance of getting a top-quality MBA rather than just any MBA.

INCREASED PAY

The better the reputation of a school, the more its graduates earn. For example, it is clear that graduates from one of the top five schools in the United States can expect, on average, to earn 50 to 100 percent more than graduates from schools ranked nearer to number 50. This pay gap increases dramatically as one goes further down the rankings, to those schools near the bottom of the 800 or so that grant MBAs in the United States.

CAREER CHOICE

Some professions are virtually off-limits to graduates of lesser business schools (let alone those without MBAs). These include investment banking and corporate strategy consulting. The most desirable companies to work for, such as major consulting firms and investment banks, would no more think of recruiting at "Acme" University Business School than they would of giving this year's profits to the Flat Earth Society. These firms look to hire the best and the brightest, and they know that the best and the brightest are to be found at the world's leading business schools.

The same is true, albeit to a somewhat lesser extent, in other fields. Making it into consumer marketing positions of responsibility at the world's leading firms also typically demands that you have an MBA from a top school.

STATUS

This category nearly speaks for itself. Whether for personal or business reasons, being a graduate of Stanford conjures up entirely different impressions and reactions among people you encounter than does being a graduate of Acme U. Status is partially related to the other items listed here, such as salary, but it also reflects the fact that Stanford admits only people who are highly regarded to begin with.

CAREER FLEXIBILITY

The benefits of going to a top school are not limited to your initial job upon graduation. If you decide to change careers in the future (which is becoming more and more common), the quality of your education will be one of the determining factors in your ability to make the switch successfully, and it will also determine how other people rate your chances (and whether they will risk hiring you). The alumni network, and your own personal network from business school, will also be important determinants of your ability to switch. With a strong network willing to help you, your chances are automatically better.

BEST POSSIBLE EDUCATION

The result of being taught by the most accomplished professors, in the company of the most accomplished classmates, is a superior education, one that lesser schools do not match. Curiously, this is perhaps the least often acknowledged benefit of attending a top school.

FINANCIAL CONSIDERATIONS

Getting an MBA represents an extremely large investment of money, as well as time and effort. The tuition for a two-year program may be $75,000 or more, and the income forgone may be $100,000 or more for the two years. Books, computer hardware and software costs, travel to and from the program, and other assorted expenses may add thousands more. The cost of a two-year program is thus likely to be upwards of $200,000 or more. A one-year program may cost 50 to 70 percent as much as this, given the often higher annual tuition at such programs.

Is an MBA worth this large sum? Although not everyone will be financially better off from getting an MBA, those attending the top MBA programs are highly likely to be. In fact, almost no one who attends a top program ends up regretting the experience. An interesting contrast is provided by American law schools, of whose graduates a majority are sorry they ever went.

The payoff is partly a matter of increased earnings. It is also a matter of increased career options, increased confidence that one can do a given job extremely well, increased security (no matter what happens, there are jobs available for people from top schools), and increased status. In addition, most people feel they lived life more intensely at business school, met the most interesting people they have ever known, and formed their closest friendships there. It is therefore probably a mistake to view the decision to get an MBA on a purely financial basis, despite the sums involved.

WHO HIRES MBAs?

The traditional employers of MBAs have been firms in financial services, management consulting, and consumer goods. They remain the biggest employers of MBAs to this date. The trend in recent years, however, has been for technology, health care, and nonprofits to recruit aggressively, and for graduates to start their own firms. Governmental units have joined the fray, too, often preferring MBAs to those with master's degrees in public administration, public health, international relations, and so on. The mix of employers varies from year to year, depending largely upon the health of their own industries.

> **CAREER PLANNING**
>
> This book is avowedly not a career planning manual. It is important to note, though, that you should view the decision to pursue an MBA as an important career decision, and one that merits considerable thought. The starting point for your decision making should be an evaluation of where you want to go and how best you can get there. If this is a complete mystery to you, by all means consult the career literature, which is abundant.

IS AN MBA RIGHT FOR YOU?

If any of the reasons for getting an MBA that were listed at the start of this chapter struck a responsive chord, an MBA is probably right for you. If you intend to be a better manager, progress rapidly in your current company, start your own business, give yourself better career options, or just earn more money, an MBA is likely to be a sensible investment.

Even after you have decided to get an MBA, however, you have not finished making important decisions. Major issues you will face include: Do you want to pursue the degree now or later? Do you want to go to a full-time or a part-time program? Do you want to go to an American or a European (or Asian or Latin) school?

The question of timing is likely to be the first one you face if you have not already made up your mind that now is the time. Chapter 7, "Making the Most of Your Credentials," discusses the amount of experience that is appropriate to maximize your attractiveness to schools.

2

TYPES OF MBA PROGRAMS

— EXECUTIVE SUMMARY —

Full-time, part-time, and executive MBA programs offer
a wide range of courses.
—The advantages of each type of program are marked.

The European MBA model offers a contrast to the American model.

Be sure to choose the type of program best suited to your personal needs.

T here are now many different types of MBA programs, as well as different means of delivering a given type of program. Thus, the business school applicant can choose from full-time, part-time, modular, or distance learning (i.e., by television, video, Internet, and mail) programs. Rather than discuss all of the many different possibilities, however, this section focuses on the major program types: traditional full-time programs (both American and European versions), part-time programs, and executive programs.

THE TRADITIONAL, FULL-TIME AMERICAN MBA

The American MBA has been around for a century now. The initial assumption was that it was to provide training for someone without prior business study, so it was made a two-year degree, with the first year providing an introduction to business fundamentals. Although there have been innumerable changes in the typical program, it retains certain core characteristics. It is still, almost without exception, a two-year program. It has a set of core courses that are required for all or most students. Most students are still relatively young, with the typical age upon entrance currently being 26 or 27. Many schools once accepted a majority of their students straight from undergraduate studies, but now schools require two or more years of experience from most of their students. In the last few years, however, the top schools have once again opened their doors to a modest number of applicants lacking substantial experience in the belief that true "stars" should be found and nurtured very early in their careers.

American schools have always been the intellectual leaders in business education, and they remain, collectively, a bastion of serious research. (The leading European schools have closed this gap, but relatively few of them are truly serious research institutions.) American professors at the leading schools therefore tend to be at the forefront of their fields. This is especially true now that American schools have emphasized developing closer links with industry, so most leading professors spend part of their time consulting to industry in addition to doing research. In fact, the two activities are closely related.

American schools have dramatically changed their programs to integrate the core subjects, incorporate softer skills, and internationalize their focus. These changes are continuing. Different schools have approached the need for change in different ways, as the contrast between the programs at the Darden School (at the University of Virginia) and the University of Chicago Graduate School of Business illustrates.

PROGRAM STRUCTURE

The Darden School provides an example of a traditional program structure. The academic year is split into two terms.

Fall Term	*Spring Term*
Decision Analysis	Financial Management
Management Communication	Global Economies and Markets
Accounting	Strategic Thinking and Action
Operations Management	Leading Organizations
Marketing	Business Ethics

In the second year, students take twenty quarter-length (i.e., half-semester) elective courses. A similar structure is evident in other programs—with most required courses completed in the first year, and the second year largely devoted to electives—although many schools have a two- or three- rather than four-term structure.

At the other end of the spectrum, the University of Chicago Graduate School of Business ("Chicago") has created a curriculum that offers dramatic freedom of choice to students. Only one course—an introductory leadership–soft skills course—must be taken by everyone. Students must take courses in a variety of fields to meet a distribution requirement, but the specific courses are to be chosen by each student. This structure is highly flexible; only one course out of twenty-one is mandated, and the rest are to be chosen to fit a student's own needs.

Most American schools are closer to Darden than Chicago in their curricula. Although a good deal of freedom of choice of electives is offered, the set of required courses remains at about 40 to 50 percent of the total program. Whereas some schools allow students to waive some required courses, most case-oriented schools (like Harvard and Darden) do not. They feel it is essential to have highly knowledgeable students in these courses because these students will effectively end up teaching the novices, through their comments in class and their work in study groups.

Advantages of a Traditional Full-Time Program (relative to other methods of obtaining an MBA)

- Traditional (in the U.S.), well-understood method of getting the degree
- High student satisfaction with most programs
- High interaction with other students in and out of class, and (often) with faculty
- Ability to take numerous elective courses as well as to do (lengthy) exchange programs abroad
- Opportunity to participate in student organizations, study trips, and other out-of-class offerings
- Appropriate for people changing careers who need courses, a summer internship (between years) in a field related to their chosen field, and time to make the change
- Potentially able to work during second year (albeit not at the most intensive programs) to earn money and gain experience
- Opportunity for in-depth study, to become a functional specialist
- Time to reflect upon one's career future and to explore career options

Disadvantages (relative to other methods of obtaining an MBA)

- Expensive
- Long time away from work
- Student body typically largely American rather than mixed

THE EUROPEAN MBA

AMERICAN VS. EUROPEAN MODEL

At one time there were two relatively distinct models of MBA education. The American model differed from the European model on several grounds:

	AMERICAN	EUROPEAN
Length	Two Years	One Year
Primary Driver	Professorial Research	Industry Connections
Course Focus	American	Global or European
Skills Emphasized	Quantitative	Soft Skills
Student Body	Largely American	Mixed (but largely European)
Selection Criteria Emphasized	Test Scores, Grades	Work Experience and Success
Age of Students	Mid-twenties	Late-twenties or Older

There were other differences, too, although this chart covers the major issues. Moreover, not all programs fit the predominant pattern in either case. In the United States, Thunderbird was (and remains) very similar to the European programs, with its global focus, emphasis upon languages, and the like. In Europe, London Business School, Manchester Business School, and IESE (Barcelona) were (and remain) a mixture of the American and European models—a "mid-Atlantic" model, perhaps.

The differences between the two models have blurred in recent years as the American programs in particular have made substantial changes. Most, if not all, of the top American programs have greatly increased the role of such "soft skills" as leadership, negotiation, and teamwork. Related to this, they have tried to improve their connections to industry, to make their courses more relevant and less driven by professorial interest (some would say whim), and also to benefit from being able to place students as interns undertaking projects for companies. They have also worked hard to examine the issues in managing in a global environment, although they generally lag behind the top European programs in this regard. The American programs have sought people with more work experience, rather than those who have only academic credentials. Some things have remained the same, however; most American programs remain resolutely two years long. The European schools have changed less, although the leading programs in particular, such as INSEAD (outside Paris) and Rotterdam, have joined London Business School in incorporating a more quantitative focus to their programs.

The old stereotypes—American schools are intellectually rigorous but their graduates lack managerial and interpersonal skills, whereas European schools produce fine managers who understand the languages and cultural context of different countries but lack substantive skills—clearly no longer apply. But before dismissing the issue, it should be said that some of the old differences between American and European programs remain. American schools still spend a majority of course time on American cases and issues, whereas European schools do not focus so heavily on any one country. American student bodies are still largely American (only 20 to 45 percent come from other countries), whereas few leading European schools have more than a substantial minority from their home countries.

EUROPEAN PROGRAM STRUCTURE

Some European one-year programs are divided into four terms, while others are divided into five or six terms. Some have a compulsory project or thesis in the last term or two, whereas others offer taught courses for the entire year.

Spain's Instituto de Empresa (IE) is an example of the latter approach. Its thirteen-month program begins with a one-week preprogram, after which the year is divided into five terms.

Term I

Case Method

Action Learning

Team Building

Organizational Behavior

Financial Accounting

Quantitative Analysis for Business

Opportunity Ideas and Entrepreneurial Market Assessment

Term II

New Venture Creation Process

Marketing Management: Fundamentals, Market, and Price

Cost Accounting

Economic Environment

Financial Management

Information Systems

Operations Management

Term III

Venture Creation Laboratory

Marketing Management: Distribution and Communication

Advanced Financial Management

Human Resource Management

Strategic Management

Operations Management

Term IV

Marketing Strategy and Plan

General Management

Business, Government, and Society

Management Control Systems

Country Economic Analysis

Supply Chain Management

Term V

Elective Courses

Exchange Programme

Final Oral Exam

Business Plan Presentation

The ratio of required-to-elective courses is a bit more than four-to-one, which is a bit higher than average for European one-year programs, although several leading schools offer almost no choice of electives. All courses are essentially set—with no waivers or options available. The shortness of the program and the consequent high percentage of required versus elective courses differ from the longer American programs.

The advantages and disadvantages of attending a European school as described below are based upon one-year programs. Those interested in the fifteen-month to two-year programs at such schools as London and IESE are advised to use this list with caution, and to consider the above pros and cons regarding American two-year programs as well.

Advantages

- For those with substantial business experience, one year may be all that is necessary to broaden horizons and improve skills.

- The time spent away from one's career is limited.

- Good industry connections mean that the best schools do very well in placing their students.

■ The internationalism of the top programs, especially regarding the mix of nationalities in the student body, is remarkable.

■ Emphasis is placed upon learning languages.

■ Teaching of soft skills is often superb.

Disadvantages

■ A one-year program is too short for some to develop enough new skills and contacts to make dramatic career shifts.

■ Some programs are too small or too structured to offer much choice of electives.

■ The underlying presumption that students have substantial business experience means that some of the introductory courses move at too fast a pace for novices.

■ Some programs do not force students to acquire substantial quantitative skills, requiring a conscious choice of quantitative elective courses in order to develop these skills.

■ There is little time for career reflection or exploring career options.

The European model is attractive to those who intend to work in Europe or for European companies. As with the leading U.S. schools, leading European schools offer worldwide employment opportunities and first-class learning environments. Top American firms that operate worldwide, such as the management consulting and financial service firms, are among the top recruiters of students from these schools.

It is indeed unfortunate that so few Americans (perhaps 3,500 per year) attend these programs, although an American who wishes to work for a Kansas City firm doing business only in the Kansas City region admittedly has little need to cross the Atlantic for an MBA. The fact remains, however, that fewer and fewer applicants can correctly assume that their careers will lack international dimensions, whether that means working abroad, working for a foreign company in the United States, managing foreign employees, or competing against foreign companies.

A handful of American schools now offer programs that mirror the one-year feature common to European schools. These include:

■ Goizueta/Emory

■ Johnson/Cornell

■ Katz/Pittsburgh

- Kellogg
- Mendoza/Notre Dame
- Warrington/Florida
- William & Mary

Some are open to anyone; others only to those with special qualifications. Thus, Kellogg offers its four-quarter program to those with undergraduate degrees in business or comparable experience. Johnson (Cornell) offers its one-year program to scientists and engineers switching into management. In each case where entry is limited to those with special qualifications, the entering group is expected to be able to study the introductory material at an accelerated pace. At Kellogg, for example, the four-quarter-program students condense the whole of the regular program's first year into a summer of study, then join the six-quarter-program students for the "second year" of elective courses. This structure is radically different from that common to the European schools. Rather than have two-thirds or more of the year devoted to required courses, as in Europe, these American programs devote the bulk of the year to elective courses.

PART-TIME MBAs

Part-time MBAs have become more popular both because they offer the opportunity to remain at one's job while also attending school and because more top-quality schools now offer part-time MBA programs. The typical program involves taking one or two classes per term, thereby prolonging the time it takes to get a degree. Those pursuing an American MBA, who would take two years in a full-time program, will take three years or more in a part-time program.

The people who find these programs attractive are likely to be older, with more experience, and many have financial obligations that prevent them from attending a full-time program. Others are unable or unwilling to leave their current jobs and choose a part-time program as the only realistic means of furthering their business education.

PROGRAM STRUCTURE

The structure of a part-time MBA does not differ significantly from that of a full-time MBA. The same core courses are generally required, although they may be taken in a slightly different sequence due to the scheduling difficulties that result from students proceeding through the program at varying speeds. The number of courses that must be completed in order to graduate will almost invariably be the same.

For a discussion of the advantages and disadvantages of part-time MBAs, see the end of the Executive MBAs section, which follows.

EXECUTIVE MBAs

Executive MBAs (EMBAs) are a relatively recent addition to the offerings of most graduate business schools. For years, the only such program was offered by the University of Chicago. Now there are dozens of executive MBA programs offered by many of the top business schools in the world.

Executive MBAs are to be distinguished both from regular MBAs and from other executive programs. Full-time MBA programs, of course, meet daily and last up to two years. Part-time programs tend to have classes in the evening and last for substantially longer than full-time MBA programs, largely because students are meant to take only one or two courses per term (whereas full-time students take many more per term). EMBA programs offer the best of both the full-time and part-time programs: they generally last about as long as a full-time program but—by scheduling classes in such a way that students with understanding employers can continue to work while still attending class—do not force students to give up their jobs. (Other executive education programs, in contrast, may meet for one to ten or twelve weeks but do not confer an MBA upon completion.) On the other hand, not all EMBA programs offer the rigor or dedicated learning environment of their full-time analogs. Furthermore, continuing to work while studying at the intense pace of an EMBA program places very substantial demands on students.

The number of EMBA programs has grown dramatically in recent years. There are several factors underpinning this growth:

■ The degree continues to meet the needs of the many people who need to keep drawing a paycheck while attending school.

■ New scheduling options (see below) have increased the flexibility of the degree, making it possible for more people to attend EMBA programs. Underlying this new flexibility is increased use of the distance-learning possibilities offered by the Internet.

■ New types of programs have developed. It is now possible to do a specialized degree in finance (Stern/NYU), health care (Fuqua/Duke), or other fields. Just as importantly, some of the newer programs attempt to mimic the full-time programs by offering a similar number of contact hours (in class, with professors and other students) and similar rigor (really teaching the nuts and bolts of accounting and statistics, for instance).

■ Courses mimicking full-time programs have often opened their doors to much younger applicants than the traditional programs welcomed. Wharton, for example, considers applicants in their late twenties to be perfectly acceptable candidates.

PROGRAM STRUCTURE

Fortunately, there is no agreement as to what constitutes the ideal structure for an EMBA program. Although many programs last approximately two years, many are much shorter (little more than a year) or longer (up to four years). Some are lockstep (the whole cohort takes the same classes together), whereas others offer multiple options as to starting dates, speed at which to complete the program, and course electives.

The scheduling of courses likewise varies enormously. For instance, UCLA's program meets every second weekend (Friday and Saturday) for twenty-four months. The TRIUM EMBA (the joint offering of Stern/NYU, the London School of Economics, and HEC/Paris) is structured in modules: a twelve-day module in London; a twelve-day module in New York; an eight-day module in Asia; a twelve-day module in Paris; an eight-day module in an emerging market; and a twelve-day module in New York, spread over sixteen months. Different formats for executive courses continue to evolve.

COURSES ON OFFER

The range of EMBA programs—and locations—is now stunning. Wharton offers a program in Philadelphia and another in San Francisco. Chicago continues to offer programs in Chicago, London, and Singapore. Kellogg offers programs in Chicago and Miami and, through partner schools, in Canada, Germany, Hong Kong, and Israel. Johnson's (Cornell) program involves less of a geographic stretch than these others: It is offered both in New York City and in its Ithaca home.

Whereas American programs are generally about two years long, European EMBA programs tend to be shorter. INSEAD's program, for instance, lasts fourteen months; Instituto de Empresa, in Madrid, has a thirteen-month program. IMD's program can be completed in as few as fifteen months or stretched out over as many as forty-eight.

Columbia and London Business School, which continue to offer their own executive MBAs, also offer a joint degree program under the EMBA-Global label. So, too, do Stern (NYU), the London School of Economics, and HEC (Paris), under the TRIUM name. Five schools—Rotterdam, Kenan-Flagler (North Carolina), EGADE-ITESM (Mexico), FGV-EAESP (Brazil), and the Chinese University of Hong Kong—across four continents, have joined to offer "OneMBA," while the various constituent schools still offer their own EMBA programs.

London Business School, Sloan (MIT), and Stanford still offer the venerable Sloan master's programs, which are unlike a normal executive program insofar as they require full-time attendance for ten months (although MIT now offers a part-time, two-year option as well) but are still aimed at seasoned executives.

EMBA programs continue to multiply and evolve. The selection below illustrates that the variations among programs are far greater than those seen with part-time or full-time MBA programs. Whether it's price, starting date, location, duration, number or frequency of residential sessions, age of participants, or admission requirements, this is a dog's breakfast. And as the EMBA market evolves, expect more rather than less variety.

The chart on the next page shows a bit of the range of courses now on offer.

SPONSORSHIP

Corporate sponsorship can mean, at a minimum, giving you the time off to attend an EMBA program or, at a maximum, paying your tuition, fees, and travel to attend a program. Virtually no EMBA program requires that you be financially sponsored by your company, but all require that your employer guarantee you suitable time to attend and complete the program. Of course, even though financial sponsorship is not a requirement for admission, having your employer pay all or part of your expenses would be nice. Your organization is likely to be concerned, however, about your time away from work, the level of financial investment required, and the possibility that you may jump ship once you have your degree.

The first step in lining up sponsorship is to determine whether your organization has an explicit policy regarding EMBA sponsorship. Even if it does not, perhaps it has paid for someone to attend an EMBA program or something similar. Next, think about how your company can benefit in general terms by sponsoring appropriate highfliers. Potential benefits include:

- Retaining the services of highfliers while also developing their skills
- If you have elective options available, your learning can be tailored to meet your organization's needs

SELECTED EMBA PROGRAMS

School/Program	Location(s)	Duration (Months)	Frequency (Residential Periods)	Start Dates	Tuition	Average Age	GMAT Required?	Percentage of Coursework Required
Anderson/ UCLA	Los Angeles	24	Alt. weekends	August	$45,570*	38	Yes	75%
Columbia	New York	20	Alt. weekends	Sept. or Jan.	$120,000*	33	Yes	40%
Fuqua/Duke *Global*	Durham	18	5 2-wk modules	May	$115,700*	38	No	100%
Johnson/ Cornell *Boardroom*	NY, OH, WA, DC, Canada possible	17	3 2-wk modules + 3 Sat/month	July	$92,000*	37	No	100%
McCombs/ Texas *Mexico*	Mexico City	22	Alt. weekends	August	$50,000*	27	Yes	100%
Stern/NYU/ LSE *TRIUM*	NYC, London, Paris, Shanghai, & 1 other	16	4 2-wk modules 2 1-wk modules	September	$111,300*	40	No (unless <15 years' experience)	100%
IESE	Madrid	18	Alt. weekends	September	€53,600	30	No (IESE exam)	100%
INSEAD	Paris & Singapore	14	8 1- to 2-wk modules	November	€86,000	36	Yes	100%
London/ Columbia *Global*	London & New York	20	20 4- to 6-day modules	May	$120,000	32	Yes	60%

*Tuition amount listed includes lodging, albeit only partial lodging for the McCombs program.

■ Even in required courses, you may be able to select projects that focus on your organization

■ Some programs require an in-company project (which can be tailored to your organization), which means that the program's resources (faculty, for instance) can be devoted to a key issue facing the company

■ Motivating highfliers; in this regard, EMBA programs can be part of an overall management development plan for highfliers

Then consider how these potential benefits could apply in your case. In building your case, be realistic not only about the benefits but about the hurdles as well. Being flexible about your choice of program—its location, its duration, the time courses meet, and so on—can certainly help. So, too, can a willingness to tie yourself to your company for a set time after the EMBA, to alleviate concern that you will leave immediately upon graduation. One way to do this is by taking out a company loan that is forgivable over time.

Most EMBA programs have substantial experience helping applicants negotiate with their employers, so seek their counsel when it comes time to pitch to your company.

FULL-TIME AND EXECUTIVE MBA PROGRAMS AT A GLANCE		
	Full-Time	*Executive*
Average Age (at start of program)	26–30	33–39
Total Fees	$50–85,000	$60–125,000
Acceptance Rates	10–35%	20–50%
Electives as Percentage of Total Courses	45–95%	0–50%

Advantages of Part-Time and Executive MBAs

■ An employer is more likely to pay your tuition if you can keep working while attending the program.

■ If you stay in your current field and continue to work for your current employer, the chances of being able to deduct the cost of the program (from your taxable income) are good.

■ By staying on the job, you can eliminate the cost and risk of searching for employment at the end of your program.

■ You keep getting paid during your studies.

- You do not have to relocate for your studies.

- You can often employ what you learn on the job as you learn it. Conversely, you can draw upon your ongoing relevant work experience to enhance your performance in the program.

- The students are generally older (especially in an EMBA program) than those in the full-time program, so they should be fonts of information and skill. They also represent a great networking opportunity.

Advantages of Executive MBAs

- Executive MBA programs are generally relatively short, so you can complete the degree more quickly than you can a part-time program. You may even be able to complete it more quickly than you could a full-time program (although it is an open question whether you can learn as much in such a situation).

Disadvantages of Part-Time and Executive MBAs

- You may not be able to commit yourself to your studies and to your classmates the way you could if you attended school full-time. The result may be failing to master as many of your courses as you would have had you been a full-time student.

- It can be hard to develop a solid network without attending full-time.

- Your job performance may suffer so much, due to the effort you must make for your classes, your unavailability to travel on certain nights, and so on, that you will not increase your responsibilities or salary as you would if you could devote yourself more fully to your job. (Your company, aware of this possibility, may resist your attending the program in the first place.)

- Your classmates are likely to be from the surrounding area, meaning that you may have few from other countries—and many from just a few companies.

- Scholarship aid is seldom available (although loans often are).

- If you receive any sponsorship from your company, you may be precluded from using many career services, especially the opportunity to interview on campus with other companies.

- When you have completed all or much of your program, your company may not recognize that you have improved your skills and thus may be unwilling to promote you or increase your pay. (On the other hand, the company may fear that you are going to leave, given that you have improved your résumé and your visibility.)

- Not all employers value part-time and executive MBAs as highly as they value full-time MBAs. This is particularly true of EMBAs, which were once widely regarded as vastly less rigorous than their big brothers, the full-time programs.

- Some programs, especially EMBAs, are indeed less substantial than the full-time programs at the same schools, especially if they have a different faculty and dramatically fewer contact hours. Similarly, some have far fewer elective courses available, making it very hard to customize a program to your needs or to become a functional expert.

- It is hard to participate in the same range of out-of-class activities as full-time students easily manage.

Disadvantages of Part-Time MBAs

- Part-time programs take substantially longer to complete than do full-time programs.

- If you want to transfer into the school's full-time program, note that this is quite difficult at many schools.

- It is hard to get to know your fellow students well enough to profit from extensive networking opportunities.

Disadvantages of Executive MBAs

- The relative shortness of many executive MBA programs means that you will simply learn less than in a longer, more intensive full-time (or part-time) program.

TIPS FOR CHOOSING THE RIGHT TYPE OF PROGRAM FOR YOU

Your individual situation is likely to involve multiple factors relevant to choosing the type of MBA program that will best fit you. The discussion above, however, leads to the following tentative conclusions:

➤ Consider the advantages and disadvantages of each program type discussed above; determine which apply to you—and to what extent. Thus, if you think your employer would fund you for a part-time program, ascertain for certain just how much financial support you can count on. Then, determine what amount of financial aid you could get from a full-time program (although this may require actually applying to such a program).

➤ The older you are, the more you should consider doing a one-year (European) MBA or an executive program.

➤ If you are very young, consider applying to a program that will accept you now and defer your entry for another year or two.

➤ If you need only to develop a narrow expertise, give some thought to the MBA alternatives listed below.

➤ If you want to change careers, favor a two-year full-time program.

➤ If you are currently in your mid-twenties and ready to get an MBA, it may not be a good idea to wait ten years to get an EMBA. Delaying getting a degree means that you delay its benefits as well—not only monetary benefits but also those involving expanding career choices and options.

➤ If you intend to stay in your career, consider an alternative to a full-time two-year program: a part-time, an executive, or a one-year MBA.

➤ Favor a part-time or executive MBA to the extent your current job pleases you and permits combining work and study, as long as you are fortunate enough to have a top-quality program available.

➤ If you want to move to another country or work in an international field, consider attending a school abroad.

➤ If you intend to work in a traditional MBA glamour field such as strategy consulting or investment banking, you are probably best off attending a full-time program at the highest ranked school you can.

➤ The quality and reputation of the program you attend matters as much as the type of program. If you live in Chicago and are admitted to the part-time program at either the University of Chicago or Kellogg, for example, you should consider long and hard whether to attend a full-time program at a school not ordinarily considered to be in the global top 20.

➤ Check with prospective employers to determine the appropriateness of different programs—and program types. (See Chapter 3 for more about this.) It is unclear, for example, whether employers value part-time and executive MBA programs as highly as they do full-time MBA programs.

SPECIALIZED MBAs

In the past, an MBA was resolutely a generalist degree. Even though the last portion of the program generally featured elective courses, thereby offering a chance to gain expertise in a specific field, there was no presumption that a student would enter any specific field. A large number of schools have changed this. There are now specialized MBAs designed for those who wish to enter fashion management, health care, luxury goods marketing, defense management, church management, and so on. A conservative count would put the different subjects on offer at fifty or more.

As with the master's degrees in single subjects, one key question is whether you need a broad range of training or simply need to develop expertise in a more limited realm. If you are clear that you will remain in or enter a given field, there is no reason to avoid an MBA geared to that field. Both the structured curriculum and the networking possibilities are of potential value. Note, however, that many of the leading business schools have eschewed such specialized MBAs. Consequently, you should be in no hurry to attend a specialized course at a lesser school if you can get into a reasonably flexible program at a leading school.

OTHER EDUCATIONAL OPTIONS

An MBA is not the only option for those who wish to do graduate business study. If you are interested in developing your skills in essentially one area only, you can do, for example, a specialized master's degree in accounting, business economics, information systems, marketing, operations, and numerous other fields. The following list, which is hardly exhaustive, is simply meant to give the flavor of the range of subjects on offer and the quality of the schools involved:

School	*Master's Degree Subject*
Bocconi (Milan)	International Health Care Management; Economics; and Policy
Carnegie Mellon	Computational Finance
London Business School	Finance
London School of Economics	Accounting and Finance; Management and Regulation of Risk; and a host of others
MIT	Real Estate

Princeton   Finance

Stanford   Engineering Management

The list could be readily expanded to cover offerings at Berkeley, UCLA, Northwestern, Harvard, Chicago, Columbia, Oxford, Cambridge, and a dozen other leading schools. The point is that there are many courses on offer that might be a sensible alternative to an MBA. It must be emphasized, however, that these degrees are not generally suitable for those who wish to receive training in the usual core courses of an MBA program, pursue advanced training in multiple fields, or become general managers.

RESOURCE

Those wishing an in-depth look at management education, albeit from the perspective of companies considering how best to develop their key managers, are advised to consult Michel Syrett and Jean Lammiman's *Management Development* (Economist Books, 1999), for a well-written, sophisticated analysis of the possibilities.

THE CAREER SERVICES DIRECTORS DISCUSS PART-TIME, FULL-TIME, AND EMBA PROGRAMS

Part-Time versus Full-Time Programs

➤ Those who elect the part-time program generally do so because they want to keep their stream of income or figure that they will be able to apply what they learn in class to the workplace the next day. Those opting for one of the full-time programs (the four-quarter or six-quarter) are looking for a different kind of experience. They want to be able to focus totally on the experience, both academic and social. They also want a chance to step back and rethink what they want to do in their careers. *ROXANNE HORI, KELLOGG*

➤ Our part-time and full-time programs have the same faculty, and many students cross-register for courses in the other program. Partly as a result, the two degrees are viewed the same by the top employers—but you do get a different menu of support services from the school. *GLENN SYKES, CHICAGO*

➤ A part-time or executive program is for people with substantial experience who want to continue either with their same company or career. A full-time program is really to help people at the beginning of their careers or those who are looking to change careers. *EVERETTE FORTNER, DARDEN*

➤ The part-time population is focused on developing technical and analytical skills. To a certain extent these students also look to participate in some co-curricular and extracurricular activities, but obviously their work-life balance places some limitations on these. Career-wise, they are likely to be looking to enhance their skills within their same firm or industry. *Pamela Mittman, Stern (NYU)*

➤ Changing careers is not as easy if you do a part-time program. People on part-time programs are generally working during the day, which greatly constrains the amount of extra time they have to work on extra projects outside of their academics. Also, they're still building up their résumés in their current careers in terms of who they are and what they can do. The longer you stay in the same kind of job doing the same kind of thing, the more difficult it is for an employer to be convinced you can do something different. *Andy Chan, Stanford*

➤ The obvious lifestyle issues affect the part-time versus full-time choice, of course, but there's not much difference between the two programs here. For example, virtually the same faculty teaches in each program. The experience is different, however, given that you can keep working while doing the part-time program (and employers are more willing to pay for it), whereas full-time students can more easily access all of the activities outside the classroom—student organizations, speakers, and so on—as well as spend much more time with their peers. *Michele Rogers, Kellogg (Admissions Director)*

One-Year versus Two-Year Programs

➤ The four-quarter program (4Q) is for those with undergraduate degrees in business or comparable work experience, who can do the core courses on an accelerated basis. The screening process for the 4Q and the six-quarter program are the same, as is the faculty. Not surprisingly, employers value the two programs equally. *Roxanne Hori, Kellogg*

➤ There is a greater opportunity to make a successful change in a two-year program. Students are exposed to more industries and functions over the longer course. In addition, they have time to develop more substantial relationships with their classmates, who are potentially very important career resources for them immediately and down the road. *Peter J. Degnan, Wharton*

➤ A one-year programme is a more intense experience. You forego less salary, but have less opportunity to do projects and internships. A two-year programme offers more time for reflection. You can experiment with your career (via project work and internships), plus you can study in more depth. *Graham Hastie, London*

Choosing Between American and European Programs

➤ *Americans:* Going to an international school increases the chances of being able to work internationally in the near-term after business school. For one thing, there are more international employers recruiting at international schools, so you're more likely to be considered. Also, the exposure—in terms of the academics, the faculty, and the environment (and hopefully you're working on your language skills)—and the student and alumni network there can be very helpful. . . . At the top U.S. schools, an American student will have the potential opportunity to work abroad, but it's not easy if you don't have much in your background showing you're international by nature—either by language skills or by experience working abroad. In that case, there will be other people at the school who have that background and will be more competitive for getting that sort of job. *ANDY CHAN, STANFORD*

➤ *For Europeans making the choice:* Leading European programs have both multi-national and American recruiters coming to their schools, so your chances of getting a job in the U.S. are good. Of course your chances of initially getting a job in the U.S. are better at a U.S.-based business school. So if you're European and you want to start your career in the U.S., you probably have a slightly higher probability of doing so if you attend a U.S. business school. *For Americans:* You can apply the same logic in reverse. *EVERETTE FORTNER, DARDEN*

➤ The couple top European business schools have a more international makeup of their student body and of their faculty, so if you're looking for a truly international degree, a European school might be a good choice. *EVERETTE FORTNER, DARDEN*

➤ Multinationals recruit here, but the more parochial American companies do not. If you want to work for Goldman in New York, there's no problem, but there may be if you want to work for Boeing, Gillette, or Kraft. To work for the latter type of company, it would be better to do business school in the States—although we do have reciprocal career center arrangements with top U.S. schools, some of which even allow our students on-campus interviewing privileges. We have a lot of Americans on the program (perhaps 20 percent, in fact), two-thirds of whom choose to remain in Europe to work. *CHRIS BRISTOW, LONDON*

➤ It's no problem at all for Americans to get a job back in the U.S., but most of the Americans doing the program want to stay in Europe rather than return to the U.S. *KATTY OOMS SUTER, IMD*

Choosing Between EMBA and Full-Time MBA Programs

➤ You need to really think about the choice. What kind of experience would you like to have? If you would enjoy the full-time MBA experience, including its social aspects, can take two years off to pursue the degree, and can't imagine combining work and study, then it's easy to choose. *LING TEE, IESE/SPAIN (ADMISSIONS DIRECTOR)*

➤ Company-sponsored EMBA students do not have access to on-campus recruiting unless their employer permits it. The self-sponsored do have access, of course. *REGINA RESNICK, COLUMBIA*

➤ Executive MBA students average thirty-seven years old, with eight to ten years of management experience. All are very successful but are now ready to learn the "theory" behind their gut reactions. Due to the amount of experience these students have had, they are at a different professional level than most of the day (full-time) students. A major reason for students to apply to the executive MBA program is that they will learn a great deal from each other and their corporate cultures. As with the day students, networking is ever important. *ROXANNE HORI, KELLOGG*

➤ The major differences between full-time and executive MBA programs are where the students are coming from and what their goals are. Students in the full-time program are early in their careers: They're generally still trying to figure out where they're headed and how they're going to get there. Students in the EMBA program, however, are older and much more comfortable in their careers. Because ours is a general management program, the students are likely to be functional specialists who are here to acquire the tools to become general managers—CFOs, CEOs, and so on. The two groups of students are very different, meaning that class discussions are inevitably very different. *PATTY KEEGAN, CHICAGO (ADMISSIONS)*

➤ EMBA students never leave their professional environments, so they don't change the way they think. The MBA students, however, have a contemplative experience; they're immersed in the academic environment for two years. They have to do a project for a real company, and they shadow a real executive. The social connections with other students are also deeper. . . . The Sloan programme, for people in their late thirties, with a substantial career behind them, is different from the other programmes. Many Sloan students will already have done an MBA, perhaps ten years before. They want to take a sabbatical and reflect on where they are headed. *GRAHAM HASTIE, LONDON*

➤ People who choose executive MBA programs want to do their degree whilst working in a challenging career full-time. In the main, they're going to be older and more experienced than full-time MBA students. They're going to feel they're on a career path that is taking them somewhere and will be reluctant to interrupt this progression. They may wish to make an immediate impact on their performance or on their company's performance. They want to have an injection of knowledge, skills, energy, and the rich experience of an MBA while still pursuing their careers. LYN HOFFMAN, LONDON (ADMISSIONS DIRECTOR)

➤ Many companies like to recruit EMBA students because they can start work immediately (rather than six or eight months later, as is the case with full-time students recruited in November to start work in July). Most companies that hire here have hired EMBAs as well as full-time MBAs. CHRIS BRISTOW, LONDON

MBA versus Specialized Master's Degrees

➤ A specialized degree tends to lead you to a specialized set of career options, whereas an MBA gives you a variety of skills that lead you eventually to general management and give you flexibility as to the career paths you can choose. A master's degree will make you smart in that discipline, so the companies that need in-depth knowledge in that discipline will be interested in hiring you, but they will be relatively few. Your career choices will be much more limited than with an MBA. EVERETTE FORTNER, DARDEN

➤ The Master's in Finance degree is much narrower, much more focused, than the MBA. It's appropriate if you are very clear that, for instance, investment banking is for you. The MBA is a general management degree; it's a much more flexible qualification, allowing you to explore different career options. Interestingly, some of the people who do the Master's in Finance have previously done MBAs at second-tier schools; some go on to do MBAs afterwards. CHRIS BRISTOW, LONDON

Blue-Chip Firms' Hiring

➤ They really look at the candidates and their career goals rather than whether they are in the part-time or full-time programs. The larger firms are interested in both populations: they're looking for as many talented individuals as possible. . . . The full-time program does have more students who are interested in changing careers and beginning formal associate programs. Many of our part-time students here may be a bit further along in their careers and therefore a bit more reluctant to take a cut in salary or title (in starting over in a new field). Thus, the consulting firms and banks, who are looking to fill Associate Programs or training classes, may find more full-time students interested in starting post-MBA careers with them. PAMELA MITTMAN, STERN (NYU)

➤ Consulting: It's an apprenticeship model, so they like you to start at a set entry level. They hire primarily from the MBA programme, but may consider the EMBA or M.S. Finance programmes. Some people within each firm care more about experience (to distinguish firms with clients); others care more about native talent. There are also a small number of specialist positions for which firms seek more experienced people. *GRAHAM HASTIE, LONDON*

➤ Investment banks: The MBA and Masters in Finance programmes are obvious places for them to look. They look for people with experience in banking to move to more senior levels. There is some willingness to take in lateral hires (from the EMBA and Sloan programmes). But these are individual hires—bespoke hiring on a one-off basis to fill very specific needs. *GRAHAM HASTIE, LONDON*

Appendix I

WHAT TO EXPECT AT BUSINESS SCHOOL

*T*his appendix is designed to give you a feel for what business school will be like in a full-time program. Part-time and executive programs are similar in most regards, with the obvious differences caused by the fact that students are not spending all of their time in the programs. As a result, the first year is not so overwhelming, and students' social lives tend not to revolve around the school.

TYPICAL REQUIRED COURSES

Nearly all schools traditionally require the following courses:

- Financial Accounting
- Managerial Accounting
- Economics
- Finance
- Information Systems

- Marketing
- Operations
- Organizational Behavior
- Quantitative Methods/Statistics
- Strategy/Business Policy

Some schools have changed their core curriculum, however, so you might find that some things have been added to this list, such as leadership or communication skills. The specific courses required at each school will differ, but the listings of those required at Darden, Chicago, and Instituto Empresa, noted earlier, should give you an idea of the range of courses required at different schools. For further information about the content of the most typical core courses, see Chapter 14, "What to Do Once You Are Accepted," which discusses how to prepare for these courses.

TEACHING METHODS

Four types of teaching are widely used in business schools: lecture, the case method, computer simulation, and in-company project. The traditional lecture method, in which students listen and take a great deal of notes but generally participate only infrequently, is still the most common method of teaching. The other traditional method, termed the case method, has been the primary teaching vehicle at Harvard, Darden (University of Virginia), and several other programs for a long time. Computer simulations and in-company projects are relatively recent additions to most schools' teaching. (The last three teaching methods, which may be unfamiliar to you, are discussed below.)

THE CASE METHOD

The case method is quite unlike the teaching used in most undergraduate courses. In its purest form, it involves reading a case—a write-up of a real or hypothetical situation at a company or other organization—and determining what one or another of the participants is best advised to do and why. Complex cases can involve dozens of pages of background reading and dozens of exhibits. The latter may lay out, for example, the cost of components used in a dozen products at each of a dozen different production sites, plus the company's financial results over the last ten years. Students are expected to analyze the case from the perspective of what would be best for the company, for one or more departments, and for one or more individuals, and to determine how best the various options could or should be realized. This involves a great deal of analysis, much of it of a "what-if" variety. ("What if we transferred all model X production to our Ireland plant, shut the Greensboro facility, and exited the Canadian market? Would this make sense? What are the likely production, marketing, organizational, and—ultimately—financial results of this policy?") This method is good for teaching students how to structure the analysis of complex problems; set forth options showing what they plan to do; and sell the chosen option to a group of doubting, difficult peers. The drawback to it is that it is not suited to learning basic, technical disciplines such as accounting, which are more easily learned by reading structured textbooks and doing relevant exercises.

*The following points are generally made **in favor** of the case method:*

➤ It fosters high involvement on the part of students.

➤ The case, and its lessons, are highly memorable—and thus of value when one encounters a related problem in the future.

> ➤ It is realistic in mimicking the real world rather than just theorizing about it.
> ➤ Students have the chance to see what people in different jobs and industries actually do.
> ➤ It compresses many career experiences into a short period of time.
> ➤ The overabundance of material forces students to develop efficient time-management techniques and to learn to choose what analysis to do and what to skip.
> ➤ The nature of the case method requires active class participation, and thus develops presentation skills and the ability to "think on one's feet." It thereby helps build confidence in oneself.
> ➤ It encourages students to think like general managers, examining a problem from an overall, "big picture" perspective.

*The following are among the points made **against** the case method:*

> ➤ It is inefficient for teaching theory that underlies the material.
> ➤ It tends to overlook the human side of management.
> ➤ It encourages ultracompetitive behavior in the fight for class "airtime" (a particularly important problem for the reserved and for those whose English is not truly fluent).
> ➤ The packaged information in the cases obviates the need for students to go out and find or develop their own data.
> ➤ The general management perspective that students tend to adopt for case analyses results in their not being prepared to work at a lower level when they graduate.

A consensus view appears to be that a substantial use of cases, especially to teach advanced marketing, strategy, finance, and organizational development, is highly desirable. For one thing, the drawbacks of the method are minimized in those settings; for another, at least some use of it helps develop the ability to mine cases for the most relevant information, package it quickly, and respond to wide-ranging questions in a coherent and powerful manner. In addition, the advent of multimedia cases has breathed new life into the method. Having interviews with key decision-makers, facility tours, and the like available for viewing enlivens and enriches the case experience.

Computer Simulation

A relatively new teaching method is computer simulation, in which students can run a company or act as head of a department, and get quick feedback about the appropriateness of their decisions from the results of the game. Team competitions, in which students are divided into teams of three to six, are common, especially for the (often required) business strategy course. Teams feed their decisions about a host of variables into the computer at set times. The outcomes of the competition depend not on what has happened in the industry in the past but on what the respective teams have chosen to do. For example, if nearly every team decides to boost volume, cut price, and push for as much market share as possible, the winner might be the team that has decided to focus on a high-price, high-quality (and thus low-volume) niche that it alone will occupy.

In-Company Projects

In-company projects, which have long been used in Europe, are now common in the United States as well. Students get a chance to put into practice their newly acquired skills in a real company. Good projects require that students tackle suitably important issues, not just make-work or trivial problems. The usual problem is not student dissatisfaction with projects, but finding enough companies willing to hand large projects over to students. From the company perspective, such projects require getting students up to speed on their company and industry, and then sharing confidential data with them, as well as soothing the employees who would otherwise have had their own chance to make a mark with the same project. Not surprisingly, most schools suffer from a dearth of ideal projects. The exceptions tend to be the most prestigious schools that are also located close to the headquarters of numerous major companies.

WORKLOAD

Top MBA programs demand a remarkable amount of work. During the first year of a program (or the first two-thirds of a one-year program), the demands are particularly great. There are several reasons for this. The first is that the schools are trying to teach all of the major functional areas of business, plus an understanding of micro- and macroeconomics and numerous skills, such as communications, leadership, and teamwork. This is a large amount to learn in a very short time, so the workload is inevitably high. (The second year—or last one-third of a one-year program—is less intense, both because students have learned how to play the business school "game" and because they are taking elective courses suited to their interests.)

Another important reason for the time pressure is that the workload of a senior executive or an entrepreneur can be grueling. The MBA program is structured to simulate that load, so that students are prepared for it later on. The excessive amount of work forces students to learn how to manage their time, one of the key skills a senior manager must acquire. Thus, a student will almost certainly have to learn to prioritize—to determine which bits of work to do, which to glance at, and which to ignore—as well as how to do all of this efficiently. Furthermore, a student's coverage of material can be greatly enhanced by working with a group of other students, so the excessive demands of the program encourage formation of student study groups. Getting the most out of a study group requires good teamwork skills, something that programs explicitly wish to foster.

So how demanding are these programs? In fact, they are so demanding that it is more appropriate to describe the amount of time a typical student is *not* working rather than the other way around. Unmarried students typically take off one or two evenings per week, enough time each day for a physical activity, plus the occasional hour or two to relax. Married students generally spend a bit more time away from their books, but not a lot. Obviously even an understanding spouse and family are likely to be put out by this sort of schedule.

STUDY GROUPS

Study groups, whether formed to prepare for exams or to do a specific project, are among the staples of business school life. The ideal group consists of students with both professional competence in a wide range of fields and the temperament to work well on teams. Most students find that their own group or groups fall far short of the ideal, so learning how to manage team interaction is of great importance to them.

Groups in some schools are chosen by the students themselves, but it has become more common for the schools to form the groups used in the first half of the program to assure everyone of a place and to make sure students have to confront the usual problems that result from highly diverse membership. For example, how should the lazy or quantitatively underprepared student be treated? Should one person be allowed to dominate discussions? And so on. From the school's perspective, this mirrors the usual problems in working on teams in the real world. Students tend to find group work a valuable experience but extremely frustrating, which bears out the school's view.

CURRICULUM

THE PREPROGRAM

Many programs start with a preprogram, which may last for as little as three days or as long as a month. Some programs are designed only to review subjects such as statistics, economics, algebra, or calculus. These programs are ordinarily optional, with those who have not had prior coursework in these fields being strongly encouraged to take them. Other programs have various team-building, "bonding," and socializing courses and events. The second type are generally mandatory for all incoming students.

THE FIRST YEAR

The first year (or first terms in a one-year program) is likely to be overwhelming unless you have had a very good preparation for it. By very good preparation, I mean that you have already done a bachelor's degree in business, or have worked in the type of environment that in many respects mimics business school, such as a management consulting firm. There is so much work to do, so many new concepts to learn, that you are likely to feel you are drowning. Not only do you have a great deal to learn, but you also have to learn how to learn. As time goes on, however, you will figure out how to cut through the massive amounts of reading and detail to focus on the key aspects, whether of textbooks and articles or of cases. Whereas a full case analysis, for example, might take you eight or ten hours initially, you might manage a similar case in just three hours in the second term. Most students feel that the first term is infinitely more difficult than the second, and the following terms are more or less a breeze.

THE SECOND YEAR

The second-year (or last term of a one-year program) curriculum generally has few if any required courses, allowing students to choose the electives that fit their interests. The second year is inevitably quite relaxed relative to the pressure of the first year, and most of the emotional focus will be on getting the right job rather than surviving your courses.

STUDENT BODY

The student body at most schools looks much as it has for years, albeit with a slightly more international and ethnic flavor. The vast majority of students are male—many schools having seen a decline in the enrollment of women since the late 1980s. A large percentage of students come from engineering, financial services and accounting, management consulting, and marketing. These fields, not surprisingly, are also the biggest employers of MBAs. Despite this, the mix of jobs held by the other third or so of the class—the group that has not come from the standard pre-MBA positions—is quite stunning. It is not unusual to have such classmates as a former navy commander, a Peace Corps volunteer, a fashion photographer, an inventor of a new machine, a television producer, and someone who sailed the Atlantic in a minuscule sailboat.

Much of the learning experience in a high-quality program comes from your fellow students, who can give real-life insights into problems, based upon their recent experiences in similar situations. The range of different jobs, companies, industries, and countries represented by students in the top programs makes for rich classroom discussions and study group sessions.

Whatever their work backgrounds, the different students have several things in common. They are invariably motivated as well as intelligent, and have been highly successful in whatever they have done so far.

These are not just the people you will work with, and compete with, for your time together in business school. You will form lifelong friendships with some of them and may well form a company with some, too. Your business school colleagues represent your future network of contacts, the people who will be your clients and partners and sources of job information when you consider switching companies.

SOCIAL LIFE

Some suspect that the only way MBA students manage to have much of a social life is by sleeping very little. There is a lot of truth in this. The time pressure inherent in demanding programs ensures that only the truly energetic can manage a social or family life in addition to their studies. The bulk of MBA students, however, are energetic enough to live at least a moderately social existence.

Social life differs greatly from one program to the next. At all schools, however, student organizations will be the focus of substantial time and effort. Many of these are preprofessional clubs designed to help students get jobs in their chosen fields. A management consulting club, for example, would help members get jobs in consulting by inviting speakers and recruiters from consulting firms to visit and discuss the field, and their respective firms, with interested members. Larger schools tend to have a magnificent range of such clubs, covering everything from consumer marketing to nonprofit management.

Not all student organizations are an extension of the job search. Many sports and activities clubs can be found on the typical campus. These in particular are likely to be open to spouses and even children. Like their preprofessional analogs, these offer the opportunity to demonstrate leadership and other desirable attributes along with simple energy and love of a given activity.

American two-year programs tend to be better at providing student-run clubs than do the European one-year programs. This is due partly to the American undergraduate ethos, which holds that extracurricular involvement in student activities is part and parcel of an educational experience, and partly to the greater amount of time available in a two-year program. (Some American schools seem to have nearly as many clubs as students, perhaps to give every student the chance to be president of something.)

Not all student social life revolves around clubs. Student parties fortunately are a staple of MBA programs, with the excuse for holding one varying from the need to get away from studying when the pressure is greatest to the need to take advantage of the opportunity when the pressure is lowest. In addition, students find innumerable ways to enjoy informal activities with their fellow students and outsiders, although the more isolated campuses make interaction with non-students rather problematic.

3

HOW TO CHOOSE THE RIGHT SCHOOL FOR *YOU*

— EXECUTIVE SUMMARY —

The first step in choosing a school is to know well what you want from an MBA.
—Consult Appendix II in this chapter to understand the key variables relevant to your choice.

Researching schools is a time-consuming, involved process.

Start with the recommended guidebooks, then investigate specific schools in depth.
—Consult the relevant rankings, but do not regard them as gospel.

Your search will not be complete until you have:
—Visited the most likely choices.
—Checked out these schools with leading firms in your chosen field.

Apply to an appropriate number and range of schools.

*Y*our selection of a school should be driven by two actions: (1) analyzing yourself and your needs well enough to determine what programs will be most appropriate for you, and then (2) getting into the highest quality, best reputed of these programs.

It is essential that you really get to grips with both sides of this equation. Your reasons for getting an MBA will help pinpoint which schools are right for you. If you carefully analyze your own needs, you are likely to opt for the right program. By the same token, if you do only a cursory analysis of the different programs, looking just at their slick websites or brochures, you are likely to choose the wrong program.

KNOW YOURSELF—AND WHAT YOU WANT FROM AN MBA

Your decision to go to business school represents a milestone, and few decisions will equal this one in significance. You want to get it right. The starting point is knowing what you want to accomplish by getting an MBA. Chapter 1, "Why Get an MBA?" discussed some of the more common reasons for getting an MBA. What are yours? Do you want to change from sales to marketing, from nursing to hospital management, from being a research associate at a consulting firm to being a managing partner at the same firm, or from one industry to another?

Your reason for getting an MBA will color your choice of schools. In some cases, your reason will narrow your range of choices to a mere handful. For example, if you intend to move to Spain to be near your wife's family, you may want to attend a Spanish business school to improve your Spanish, learn about the local market, and make good contacts there. If so, you may want to look at IESE, ESADE, or Instituto de Empresa, the three leading Spanish business schools. Attending a comparable quality school, of comparable reputation, elsewhere in the world is unlikely to be as useful to you. If you do attend a leading business school elsewhere, you may want one that will allow you to do an exchange semester at one of these same Spanish schools.

Your relative ability—your strengths and weaknesses where business schools are concerned—will also help you narrow your choices. If you are among the world's top five or ten thousand candidates, you will probably focus your attentions on the top 10 or 20 schools.

AN ITERATIVE PROCESS

The process of choosing schools to apply to is likely to be an iterative one. As you understand better what you are looking for in an MBA program, you will be able to choose programs that better meet your needs. And as you research schools and learn what they have to offer, you may change what you are looking for from an MBA and thus what you will demand in a program.

RESEARCH THE SCHOOLS

STEP 1: DEVELOP GENERAL KNOWLEDGE ABOUT MBA PROGRAMS

Before narrowing your search to a handful of schools, you should become acquainted with what the various MBA programs have to offer.

1. Take a look at Appendix II to this chapter, where several dozen possible criteria for choosing a school are discussed. This will introduce you to the wide range of factors that might be relevant to your choice of schools.

2. Read several of the publications devoted solely to the question of which school to choose. The best of the guides are listed at the end of this chapter, along with a brief description of their contents. They provide good overviews of numerous programs, covering the quantitative (such as the number of students and the most popular concentrations) and the subjective (such as what the programs are most famous for).

3. You should also read the rankings produced by the *Financial Times*, *Business Week*, *U.S. News & World Report*, and other organizations to get a rough approximation of the reputation of the different schools. See Chapter 4 for more information on the different rankings.

STEP 2: START GETTING INFORMATION ABOUT SPECIFIC SCHOOLS

Your initial efforts should have generated a preliminary list of schools that might be appropriate for you. Now you should start to investigate these schools more seriously.

1. Look more carefully at the information contained in the various guidebooks to business schools. Consider which criteria are most important to you. Three criteria should weigh heavily in your thinking at this point. (1) What do you intend your concentration to be? If you intend to study marketing, you may be safe going to any leading school, since they all offer numerous courses in marketing (although some of the leading schools

are more famous for it than are others). If you intend to study health systems management, however, some schools will offer many relevant courses whereas others will offer none. (2) What type of learning environment is best for you? Some people need to get their adrenaline flowing through competition and fear. If so, there are several schools that should be ideal for them. For other people, these schools would be disasters because these people learn best in collegial, supportive environments. If one of these environments would be much better than the other for you, be sure you know which schools fall in which category. (3) Consider what additional criteria are particularly important for you. The most likely criteria include location, size, teaching method and quality, program length, starting date, and cost.

2. Get information from the schools themselves. Have each send you its brochure, which will explain the school's philosophy, what it seeks in applicants, and what makes it noteworthy. (Do not, however, believe all that you read.) Check each school's website, noting what courses are being offered this year. (Brochures often list courses that are not actually offered, so check to make sure that courses you will value actually exist.)

3. Learn when you can meet the schools' representatives. They will travel to MBA forums, which are gatherings held at cities around the world, at which schools set up booths and give out information about their programs. The MBA forums are convenient affairs for meeting representatives from a large number of schools, but they can be too crowded and hectic to provide good opportunities for lengthy questioning of any one representative. Schools also send their representatives around the world to do "dog-and-pony shows" to sell their programs to potential applicants. These information sessions are often less hurried than the MBA forums, thereby providing the opportunity to question representatives at greater length.

STEP 3: FOCUS ON THE MOST INTERESTING SCHOOLS

By the time you have finished the first two steps, you should have a good understanding of which schools are most likely to meet your needs. It is now time to investigate these schools carefully.

1. Talk with each school's alumni to learn more about the schools. Schools are generally glad to give you the names of alumni living near you who have volunteered to discuss the respective programs. Recent alumni, in particular, can be good sources of information about the atmosphere of the school, its academic strengths and weaknesses, the ease with which

they did (or did not) get a job in their chosen field, and the types of students who seemed most pleased by their selection of this school.

2. Talk with a school's competitors to learn what the weak aspects of a school might be. (Take these comments with at least one grain of salt.)

3. Do a search on the Web to find whatever articles have recently been published about each school. These will alert you both to recent school initiatives and problems large enough to have hit the press. For example, the issue of sexual harassment at one major American school was written up in a major business journal while the scandal was still ongoing.

4. Examine the résumé books of schools that interest you. Each school prints a book of résumés of its current students to send to potential employers. (If a school does not post them on its website, or give them out for the asking, you may need to resort to a ruse, such as having a friend in the human resources department of a company request one on your behalf. Note, too, that many school clubs, such as Harvard's Management Consulting club, compile books of their members' résumés.) The résumés of the students will provide you with a very detailed picture of the student body, thus giving you an understanding of the quality and nature of students attracted to the program.

5. Visiting the school is an important part of your research. See Appendix IV to this chapter for a discussion of how to conduct such visits. The importance of such visits can hardly be overstated. Sitting in on a class, for example, is critically important. You should be certain that the classroom atmosphere is one in which you will thrive, and there is no way to be sure of that short of seeing one, or preferably several, in action. The classes of different schools tend to differ substantially, so do not assume that what you see at one school will be duplicated at another.

    You should also talk with a representative group of students. If you attend this school, you will soon be spending all of your waking hours with people just like them, so be sure they are people with whom you would be comfortable. I suggest that you not limit yourself to those students the admissions office arranges for you to meet, because those who volunteer to do this may not be entirely representative of the student body. You can meet plenty of students by just going to the school's cafeteria and joining a group of students who will certainly remember when they were going through the same process, making it quite likely that they will spend whatever time they can with you.

6. Most important, if you know what field you intend to enter, contact the leading firms in it. Be sure to include the firms you would most like to

work for. Ask the human resource people most responsible for hiring at which schools they actively recruit. Have them explain why they choose these schools, their impressions of strengths and weaknesses of the respective programs, what types of people they choose from each (to the extent that this differs by school), and how many individuals they generally hire from each school. Ask them which other schools they would be particularly happy to receive résumés from. (They might not recruit at some schools for logistical reasons and would be glad to hear from students at those schools. Similarly, they might be glad to hear from the best students at certain schools that they feel produce strong graduates but in too small a number to warrant proactive recruiting efforts.)

This is a critical step to finding the right school for yourself, but the one most frequently skipped because it involves a bit of honest effort. By the way, the connection you make with these firms' human resource people should be viewed as an advance networking effort, so treat these folks well and keep in touch with them.

I recommend that you not start your efforts with the human resource professionals because you will be imposing upon their time as it is, and to do so without knowing anything about schools will prove embarrassing. Approach them for such a favor when you have some reasonable idea of what's what in MBA programs and can thus use their time efficiently.

DETERMINE HOW MANY SCHOOLS TO APPLY TO

Some people want to go to a specific school and would not even think about going to one of its rivals. This may or may not be shortsighted, but those who feel this way do not face any problem in determining how many schools they should consider. If you would be content to attend one of a number of schools, you must consider how many applications you should file. This will depend upon several factors:

- Are you determined to go this year? If so, you must apply to enough schools to be sure of getting into at least one of them.

- What are your chances at the schools you favor? If your credentials are better across the board than those of the average student accepted at these schools, you need not do a great number of applications. If your credentials are not superior, however, be prepared to do more applications.

- How many applications can you do without sacrificing the quality of essays, and so on? Conscientious applicants who prepare for the first application by gathering the necessary information about themselves and establishing how to market themselves effectively generally find that the first application takes about the same amount of time and effort as the next five applications altogether. (There is a large "fixed cost" to starting the process, but after that, by the time you are doing a fourth or fifth application, you have already, for example, responded to many of the same essay questions and know a great deal about how to market yourself.)

- How many applications can you afford, given the fees schools charge for applying?

Many serious applicants apply to about six to ten schools. For all but the very strongest candidates (who will apply only to the most demanding programs), it is appropriate to spread your applications across a range of schools. Thus, you can apply to one or two "likely" schools, two or three "possible" schools, and two or three "stretches." *Likelies* are schools to which you are likely to be admitted. These are schools at which admittees have substantially lesser credentials than you possess. For example, your GMAT score is 40–50 points higher than the school's average, your undergraduate grade point average is 0.4 points higher (and was achieved at a particularly strong institution), and your career progression has been much faster—your level of responsibility and title are common only among those two years older than you. *Possibles* are schools where your credentials are about equal to the average for those admitted. *Stretches* are the flip side of "likelies": Your credentials are substantially lower than those of the average person admitted. Your GMAT score might be 40–50 points lower, your grade point average 0.5 points lower, and your career progression somewhat less impressive.

Why separate schools into these three categories and apply to some in each category? If you apply only to schools in one category, you are likely to miss out on an opportunity. If you do not apply to some "stretches," you may not get into the highest quality school possible. If, on the other hand, you do not apply to a "likely" or two, you risk not getting into any school at all.

Given that schools do not just look at quantitative data in determining which applicants to accept, you should try to understand your chances at different schools beyond the raw numbers mentioned above. The easiest way to do this is to examine the résumé books mentioned earlier in this chapter. Looking at the résumés of individual students at a given school, when combined with the quantitative data such as GMAT scores, should make it clear where you stand relative to the typical admittees.

THE ADMISSIONS DIRECTORS* DISCUSS
HOW TO CHOOSE THE RIGHT SCHOOL

➤ If I were giving my daughter advice on how to choose a school, I would suggest that she start by considering what industry she wanted to be in. Then she should talk with as many people in that industry as possible and see which schools they recommend and which they attended. It is also important to look carefully at placement statistics: who recruits these students, which companies hire them, and how many are placed and at what salaries. Visiting the campus and talking with the professors and students should be an integral part of her decision-making process. Other questions that are important for her to have answered are: Is the student body diverse? Will I be comfortable there? Does it represent the real world? And does it have a strong international program? In today's business world, this is imperative. *LINDA MEEHAN, COLUMBIA*

➤ Analyze yourself first. Consider why you want an MBA, what you want to do afterwards, and what you're willing to risk. For example, if you are unwilling to take large risks, you'll lean toward a local program, maybe a part-time one. Are you willing to move? Should you do your MBA in the U.S. or Europe? How much can you afford? Once you've answered these questions, look for schools that fit your needs. *ROSE MARTINELLI, CHICAGO*

➤ I think that the first step is self-assessment. Take the time to truly understand why you have made the choices you have and what you want to do with your future. This upfront investment will allow you to determine your criteria for an MBA program. The second step is to do your own firsthand research. Visit each school, attend classes, and speak to current students and alumni/ae. While business schools may seem the same on the surface, we are quite different in reality. Find the best program for you according to your criteria and then apply. *BRIT DEWEY, HARVARD*

➤ Look beyond the "spin" of the institution. See where people are headed on their way out of the institution, for example. Look carefully at the placement statistics. *PETER JOHNSON, HAAS*

➤ It's important, if not absolutely necessary, that someone knows who and what we are because we are so different from so many of the other schools. We want to be sure people know that they cannot come here and fail to be engaged. *SALLY JAEGER, TUCK*

➤ If someone has professional goals that require an MBA, the only smart thing to do is to apply to multiple schools. I would be concerned if someone were applying only to our program; I'd question how serious they are about getting an MBA. *PETER JOHNSON, HAAS*

➤ Once you're admitted to a number of schools, talk to as many of their students, alums, and so on, as you can. Visit the schools and go to classes. The top schools tend to teach similar materials but in very different ways. Some emphasize the case method; others, textbooks or field research. Small classes are the rule at some; teaching the whole cohort the rule at others. Consider how you want to learn. At some schools, but by no means all, people really enjoy their experience. Look for a school where you fit in comfortably but are challenged intellectually. Remember that you're picking a group of people and a name with which to affiliate yourself for the rest of your life. SHARON HOFFMAN, STANFORD

➤ If you're looking for a broad-range, general, international MBA, then look at the European schools. For the more specialized programs, consider looking Stateside. ALISON OWEN, SAÏD (OXFORD)

➤ Many people, with five or six years of experience, begin contemplating doing an MBA. They may not yet be sure of what they want to do, but they do know what they don't want to do. I suggest they create a detailed mental image of where they see themselves post-MBA. Then, when they start researching schools, they can see how the schools measure up to their individual needs, evaluate how the MBA program meets these needs and how the program can help them to reach their goals. "Fit" and "feel" are very important to the decision. Applicants need to explore a few programs. Visit the school and meet the people. Get a feel for the school. Then contact the school's alumni to see how they leveraged their MBA. The most credible answers are going to come from the alumni. KIRT WOOD, ROTTERDAM

---

*The term "admissions director" is used generically, as a catchall title, to denote those in charge of the admissions process at their respective schools, as most people quoted in this book are, whatever the specific title accorded them.

THE CAREER SERVICES DIRECTORS DISCUSS HOW EASILY INTERNATIONAL STUDENTS CAN REMAIN IN THE UNITED STATES TO WORK, POST-MBA

➤ A lot of firms, particularly in certain industries, are willing to assist with visas and work authorizations, but you need to look carefully to see whether a given firm will do so. Fewer firms will do so, however, when the economy is slow. REGINA RESNICK, COLUMBIA

➤ The likelihood of a foreign student being able to stay on to work in the U.S. after business school depends upon the state of the job market. When it's a students' market and employers have a harder time finding talent, they'll go further and work harder to get someone on board. *ROXANNE HORI, KELLOGG*

➤ That depends on a number of factors. First of all, it depends on the interest level and enthusiasm of the student regarding where they want to work. The passion to work in a particular place for a particular division will shine through in an interview and affect the results. The overall economy and the job market also need to be taken into account. This year, over two-thirds of our international students secured job opportunities in the U.S.—but I emphasize that this varies from year to year. The majority of those students chose to go into investment banking or consulting. The largest investment banks and consulting firms are able and willing to provide support for U.S. work authorizations. *PAMELA MITTMAN, STERN (NYU)*

➤ It's not necessarily easy to get a job outside your home country even if you do a degree where you'd like to work, given the possible visa and work authorization issues you'll face. Understand these constraints before you apply and enroll. Plan to work hard in your job search to make it happen. *ANDY CHAN, STANFORD*

➤ Our international students are as successful as our U.S. students in getting work in the U.S. (and 95 percent of our placement is in the U.S.). It's not easy: it's more work for an international student to get work in the U.S. than it is for a domestic student, but I'm confident that international students can get a job here if they work hard at the search. *EVERETTE FORTNER, DARDEN*

AVOID THE LIKELY PITFALLS IN CHOOSING A SCHOOL

Some warnings to keep in mind as you go through the search process:

• Start the process early, because you need to gather a lot of information, and you should give yourself time to reflect on what you learn at each step.

• Do not take the rankings too seriously. They are no better than rough proxies for a school's quality and reputation. (See Chapter 4 for more on the limitations of business school rankings.) They obviously do not take into account your specific set of key criteria. Look for high-quality programs that will satisfy your needs.

• Be wary of schools with learning environments that are not hospitable to *you*. Do not put yourself through months of hell and the disappointment of performing poorly due to a bad match between you and the learning environment of a school. For example, if you are a reserved person, the free-for-all quality of a case method program may not be appropriate.

- Be aware that your interests may change as you go through the search process, because you can alter what you want to do and better understand what would help you. As a result, your criteria for schools should change to reflect your changed interests.

- Do not be swayed by spiffy school brochures. The quality of a school is not directly related to the quality of the pictures in its brochure.

- Do not be swayed by warm (or cold, or inefficient) admissions people. They are not the ones who will be teaching you or helping you to get a job upon graduation.

- Pay attention to the quality of the career services department, because your job fate can be dramatically improved by a top-notch department.

- Remember: Eliminate schools that do not offer the curriculum you need. Eliminate those with inappropriate learning atmospheres. Eliminate those with other important negatives for you. Include the highest quality schools you believe you can get into (and, yes, pay attention to consensus views of the rankings).

- Ultimately, any of dozens of schools can give you a great learning experience and help your career prospects dramatically, but it is up to you to take advantage of the opportunities afforded you. (For more, see Chapter 15.)

FINAL DECISION CRITERIA

The most important criteria for each applicant will, of course, differ substantially. Some applicants will be greatly cost-constrained, leading them to choose schools that have lower tuition or offer financial aid. Others will choose schools only in a given area. Others will look for the best quantitative finance school they can get into.

No matter which criteria are relevant to you, it would be highly appropriate to determine which schools will give you the courses you most want, in an atmosphere in which you think you could thrive (collegial vs. competitive, lecture vs. case method, faculty open door vs. isolated, etc.), and in a location that is appropriate to your current circumstances and future goals. Having taken account of these and the other criteria you regard as most important for you, the final choice among those schools that meet these criteria should probably come down to the school's reputation. If you were a financial economist considering Chicago and

Simon, for example, it would be peculiar to choose Simon if you were admitted to both. Although Simon is very well regarded, it is not a contender for the mantle of best business school in the world, as is Chicago. Reputation is not everything, but among schools that do not differ dramatically in their ability to deliver what you are looking for, reputation should ordinarily be the critical factor.

Recommended Readings

Note that you can find an up-to-date listing of appropriate guidebooks on my website, www.degreeofdifference.com, as well as further comments about the respective strengths and weaknesses (including length and price) of these and other books.

➤ George Bickerstaffe, *Which MBA?* (The Economist Intelligence Unit, Pearson Education). A particularly sensible view of full-time, part-time, and executive MBA programs at over one hundred schools across the world. Also provides detailed rankings of the schools. (In the spirit of declaring interests, note that I wrote the book's brief summary regarding how best to market yourself to schools.)

➤ Betsy Gruber and Elizabeth Garone, *Business Week's Guide to the Best Business Schools* (McGraw-Hill). Generally read for its well-known rankings of America's top schools (and a handful of non-American programs), but more valuable for its in-depth discussions of the schools themselves.

➤ Ronald Alsop, ed., *The Wall Street Journal Guide to the Top Business Schools* (Simon & Schuster). Gives a helpful overview of one hundred schools worldwide, including specialties and rankings of academic concentrations, substantial recruitment data, and comments by recruiters. (And once again I have an interest to declare: the *Online Journal* uses an abbreviated version of my comments about "preparing for business school," a fuller version of which is available in this book in Chapter 14.)

Recommended Websites

There are a substantial number of websites devoted to education, but the two most useful for our purposes are www.businessweek.com (for American business schools) and www.financialtimes.co.uk (for non-American business schools).

Chat Rooms

Many applicants follow the discussion of specific business schools or hot admissions topics all day, every day, in one or another chat room. It is hard to think of a sillier way to waste time. Beware that a large percentage of the comments are misleading or represent a sharing of misinformation (and panic).

Appendix II

CRITERIA FOR ASSESSING MBA PROGRAMS

Few people will consider all of the following criteria to be important, but they are listed here to spur your thinking about what you would most like in a program. The most important criteria will depend upon your specific needs, but on average they include course offerings, school reputation, location, academic atmosphere, school size, facilities, and teaching quality. The two items that applicants tend not to weight heavily enough are the learning atmosphere, for reasons discussed in the body of the chapter, and the quality of the career services function, because schools of equal quality and reputation tend to have very different rates of success in placing their graduates in desirable companies and positions.

GENERAL CRITERIA

REPUTATION. Is the school considered one of the best schools in the world, especially in your particular specialization? Is it particularly well known and respected where you would most like to work? As Chapter 4 discusses in detail, the various school rankings should not be considered definitive. Pay at least as much attention to the opinions of those in charge of hiring at companies of the type you wish to work for.

SIZE. Smaller schools often engender a friendly, family atmosphere. Large schools, on the other hand, are able to provide large numbers of both elective course options and skilled professors. (Smaller schools tend to be better rated by students; larger schools by employers.)

LOCATION. The appropriate location for you is likely to depend upon a host of factors, including, of course, personal preference. If you prefer a small town to a global city, you will lean toward Hanover, New Hampshire, rather than New York City; Cambridge rather than London. If you intend to work part-time during the latter part of your program, however, you might prefer large cities to small, given the greater employment opportunities.

The school's location will also have a major impact upon your spouse's (or significant other's) employment options. A corporate strategy consultant will have a relatively easy time finding appropriate employment in a major city but not in a small town. Similarly, your spouse's educational options are likely to be greatest in a city with numerous major universities rather than in a one-university town. By the same token, your children might have a tougher time socially and educationally in a large city than in a small town, or vice versa.

The location of a school helps determine its social environment. Schools in large cities tend not to foster the degree of social bonding among classmates that schools located in small towns do, largely due to the lack of other entertainment options in small towns.

The question of whether to go abroad is often a matter of whether you intend to work in the country where the school is located. Other compelling reasons to attend business school abroad include wanting to work for a target company based in the other country; wanting to improve a foreign language; wanting to experience another culture in order to be ready to work in international business; or wanting to attend a better quality school than is possible at home.

One additional locational factor to consider: How important is it to be close enough to your home to allow easy visits?

QUALITY OF LIFE.   Student lifestyles may vary a great deal, of course, depending upon both the program and the student. A program in New York City may influence a student's life less than one in the country. At a school like Duke, in a small city, most student socializing is done with other students, both because the students tend to get on well with one another and because Raleigh-Durham offers limited enticement to pull students away from the business school.

Note that some schools treat spouses and families much better than do other schools. Some allow spouses to sit in on courses as a routine matter, whereas others have never heard of the idea. Again, some but not all schools include families in the school's social life and go to great lengths to help them find child care and jobs, whether in the business school (or university) or in the surrounding area.

Be sure that your favorite activities (including those typically organized as a business school society or club) are available, whether at the school itself or nearby.

SAFETY.   Related to the location issue is the question of safety. Be sure that the school environment is, and feels, safe. In assessing safety, make sure you see the school and its environs (wherever students spend time), and do not assume that what appears safe at noon will also be safe at midnight. Discuss the matter with school officials, of course, but do not take their comments on faith. Be sure to discuss your concerns with students physically like you. (Your notion of a safe environment will not necessarily be the same as that held by a 250-pound world karate champion or a tiny, fragile arthritis sufferer.)

FACILITIES.   Check to be sure the school has top-quality research facilities, including a traditional library and extensive online services. In particular, note whether the library and study rooms are comfortable for extended work efforts. Check, too, for facilities of unique importance to you, such as a simulated trading floor.

HOUSING.   Housing can be a major concern, especially in your first year. Look at the school's student housing (dormitory or apartment). Examine the price and availability of off-campus housing. Note also what transportation options you will have (and their safety implications).

MISSION.   Some schools view their job as training general managers. Other schools look to train functional specialists. All want to train people who intend to get to the top of their chosen fields. Related to this, some schools require that students specialize in a field of their choice, meaning that they must take at least a set number of courses in that field. Others permit a free choice of electives. These differences can have a major effect upon your fit with a program and the students who have chosen to attend it.

PROGRAM

TERM LENGTH.   Long semesters lift the pressure of constant examinations and papers, but shorter terms make it possible to sample a wider variety of courses.

PROGRAM LENGTH.   A shorter program is generally more appropriate for those well advanced in their careers, especially those who do not wish to change fields. Longer programs are more appropriate for those with lesser business backgrounds or a desire to switch fields.

COURSES IN OTHER BRANCHES OF THE UNIVERSITY.   Those studying many different areas of business can benefit from taking courses in other parts of the university. Thus, someone intending an investment banking career in corporate finance or mergers and acquisitions might profit from courses in securities regulation offered by the law school. Many business schools severely limit the number of courses that may be taken for credit in other parts of the university. Chicago is a notable exception, allowing students to take up to six courses in other university departments. Some European business schools, of course, are stand-alone schools unaffiliated with a university; thus, they offer no opportunity to take courses in other parts of a university.

JOINT DEGREES.   The number and variety of joint-degree programs on offer at some schools is very impressive. For example, various schools offer the chance to do a master's or doctoral degree in a related subject of interest, such as economics, engineering, international relations, law, medicine, urban planning, and so on. (This is likely to be possible only if the school is part of a university.) The leading American business schools have long offered this possibility, but it is rare in Europe apart from the British universities.

The most popular option in the United States remains the JD-MBA. Joint law and master's degree programs generally require four years of study, thereby decreasing the amount of time that would be required to do each degree independently by one year. (An exception to this is Northwestern's JD-MBA program, which can be completed in three calendar years rather than four.) Most schools require you to apply to and be admitted by each program separately.

The reputation of the "other" degree program may be more important than the reputation of the MBA program, depending upon your future career path. For instance, if you are pursuing a JD-MBA and intend to work in a corporate law firm, the reputation of the law school will be paramount; if you intend to work for an investment bank, however, the reputation of the business school will weigh more heavily. Note that although many top business schools are ranked at approximately the same level as their affiliated law schools, there are some prominent exceptions. Yale's MBA program is ranked lower than its powerhouse law program (the same is true for NYU), whereas Northwestern (Kellogg) and the University of Pennsylvania (Wharton) have higher-ranked MBA programs.

INTERNATIONALIZATION.   It is not easy to gauge a program's degree of internationalization. Consider the extent to which cases and courses focus on international management issues, whether the students and professors come from a variety of different countries, the ease with which one can do projects and exchanges abroad (see below), and the degree of emphasis placed upon language learning. Or, rather than assessing these input factors, you could look at factors that actually measure the programs' outputs—the percentage of graduates who take jobs abroad or jobs that include a large international component.

EXCHANGE PROGRAMS. Those interested in an international dimension to their studies might benefit from a term at another top school, one that offers the opportunity to study in another language and (business) culture or pursue a specialized topic in greater depth. Consider the number and quality of exchanges on offer at a given school (and how many students actually participate), but also make sure your particular interests are catered to. Note that some schools, such as London Business School and Anderson (UCLA), have exchanges established with dozens of foreign programs, whereas Harvard and Cambridge have none.

VISITING EXECUTIVES. Schools should bring CEOs and other senior executives to campus as executives in residence and guest speakers. The quality and location of the school will tend to determine the number and nature of such visitors.

CURRICULUM

PREPROGRAM. If you need help in algebra, calculus, statistics, computer usage, or languages, try to prepare yourself as best you can before the program begins. Note, however, that schools now offer preprograms that range from a few days' social introductions to a month's instruction in core (especially quantitative) subjects.

CORE COURSES. Some schools allow you to opt out of or substitute advanced courses for any core courses about which you are already knowledgeable. Two problems can result from this. One is that this is a detriment to less-well-prepared students, who have to do without the benefit of your contributions in these courses, and vice versa when you are the neophyte and others are the experts. Another is that the program will have less of a community feel. In fact, some schools do not permit waivers of introductory courses in order to keep a cohort or group together. Case method schools in particular feel that much of the teaching comes from students who are knowledgeable about the specific subject matter, so the school must keep those who are already expert in a subject in these classes to teach the novices. Whether this is a key issue for you will depend upon your background. Undergraduate business majors with work experience in a management consulting firm, for example, may prefer programs that allow them to substitute advanced courses for the basic courses in the core program.

"TOUCHY-FEELY" COURSES. Check that the program offers courses that capture the non-mathematical elements of management in as rigorous and productive a fashion as possible. Note that graduates ten years out of business school almost invariably describe courses in negotiation, communication, team-work, leadership, interpersonal skills, and other soft skill areas as being of great and continuing importance to them.

INTEGRATION. In the past, most schools taught courses that were neatly divided into functional areas. Thus, a marketing course resolutely stuck to marketing topics without, for example, considering the impact of marketing decisions upon manufacturing operations. It is now generally recognized that such compartmentalization is not only artificial but also harmful to students who fail to integrate their knowledge of different functions. Although schools recognize the nature of the problem, not all of them have succeeded in devel-oping truly integrated programs.

ELECTIVES. Make sure the school offers sufficient electives in your cho-sen field. Note, too, whether the course offerings reflect recent developments in the field. Be sure courses listed in the catalogue or on the website are given annually. Some schools list all the courses they have given at some point in re-cent years, or hope to give, rather than those that will indeed be offered. Be sure, too, that more than one professor provides them, so that your education will not be savaged by one professor choosing to take a sabbatical during your second year.

Note that some schools have definite specialties (and reputations to match). For example, Chicago, London, and Stern (NYU) are famous for finance; Carnegie Mellon, Cranfield, and Sloan (MIT) for supply-chain management. Some schools offer few electives; others offer many.

NONBUSINESS COURSES. Consider to what extent a school will allow you to take (for credit) courses offered in other departments of the university. Note that many American schools do not give credit for language courses—hardly appropriate for those that claim to be educating global managers. Among the honorable exceptions are Columbia and Texas.

PROJECTS. Numerous courses will offer the chance to perform consult-ing projects for credit with local companies. The teams will include executives of the company as well as other students, thereby giving you a chance to put your learning into practice while making valuable contacts. These projects also serve as helpful integrating devices, both for showing how different functions relate and for demonstrating the value of soft skills. These projects tend to be more readily available in schools situated in a region that is home to many companies; schools in splendid rural isolation tend to find it difficult to place students in good consulting projects due to the lack of local firms.

PEDAGOGICAL ISSUES

TEACHING METHODS. Teachers can use lectures, the case method, computer games/simulations, or company projects in a course. Some courses lend themselves to one method rather than another. Thus, many schools use a variety of methods, depending upon course focus and professorial preference. Many professors mix teaching methods, including lectures and cases or projects, for example, in a single course.

The case method, however, remains the single most important and most common teaching method in top business schools. It is arguably not at its best for introductory economics, statistics, and accounting classes. By the same token, a consensus view appears to be that at least some use of cases—especially in advanced marketing, strategy, organizational development, and finance classes—is highly desirable. The drawbacks of the method are minimized in those settings, whereas at least some use of it helps develop the ability to mine cases for the most relevant information, package it quickly, and respond to wide-ranging questions in a coherent and powerful manner.

Schools noted for their extensive (or exclusive) use of the case method include Harvard, Darden, Kenan-Flagler (North Carolina), Ivey (Western Ontario), ESADE (Barcelona), Instituto de Empresa (Madrid), and IESE (Barcelona).

TEACHING QUALITY. Even apart from the question of what would be the best method for teaching a given subject, quality is remarkably uneven and hard to assess (especially from a distance). It varies mightily from school to school and professor to professor, yet few students take enough courses at multiple business schools to be able to render a judgment about the relative merits of the schools' teaching. As a result, the best way to gauge a school's teaching is by examining the ways in which it promotes good teaching. Kellogg, for example, which is noted for good teaching, has a number of procedures in place to facilitate good teaching: "Professors are held to high standards in the classroom. Each new faculty member attends an orientation, is assigned a mentor, and is invited to a session on teaching techniques especially designed for Kellogg. New faculty do not teach in their first quarter, so that they may observe more senior colleagues and become familiar with the Kellogg environment. Every class is evaluated by students, and the evaluations are posted publicly. Tenure and promotion decisions are partially based on teaching quality." Note that student course evaluations, which are produced at perhaps half of the top schools, offer a chance to judge the teaching in departments of greatest interest to you (even if such guides do not allow you to judge the school's overall teaching quality). Such guides are typically available only if you visit the campus or have a friend in the student body send you one; few schools are willing to send them out to applicants.

WORKLOAD. All of the good schools require substantial work, but there is still a large disparity between the load at the least and most demanding schools. This is partly a function of the degree of competition at the school rather than the actual demands of professors. To this extent, your workload is under your control; you do not have to work one-hundred-hour weeks simply because most people around you are doing so. Still, the more easygoing the academic atmosphere, the less hard you will need to work for a given rank-in-class or the possibility of impressing the most demanding of prospective employers. (Be careful in asking about this, by the way, because doing so may mark you as someone insufficiently determined. Rely in part on the various guidebooks for this information, and pay close attention at school information sessions when someone else is silly enough to inquire about it. When visiting a school, ask students how hard most people work, but do not take their replies at face value because students love to complain about how hard they need to work.) Note that case method schools tend to involve heavy workloads, although students also tend to enjoy their work.

MATHEMATICAL SOPHISTICATION. Some schools require substantial mathematical sophistication of incoming students, whereas others require little more than a passing familiarity with differentiation and regression. Be aware of the level of quantitative knowledge required—for the school generally and your proposed course of study particularly—and assess your own skills carefully. Do not, for instance, blithely assume that you will easily recall math you have not studied for a decade.

There are obvious advantages to attending a school that uses advanced math in any course that can be taught better and faster with it. For the mathematically desperate, however—the so-called "poets"—these advantages will not be readily available.

CLASS SIZE. Smaller classes offer students the benefit of substantial interaction with, and attention from, the professor as well as a chance to participate relatively frequently. On the other hand, with more students you find a greater likelihood of students with relevant current experience commenting on matters. Small classes offer no chance to be anonymous and to hide, whereas larger classes—especially in courses using the case method—force students to compete for airtime. On balance, however, most students prefer small to medium-sized classes.

In addition, it is valuable to have available seminars in your field, not just for the in-class attention you can get from professors but also for the opportunity to get to know professors in your field out of class.

PROFESSORS. The ideal professors would combine three related features. They would be dedicated to teaching, and would always be available in their offices for conversation and assistance. They would also be world-famous consultants who spend a great deal of time with companies spread across the world, thereby increasing their knowledge and making contacts that might be useful when it comes time to help you find a job. Ideal professors are, moreover, people who devote substantial energy to research and publishing, to increase their fame and that of the school.

Although it is impossible to square the circle and have professors both be readily available and be international consultants and prolific authors, a school can foster an open-door policy that encourages professors to be on campus and readily available to students for at least some portion of each week. Students routinely prefer teachers who teach well over those who do high-quality research at the expense of quality teaching. At a minimum it is possible to say that teachers who only teach in the executive program, whose courses are so oversubscribed that you will be unable to enroll in their classes, or who are on sabbatical while you are attending the school, are likely to have little impact on your learning. The greatest danger exists for someone who chooses a school because one or two famous professors are there. The student may be unable to get a class with either of them, or may change his intended field of concentration and thus choose other professors for study after all.

It is important that a school have full-time professors in your field, not just adjunct professors or lecturers whose full-time occupation is actually practicing in the field. Such adjunct faculty can provide a wonderful view of current issues and practice, but they are less likely to remain at a school for an extended period (thereby risking leaving you high and dry) and may not be available on campus for out-of-class discussions.

LANGUAGE OF INSTRUCTION. A number of European programs offer the opportunity to do either a bilingual or an English-only program. Some start students in one language and require them to learn a second language during the program and to take business courses in that language during the second half of the program.

STUDENTS

STUDENT BODY. The composition of the student body will have a major impact upon your learning experience, your enjoyment of the program, and even your ability to get desirable jobs in the future. The large amount of teamwork embodied in most programs guarantees that much of your time will be spent discussing classroom issues with other students. The other students should be experienced enough that you can learn a great deal from them. On the other hand, they should not be so skilled, relative to your own level, that you will be unable to compete with them. One thing that they definitely should be is friendly and willing to share—both their time and their knowledge.

You risk being isolated and miserable if you do not fit in with the typical students at a school. Make sure you have spent some time with current students or those who have recently graduated to make sure you will feel comfortable at a school.

You can determine a lot about the nature of a school by looking at the makeup of its student body. The University of Texas, for example, has a strong technology management program and thus has many engineers and others with technology backgrounds in its student body. However, nearly one-third of its student body have liberal arts degrees. This is in contrast to Carnegie Mellon's Tepper School, at which only approximately 15–20 percent of the student body comes from a liberal arts background. If you have a liberal arts background, Texas might be a better bet if you are worried about being able to handle the curriculum successfully. Schools want students who will fit in, and you should probably choose schools on that basis as well.

Other aspects of the student body that might be of keen interest are the types of jobs people have held before business school, the age range, the percentage of women students, the percentage of minority students, and the percentage of international students. In general, the more diverse the student body, the more you will be able to learn.

It is, of course, one thing to have a number of students who are like you in some aspect you regard as critical. It is another to see how such people are treated. If you are foreign, for example, you should check to see whether foreigners are well integrated into campus life rather than being a distinct subgroup that mixes little with others.

COMPETITION.   Although most students would prefer an atmosphere that emphasizes cooperation more than competition, that is not true for everyone. Some people are inspired to work harder and perform better in a competitive environment. In assessing schools, note that six factors tend to determine the degree of competitiveness among students. Large schools, and those that have a high percentage of case method courses, are prone to a high degree of competition. On the other hand, the more work that is done in teams (and graded on a team basis), the less competitive the atmosphere is likely to be. If students' grades and class rank are displayed to the class and to potential employers, the atmosphere is likely to be more competitive. The use of a mandated grading curve inspires competition, since an improvement in one student's grade means another's must suffer. Last, the number of students who are flunked out of the school has a large impact. Many, but by no means all, schools try to retain every student they enroll, thereby easing student fears.

STUDENT-FACULTY RELATIONS. The student-faculty ratio, at the extremes, can have an influence upon the relations between the two groups. Thus, at a school with a 20:1 ratio, getting to know professors may be more difficult than at one with a 7:1 ratio. But this simple ratio is likely to conceal as much as it reveals. The relative numbers of students and professors tend to have less impact upon relations between the two groups than do other factors. Most important is the attitude professors have toward students. Some schools have a traditional closeness between students and faculty; faculty routinely invite students for coffee or drinks, join them for lunches, and so on. At other schools, professors do little more than hold periodic office hours. One determinant of the tradition is the school's geographic situation. Schools that are isolated tend to have closer faculty-student relations than those in the midst of major cities. Another determining factor is the size of the business school. Smaller schools tend to have closer relations than large schools.

JOBS

JOBS. The more highly employers regard a school's graduates, the more job offers will flow. Specific offers depend upon more, however, than just a school's general reputation. Some schools are much more successful placing graduates in one field rather than another. Consider Columbia and INSEAD, for instance. In one recent year, Columbia placed 50 percent of its graduates in finance and 20 percent in consulting, whereas INSEAD placed 24 percent of its graduates in finance and 38 percent in consulting.

Check whether people get jobs that you would like to have. In addition, check what credentials they had. In general, distinguish between the job prospects of those at the top of the class and those at the middle and the bottom. The top graduates of the elite schools can be expected to get highly desirable jobs. The differences among schools become more marked as you work your way down their class rankings. Those at the bottom of the class at Stanford or Harvard, for instance, tend to do quite well, getting jobs at well-known firms. At less highly regarded schools, this is by no means necessarily the case.

To assess whether a school's degree "travels" to whatever area is of interest to you, consider both where recruiters come from and where graduates end up working. Similarly, to assess the school's overall success in placing graduates, consider not just which jobs graduates take but also the nature and number of recruiters pursuing graduates (and summer hires). Precise calculations, such as the number of recruiters per student, should not be taken as definitive, just suggestive of the school's success.

CAREER SERVICES. A good career services department will provide in-depth assistance to you at each stage of the career assessment and job search process. The stages include assessing your skills and interests; determining precisely which field, then which type of employer, you should consider pursuing; mastering résumé and cover-letter writing, interviewing, and "call-back" interviewing processes (including those specific to your chosen field, such as investment banking); sorting through job offers and negotiating the best deal; and learning how to succeed in the first months (or years) on the job.

Good departments offer presentations—and extensive one-on-one assistance—regarding each step of the process. They also offer "brown bag" lunches, for instance, where you can hear from graduates about work in large consulting firms versus small firms, job opportunities in a given field or city, and so on. They should intervene early to help those who intend to make dramatic career changes. They should have a database of alumni that can be easily searched by location, graduating class, function or specialty, nature of employer, and so on. (Alumni, as discussed on page 69, are potentially highly valuable in your career assessment and search as well as your career success later on.) These services should be available to alums, too, because you may need them more when you are out of business school than when you are in.

To assess a career services department, compare the programs it offers for each of the aspects mentioned above. Note what is available only on a group basis and what is available one-on-one with career service professionals. Good departments will have specialists devoted to each major employment sector, such as strategy consulting, investment banking, and so on. The department's assistance should not be limited just to the traditional employers of MBAs, however, or to the most popular or closest cities. Thus, a truly international school will have international career services officers. Discuss both the effectiveness of the various programs and the availability and professionalism of the staff with a variety of students. Although the number of professionals working in a career services department is no more than a very rough approximation for the value of the service, it can still be helpful to know how many there are at a given school (adjusted for the number of students).

THE CAREER SERVICES DIRECTORS DISCUSS
HOW TO EVALUATE A CAREERS SERVICE

➤ Look at four things. (1) Understand the strength of the on-campus recruiting program and how it fits with the things you want to do. If it's not a good fit, consider what other resources are available to help you meet your goals. (2) Look at the career management program and determine what is available to you—and how individualized it will be. (3) Understand also the background of the people in the department. It's best if there's a mixture of business and counseling experience. (4) You'll also want to learn what employers think of the operation; this shows how the school manages relations with employers, which is an important element of the career management process. *Glenn Sykes, Chicago*

➤ A growing number of people in career management come from the outside—from positions of real business experience rather than human resources experience. The veteran brand manager is better able to give students a real sense of what a brand management position entails than an H.R. person can. Similarly, the ex-brand manager is better able to speak the language and understands the inner workings of the specific functions inside the hiring companies, and can better match their needs as a result. *Peter J. Degnan, Wharton*

➤ There are a couple of broad areas you should look at. *First* is the resources they put at your fingertips: online services, the library, the consultants, the alumni—and in particular how you are permitted to access alumni. *Second* is to try to understand the career preparation program they have. There are two broad areas that distinguish schools. One is the career assessment side. You want to find a school that will really help you dig into what you're passionate about and what you have the skills for. If you're changing your career, which 80 percent of full-time MBA students are doing, you want an assessment part that will really help you understand the variety of options you have and how you might best fit in terms of those options. The second side is career preparation. Consider whether it is required and whether it is part of the curriculum. How in-depth is it? Is it done by professional staff members, by alumni, by students, or by a combination? A *third* area, which is somewhat less important, is a broad look at the companies associated with the school. You want to look beyond the companies that come there to recruit because that no longer reflects how and where students get jobs. A better list would be that of companies that hired (or interviewed) students last year. *Everette Fortner, Darden*

➤ Most schools have designed their career center to match the needs and expectations of the students (and recruiters) who have, historically, come to that school. One way to gauge this is to look at the kinds of jobs students get at a given school and ask whether those are the kinds of companies and jobs that interest you. If so, then you need to understand the process by which students go about getting these jobs. Given whatever that process is, will you be comfortable with that and will you be able to take advantage of both that process and the resources available to achieve your goals? *ANDY CHAN, STANFORD*

➤ A good careers office will have people knowledgeable about different job functions and industries. In addition, it is essential that counselors be readily available on an individual basis. *ROXANNE HORI, KELLOGG*

➤ Look for a mix of professional backgrounds among the personnel, including both psychology and counseling on the one hand, and corporate and professional on the other. Look, also, for an in-depth knowledge of a range of different professions and industries. Make sure that you'll be given access to the companies that matter to you. *REGINA RESNICK, COLUMBIA*

Key Elements of Career Services

➤ We've instituted a number of new approaches in recent years. We now have a structured career development program for students. This is a two-year curriculum that begins even before classes with an assessment process and continues throughout the academic year with workshops and informational panels about various industries and functions, networking techniques, résumé review, informational and mock interviewing, and so on. We've also balanced our staff. Our team includes both career counselors, who have years of MBA coaching experience, as well as people from industry, who understand the corporate perspective and have had experience in specific industries of interest to students. Finally, we provide lifelong career-service support through our Career Center for Working Professionals. *PAMELA MITTMAN, STERN (NYU)*

➤ At Stanford, about one-third of the students actually get their jobs through traditional, on-campus recruiting. (More will get offers through on-campus recruiting, but only about one-third accept one.) That may sound like a low number, given that at some schools the number will range from 50 to 70 percent. But the reason is that the jobs Stanford students have decided are of interest are at the sort of companies that do not typically come to campus. So we've designed our career center to get to know each student and provide each one with specific resources to help them network with both alumni and recruiters on their own time and be able to go out and market themselves effectively. We have over one hundred workshops during the year designed to help them get those jobs. And ultimately they go out and get very unique jobs. At some other top-tier business schools, on the other hand, 60 or 70 percent of the students get jobs in consulting or investment banking, so the way that office has set up their career center matches the way those students get their jobs (i.e., via on-campus recruiting). *ANDY CHAN, STANFORD*

➤ We spend more time now than we used to on the independent search process. The mass-recruiting process—hiring students on-campus in November for jobs that begin in July—is fading, given the difficulty of forecasting needs that much in advance. *CHRIS BRISTOW, LONDON*

ALUMNI. Alumni can be useful in providing pointers to jobs, or indeed to jobs themselves. They can also mentor students while the latter are still in school, offering advice and contacts that can help establish them in their careers. In addition, alumni affect the ranking of the school by virtue of their comments about it, their degree of career success, and the amount of money they raise for the school. It is easy for you to determine the number of alums—the bigger and older the school, the more alums it has. To determine their dedication to the school, look at the amount of money they raise, the percentage of alums who donate, their willingness to come back to the school to sit on panels offering advice to current students, and so on.

LOCAL CONNECTIONS. Schools tend to do very well in placing their graduates in nearby firms. If you are sure of where you want to live and work, consider the extent to which a local school's connections may balance the appeal of a slightly more prestigious but distant rival. For example, the University of Southern California (located in Los Angeles) has a network of graduates in Southern California not easily matched by even the most prestigious of its rivals.

PRICE

For how to factor the cost of business school into your decision-making, see Chapter 16, "Financing Your MBA."

Appendix III

CHOOSING A PART-TIME OR AN EXECUTIVE MBA PROGRAM

*C*hoosing a part-time or executive MBA program is necessarily somewhat different from choosing a full-time program. Your choice of program will probably be limited to those within your immediate area, or within an easy airplane commute—for those with the means or the understanding employer. Therefore, some of the criteria used for determining the most appropriate full-time program, such as available housing, will no longer be relevant because you will probably not be moving. Some of the other criteria may be less important than would the case be if you were to attend a full-time program. The career services office may be unimportant for you if you intend to remain with the same employer after you complete your degree.

Other criteria are likely to be more important. A program's schedule may not fit within your own, thereby eliminating it as a possibility. For example, an executive program that requires your attendance for several weeks in the summer right when you will need to attend your industry's most important trade fair in a distant city may make it impossible to attend that particular program.

In spite of these differences, choosing a part-time or executive program still closely resembles the selection process for a full-time program. The courses must be of value to you, with an academic atmosphere suited to your desires. When you are choosing between several schools that offer what you want, reputation is still likely to be the most important criterion.

The differences between part-time and full-time programs are much less substantial than the differences between EMBA and full-time programs. Accordingly, the following discussion focuses on choosing an EMBA program.

CHOOSING AN EMBA PROGRAM

The proliferation of EMBA programs, and the substantial differences between them, means that you have a real choice to make. EMBA programs differ on a number of key dimensions:

PROGRAM

Schools' *missions* differ dramatically. Some aim to duplicate the full-time programs' teaching of fundamental skills (before building on them to teach more advanced skills). Others assume that they should teach very different material to their 40-year-old managers than they would to 27-year-olds. The emphasis in the former tends to be on academic rigor; in the latter, on thematic understanding. Thus, if you believe you would benefit from learning how to perform accounting, statistical, or financial calculations, the former type of program would best suit you. (Those looking to change careers are also likely to be best served by such a program.) Those with mastery of their function looking to transition to general management might prefer the latter, with more emphasis on senior management responsibilities.

Some programs rely heavily on adjunct *faculty* rather than using the same faculty that teaches their full-time programs. This is not as common as it used to be, however, which has helped dispel the notion that EMBA programs are less rigorous than other means of earning an MBA. (Similarly, many schools now offer the same degree—an MBA rather than an "Executive MBA" or "MBA for Executives"—for both full-time and executive programs, thereby equating the two degrees in another fashion.)

EMBA programs also vary greatly in terms of the number of *contact hours* (time in a classroom, with professor and other students present) involved. At Fuqua (Duke), for instance, one program features 85 percent of its teaching in a face-to-face setting; another program features 25 percent face-to-face teaching, with the balance delivered via the Internet.

Some programs, especially those aimed at more experienced managers, offer the chance to take few if any *electives*. Other programs allow up to 40 or 50 percent of courses to be chosen by the students. Similarly, some programs are generalist by nature, whereas others focus on a particular field (such as Stern's finance-oriented program) or allow students to concentrate on a given field via their choice of electives.

One of the biggest drawbacks of EMBA programs used to be their lack of *internationalism*. This is no longer the case with many. Some, via partnerships with foreign schools, offer or require attendance abroad for part of the program. Others achieve the same with their own campuses abroad. Similarly, some have mandatory study trips abroad. (Be careful that these are not just "managerial tourism," though, with more focus on having an enjoyable time than on having an in-depth learning experience.)

STUDENT BODY

A program may draw students just from the local area, which can limit the mix of industries and nationalities represented, especially if it is not located in a major metropolitan area. Even if a program draws from a wider area, check to see whether a few companies dominate.

The nature of an executive program tends to cause a very hefty percentage of the learning to come from interaction (in-person and on-line) with the other students. In addition to assuring that your classmates are a suitably diverse group in terms of industry, nationality, and function, make sure that there is an appropriate level of experience represented in the program. If your experience level (and nature) differs substantially from the norm, do not expect the other participants to share your learning goals and concerns.

ADMISSION REQUIREMENTS

Schools' admissions policies vary dramatically. Some, especially those that regard themselves as close substitutes for full-time programs (and are thus rigorously academic in nature), require the GMAT. A slim majority of programs do not require an undergraduate degree, although even they prefer at least some college coursework. The nature and amount of experience required also varies enormously. One program offered by Fuqua (Duke), for instance, requires a minimum of five years of professional work experience whereas another Fuqua program requires ten years. Be aware that the stated experience requirements are often meant more to signal what sort of applicant a school wants to attract than to serve as absolute cutoffs.

One of the biggest differences amongst programs is the degree of employer sponsorship required. In the old days, schools expected employers to pay the entire cost. Now, however, at least one-third of participants in a program are likely to be self-paying, and of those who receive financial support, many will still pay for a majority of the cost themselves. At a minimum, schools want a signed letter from an employer indicating that it supports your educational efforts and will grant the necessary time off to attend classes. When considering applications from candidates whose companies willingly fund some employees, some schools take the level of support offered as an important indicator of how strong the candidate is. Thus, someone without financial support on offer from an employer that never funds candidates will not suffer in the admissions process, but someone lacking support from a firm that supports some candidates will have his candidacy weakened.

LOGISTICS

In the past, many programs met on Friday one week, Saturday the next. That schedule is less common now. Instead, there are numerous other possibilities, including meeting on both Friday and Saturday every second week, for a long (three- or four-day) weekend once a month, or for a weeklong residency periodically. Many programs schedule sessions not just at their own campus but also at those of partner schools (often abroad) or even in regions of managerial interest. Thus, trips to Shanghai or Guangzhou to observe Chinese industry at work are a staple of some programs. Some programs offer the chance to attend a session in one or another of their locations. INSEAD students, for instance, can attend a session in Fontainebleau one week or in Singapore another week, depending upon which best fits their schedule. (Consider that this can, however, have a deleterious impact upon group cohesion.)

Commuter programs (in which participants return home each evening) tend to be very convenient and cost-effective for participants, but there is generally less bonding amongst participants than in programs where everyone is booked into the same hotel or residence during each program segment.

COSTS

Consider the full costs of attendance: tuition, other course fees, books and materials, travel to and from (flights, taxis, etc.), and lodging during the course. Some course fees are stated inclusive of lodging, for instance, whereas other schools' figures are not. Note, too, that your employer may be willing to provide financial support for some programs but not for others.

CAREER SERVICES

Access to the various career services offerings is a major issue at nearly every EMBA program. Employers sponsoring students do not want them to be able to shift employers with the aid of the program for which they are paying. Most programs honor employers' wishes, granting supported students access only to general workshops about career development and the like, while forbidding access to everything from résumé and cover letter workshops to actual job interviews. Sponsored students can generally gain access to the full range of career services with the explicit approval of their employers. Be aware that "sponsorship" is generally considered to be any financial support, however minimal. Some students therefore decline any but substantial support from their employers so as to keep their options open. (A few schools define sponsorship even more broadly as including giving a student time off to attend classes, whether or not any financial support is involved.)

Even if you gain access to the full range of career services, do not expect to find the same set of opportunities to interview for new jobs that you would with a full-time program. Employers hiring people by the dozen for beginning jobs (such as analysts in consulting or investment banking) are more likely to find a large number of students with suitable experience levels, backgrounds, and interests in the full-time programs than in an EMBA program.

TESTING THE WATERS

Admissions directors at many EMBA programs, unlike their counterparts at full-time MBA programs, will discuss your chances of admission before you formally apply. They recognize that it can be awkward to approach your supervisor for a recommendation, or your firm for financial support, and thereby take the risk of falling out of favor without knowing whether you have a realistic chance of acceptance. By all means take advantage of their willingness to discuss your situation before committing yourself to applying.

THE ADMISSIONS DIRECTORS DISCUSS EMBA PROGRAMS

Program Philosophy

➤ There are two schools of thought about the content an EMBA program should provide. One says that people with substantial experience don't need the same things from a program that less experienced people doing a full-time MBA need. The other, to which we subscribe at Wharton, is that even experienced managers do need to learn the same skills with the same academic rigor. *HOWARD S. KAUFOLD, WHARTON*

➤ The average age of students entering our program is 39. We therefore think that our curriculum should be substantially different than that of the full-time program, which is designed for students 27 years old (on average). We aim to teach some of the accounting basics, for example, but more to help senior executives spot red flags in the annual report than to be accountants. Similarly, we teach upper-level skills such as how to work with the media or corporate analysts as part of our professional development program. *DAVID ARDIS, MICHIGAN*

➤ Our Global Executive program students have an average of fifteen years of experience. They have typically come up through a functional specialty, but now have broader responsibilities. They generally have learned from the school of hard knocks, but want to be able to do a better job of what they're currently doing or what they've been identified to do in the future. Our program is not designed to develop functional expertise but to give them sufficient knowledge in a given field so that they can be better overall leaders. *KELLI KILPATRICK, FUQUA (DUKE)*

➤ The ten core courses you take in the traditional MBA program you also take in the Executive MBA program. That's similar. On the other hand, you have more emphasis on strategy, leadership, management communications, and ethics in the EMBA program. So even in the core courses, the volume of class time focuses more on issues of strategy, leadership, and so on, than is the case in the traditional MBA program. . . . . It takes more of an enterprise perspective. So in some respects it's similar (to a traditional MBA), but it's geared to someone at a different point in his or her career. In the traditional program we'd devote substantial time to teaching how to do accounting calculations, whereas in the EMBA program we do only a little bit of that. Instead, we help EMBA students understand what the accounting data is telling them and how they can use it to make good decisions. *BARBARA MILLAR, DARDEN*

➤ Our typical student is currently managing a region for a multinational, who realizes his technical expertise (in engineering or marketing, for instance) is not going to be enough for him to manage the challenges now facing him—or an entrepreneur who looks to take his business global. Our program is designed—and we look—for people who need to understand global strategy, which is our greatest strength. *ERIN O'BRIEN, TRIUM (HEC/PARIS, LSE, STERN/NYU)*

➤ Our overarching philosophy is about total diversity. We're targeting the international expatriate community (for our EMBA), which is a very large one here, to add to the diversity of our student body. Most of our students have had a host of international experiences, and they speak multiple languages. Another essential part of our program is awareness of societal issues, particularly sustainable development. *KIRT WOOD, ROTTERDAM*

The Admissions Process

➤ The admissions process for the EMBA program is similar to that for the full-time program. We require essays, recommendation letters, transcripts, an interview—just like in the full-time program. The EMBA application volume is less. This allows our admissions process to be very personal. *PATTY KEEGAN, CHICAGO*

➤ The full-time program has to process thousands of applications, being sure to keep applications high and acceptances low for the sake of the rankings. Our EMBA programs have a very different model. Because candidates have to take the risk of revealing their interest in doing a degree early in the process (by requesting a letter of support from the company and a recommendation from a supervisor), we encourage them to participate in a prequalification process. Before they need to approach their company, they can discuss the strength of their application with us. We'll look at their credentials (résumé, transcript, perhaps their GMAT score) and give them a sense of the likelihood that they'll be accepted. In this way we encourage those likely to be admitted to apply—and indirectly discourage those unlikely to be admitted. This intensive, relationship management model of recruiting is possible only because the numbers involved are in the hundreds rather than the thousands. *KELLI KILPATRICK, FUQUA (DUKE)*

➤ Unlike those applying to full-time programs, EMBA applicants tend to apply to only one or two programs. *KATHERINE LILYGREN, ANDERSON (UCLA)*

➤ We recognize these are busy people, with demanding jobs, on an accelerated path within their organizations. They may have full home lives as well. So we try to make it easy for them to apply. Before they submit a formal application we encourage them to come in to interview with us, to meet with one of our admissions directors, to probe the fit of the program. We also encourage them to come to an information session as well as to visit a day of classes, where they are hosted by a current student. We encourage them to experience the program rather than just hearing about it. *JAKI SITTERLE, STERN (NYU)*

➤ We offer a preadmissions process where you can submit a résumé to us and have us evaluate it before you ask your company for recommendations or sponsorship. We want to make sure there's a good match before you go public with your desires. We look at your career history and objectives, your academic objectives, and we make sure you understand what Darden will deliver—to make sure this is what you want. We also require two evaluative interviews, one with a professor and one with an admissions officer. *BARBARA MILLAR, DARDEN*

➤ We use the same sort of process and criteria as the full-time program. We require applicants to write serious essays, score well on the GMAT, and so on. The major difference concerns the interview. We expect everybody who is short-listed for our executive MBA program to be interviewed here in London. Bringing them to the school means that they get a clear sense of us and we get a very clear sense of them, including what contribution they'll make to everyone else's learning. We go through an interview process with two alumni and very often a member of the admissions team or admissions committee as well. The full-time program also interviews short-listed candidates, but it does so all around the world because it's not easy for people living far afield to get to London. *LYN HOFFMAN, LONDON*

➤ The process is largely the same as for the full-time program. One difference, however, is that we ask candidates more about their past experience and less about their future plans because our candidates have so much more experience than those applying to the full-time program. We also ask about their current job, as they will keep working while doing their MBA. *GAMALIEL MARTINEZ, INSTITUTO DE EMPRESA (SPAIN)*

➤ We interview all of our EMBA candidates. The interview is particularly important for this program. . . . We need to ensure that the student will fit in with our cosmopolitan ethos and international approach and that we will meet the learning needs of the student. *KIRT WOOD, ROTTERDAM*

➤ The EMBA admissions process is much more individualized. We deal with many fewer candidates, so we don't need to be process-driven. This allows us (unlike the full-time program) to work one-on-one with a candidate starting even before he or she submits an application. We get into detailed conversations with them from the beginning to help them determine whether this is the right program for them and to help them submit the most persuasive application. . . . We are more willing to accept GMAT waivers. You can't force someone with a CFA or working as a CFO to prove his analytical abilities with a GMAT score. *LING TEE, IESE (SPAIN)*

➤ Our admissions process is similar to that of the full-time program. The one difference is that interviews are conducted by a faculty member rather than an MBA student (or admissions officer). *JANINE SERIEYS, INSEAD*

Admissions Criteria

➤ We have four different MBA programs here, the full-time program and three executive programs. We're strict in our guidelines regarding who qualifies for each. We're reluctant to admit someone who's outside the experience norms for a given program, whether it's substantially more or substantially less than other participants have. Someone with fifteen years of experience, for example, is likely to be bored in the Cross Continent program, where the average amount of experience is just six years. *KELLI KILPATRICK, FUQUA (DUKE)*

➤ We don't require the GMAT, although candidates with weak quantitative backgrounds are encouraged to take the test. Quantitative skills are very important in any MBA program, and those who are not prepared or comfortable with the numbers side of business are at a disadvantage. *KATHERINE LILYGREN, ANDERSON (UCLA)*

➤ We don't require the GMAT. Instead, we focus on management and supervisory experience. We look at candidates' track records, career progression as well as their current level of responsibility, and their future growth potential within their organization. We have an official minimum of ten years of work experience, but that is really meant more to indicate the sort of person we want than to be a strict cutoff. Our average experience is fourteen to fifteen years. *DAVID ARDIS, MICHIGAN*

➤ EMBA applicants are older and more seasoned than the applicants to the full-time program. As a result, we have more information about their careers available to us. Therefore, we pay more attention to their career success and less to the criteria that matter so much to the full-time program: GMAT scores, undergraduate GPA, and so on. We don't require the GMAT, nor do we necessarily require an undergraduate degree although it is strongly preferred. We do like to see at least some college coursework, however, and we may ask someone without a degree to take the GMAT or CLEP exam.

We look for significant management experience, whether that means managing people or projects. We expect to see a steady progression in the amount of responsibility assumed. We also look for the potential for substantial future growth. To assess the quality of work experience, we look at the career path to date, including salary and title progression, which are helpful indicators of career progress. We examine the candidate's recommendations, of course, and also discuss the issue with the candidate. *PATTY KEEGAN, CHICAGO*

➤ The GMAT is required, although in exceptional cases we will grant a waiver. The people who have qualified for this waiver in the past have tended to have very substantial experience and to be highly educated in their fields, such as having a doctorate in biomedical engineering science. . . . The average age is 35, but we look not only for number of years of experience and age but also number of years of management experience. Those with substantial breadth and depth are often the most valuable contributors to the classroom conversation and to the study group dialogue. We look for those with international experience as well, because they bring that added dimension. And it's not just considering each individual; it's considering the composite of the class, which is just as important. We wouldn't want everyone to be from the same industry or background. *JAKI SITTERLE, STERN (NYU)*

➤ We require the GMAT of everyone. *BARBARA MILLAR, DARDEN*

➤ Our bare minimum of experience required is ten years, at least five of which must have been spent in a managerial role. Our recent class has ranged in age from 31 to 55, with most students being between 35 and 45 (and an average of 40). We had fifty-seven students from twenty-nine countries in the 2008 class, based across the globe. In fact, most of our students have worked overseas and currently have global responsibilities. *ERIN O'BRIEN, TRIUM (HEC/PARIS, LSE, STERN/NYU)*

➤ There is no age limit for the program, but we require three years in a management position. This usually translates into eight or nine years of professional experience after university. . . . We don't see many people with prior MBAs, but we do have a number of people who already have specialized master's degrees, such as in finance or economics, or even Ph.Ds. *GAMALIEL MARTINEZ, INSTITUTO DE EMPRESA (SPAIN)*

➤ Our minimum number of years of work experience is seven, but the average here is fifteen. The range is seven to thirty years. There is no age limit per se, but we look at the whole package. Good work experience is very important, yet we find that in some countries people start serious work very young. In

Russia, for instance, it's common for 28- or 29-year-olds to have been working for ten years. Because of the growing economy, such candidates may be given substantial responsibility early on and now be leading a team of more than twenty. *LING TEE, IESE (SPAIN)*

➤ The vast majority of our interest is in their professional and life experience. We're looking less at their ability to function in a corporate finance class than in their ability to leverage their vast experience, their skills, and their networks. *KIRT WOOD, ROTTERDAM*

➤ Work experience counts for a lot more than GMAT scores. With the average applicant having more than ten years of experience, their work history provides more information than it does for much younger candidates. . . . It's not very common, but about two out of our class of forty are likely to have done an MBA previously, usually right after their undergraduate studies. They probably approached it from a very academic perspective. The pace and focus are very different in this program. The peers and class exchanges are very different when the average participant has ten to fifteen years of experience instead of zero or one. *LING TEE, IESE (SPAIN)*

Evaluation of Younger Applicants

➤ For younger applicants, we like to see that they belong in the program because they've accomplished more than others their age. This is most often seen in entrepreneurs or people in family businesses, whose responsibilities often exceed those in Fortune 100 companies with comparable years of work experience. *DAVID ARDIS, MICHIGAN*

➤ We consider their ability to contribute substantively not only to study groups but also to the classroom discussion. Do they show sophistication beyond their years? This will tend to show up in both their interviews and their essays. Have they had formative experiences that will give them deep insights? We want to make sure the level of the dialogue is consistent with that of their older, more experienced classmates. So we look at younger candidates in part from the perspective of the older candidates and the professors. *JAKI SITTERLE, STERN (NYU)*

➤ We believe we can spot leadership potential based on a combination of your career progression and what you tell us in an interview and in your essays. We're looking to see whether you are on your way. *BARBARA MILLAR, DARDEN*

➤ We look for a clear fast-track background, so we consider the kind of organization they're in and the way they've progressed within that organization— albeit in a short period of time. The other thing we test very rigorously is the question of contribution. In other words, what is this person going to bring that is going to add value to the 40-year-old, if you like. The third thing we examine is interpersonal skills: Will this person be able to work well in a very bright, highly motivated, nonhierarchical study group, for instance? Do they have the right kind of approach, self-knowledge and awareness, sensing of other people, and cultural sensitivity—given the diversity of our student body—to be able to work effectively in their study group? *LYN HOFFMAN, LONDON*

➤ First, we want to see that they have a good position in their company. Second, we want them to have a variety of experience in the company. Someone who has just done finance, for instance, will have too narrow a perspective on their company. Unless he or she has also had another role, whether in operations, marketing, or something else, we won't accept him or her. Third, we want to be sure they have sufficient motivation to do the program because it will be harder for them than it is for more experienced candidates. *GAMALIEL MARTINEZ, INSTITUTO DE EMPRESA (SPAIN)*

➤ We look particularly hard at their maturity level. We also study their career progression. We want people who have been highly successful, with clear progression to their careers. Part of this is that we want to identify those with sufficient ambition and drive to complete the program (while working full-time). *LING TEE, IESE (SPAIN)*

Sponsorship

➤ Even students whose companies don't pay for them are supported by being given time off from work, assuming that they don't use their vacation time for classes. If they receive either financial assistance or time off, we consider them to be "sponsored," which means that we have two customers to service. Sponsored students are required to disclose what career service functions they propose to use to their employers. *KELLI KILPATRICK, FUQUA (DUKE)*

➤ Some students aren't interested in being financially sponsored by their companies because of the additional strings companies attach. These students want the format and flexibility our EMBA offers, which allows them to keep working, so they are willing to pay their own way. *KELLI KILPATRICK, FUQUA (DUKE)*

➤ The trend is certainly moving away from full financial sponsorship. *JAKI SITTERLE, STERN (NYU)*

➤ Two-thirds of our students are self-sponsored, which is more than at most programs. One of the reasons is that we have a substantial number of entrepreneurs in the program. Another is that many students don't even ask their companies for funding, figuring the money would simply be taken out of their bonuses anyway. *ERIN O'BRIEN, TRIUM (HEC/PARIS, LSE, STERN/NYU)*

➤ As having the support of one's firm is critical to our students' success, all TRIUM students must have sponsorship for time. Approximately half of TRIUM students have full or partial financial sponsorship, and half are self-sponsored. *ERIN O'BRIEN, TRIUM*

➤ Our last class had 60 percent sponsored: 31 percent fully sponsored, 29 percent partially sponsored. Forty percent were self-sponsored. That fluctuates every year, but sponsorship has been slowly declining. *LYN HOFFMAN, LONDON*

➤ Nearly 85 percent of our students are financially sponsored by their companies; most are fully sponsored. *KIRT WOOD, ROTTERDAM*

➤ One-third of our students are fully sponsored, one-third are partially sponsored, and one-third are self-financed. *LING TEE, IESE (SPAIN)*

Individuals Rather Than Companies Seek Out Programs

➤ These days it's rare that a company makes a decision to send someone to the program. It's usually the individual who comes up with the idea of attending the program and then sells it to the company to get its support. *PATTY KEEGAN, CHICAGO*

➤ It all starts with the individual, who says I'm ready for this and I'm ready to make the necessary commitment. If it were the company pushing it, I'd be concerned about the student's level of commitment. I don't think many corporations are identifying an individual and saying, "OK, go for an MBA." *BARBARA MILLAR, DARDEN*

➤ In my experience, the vast majority of the decision-makers are the students themselves. They go back to their organizations and say, "This is what I want to do. Will you sponsor me? And this is why you should." It's only rarely that the organization comes to us, although people do sometimes say, "My boss suggested this." *LYN HOFFMAN, LONDON*

➤ Over 90 percent of our candidates have initiated the idea of an executive MBA themselves. It is very uncommon for a company to do so. Once candidates contact us, we work with them to convince their companies to provide financial support. *LING TEE, IESE (SPAIN)*

Impact of Sponsorship Upon Admissions Decisions

➤ We don't know when candidates apply whether they will be sponsored or not. It would not affect our admissions decision in any event. *KATHERINE LILYGREN, ANDERSON (UCLA)*

➤ Some programs require full financial support for admission. At Wharton, the percentage of support generally doesn't affect a student's chances. If someone works for a company that normally sponsors people but the company is not sponsoring him (or her), we consider what this says about the applicant's importance to the employer. *HOWARD S. KAUFOLD, WHARTON*

➤ For a candidate who is strong in each area we consider, the question of whether he (or she) is to receive financial sponsorship has no impact upon our admissions decision. For those who are weak in one or more areas, we do consider whether he will be supported by his company. If not, we worry that he may not be the sort of high potential candidate we look for. *KELLI KIL-PATRICK, FUQUA (DUKE)*

➤ It's not taken into consideration. We're looking at the contribution the student will make to his classmates and to the whole enterprise and the value we will add to the student and, hence, the value he will add to his institution. *BARBARA MILLAR, DARDEN*

➤ We evaluate candidates on their own merits. How they will finance the program has no bearing on the admissions decision. *LING TEE, IESE (SPAIN)*

➤ If a company is prepared to sponsor a person, that gives us lots of signals about their performance, their potential, and their capacity for senior roles and leadership. But that's all we take from it. We certainly don't accept people because they have company sponsorship. *LYN HOFFMAN, LONDON*

➤ It's valuable for us to know that a company trusts a candidate's future enough that it will pay for his International Executive MBA. However, we worry more about the quality of the individual candidate than we do about the fact of sponsorship. *GAMALIEL MARTINEZ, INSTITUTO DE EMPRESA (SPAIN)*

➤ Whether or not someone is sponsored has no impact upon the admissions decision. *KIRT WOOD, ROTTERDAM*

Sponsorship and Career Services

➤ Each year fewer candidates receive financial support from their companies. The tension regarding how much career assistance to give them continues, but over time we've liberalized our policies. *DAVID ARDIS, MICHIGAN*

➤ Students who are unemployed or not sponsored financially by their companies are allowed to use the career management center just as the full-time students do. This is also true for sponsored students who get letters from their companies permitting them to do so. On the other hand, the time schedules of MBA for Executive students make it difficult to take advantage of all that our career management center can offer. They're here all day on every other Friday and Saturday, in class throughout the day except for their lunch breaks, which makes it very challenging to provide access to all services, including the vast array of on-campus presentations, which typically occur Monday through Thursday. *PETER J. DEGNAN, WHARTON (CAREER SERVICES DIRECTOR)*

➤ We have opened up career services almost wholly to executive MBA students, without regard to whether they are being sponsored. The only exception concerns hiring companies that will not recruit students who work for their clients. *LYN HOFFMAN, LONDON*

➤ We focus on career management rather than helping people find new jobs, but a sponsored student who wants help from career services to find a new job will need his company's endorsement. *LING TEE, IESE (SPAIN)*

➤ There are no limitations on use of the careers department. Everyone (including alumni—this is a lifetime service) is welcome to use it. On the other hand, many companies have separate agreements with employees they're sponsoring, requiring, for instance, that if they leave before working another two years, they have to pay back the money the company spent. *GAMALIEL MARTINEZ, INSTITUTO DE EMPRESA (SPAIN)*

Career Changers

➤ Personally, I prefer people who are happy in their careers and are looking to progress within their fields. I am concerned when applicants think an EMBA program will allow them to make wholesale changes in their careers, such as a 40-year-old engineer looking to become an investment banker. Unrealistic expectations lead to unhappy students. *KATHERINE LILYGREN, ANDERSON (UCLA)*

➤ I'd advise them to think about a traditional MBA program, where 85 percent of the people are career changers. So recruiters understand that and understand what that means in terms of transferability of skills, etc. Faculty and alumni also understand it. It's just a different animal. That's really not what we're designed to do. Like other EMBA programs, we don't have a long line of employers coming to recruit graduates, let alone more seasoned managers looking to change careers. *BARBARA MILLAR, DARDEN*

➤ Now that we have 40 percent of our students self-sponsor, it's clear that this is seen as a career-changing opportunity. Of course, they need to spend more time focusing on the career services part of what we offer. *LYN HOFFMAN, LONDON*

➤ (This) is a good program for those looking to change careers. Of course it's critical to prioritize getting to know people who can help you make contacts in your target industry rather than just studying. It's also ideal for changing jobs within your company. We had the VP of IT of a French company, who was considering to change career within his company, do an International Executive MBA here in order to overcome his company's resistance to making this change. *GAMALIEL MARTINEZ, INSTITUTO DE EMPRESA (SPAIN)*

➤ We're wary of people further along in their careers wanting to make a radical career change. Many have unrealistic expectations, such as a salesperson in an engineering firm (age 35–40) who wants to become a financial analyst. People far along in their careers are less willing to start at a low level in a new career, plus they have substantial salary expectations. Combine those factors with the fact that many firms look to hire people new to the industry only if they're relatively young and you have a major problem. But we also have career changers who can leverage their prior experience to change careers successfully. For instance, the neurosurgeon who needs to leave the practice because a bad knee prevents him standing for a long period in an operating room who, after an MBA, becomes a hospital manager. *Ling Tee, IESE (Spain)*

Financial Aid

➤ Approximately 70 percent of our students get financial aid, but this is almost exclusively student loans rather than scholarships. *Katherine Lilygren, Anderson (UCLA)*

➤ We only have loans available, either the Stafford Federal Loan or a private loan through the school. *Barbara Millar, Darden*

➤ We offer a limited number of merit-based scholarships. Financial aid is available, in the form of federal and private student loans. *Jaki Sitterle, Stern (NYU)*

➤ We have scholarships available in three main categories: for women, for managers from emerging economies, and for entrepreneurs. *Ling Tee, IESE (Spain)*

➤ If someone is not corporate-sponsored, we do have a number of partial scholarships available. *Kirt Wood, Rotterdam*

➤ We're trying to increase the number of women in the program. We have four half-scholarships that we allocate solely to women. That is the only financial aid we offer, but we do have a generous loan scheme via HSBC. *Lyn Hoffman, London*

➤ We have a lot of scholarships available—some sponsored by the IE foundation, some sponsored by other organizations. We also offer attractively priced loans through arrangements with various banks. *Gamaliel Martinez, Instituto de Empresa (Spain)*

Other

➤ Students attend school here on Fridays and Saturdays, which means that the sacrifice is shared. The companies agree to free up participants on Fridays; on Saturdays, the students sacrifice weekend time. *Howard S. Kaufold, Wharton*

➤ Applicants considering global EMBA programs should be wary of programs based on a "parachute" model, where the school's students and professors are shipped abroad and dropped into a foreign environment for a week or two. Our own program was designed to avoid this approach and to draw heavily on local expertise instead. So in our module in China, we draw on faculty from top Chinese schools such as Tsinghua and HKUST and local experts from both government and industry to bring together "the best of the region." *Erin O'Brien, TRIUM (HEC/Paris, LSE, Stern/NYU)*

➤ Our complete elective course portfolio is open to executive MBA students: if they have flexibility over time-tabling, they get the same choice as full-time MBA students. This is probably unique among EMBA programs. *Lyn Hoffman, London*

➤ We can have only so much influence on (companies failing to make use of graduates' new skills). Several times a year, though, we do have events to which we invite sponsoring companies. We also have a major employers' event to which we invite all people who sponsor students, whether that is a line manager, HR director, or CEO. We get an interesting faculty member to do a seminar which has broad appeal and might be particularly topical. Students often say that the learning from the seminar was taken back to the organization and has changed the organization. As a result, the organization has a better idea of what the students can bring to it. Of course, reintegration is never going to be easy when someone is a different or more effective person than was the case at the start of the program. *Lyn Hoffman, London*

Appendix IV

VISITING BUSINESS SCHOOLS

*V*isiting a business school is an extremely important part of your research. The visit brings to life a school that has heretofore been only an imaginary place fashioned by rumors, hearsay, website information, guidebook and brochure blurbs, and statistics. In addition to partaking in the usual tours and information sessions, you should attempt to understand both what daily life is like for students and whether the academic and social experience is what you seek. Business school visits also offer opportunities to improve your admissions chances: Knowing well the school to which you are marketing yourself and showing yourself as interested enough in it to have undertaken a substantial visit are two ways in which you can distinguish yourself.

WHEN TO VISIT

It is best to visit a business school when it is in session so that you can get the right feel for student and academic life. If at all possible, visit when classes are in session, but not during exam period. Attending when school is in session will give you an opportunity to interact with students, who are the best reflection of a school and what it is all about. At exam times, however, students will have little interest in discussing the school (or anything else) with you, so you will be unable to gain an in-depth understanding of the school.

Try to visit on a weekday in order to get the best sense of the school. Weekday visits will allow you to see students interacting and to attend several classes; they will also ensure an opportunity to visit with admissions staff. Even if the school does not conduct formal interviews, you may be able to leave a favorable impression with admissions officers, which can work to your benefit.

It is not particularly important that you visit immediately before applying. Even if you visit a year (or two) beforehand, your understanding of the school will stand you in good stead as long as your key criteria for selecting a school have not changed substantially in the interim. By the same token, it is not a bad idea to revisit schools you are seriously considering after you have been accepted in order to arrive at a final decision.

BEFORE THE VISIT

Plan to visit a range of schools. If you are not certain what you are looking for, this part of the application process is extremely important. Visiting different kinds of schools is a smart move even for those who think they know what they want. You might be certain, for example, that you want to attend a small, suburban school because you had such a good experience at just such a college. Upon visiting a range of schools, however, you might find that you would now be better served by a much larger environment, both business school and city. Visit small and large, public and private, urban and rural schools. Also, be sure to visit schools that represent a range of selectivity. You need to visit not just your *stretches* but also your *possibles* and *likelies*.

Note that you will learn about business schools—and about business school *visits*—as you tour schools. After you have visited several schools, you will know what items are most crucial for you to investigate as well as how best to gather the information you need. Therefore, do not plan to visit your likely top two choices first. Instead, try to visit several schools about which you are not certain as a means of familiarizing yourself with the visiting process.

Keep these additional guidelines in mind when planning your itinerary:

- Familiarize yourself thoroughly with the schools you will be visiting. (See the body of this chapter for specific information sources.) You should be familiar with all the basic facts about a school before getting to the campus, where your job is to refine your impressions and conduct a more detailed investigation—not to learn the absolute basics.

- Visit no more than one school per day. The amount you need to do on campus necessitates a full day, not just two or three hours. The more you value a given school, the longer you should plan to spend at it.

- Arrange meetings ahead of time with individuals in areas of interest to you, whether professors, career services professionals, or financial aid officers.

- Arrange for a formal interview (if this is part of the admissions process for that school).

- Compile a list of the questions you intend to ask at each school, along with any which are specific to that particular school. (See page 92 for suggestions.)

WHILE ON CAMPUS

Your visit can include general information gathering and efforts targeted at specific areas of interest or concern to you. Thus, you can take a campus tour or spend time talking with various finance professors. The time you have available is likely to determine much of what you do. If you have very little time, a great need for financial aid, and a keen interest in marketing, and you have already visited a number of other schools, you would be silly to spend most of your time taking a general campus tour. Instead, you would probably want to spend time with a financial aid officer, talk in depth with marketing professors, and discuss the school and the marketing department with several students.

THE CAMPUS TOUR

You can take a general tour of the university or, perhaps, a tour of just the business school. These tours are a pleasant way to get your bearings; they can also give you the chance to size up the atmosphere of the campus. The students who lead such tours are, of course, salespeople for the school, so do not expect to get a forthright perspective on the school's strengths and weaknesses from them.

INFORMATION SESSION

A group information session is essentially a school's sales pitch. It is, however, a useful tool for gaining basic information about a school. These sessions generally give an overview of the school's tradition and philosophy as well as the multitude of academic, extracurricular, and other opportunities available there.

Although admissions officers often lead these sessions, this is seldom a time to try to stand out from the crowd in order to impress them. Those who try to dominate sessions or gain attention with too many questions that are not of interest to other applicants are frowned upon by admissions officers. If you are lucky enough to be one of only a couple attendees, however, keep in mind that your efforts may improve your admissions chances (as the next section discusses).

THE ADMISSIONS OFFICE

At many schools, you can visit the admissions office and ask to speak with an admissions officer, even if you have not arranged an interview. (Do not expect to be given a formal interview, however, unless you have arranged one in advance.) An officer might be willing to give you a few minutes of his or her time to answer questions and address concerns. Express your interest in the school and ask questions that show you to be serious.

You have the chance to impress the admissions officer in a positive way. Be on your best behavior and be sure your questions and comments show your overall knowledge of the school, your general intelligence, and your poise. Even at schools that do not conduct formal interviews, it is common for admissions officers to make notes of any substantive interactions with applicants.

THE FINANCIAL AID OFFICE

If you intend to seek financial aid, you are likely to have numerous questions about how this school handles financial aid matters. Arrange in advance to speak with a financial aid officer; twenty to thirty minutes is likely to be enough time if you are well organized. See Chapter 16 for a discussion of what you will need to know about financial aid.

THE CAREER SERVICES DEPARTMENT

Relatively few applicants pay sufficient attention to the value a good career services department can add to a school—and to their own career prospects. Visiting the career services department at each school you visit will quickly show you which are the most able where your interests are concerned. Take twenty or thirty minutes to discuss what they offer (in light of the discussion on prior pages of what a good career services department can do).

CLASSES

Upon contacting the admissions office to arrange a visit, ask about the possibility of sitting in on classes. This is your opportunity to get a feel for the professors, the students, and the nature and quality of teaching at the school. If you have time, try to sit in on a variety of classes. Consider sitting in on a first-year (core) course as well as an advanced course in a subject of particular interest to you. Try to sit in on a course for which the admissions office does not make the arrangements. Given that the admissions officers want to sell their school, you can expect them to try to route you to the best instructors. To see what an ordinary professor is like, ask students for a suggestion in your chosen field. Then approach the professor of the course and see whether he or she will permit you to sit in. Most will accommodate you without hesitation.

BE AWARE OF YOUR PREJUDICES

Many things can skew your impressions of a school for better or for worse, thereby affecting your ability to evaluate it. Therefore, pay attention to these points:

- Do not let your like or dislike of a single person (such as an admissions officer) influence your overall impression of a school.

■ Bear in mind that weather is a transitory matter, and you might be visiting a school on the rare sunny (or rainy) day.

■ Depending upon when in the term you visit (i.e., at the beginning of the term or during midterm or final exams), students may be more or less enthusiastic about their choice of school—and about spending time with you.

■ If you sit in on an advanced class, do not be surprised if the material and the class discussion are beyond your comprehension.

■ Remember that school officials are more likely to try to sell you than are students. Try to talk with as many different types of people as possible to build up the most complete and accurate picture of the school.

■ Pay particular attention to those students who most resemble you in terms of their background and goals. Whenever you encounter someone who reminds you of you, dig in. Pump her, and all of her friends, for as much information as you can get regarding what they think the school does and does not do well.

■ Appreciate and observe the school for what it is rather than obsessing about your chances of admission there. If you focus too much on the latter, you will limit your ability to assess the school.

■ Keep in mind that even though a school might have a prestigious name, it is not necessarily the best school or the best school for you. Keep in mind the criteria you have established for determining the best school for *you*.

Remember that choosing a business school is an iterative process. As you visit and examine schools, you should learn more about your own needs; and as you learn more about your own needs, you will refine your criteria regarding which schools are best for you.

THINGS TO NOTE ON YOUR CAMPUS VISIT

➤ Are the students happy or glum? Engaged or apathetic? (Remember, though, that the timing of your visit can affect the way students are acting.)

➤ Do different ethnic and national groups interact? On campus and off?

➤ Do professors interact with students? (Look outside of classrooms, especially in cafeterias, the student union, and local watering holes.) Do professors, especially older ones, seem weary and bored with their material—and the prospect of teaching mere students—or are they energetic and uplifting?

➤ What is the atmosphere like in the classes you sit in on? Are students engaged?

➤ Are the library and computer facilities well used? Comfortable? Are there sufficient private carrels and areas for group meetings? Is the atmosphere conducive to studying? (Given that some students work best in absolute quiet, whereas others prefer a buzz of noise and activity, check that the school's facilities meet your requirements for effective study space.)

➤ What is the pulse of the school? What sorts of activities and events are advertised on bulletin boards? What issues are important to students? (You can discover the latter by talking to students, listening to conversations in eating facilities, and reading the school newspaper.) What is the overall "feel" of the school?

➤ Is there a student course-evaluation booklet available?

➤ Where do most business students live? Do the housing options fit your needs?

➤ How much interaction is there with other departments and schools of the university? With the surrounding town?

➤ Does the area feel safe, both during the day and at night?

➤ How readily available are restaurants, cafés, bars, theaters, and the like?

➤ Are the athletic facilities of good quality? Available at useful times?

UPON LEAVING CAMPUS

RECORD YOUR IMPRESSIONS

Keep detailed notes of the schools you visit. Note what you can during the course of your visits. Be sure not to let the day of a visit end without completing your written record. If you visit multiple schools on a single trip, failure to complete your notes on one school before you visit the next will almost surely cause you to forget important things about the first or muddle together your impressions of the various schools.

SEND THANK-YOU NOTES

Send thank-you notes (or e-mails) to key people with whom you interacted. This can include interviewers, financial aid officers, and professors or other faculty who took time to chat with you. It is not necessary (or worth your time and effort) to send notes to people who conducted large information sessions or tours—these people are not likely to remember you, and there is no reason to send a note to thank someone for this kind of routine group treatment. It is individualized attention that needs to be addressed with letters of appreciation. Tradition, by the way, dictates that these be handwritten.

Be sure to note the names, titles, and addresses of individuals while on your visits—and be sure to get all the spellings correct. If you are unsure of any spelling details, you can always call the admissions department (for the names of admissions officers), the financial aid office (for the names of financial aid officers), the student telephone directory (for the names of students), or academic department offices (for the names of faculty or administrators) to make sure you are correct. Although sending thank-you notes will not guarantee your admission, it is nevertheless a nice gesture and will be appreciated by the recipients.

QUESTIONS TO ASK WHILE ON CAMPUS

Do not be merely a silent observer of a business school scene. Instead, ask the people you encounter whatever questions are important to you. Asking the same question of a variety of people will often give you different perspectives on an issue.

➤ What do you particularly like, and what do you particularly dislike, about the school? What do you see as its benefits and shortcomings?

➤ If you could change one thing about your school, what would it be? (This question will help you gauge the honesty—and grip on reality—of the person responding. If she cannot think of anything that she would like to change, assume that you are dealing with a shill for the school or a Pollyanna. In either case, you would do well to spend your precious time questioning others.)

➤ Which professors do essentially no teaching?

➤ Which professors are excellent teachers? Terrible teachers?

➤ Is it common for students to have close relationships with their professors? What opportunities exist for students to foster such relationships?

➤ What do students do for fun?

➤ What are the most popular courses? Which courses are difficult to get in to?

➤ What are the strongest and weakest fields?

➤ What are the most popular student societies and clubs?

➤ How competitive are the students?

➤ What do you consider the strengths of this school relative to its competitors? (For students only: Why did you choose this school over others?)

➤ How many students work part-time off-campus? What is the usual pay?

➤ What is the quality of the career services department? Are there career services professionals who specialize in (your area of interest)? (Ask the career services people what their backgrounds and specialties are.)

Questions Not to Ask

➤ Avoid asking questions about admissions requirements or any other questions to which you can find answers on your own by simply consulting the school's website or reading admissions brochures and standard publications.

➤ Avoid grilling anyone only about the school's weaknesses. Asking about weaknesses shows that you are doing serious investigative work and that you are appropriately concerned about your future, but remember also to be positive and ask about strengths as well.

THE ADMISSIONS DIRECTORS COMMENT ON THE VALUE OF VISITING SCHOOLS

➤ We strongly recommend that people come and visit the campus and sit in on classes. There are a ton of misperceptions about it in the press, but if you visit it you can find out for yourself what it's really like. This is an investment like buying a house. I wouldn't buy a house without seeing it. People go to extraordinary lengths when buying a house, but only to superficial lengths when choosing a program. *JAMES MILLAR, HARVARD*

➤ You should visit the three or four schools you think are great fits for your needs. See whether the buzz, the atmosphere, is right for you. You can interact with current students on an online bulletin board. Knowing what the school values in its students not only helps you determine whether it's right for you but also helps you write your essays for it. *ROSE MARTINELLI, CHICAGO*

➤ After examining brochures, websites, and books, the next step is to visit the school. I'm a big believer in seeing the school, chatting with students, meeting professors, and sitting in on classes. An MBA program is such an important life decision that it's worth the investment of visiting. *DAWNA CLARKE, TUCK*

➤ Visit the school when it is in session. Talk to students and alums. If you're miserable at a school, your education will suffer, so be sure you'll be comfortable and will thrive in a given school's environment. *ANN W. RICHARDS, JOHNSON (CORNELL)*

➤ Narrow your choices down to three to five schools, then visit them. You can only get a sense of what a school is like by visiting it and talking with people on the program (and the alums). *KATTY OOMS SUTER, IMD (SWITZERLAND)*

➤ It's important to get a sense of the place and especially of the people. You'll be investing considerable time, much of it spent intensely with fellow students, so it's vital to know that you'll enjoy working with them. Even though we offer a lot of virtual ways to get to know the school and the program, there's no substitute for an actual visit. We therefore have open days at least once every two months, when we schedule a full day of activities, including an information session, a teaching simulation, meetings with students, and so on. *DAVID BACH, INSTITUTO DE EMPRESA (SPAIN)*

➤ We strongly suggest that our candidates find the way to visit our school: It's a very good opportunity to experience . . . Bocconi MBA life by sitting in on a class session; by having the chance to talk to faculty members and current students; and, of course, by scheduling an individual orientation meeting with the school's staff members. Before deciding to go for an intense one-year MBA program you want to be sure of your choice, which is not just based on the course contents but also on its environment. *ROSSANA CAMERA, BOCCONI (ITALY)*

4

How to Use the Rankings

— EXECUTIVE SUMMARY —

■

Schools in the United States, Europe, and elsewhere are routinely ranked by various authorities.

■

These rankings provide handy guides to the reputations of different programs, but are subject to many qualifications.

■

Consult them, but do not rely on them.
—Recognize their limitations as well as their strengths.

*T*he purpose of this book is not to rank schools, nor to place school X on a list of "top" schools and relegate school Y to the list of also-rans. Other publications devote substantial effort to doing just this, and the field will be left to them. This chapter will examine some of the more important rankings and discuss the methodologies they employ to reach their conclusions.

Formal rankings have been made for American full-time programs, part-time programs, and executive programs; Canadian full-time programs; British full- and part-time programs; European executive and full-time programs; Asian full-time programs; and, to a very limited extent, programs in the rest of the world. No doubt other rankings exist, but this chapter will focus on those that are the best known and most useful.

There is another important, albeit highly unofficial ranking—that provided by word of mouth and received wisdom. In the United States, for example, whereas some people would refer to the specific rankings of a school in one or another guide, others would take into account the "traditional" ranking of a school, which often amounts to a combination of the fame of the school's parent university, the ranking of the business school in the past, and the fame of the school in the local area.

USING THE RANKINGS

The ranking of business schools is a very uncertain science. Organizations that undertake these rankings are confronted by daunting methodological problems. For example, how important is it to have a library of 5,000,000 volumes rather than 600,000 volumes, and how does that compare with having a student body GMAT average of 660 rather than 680? Is the school with 5,000,000 volumes and a GMAT average of 660 better than, equal to, or worse than the school with 600,000 volumes and a GMAT average of 680? It is not obvious how the two schools should be compared, even when two relatively simple quantitative measures are employed. The problem is made infinitely more complicated when numerous other factors are considered, especially because many of these are inherently subjective rather than easily and objectively quantifiable.

Several bypasses are available to the ranking organizations. They can examine the opinions of those doing the hiring at major firms, taking the likely employers of MBAs as the ultimate arbiters of worth. (To an extent this assumption is correct, of course, insofar as MBAs tend to view the value of their degree in large measure as a matter of what employment doors it opens.) Another possible shortcut is to examine the earnings of the graduates of each school, relying again on the market as the arbiter of the value of MBAs from the various schools. Unfortunately, these shortcuts also suffer from limitations. Some drawbacks are due to the fact that an overall ranking for a school does not distinguish between how its finance graduates do in the market and how its human resources graduates fare. Nor does it take account of the fact that its graduates may do very well locally but not in another region or country. Thus, if a school is rated highly because its finance graduates make a lot of money, but you intend to go into human resource management, this school may not boost your salary more than another school would.

SOME WARNINGS

Rankings are useful as a very rough guide to the reputation and quality of different programs. Most people take them far too seriously, however, when considering where to apply. It is inappropriate to take the latest *Financial Times* or *Business Week* rankings and limit yourself to the top 5 schools on their list. The schools differ enough in their goals, programs, and atmospheres that a person who will be well served by one may be very poorly served by another. To take an obvious example, a person who is determined to be managing the "factory of the future" and is not particularly interested in general management should probably be looking at MIT's Sloan School rather than Harvard. Both are superb, but their missions are quite different.

Chapter 3, "How to Choose the Right School for *You*," lists several dozen criteria that are relevant to choosing the right program. Not all are equally significant, and admittedly reputation is critically important. But it would be silly to opt for a school ranked fourth by *U.S. News* or *Business Week*, rather than one ranked sixth solely because of these rankings if the first had an unsuitable atmosphere, had few electives in the field you want to enter, or suffered from one of a number of other defects that may also be important to you. There is no precision to these rankings; the same publication may reverse the rankings of these same schools the following year! The imprecision and variability of the rankings is one reason for being cautious in using them; another reason for caution is that one school will be able to offer you a program geared to your needs whereas another will not. Yet another potential issue is that schools do not have the same reputation everywhere. A school that is highly regarded in the United States might be virtually unknown in Austria.

These concerns give rise to some guidelines for using rankings:

1. Look at as many rankings as possible and consider the *consensus* rather than any one ranking.

2. Consider even this consensus view as only an approximation of the appropriate tier for a school. Thus, a school that is ranked about tenth to fifteenth in various rankings should be regarded as a very fine school, but whether it really should be ranked in the top 5 or merely the top 25 is not determinable.

3. Since you should be looking for the best program to meet your specific subject and other needs, with an atmosphere in which you will thrive, the rankings have only a modest part to play in helping you find this program. They have little to say about which school will provide the courses that will be most useful, the connections that will matter most for the job and region in which you wish to be employed, the academic and social environment there, and other key factors.

4. When rankings are suitably detailed, as is true of the *Financial Times* and *U.S. News* rankings, examine them to see what questions are raised in addition to what answers might be provided. For example, if a school's graduates boost their salaries after the program (relative to their salaries before the program) less than a peer school's graduates, you should investigate what underlies the disparity.

5. Check whatever rankings are done (or even republished) by reputable business-oriented newspapers and journals in whatever country you intend to study or work. For example, if you are considering attending a business school in France, find out how well it is ranked by *Le Figaro*, *Les Echos*, and other local publications. If you are considering working in France after attending a business school in the United States, do the same.

6. Go well beyond consulting various rankings. Conduct in-depth research to evaluate specific programs, as is discussed in detail in Chapter 3.

THE RANKINGS

The rankings that follow are reproduced on a strictly geographic basis. Thus, American schools are classed together, as are Canadian, European, and Asian schools. The same is true regarding type of MBA program: full-time, part-time, and executive programs each merit a separate listing.

FULL-TIME MBA PROGRAMS—AMERICA

The five rankings on the following chart are the most useful, and most commonly referenced, of those currently in circulation.

	FINANCIAL TIMES	BUSINESS WEEK	U.S. NEWS & WORLD REPORT	EIU*	WALL STREET JOURNAL
Wharton	1	2	3	12	7
Harvard	2	4	1	5	14
Stanford	3	6	2	2	18
Columbia	4	10	7	9	4
Chicago	5	1	6	3	11
Stern (NYU)	6	14	13	6	17
Tuck (Dartmouth)	7	11	9	1	2
Sloan (MIT)	8	7	4	13	10
Yale	9	19	15	15	9
Ross (Michigan)	10	5	11	7	1
Haas (UC Berkeley)	11	8	7	8	5
Kellogg	12	3	4	4	6
Anderson (UCLA)	13	12	10	11	19
Darden (Virginia)	14	15	13	10	13
Fuqua (Duke)	15	9	11	19	12
Kenan-Flagler (North Carolina)	16	17	20	25	8
Broad (Michigan State)	17	29	23	—	—
Tippie (Iowa)	18	—	—	42	—
McDonough (Georgetown)	19	22	34	30	—
Johnson (Cornell)	19	13	16	14	16
Tepper (Carnegie Mellon)	24	16	16	18	3
Goizueta (Emory)	25	23	18	16	—
Olin (Washington University)	29	27	26	23	—
Marshall (South California)	31	21	29	31	15
Texas	39	20	18	32	—

*Economist Intelligence Unit

There is clearly no agreement as to which school is the best, nor which one is the seventeenth best. There is some reasonable agreement, however, as to those schools considered the real elite of American schools. The following schools (listed in alphabetical order within each subcategory) were highly ranked by multiple rankings:

Ranked in top 10 by at least three:		*Ranked in top 15 by at least three:*	
Chicago	Columbia	Anderson (UCLA)	Darden (Virginia)
Haas (UC Berkeley)	Harvard	Fuqua (Duke)	Stern (NYU)
Kellogg	Ross (Michigan)	Yale	
Sloan (MIT)	Stanford		
Tuck (Dartmouth)	Wharton		

Ranked in top 20 by at least three:

Johnson (Cornell)

Kenan-Flagler (North Carolina)

Tepper (Carnegie Mellon)

PART-TIME MBA PROGRAMS—AMERICA

	U.S. News & World Report
Stern (NYU)	1
Chicago	2
Kellogg	3
Anderson (UCLA)	4
Haas (UC Berkeley)	5
Marshall (USC)	6
Robinson (Georgia State)	7
Ross (Michigan)	7
Carlson (Minnesota)	9
Cox (Southern Methodist)	10

EXECUTIVE MBA PROGRAMS—GLOBAL

The EMBA rankings are a bit of a mess, largely because the various magazines approach them from substantially different perspectives. The *Financial Times* considers programs rather than schools. Thus, it rates each of Kellogg's various programs (in different countries) separately. *U.S. News* considers schools rather than programs, and *Business Week* seems to be in between the other two, generally ranking schools, but occasionally ranking separate programs of a school. To add to the confusion, the *Financial Times* and *Business Week* rank programs or schools on a global basis, whereas *U.S. News* considers only American programs. Similarly, the first two organizations rank twenty-five or more schools, the latter only ten. The result is a slightly unwieldy list, with no attempt (as in the ranking of full-time programs) to derive a consensus view from the set of rankings.

	FINANCIAL TIMES	BUSINESS WEEK	U.S. NEWS & WORLD REPORT
Wharton	1	2	3
Columbia/London Global	2	—	—
Kellogg/Hong Kong UST	3	—	—
TRIUM (HEC/LSE/Stern)	4	—	—
Instituto de Empresa (Spain)	5	—	—
Chicago	6	3	2
London Business School	7	25	—
Olin (Washington University)	8	—	—
Fuqua Global (Duke)	9	9	4
Kellogg Executive	10	1	1
Columbia	11	—	6
Purdue/TIAS/CEU/GISMA	12	—	—
Kellogg/WHU Beisheim (Germany)	13	—	—
Warwick (UK)	14	—	—
Chinese University of Hong Kong	15	—	—
Cass (City, UK)	15	—	—
CEIBS (China)	17	—	—
Stern (NYU)	18	19	5
Johnson (Cornell)	19	17	—
IMD (Switzerland)	19	7	—
IESE (Spain)	21	15	—
Tanaka (Imperial, UK)	21	—	—
Australian Graduate School	23	—	—
Merage (UC Irvine)	24	—	—
Ivey (Western Ontario, Canada)	24	22	—
Goizueta (Emory)	27	6	10
Texas	30	12	—
Marshall (Southern California)	32	8	9
Anderson (UCLA)	32	14	8
Kenan-Flagler (North Carolina)	50	5	—
Fisher (Ohio State)	71	13	—
Ross (Michigan)	*	4	7
McDonough (Georgetown)	—	10	—
Fuqua Weekend (Duke)	—	11	—

*Too new to qualify for the *FT* rankings

FULL-TIME MBA PROGRAMS—CANADA

	FINANCIAL TIMES	BUSINESS WEEK	EIU
Schulich (York)	1	4	1
Rotman (Toronto)	2	3	*
Ivey (Western Ontario)	3	2	*
McGill	4	—	—
Sauder (British Columbia)	5	—	2
Queen's	6	1	—
Alberta	7	—	—
HEC (Montreal)	—	5	3

*Did not participate in EIU survey.

FULL-TIME MBA PROGRAMS—UNITED KINGDOM AND CONTINENTAL EUROPE

	FINANCIAL TIMES	BUSINESS WEEK	EIU
London Business School	1	2	7
INSEAD (France)	2	3	9
Instituto de Empresa (Spain)	3	—	5
IESE (Spain)	4	5	1
IMD (Switzerland)	5	1	2
Saïd/Oxford (UK)	6	—	13
HEC (Paris)	7	—	18
Manchester (UK)	8	—	23
Rotterdam (Netherlands)	9	—	33
ESADE (Spain)	10	4	12
Lancaster (UK)	11	—	19
Bocconi (Italy)	12	—	38
Judge/Cambridge (UK)	13	—	3
Cranfield (UK)	14	—	6
Tanaka/Imperial (UK)	15	—	36
Cass/City (UK)	16	—	17
Warwick (UK)	17	—	11
Ashridge (UK)	18	—	8
Bradford/NIMBAS (UK, Neth., Germany)	19	—	26
Leeds (UK)	20	—	15
Vlerick Leuven Gent (Belgium)	—	—	10
Henley (UK)	—	—	4

FULL-TIME MBA PROGRAMS—AUSTRALASIA

Three major organizations rank Australasian MBA programs. The *Financial Times* ranked only five of the region's schools in its most recent worldwide top 100 listing, clearly suggesting that the top Asian programs are not yet competitive with the leading North American and European programs.

	FINANCIAL TIMES	EIU
CEIBS (China)	1	—
Hong Kong University of Science and Technology	2	1
Melbourne (Australia)	3	6
Australian Graduate School of Management	4	—
National University of Singapore	5	11
University of Hong Kong	—	2
Monash (Australia)	—	3
Nanyang (Singapore)	—	4
Macquarie (Australia)	—	5
International University of Japan	—	7
Curtin (Australia)	—	8
Otago (New Zealand)	—	9
Indian Institute of Management (Ahmedabad)	—	10

Asia Inc. magazine no longer ranks schools across Asia, preferring to name a top three in each of four Asian regions:

- Southeast Asia: National University of Singapore; Nanyang Business School (Singapore); Asian Institute of Technology (Thailand)

- East Asia: Chinese University of Hong Kong; University of Hong Kong; Antai (Aetna) School of Management (Shanghai)

- Australia/New Zealand: Australian Graduate School of Management; Macquarie (Australia); Monash (Australia)

- South Asia: Indian Institute of Management (Ahmedabad); Indian Institute of Management (Bangalore); Indian Institute of Management (Calcutta)

BUSINESS SCHOOLS IN THE REST OF THE WORLD

Schools in Latin America, Africa, and the Middle East hardly feature among the world's very best. The *FT*'s global rankings, for instance, include only Cape Town from South Africa, Incae from Costa Rica, Coppead from Brazil, and Ipade from

Mexico in its top 100—and not one makes the top 50. (For the most important rankings of Latin American schools, consult *América Economía*.)

WHAT DO THE RANKINGS NOT COVER?

The primary rankings of the business schools, noted above, tend to let some programs fall between the cracks. In particular, they tend to miss the outposts of schools such as INSEAD, Chicago, and Kellogg, which have satellite programs outside their home countries. For instance, INSEAD's Singapore program does not show up in many Asian rankings, nor does Chicago's executive MBA program (one of the bases of which is Singapore). Similarly, most rankings consider only the flagship MBA program of those schools that offer more than one. Thus, the one-year programs at Kellogg and Johnson (Cornell) are generally overlooked by the various rankings, which consider instead their larger two-year programs.

THE TOP IN EVERYTHING?

DEPARTMENTAL RANKINGS

Are the top schools the best in terms of everything they do? Not necessarily. Although the overall reputation of a school might guarantee that a graduate will be taken seriously, it does not guarantee that every specialization the school offers is of equal quality or renown. If you want to study a particular subject, especially an unusual one, you will want to consider the quality and reputation of the relevant department and its course offerings at different schools.

The *Financial Times*, *Business Week*, the *Wall Street Journal*, and *U.S. News* list top schools in a host of different specialties:

	U.S. NEWS	*BUSINESS WEEK*	*WALL STREET JOURNAL*	*FINANCIAL TIMES*
Accounting	x		x	x
Economics				x
Entrepreneurship	x	x	x	x
Finance	x	x	x	x
Information Systems/Technology	x		x	
International	x		x	
Management	x	x	x	

	U.S. NEWS	BUSINESS WEEK	WALL STREET JOURNAL	FINANCIAL TIMES
Marketing	x	x	x	
Nonprofit	x			
Operations Management	x		x	
Organizational Behavior				x
Strategy			x	
Supply Chain Management	x			

Note, however, that these departmental rankings are done in a much more casual fashion than are the rankings of overall MBA programs. Thus, *Business Week* simply asks business school deans and program heads to list what they consider top departments, instead of surveying thousands of students and employers and calculating an intellectual capital quotient. (See the discussion below.)

In addition to these generalist publications, specialist journals in fields ranging from information technology to entrepreneurship rank schools, focusing on such matters as the percentage of their graduates taking jobs in the relevant field or the number of courses offered in the field. Although these can be helpful in your search to find appropriate schools on which to focus, beware that many of the specialist publications put little effort into these rankings. Pay particularly close attention to their methodologies in light of the methodology discussion below.

LIMITATIONS OF THE RANKINGS' METHODOLOGIES

Rankings of schools can be based on different factors. Simple rankings may measure nothing more than one statistical feature of the school, such as the average salary of graduates or the average GMAT score. Others may combine various statistical features. Another approach is to rank schools based upon informed opinion. Business school deans, recruiters of business school graduates, and students at the schools themselves are the most commonly utilized "experts."

The rankings are neither precise nor totally accurate in measuring the quality of programs. They do, however, influence the number and quality of applicants to specific programs and, as a result, the number and quality of recruiters hiring graduates of the school.

There are dozens of individuals and organizations that publish rankings of MBA programs. Due to space limitations, it is not possible to analyze the methodologies employed by all of them. Five rankings that use very different methodologies, and so reach different conclusions about the relative value of different schools, are the *Financial Times*, *Business Week*, *U.S. News & World Report*, the *Wall Street Journal*, and the Economist Intelligence Unit. These provide an opportunity to examine some of the methodological issues that bedevil the rankings business.

In general, it is clear that there are a number of problems any rater of schools must address. What does "best" mean? Is it the school that conveys the most technical knowledge, is most up to date, best prepares someone to be an entrepreneur (or senior manager for a large multinational), nets graduates the highest salaries, most increases students' earnings (versus their pre-MBA salaries), best prepares someone in a particular field, or is the least painful to get through? A rater who chooses any one definition to the exclusion of all others is still faced with potentially insurmountable problems. For example, how is the rater to measure which school is the best today at preparing entrepreneurs whose success may not be fully visible for another thirty years? (And, of course, even if the rating is generally accurate, it does not mean that the number-one school will be the best one for you in particular.)

FINANCIAL TIMES

Methodology. The *Financial Times* ranks MBA programs each year in late January. It ranks the top 100 programs in the world on the basis of some twenty factors, both objective and subjective. Not only does it take account of more factors than does any other major ranking, but it is also one of the only major rankings that directly compares schools from different regions of the world.

Advantages of the approach. In comparing schools from different regions (and traditions), it is particularly appropriate to take account of a large number of factors; any one might produce highly skewed rankings favoring schools from one country, region, or tradition. (See the discussion below for more about this.) As more and more applicants cross borders for their business educations, it is very helpful for these applicants to have rankings that compare schools from different countries and continents.

Limitations of the methodology. The *FT*'s approach is to try to measure three broad elements of an MBA: its graduates' career progression, the diversity of their experience in the program, and the school's research quality. One can certainly argue about whether this is the right set of elements to measure, but it is at least a reasonable one. However, even if one accepts that these are the three most important elements of an MBA program, there are inevitable difficulties in finding appropriate ways to measure them and inevitable arbitrariness in assigning weights to the different factors. (Should the percentage of women in the program be 2 percent of a school's total score, as it is here, rather than 1, 3, or 6 percent?)

A *program's "performance"—its impact upon the careers of its graduates*—accounts for 55 percent of its score. Eight criteria are used to assess performance, with salary (at three years after graduation) and salary increase (from the beginning of the program) being the most heavily weighted. Salaries are standardized by converting to U.S. dollars at purchasing power parity exchange rates, which takes into account countries' different price levels but ignores different levels of taxation. Each school's salaries are weighted according to an average distribution of jobs by sector. Thus, it has been assumed that 29 percent of alumni are employed in finance, 14 percent in consulting, and so on. If 80 percent of a school's graduates were actually employed in finance, however, this standardization would produce data of questionable relevance.

A host of other, mainly subjective, factors are used to measure graduates' success. For example, alumni are asked to what extent they fulfilled their goals for doing an MBA and how helpful the career services office was to them. Such views are clearly open to "gaming"—reporting whatever one thinks will be most helpful to one's school rather than what might be true. There are other potential problems here, too. Judging career progress by the size of the company in which graduates are employed—at a time when many people pursue MBAs in order to work for (or found) smaller, more entrepreneurial organizations—seems misplaced. (See the *U.S. News* discussion below, regarding other problems in measuring placement and career success.)

The *diversity of experience* a student enjoys during the program comprises 25 percent of the total score. The more international the student body, faculty, and board, the better a school does. (Ditto for women in the student body, on the faculty, and on the board.) In addition, schools are credited for such things as the number of languages required of graduates and the international mobility of graduates (i.e., taking jobs outside one's own country or country of the school). Although the emphasis upon the international dimension, for instance, is praiseworthy, there is inevitably an arbitrary element to how it is measured. Thus, awarding points for the percentage of alums who work outside the country in which the school is located clearly rewards schools in small countries. Graduates of a school located in Switzerland (about 1 percent of the world economy) are clearly more likely to be tempted to take jobs elsewhere than are graduates of schools located in the United States. Similarly, a finance graduate of a Dutch school who wants the most sophisticated, challenging job possible is likely to work in New York or London at some point. A graduate of an American or British school, on the other hand, cannot be said to be ducking challenges (or even an international dimension to his career, for that matter) by taking a job in his home country.

Three criteria are used to measure the school's *performance in research* (20 percent of the total). These criteria include the percentage of the faculty having a doctorate, the number of doctoral graduates produced by the school, and a rating of faculty publications in major journals. Arguably the most questionable of these submeasures is the first. Considering the percentage of faculty with doctorates is no doubt highly useful when evaluating lesser schools (which might otherwise look to hire masses of underqualified and uncredentialed instructors), but it is unlikely to be so valuable when judging the very elite. For instance, some schools like to bring in a few practitioners of whatever is hot at the moment, such as the latest financial engineering approach, even if (gasp!) they have only an MBA rather than a Ph.D. Penalizing a school for doing this seems strange. It is also unclear to what extent an MBA graduate benefits from a school producing Ph.D. graduates—and, if the benefit is substantial, whether or not it is captured in the career progression data that features so heavily in this survey. (That is, if a graduate has more finely honed skills as a result of having worked with professors who are developing doctoral students at the same time, won't these skills command higher compensation in the job market?)

SOME IMPLICATIONS OF THE *FINANCIAL TIMES*'S METHODOLOGY

A savvy admissions director trying to boost her school's position in the *FT*'s rankings could make a few simple moves that would produce large results. First, she would try to accept as many applicants as possible from the nonprofit and governmental sectors, in order to minimize the average salary of the incoming class (so that the resulting post-MBA salary "step-up" would thereby be maximized). The same goes for younger candidates: They tend to have lower salaries before business school than do older candidates. Candidates serving in the armed forces with technical backgrounds, who would be suitable candidates for consulting jobs after business school, would be ideal. (Their current salaries are below market, making the step-up effect all the greater.) She would also try to ensure that all candidates would head to the highest paying professions, notably consulting and investment banking, and would shy away from those who would start up their own companies or go into the nonprofit or governmental sectors—again, to maximize the step-up effect. Similarly, she would favor applicants who would head to the United States or Switzerland (where salaries for managers are highest) rather than harming the school's ranking by going somewhere offering lower salaries.

But a savvy admissions director could go much further than this. By getting the school's dean to replace the current board of directors with foreign women, and by maximizing the number of foreign women in the program itself, she would maximize the school's "internationalization" score.

And so on.

This somewhat tongue-in-cheek response to the *FT*'s rankings is not meant to be highly critical. In fact, the *FT* offers a valuable and sensible set of rankings. On the other hand, no ranking is perfect—as the above comments suggest.

BUSINESS WEEK

Methodology. Business Week magazine rates MBA programs every even-numbered year in a late October issue of the magazine. It then incorporates these views in its companion book, *Business Week's Guide to the Best Business Schools*. It rates the top 30 schools based upon surveys of two "consumers" of business school services: the students who attend and the employers who hire graduates of these schools. In addition, it considers the "intellectual capital" of the school itself by examining the extent to which the school's professors are published in the major business journals or reach a wider audience. The rating of each school is based upon its combined score; the students' and employers' opinions each represent 45 percent (90 percent together) of the total; the intellectual capital score only 10.

Advantages of the approach. It is obviously appropriate to know what the two major consumers of business school services—the students who are trained by the schools, and the employers who hire their graduates—think about the programs. Student views of the total experience—of teaching quality, academic atmosphere, career services, and so on—are clearly relevant. Similarly, the views of likely employers concerning the quality of a given school, and its graduates, are important when trying to assess how useful a degree from that school will be.

Limitations of the methodology. Business Week has made substantial changes in its methodology in recent surveys. The biggest change is that it now includes a measure of the intellectual capital of a school. In other words, to what extent is the intellectual debate in a field such as finance driven by the faculty at school X rather than the faculty at school Y. There are two problems with this approach. First, the means chosen to measure intellectual capital are questionable. As just one example, in looking at articles that appear in the major professional journals, points were assigned on the basis of the articles' length! (Why anyone would want to encourage business academics to write longer articles is entirely unclear to me.) Second, and more important, the underlying principle of *Business Week*'s approach to ranking has been predicated upon the idea that all relevant information is to be found in the opinion of a school's students and recruiters of those graduates. Thus, rather than look at a school's acceptance rate, average GMAT score, or other data about the students, *Business Week* chose to consider the view of recruiters. The rating recruiters gave a school, it was assumed, incorporated all of these data. Therefore, *Business Week* did not double count GMAT data by including recruiters' opinions of graduates as well as a separate rating of the school's average GMAT score. Presumably the same is true regarding intellectual capital; a student exposed to the finest finance minds is presumably a more able graduate and valued as such by recruiters, who rate the school highly in consequence. Therefore, it is unclear why *Business Week* has decided to double count intellectual capital—and no other measure.

It is important to note at this point that both student and employer surveys are subject to significant sources of potential bias. The student survey, for example, is very open to being "gamed." If you were a student at good old Acme Business School, and you knew that your employment options and starting salaries depended to some substantial degree upon the rating of your school, wouldn't you consider rating the school as better than perfect in every survey category so as to improve your employment prospects? Another potential source of bias concerns the nature of the students who choose to attend different schools. It is quite possible that those attending Harvard are sophisticates who demand the best, who went to Harvard expecting to have the best possible professors for each and every course, and who would be disappointed if they did not have the most famous and pedagogically able professor for each course. Students who go to Indiana University, in the unpretentious town of Bloomington in the middle of America's corn belt, might have very different, very reasonable expectations. Thus, the ratings by these different groups of students might not be readily comparable.

The employer survey suffers from a similar potential problem. Employers hiring from Harvard and Indiana might be hiring for very different positions and expecting very different people from each school. They might pay Harvard graduates $150,000 and expect them soon to be running a region, whereas they might hire an Indiana graduate for $80,000 and expect him to be a solid contributor who will take twice as long to get a promotion as the Harvard graduates. Once again, are employer's ratings of the schools truly comparable?

There are also the usual problems with the selection of the employers for the survey. For example, there is an apparent bias toward larger employers, even though more and more MBA graduates are being employed by smaller, especially high-tech, firms. Similarly, there is the problem of potential nonresponse bias—which puts entrepreneurially focused schools at a particular disadvantage. (Would-be entrepreneurs are disproportionately likely to be "unemployed" when they graduate, trying to get their company up and running.)

In addition to all of these issues, the *Business Week* survey arguably asks the wrong question of employers. It seeks to learn whether employers were satisfied with their recruitment effort at a given program. If the employer says "no," the survey does not ask for an explanation. Instead the "no" response is counted against the program, even if the underlying reason for the dissatisfaction was that the employer was unable to hire students it dearly wished to employ. In other words, an employer's inability to attract a student could undermine a program's ranking, even though it was the employer that was found wanting.

(The *Wall Street Journal* survey discussed below also depends upon employers' rankings of schools for its results; thus, its methodology suffers from many of the same inherent problems and limitations.)

One further note: Rather than pay attention to the self-serving comments of students about their own programs, why not emphasize where the best applicants choose to apply and enroll? For example, of those students admitted to Harvard, MIT, Stanford, Chicago, and Wharton, what percentage choose Stanford? "Voting with their feet" is a more reliable indicator of what students think about different programs.

U.S. NEWS & WORLD REPORT

Methodology. U.S. News & World Report magazine rates business schools each year in March. Its methodology is much more complex than that of *Business Week. U.S. News* considers three factors: a school's reputation, placement success, and admissions selectivity, each of which is composed of multiple subfactors.

Advantages of the approach. The virtues of this approach are clear. First, by explicitly taking many more factors into account than does *Business Week*, it may well do a more thorough job of measuring what makes a business school great. (*Business Week* could retort that its own methodology implicitly takes these other factors into account insofar as its survey respondents—students and employers—evaluate whatever factors they consider relevant.) Second, the ratings that *U.S. News*'s methodology produces are quite stable over time, with essentially none of the extreme jumps and falls in individual ratings that have been so marked in the *Business Week* ratings. This is presumably a reflection of reality, insofar as it is highly unlikely that the actual quality of many business schools would change dramatically in a short period of time.

Limitations of the methodology. A school's reputation counts for 40 percent of its score. This comprises results from two separate surveys. The first is a poll of the deans and program directors of America's accredited business schools; the second is a poll of the corporate recruiters who recruit from top-ranked programs. Both of these polls are subject to potential bias. It is highly unlikely that even a well-informed business school dean will know the operations of other schools so thoroughly that he or she can accurately rate many dozens of them. This is likely to be even more true of recruiters, who are not even in the education business. The likely impact of this is that both groups might tend to overrate schools that are already famous or those that make the biggest splash (perhaps due to their faculty's publications).

Placement success counts for 35 percent of a school's score. This comprises the percentage of students who are employed at the time of graduation and three months later, and the average starting salaries and bonuses. The possible biases here are several. Average starting salaries are highly industry- and location-dependent. Investment banking pays more than industry, so schools that turn out investment bankers will be favored relative to those that turn out people who go into industry. The same is true of schools that send graduates to New York rather than to Durham, North Carolina. The salaries in the former will tend to dwarf those in the latter for the same job, given the different costs of living and other factors. Thus, Columbia and NYU in New York City will have an advantage over the University of North Carolina. The other possible bias concerns the fact that the data are reported by the schools themselves, and it is quite possible that some "cook" the numbers. In reporting starting salaries, for example, will a school include those who take jobs out of the United States? If the dollar is high, and foreign salaries when translated into dollars appear low, the school might choose to forget to include them. When the dollar is low, perhaps the school will remember to include them. The other data can also be manipulated by excluding various categories of students or simply by lying.

Student selectivity counts for 25 percent of a school's score. This comprises the undergraduate grade point averages, average GMAT scores, and percentage of applicants the school accepts. Since these are all reported by the schools themselves, they are all open to manipulation. A school can include or exclude various groups of students to manipulate its numbers. For example, should a school include only American students in calculating its undergraduate grade point averages if only the Americans have been graded on the traditional 4-point scale? On the other hand, perhaps it should include the non-American students, too; but in that case, how should it translate the French 20-point scale or someone else's 100-point scale into an American equivalent?

Student selectivity measures can be gamed in another fashion. Columbia, for instance, goes to great lengths to determine whether an applicant will accept the offer of a place before deciding whether to admit him or her. It thereby greatly reduces the number of students it needs to admit in order to fill its class. Other schools make it easy to apply by waiving the application fees for various applicants, just as some schools encourage even no-hopers to apply, all in order to improve the numbers they report to the AACSB (which accredits American and other programs), *U.S. News*, and other rankings.

And, frankly, even legitimate numbers may have limited information value. Undergraduate GPAs are not comparable from one major to another at a given school, let alone from school to school (or country to country). In fact, grade inflation (and, thank goodness, grade deflation) can make GPAs hard to compare over time—even for someone taking the same courses at the same university.

WALL STREET JOURNAL

Methodology. The *Wall Street Journal* rates business schools annually. It surveys two thousand-plus recruiters to assess three equally weighted factors: their perceptions of schools and their students, the likelihood that they will recruit from these schools in the near future, and the number of recruiters from each of these schools.

Advantages of the approach. The opinions actual recruiters have of the schools (and their students) from which they recruit are clearly relevant to prospective students who would like to understand the employment value of attending one school over another.

Limitations of the methodology. Any employer ranking of programs faces inherent difficulties, some of which were noted above in the discussion of the *Business Week* rankings. The *Wall Street Journal*, however, has compounded these problems with some self-inflicted wounds.

When it first started ranking schools, the *Journal* ended up with extraordinarily anomalous results. A stunning roster of the world's leading schools failed to make the top 25, including INSEAD, Stern (NYU), Darden, IMD, Anderson (UCLA), Sloan (MIT), London, Fuqua (Duke), and Stanford. In their place were schools like Purdue and Michigan State. Ironically, when the same recruiters who put Stanford 45th were asked to list the school they themselves would choose if they were to get an MBA, they plumped for the usual top schools. Thus, they placed Stanford 2nd, not 45th. Similarly, Purdue, which had ranked 6th in the basic survey, was nowhere to be seen among the recruiters' own rankings.

The mistake was to ask recruiters about their past hiring success with a given school, including:

- The number of graduates they have hired from that school.
- The willingness of the school's students to relocate to the job location recruiters require.
- The success they have had retaining students hired from the school.

Even if one asks these questions only of recruiters at top investment banks and consulting firms aiming for the best and brightest, the results will be peculiar. For instance, whether students at INSEAD (outside Paris) or Columbia (in New York City) are willing to relocate to a firm's new office in Frankfurt (let alone Lagos) hardly answers the question of whether these are great business schools. Graduates of the top schools can afford to be very particular about the firm and the location they choose. Thus, it is not clear whether a recruiter having good things to say about a school's graduates' willingness to relocate is a sign that the school is a top school—or an also-ran. The problem is compounded when the question is asked of lesser firms in lesser industries. A cement company in Middle-of-Nowhere Iowa or Siberia will surely be unable to get the world's top graduates to queue for its positions. As a result, it is likely to value middle-tier schools rather than top schools. From this perspective, it is clear why Stanford was at the bottom of the rankings: Its graduates are too highly sought-after by better firms in better locations to take such jobs.

The *Journal* has dropped some of its problematic questions, but it still asks about "willingness of the school's students to relocate" and "overall value for the money invested in the recruiting effort." In addition, fully one-third of a school's score is based on firms' statements as to where they intend to recruit in the future. Thus, a large part of what the *Journal* is ascertaining remains similar to asking the least popular boy in high school which girls offer him the best chance for dates: the extremely popular, attractive, intelligent, interesting ones, or those who have to take whatever offers they can get.

The appropriate question would have been something akin to "Which schools produce the best graduates—the ones that you would most like to land?" Instead, recruiters are asked to indicate where graduates are the most undervalued. (It is tempting to ask whether the inability of graduates to realize their full value in the marketplace is the hallmark of a top school.)

This is not the only problem with the *Journal*'s approach. One-third of a school's score comes from the total number of recruiters participating in the survey who say that they recruit from the school. This measure faces numerous problems. For one thing, it clearly favors large schools, which—other things equal—will attract more recruiters than will small schools. For another, the accuracy of the data is suspect. Rather than asking the subset of firms that have been contacted to participate in this survey—and have agreed to do so—which schools they recruit at, why not use actual data regarding the number of firms that have recently hired a school's graduates?

ECONOMIST INTELLIGENCE UNIT

Methodology. The Economist Intelligence Unit (or "EIU") sends detailed questionnaires to business schools and students around the world. Numerical data from the schools (such as the percentage of women in the program) is combined with student opinions to rank schools according to four criteria: the ability to (1) open up new career opportunities or further a current career, (2) increase salary, (3) network, and (4) develop personally and educationally.

Advantages of the approach. The EIU's emphasis on student opinion is a welcome complement to the *Wall Street Journal's* focus on what recruiters have to say. The four criteria chosen by this survey are eminently reasonable ones for ranking schools insofar as they do reflect major applicant concerns. Understanding what is most important to students, and then attempting to evaluate how business schools stack up on each of these four criteria, is highly relevant to choosing a program.

Limitations of the methodology. This survey is too riddled with issues to attempt to catalogue all of them. One problem is that various major schools, including Harvard and Wharton, refuse to participate in this survey, forcing its authors to estimate data for them (or even leave them out of the survey entirely). Another problem is one common to all student surveys: Most students experience only one program, so their ranking of it may reflect more about their own expectations than about the school's actual performance. By the same token, all student surveys run the risk of being gamed by students desirous of promoting their schools (and, not coincidentally, their own career prospects). These issues are exacerbated by the nonresponse bias of such surveys: Are the opinions of those who choose not to participate the same as those who do respond?

A brief look at the first criterion examined by the EIU—the extent to which a school "opens new career opportunities," which is accorded 35 percent of a school's total score—illustrates the nature and problems of this ranking. One-quarter of the "new career opportunities" score is determined by the diversity of recruiters at a school. This is defined as the number of industry sectors recruiting at it, which clearly favors large schools (as well as those not choosing to focus on particular industry sectors). Another quarter of the score is based on the extent to which students get their ultimate jobs via the schools' career services. This is most peculiar. Shouldn't the standard be the quality of the job obtained (and the extent to which it is what the student wanted), by whatever route? Similarly, this measure penalizes schools whose students start their own businesses or head to their own family businesses. Yet another quarter is based on the percentage of graduates in jobs three months after graduation. This statistic tends to reward those schools whose major regional markets are booming as much as it distinguishes top schools from lesser competitors. The remainder of the score is based on student opinion.

Put simply, the results of the EIU survey tend to be highly anomalous as well as volatile. For instance, Vlerick Leuven Gent (in Belgium, now that you ask) jumped from 47th in the world to 15th in a recent ranking. The idea that a school could improve to this extent in one year (short of buying Harvard's faculty in the interim) is preposterous. The idea that schools which attract much less qualified students are better than rivals that get first choice of both students and professors seems to me highly questionable. Much of the substantive learning in a program comes from other students; so, too, does the value of networking amongst one's classmates.

OTHER RANKINGS

Obviously, the published rankings do not necessarily cover all of the issues and concerns you might have about business schools. This leaves you with room to make your own rankings, tailored to whichever criteria you deem to be most important. Following are a few of the "rankings" you might consider helpful.

JOINT-DEGREE RANKINGS

If you are considering getting a joint degree, pay attention to the ranking of the other program. Depending on your intended career path, the reputation of the nonbusiness program may be the more important of the two.

NUMBER OF GRADUATES HIRED BY YOUR TARGET EMPLOYER(S)

If you want to work for a bulge-bracket investment bank, consider where they recruit. For instance, if you want to work for Morgan Stanley, Merrill Lynch, or Goldman Sachs, note how many students they have recruited from each school in each of the last three years. Then, adjust for the size of the graduating class at each school. Do not, however, take the resulting figures at face value. Consider two additional matters:

- Were the graduates hired only for the local office?
- Were graduates hired for the most prestigious positions (such as mergers and acquisitions)?

OTHER POSSIBLE RANKINGS

Nothing stops you from ranking schools on the basis of what most interests you. For example, you might choose any one or more of the following:

- Percentage of women (or minorities, or Asian Americans, or foreigners, or married people)
- Percentage of incoming students with more than five years' experience (or over the age of 30)
- Salary (which *Forbes* magazine uses as the sole criterion of its annual ranking)
- Number of *Fortune* 100 (500) firms run by graduates of the school (perhaps adjusted by number of graduates)

- Percentage of graduates entering a specific field (consulting, investment banking, and so on)
- Number of alums living in a given city
- Number (or percentage) of courses in your chosen field

Each of these criteria could be a valid measure for what you most desire. The first two measures, for instance, are means of determining whether you will have classmates who are most like you—or most unlike you, if you look to learn from those who least resemble you. There are innumerable other possible bases for rankings, depending upon what you seek from your business school education.

Note that the primary rankings discussed above (such as *Business Week*'s) allow you to sort or rank schools on the basis of various criteria that you select, making the job of producing your own rankings all the easier.

THE ADMISSIONS DIRECTORS DISCUSS THE RANKINGS

Appropriate Use of Rankings

➤ Rankings certainly sell magazines. The raw data that accompanies some of the rankings *does* offer a chance to learn something useful about the programs, such as the ratio of recruiters to students, or courses offered at a school. However, when it comes to the overall conclusions and weightings of what matters, applicants really need to do this on their own. SHARON HOFFMAN, STANFORD

➤ Rankings are beneficial if used as a starting point for exploration. Too many people, however, due to a lack of time, use them as an end point. They should not represent the full extent of your exploration of schools. ANN W. RICHARDS, JOHNSON (CORNELL)

➤ It's fine to use the rankings to learn what schools are out there, but you need to do your own research. THOMAS CALEEL, WHARTON

➤ Research we've done shows prospective students are very strongly influenced by rankings. One can correlate a school's rankings with its number of applications. . . . But applicants should be looking beyond rankings. The different cultures and focuses of programs bear deep and careful research. The best way to do this is by talking with students and alums to find out what a program is really like. DR. SIMON LEARMOUNT, JUDGE (CAMBRIDGE)

➤ I recommend that applicants use the rankings primarily to distinguish between first-tier and second-tier programs. But look at them as a form of accreditation, not as a precise quality measure—and be sure to see whether its priorities are your priorities. MARY GRANGER, ESADE (SPAIN)

Limitations

➤ Rankings are a very interesting research tool—up to a point. They're a great place to start to narrow down your focus. *ROSE MARTINELLI, CHICAGO*

➤ In a broad-bucket sort of way, it's reasonable to choose schools on the basis of reputation. That's to say there is a massive difference between schools normally ranked in the top ten or twenty and those not listed within the top hundreds. It's not reasonable, however, to choose a school ranked sixth over another that's ranked seventh, solely on the basis of the survey. *SHARON HOFFMAN, STANFORD*

➤ You should recognize that rankings are used to sell magazines, not to judge programs in an equitable fashion. *ROSE MARTINELLI, CHICAGO*

➤ Schools have dramatically different cultures and ways of learning. If you go to a school that's wrong for you, it can be a disaster. If you aren't comfortable at a school, you'll fail to learn as much as you could, just as you'll fail to make the friendships and lifetime connections you should. When it comes time to get a job, having an MBA from a highly ranked school will open a door for you, but it's up to you to cross the threshold. You need the skills and abilities you should have developed through wholehearted engagement during your MBA program to do so. *THOMAS CALEEL, WHARTON*

➤ The rankings are dominated by those emanating from the United States. For programs outside the United States, the accuracy of rankings diminishes enormously. *KIRT WOOD, ROTTERDAM*

CONCLUSION

The discussion of the limitations of the various ranking methodologies should not be viewed as a severe criticism of these surveys. In fact, each survey offers useful information, and taken together, a group of surveys offers a great deal to prospective applicants. I urge you to consult the items described above, but I also urge you to be cautious in using them. Remember that such rankings should be the starting point of your investigation of which schools are likely to be right for you, not the end point.

Sources

América Economía: www.americaeconomia.com

Asia Inc.: www.asia-inc.com

Business Week: www.businessweek.com

Economist Intelligence Unit: www.eiu.com

The Financial Times: www.ft.com

Forbes: www.forbes.com

U.S. News & World Report: www.usnews.com

The Wall Street Journal: www.wsj.com

Die Zeit: www.zeit.de (for a German ranking of schools)

THE ADMISSIONS PROCESS

— EXECUTIVE SUMMARY —

▪

Most schools have more than one person read your file, guaranteeing that you will not be rejected by someone who is having a bad day.

▪

Admissions professionals, mindful of the need to fill classes with human beings rather than data points, seek to understand who you are as well as what you have accomplished.

▪

In addition to admissions professionals, some American schools involve students and alumni in admissions decisions, whereas most European schools also use faculty members.

*T*his chapter describes the mechanics of *how* schools make their admissions decisions and *who* makes them. Chapter 7, "Making the Most of Your Credentials," analyzes the criteria the schools apply, whereas this chapter is devoted to explaining the admissions *process*.

A school's admissions professionals will determine whether or not to admit you based upon the whole of your application folder—your job history, educational achievements, extracurricular and community involvements, honors and awards, essays, recommendations, and interview evaluation. Not every admissions officer will weight the different elements in the same way—or, for that matter, grade them in the same way—but the way the process is followed will hold true for each and every applicant to a school. And while the admissions process at different schools varies somewhat, it varies much less than might be expected—partly because admissions officers at the various schools talk with one another about what procedure each follows—but probably owing more to the desire schools have to be thorough in their evaluation of candidates. Schools go to great lengths to be sure they have given every applicant a fair chance.

"ROLLING" VERSUS "ROUNDS" ADMISSIONS

Applications can be processed in either of two ways. Schools using *rolling* admissions evaluate applications as they are submitted, on a "first come, first served" basis. For example, if George's application is complete on November 1 and Martha's on November 28, the admissions officers will start the process of reviewing George's application before they start reviewing Martha's. They will start on George's application when they get the chance, whether that means beginning on November 1 or December 9. In either event, the one certainty is that they will start to process George's file before they start on Martha's.

The process for schools using *rounds*, however, is quite different. These schools split the application period into multiple mini-periods. For example, a school might have deadlines on November 10, January 20, and March 30. All applications received on or before November 10 will be held, without any admissions actions being taken, until November 11 (or thereabouts). At that time, all of the applications in this batch will begin to be evaluated (a process that of course takes at least several weeks).

Please note that your application will receive no attention from admissions officers until it has been completed, meaning that *everything* that is required has been received by the school. Thus, if your second recommendation has not yet been submitted, the admissions staff will keep your file open until they receive the recommendation, at which time your application will be ready for evaluation.

THE STANDARD (AMERICAN) MODEL

WHO ARE THE ADMISSIONS OFFICERS?

The director of admissions is typically someone who has worked in business school admissions for some years. *At the top schools*, this generally means someone who has had substantial experience as a more junior admissions officer at the same school, or an equivalent amount of time in charge of admissions at a less prestigious school. He or she may not have an MBA, but in this case will probably have a human resources background.

Directors *at other schools* are likely to include those with similar backgrounds in human resources, and recruitment in particular, and those who have recently graduated from the school's MBA program. All schools like to have some of the latter involved to provide a realistic flavor of the program to applicants who attend school information sessions, and also because these recent graduates have a potentially different appreciation of which applicants will fit well and contribute significantly to the program. What all the admissions officers share is dedication to their schools and a concomitant drive to admit only the most qualified group of applicants they can find.

HOW ARE DECISIONS MADE?

Most American schools follow a similar procedure, known as a "blind read." Two admissions officers are given copies of an applicant's file and asked to categorize it. Although it is possible for a school to use more categories, for simplicity's sake I will refer to just three: "accept," "reject," and "don't know." If both admissions officers rate the applicant as an "accept," then no more work needs to be done: She is accepted. Similarly, if both admissions officers rate her as a "reject," she is rejected. In some schools, the process works in the same manner except that the admissions director may quickly scan each file, including those that were rated a clear "accept" or "reject" by the two initial readers, to make sure nothing is amiss in the process.

On the other hand, if the two admissions officers disagree about her or rate her as a "don't know," then her file will be considered further. At this point, some schools have the admissions director make the final decision whereas others have admissions officers decide as a group.

The mix of different backgrounds and talents on the part of the admissions officers leads to occasionally spirited discussions about how to rate a given applicant, but this is generally viewed as a positive because the school is looking for a diverse group of students and wants an admissions team that is appreciative of a range of different backgrounds and talents.

Recently, the career services departments at certain schools have become involved in the admissions process. Although it is easy to find jobs for the typical applicant, such as an engineer who wishes to enter management in the same industry he has worked in for the last four years, it may be difficult to help an atypical applicant find a job. In such cases the admissions director is likely to chat with the career services director to get his or her opinion regarding the employability of such applicants. (The candidate who intends to change careers is thus well advised to make it clear that the proposed change is a realistic one that suits her talents, and is one that she will pursue vigorously and intelligently.)

THE CRITERIA

Admissions officers have a lot of information about you when it comes time to make their decision. Most applicants assume that the admissions process is devoted to weighing applicants' grade point averages, GMAT test scores, and number of years of work experience, and they thereby make a fundamental mistake. (See Chapter 7 for an in-depth discussion of the admissions criteria.) Admissions committees are made up of human beings, generally those who have chosen to work in a human resources capacity, and consequently they are particularly interested in admitting real human beings rather than a set of statistics. You will find it hard to gain admission if you are just so many data points on a page. (Applicants who can make themselves real—that is, human—are more likely to gain supporters among the admissions officers. You should therefore take every opportunity to distinguish yourself from the mass of the applicant pool and make your human qualities apparent.) It takes a lot of time and effort to accept or reject a given applicant because admissions officers try very hard to understand her, not just to glance at her test scores.

THE TIMING

The average decision period is approximately eight to ten weeks at American schools, although this period varies according to circumstance. In years with a particularly large number of applicants, it can stretch to twelve weeks or more. The European schools generally decide more quickly; the smaller programs often make decisions within a month.

THE STUDENT-INVOLVEMENT VARIATION

The student-involvement model of the admissions process is essentially identical to the standard American model, but with one important exception: the involvement of students in the process. Kellogg and Wharton are well known for this practice. The usual way in which schools make use of students is in interviewing applicants, although some have begun to involve them in the evaluation of files—and even in making final decisions about them.

The use of students is confined to second-year students, who are trained how to interview and/or evaluate files. There are several reasons for not using first-year students. It would be inappropriate for them to be in classes and activities with people who might have bared their souls in the admissions process. Second-year students, however, will have graduated by the time the applicants whom they interviewed or whose files they evaluated enroll, thereby eliminating such confidentiality concerns. In addition, it would be inappropriate to have students evaluating applicants before they (the students) themselves know what business school is all about.

Schools use students not just to share the workload, to get free labor, or even to deepen the involvement of these students with the school. These students are relatively fresh from the jobs they held before business school as well as actively involved in deciding which job they will take upon graduation. As a result, they are well placed to evaluate how well applicants have done in their jobs, how well employers will regard them in the future, and how well they will be able to contribute to classes and study groups.

Note: Many schools involve alumni in the interviewing process. (See Chapter 12 for a discussion of this process.)

THE EUROPEAN VARIATION

Most European schools eschew the American practice of having admissions professionals make admissions decisions. These schools have their admissions professionals prepare the files on each candidate and then present them to the admissions committee, which is made up of professors from a variety of disciplines. The admissions officers therefore act more as advisors than decision makers.

The procedures of these schools tend otherwise to resemble those at American schools. Many, for example, use the "double blind" reader approach, in which two professors on the admissions committee read an applicant's file and categorize it as "accept," "reject," or "don't know." Those rated by both professors as "accept" are indeed accepted; those rated as "reject" are rejected; and in cases where the two professors disagreed or marked "don't know," the file is handed to a third professor or, more often, the whole committee for a final decision.

(Using professors to make admissions decisions might be expected to elevate the importance of academic credentials, but this appears to be true to only the slightest extent. Whether this outcome is due to the influence of the admissions professionals in the process is unclear.)

The use of professors to make admissions decisions is quite rare at the leading American schools, hence my designation of the practice as the "European variation."

THE ADMISSIONS DIRECTORS DISCUSS THE ADMISSIONS PROCESS

How Their Schools Process Applications

➤ Each application is thoroughly evaluated by at least two members of the MBA Admissions Board. Due to the size of our applicant pool, we are unable to interview all candidates. Interviews are conducted by invitation only, at the discretion of the Admissions Board, after all applications have been submitted and reviewed. *BRIT DEWEY, HARVARD*

➤ Our first reader summarizes the application and gives grades of one to five (one is the top grade) on academic credentials, professional experience, personal qualities (leadership, for example, and the interview are important here), and overall. The second reader also grades the application. It is then classified according to the higher of the two graders' marks. We then review the applications as a committee, starting with those having the highest and lowest grades and working toward the middle (where the decisions are hardest). It's an extremely thorough and extremely fair process, even though it is subjective rather than scientific. *SALLY JAEGER, TUCK*

➤ The first reader comments on the application and recommends that we admit, wait-list, deny, or interview before making a decision. The second reader also makes a recommendation. If both agree, we generally do what they recommend, albeit after a brief look by the admissions committee. If they disagree, a third reader reviews the file, and then the candidate is invited to interview. After that, the case goes back to the admissions committee for a decision. *PETER JOHNSON, HAAS*

➤ The first reading of the file is done by one of our trained second-year students. The second reading is conducted by an admissions officer. If both of them feel that the candidate should be rejected, the file is examined by another two or three admissions people to be sure that rejection is the right option. If, on the other hand, either of the first two readers believes that the candidate might merit admission, we invite him or her to interview. After he or she is interviewed, the admissions committee decides whether or not to offer admission. *ANN W. RICHARDS, JOHNSON (CORNELL)*

➤ Each applicant is interviewed before the application is submitted. Afterward, each one is assigned to one of three account managers. So if they have questions, or have information to share later in the process, they'll have someone specific to contact. Once the application is complete, it is read by a minimum of three people before a decision is made. *SARAH E. NEHER, DARDEN*

➤ We start by printing out the application. Then, one of our sixty-plus highly trained, second-year students does the first reading of the file. He or she prepares a "case sheet" that summarizes the application, with comments on everything from the essays to the recommendations, along with the GMAT results and so on. Next, the file goes to one of our full-time admissions committee members, who reads it cover to cover and also makes notes on it. At this point the files are separated into two piles: the "invite to interview" and "do not invite" piles. I then review both piles, reading each of the "no interview" applications thoroughly. After an applicant is interviewed, the file—including the interview evaluation—is read by an admissions committee member. Then I read the entire file. The last step is that it goes to the admissions committee for a final decision. *THOMAS CALEEL, WHARTON*

➤ We take a one-on-one counseling approach to applications. We create many opportunities for a dialogue with each applicant. Ideally we can work with people before they apply—to talk both about financing strategies and about how to improve their application. . . . Once an application is complete, our committee decides whether to invite the applicant to interview. We request either one or two interviews, depending upon how much we feel we need to evaluate the candidate. Once we have the interview information back, the file again goes to committee. Some seven to ten people will end up evaluating the candidate (since we involve people from throughout the school—academic directors, alumni, career services, program directors . . .). The whole process usually takes four to six weeks, after which applicants get our response. *KIRT WOOD, ROTTERDAM*

➤ The process starts with the five-person admissions committee, which consists of faculty members and the MBA Director, evaluating people's files. Some people are rejected at this stage; others are invited to interview. The interview is usually done at Oxford by the MBA Director or a faculty member, although we do hold interview events around the world (and will even interview by telephone if necessary). The committee makes a final decision based on the file and interview comments. *ALISON OWEN, SAïD (OXFORD)*

➤ One admissions person reads the application, and then decides whether to invite the candidate for an interview. A member of the admissions team conducts the interview. Then the file goes to the admissions committee, where at least three people will read the entire file. *Mary Granger, ESADE (Spain)*

Advice on How to Communicate with the Admissions Office

➤ The best piece of advice is that timing is everything. There are times when admissions officers are busy and have no time to talk. The worst time to contact us is when we are on the road interviewing or when we're reading applications. *Rod Garcia, MIT*

➤ I'm outside the norm: I really love the contact with people, so I don't mind candidates contacting us during the process. *Sally Jaeger, Tuck*

➤ It's good that applicants contact us more often via e-mail than phone. We know they're anxious, so we now release decisions just as soon as they're made. Applicants can go on-line to check their status at any time. *Anne Coyle, Yale*

➤ I don't think there's ever a point in the process when applicants need to call us. We are proactive in supplying them with information on-line regarding the status of their files. *James Hayes, Michigan*

➤ A short thank-you note after meeting one of our people is fine. A convoluted, multilevel question meant to dazzle us is not. *Thomas Caleel, Wharton*

➤ We pride ourselves on getting to know our applicants very well. We look at the total presentation of the person. So how you behave in an interview or information session, the tone of your e-mails, or interactions with our customer service professionals definitely speaks to you as a person. So you want to make sure all of your interactions put you in the best light. Be professional, civil, polite, and understand that being pushy or rude is not well received. *Isser Gallogly, Stern (NYU)*

➤ It's useful to stay on top of the process without being overbearing. *David Bach, Instituto de Empresa (Spain)*

➤ We're happy to talk to applicants with questions that they can't find the answers to on our website. *Katty Ooms Suter, IMD (Switzerland)*

➤ If an applicant faces a specific deadline by which he or she needs to respond to another school's offer of admission, it is perfectly fine to contact us to see whether we will be offering admission. *Mary Granger, ESADE (Spain)*

6

APPLICATION TIMETABLE

— EXECUTIVE SUMMARY —

▪

Start the process as early as possible.

—Assess what you want from an MBA.

—Gather information about programs to determine where you should apply.

▪

Apply as early as you can without sacrificing the quality of your application.

—Applying early improves your chances.

—It also gives you some slack if factors beyond your control delay some aspect of your application.

▪

Track your progress with the Master Application Organizer.

Schools basically use one of two types of admissions decision cycles. "Rolling admissions" involves considering applicants whenever they apply within the several-month admission cycle, and responding soon after receiving a completed application. "Rounds admissions" means that they establish multiple deadlines and wait until each to look at an entire group of applicants.

WHEN SHOULD YOU APPLY—EARLY OR LATE IN AN APPLICATION CYCLE?

The application cycle refers to the period of time during which a school accepts applications for a given class. In other words, a school might accept applications from November 1 through April 15 for the class beginning in September. This raises a question. Should you apply early (in November, for example) or late (in April) if you wish to maximize your chances of getting in?

WHAT ARE THE BENEFITS OF APPLYING EARLY IN THE APPLICATION CYCLE?

There are several benefits to applying early in the application cycle. Assuming that the application is well written, an early application suggests that you are well organized. It also suggests that you are serious about getting into business school rather than applying on a whim. Another benefit can accrue if the school underestimates the number or quality of applicants it will eventually get this year. If this is the case, early applicants will have an easier time getting in than they otherwise would.

Certain types of applicants, of course, can benefit (from applying early) more than others. If you are a "cookie-cutter" candidate, who is not readily distinguishable from a large number of other applicants in his part of the applicant pool, your file will be less likely to inspire yawns if yours is one of the first of its kind to be read. For instance, if you are an analyst from a major investment bank or an electrical engineer from India, you should apply as early as practicable. A second type of candidate who stands to benefit from applying early is someone who has a complicated message and who therefore must give the admissions committee the time and mental energy to read his or her application. Admissions committees tend to lack this time and lose energy as the application season progresses. (International students should seek to apply as early as possible since international credentials may add complexity to their applications.)

The *most important benefit* of applying early, however, is that schools make it easier to get in early than to get in near the end of the application cycle. They "set the bar lower" for early applicants largely for internal reasons. Even if the ideal process (in terms of getting the best possible group of students) might be to apply the same standard throughout the process, rather than accepting a slightly lesser candidate early in preference to a slightly better candidate later on, human factors push for somewhat lower standards early on. The admissions director, MBA program director, and dean of the business school can sleep better in January if they know that they have already filled 75 percent (rather than 40 percent) of the class. The degree to which schools raise the bar through the course of the application cycle, however, varies substantially. Wharton, for instance, tends to raise the bar very substantially; Chicago, much less so.

THE ADMISSIONS DIRECTORS DISCUSS THE BENEFITS OF APPLYING EARLY

➤ It's easier to stand out early in the process—as the twentieth investment banker we look at rather than the two-hundredth. Besides, you can learn about financial aid and look for housing earlier on, too. *DAWNA CLARKE, TUCK*

➤ Apply as early as you are ready. Don't rush to get the application in if it's not competitive. Make your most competitive application, and if that needs to be somewhat later, so be it. *ISSER GALLOGLY, STERN (NYU)*

➤ Early Decision was designed specifically for our purposes—an opportunity for us to read applications for the September (start-date) program before reading applications for the January program. . . . A good applicant's chances in the Early Decision round are far better than they would be applying later on. *LINDA MEEHAN, COLUMBIA*

➤ The criteria remain the same throughout the process. But one of the criteria concerns applicants' fit with the Darden community. We determine that in part via their level of understanding of Darden and the case method. And the earlier you apply, the more we feel you understand what we're offering and want to be a part of it. *SARAH E. NEHER, DARDEN*

➤ We have three rounds. There is absolutely no difference between the first and second rounds. We separate them simply for administrative ease. In round three we always have room for highly qualified candidates, but they need a reason to be applying late in the process. "I've been busy" isn't a valid excuse. Other busy people have managed to get their applications submitted in the first or second rounds. On the other hand, an unexpected liquidity event for an entrepreneur would justify a third-round application. *THOMAS CALEEL, WHARTON*

➤ Setting up living arrangements in a European (socialized) country involves an enormous amount of paperwork. So applying early allows you to become part of the system and set up your life regarding housing and so on. It also allows us to provide a better support system for you. *KIRT WOOD, ROTTERDAM*

➤ You apply to the program, not to a specific starting date. Once you are admitted to the program, you then register for whichever starting date in the next two years best fits your needs—assuming there is still space available for it. So although applying early in the process doesn't help you get admitted, you do increase the chances you'll be able to get your preferred starting date. *DAVID BACH, INSTITUTO DE EMPRESA (SPAIN)*

➤ Applying early gives you the best chance of getting into the intake (i.e., starting in September or January) and campus (Fontainebleau or Singapore) of your choice. *JOELLE DU LAC, INSEAD (PARIS)*

➤ Applying early gives us the time to read through the application and clear up any doubts we might have. *MARY GRANGER, ESADE (SPAIN)*

WHAT ARE THE BENEFITS OF APPLYING LATE IN THE APPLICATION CYCLE?

There is only one substantial benefit to applying late in the cycle. An applicant has the opportunity to continue to build her credentials during the few months involved. This can be significant for someone with the potential to transform her application. For example, someone who expects a major promotion and salary increase might wish to apply after getting them rather than before.

A second potential benefit can occur if the school has misjudged its popularity and finds that fewer good applicants have applied than it expected earlier in the cycle, resulting in reduced admissions criteria for those applying later. This is an unpredictable factor and not likely to happen to any substantial degree, however—particularly at the very top schools.

SO, WHAT SHOULD YOU DO?

Most people will benefit by applying early in the admissions cycle. In general, the most important timing criterion is to get the application done well as soon as is practicable. The earlier it is started, the more opportunity there is to rewrite and reconsider, to allow recommenders to finish their work—and even to have others help out by reading the finished product. The only group that should purposely apply late in the cycle consists of those who can substantially improve their credentials in the meantime.

So, unless you are in the small minority expecting such credential improvement, apply as soon as you can finish a truly professional application.

HOW LONG WILL IT TAKE TO DO YOUR APPLICATIONS?

Most applicants underestimate the amount of time that a good application requires, thinking that they can do one in a long weekend or two. The reality is that many of the necessary steps have a long lag built into them. For example, approaching a recommender, briefing her on what you want done, giving her time to do a good recommendation for you, and ensuring that she submits it on time calls for months rather than days of advance notice. This is all the more true when you apply to six or ten schools rather than one; you have more application forms to get, more essays to write, and more recommendations to get submitted. Although work does not increase proportionally with the number of applications, the increased complexity as well as the number of additional things you need to do will inevitably increase your efforts.

The application process should start *at least one and a quarter years in advance* of when you would like to start business school. Thus, if you wish to start a program in September, you should start work in June of the preceding year. This may sound excessive, but the timetable in this section makes it clear that this is an appropriate time to get serious about the process. One of the reasons this process takes so long is that schools generally require that applications be submitted three to nine months in advance of the start of the program, meaning that you will have six to twelve months to complete the process if you start at the suggested time.

Starting the application process late, or failing to work seriously at it until deadlines approach, leads to the typical last-minute rush and the inevitable poor marketing job. This book presents an enlightened approach devoted to the idea that applicants can dramatically improve their admission chances if they do a professional job of marketing themselves. This timetable is meant to reinforce the message that time is required for a successful marketing effort.

It is useful to establish your own timetable for applying. Ideally, you will be able to start about fifteen months before you begin your MBA program. Don't panic if you can't, since many people will, like you, need to condense their work efforts. It is still useful, however, to make sure you use whatever time you have to your greatest advantage.

THE APPLICATION TIMETABLE

The following is a typical schedule for someone applying to schools that begin in September, with interim application deadlines starting in October and a final deadline in March. It is intended not as an exact timeline for you to follow but rather as an illustration of the tasks and deadlines you will want to track.

Early Spring (More than fifteen months in advance of the program)

- Start considering specifically what you want from an MBA program, and whether an MBA is indeed appropriate.

- Develop a preliminary list of appropriate schools. Read several of the better guides, look at the most recent surveys printed in the leading business and popular magazines, scrutinize the course catalogues and websites of the schools themselves, and talk with people knowledgeable about the schools.

- Examine several schools' application forms, even if they are a year out of date, to see what the application process will involve.

- Consider who should write recommendations for you (and be sure you treat them particularly well from now on).

- Start putting together a realistic financial plan to pay for school. Research financial aid sources and your likelihood of qualifying for aid. (Identify necessary forms to be completed and their deadline dates.)

- Consider how you will prepare for the GMAT. Start by getting the *Official Guide for GMAT Review* and subjecting yourself to a sample exam under realistic conditions. If you are not a strong standardized test taker, are unfamiliar with the exam, or just want to save yourself the bother of preparing on your own, figure out which test preparation course you will take and when it will be available. International students will want to do the same regarding the TOEFL exam.

- Take a GMAT (and TOEFL) prep course or begin an intensive GMAT self-study regimen. Take the exam(s) itself, when ready.

- Start filling out the Personal Organizer in Chapter 8 to get a jump on the essay writing. Glance at the chapters covering what the schools want and how to write the essays (Chapters 7, 9, and 10) so that you have some idea of what will be required in writing the essays.

- Start planning school visits.

August/September

- Request interviews at those schools permitting you to do so prior to completion of your applications.

- Look at the online application options. (If a school's application is not yet available, examine last year's form. The application tends to change very little from one year to the next, so even last year's form will give you a good idea of what to expect from the new application.)

- Retake the GMAT (and TOEFL) exam, if necessary. (Do not wait until the autumn to take the exam; you will have your hands full doing your applications.)

- Read the chapters in this book regarding the essay questions, and the essay examples in Part IV.

- Develop a basic positioning statement; write a preliminary essay regarding where you are headed and why you want an MBA. Then, do a rough draft of at least one school's set of essays.

- Start visiting school campuses based upon a "short list" of preferred schools.

- Request transcripts from the relevant schools, get military discharge papers, and so on.

- Establish a file folder system—paper or electronic—for each school, and note specific deadlines for each.

- Approach recommenders—but only once you understand your own positioning, which is unlikely to be before you have done at least a rough draft of one school's essays. (Assume the average recommender will take at least one month to finish the recommendations.) *Note:* The more time you give a recommender, the more willing she will be to support you.

October/November

- Attend MBA fairs. Continue to visit schools.

- Submit applications for financial aid to third-party institutions (i.e., sources other than the schools themselves).

- Request interviews at those schools that require you to complete an application first.

- Revise your essays. Have a friend (or your consultant) read them over. Then, submit them.

- Submit loan applications (for school loans) and any forms necessary for institutionally based scholarships or assistantships.

- Contact recommenders who have not yet submitted recommendations.

- Prepare for interviews by reading Chapter 12 and by staging mock interviews with other applicants, friends, or your consultant.

December/January

- Thank your recommenders.

- Contact schools that have not yet acknowledged your complete file.

- Finish remaining school interviews.

Once You Have Been Accepted (or Rejected)

- Notify your recommenders of what has happened, and tell them what your plans are. Thank them again for their assistance, perhaps by getting them a bottle of champagne or flowers.

- Prepare to leave your job, and get ready for business school. (See Chapter 14, which discusses both of these points in detail.)

- Notify the schools of your acceptance or rejection of their admissions offers, and send your deposit to your school of choice.

- If you have not gotten into your desired school, what should you do? Consider going to your second choice, or perhaps reapplying in the future. (See the discussion in Chapter 13.)

August/September

- Enroll.

Each point made above is discussed in detail elsewhere in this book; refer to the in-depth discussions as appropriate. The timing set out in this schedule is of necessity approximate, since everyone's style of working and personal circumstances will vary. For example, if you are working in a liquefied natural gas facility on the north shore of Sumatra, you will probably have to allow more time for most of the steps listed here. Using this schedule as a starting point, however, should give you a good idea of the sequence to follow, as well as the approximate timing. It should also go without saying that doing things in advance is always a good idea.

SPECIAL NOTES FOR INTERNATIONAL APPLICANTS

GMAT test preparation is not readily available outside the United States, so check carefully to determine where and when you can take a course. Because you must provide official translations of transcripts, recommendations, and the like, you should allow extra time. The slowness and lack of reliability of international mail should also be factored into your timetable, both for tests and for the other elements of the application process.

Also notify the school you have chosen to attend as early as possible so that you can begin the student visa application process. Depending upon your nationality and individual circumstances, this process may be either short and simple or lengthy and complicated.

WHERE ARE THINGS MOST LIKELY TO GO ASTRAY?

You should be aware of three problem areas: (1) Some schools fail to send out a substantial percentage of transcripts upon a first request, or do so with a lengthy delay. The obvious solution to this is that you start requesting them early and stay on top of the situation. (2) Your recommenders are busy people who, despite their best intentions, are all too likely to need prodding to get the recommendations turned in on time, especially if they elected to write them themselves. As Chapter 11 suggests, you will want to make their job as easy as possible, and then stay on top of the situation. (3) Your essay writing is all too likely to fall behind schedule, leading to last-minute rushing and poor writing. Start the whole essay-writing process early, and continue to give yourself time, on a regular basis, to work on them. You must be disciplined about this if you want to maximize your chances.

Appendix V

APPLICATION ORGANIZER FOR EACH SCHOOL

SCHOOL

ADMISSIONS AND APPLICATIONS DETAILS

Address

Telephone

Fax

E-mail

Website

Admissions Director

Admissions Officer Contacted

   Under What Circumstances

Application Fee

Application Deadline Date

Financial Aid/Scholarship Deadline Date

ACTIONS REQUIRED

☐ School's application, course catalog, and publicity materials requested

   ☐ Received by me

- ☐ Secondary research completed
  - ☐ School website
  - ☐ School brochure, catalogue
  - ☐ Books
  - ☐ Articles
- ☐ GMAT scores requested
  - ☐ Received by school
- ☐ Transcripts requested
  - ☐ Received by school
- ☐ Recommenders approached
  - ☐ All necessary material sent to them
  - ☐ Recommenders' progress checked
  - Recommendations received by school: ☐ #1 ☐ #2 ☐ #3
- ☐ Application data form filled in
- ☐ Application short answers completed

Application essays:

	rough draft completed	*outsider reading completed*	*final draft completed*
Essay 1	☐	☐	☐
Essay 2	☐	☐	☐
Essay 3	☐	☐	☐
Essay 4	☐	☐	☐
Essay 5	☐	☐	☐
Essay 6	☐	☐	☐

- ☐ Completed application photocopied
- ☐ Application sent (by Federal Express or similar firm)
  - Date/routing number

Interview status

Required?

Date requested

Date of interview

Interviewer's name

Interviewer's title

Interviewer's address (for thank-you notes)

☐ School notified me of file completion

FINANCIAL AID

Financial Aid/Scholarship Form

☐ Requested

☐ Completed

☐ Mailed

☐ Checked with financial aid office that financial aid file is complete

Note: Make copies of this template, then place one in the folder you keep on each school—or retype the text to keep an electronic filing system.

Part II

MARKETING YOURSELF SUCCESSFULLY

7

MAKING THE MOST OF
YOUR CREDENTIALS

— EXECUTIVE SUMMARY —

■

Admissions committees look for four things: academic ability, managerial
and leadership potential, character, and solid career goals.

■

They examine everything from your undergraduate record to your
work experience to determine whether you have what they seek.

■

You can improve your credentials.

■

You can maximize the value of your credentials by
presenting them in the best light.
—To do so, understand what admissions committees
value most highly.

QUALITIES SCHOOLS LOOK FOR

Stanford has explained what it looks for in candidates: "In reviewing applications, the admissions officers are guided by three key criteria: All admitted applicants must demonstrate solid academic aptitude coupled with strong managerial potential; in addition, diversity among students is sought in assembling each incoming class.

> "*Solid academic aptitude.* A candidate's academic ability is evaluated on the basis of proven academic performance as well as skills evidenced by scores on the Graduate Management Admission Test (GMAT). The Business School seeks applicants with intellectual curiosity who have the desire to stretch themselves intellectually in a rigorous academic program.

> "*Strong managerial potential.* Managerial potential is considered in the context of full-time and part-time employment experiences, as well as experiences in non-work settings and undergraduate extracurricular activities. The School looks for evidence of leadership and interpersonal and communication skills, as well as maturity and the ability to fully utilize opportunities. Letters of reference are relied upon to add insight in the evaluation of these areas.

> "*Diversity among students.* Diversity is a critical ingredient in the makeup of each MBA class. Students come from a wide variety of educational, experiential, and cultural backgrounds. The Business School attempts to identify and encourage applications from minorities, women, and residents of countries outside the United States. Having applied, however, members of these groups must meet the competition from the entire applicant pool.

"[In addition,] candidates are accepted partially on the basis of their ability to benefit from and contribute to the learning environment."

Other schools look for similar qualities. One easy way to learn what the top business schools want is to look at the recommendation forms they use. These typically ask a recommender to check boxes in a grid, indicating whether the applicant's analytical ability, for example, is in the top 2 percent, 5 percent, 10 percent, 25 percent, 50 percent, or bottom half of those the recommender has seen at similar stages in their careers. Leading schools, whether American or European, ask recommenders to evaluate similar sets of qualities. The schools in the following chart ask their recommenders to rate applicants on the qualities indicated.

SCHOOL

QUALITY	HARVARD	WHARTON	TUCK	CHICAGO	UCLA	DUKE	HAAS	LONDON	IESE BARCELONA	INSEAD PARIS
Intellectual/Analytical Ability	x	x	x	x	x	x	x	x		x
Imagination & Creativity	x	x	x	x	x	x	x		x	x
Motivation & Initiative	x	x	x	x	x	x	x	x	x	x
Maturity	x	x	x	x	x	x	x		x	x
Organizational/Admin. Skills	x									
Ability to Work with Others	x		x	x	x	x	x	x	x	x
Leadership Skills/Potential	x	x	x		x	x	x	x	x	x
Self-Confidence	x	x			x	x	x	x	x	
Ability in Oral Expression	x	x	x	x	x	x	x	x	x	
Written Communication			x	x	x	x	x	x	x	x
Managerial/Career Potential		x		x	x				x	x
Sense of Humor		x	x		x		x			
Quantitative Ability	x				x		x	x		
Integrity	x					x	x			x

The picture that emerges from this chart suggests that each school is look-ing for candidates who are quite similar to the Stanford profile—possessing brains, demonstrated business talent, and outstanding personal characteristics. In fact, this chart understates the extent to which this is true, insofar as the schools often use different approaches (and phrasing of questions) to get at the same qualities. For example, London Business School does not ask about a candidate's motivation and initiative, but does ask about a candidate's ability to make decisions and solve problems.

Schools obviously want people with the above-mentioned characteristics, but they also want something more. No matter how talented someone is, he or she is unlikely to fully realize his or her potential without a sensible *career plan*. Those who know (at least in broad terms) where they are headed, and how an MBA will help them get there, will take fullest advantage of the program's opportunities. Their drive and self-knowledge make them more likely to get to the top, making them sought-after MBA candi-dates.

THE EVIDENCE SCHOOLS EXAMINE

Where do admissions committees look to find out whether you have the brains, managerial potential, personal attributes, and sensible career plan they con-sider necessary?

	PRIMARY SOURCES	*SECONDARY SOURCES*
BRAINS	Undergraduate record GMAT scores	Work experience Additional coursework and degrees, if any Essays Interviews
MANAGERIAL POTENTIAL	Work experience	Extracurricular and community activities
PERSONAL ATTRIBUTES	Essays Recommendations Interviews	Extracurricular and community activities
CAREER PLAN	Essays Interviews	Work experience Recommendations

UNDERGRADUATE RECORD

WHAT ARE ADMISSIONS COMMITTEES LOOKING FOR?

Your academic record refers not just to the grades you received in college but also to the quality of your university and the substance of the classes you took. It does not particularly matter what you majored in at college. More important is that you excel at whatever you do. This does not mean, however, that your selection of courses is irrelevant. Taking the easiest courses will arouse suspicion about your ability to do top-level graduate work. Similarly, all MBA programs, and most especially those that are quantitatively oriented, will look for success in undergraduate quantitative courses.

HOW IMPORTANT IS IT?

Admissions officers view your undergraduate record as a key indicator of your intellectual ability and your willingness to work hard. The less work experience you have, the more important your college record will be. A strong undergraduate record earned at a leading university will demonstrate that you can make it through business school, especially if you have had a mixture of quantitative courses and courses demanding substantial amounts of writing. Schools want people who can crunch numbers as well as communicate, as the aforementioned chart shows, so doing well in both quantitative and writing courses is a useful means of demonstrating your suitability for an MBA program. The ideal undergraduate record would thus exhibit all of the following:

- Top-quality school
- Demanding course load
- Top grades throughout
- Courses in economics, mathematics (including calculus and statistics), and writing

INTERPRETING YOUR RECORD

Not every successful candidate has graduated with a 4.0 from MIT or a First from Oxford in mathematical economics and modern history, of course, so admissions officers are accustomed to examining undergraduate transcripts with a practiced eye. A given grade point average is more impressive if achieved in demanding courses, with the better grades received in the junior and senior years. A candidate with high grades in introductory courses and low grades in more advanced courses will be considered less favorably.

In addition to getting the best possible grades, it is helpful if you can show that you have taken a real interest in your studies and have gotten a lot out of them. You have thus not wasted an opportunity. Taking extra courses in your major or in complementary fields can help to show this dedication, as can a successful thesis.

IMPROVING YOUR CHANCES AFTER THE FACT

If you have already graduated from college and do not possess a sterling record, is it too late for you to do something to help your candidacy? No. You may not be able to do anything about the grades you got as an undergraduate, but you can always take courses at night or on weekends to provide another set of grades—more recent and thus potentially more reflective of your current ability—for business schools to consider. Admissions officers call this "building an alternative transcript." If you have not yet taken any quantitative courses, for example, why not take some statistics, calculus, financial accounting, and microeconomics courses at a local community college or continuing education division of a nearby university? To achieve the maximum possible benefit from these courses, you will need to get excellent grades in them. Taking these courses may show that you are interested in improving your background but getting mediocre grades will arouse serious questions about your ability to do outstanding work in a graduate business program.

Although the business schools are capable of interpreting the meaning of good grades received in courses at a well-known, demanding graduate-degree program, they may not know how to interpret your record in coursework from lesser-known programs. This is especially true for continuing education programs. Be sure to do all you can to help them understand what your new record means (assuming, of course, that you have performed well in a highly regarded program). For example, relate to the admissions committees what it takes to get into the program, the program's ranking or standing in its field, the average grades achieved in the program compared with your own grades, or even the average grades achieved course by course if that helps show that your record has been superb.

**THE ADMISSIONS DIRECTORS TALK ABOUT
ACADEMIC QUALIFICATIONS**

Evaluation

➤ We look for accomplishment and success. We do, however, look beyond the numbers to see the trends. For example, someone with a 3.6 GPA might have gotten that in three very different ways. She might have started at 3.0

and ended at 4.0, or the reverse—starting with a 4.0 and ending up with a 3.0. Or she might have been static, with a 3.6 throughout college. These are three very different stories. We look for intellectual curiosity. What does an economics major take outside his major? To what extent does he take courses outside his comfort zone?

We're impressed by someone who is the first in her family to get a university degree, just as we are by someone who pays for his entire education. We look differently at a person from privilege who just coasted through his education and another person who really dug in (metaphorically) with her cleats and made it happen for herself. *Sharon Hoffman, Stanford*

➤ If you've been out of school for ten or twelve years, we'll take your GMAT score as more predictive of your academic ability than your undergraduate grades are. But we still look at it in the context of your undergraduate performance. *Rose Martinelli, Chicago*

➤ We like to see evidence of quantitative skills. We also want someone to have taken challenging courses, to have stepped outside his or her comfort zone. When looking at course selection, we like to see someone who is well-rounded. *Peter Johnson, Haas*

➤ We'd rather take someone who had a 3.2 GPA but was juggling other significant involvements while at college than someone who had a 3.4 but did little other than study. *Dawna Clarke, Tuck*

➤ We look for solid performance, coupled with some balance in your undergraduate career. Thus, we prefer the B student in engineering who participated in student government or band than the A student who never got involved in any activity. We also understand that some majors are more demanding than others. Someone with a B average in nuclear engineering will probably be rated more highly here than someone with an A average in theater. Frankly, the type of work done at the Johnson School is such that the former student will be better able to jump right in and succeed. *Ann W. Richards, Johnson (Cornell)*

➤ We want to be sure someone can succeed academically. Not everyone goes to a name-brand undergraduate school. We take a look at the whole academic package. We look at the undergraduate transcript, any other academic work (like a master's degree), the GMAT score. We try to make a holistic assessment of whether someone is going to succeed in our academic environment. *Isser Gallogly, Stern (NYU)*

➤ We get applications from literally all over the world. It's difficult to compare someone from Seoul National University to someone from an American university. Similarly, the Dutch, German, and Italian systems are quite different from each other. This means that we spend a lot of time looking at both the nature of their studies and their grades. *Kirt Wood, Rotterdam*

Uses

➤ Every school wants to know that you can do the program successfully. They don't want to have to worry about your academic potential—they want to get beyond that issue as fast as possible. *ROSE MARTINELLI, CHICAGO*

Quality of Undergraduate University

➤ We look for what you've done as an undergraduate, not what institution you attended. Someone who took challenging courses and did very well at Eastern Michigan University—great; someone who just cruised through a top-ranked school, taking the easiest courses and getting B-minuses—not the best candidate. We also look closely at your involvement during undergrad—did you work while attending school or participate in activities, sports, etc. Leadership and service come in many different forms, and we look for applicants who have shown an ability to excel academically while making a contribution to the school community. *THOMAS CALEEL, WHARTON*

➤ At the Sloan School, we have a good mix of people who went to American public and private universities. We take pride in finding talent from a list of settings. Going to a recognized or top university is valuable, but it doesn't get you in: You need to do the work. We look at the courses taken, major, and grades received—and, in an American context, what else you did (such as starting a club, working while still in school, and so on). We consider the grading system at your university: we know which ones are hard and which are not. *ROD GARCIA, MIT*

➤ The less well known your school, the better your other qualifications have to be. *PROFESSOR LEO MURRAY, CRANFIELD (ENGLAND)*

➤ If you are applying two years out of university, the quality of school you went to will count heavily, but if you're applying ten years out, with a successful career under your belt, it really doesn't matter—it fades into the background. *ANDREW DYSON, MANCHESTER (ENGLAND)*

Trend in Academic Record

➤ If someone did badly early in college, he can point to his later performance whether at the end of college or in courses that he takes after college. He can explain his early failures by saying that "back then I was a C student but now I am an A student." This sort of person will probably need to work longer too, though, to confirm that this reformation has truly taken hold. *JUDITH GOODMAN, MICHIGAN*

➤ Explain the trend in your performance. Otherwise we're left to our own devices to try to understand it. The optional essay is a great place to provide more information. *ISSER GALLOGLY, STERN (NYU)*

➤ If someone had a terrible first two years but strong last two years, we may well think highly of him, especially if he's taken the trouble to explain the reason for the weak initial performance. *Ann W. Richards, Johnson (Cornell)*

Quantitative Ability

➤ Applicants who have not demonstrated their abilities with quantitative concepts are strongly encouraged to complete introductory coursework such as accounting, finance, economics, and statistics prior to matriculating at HBS. Strong results can reinforce an applicant's case for demonstrated academic ability and give the Admissions Board confidence in their ability to handle the academic rigor of the MBA program. *Brit Dewey, Harvard*

➤ We look at what they studied and where they studied. We examine the rigor of the courses they took and whether they challenged themselves. Tuck's is a quantitative program, so we definitely look to see whether they can handle the quantitative side. *Sally Jaeger, Tuck*

➤ We're looking for raw quantitative ability—to determine whether someone can do the work here. Given that we get applicants from such a wide range of backgrounds, we get very granular in looking at the courses they took as undergraduates, their grades, etc. A history major who took both stats and calculus courses freshman year and got *A*s in them, for example, will be fine. *Thomas Caleel, Wharton*

➤ You can do our program with just a high school math background. You need not have done a university degree with a quantitative component to it. Our one-week quantitative methodology precourse will help you get back up to speed. You can do it here in Madrid or online. *David Bach, Instituto de Empresa (Spain)*

➤ The European MBA model is extremely intensive. We don't do extensive brush-up periods. The pace of the Rotterdam MBA is relatively rapid, so we want to be sure they can keep up with a pretty high level of mathematics—especially in the first semester. *Kirt Wood, Rotterdam*

➤ We consider both the academic record and GMAT score. For someone with a low GMAT quantitative score, we look at the type and quality of academic quantitative work. *Mary Granger, ESADE (Spain)*

Repairing a Weak Undergraduate Record

➤ If you've been out of college for five or six years and are burdened by a weak undergraduate record, it can be a good idea to take a couple of courses to improve on it. We see you applying yourself, committed to continuing education. In addition to this, address what happened before. Was your poor performance due in part to immaturity, working in college, family trouble, or what have you? Don't give us an excuse—just an explanation.

Be sure, also, to show us what you have done since then to address the situation. *ROSE MARTINELLI, CHICAGO*

➤ In some instances you may need to create an "addendum" to your transcript. If you encountered academic difficulties in quantitative courses during your undergraduate years, retaking a calculus course or a statistics course may improve your chances. Achieving *A*s in these courses indicates a level of competence as well as a commitment to pursuing an MBA. We are more willing to give the benefit of doubt to someone with a borderline GMAT quantitative score if he or she takes the initiative to address a deficit. It is also beneficial to enroll in business-related courses (i.e., microeconomics, accounting, or statistics) should you not have any prior exposure to these core courses. Again, your pre-MBA preparation can say a lot about your determination and commitment. *LINDA BALDWIN, UCLA*

➤ If you take courses after graduation in order to beef up a mediocre transcript, be sure that you take them at reputable institutions. Do not duck challenges; take demanding courses at demanding institutions. If you must attend a lesser-known institution, consider adding supplemental materials to show the quality of what you've done. If necessary, send a copy of the text used, the faculty member's name and credentials, and a course description. *ANN W. RICHARDS, JOHNSON (CORNELL)*

➤ It may be a matter of personal issues interfering, or of having to work to support one's family. Unfortunately, you can't repair a poor GPA, but we would hope you would do really well on the GMAT. If you don't, consider taking some courses in the years after college to show what you can do. Presumably you'll also write an optional essay explaining—without complaining or whining—that there were other things going on preventing you from just going to school. *LINDA MEEHAN, COLUMBIA*

➤ When someone has underperformed as an undergraduate, their GMAT score becomes proportionally more important. We've accepted people without undergraduate work, but they've had exceptional work experience. *DR. SIMON LEARMOUNT, JUDGE (CAMBRIDGE)*

➤ If you have a proven work record—especially if you did well in a position that required real intellectual ability—and scored well on the GMAT (or on our own test), a weak undergraduate record will not automatically sabotage your application. Of course, it's necessary to be able to demonstrate your success, through interviews, essays, etc. *DAVID BACH, INSTITUTO DE EMPRESA (SPAIN)*

➤ We take a holistic look at a person's record. We try to understand why they struggled. Since we're looking for people with four to six years of experience, we have the opportunity to see how well they've progressed in their careers. We also look at their GMAT scores, particularly their quant scores, to see whether they'll be academically sound enough to handle the program. . . . We do factor in additional coursework someone does after a degree, much as we do an internship. We don't value an internship as highly as we do full-time work, nor do we value continuing education coursework as highly as we do the undergraduate degree coursework. *KIRT WOOD, ROTTERDAM*

International Applicants

➤ Consider adding supplemental information about your institution if you can provide appropriate documentation, such as governmental rankings, major newspaper rankings, incoming or outgoing student test results, or statistics regarding the number of applicants per place and school yields. *ANN W. RICHARDS, JOHNSON (CORNELL)*

➤ We recognize that there is more than one top university in most countries. One reason we interview abroad is to acculturate members of our admissions committee to the quality of different schools. *ROD GARCIA, MIT*

➤ Comparing undergraduate credentials for people from fifty-five-plus countries is nearly impossible. That's why we rely heavily on interviews, references, essays, etc. *DAVID BACH, INSTITUTO DE EMPRESA (SPAIN)*

THE GMAT

WHAT IS THE GMAT?

The Graduate Management Admission Test (GMAT) is a computerized examination that combines essay and multiple-choice formats. This exam, created and administered by an American firm called Educational Testing Service (ETS) on behalf of the Graduate Management Admission Council (GMAC), is required by virtually every leading business school in the world. The GMAT is designed to measure your ability to think logically and to employ a wide range of skills acquired during your prior schooling, including the ability to write persuasively and well. The GMAT does not attempt to measure your business competence or knowledge, nor does it require specific academic knowledge beyond that of very basic mathematics and grammar.

THE TEST FORMAT

The test is now given in most of the world in a computer-adaptive format, although the traditional paper-and-pencil version is still on offer in some remote regions. The test begins with two half-hour essays, which constitute the Analytical Writing Assessment (AWA) section. The two essays are similar to one another: one is termed "analysis of an argument"; the other, "analysis of an issue." The former asks you to assess the validity of someone's position, or "argument," in light of how persuasively the writer marshals argument and evidence in support of that position. The latter asks you for a more personal response to an issue that is not resolvable—not a matter of right or wrong—but something you can discuss at length based upon your personal experience.

Next come the two (75 minutes each) multiple-choice sections: one "quantitative"; the other "verbal." In the computer version, the multiple-choice sections adapt to your performance. You are given one question at a time, which you must answer in order to move on to the next question. Your first question is of medium difficulty. If you answer it correctly, the next question is more difficult; if you answer it incorrectly, the next question is easier. The exam thus homes in on your ability level.

The multiple-choice questions are of five types. The quantitative section includes:

- Problem-Solving—Involving arithmetic, basic algebra, and geometry.

- Data Sufficiency—Similar in scope to the problem-solving questions, but more abstract in nature.

The verbal section includes:

- Reading Comprehension—Testing your ability to comprehend and analyze the logic, structure, and details of densely written materials.

- Critical Reasoning—Testing your ability to evaluate the evidence and logic used in short arguments or statements.

- Sentence Correction—Requiring you to recognize clear, concise, and grammatically correct sentences.

HOW TO REGISTER FOR THE GMAT

Contact the Graduate Management Admission Council at:

Website:		www.mba.com
Telephone:	Americas	(952) 681-3680
	Asia Pacific	(+61) 2 9478 5430
	Europe/Middle East/Africa	+44 (0)161 855 7219

The exam is given throughout the year. To be sure you will be able to take the exam at the site you prefer, plan to register several months before your desired exam date.

WHAT YOUR SCORE MEANS

You will receive four scores: three regarding your performance on the multiple-choice questions and one regarding your essay writing. Your multiple-choice "overall" score will be reported on a 200–800 scale. Business schools consider this to be the most important of the four scores. The exam is designed to produce an average score of 500, with one standard deviation equaling 100 points. Thus, someone scoring a 700 is meant to be two standard deviations above the mean (average)—that is, 97 percent of the scores were below this. Your "percentile ranking" shows precisely this—the percentage of people scoring below you.

Top schools have average scores in the high 600s or low 700s, meaning that their students are typically in the top 5 to 10 percent of test takers. The range of scores is substantial, however, so a score of 650 need not be cause for despair.

You will get two other scores based upon your performance on the multiple-choice sections. Your verbal score will give you a percentile ranking for the verbal portion of the exam, whereas your quantitative score will give you a percentile ranking for the math portion. Schools are generally more interested in your overall score than how you achieved it, albeit with some notable exceptions. Quantitatively oriented schools will want to be sure that students can handle numbers, so applicants without prior coursework in quantitative fields or other evidence that they can handle numbers will find their quantitative performance on the GMAT closely scrutinized. (At more than one top school, candidates with quantitative scores below the 90th percentile are subjected to substantial additional scrutiny. An admissions officer urging admission of someone with a lesser quantitative score will find herself pressed by the admissions director to explain why he should be accepted.) Similarly, those candidates who are not native speakers of English will find their verbal scores closely scrutinized (along with their TOEFL scores).

The fourth score is based solely upon the Analytical Writing (or essay) portion of the exam. One grade is given, on a 0 to 6 scale. The average grade is about 3.5–4.0 (scores are reported in half-point increments). Schools typically consider a 4.0 or 4.5 to be acceptable and anything higher, a good performance. Copies of the essays are sent to the schools for them to read if they care to, but there is as yet no consistent use of the actual essays. Some schools examine both, some read only the Analysis of an Argument (in preference to the Analysis of an Issue) essay, some read the Issue rather than the Argument, and some read neither, taking into account only the quantitative grade. As you would expect, the weight given to the writing score will depend heavily upon the nature of the candidate involved. Someone who graduated *summa cum laude* from the journalism program at Columbia and then worked as a *New York Times* reporter is unlikely to be rejected as a poor communicator due to a 3.5 score, because he has already demonstrated many times over that he can think and write well under time pressure. On the other hand, an Italian engineer who has never worked in English before may be viewed with doubt if she does not score at least a 4. Schools occasionally make use of the essay results in another way. If your application essays are brilliant pieces of literature, but your Analytical Writing efforts on the GMAT are disturbingly shoddy, the discrepancy may be noted. The admissions committee may question whether you actually wrote your application essays.

WHAT ARE THE ADMISSIONS COMMITTEES LOOKING FOR?

Business schools use the GMAT in two different ways. First, and perhaps most important, business schools publicize the average GMAT scores of their students to demonstrate the quality of their programs. (Rankings that use GMAT scores do the same, reinforcing the interest of schools in enrolling applicants with the highest scores.) Second, schools use the scores for two related purposes: to predict which candidates will do well in business school and to rank students.

The GMAT score provides business school admissions officers with a standardized measure to use in assessing all candidates. Admissions officers tend to rely on it most when analyzing students from unusual backgrounds, or when comparing people from substantially different backgrounds. If you went to a university not well known to the admissions officer, for example, you can expect extra emphasis to be placed upon your GMAT score. The GMAT will likewise be used to compare someone at the very top of her class at a weak university with an applicant who did less well at a leading university.

Note, too, that the value of your score will depend upon the part of the applicant pool in which your application places you. If you are an electrical engineer from India, you face some of the stiffest possible competition at leading American schools. A school with an overall GMAT average of 700 might have an average of 740–750 for electrical engineers from India. A human resources consultant would not face such stiff competition in this regard.

HOW TO PREPARE

It is not easy to prepare for the GMAT at the same time you are investigating schools and preparing your applications. To avoid this problem, and to give yourself the time to prepare properly, try to take the exam before you begin your applications and school visits. Besides avoiding scheduling conflicts, you will have the chance to prepare better and retake it if necessary.

You have two options if you wish to prepare seriously for the GMAT: You can prepare on your own using specially designed preparatory books, CD-ROMs, and online materials, or you can take preparatory classes. Self-preparation has several substantial advantages. It is (relatively) low cost, offers complete flexibility of schedule, and allows you to tailor your preparation to suit your own needs. On the other hand, preparatory classes also offer several advantages. They force you to start preparing in earnest well in advance of the exam, they guide you through the mass of potential preparatory material, they offer you an expert on call when you have questions, and they give you the opportunity to study with other people (and compare yourself with them). Finally, their price and inconvenience will be outweighed for some people by the higher scores they are likely to produce.

The appropriate choice for you will depend upon the kind of person you are, your financial resources, your goals, and other variables. Those who should almost certainly take a prep course are those who:

- Have not taken similar tests before, or have not done so in many years
- Tend to test below their overall ability level
- Lack the self-discipline necessary to prepare on an individual basis
- Need substantial help on one or more parts of the exam, such as those who have let their math muscles atrophy

GETTING THE MOST OUT OF YOUR PREPARATION

If you decide to follow the self-study route, make sure you do two things. First, buy and use several of the popular prep books, because no one book on its own contains sufficient discussion of the strategies, techniques, and fundamentals required. Second, be sure you practice on past GMAT exams rather than on the very different exams created by the various prep book authors. Old exams are available from only one source, *The Official Guide for GMAT Review* (Graduate Management Admission Council), making it required reading. (Be sure you practice on the computer, too, in order to get used to a format that bears little resemblance to pen-and-paper test-taking. By using GMAC's software, *PowerPrep*, you can also become accustomed to answering questions that adapt to your ability level as the real test will.)

You will need to keep to a regular review schedule—such as spending two hours a night, twice a week; and six to eight hours on weekends—for six to eight weeks before the exam. Having a study partner can ease the strain and provide you with someone who can explain something that mystifies you (and vice versa). The best partner is likely to be someone with the opposite strengths to yours. Thus, if you are strong at math, find someone strong at verbal questions.

CHOOSING A TEST-PREP COURSE

Test-prep courses tend to cost a lot of money, so be sure you will get what you pay for. The best value, and best instruction, may not come from the internationally known firms. There are several reasons to look at the full range of test-prep companies rather than opting for the default choice of one of the famous providers. First, the major companies' claims that they have ultra-sophisticated materials, embodying the otherwise unknowable secrets of the exam, are spurious. The fact is that employees of each company, large and small, monitor the efforts of their competitors and readily incorporate each other's best ideas. Thus, courses are more alike than different. Second, although the major companies can boast enormous libraries of materials on which to practice, few students utilize more than a modest fraction of these materials. Third, the major companies inevitably (given the huge numbers they employ) take on many instructors of modest ability (including out-of-work actors, waiters, and so on), provide them with limited training, and suffer from high instructor turnover. The best of the smaller companies can avoid such difficulties. By the same token, if you do opt for one of the major firms, be careful to select the specific course on the basis of the instructor teaching it. To do so, inquire of others who have already taken courses there, and check with the firm's clerical staff, too.

RECOMMENDED GMAT PREP FIRM

In recent years I have been recommending Manhattan GMAT to my clients as the best of GMAT prep firms. It has offices in various cities (not just New York) and a substantial on-line prep service as well. Contact them at www.manhattan.gmat .com/mba or (212) 721-7400. Please note that I have negotiated a substantial *discount* on behalf of readers of this book. Anyone entering the code MONTAUK upon registering will get $100 off the price of a course or tutoring package. My clients have given me a great deal of feedback about the service, but I ask that readers do the same. Please let me know whether or not you have received high-quality service, so that I can continue to help future readers with an appropriate recommendation. I can be contacted at www.degreeofdifference.com.

RECEIVING YOUR SCORE

Within two weeks of completing the exam, your scores will be sent to the schools you designate. You will be given your multiple-choice scores, however, as soon as you finish the exam. (Your Analytical Writing score will not be available immediately because it takes some time to grade this section.)

THE ADMISSIONS DIRECTORS DISCUSS THE GMAT

Its Uses

➤ A study we conducted regarding the GMAT quantitative score suggested that when someone scored below the 75th percentile, he or she was much more likely to have trouble with our program. We use this as a watermark, not a cutoff. If someone scores below the 75th percentile, we examine his quantitative coursework and his professional work (to what extent he's been using numbers and formulas), and pursue the matter with him in the interview. If we like someone, we may admit him conditional upon his completing appropriate coursework. *Sally Jaeger, Tuck*

➤ Its most valuable function stems from its being a standardized measure that everybody takes, which provides a good indication of how someone is going to perform academically in the first year of the program. Beyond that, it depends on the context. For someone with a great quantitative background, such as an engineer, we're not going to worry as much about the quantitative section. For a liberal arts major who works in the arts, though, we're likely to pay more attention to it to make sure this is someone who can handle the economics, finance, and statistics classes as well as the management and marketing classes. So we use it in concert with the transcript. *Isser Gallogly, Stern (NYU)*

➤ After a certain (high) score, it just doesn't matter much to us—we start to focus on other aspects of your application. *Rose Martinelli, Chicago*

➤ We might not really look at the total score: we might concentrate on either the verbal or quantitative score, depending upon the person's background. For an engineer, we might look at the verbal score to make sure he has the necessary skills. For a foreigner, we might want to see a 35 or 40 verbal score. The total score can be a matter of someone excelling on just one-half, so we want to make sure that that's not the case. *Rod Garcia, MIT*

➤ By themselves, GMAT scores don't mean a lot. We compare applicants' scores to their transcripts. For example, if someone is at the 60th percentile in quant and weak in undergraduate math courses, there's a problem. If one or the other is a standout, it's of less concern. *Peter Johnson, Haas*

➤ Someone's GMAT score isn't make or break to an application. Significant work experience can compensate for a relatively low GMAT. We care a great deal about putting together a whole class, so we value someone who can bring something unique, whether that's an unusual language or work experience or something else. That uniqueness matters more to us than a GMAT score. *Mary Granger, ESADE (Spain)*

➤ The GMAT is just not very important for us. You need a minimum score to convince us you know English and can do math, but that's about all. A weak score can therefore keep you out, but a good score doesn't get you in. With seven years' average experience on the part of our applicants, we have a lot more to consider. *Katty Ooms Suter, IMD (Switzerland)*

Multiple Scores

➤ If your first score was below your ability, retaking the GMAT shows appropriate self-awareness. We certainly won't hold multiple scores against you. That said, we are concerned when we see applicants retaking the GMAT every month just to gain a few extra points. *Thomas Caleel, Wharton*

➤ We take the highest score. We're looking at potential, so we want to see people on their best day. *Isser Gallogly, Stern (NYU)*

➤ We look at each set of scores, but we pay more attention to the highest score. *Peter Johnson, Haas*

➤ When someone has taken the exam more than once, we give the applicant the option to report the score or scores they would like us to consider. *Rod Garcia, MIT*

Analytical Writing

➤ If someone's AWA score is low and her essays are perfect, we'll read the AWA essays to see whether different people wrote them. *Ann W. Richards, Johnson (Cornell)*

➤ Unless the AWA is really weak, it usually is not a significant factor in the admissions decision. If it is really weak, I may read the GMAT essays themselves to see what's wrong. We haven't found the AWA score to be terribly predictive of performance. On the other hand, we've found the quantitative score to be very predictive. *Peter Johnson, Haas*

➤ We look at the scores. We also occasionally read the AWA essays, particularly when the essays in someone's application are poorly written and hard to understand. *James Hayes, Michigan*

➤ We tend to look at the scores, not the essays themselves. We have other proxies (essays, recommendations) for someone's analytical writing ability. *Thomas Caleel, Wharton*

➤ We don't put a lot of emphasis on it because we do a lot of our own language-based testing through the interview process, etc. We might read the GMAT essays if there were questions about an applicant, but we generally prefer to concentrate on our own application essays. *Kirt Wood, Rotterdam*

➤ We use the AWA score as supplementary information in cases when we doubt their language ability. *Mary Granger, ESADE (Spain)*

➤ We read many of the essays, mainly to help determine whether the person can string together a logical argument. *Julia Tyler, London*

Advice for Preparing

> ➤ Many applicants do not adequately prepare for the GMAT. Excusing poor performance by saying that you just don't test well or that your job is too demanding to permit time for study won't work. We allow you to take the GMAT twice, and we will consider the higher score. If you have trouble on the first take of the GMAT, it is not advisable to simply retake it without analyzing your weaknesses and/or taking action—whether it means enrolling in a college algebra/geometry class, signing up for one of the test-preparation services, or embarking on an intense self-paced test prep. *LINDA BALDWIN, UCLA*

> ➤ It's become standard practice just about everywhere to do a prep course. Anyone who's worried about his or her ability to score well on standardized tests should consider taking a course, whether in person or online, getting tutoring, or doing the equivalent via self-study. *LINDA MEEHAN, COLUMBIA*

> ➤ The GMAT is a very important indicator of class performance. Therefore we advise our applicants to spend time (at least two or three months) preparing for it so that their result will best reflect their true abilities. *ROSSANA CAMERA, BOCCONI (ITALY)*

International Applicants

> ➤ We have come to expect different GMAT scores from different parts of the world. From India and China, for example, we generally see pretty high scores; from other parts of the world, substantially lower scores are not uncommon. *JAMES HAYES, MICHIGAN*

> ➤ We expect non-native speakers of English to get lower scores. For the Scandinavians and Dutch, maybe 20–30 points lower; for others, maybe 50 points lower, but we wouldn't "credit" someone with more than 50 points. *ANDREW DYSON, MANCHESTER (ENGLAND)*

Other

> ➤ If someone has trouble taking standardized tests, we expect them to deal with this at the test-taking level by arranging (with GMAC) for extra time, for instance, to take the exam. *ANNE COYLE, YALE*

RETAKING THE EXAM

If your score will not get you into a program of the quality you want, then you may need to retake the exam. Before deciding that this is necessary, however, you should analyze your application to see whether your GMAT score will actually handicap you significantly. Remember that many people with scores in the mid-600s (and even lower) get into top programs because they marketed themselves well (and had something worth marketing). You may be better off applying the time you would otherwise spend studying for the GMAT working on your essays or improving your other credentials.

Given that schools will generally take account of the highest score you receive, rather than averaging them or just considering the first one, you may wish to improve your position by retaking the exam. If your original score was mediocre rather than disastrous, consider sending it out to all of the schools to which you intend to apply. When you register for your second try, do not list any schools to receive the second score. If your second score exceeds the first, by all means have the new scores sent out. Otherwise, do not bother to send your second score; let the business schools live in blissful ignorance of your disappointing second effort.

WORK EXPERIENCE: REGULAR APPLICANTS

WHAT ARE ADMISSIONS COMMITTEES LOOKING FOR?

Work experience is probably the single most important substantive element of your application. Schools are trying to assess your management potential, and the best way to do so, in their opinion, is to determine your managerial success to date. In other words, the best predictor of your future success in management is your past success in management.

You are expected to have worked for at least a couple of years prior to applying. The appropriate amount of experience will differ according to the school you are applying to, of course, with some European schools expecting double or triple the experience required by most of the American programs. (Some top American schools are willing to accept a small number of applicants straight from college, although their actual matriculation may be delayed until they have worked for several years. The schools' willingness to accept these younger applicants comes and goes in cycles.)

The amount of work experience, beyond the required minimums, tends to be much less important than the nature and quality of the experience. Those applicants whose undergraduate performance was comparatively weak, however, should consider working a little longer in order to lessen the currency of those grades and course selection, and to increase the amount of good information to be able to show to the admissions committee.

NATURE OF EXPERIENCE

It almost does not matter what type of managerial or professional experience you get! Many successful candidates take the tried-and-true path to business school by working in a traditional feeder industry. Thus, they work for accounting firms, consultancies, investment banks, or advertising firms, or work in marketing for consumer goods firms. They get good training in these companies, and because these firms recruit MBAs heavily, they are very welcome at business schools, which always want to produce graduates who will be in demand.

These candidates tend to compete among themselves for places at the top schools. They are reckoned to be smart, hardworking, and well-trained, which should get them a place at a top school, but the fact that there are so many of them with similar credentials means that schools limit how many will be taken. This is also increasingly true of candidates who have worked for entrepreneurial start-ups (in high-tech and other industries). Schools look for diversity in their applicants, including people with different work experience. This opens the door for people who have been journalists, government administrators, managers of art galleries, research scientists, and everything else under the sun. These backgrounds bring an unusual perspective into the business school, something that is highly valued. Consequently, it is not clear which type of background, the usual or the unusual, is the more likely to help you gain acceptance.

LENGTH

The optimal amount of experience depends upon the school and the nature of your job. American schools generally take younger applicants than do European schools. Whereas students in American schools are typically 26–27 when they begin, students in some European programs average 30 or older. Thus, whereas the candidate for an American program might "peak" at four to six years of work experience, that same candidate might be better off applying to some of the European programs after six to ten years of experience. (See the discussion in Chapter 2 regarding executive MBA programs, which look for more experienced students.)

Schools see a certain amount of high-quality experience as necessary to:

- Understand how complex organizations work (and how you might fit in them)

- Have had the opportunity to take initiative to solve technical and organizational problems

- Know where you are headed

- Know which classes to take in business school
- Have relevant comments to make in class and in study groups (and thereby teach other students)

Too much experience, according to this analysis, would be impossible. On the other hand, an MBA is meant to provide help to people early in their careers, and recruiters come to schools looking for students at a relatively early stage in their careers. Therefore, schools want to have candidates who have some, but not too much, experience.

The optimal amount of experience also depends upon your specific job. If it takes four years to get a valued professional credential, such as becoming a chartered accountant, applying to business school long before reaching this point might be silly. On the other hand, it is nearly always considered acceptable to apply once you have reached the natural break point in a career, such as after your four-year military enlistment has expired.

The weaker your other credentials, the longer you should work before applying, because you will need more impressive work experience to show that your real talent was not properly reflected, for example, in your undergraduate grades.

ACHIEVEMENT AND IMPACT AT WORK

The key to impressing admissions officers with your work experience is not a matter of your specific job or industry, or even of how long you have worked. What you accomplish is the key. Admissions officers want to see people successfully take on responsibility; manage people, projects, and assets; perform complicated analysis; wrestle with difficult decisions; and bring about change. They want people to progress in their jobs and develop relevant skills, with consequent improvements in responsibilities, salary, and title. People who meet these criteria will be highly valued no matter what industry they come from.

To impress admissions people with your work experience, demonstrate as many of the following as possible:

- First and foremost, you have been successful at whatever your job involves. (The easiest way to demonstrate this is to be given significant salary increases and promotions.)
- You have worked well with other people.
- You have managed other people. Managerial experience is important insofar as it allows you to show that you are able to do what is, after all, the one thing required of people who wish to get to the top of companies, whether large or small.

- No matter what your job has required of you, you have done more (and exceeded your boss's expectations).

- You have achieved meaningful results.

- You have had a wide range of experiences, each one requiring different skills (analytical, interpersonal, etc.).

- You have acquired substantial skills in your job, both technical and interpersonal.

- You have done a better job than anyone else in a similar position; you stand out from your peers.

The sum total of this list is that you present a picture of someone with senior management potential, a person who has not only already accomplished things but also built a strong foundation for greater future success.

As you will see in later chapters, these components of work experience are exactly those about which the business schools will ask you to write essays and your recommenders to comment. These same facets are even what you are likely to be asked about in interviews. The application examples throughout this book, in Chapter 8 and Part IV, show people who have looked for and taken advantage of opportunities to do more than what was simply inherent in their positions.

If your work experience gives you little to write about, you face an uphill battle in your applications. Consider waiting a year and devoting that year to making an impact in your job. Focus on developing your skills, assuming new and different responsibilities, and impressing one or more potential recommenders to maximize your chances of success when you do apply.

WORK EXPERIENCE: YOUNGER AND OLDER APPLICANTS

The bulk of applicants to major American business schools tend to be in their mid to late twenties, with perhaps four to six years of experience. (The comparable figures for European schools are late twenties to early thirties, with comparably more experience.) That does not mean that all applicants are, or should be, within these ranges. The opportunity—not to mention the frequent need—to make money during college, along with the proliferation of opportunities to have a meaningful impact upon all sorts of organizations during college, means that many young applicants may be qualified to start a major business school straight from or soon after college. Thus, America's leading business schools are again doing what they routinely did thirty years ago: accepting applicants with little full-time work experience. In the 1970s, however, that meant accepting large numbers of them, whereas today it means filling only a couple dozen seats with young applicants.

The increase in the number of older applicants is due to a somewhat different set of factors. Rapid economic change means that many need to increase or change their skills dramatically long after initially entering a field. Such change also means that some fields evolve into professions quite unlike what individuals entered a decade or two before, causing some people to want to leave their now hard-to-recognize fields. Similarly, it means that opportunities are available for the nimble, those willing to retrain in midcareer. And the increase in individual wealth means that more people will indulge their desires to try their hand at something new because they can afford to do so.

The two age (and experience) groups face very different challenges. *Young applicants* may be regarded as:

➤ Emotionally immature

➤ Lacking in organizational experience and savvy

➤ Unused to working with older people

➤ Undesirable classmates, especially in case method classes, where students learn much more from classmates than from professors

➤ Undesirable case team members, given their limited real-world experience

➤ Lacking knowledge about themselves and the world of work—and therefore unable to choose an appropriate career direction

➤ Unwilling to get into the cut-and-thrust of business life without the safety cushion of a graduate degree

➤ Spoiled and unwilling to wait until a later and better time to get an MBA

➤ Hard to place, since many business school recruiters look for the typical graduates

The less full-time work experience an applicant has, the more she will need to demonstrate that she has had reasonably comparable experience through internships, entrepreneurial efforts, college organizations, a family business, or other involvement. Being able to eliminate any (let alone all) of the above concerns will be very helpful. For instance, showing a sensible career plan based upon substantial internships in a given field can reduce the career concerns noted above. But even when many of these concerns are reduced or eliminated, young applicants are unlikely to have the same sort of career track record that older applicants possess. As a result, admissions decisions will rest more heavily on the data that is available: GPA, course selection, quality of undergraduate institution, GMAT score, and the like. Any weaknesses in these will be especially harmful to a young applicant's admissions prospects given the lack of countervailing work experience as well as the fact that little time has passed since these occurred. And no matter what the quality of the credentials, these applicants will need to be able to explain why getting an MBA now rather than later is a good idea.

Older applicants, on the other hand, may be regarded as:

➤ Stuck in a dead-end job

➤ Running away from a poorly chosen field

➤ Unlikely to be able to work with youngsters

➤ Unwilling to do the hands-on work of setting up spreadsheets and other tasks that they have had junior employees do for them until now

➤ Likely to want to pontificate about their experience

➤ Out of touch with the classroom and the fundamentals (statistics, for instance) necessary for business school success

➤ More suited to an executive MBA

➤ Unrealistic about being able to make a substantial career change

The older and more experienced someone is, the larger these concerns will loom. Similarly, the more someone is looking to change directions rather than build on what he has already done, the greater the concerns.

Note that some schools are simply unwilling to accept older applicants into their full-time MBA programs. Many will try to push older applicants into their executive MBA programs instead. This is particularly true for some of the European programs. Even though they may have an age profile several years older than that of their American counterparts, they tend to have a much narrower age range. Thus, targeting schools open to older candidates is likely to be an important part of the application process for many applicants.

Another important aspect is understanding that their experience may sell at a discount. Many older applicants assume that their greater experience is a big plus. In fact, the longer they have done something not relevant to their prospective future careers, the harder it will be to find work in that new field. Also, schools do not look to maximize the amount of experience in a class; if they did, schools would be filled with octogenarians rather than 27-year-olds.

WHAT THE ADMISSIONS DIRECTORS SAY
ABOUT WORK EXPERIENCE

Why It Is Important

➤ We want a depth and breadth of experience in the first-year class. DAWNA CLARKE, TUCK

➤ Business school is a great place to take the next step in your career, whether that means taking a significant step forward in your current industry and function or making a transition to an industry and function that you think you'll enjoy more. Some work experience may help you with making that decision. Work experience may also help you get more out of the classroom. For example, when there are classroom discussions about leadership and you haven't had to lead or manage a team, it's harder to add to that discussion. There is also a career-placement dimension. You'll be competing for jobs with classmates and others who have had work experience, so you may put yourself at a disadvantage in trying to achieve your career goals. ISSER GALLOGLY, STERN (NYU)

➤ There are three aspects to this. One is because we rely heavily on the case method. The professor's role is to get students to share their knowledge, in a structured fashion, with the class. So diversity is a means to an end: the classroom experience is much richer if students have a variety of professional (as well as cultural) backgrounds. Second, we emphasize teamwork, so students who are good at it are valuable. Those who are able to motivate and work with others help other students learn. We find that students with substantial work experience are more likely to have developed these teamwork skills. Third, it helps us evaluate candidates. Also, our students want their fellow students to have substantial work experience so they can maximize their learning in the program. DAVID BACH, INSTITUTO DE EMPRESA (SPAIN)

➤ An MBA prepares you to become a general manager, a successful leader. That's why the MBA requires constant and active participation, and that's also why we strongly encourage our candidates to enter the course with some years of work experience. In this way, they can exploit to the full their MBA life because they are "participants" and not simply "listeners"; they do not come from a purely academic environment but are, instead, already familiar with company processes and functions. They can compare what they are being taught with their previous professional experience, which therefore becomes part of the learning process for the whole class. ROSSANA CAMERA, BOCCONI (ITALY)

➤ It is hard to apply theories from the program without having had real work experience. Plus, there are job skills (teamwork, for instance) and maturity that one only gets on the job. MARY GRANGER, ESADE (SPAIN)

What Type of Work Experience Is Most Desirable?

➤ There is no perfect pre-MBA job. Instead, it's what you make of it. We look to see how you learn and develop, how you contribute, and what impact you have. *Rose Martinelli, Chicago*

➤ When deciding between two different jobs, take the one you're more excited about. You'll do better at it, and that's what we care about. We don't care whether you manage a sports team or go into private equity—just do it *well*. *Sharon Hoffman, Stanford*

➤ We look for achievement within a position, progression within a career, and—in terms of career goals—a sense that you know what is possible. That, of course, requires some self-assessment. *Michele Rogers, Kellogg*

➤ What kind of experience and teamwork have they had? Have they had leadership experience in a team environment? Managerial supervisory experience? *Sally Jaeger, Tuck*

➤ We would ideally like to see managerial responsibility, but that is not always possible. Someone in sales, for example, might not have any. *Ann W. Richards, Johnson (Cornell)*

➤ We look for candidates with a demonstrated ability to have a positive impact upon an organization. We don't prefer experience in finance to experience in marketing, or vice versa. *James Hayes, Michigan*

➤ We really look for people to have the drive and passion to excel at whatever they have tackled, whether as an analyst at an investment bank or working as a Teach for America Corps member. *Anne Coyle, Yale*

➤ We have a very open mind about this. What is most important is that you've accomplished things, that you've been successful and progressed in your career, and that you've demonstrated leadership potential. And whether your experience fits with your plan for the future. *Isser Gallogly, Stern (NYU)*

➤ Not a specific one: we care for the professional and personal growth of our candidates, and we consider the kind of responsibilities they have had, the team spirit shown, and the problem-solving approach possessed. *Rossana Camera, Bocconi (Italy)*

➤ Those with science backgrounds, especially in biology and chemistry, are most sought after by recruiters. *Mary Granger, ESADE (Spain)*

➤ It doesn't particularly matter which company someone's worked for; what matters is to what extent he or she has made the most of the opportunities there. *Julia Tyler, London*

➤ We look for progression in responsibilities and the position held—that's the key. *Alison Owen, Saïd (Oxford)*

The Appropriate Amount of Experience

➤ Business schools go through phases regarding how much they value experience. Twenty or thirty years ago the top schools took people right from college. Then, they developed a taste for those with some experience. Now, the pendulum's swung back a bit. It's OK to come here at any point in a career. In fact, we particularly look for young professionals shot out of a cannon. We want quality, not quantity of work experience. What's been your trajectory on the job—and how many passionate fans have you earned? *SHARON HOFFMAN, STANFORD*

➤ We look for quality rather than quantity. We certainly prefer seeing someone who has progressed up the ranks quickly than someone who has been in the same position for four years and now says, "I guess that it's time to go to business school to get out of this rut." *ANN W. RICHARDS, JOHNSON (CORNELL)*

➤ The appropriate time to apply depends upon your goals and what you have already done. If you want to go into investment banking, two years in an analyst program is enough. If you want to go into brand management, two years of teaching experience is not enough. *ANN W. RICHARDS, JOHNSON (CORNELL)*

➤ There is no right amount. Previously we said you needed four years of work experience, but not anymore. For example, analysts who will rotate off a two- or three-year program in investment banking no longer need to find another job before applying. This year nearly 3 percent of the incoming class has zero to two years of work experience, including several coming to Wharton straight from undergrad. *THOMAS CALEEL, WHARTON*

➤ It depends on your plan for the future. If you've done your homework, you know the typical profiles for people going into post-MBA career fields and how well you fit them. *ISSER GALLOGLY, STERN (NYU)*

➤ It depends on the individual. Our average is seven and a quarter years—and we prefer more rather than less. As a one-year program packing in two years' worth of work, we rely on people being able to grasp concepts and turn them into practical examples. This is easier for those with substantial work experience. In fact, we look for applicants with substantial managerial experience. (In the United States, on the other hand, candidates are typically looking for their first managerial experience after they graduate.) *DR. SIMON LEARMOUNT, JUDGE (CAMBRIDGE)*

➤ We generally prefer more experience rather than less, but someone who wants to totally change careers will be worse off the more experience she has. She's better off making the career switch as soon as possible. *GEA TROMP, ROTTERDAM*

Concerning Inexperienced and Younger Candidates

➤ We evaluate young applicants, such as those still at college, differently from those with substantial experience. If they're really talented and ready for business, we don't want to see them idling. We do worry about whether they've thought through why they want to do an MBA and what they can contribute in class. *SHARON HOFFMAN, STANFORD*

➤ It's substantially more competitive to get in without several years of full-time work experience. *DAWNA CLARKE, TUCK*

➤ For someone with two and a half years of professional experience, for example, rather than six years, we'll care about the applicant's level of maturity and amount of relevant useful experience. This is particularly important in our program because we have a lot of case teaching and group work. So someone without a lot of experience needs to do the best possible job of presenting his professional abilities and successes. *PETER JOHNSON, HAAS*

➤ Younger applicants need to be able to portray their experiences to date, to talk about their role on projects and so on. This shows they'll be able to contribute in class and in their study groups. They'll also be able to tell their story to recruiters when the time comes. Therefore, we look at the way they put together their essays and their résumé, to see how recruiters will view them. *ANNE COYLE, YALE*

➤ We want someone to share in the classroom the experience they've gained in the workplace, so fellow students can benefit from it (rather than just listening to the professor). For this to happen, younger students in particular need self-confidence and assertiveness—an ability and willingness to challenge more experienced classmates when appropriate. We also look for the interpersonal and communication skills that are necessary to do this. *JAMES HAYES, MICHIGAN*

➤ It is very tough for college seniors to show that they have accomplished a great deal when they have no professional track record to lean on; it's hard for them to beat out people who do have a substantial track record. *MICHELE ROGERS, KELLOGG*

➤ We don't require any work experience at Columbia. We're looking for talented leaders, whether or not they've had business experience as such. The people we take straight from college, however, are outstanding on every level—leadership, academics, involvement, risk-taking—and have at least been exposed to business. Some have been working in a family business; others have just grown up in a business environment and have a good idea of what business is about. They may have done various internships or started their own business while in school. In other words, they're not as green as they might appear. In fact, it's important they have something they can relate their classroom learning to; they need to understand the context in which ideas will be applied. *LINDA MEEHAN, COLUMBIA*

➤ For younger candidates in particular we ask: Do they know themselves? Do they understand the traits and skills they've accumulated? Do they know how they'll apply these to reach their future goals? We want them to be able to apply their past experiences, whatever sort they may be, to classroom discussions and working on a case with their team. They need to be able to contribute in class and help others learn; they also need sufficient context for the business school experience to be meaningful (to themselves). *LINDA MEEHAN, COLUMBIA*

➤ Someone without full-time work experience needs to be outstanding in other regards: impact on campus, exemplary academics, and real internships. He or she also needs to articulate clearly why now is the right time to do an MBA. *THOMAS CALEEL, WHARTON*

➤ Get the GMAT out of the way while you still remember how to take tests. And then do your homework about a career. So many people are focused on getting into business school, but they should really be focused on figuring out their career instead. Business school is not the place to figure out your career; it's the place to achieve it. Your résumé is due in the first week, the recruiters come to NYU Stern in the first month, and interviews happen at the end of your first semester. *ISSER GALLOGLY, STERN (NYU)*

➤ Maturity. Meaning they have a global perspective. They'll be facing some pretty tough recruiters when they finish the program, so they'll have to talk a pretty strong story. I would encourage them throughout the programme to get some leadership experience here. . . . Given the experience level of others in the class, younger applicants need real confidence in their professional abilities in order to thrive here. *KIRT WOOD, ROTTERDAM*

➤ We take about 10 percent of our class each year with little or no experience, and they need to be really exceptional—first-class degrees and extracurriculars and perhaps some informal business experience. *ANDREW DYSON, MANCHESTER*

➤ It's very rare to see someone quite young having progressed sufficiently to be valuable to our program. One exception, however, is a person from a family business, going to school at the same time he or she is working in the business. He can pile up a lot of relevant experience. *ALISON OWEN, SAÏD (OXFORD)*

➤ Ours is a ten-month program, so there is no time to get up to speed. You need to show that you are mature enough and have enough work experience to hit the ground running—and to contribute while you're here. *JOELLE DU LAC, INSEAD*

Concerning Older/More Experienced Candidates

➤ Those with twenty years of experience need to think carefully about whether they should do a part-time or executive MBA program rather than a full-time one. Do they really want to sit in a classroom with 26-year-olds waxing on, pontificating on the basis of their "vast" experience? *Sharon Hoffman, Stanford*

➤ If your goals and background align well, you're potentially a good fit here regardless of your age. *Michele Rogers, Kellogg*

➤ With older candidates, we look to be sure that they are ready to carry their own weight rather than having others do the laborious work for them. Some highly experienced candidates are accustomed to having people working for them do the number crunching, for instance, and expect this to continue on their project teams. This obviously leads to trouble, so we try to make sure that an older candidate is prepared to do hands-on work. *James Hayes, Michigan*

➤ The people coming to recruit at Columbia and other top business schools are looking for people with certain backgrounds to fill the jobs they have. Someone with extensive experience, such as someone in his late thirties, is not going to be the typical graduate coming out of this sort of program. In fact, someone with a huge background in his or her current field will generally have a difficult time trying to make a major career change given that recruiters are not looking for such a person. Their opportunities for employment are going to be more self-directed than provided by the institution. They need to be realistic about what an MBA is going to do for them—whether it will accomplish what they want. If so, they may be a great applicant. . . . In other words, it's not about their age but about what they want to do and how they expect an MBA to help them accomplish this—and whether or not they have realistic goals. *Linda Meehan, Columbia*

➤ They need to describe why a two-year intensive program suits their needs better than continuing to work or doing an executive program would. *Thomas Caleel, Wharton*

➤ Make sure this will do for you (career-wise) what you want it to. If you're thinking of starting as an investment bank analyst—and they usually have two to six years of experience while you have sixteen—that may be a concern for you. Make sure you've spoken with people in the industry to be sure you are an attractive profile for those recruiters. Make sure an MBA is a good path into this field. *Isser Gallogly, Stern (NYU)*

➤ It's risky for a highly experienced candidate to look to change careers: Companies may be unwilling to hire someone without experience in the relevant field. We might redirect such a candidate if we feel that we can't offer what will be necessary to make the career change he or she desires. *Mary Granger, ESADE (Spain)*

➤ It's a harsh labor market out there. The older someone is, beyond his early thirties, the fewer the job offers he'll get. We don't want to take someone who'll do the program and then find that he can't get a job. *Julia Tyler, London*

➤ People with too much experience do not belong in an MBA program. Instead, they should be in an executive MBA program. We look at the number of years of business experience rather than age in determining whether someone will fit. *JOELLE DU LAC, INSEAD*

Other

➤ We want to understand whatever transitions an applicant has made. If someone started with one job and then changed job or company, we want to understand why. What was he thinking? What sort of opportunity or challenge was he looking for? *DAWNA CLARKE, TUCK*

THE CAREER SERVICES DIRECTORS DISCUSS YOUNGER AND OLDER APPLICANTS

Younger Applicants

➤ On the positive side, at the top schools there are only a small number of these students, so some recruiters regard them as pretty special—as being incredibly hardworking and incredibly intelligent. For some recruiting firms, this is very attractive. Oftentimes you'll run into certain types of firms that value people who are extra smart and are willing to overlook other things. But I wouldn't say that is the typical MBA recruiter. On the negative side, the student without a lot of business experience who's being compared to classmates with experience has to be prepared to explain to the recruiter, "Here's why I would be a great employee at your company. Here are the professional skills and capabilities I have that match what you're looking for—and these are the reasons I managed to get into this business school." They have to say it with conviction and without defensiveness—without the feeling they are being overly judged. *ANDY CHAN, STANFORD*

➤ As a case method school, we depend on students teaching each other, which is based on the experience they bring. Younger students generally have less experience to draw on. Forty to 50 percent of your grade in many classes is based on class participation, so that can be difficult. *EVERETTE FORTNER, DARDEN*

➤ Many of them have worked hard through college to get in, but business school isn't the time to let up on the accelerator and ease back. A major source of jobs, as well as personal happiness and friendships, is your business-school network. Yet the 22-year-olds are quite different from the 27- or 28-year-olds in that they can be readily put in the box of being too young and lacking in their own networks for the other students to spend time with. It's very important for young or inexperienced students to be strategic about making a positive impression on their classmates, whether that be through positively contributing in class or being an active leader in study groups, student government, or student clubs. *ANDY CHAN, STANFORD*

➤ On the career front, some general management programs wouldn't look at younger students. Those we admit more or less straight from college, however, do have deep, meaningful summer experiences prior to coming here, or they have had substantial leadership experience in college. This helps them contribute in the classroom and is also meaningful to the recruiters coming here. *EVERETTE FORTNER, DARDEN*

Older Applicants

➤ Many companies prefer candidates with just three to five years of experience rather than many more years. Such companies tend to be more comfortable being able to mold their recruits, which is easier with less experienced candidates. In addition, younger candidates are likely to be more comfortable around the others undergoing training insofar as the others will be of a similar age. . . . Older students need to rely more heavily on their existing and newly expanded network of contacts in order to find the one-off position that will fit them rather than what is on offer to the younger students through the on-campus recruitment process. *PETER J. DEGNAN, WHARTON*

➤ There are several different types of older students. The hardest ones to help are the absolute career changers who are a bit older, especially those who want to do something like investment banking. Investment banking has a pretty clear model of the person they want, and an older applicant might not fit that profile. But for general management programs and even some types of management consulting, the older applicant may have a body of experience that those types of firms may be looking for. Statistically, we don't see any difference at all in number of job offers by age at graduation. *EVERETTE FORTNER, DARDEN*

➤ To the extent people want to make a career change, it is very important that they take on projects, take relevant new classes, and get involved with the appropriate clubs, so that they can get this information placed on their résumé. It can reframe who they are: what their interests are and what they're good at. The more information they have on their résumé that makes them look like they are, for example, a consumer-marketing manager-type person, when they'd like to become a hedge fund analyst, the more it hinders them. They need to find a way to get information on their résumés that shows they're really a hedge fund analyst: they have the skills and desire to be one, and that's what they're determined to do. *ANDY CHAN, STANFORD*

➤ Generally they'll be in a different life stage than younger students. They're more likely to be married, and more likely to have children. The older students' struggle is trying to balance work and life. That should be the problem for 28-year-olds, also, but normally they have fewer things to juggle. Also, we deliver a highly quantitative, rigorous program, and an older applicant has been out of school longer, so it takes a little while to get back into the right study habits and to remember the analytical things learned as an undergraduate. *EVERETTE FORTNER, DARDEN*

➤ Older candidates might want to look at schools where the average age of the students is older. The hiring regime at these schools is more geared to these students, which works to their benefit. *CHRIS BRISTOW, LONDON*

EXTRACURRICULAR ACTIVITIES DURING COLLEGE

WHAT ARE ADMISSIONS COMMITTEES LOOKING FOR?

Admissions officers hope to see a pattern of substantial involvement and increasing responsibility in one or more extracurricular activities. Top business schools want to admit people who are (and will be) successful leaders of groups. Activities offer an ideal opportunity to demonstrate leadership inclinations and skills.

The specific activity is not particularly important (although American schools admittedly retain a triste attachment to varsity sports). What matters is that you cared enough about it to pursue it throughout college and to contribute significantly to it. The depth and impact of your involvement will also be more important than the number of activities in which you participated. If you were a member of the college film society, for example, writing the monthly newsletter and serving on the board of directors will demonstrate that you were actively engaged in it. It would be even better if you were the president, of course, especially if you managed to increase the number of films shown from three to twelve per week, which conveniently demonstrates a quantitatively measurable impact.

Extracurricular achievement is particularly important for those with limited work experience. As Yale notes, "Full-time post-college work experience is highly desirable, although students whose extracurricular accomplishments demonstrate exceptional organizational and leadership abilities may sometimes be admitted directly from college."

COMMUNITY AND OTHER ACTIVITIES

WHAT ARE ADMISSIONS COMMITTEES LOOKING FOR?

Schools expect people without particularly heavy job responsibilities to be involved in more than just watching television every evening. Schools prefer "joiners" to loners. The MBA is not a degree for people who dislike being involved in group activities. Schools do not particularly care which activities you pursue, as long as you are active in something. If you take on responsibilities and leadership roles, of course, you will be viewed even more favorably. The same is true if you show a dedication to excellence in what you do.

The importance of outside activities varies according to your circumstances. If you intend to be involved in nonprofit management, you will be viewed with suspicion if you have not been involved in substantial community activities. On the other hand, those working in jobs such as investment banking and strategy lack the time for substantial outside activities due to the long hours and extensive travel. In such cases, a lack of outside activities since college is generally excused as long as the applicant was an active extracurricular participant during college. The candidate who is working as many hours as possible to support her destitute family, or to raise enough money to get her family out of a war-torn homeland, will certainly not be expected to have donated her very limited free time to charity work. (Note, however, that these circumstances must be explained in the application.)

Schools are not particular as to the type of outside activity in which you involve yourself. Playing sports, making movies, working for a professional or industry association, or acting in local theatrical productions could be excellent choices for you. Schools are particularly pleased, however, to see at least some involvement in community activities because it suggests that your heart is in working order.

GETTING MAXIMUM VALUE FROM EXTRACURRICULAR, COMMUNITY, AND OTHER ACTIVITIES

Although the particular activities you choose will not matter, keep in mind that the following will help you maximize the value of your outside activities:

➤ *Depth of involvement:* You want to be able to show that you have been seriously committed to one or more activities for a length of time, preferably several years.

➤ *Leadership:* Show that you have taken an important leadership role in at least one activity. This means founding a club or group, becoming an appointed or elected high officer of a group, or directing a group's efforts in one area. Show that you can motivate others around you to contribute their best efforts to a common cause.

➤ *Avoid reinforcing doubts:* If your profile features a job without an apparent social or team dimension, for example, be leery of activities that are essentially solo pursuits. Thus, a test pilot or fashion industry spy will face additional doubt about their candidacies if their outside activities involve writing movie reviews or playing the piano (alone). Try, instead, to augment your admissions profile by reducing doubts, bolstering your positioning, or highlighting underappreciated aspects of your candidacy. (See Chapter 8 for more on positioning.)

➤ *Something unusual:* Not everyone has the interest or resources to do something really out of the ordinary, but beware of the monotony of what admissions committees see. Applicants who have pounded nails for Habitat for Humanity, tutored children, helped Junior Achievement, or ladled at soup kitchens are unlikely to win points for uniqueness.

➤ *Possession of at least two dimensions:* You want to present yourself as a focused individual with a memorable profile, not someone who dabbles in everything without much commitment to any one particular activity. But this does not mean you should be regarded as obsessed with just one aspect of life. Be sure there is at least one activity you can point to that stands out as not fitting into your main marketing scheme. (This is critically important for the candidate who is, for example, a would-be financier whose only leisure activity is reading biographies of successful financiers.)

➤ *Something that you truly enjoy:* Logging hours in an activity that you do not really like is a recipe for boredom and frustration. Try to choose activities that are truly enjoyable—so much so that even if you decided not to attend business school, you would still be pleased that you had participated.

RECRUITING RECOMMENDERS

Doing voluntary work is an excellent way to develop good references. You will be working in a hand-picked activity in which you will be able to control your environment. You can choose a position that is just right for you, or you can create a position that offers some benefit to an established organization. Charitable organizations are not like regular corporations; they know they are highly dependent upon volunteer workers and consequently are willing to go out of their way for anyone who makes a difference in helping their constituency.

If you have not had substantial leadership experience in your job, community activity presents an important possibility for developing the necessary experience and skills to convince an admissions officer that you have leadership and managerial potential.

USE YOUR ACTIVITIES TO HIGHLIGHT YOUR PERSONAL SIDE

Your extracurricular and other activities can also be used to highlight the personal side of you. As noted elsewhere in this book, you should show who you are, not just what you have accomplished. Many use their application essays simply to retell the elements of their professional résumé or brag about their accomplishments, without ever reaching beyond such matters to let admissions officers understand who they really are. This is generally a mistake. Take the opportunity to win over these people-oriented officers; show them you have the warmth, generosity of spirit, and concern for others that will make you a truly valuable member of the incoming class. Show that you have a positive impact that reaches well beyond your own narrow interests. By doing so, you will cause admissions officers to interpret your credentials in a positive light.

WHAT THE ADMISSIONS DIRECTORS LOOK FOR IN EXTRACURRICULARS AND COMMUNITY SERVICE

➤ We're looking for people who step up and take a leadership role. They'll need to take leadership roles while they're here and after they leave. What's not highly valued is peripheral involvement in an activity. We often see involvement that started when the candidate decided to apply to business school. If it's a recent involvement, they need to explain it to us. *Sally Jaeger, Tuck*

➤ We're not impressed by someone who starts dabbling with Christmas in April and Habitat for Humanity three months before applying to business school. Instead, we look to see whether someone is passionate about a few activities. We're excited to see someone who has started something and run with it, who has inspired others to join in, who has had a real impact. *Sharon Hoffman, Stanford*

➤ We look for quality rather than quantity. We prefer leadership in one to membership in ten. We look to see leadership and impact. By the way, we don't look for accomplishment just in professional or organized activities. If you have a grandparent in a care facility, for example, and have regularly visited another of the patients there, tell us about that. We simply want to see whether the activity has some meaning to you and whether your commitment to it has been substantial. *Ann W. Richards, Johnson (Cornell)*

➤ We're looking for people who want to be engaged. This program is designed to mentor leadership and provide opportunities through our extensive set of clubs and organizations. Someone who has not been involved before is less likely to get involved here. Of course, we understand that a consultant who lives on airplanes may not have much current involvement outside of work, but we would hope that that person has a background of involvement before starting to live on airplanes. . . . Given the premise that you learn as much from other students as you do from faculty, we like to see people who have been involved in activities outside of work—it makes them that much more interesting and valuable. *Linda Meehan, Columbia*

➤ This is an opportunity for them to showcase how they've been leaders and contributors outside their industry and how they might get involved here. It's also a chance to show who they are as people, not just professionals, because ultimately we're admitting people rather than just students or professionals. *Isser Gallogly, Stern (NYU)*

➤ We pay a lot of attention to them. We want someone contributing broadly to society. However, we see a lot of people talking up their activity, which becomes clear in the interview. We prefer straight talk rather than embellishment of what they've done. *Dr. Simon Learmount, Judge (Cambridge)*

➤ It's important that you be passionate about more than work. It's better to have one concrete passion than to dabble in a bunch of activities—and, by the way, CV fillers don't fool anyone. *Joelle du Lac, INSEAD*

➤ It's not a requirement that someone has participated in activities, but we do like to see someone who has focused on more than one aspect of life. An accountant who has done nothing but accounting will not be as interesting to us as one who has excelled at a sport and led a nonprofit organization. *Katty Ooms Suter, IMD (Switzerland)*

➤ We'll look at a significant extracurricular activity to evaluate someone's leadership abilities. We also use knowledge of people's extracurricular activities during interviews, recognizing that this is what they are likely to be passionate about. As such, it is a way for us to get to know them as people. *Mary Granger, ESADE (Spain)*

➤ Extracurricular activities are generally not considered in the admissions process unless someone is borderline, in which case we'd look for leadership activities and initiative in outside activities. *Alison Owen, Saïd (Oxford)*

YOUR PRESENTATION

The first part of this chapter examined the credentials business schools are looking for—in other words, the substance of your application. Now it is time to consider the way in which you present yourself. How much difference does it make if you write marvelously and make the strongest possible case for yourself? How much does it matter if you get impressive people to write persuasively on your behalf? How important is it that you come across well in person?

THE ESSAYS, RECOMMENDATIONS, AND INTERVIEWS

The credentials you bring to the application are one thing; your presentation of them is another. Your presentation matters greatly for several reasons. You have the opportunity to color the interpretation of all the objective data by explaining its context and how all of the different pieces fit together. In addition, sharp admissions officers will cross-check your essay assertions, for example, with what you say (and how you say it) in your interviews, to get as honest a picture of you as possible. Your performance also provides important additional data for the admissions decision. The essays, for example, reveal your writing ability and your ability to sustain a closely reasoned argument. The recommendations reveal the extent to which you have impressed some of the most important people you have worked and studied with. The interviews reveal not only your oral communication skills but also your presence and other important leadership attributes. (In fact, these communication vehicles demonstrate much more than these qualities; for an in-depth view of them, refer to the individual chapters in Part II.)

Although it is always easier to make an impressive presentation when your substantive credentials are strong, the extent to which you take full advantage of the opportunity to present your case as effectively as possible will tell the admissions committee an immense amount about your abilities and your willingness to work hard to attend their program.

SHOW WHERE YOU ARE HEADED

If you have a clear idea of where you are headed, and why, you can add substantially to the value of the credentials you possess. This is particularly true for candidates whose pasts look like a dog's breakfast. If you have had six jobs in four years, you will maximize the negative impact this messiness has on your application if it looks like you still do not know where you are headed. On the other hand, if you can show that your bouncing around was part of a plan to sample different jobs and industries in order to learn about your own fit with the world of work, you can lessen this negative impact—that is, you can if you at least present a sensible plan for your future based upon having learned useful lessons from this bouncing around.

The truth is that the vast majority of applicants do not know where they are headed after business school—or, if they think they know, it turns out they end up doing something quite unexpected. This is partly because the year or two away from their current jobs offers time to figure out what they really want in life. Many candidates know that their prior careers have been less than fulfilling, so they ache to make a change. Clever applicants, however, will not visit their angst and indecision upon admissions committees. Highlighting your uncertainties suggests that you might be too much of an emotional basket case to contribute effectively at business school. It also subtly undercuts the value of what you have already done; people tend to be good at what they enjoy (and vice versa). If you have not enjoyed your career to date, this suggests that maybe you were not really as successful as might otherwise be assumed. It also suggests that you may be a perpetual malcontent.

MAKING THE ULTIMATE DECISIONS

THE CRITERIA TRADE-OFF

The question inevitably arises: How do admissions directors determine whom to accept, given that some applicants will have outstanding job records but unimpressive grades and GMAT scores, whereas other applicants will have the reverse set of strengths and weaknesses? In other words, how do admissions directors trade off the different admission criteria? There is no set answer to this question. There are, however, three considerations to keep in mind.

First of all, it is important to understand that the top schools do not need to make many such trade-offs. The Stanfords, Whartons, and London Business Schools are in the enviable position of having many applicants with sterling undergraduate records and impressive work experience, which reduces the need to trade off criteria.

Second, schools will weight criteria differently depending upon the applicant. For example, someone who has worked for only two years can expect to have his undergraduate record, extracurricular activities, and GMAT scores count very heavily because his work experience is too slight to provide a great deal of information about him. Someone with seven years of work experience can expect that somewhat less weight will be placed on the academic measures; her extensive experience provides a great deal of information about her, making her experience a much more important indicator of her potential than it was for the two-year man.

Third, different schools will have different priorities, causing them to apply a somewhat different set of criteria, and criteria-weighting, to the process. A school like IMD (in Lausanne) considers work experience to be far and away the most important criterion. INSEAD (outside Paris), which takes a younger group of students, places relatively less weight on work experience and more on the undergraduate record and GMAT scores (although work experience is still its most important criterion).

FILLING THE CLASS

Business schools have come to believe in the virtues of diversity. They feel that a mixture of nationalities, industry, and job backgrounds in their student body enhances the learning process and also makes for a more attractive group of graduates, given that employers need a wide range of potential recruits. Schools have responded to their relatively newfound desire for diversity mainly by marketing intensively to hard-to-attract groups rather than by dramatically reducing their admissions standards for them.

THE TARGETED GROUPS

The groups targeted vary somewhat by area. American schools are always concerned about getting sufficient minority students, European schools tend to monitor their geographic balances closely, and programs throughout the world would like more female students. Targeted groups may have a slight edge in the admissions process, but it is not pronounced (except in the case of American minorities). Most admissions officers would concur with Harvard's Brit Dewey, who notes, "We don't have a certain number of places reserved for specific types of applicants. We admit each candidate individually, choosing the most compelling candidates among the entire pool."

THE ADMISSIONS DIRECTORS DISCUSS DIVERSITY AND UNDERREPRESENTED GROUPS

Diversity Desired

➤ You don't have to be a consultant or investment banker to apply here. We care about people who want to manage things and lead other people. *Sharon Hoffman, Stanford*

➤ We look to assemble a class that has a good balance in terms of gender, ethnicity, nationality, geography (within the U.S.), age, and so on. This is driven by the interests of our recruiters, who look for this kind of diversity. *JAMES HAYES, MICHIGAN*

➤ We look to create an environment in which people from a lot of different backgrounds and cultures and experiences come together to share with each other. It's reflective of our city. There is no cookie-cutter definition of a Columbia student. We're looking for people from all over the world. The incoming class has about sixty countries represented, with equal numbers from Latin America, Europe, and Asia. Similarly, we don't have just finance people here—contrary to popular belief. We get lots of people targeting media, real estate, marketing, and management. We also get a lot of entrepreneurs. *LINDA MEEHAN, COLUMBIA*

➤ I think broadly about diversity. Class participation is 40–50 percent of your grade, so I hope you'll have something unique to add to the discussion. I also think concretely about ethnic, gender, work experience and industry, and geographic diversity. *SARAH E. NEHER, DARDEN*

➤ We look for good gender mix and good sectoral representation on the programme—and not just from the usual MBA industries like investment banking and consulting. We look for people from the nonprofit sector and spend a lot of time marketing the idea of an MBA to them. And it goes without saying that we look for national diversity. We have 110 students representing, typically, about forty countries, no one of which accounts for more than 10–12 percent of a class. *DR. SIMON LEARMOUNT, JUDGE (CAMBRIDGE)*

➤ We don't have an ideal profile, except to say that we want candidates with the ability to become real leaders. We look for overall excellence first, and then we look to put together a highly diverse class. We look at nationality (which is how we have forty nationalities in a class of ninety), function in a company (we try to get the maximum number of different functions), and industry in building our class. *KATTY OOMS SUTER, IMD (SWITZERLAND)*

➤ Companies across the board, from industrial firms to consulting firms, are concerned that business schools are in danger of getting only stereotypical candidates. In other words, the person who understands how to manage his career very well—how to trade off length in job vs. salary and so on—but who as a result is never going to take real risks. We now have a scholarship from L'Oreal to attract people from off the beaten path. That diversity is something that companies want and appreciate. *LUDO VAN DER HEYDEN, INSEAD (PARIS)*

Underrepresented Groups

➤ We want to see more women here. It's a very hospitable environment. And business is at least as good a field for women as law or medicine. With a Stanford MBA, you'll be more marketable for the rest of your career—and able to contribute more, whether in the private or nonprofit sectors. You can drop in and out of the workforce, as well; you maximize your flexibility with this degree. *SHARON HOFFMAN, STANFORD*

➤ Like most business schools, we have a large number of people from engineering, consulting, accounting, or banking backgrounds, but the people from less typical backgrounds do enrich the class. They come in with the ability to actually question those consultants and say, "It doesn't work like that if you're managing a hospital" or whatever. That adds a bit of grit, which makes the pearl in the oyster better. *JULIA TYLER, LONDON*

➤ We don't have national or other quotas. We find that we attract such a wide pool of applicants that diversity takes care of itself. *JOELLE DU LAC, INSEAD*

➤ Like everyone else, we would like to have more women. In general, we like to see applicants from diverse backgrounds, such as from the sports and entertainment industries. *KATTY OOMS SUTER, IMD (SWITZERLAND)*

THE ADMISSIONS DIRECTORS SPEAK ABOUT WHAT THEY REALLY LOOK FOR

In General

➤ **HARVARD:** HBS is looking for leaders who will contribute to the well-being of society, who are guided by strong values and high standards, and who inspire trust in others. Our selection process emphasizes leadership potential, strong academic abilities, personal qualities and characteristics, and demonstrated excellence. We are looking for applicants who have been leaders in a variety of settings: in their extracurricular activities while at college or university, in their workplaces, and in their communities. We are looking to learn about your personal qualities and characteristics that have contributed to your success as a leader and to understand how you intend to use the MBA experience to reach your career goals. The HBS community maintains high standards of personal excellence; therefore, we are looking for candidates who have demonstrated excellence in their lives. *BRIT DEWEY*

➤ **CHICAGO:** We look at the whole package. We want to see who you are, where you're going, and why. The why's are more important than the what's.

    We look for performance over pedigree; passions and motivations over accomplishments. We look for leaders, in a team context, who inspire, motivate, and mentor. We want people who respect and enjoy others and still get the job done. We look for collaborators who aim to make the whole unit, not just themselves, great. We want people who are comfortable in multicultural environments and in a variety of socioeconomic contexts. Finally, we recognize that those who do well at Chicago are self-directed and intellectually curious, people who push themselves to keep learning. *ROSE MARTINELLI*

➤ **STANFORD:** We always say we look for academic achievement, leadership potential, and, also, bringing an element of diversity to the program. But what we really search for is "wow." There is academic wow, professional wow, diversity wow—and, of course, all sorts of wow we don't want. *SHARON HOFFMAN*

➤ **COLUMBIA:** We are looking for people with professional promise. We assess this by looking at the applicant's résumé and recommendations. We do need to ensure that people will get through the program, so we look for competitive undergraduate schools and grade point averages, and meld these with the applicant's GMAT score. Some of our competitors are more focused on GPAs and GMAT scores. *LINDA MEEHAN*

➤ **ANDERSON/UCLA:** We look for responsible people who take risks and enjoy taking the lead. Intelligence, a strong commitment to achievement, and positive interpersonal skills are highly valued. We have an interest in individuals who have a comfort level interacting and communicating with a wide range of people. Breadth in academic background and life experiences often facilitates discourse among diverse groups. *LINDA BALDWIN*

➤ **MICHIGAN:** We believe that getting an MBA is a rigorous two-year effort. We want candidates who demonstrate a good understanding of themselves, know why they want an MBA, and understand how important it is to find the program that's right for them. Our approach to management education is based on action learning, tying theory to practice. We want students who understand and appreciate that and want it to be a major part of their MBA experience. . . . (Also,) we don't want to admit people we won't be able to place upon completion of the program. When we have questions about whether someone will be placeable, we discuss the case with the Office of Career Development. *JAMES HAYES*

➤ **YALE:** Our program is definitely mission-driven. Our mission is to educate leaders for both business and society, so we look for applicants who want to make a real difference in whatever realm they're aiming for. (There's a misconception that we are somehow just public-sector-oriented, but 95 percent of our graduates go into the for-profit sector.) We like applicants who see how the different sectors interact and affect each other. *ANNE COYLE*

➤ **SLOAN/MIT:** We use a competency model—and look for very specific competencies. To use an iceberg analogy, we look at the above-the-water-line attribute of demonstrated success. This can be seen through grades, work experience, and so on. We also look beneath the water line, at personal attributes. These innate qualities are visible essentially from the essays and the overall pattern of experience presented. The above-the-line attributes are the obvious things, which can be easily influenced by one's education. The below-the-line attributes are less obvious, and are not readily changed by education. *ROD GARCIA*

➤ **DARDEN:** Darden's mission statement is to develop leaders in the world of practical affairs, so it's important to find leadership experience and potential in our candidates. We look for leadership in three realms. First, we look for leadership in the workplace. We examine your work experience, advancement and career potential, innovation, and teamwork experience. In general, we want to see that you've exceeded expectations. Second, we look for leadership in the community. This may come through volunteerism or membership (or board participation) in organizations. It may also be a matter of articulating what you want to do with an MBA, even if you haven't had the opportunity for substantial community involvement yet. We want to see that your end goal is not just about yourself. This is partly because of our use of the case method. Given that this is a small community, everyone needs to be equally engaged for people to get the maximum benefit from the program. Third, we look for leadership in the classroom. Once again, this is partly due to our use of the case method. We look for candidates with high intelligence and communication skills (which is why we require an interview as part of the application). *SARAH E. NEHER*

➤ **WHARTON:** We're looking for intellectual curiosity, a demonstrated record of achievement, and passion. We want people who are going to make a difference. We get many valedictorians applying, but it's not simply a matter of brain power. *THOMAS CALEEL*

➤ **STERN/NYU:** The three main things for us are academics, career, and fit. Can you do the school work, can you do the work work, and are you going to be successful in the Stern environment? . . . We say that we're "downtown, down-to-earth, and down to business," so we like people who are doers, who know what it takes to make things happen. *ISSER GALLOGLY*

➤ **JUDGE/CAMBRIDGE:** We look for curious people—people who know they don't know it all. This often means they're exceptionally good listeners. Their curiosity also causes them to ask the right questions. We want people with ambition and drive, but not egocentric types. Our students are often very competitive but also collaborative, wanting to excel for themselves and for others around them. We also want well-rounded people rather than those who have excelled in only one regard and failed to develop other important parts of themselves. *DR. SIMON LEARMOUNT*

➤ **INSTITUTO de EMPRESA (Spain):** We want our students to be entrepreneurial and to create value, not just for themselves and their companies, but for society as a whole. *DAVID BACH*

➤ **ROTTERDAM:** We want to produce executives with broader social awareness, who are adaptive, who are critical/conceptual thinkers, who make informed decisions, and who can implement. *KIRT WOOD*

➤ **CRANFIELD:** It's also a question of what we don't want. It's important to have people who will gain from the program *and* contribute to it. We don't want people who'll just go through the motions in order to tack three little letters after their names. We don't want people who'll be complete pains in their study groups. When we accept an accountant, we want someone who can get his study group through accounting. It is an important learning issue. The personalities of people are quite important to us. *PROFESSOR LEO MURRAY*

➤ **IMD (Switzerland):** We have five major criteria:

1) Prior business experience. In a class of ninety, everybody has to contribute. (We aim for the best combination of ninety people, not the ninety best people, by the way.)

2) Willingness to take a certain amount of risk. In today's business environment, the ability to innovate is essential.

3) Burning desire to lead. It isn't essential that people want to be business leaders; they could be leaders in politics, nonprofits, or other fields, but the entire program is focused on leadership. (We offer our MBAs the opportunity to take one-on-one coaching to help them understand and improve their leadership style and skills.)

4) Clear sense of their goals. Unlike the American schools, ours is a short program (just ten months), so there isn't time to consider what sort of job to seek, how to go about finding it, and so on, all prior to actually carrying out the effort. We encourage our students to build on their prior careers.

5) International work experience and/or interest. Only about 5 percent of students are Swiss, so people need to appreciate and value how international the experience is. *KATTY OOMS SUTER*

➤ **INSEAD (Paris):** We look for four things in addition to career success. This has become a very international, not just European program, with the opening of our Singapore campus and our linkup with Wharton, with its two U.S. locations. Consequently, we want to see an *international perspective*. You need to show cultural sensitivity; not everyone, after all, is comfortable working in a multicultural environment.

We look for the *appropriate personality*, someone who works well as a leader and as a team player. So much of the work here is group work, and the groups are so diverse that you need to be ready to learn from a range of different people.

You need two *languages* to be admitted, although not necessarily to apply. Before you can start the program you need to prove your second language ability. To graduate, you need a third language. Instruction is in English, so you obviously need fluent English. (A TOEFL score of 260 is required if English is not your native language.)

To gauge *academic ability*, one of the things we look at is the GMAT score. (Our average is about 690.) We look at it in the context of the whole application. It's the only common measure available to us, which is particularly important for us, given that we have such a diverse group of applicants, schooled in every conceivable school system. Of course, we also look at other things, such as the applicant's undergraduate performance and the quality of his or her undergraduate institution.

A good candidate is probably great in one area and at least good in the other three. If you're really weak in one of the areas, it is probably enough to eliminate you. *JOELLE DU LAC*

➤ **SAÏD/OXFORD:** We look for a first degree with a 3.5 GPA (or equivalent). Non-native English speakers should have at least a 250 TOEFL score. Normally, we expect a GMAT score in excess of 630 and at least two years of work experience at the managerial level. *ALISON OWEN*

➤ **MANCHESTER:** We won't rule out anybody because of one factor. We look first to make sure the person can do our program, then we look at motivation and character and whether our quite different program is right for them. So we start with the undergraduate record and GMAT, then we go on to the essays and recommendations and such. You do not need to be Einstein to complete an MBA—the threshold is quite low. So we look at other things: progress on the job, motivation for doing an MBA, career plans. *ANDREW DYSON*

➤ **LONDON:** We want people who are extremely intelligent, who are very motivated, and who can see that it's to their benefit to work in groups, however difficult that may be. We put a lot of emphasis on group work. So we aren't necessarily looking for somebody who'll come in with highly polished group skills, because that's something we help people with, but we want people to whom this challenge is not just absolutely frightful. *JULIA TYLER*

OTHER FACTORS

Value of Legacy Status

➤ Being a legacy (son or daughter of someone who went to Harvard) has absolutely no impact on your chances of being admitted. *BRIT DEWEY, HARVARD*

➤ Legacy status does not earn someone a spot in the class; it's not a free ticket. Only in the case of two equally qualified applicants would it make a difference to a decision. It does merit closer attention, however, and a rejection is likely to be handled with a telephone call rather than an e-mail. In other words, there is a more personal dimension to how we handle things. *ROD GARCIA, MIT*

➤ There is no admissions benefit to being a legacy here. *PETER JOHNSON, HAAS*

➤ (We consider legacies to be applicants whose parents attended Columbia Business School.) For us, the value of legacies is that they know the program, the school, and the city, and choose to seek us out. The fact that a parent attended the Business School isn't going to open the door for you, but it does mean something because your parents are part of this community. However, you need to be qualified to be in this program: you need to be able to get through the program and seize the opportunities here, while contributing to it. *LINDA MEEHAN, COLUMBIA*

➤ You need to know we're a Quaker university and we value the idea of performance over pedigree. You have to earn your spot here. We admit the 800 best and brightest candidates from around the world. *THOMAS CALEEL, WHARTON*

➤ None whatsoever. However, parents who've been through the Cambridge system tend to value it and encourage their sons and daughters to give it a go. *DR. SIMON LEARMOUNT, JUDGE (CAMBRIDGE)*

➤ Legacy status has no value at all in our admissions process. *KIRT WOOD, ROTTERDAM*

➤ There is no such thing as a legacy here. There is no room for someone with lesser abilities in a class of ninety. The others in the class would immediately identify someone who didn't fit and question how he was admitted. *KATTY OOMS SUTER, IMD (SWITZERLAND)*

Articulation of Future Goals/Career Focus

➤ Past experience is crucial to formulating future goals. A general sense of where one is headed is very important; a specific one, not at all. Candidates should have a sense of where they see themselves in the future—in general management/consulting, in technology, in finance, or what have you. To think about this and put a plan together is very useful. However, we're more concerned with the thought process than the result—with how it fits together. *SALLY JAEGER, TUCK*

➤ Most people don't know precisely where they're headed; instead, they have general ideas. Of course, it's easier in many respects if they know exactly where they're headed—for one thing, knowing that makes it easier to get there. *MICHELE ROGERS, KELLOGG*

➤ People who lack direction worry us if their history reflects bad decision-making to this point. For example, someone who has changed schools and majors multiple times and had three jobs in four years may be applying to business school on a whim. Plus, two years at business school provides less time for career exploration than you'd imagine. *ANN W. RICHARDS, JOHNSON (CORNELL)*

➤ If you intend to change careers, do your homework. A person who has practiced law for several years and wants to get out of it because he's sick of the effort and the long hours looks like a fool when he says that he wants to go into investment banking. Use your college networks to contact people in your desired field; pursue informational interviews with people in it. *ANN W. RICHARDS, JOHNSON (CORNELL)*

➤ We are the only school that doesn't dwell too much on the specifics of your goals. It's not a competency we look for. You certainly need to exhibit thoughtfulness in your cover letters and have a realistic sense of what your skills and ambitions are, but we know people change their lives, and therefore their goals will change, too. Rarely do people go through our program without changing their goals, due to the people they meet and opportunities they didn't expect. *ROD GARCIA, MIT*

➤ A large portion of the people graduating from Columbia end up being career changers, whether or not that's what they intended when they applied. Obviously, we don't hold them to what they wrote about their goals in their applications. What we're really trying to evaluate is how well you know yourself. How well can you articulate that what you've achieved so far has laid a foundation for your next steps? Are you realistic about who you are and what you've accomplished—and what you'll be able to achieve with that background? We're not trying to determine whether you know exactly what you're going to do. But the last thing we want to do is to bring people into an MBA program who have no knowledge of who they are and whether they can actually achieve what they want to do. *LINDA MEEHAN, COLUMBIA*

➤ The two-page essay about your career should be effortless. The essay about Stern should only be hard because they've done so much research that they may have too much to say. Lots of people haven't thought it through: they haven't done enough homework on their career, themselves, or the school. It shows, and it does hurt them. I don't consider that I'd be doing them a favor by admitting them before they are ready for the program. *ISSER GALLOGLY, STERN (NYU)*

➤ We want to understand the reasoning behind peoples' goals. We understand that in 65 percent of cases these goals will change, that while at Cambridge they'll realize they have additional options available. So we want to understand the underlying motivations more than the specific goals. . . . The quality of their thinking matters more than having a clearly delineated career path to McKinsey or J. P. Morgan. *DR. SIMON LEARMOUNT, JUDGE (CAMBRIDGE)*

➤ Essential. For instance, if you tell me you're targeting consulting, I'm going to ask how you're going to get your job. "Who do you know?" "What are the steps you're going to take to accomplish that?" *KIRT WOOD, ROTTERDAM*

➤ A candidate with clear career goals shows good motivation for the MBA Program. . . . Of course, an MBA may also mean undergoing a thorough personal and professional change; you might enter the program with certain career plans and end it with completely different perspectives. Hence, together with clear objectives, candidates must also show a certain open-mindedness and flexibility. *ROSSANA CAMERA, BOCCONI (ITALY)*

➤ If someone hasn't a clue where he's headed, we'll be uncertain as to why he wants to do an MBA. *ALISON OWEN, SAÏD (OXFORD)*

➤ We want to be certain that applicants have thought about their futures even if most won't do what they say. It's how you say what you intend to do, and how you structure your plan to move along to your goal, that matter. Those who take a structured view of the process end up doing better in the long term. *JOELLE DU LAC, INSEAD*

Value in the Program

➤ We particularly value someone who takes advantage of the full range of what's on offer here. We look not just for someone who's a strong leader or who's brilliant and can show up from nowhere and ace a test. We want people who will be actively involved in the program as cocreators (with us) of their MBA experience, customizing it to their own needs. *JAMES HAYES, MICHIGAN*

➤ Being a good member of the collaborative Stern community. Part of that is looking to succeed, but never at the expense of someone else. Our students are always helping one another, whether it's helping someone on a case study at 2 a.m. or doing interview prep together at a McKinsey callback. People come here expecting they'll find little sense of community—that folks won't stay on campus, given that we're in the midst of New York City. They're surprised that we actually have an incredibly tight community. Students stay on campus, do hang out with one another, become close friends, and end up traveling together and being in one another's weddings. We expect people to be engaged, active partners in the Stern community. We expect them to come in here with new ideas and partner with us to make them happen. *ISSER GALLOGLY, STERN (NYU)*

➤ It's someone who's prepared to risk himself or herself. Any great business school provides a challenging but safe program in which to explore ideas, but for that to work well, a person has to be willing to put forth his ideas and be challenged by others. *DR. SIMON LEARMOUNT, JUDGE (CAMBRIDGE)*

➤ What makes somebody good whilst they're here? They're involved not just in their learning but also they join the sports tournament and go off to Paris for the tug-of-war contest or whatever. It's somebody who recognizes that there's a community here. They're people who are active in getting clubs going. They're people who'll get someone good to come in and speak at their affairs. It's somebody who, on their weeklong shadowing project (on which they follow a senior executive for a week to understand what he actually does and how he does it) say that it shouldn't stop at a week and convince the sponsoring company that they should actually be paid to go with the executive to China because it's so interesting. So the way to put it is that they're engaged. *JULIA TYLER, LONDON*

Company Sponsorship

➤ It's no more than a clear indication that a company values someone, so it functions like a good recommendation. *THOMAS CALEEL, WHARTON*

➤ It isn't. We make decisions on a need-blind basis. *DR. SIMON LEARMOUNT, JUDGE (CAMBRIDGE)*

➤ A company's willingness to sponsor (i.e., pay for) a candidate shows that it is willing to invest in the person, which is one more positive thing about the candidate, albeit not a major consideration for us. *JOELLE DU LAC, INSEAD*

Residence

➤ Being a California resident has no impact upon one's chances of admission, except that we try not to have too many people from any one industry background or geographic area. *PETER JOHNSON, HAAS*

➤ Residency is not a factor in the admissions decision. *JAMES HAYES, MICHIGAN*

➤ Being a Virginia resident has no impact on the admissions decision. *SARAH E. NEHER, DARDEN*

FOR INTERNATIONAL APPLICANTS

This section is designed to provide applicants from outside the United States with information about the special difficulties they face when applying to American programs. For example, top American schools will generally accept only certain degrees earned at certain types of foreign institutions.

Although this section is designed explicitly for non-American applicants applying to American schools, the concerns it addresses are common for anyone applying outside his or her own region. Thus, an American student applying to a European school may face similar concerns about the validity of his or her degree or college. So if you are applying outside your region, this section may alert you to the key issues you will face in addition to the normal ones faced by all applicants.

ADMISSION POLICIES

Most of the top MBA programs require that students have a minimum educational background roughly equivalent to an American bachelor's degree. A number of European schools, however, will accept applicants who have not completed the equivalent of a bachelor's degree but who have made up for this deficit by acquiring substantial work experience or professional credentials, such as membership in the Institute of Chartered Accountants. These schools generally require at least five years of work experience before they will consider such an applicant.

For those American schools that want educational credentials similar to an American bachelor's degree, however, the following list gives a rough indication of what level of education is likely to be deemed acceptable. Be sure to double-check with each institution you are interested in because substantial differences in criteria do exist.

Australia and New Zealand. See United Kingdom and British-styled systems.

Canada. Four-year bachelor's degree from English-speaking provinces or three-year bachelor's degree from Québec are generally acceptable.

Central America. See Spain and Latin America.

China (People's Republic). Bachelor's degree requiring four years of study at a university is generally acceptable.

Denmark. Academingenior or Candidatus are generally acceptable, even in the case of Candidatus degrees requiring only three years of study.

French and French-styled systems. Degrees (diplômes or maîtrises) that require a baccalaureat plus four years of further study from a university or grande école are generally acceptable.

Germany. Magister Artium, Staatsexamen, or University Diplom are generally acceptable. Fachhochschulen graduates may or may not be eligible.

Hungary. Oklevel requiring at least four years of study is generally acceptable.

India, Pakistan, Myanmar (Burma), Bangladesh, and Nepal. Bachelor's or master's degrees requiring at least four years of study are generally acceptable, but B.A., B.Com., and B.Sc. degrees alone are often unacceptable.

Indonesia. Sarjana or Sarjana Lengka awarded after five years of study is acceptable, but Sarjana Muda (requiring only three years of study) is not.

Mexico. See Spain and Latin America.

Netherlands. The following are generally acceptable: Doctorandus, Ingenieur, or Meester. Kandidaats, Propaedeuse, and H.B.O. diplomas are often considered unacceptable.

Philippines. Bachelor's degrees requiring either five years of work or four years of work and one year of graduate study are generally acceptable.

Poland. Magister, Dyplom, and Inżynier are generally acceptable.

Russia and former states of the U.S.S.R. Diploma requiring five years at a university or institute is generally acceptable.

Spain and Latin America. Licenciado, Licenciatura, or Bacharel is generally acceptable.

Switzerland. Diplom, Diplôme, and Licence, requiring at least four years of university study, are generally acceptable. The following are often considered unacceptable: Betriebsökonom, HWV, Econ. ESCEA, Ingenieur ETS, Ingenieur HTL, and Ingenieur STS.

United Kingdom and British-styled systems. There is no general rule in effect as to British-style education, although a number of schools require an honours bachelor's degree; some schools require a First or Upper Second.

ACADEMIC RECORDS

American schools almost invariably require that records be translated into English and that the translation be officially notarized.

GRADES

The grading systems in use in your country may or may not be familiar to the admissions staff at business schools to which you are applying. If you have any doubt about this, be sure to have your school send an explanation of the grading system (in English), showing especially the percentage of students who typically get each mark. For example, if your school uses a 20-point system, the top 5 percent of students might have averages of 13–15 points. It is important to point this out because a poorly informed admissions officer might try to translate your grade of 14 into a 2.8 average in the American style 4.0 system (by simply dividing by 5). This 2.8 is a very mediocre grade, likely to place a student in the bottom half of his class. Your 14, on the other hand, might put you in the top 5 percent of your class, something you would want a school to know.

Showing your class rank can thus be very helpful. Another matter of concern to admissions officers is the overall quality of your school. Having your recommenders place it in appropriate context, or having your school note its usual place in the pecking order of local schools, can be helpful, at least if your school is generally well regarded.

STANDARDIZED EXAMS: GMAT AND TOEFL

The GMAT exam is difficult enough for Americans, so it is likely to be doubly difficult if English is not your first language. Americans have the advantage of taking the exam in their native language. The exam is also familiar to them because they take similar exams to get into their undergraduate programs. As if this were not enough of an advantage, they also have ready access to preparatory materials and classes, and those who intend to get into the leading business schools generally take extensive prep courses. If you are a non-native speaker of English, therefore, you owe it to yourself to prepare thoroughly for this exam. Although schools will take into account the fact that English is not your first language, they will not accept a dramatically lower score.

Leading business schools around the world require that non-native speakers of English be certified as competent in English. The only general exception is granted to those who did their bachelor's degree in an English-speaking country. The preferred exam is the Test of English as a Foreign Language (TOEFL), although the very similar IELTS exam is sometimes accepted in lieu of the TOEFL. There are three TOEFL formats: the original paper format, a computer format, and a new Internet format. The Internet version is the most extensive, testing reading, listening, speaking, and writing skills. Given that the three formats are scored on radically different scales, comparing scores across them is difficult. The top MBA programs usually look for top 10–20 percent scores, but higher scores are preferred. Frankly, if you are unable to reach these scores, you will not be able to succeed on the GMAT—the English requirements of which are much greater—nor will you be able to survive a rigorous MBA program.

To find out more about the TOEFL exam or register for it, contact:

TOEFL
www.toefl.org
+1 (443) 75 1-4862

ENGLISH LANGUAGE ABILITY REQUIRED

Stanford explains the level of English required in good graduate business schools: "All students must be able to understand rapid, idiomatic English, spoken in lectures and group discussions by persons of widely varying accents. Students from non-English-speaking countries must be able to express their thoughts quickly and clearly in spoken and written English, and be able to read it with ease. The quantity and quality of academic work required at the Business School cannot be accomplished without such mastery of the English language before arrival on the campus. This point must be emphasized, as the Business School expects its students to submit numerous reports, take written examinations regularly, and participate in classroom discussions."

EXTRACURRICULAR AND COMMUNITY ACTIVITIES

Extracurricular and community activities are not always a priority for applicants outside the United States. As a result, schools may not expect to see as much in this category as they do for Americans. By the same token, to the extent that you can do something significant, it will help to distinguish you from other foreign applicants and make you look like a better "fit" for an American program.

TERMINOLOGY

American usage tends to differ from that used elsewhere. In the United States, a *college* is similar to a *university* (rather than to a high school), the difference being that a college typically focuses on only one area of study and/or grants no degrees higher than a master's degree, whereas a university is typically a collection of colleges and grants degrees up to and including doctoral degrees. A *faculty* refers to the professors teaching at the school rather than to a specific department. Last, a *school*, in American parlance, refers to an educational institution of any level, from grade school (ages 5 to 12) to graduate school (ages 22 and up).

ADDITIONAL INFORMATION SOURCES

To learn more about being a student in the United States, consider contacting the United States Information Service (USIS), a government agency housed in most American consulates around the world. Many of these offices have college advisory services, and all of them have libraries that contain many books about life in the United States and about student life.

Many capital cities also have an educational advising center. These centers have a variety of names: the Institute for International Education, the Fulbright Commission, the U.S. Educational Advisory Service, or the Home Country-American Educational Foundation. These offer numerous services, including lectures about the application process, in addition to well-stocked libraries with many school brochures and guides to schools.

8

MARKETING YOURSELF: GENERAL PRINCIPLES

— EXECUTIVE SUMMARY —

Understand how you compare with the competition.

Learn how admissions officers will view your candidacy based upon their expectations of people from your field and educational background.

Capitalize on your strengths while minimizing your weaknesses, in light of their expectations.

Show how you bring unique value to the school without being so unusual as to be perceived as a risk.

Use themes to focus your marketing effort.

*T*he first part of this chapter shows you how to determine what you should emphasize in your application. Your areas of emphasis depend upon several factors: what the top business schools want, what your competition offers, and how your relevant strengths and weaknesses compare with these applicants. The second part of the chapter begins the discussion of how to capitalize on your strengths and make the strongest possible argument for your acceptance. This discussion continues throughout the following chapters, which explore the marketing vehicles you need to master: the essays, recommendations, and interviews.

DETERMINING THE SUBSTANCE OF YOUR MESSAGE

YOUR STRENGTHS AND WEAKNESSES VERSUS THOSE OF THE COMPETITION

Chapter 7, "Making the Most of Your Credentials," explained what schools seek in their applicants. You should therefore have a reasonable idea of what your own strengths and weaknesses are. This knowledge, however, is not really enough; at this point you should go one step further in determining how you stack up versus the competition.

Start your analysis of the competition you face by getting the summary data about entering students provided by every program. The information Chicago provides potential applicants is highlighted below:

CHICAGO	
Total enrollment	550
Male (69%)	
Female (31%)	
Underrepresented U.S. minority students	10%
U.S. citizens	60%
U.S. permanent residents	10%
International students	30%
Average full-time work experience	5 years
Average age	28 (age range 21–39)

(Continued)

CHICAGO	
Countries represented	53
Average GMAT	703 (80% of class scored between 640 and 760)
Average undergraduate GPA	3.5/4.0 (80% of class between 3.0 and 3.9)
Undergraduate major	
Liberal Arts and all others	35%
Finance and Business Administration	23%
Engineering	22%
Economics	20%

In the interest of saving space, I have not included a more detailed geographic area distribution.

Most other schools provide this much, or more, data on their entering classes. Some schools give more detail about the age distribution of students, their experience distribution, the fields they were working in at the time of applying, and their salaries. These "class profiles" are generally included in the information packages schools send potential applicants. Some of the guides to schools, as Chapter 3 discussed, also provide such information, as do school websites.

With these data in hand, it is a simple matter to determine how you stack up relative to the average candidates in terms of your academic credentials, GMAT score, amount and nature of experience, salary, international background, and the like. The problem, however, is that you cannot tell how you stack up relative to those in your part of the application pool. To get a sense of this comparison, you will need to go a step further. Look at the "résumé books" schools put together to help potential employers determine which students might be of interest for upcoming job openings. These books have traditionally not been given to applicants, but there are ways around this problem. For example, you can ask a human resources person at your company to request one. Some schools actually post student résumés on their websites, although a student access number may be required to view them; if you have a friend in the program at the moment, have her download the résumés for you. Many student clubs—such as Harvard's management consulting club—publish their own résumé books for distribution to potential employers.

Looking at the precise details contained in these student résumés also allows you to get a real sense of what a school is looking for. This will help you tailor your message to the school's specific interests.

A SHORTCUT TO THE STRENGTHS AND WEAKNESSES ANALYSIS

Each person will be more than just a member of a category; a person who happens to be an accountant will not be the same as all other accountants. By the same token, knowing what category you fall into, especially the job category, can help you determine how you are likely to be viewed by admissions officers. Although admissions officers will not assume that every accountant has the strengths and weaknesses listed here, these are likely to be their starting presumptions.

The following chart is intended to make this process of marketing yourself a bit easier by showing the presumed strengths and weaknesses of different categories of applicants. In terms of strengths, or reasons to admit you to a program, these may give you some ideas for things you can emphasize about yourself as good reasons to value you. If you are a member of one of the most traditional categories of applicants to MBA programs, however, recognize that just having the strengths noted here will be insufficient reason to admit you. You may need to be demonstrably stronger than others in the same category (and perhaps even freed of the category's typical weaknesses). The job/industry categories that generate large numbers of applicants include accounting, computer programming, consulting by admissions officers, engineering, finance, sales, and marketing. The chart shows what admissions officers presume to be strengths and weaknesses unless evidence is presented to the contrary.

CATEGORY	LIKELY STRENGTHS/REASONS TO HAVE THEM IN THE PROGRAM	LIKELY WEAKNESSES
Job/Industry		
Accountant	Understanding of accounting (good for study groups) Seriousness of purpose Exposed to numerous businesses and industries (if CPAs) Quantitative skills	Undynamic Not a leader Dull, no sense of humor Quiet, unlikely to engage in class discussions Lacks interpersonal and communication skills Not a risk-taker One of many candidates of this type applying
Computer Programmer	Bright Technologically up-to-date Quantitative skills Technical skills	Poor interpersonal skills Not a leader Unwilling to develop "soft" skills Not well-rounded
Consultant	Bright Smooth, good communicator Strong research and analysis skills	Just getting "ticket punched," without truly wanting to be in program

(Continued)

Category	Likely Strengths/Reasons to Have Them in the Program	Likely Weaknesses
	Integrator Leader Facilitator Big-picture knowledge	Arrogant, even by MBA standards Limited management experience One of many candidates of this type applying
Engineer	Quantitative skills Technologically up-to-date Smart Used to rigorous academic setting Team-oriented	Lacks outside interests; not well-rounded Lacks communication and interpersonal skills One of many candidates of this type applying
Entrepreneur	Determined Small business focus Real understanding of business nuts and bolts, not just theory Integrator Risk-taker	No patience for "book learning" Not team oriented Dysfunctional obsessiveness Self-serving Disruptive
Finance/Banking	Quantitative skills Understanding of accounting (good for study groups) Strong research and analysis skills Diligent	Lacks management skills One of many candidates of this type applying Arrogant Rushing into MBA
Human Resources	Social and interpersonal skills Knowledge of compensation, selection, training, and related issues Team player	Lacks quantitative abilities! Interested in business problems or just people's feelings? HR role not considered challenging Lacks guts to make managerial decisions?
Lawyer	Communication skills Accustomed to hard work Smart Analytical thinker	Lacks quantitative abilities! Unable to work with others Unlikely to adopt business perspective Arrogant Whiner Running away from law, not toward business
Marketing	Communication skills Integrator Strategic thinker Team player	Limited management experience One of many candidates of this type applying

CATEGORY	LIKELY STRENGTHS/REASONS TO HAVE THEM IN THE PROGRAM	LIKELY WEAKNESSES
Military	Good leadership training Disciplined Determined	Cultural misfit (business chaos instead of military hierarchy) Lacks business experience Lacks human compassion Limited interpersonal skills
Nonprofit	Few available in application pool Unusual perspective Qualitative skills	Lacks quantitative skills No "real world" corporate experience Lacks guts to make managerial decisions
Sales	Communication skills Interpersonal skills Understands customers Self-confident	Lacks analytical skills Lacks managerial skills So easy to get into it's easy to excel
Scientist	Bright Quantitative skills Few available in application pool Valued by biotech and venture capital firms	Interest in business? Lacks interpersonal and communication skills
Writer, Artist, Photographer	Unique perspective Creative thinker Communication skills Few available in application pool	Lacks quantitative skills! No relevant managerial experience Lacks team skills Little dedication to business Not marketable at end of program
Nationality*		
Chinese	Hardworking and determined Strong interest in technology Strong individual contributor Good quantitative skills	Weak grasp of English Likely to socialize only with countrymen Limited managerial skills and interest
German	Hardworking and determined Likely to focus in heavy industry Good team player (but only when other members are strong) Strong secondary and university education Represents a major market	No sense of humor; stiff No interest in the underdog Arrogant
Irish	Amiable Team player Good communicator	Lacks drive Romantic dreamer rather than pragmatist

(Continued)

CATEGORY	LIKELY STRENGTHS/REASONS TO HAVE THEM IN THE PROGRAM	LIKELY WEAKNESSES
Age		
Older (mid-thirties or order)	Experience and industry knowledge Willingness to share experiences	Lacks energy (especially if over 40) Unwillingness to sit through basics in class Hard to place in jobs Impatience with theory Poor fit with younger students Unwilling to participate in school community due to other life demands
Young	Energetic, enthusiastic	Lacks experience Nothing to contribute to class discussions Doesn't really know where headed in career Immature

*This listing is not meant to be exhaustive. By sampling just a few nationalities, I intend simply to highlight the significance of this factor. Note that when using the term "nationality," I do not, for example, mean German American, but one who is native-born German. (One reason for choosing Irish and German, and being very blunt about their supposed shortcomings, is that I number Germans and Irish among my own ancestors.)

Job, nationality, and age are by no means the only determinants of an admissions officer's expectations. For example, your *college major* is another. If you majored in Egyptology, an admissions officer will probably picture you differently than if you had majored in Physics. Similarly, your *family background*, even the *name of the firm* you work for, can influence expectations. If you are from a wealthy background, for example, you risk being perceived as spoiled.

COMBATING A PRIVILEGED IMAGE

Do:

➤ Participate in/lead substantial community service activities.

➤ Show that you have taken advantage of all opportunities.

➤ Demonstrate that you have crossed social and other divides or experienced the plight of (and sympathize with) others less fortunate.

Do Not:

➤ Sound arrogant, spoiled, or unappreciative of your opportunities. World-weary cynicism does not play well with admissions directors.

➤ Make a big deal out having fancy hobbies that grow out of having had wealthy parents, such as flying private planes.

➤ Discuss expensive trips you have taken or glamorous events you have attended.

CAPITALIZING ON YOUR STRENGTHS, MINIMIZING YOUR WEAKNESSES

Once you have analyzed your situation and recognize where you stand, you should be aware of what an admissions officer is likely to see as strengths and weaknesses. Your job now is to capitalize on this understanding.

First, you will want to support any of the strengths you do indeed have. You can relate stories in your essays that show you, for example, as an effective leader. Just as important, you can (and should) have your recommenders provide supporting examples. The interviews give you a further opportunity to amplify your strengths. The following chapters show you how to use these three communication vehicles most effectively.

Second, do whatever you can to minimize your weaknesses or, better yet, show that you do not suffer from them. Once again, it is a matter of addressing them through each of the vehicles at your disposal: the essays, recommendations, and interviews. In other words, you should maximize your reward/risk ratio. Schools want students who will make major contributions to their programs (i.e., provide a reward for accepting them) without involving substantial risks of academic and other types of failure. The higher the reward/risk ratio, the better your chances of appealing to a school.

EXAMPLES

People with different profiles will, of course, face very different challenges. A research associate (or, so to speak, a junior consultant) at a major management consulting firm faces a very different task from that of a commercial photographer in trying to maximize the reward/risk ratio. The *junior consultant* is likely to be regarded as very bright, with strong research and analysis skills, and a good overview of business, without being much of a risk to a program. She has already gone through the difficult screening process of the consulting firm, which was much like the screening process of a business school. After three years in consulting, she knows enough about business and about how to do business analysis that there is essentially no danger that she will fail out of a program, or lose interest in business, or be unplaceable in a good job upon graduation. She therefore looks like an absolute cinch to be admitted because she brings good experience and qualities to the program without any risk, meaning that her reward/risk ratio looks very high indeed. The problem for her, however, is that she is but one among thousands of junior consultants, all of whom bring similar qualities. To improve her chances of admission, she must show that she is quite different from these other consultants in terms of the range of her work, the depth of her understanding of a given industry (or two), the extent of her direct work with clients, her success to date, and how she intends to employ her MBA in the future (based, of course, upon a realistic scenario of how she will do so). Differentiating herself on the basis of the nature and quality of her extracurricular activities and prior academics will also help.

The *commercial photographer* is in a nearly opposite situation. In his case, the problem is not what he brings to the program. He is likely to be the only photographer applying, so he has considerable uniqueness value to start with. His problem involves the risk side of the ratio. An admissions director is likely to worry that he will be unable to handle the program's academic (especially quantitative) demands and that he will fail out of the program early on. Similarly, she may worry that he will lose interest in business and simply go back to photography midway through the program. She will probably also worry that his lack of work in a traditional field may make the employers who normally recruit at the school reluctant to hire him. To improve his chances of admission, he needs to address each of these concerns. He may, for example, want to take several quantitative courses prior to applying to show that he has the ability to do quantitative work. By taking these steps, he also shows that he is sincerely interested in business, is not applying on a whim, and is likely to complete the program. Last, he will want to show where he is headed with his MBA and how he intends to get there. This will involve explaining what skills and experiences he already has, plus showing how he will acquire other relevant skills and experiences during the business school program (through part-time work, club activities, course projects, etc.) to be able to land a job with the type of employer that interests him. Explaining this trajectory will help him clearly communicate why he wants/needs an MBA.

The junior consultant would make a terrible mistake if she were to concentrate on the risk side of the ratio; rather, she must show her unique value. The commercial photographer would, on the other hand, make a terrible mistake if he were to concentrate on the reward side of the ratio; he must reduce the risk he poses.

Essay Example

The following essays written by Joerg (some years ago) provide a good example of how to capitalize on a category's strengths and minimize the expected weaknesses. He was finishing a doctorate in mechanical engineering at a leading German university when applying. Although he had substantial work experience, in traditional German fashion it had been obtained part-time while completing his studies. If you look at the chart earlier in the chapter, you can see that a German engineer carries a lot of baggage, a lot of expectations. Joerg wanted to reap the benefits of being a German engineer, so he made it very clear that he was determined, conceptually able, well grounded in fundamentals, and a solid team player in working with other strong engineers. In fact, he was able to show that he was quite exceptional on these counts, thereby increasing the "reward" side of the reward/risk ratio. He also neutralized the potential weaknesses for someone of his profile. He showed that he was a deeply caring, humanitarian fellow in helping someone involved in political difficulties escape from China. He showed that he was not an arrogant, insular German by demonstrating his international involvement. His essays have other virtues as well, but these are the most important ones for us for the moment.

1. **Briefly describe your career progression to date. Elaborate on your future career plans and your motivation for pursuing a graduate degree at Kellogg. (400-word limit)**

   I have followed a traditional German route to a serious business career by pursuing my education in Mechanical Engineering to the doctoral level. In spring 1993 I will complete my ME education in approximately 2.5 years less than the average student requires, without sacrificing the breadth or depth of my studies and apprenticeships, even while doing this at Germany's finest engineering school.

   My engineering efforts have been meant to prepare me for a business career combining engineering and marketing skills. The marketing side of the effort started with my work for two business consulting firms in the late 1980s. I had to support myself throughout my studies since my parents are disabled. I consequently sought the highest paying outside jobs I could get which also fit my school schedule. The first of these jobs was with a computer consulting firm, Consultax. One of my projects for Consultax involved helping a marketing consultancy, Wehmeyer Marketing, develop and implement a new marketing information system.

   My work for Wehmeyer Marketing Consultancy, whose principal activity was textile consulting, convinced it to hire me away from Consultax. Wehmeyer wanted me to apply my computer and textile engineering skills, as well as the ability I had demonstrated to understand quickly the marketing dimension of a business. I ended up managing numerous projects that combined technical and marketing elements, including, for example, the analysis of potential textile suppliers in Mauritius.

Since early 1991 I have been managing a research project* at Hans Schwarzkopf GmbH to develop a new machine to measure the shape stability of chemically treated fiber and hair. This work, which will also satisfy my ME doctoral thesis requirements, should result in one or more patents once it is completed this spring.

My career, while focused upon engineering, has started to straddle the marketing area as well. I very much wish to combine my engineering knowledge with marketing and general management skills. I would prefer to do so by getting an MM at Kellogg, given its international reputation in these areas (and emphasis on teamwork). For the future, I hope to do marketing work for a technically based company, perhaps in the reinforced composite material field. And, not surprisingly, I would like eventually to run such a firm.

Described in detail in my employment history.

2. **Your background, experiences, and values will enhance the diversity of Kellogg's student body. How? (400-word limit)**

My very strong technical background, project management expertise, and international exposure will, I hope, enhance Kellogg's student body.

The strength of my technical background—which will shortly include a Ph.D. in Mechanical Engineering and already includes substantial engineering work experience in a variety of engineering disciplines—should be clear. While there will be other engineers in the Kellogg Program, I suspect that few will possess the same depth and breadth of knowledge and experience that I have acquired.

My project management experience, described briefly in my employment history, has involved the development of a device to measure the shape stability of hair and fiber. This project has required me to motivate, integrate, and control people in various parts of Schwarzkopf Co., ranging from technicians in workshops of different companies to scientists in chemistry laboratories (and even to company owners).

My international background consists of several components. I am German and have worked and gone to school in Germany for most of the last 20-plus years. On the other hand, I have also sought out opportunities to live and work abroad. These experiences have included working in a Japanese factory and doing marketing/engineering work in Mauritius, as well as being a research intern at the University of Wisconsin, Madison. In addition, I have worked in various parts of Europe.

I recognize, however, that my experience will not benefit others at Kellogg except to the extent that I am what Americans call a "team player." I certainly regard myself as precisely that, one who enjoys people of different skills and interests, and, for that matter, different nationalities. My experiences in different disciplines (from chemistry to mechanical engineering to marketing) and different countries (from Japan to Europe to Mauritius) have caused me to enjoy greatly being part of multifaceted teams. I have sometimes led such teams, as I am now doing at Schwarzkopf, but I have also enjoyed participating in research groups as a junior member. I derive great satisfaction from being able to contribute and thus hold up my own end, while simultaneously learning from others with very different skills. My enjoyment of multidisciplinary groups is actually one of the reasons that I look forward to combining my engineering skills with what I hope will be my strong marketing and general management skills in the future.

3.a. It's the year 2030 and your autobiography has just been published. What do the book reviews say? (150-word limit)

(As translated from the Japanese)

Mr. Otzen's view of the first twenty years of his career—perhaps uniquely for a German industrialist—provides a lighthearted view of his climb to the top of Du Pont's Asian operations. There is little surprise that his polymer processing background, combined with his marketing skills, led him to Du Pont. Similarly, his long-time interest in Asia explains his early posting to China. The surprises, of which there are many, come instead from his uninhibited joy in virtually all that he did. He loved the early engineering challenges which yielded his treasured patents. But he also loved the managerial side of his career, particularly working with people from every conceivable country and background. This combination appears to explain at least part of his success.

Volume 2, much anticipated by this reviewer, will cover his controversial years as CEO of Du Pont and then as Germany's Commerce Secretary.

3.b. What are your most valued accomplishments outside of work? Why? (150-word limit)

Through my long involvement in Jülich's International Club, which is dedicated to helping the foreign scientists working at the Research Center Jülich, I met Fanxia Ling,* a Chinese woman anxious to get her son out of the PRC. This couldn't be arranged until she returned to China, so she needed someone to help from within Germany.

I eventually arranged for Li Ling* to come to Germany, but only after countless interventions on his behalf. I arranged his admission, without interviewing, to Karlsruhe University. The PRC refused him a passport several times due largely to his Tiananmen Square activities, but each time I was able to convince both Chinese and German officials to intercede for him. Then I convinced the German Embassy to give him a second chance to prove his German was acceptable and to grant him a student visa.

He is now a student here, and we are friends.

These are pseudonyms; their real names, due to his/her involvement in the Tiananmen Square activities, should remain undisclosed.

3.c. For fun I . . . (150-word limit)

For fun I travel as much as I can. Of course there are other things I greatly enjoy doing, ranging from skiing to scuba diving, but the most satisfying of my pursuits is traveling.

My sort of traveling may not suit everyone. I enjoy going to stay with the people I have met through the International Club of Jülich, which assists visiting scientists and their families. I prepare for each visit by learning all I can about the history, geography, and culture of the region. By staying with friends, however, I am able to see other countries through the eyes of the local residents rather than as a tourist.

Because this discovery process exhilarates me so much, I have explored much of the United States, nearly a dozen European countries, and parts of Japan. But the most interesting thing still awaits me: to see Li Ling's family in China. (See essay 3.b.)

FIT IN—STAND OUT

Another way to think about the reward/risk ratio is, as many admissions directors put it, a "fit in—stand out" problem. *Fitting in* means that you are accepted by your classmates as belonging in the program rather than being regarded as an oddity. If you can do the coursework, subscribe to the program's goals, and get on well with the other students, you will fit in. *Standing out* means that you bring something unique to the program, something that distinguishes you from the other students. At some level, all of the programs are quite similar in terms of what would make someone fit in or stand out, but this may vary at another level. Having basic accounting skills would help you fit in at any program. Being a fluent speaker of four languages might make you stand out at Darden (which has a high percentage of American students) but would help you fit in at INSEAD, where students must speak at least three languages by the time they graduate.

The trick, obviously, is to fit in and stand out at the same time. It is not sufficient to do just one of these things. Saying that you really fit in, that you look like a composite of all the other students, gives the school no reason to want you there because you bring nothing different and therefore nothing special. Saying that you really stand out, that you do not resemble any of the other students in any relevant way, is similarly useless because you will be seen as too risky to have in the program. If you really have nothing in common with people, the likelihood of your not getting along with others in the program is high, as are your chances of failing. The way to straddle this apparent divide is to fit in on certain key dimensions and be different on other specifics. Most people will tend to fall more on one side of the divide than the other. The consultant need not worry that she will fail to fit in; her problem is showing how she stands out. The photographer need not worry about standing out; his problem is showing that he will fit in.

FASHIONING YOUR MESSAGE: POSITIONING

The admissions director for a top business school is confronted with thousands of applications for each class. He or she is meant to read the lengthy folders on each applicant, containing lists of full-time and part-time jobs with descriptions of the responsibilities, reporting relationships, salaries, and so forth; university grades and activities; plus all of the essays, recommendations, interview write-ups—and so on and so forth. As if this onslaught were not enough, every time an admissions officer ventures into a public forum, there are applicants trying to get his or her attention. One of the more bizarre sights at an MBA fair, for example, is to see dozens of people clustered about a top school's admissions staff, each of them waiting impatiently to try to get a couple of minutes with the admissions director to plead his or her case.

Most of these applicants are actually qualified, meaning that they could successfully do the academic work of the program and get something useful from it. If you are not careful, you will remain part of this undifferentiated mass of applicants. The key to standing out from the crowd is to "position" yourself appropriately.

Positioning is a marketing concept that is meant to deal with this problem of too many applicants trying to capture the attention of admissions directors who are overwhelmed by the onslaught. To cut through all of this communications haze, you must have a very sharp and clear image that is readily noticed, understood, and valued.

Let's look at an example that is dear to my heart. There are many types of whiskey, even of scotch whiskey. Nonetheless, there are a number of products that are distinctively positioned in the market for scotch. For example, Laphroaig is a single malt scotch with a peatier, more iodine taste (and "nose") than its competitors. Its unique attributes allow it to market itself to consumers who consider themselves beyond the "beginners'" scotches and who want the strongest possible taste they can find. Macallan, on the other hand, is exceptionally smooth and even bears a certain resemblance to cognac. It tells consumers that its product is aged in old sherry casks, which impart a distinctive hint of sherry in the nose.

These two products compete in the very high end of the scotch market, yet each is positioned to be completely unique. Their marketing efforts aim to make it very clear what key attributes they possess, and they are very successful. Both are held in extremely high regard by serious malt scotch drinkers, although they are considered virtually unrelated to one another. The result is that each can claim a price premium for its distinctiveness that would be impossible were they positioned to compete head-to-head.

How does this apply to you? You must distinguish yourself from others in the applicant pool who may apply to the same schools you do. Business school applicants are not all the same; your job is to show your uniqueness. By appearing unique, you increase your value. After all, if you are the same as 2,500 other applicants, what school will really care if they get you rather than one of the other 2,499? By making yourself unique, you also make yourself more memorable. Remaining anonymous will not help you. Far better if an admissions committee remembers you, perhaps even having a shorthand expression for use in discussing you. Being "the woman who runs the binational airport"—

JUXTAPOSITION

The easiest positioning effort, frankly, is simply to show that you have the traditional strengths of your category to an unusual degree, with none of the weaknesses. For example, if you are an accountant, you can try to show that you are truly an exceptionally good accountant (the best in your cohort of thirty-seven at Deloitte's Chicago office), plus you are blessed with a sly sense of humor.

It is wonderful if you can take this advice one step further. If you happen to be a stand-up comedian who has played some of Chicago's professional clubs, you can show that you actually have two generally incompatible competencies. This juxtaposition of the unlikely (how many stand-up comics work as CPAs in their day jobs?) will certainly leap out at an admissions officer and make sure that you are remembered and viewed very favorably.

as one of the people whose essays we include later in the book might have been characterized—means that you are remembered and can be discussed as a unique person. Contrast this with the sort of person who is discussed as "Which one is she? Really? Could I see that file again? I don't remember reading that one before."

GENERAL POSITIONING VERSUS SPECIFIC POSITIONING

To what extent should your positioning be different for each target school? Since no two schools are exactly the same, you might want to position yourself differently for each school. On the other hand, doing markedly different applications for each school is a lot of extra work. Not only do you need to write your essays differently, but you also need to have your recommenders write each recommendation differently. For example, if you intend to apply to MIT to study manufacturing (to take advantage of its Leaders for Manufacturing program) and to Kellogg to study marketing (to take advantage of its well-known marketing curriculum), you will face the difficulty of being a persuasive applicant for both.

Take a modified approach: Have a general positioning strategy that you can fine-tune to fit the needs of specific schools without making major changes in your applications. Emphasize different aspects of your experience for a given school; don't try to re-create yourself for it. This approach assumes that you will not be applying to one school in order to do marketing and another in order to do manufacturing. (Obviously, if you have not yet resolved what you intend to do at business school and afterwards, you may need to do very different applications for each program.)

Any positioning approach you take must be something you can reinforce via specific, powerful examples.

THE MECHANICS OF POSITIONING: USING THEMES

Positioning is meant to provide a method for presenting a very clear picture of you. A simple way to achieve this is to use several *themes* to organize your material. When writing your essays, for example, relate all or at least most of your material to your chosen themes. If your material is organized around three or four themes, your positioning will be very clear and easy to grasp.

The themes you use will be different from those others will (or should) use. Because business schools are looking for some very definite features in all of their candidates, however, you should have one or two themes that other strong candidates will also use. Chapter 7, "Making the Most of Your Credentials," showed that schools are always concerned to find people who (1) are determined to succeed and (2) will profit from an MBA now.

Business schools want people who will accomplish things, despite the inevitable obstacles they will encounter. Success in spite of difficulties is what determination is all about. At age 25 you might have had moderate success without having tried very hard or without having confronted substantial obstacles, but this good fortune is unlikely to continue for your whole career. Thus, you should show that you have accomplished things only after overcoming significant difficulties placed in your way.

Top schools believe that the education they offer is very valuable, and they want to admit students who will get the full measure of this value. Such students are those who want an MBA for the right reasons and who are at the proper point in their lives and careers to get the most out of it. This is one reason schools want students with at least several years of work experience. Those with experience are likely to know where they would like to head in their careers and what they currently lack in order to achieve their goals. This means that they are able to appreciate what an MBA offers them. It also means that they will figure out how to maximize the benefit of a program by choosing the appropriate courses, making the right contacts, and marketing themselves effectively to potential future employers. Those who have not thought through their own futures, or who do not appreciate where their talents and interests lie, are not likely to maximize the benefits of an MBA and are thus likely to be rejected by the best schools. This means that you are obligated to show *your need for an MBA*—and that it is best done *now*.

The other organizing themes you choose will be those that are appropriate to you. The essays in Part IV show some examples of what others have chosen; look at several of them from this perspective. In general, here are a few of the many possible themes around which you can organize parts of your application, and some idea of who might make use of them:

- *Number-crunching analyst:* World Bank economist
- *Warm, loving "Saint Bernard":* human resources consultant specializing in outplacement
- *All-round synthesizer:* as an architect, you have had to bring together the work of various types of engineers, interior decorators, lawyers, accountants, city planners, and clients

- *Functional specialist:* you have become an expert in tax planning for international companies, utilizing triple-tiered corporate structures based in Liechtenstein, the Channel Islands, and the Caymans
- *Polyglot:* you speak five languages fluently, with substantial knowledge of multiple cultures
- *From an unusual background:* you lived for five years in a nunnery
- *Risk-taker:* your idea of fun is scuba diving in the North Sea, or your idea of how to earn a living is going short in developing markets or starting a new business

HOW MANY THEMES SHOULD YOU USE?

There are practical limitations to the number of themes that will help you. If you use too few, you have very little maneuvering room in writing your essays because everything has to fit with just one or two organizing themes. If you use too many, you end up doing no organizing whatsoever and your positioning will no longer be clear. The trick is to balance these two factors. Using *about three to four themes* is generally appropriate because with that number you do not constrain your efforts so much that you appear boring, but you are focused enough that an admissions committee reading your application will know what you are about. The key is that a committee should be able to summarize your positioning in three or four short phrases: You are determined; you need an MBA now; you are a marvelous synthesizer; and you are a real Saint Bernard. If this is what a committee comes away with, they have you pegged in just the way that will serve you best: You are an individual to them, yet one whom they can get a handle on.

THE ADMISSIONS DIRECTORS DISCUSS HOW YOU SHOULD MARKET YOURSELF

Why Marketing Yourself Matters

➤ It's good to have credentials, but that's not enough to get you where you want to go. You need to market yourself well to get in here, in part because everyone else is trying hard to market him or herself well. It's also what you will have to do once you are here in order to get your summer job and your permanent job. It's the real world: You need to have the skills to sell yourself in an elevator pitch to the CEO. *Rod Garcia, MIT*

➤ It is extremely important for an applicant to market himself well. We get some four thousand applications; the decision on who to admit is based largely on applicants' success in distinguishing themselves from the competition. To do this requires that they know well what will appeal to Michigan. They should understand that we are not just looking at numbers, GMAT and so on. We look to form an image of the person, his personality, and what he'll bring to the program. *JAMES HAYES, MICHIGAN*

➤ The extent to which they can market themselves well to us is a good indicator of how well they'll market themselves in the job search process. *ANNE COYLE, YALE*

➤ There are a lot of fabulous people who are applying, but we can't take all of them. You may have done really well in terms of work; have great GMAT scores, undergraduate performance, and recommendations; but if you haven't done a great job putting together your application—it's sloppy, inconsistent, or unclear—you don't get in. In the workplace, if you presented yourself in that way, you wouldn't have much of a future, either. *LINDA MEEHAN, COLUMBIA*

➤ If you clearly have your act together, you're sending an important message: (1) You're showing what kind of student you'd be in the program. (2) Applicants underestimate how much schools want to build legacies. You'll be an alum for much longer than you'll be a student. So if you seem thoughtful, organized, etc., thereby showing you'll be successful after the program, you make yourself a desirable applicant. Plus, (3) you'll need this skill later on. *DAVID BACH, INSTITUTO DE EMPRESA (SPAIN)*

➤ SDA Bocconi's MBA is very much student-centered and wants to focus on each candidate's personal development. That's also why, through our admissions process, we want to be very sure to admit the right person to the right program at the right time. To do so, we need our candidates' "collaboration": especially through their essays and the personal interview, they need to convince us that we are the right school and program for them in that specific moment of their professional life; they need to well present their profile and motivation in a very focused and unique way. What we look for is our candidates' uniqueness, and should that uniqueness fit with our program, then the match can be a successful one. *ROSSANA CAMERA, BOCCONI (ITALY)*

Marketing Advice

➤ Think through why you've done what you have, where you're headed, and why. Know why you're doing an MBA. If you do this and can articulate it, you can be successful in this process. *ROSE MARTINELLI, CHICAGO*

➤ Make sure you think of your application in its entirety—as a presentation of your case for admission. If there are themes that you want to emphasize, make sure that they stand out as part of the overall case. *BRIT DEWEY, HARVARD*

➤ Every inch of the application—the two essays, recommendations, and résumé—and every one of the thirty minutes in the interview, is valuable "real estate," so be careful how you use them. *Anne Coyle, Yale*

➤ We're looking to educate leaders. They're aware of who they are, their strengths and weaknesses. They know how to compensate for their weaknesses and manage around them. *Rose Martinelli, Chicago*

➤ Good marketing and good positioning are about clear communication: clearly defining who you are and what you have to offer. If you're applying to business school, you have to have things to offer—things that make you unique, that you're proud of. You need to be able to communicate them clearly to someone else. In fact, it's almost a matter of being able to write who you are on the back of a business card. That means you're communicating clearly. . . . The application is a vehicle to communicate who you are. That's what good marketing is about. *Isser Gallogly, Stern (NYU)*

➤ The best marketing is honest and straightforward, a true reflection of that person. We think a lot about the design of our application and how we interact with candidates in hopes that we'll give them a chance to do just that. *Dr. Simon Learmount, Judge (Cambridge)*

➤ Be yourself. We're not looking for a single type; instead, we look to assemble a diverse group. So underscore what makes you different; what makes you special; why other students should be excited if you're sitting next to them in class. It's absolutely fine to discuss what you want to work on while you're here, which is presumably why you're interested in attending the program. (Someone without a weakness would have no reason to attend.) *David Bach, Instituto de Empresa (Spain)*

➤ Look at yourself in a complete fashion. Be prepared to talk about yourself as an individual, on a relatively personal level. Be open and forthright. Be prepared to discuss openly both strengths and weaknesses. Don't try to present yourself as a perfect individual who absolutely belongs here, but as a fallible human who has nonetheless accomplished some wonderful things. *Kirt Wood, Rotterdam*

➤ Don't focus on what you can get out of the program. Show what you can contribute. We're looking for people who can bring something unique and of quality to the program. *Joelle du Lac, INSEAD*

➤ The ones who impress are the ones who have thought about who they are, what they want, what an MBA can give them, and above all about the links between these things. Therefore, they can be precise and to the point, even in interviews. So it's not just somebody who has a stunning undergraduate or employment history up to now, which sits there isolated. It's the person who convinces us that he is thoughtful and reflective about what he wants out of an MBA and has thought about what aspects of himself fit, and what aspects don't, and is able to explain both. *Julia Tyler, London*

Few Applicants Market Themselves Well

➤ A very small percentage of applicants do a great job of marketing themselves. They're the ones who understand how it all fits together. *SALLY JAEGER, TUCK*

➤ Substantially under 10 percent of candidates market themselves very effectively. *PETER JOHNSON, HAAS*

➤ One percent (maybe 2 percent in an outstanding, oddball year) market themselves well, giving us a chance to see a complete person, with aspirations, passion, and vision. *ROSE MARTINELLI, CHICAGO*

➤ Less than 10 percent really market themselves well. In fact, when we get a really well-put-together application, it makes a major impact. We notice it and talk about it amongst ourselves. *DAVID BACH, INSTITUTO DE EMPRESA (SPAIN)*

Lying/Inconsistency

➤ Do not embellish your credentials. We are more understanding of someone who has gotten a few bad breaks than of someone who has fabricated achievements—which is all too often apparent. *ANN W. RICHARDS, JOHNSON (CORNELL)*

➤ We have trained all our application readers to look very carefully for inconsistencies or things that don't look quite right in each and every application they read. Each one reads an application independently, so when different readers of a given file are in committee, each one worries about being shown up by someone else having found something suspicious when he or she hasn't. We have also retained Kroll Background America to verify each and every admitted applicant. Our objective is not to catch people but to discourage those inclined to lie or cheat from applying. *ANNE COYLE, YALE*

➤ We use Kroll and Associates to check applications, which we've found to be extremely helpful. If there is falsification of information, it's very simple. We give the applicant an opportunity to talk to us about the matter, but if we're not satisfied, the offer is rescinded. We don't want them here at Columbia. This program is about honor, about an incredible brand, about an institution that has been around for a very long time. We're proud of the people who graduate from here, so we expect them to be who they say they are. If they felt they needed to embellish in order to get in, this is the wrong place for them. *LINDA MEEHAN, COLUMBIA*

➤ We have them sign a statement of integrity, stating that the application is their own work and it's truthful. We reserve the right to withdraw their acceptance before, during, or even after the program if we find they've lied. We retain Kroll and Associates to do a background check on accepted applicants, and we verify selected parts of applications in-house. *THOMAS CALEEL, WHARTON*

> ➤ We're making very extensive use of databases. We're also sharing a lot of information with cognate organizations, such as GMAT. In addition, we follow up with recommenders if we have any doubts about someone. But our key fraud-detection system is that we interview candidates carefully. It seems to be harder to maintain a lie during an interview than on paper. *Dr. Simon Learmount, Judge (Cambridge)*

> ➤ If someone wants to lie about his job experience and such, he'll have to carry that lie through for the rest of his life. And that's not easy. *Kirt Wood, Rotterdam*

> ➤ We have pretty good security. We learn a lot in our interviews, such as the actual level of English an applicant has, his/her work experience, and so on. We also frequently call one or more of an applicant's recommenders, largely to talk further about his or her leadership and team-building skills rather than to discover whether he or she lied in the application. However, we also use these conversations to probe anything that concerns us in the application. *Katty Ooms Suter, IMD (Switzerland)*

A SIMPLE POSITIONING EFFORT

"I always loved science, beginning in childhood. The only courses I loved in high school were hard sciences and math, so I ended up becoming a research scientist. I worked as a research chemist. My dedication—a willingness to work extremely hard to finish work on time—came to the attention of my boss who started to use me as a project manager. He valued my combination of technical ability and sociability; I got on well with the other researchers in the lab. I have enjoyed this project management work, but I would like it more if I felt that I had the managerial tools to do the job as well as possible. I therefore would like to get an MBA sooner rather than later."

The paragraph above is a no-frills positioning effort. It is not meant to be a realistic essay someone would write in describing her career to date, future goals, and reasons for wanting an MBA. Instead, it is meant to illustrate that it is possible in a very short space to develop some important organizing themes. We know, in just a few short lines, that this woman is a good scientist who intends to remain involved with scientific efforts. She is a determined worker also. We know that an MBA would be appropriate for her, and that she could make good use of MBA skills immediately. This mini-portrait thus shows several clear themes: technical specialization, determination, and a pressing need for an MBA. It also shows a logical progression to her career. In other words, she has the fundamentals of her positioning effort already in place.

THE MARKETING VEHICLES

You have three primary vehicles for getting your message across to business schools: the essays, recommendations, and interviews. You will need to be consistent within and across these three vehicles to gain the maximum positive impact. The following chapters will show you how to make the most of them.

CONCLUSION

The penalty for failing to capitalize on your strengths and to prepare a powerful application is, all too often, rejection. Schools have plenty of qualified applicants who took the time to figure out the process and to submit a good application. Failure to do these things suggests that you are not able to do so, or at least do not care to. In either case, you are unlikely to be viewed as showing top management potential, at least at the moment.

Your application to a top business school will be read differently from the application of an 18-year-old for a part-time job. You are competing with the best and the brightest of several continents to get into programs that offer great benefits to those who succeed. The competition for these positions is intense, and the business schools feel justified in expecting high-quality applications. Given that the applicants are expected to have some prior work experience and that they are applying to graduate programs in business, business schools expect that applicants will have at least a reasonable idea of how to market themselves. They also expect applicants to treat the process seriously insofar as the program will take up to two years of the person's life and affect his or her earning potential and career choices forever.

Appendix VI

PERSONAL ORGANIZER

(Make extra copies of this form to have additional room for describing multiple schools, jobs, or other experiences, as necessary.)

EDUCATION

School:

Degree: Date received:

Grade point average: Major/Concentration:

Minor: Relevant additional coursework:

Substantial papers written:

Activities:

Offices held/responsibilities/achievements (academic and extracurricular):

Honors and awards:

Scholarships:

Why did you choose this school? In retrospect, was it a good decision? Why or why not?

(Repeat for choice of major.)

WORK EXPERIENCE

Start with your most recent job and work backwards chronologically. It you had more than one job with the same employer, fill out separate data fields for each. Include all part-time as well as full-time jobs.

Employer: Division/Subsidiary:

Dates employed: Location:

Title/Position:

Beginning salary: Ending salary:

Bonuses/other compensation—Beginning: Ending:

Key responsibilities:

Whom did you manage?   To whom did you report?

Key accomplishments (quantify whenever possible):

Key skills that enabled you to accomplish these things:

Superiors' reviews (excerpts):

Reasons superiors feel this way about you (think in terms of your achievements, skills, actions, attitude, etc.):

In what ways do you stand out from your peer group?

Reasons for taking the job:

Reasons for leaving the job:

Ways in which the job met/did not meet your expectations:

Important stories illustrating your leadership, teamwork, analytical, managerial, creative, and other abilities:

What sources (including people) are there for developing further information about each story?

PROFESSIONAL ACCOMPLISHMENTS

Copyrights:

> Title:
> Date:
> Publisher/Publication:

Patents:

> Title:
> Date:
> Number:

Professional certification:

> Certifying organization:
> Date certified:

Professional honors and awards:

> Name: Date awarded:
> Organization awarding:
> Reason for the award:
> How competitive:

EXTRACURRICULAR (AND POST-GRADUATION) ACTIVITIES
(artistic, athletic, community, religious, political, etc.)

Activity: Dates of involvement:

Offices held/responsibilities/achievements:

Was this a voluntary position or one to which you were elected/appointed? If elected, by whom?

Reasons for your involvement:

How does it relate to your other activities and interests?

PERSONAL QUESTIONS

Who are the four or five people who have most influenced you? (How?)

What are the four or five things you most admire in others? (In whom and why?)

What are your four or five most memorable experiences, whether great or small?

What was your greatest success, and what did you learn from it?

What was your greatest failure, and what did you learn from it?

What fear have you overcome? (How and why?)

What do your friends most like (and dislike) about you?

What are the four or five (or more) key words that would describe you? What on your list demonstrates this?

Do you have a personal motto or something that you frequently quote? If so, what is it?

YOUR FUTURE CAREER

What are your career goals? What do you hope to accomplish in your life?

How has your interest in this career developed?

LEISURE TIME

What are your favorite books? Why? What have you read most recently? (Repeat for films, plays, music, etc.)

What do you like to do when given the time? Why? What do you most enjoy about it?

PULLING YOUR INFORMATION TOGETHER

At the conclusion of this exercise, list your major accomplishments in each category.

Business:

    1.
    2.
    3.
    4.
    5.

Education:

    1.
    2.
    3.
    4.
    5.

Personal:

    1.
    2.
    3.
    4.
    5.

Which events or activities represent turning points in your life (i.e., when you changed direction)?

Which events or activities reaffirmed your desire to continue your career (or education or life) in the same direction?

In what ways are you different from a year ago? Why? (Repeat for five years ago.) Think in terms of your personality, interests, personal and professional goals, and values.

How have your various experiences helped you to grow? What do they show about your abilities? What do they show about your interests?

Which of your experiences demonstrate the following characteristics? (This list is taken from the Chapter 7 analysis of what business schools are looking for in their applicants.)

CHARACTERISTIC	*RELEVANT EXPERIENCE*
Intellectual ability	
Analytical ability	
Imagination and creativity	
Motivation and initiative	
Maturity	
Organizational/administrative skills	
Ability to work with others	
Leadership skills/potential	
Self-confidence	
Ability in oral expression	
Ability in written communication	
Managerial/career potential	
Sense of humor	
Integrity	
Quantitative ability	

9

UNDERSTANDING THE KEY ESSAY TOPICS

— EXECUTIVE SUMMARY —

Familiarize yourself with the topics you need to address.

Learn how to use the essays to market yourself effectively.

Avoid the numerous traps that are built into the essays.

TAKING FULL ADVANTAGE OF THE ESSAYS

One leading business school states, "While we believe that previous academic records and standardized test results are useful tools for (our) evaluation, we find several less quantifiable indicators to be of equal or greater importance. Please keep this in mind as you complete the questions. . . . Use these short essays to show us your personality, motivation, goals, leadership abilities, and communication skills." (IESE, BARCELONA)

Essays offer you the chance to show schools who you really are. Take advantage of this opportunity. Recommenders can show only a part of who you are, since most of them are employers and have thus seen you in only one context, often for a limited time. Similarly, interviews are not under your control to the same extent as the essays, which can be rewritten and reexamined to make sure that the "best you" is presented.

Your essays can and should present a clear picture of you, but they do not need to tell all. Sketching in the main points with appropriate stories will show who you are. In fact, whenever possible, try to tell a story rather than write an essay. The task will seem lighter.

This is your chance to choose which parts of your past and yourself to highlight, and to determine how people should view them. This is a precious opportunity; take full advantage of the chance to color your readers' interpretations.

This chapter analyzes the essay questions; the following chapter shows you how to write your responses. One hundred six examples of actual essays written by applicants are available in Part IV. The chart at the beginning of Part IV shows where to find specific examples, classified by the background of the applicant, the school applied to, and, of course, the specific question asked.

WHICH ESSAYS SHOULD YOU DO FIRST?

If you will do multiple applications, an important issue is which essay or set of essays should be your starting point. Do not write essays piecemeal—one essay

228

from each of several schools' applications. Instead, complete a full set of essays for one school before tackling another essay set for another school. This will allow you to:

- ➤ Get your overall positioning strategy in place.
- ➤ Think hard about what attributes and experiences you have to offer.
- ➤ Make sure you are discussing the right stories (ones that illustrate your key points).
- ➤ Balance the professional and personal elements you discuss (about 75/25 is a good rule of thumb for a typical applicant).

In recent years, the best application with which to start has been Kellogg's. The six essays it requires call for about nine pages of writing, thereby ensuring that you will have adequate space to put across your key points and tell your most important stories. The first three essays are required of everyone; you must address such issues as why you want an MBA, why Kellogg, where you are headed in your career, what you will contribute to the program, and how you think an admissions director would view your file. These are exactly the issues that you should have in mind before doing any application, whether the school explicitly asks you to address them or not. The next three essays are to be selected from a flexible list. This gives you a great deal of freedom in choosing what to discuss, thereby forcing you to consider all that you have to offer. By doing a serious job in responding to all of these questions, and considering how they fit together, you should develop a good understanding of what to discuss in other applications.

If you are not applying to Kellogg, or its application changes dramatically, start with whichever application requires you to write the most, but try to avoid ones that force you to write either very lengthy or very short answers to each question because you will develop habits that will be hard to break when writing essays for other schools.

MBA PROGRAM TOPICS

QUESTION: WHAT ARE YOUR CAREER OBJECTIVES AND REASONS FOR WANTING AN MBA?

WHY THE QUESTION IS ASKED

Schools ask this question for a number of reasons. They want to make sure you have given substantial thought to your future career. They want to see that an MBA fits with the future you envision for yourself. They want to understand why *now* is the right time to earn an MBA.

THE TYPICAL APPLICANT

Many people apply to business school because they are unhappy with their current situations and are hoping to do virtually anything else as long as it is different from what they currently do. Too many of them have no idea of where they are heading; they just know what they are running from. Their response to this question tends to show that they do not have a realistic career plan. They either describe their hoped-for jobs in vague, rosy terms, saying that they hope to find something liberating, empowering, with substantial responsibilities and high pay, or they mention a popular career like investment banking, for which nothing in their past even remotely qualifies them.

Other applicants discuss the virtues of an MBA, including the fact that it can increase graduates' skills, salaries, and career options, which the reader in the admissions office knows quite well without having to be reminded. They forget to discuss why they want an MBA from that particular school, making it seem that an MBA from any program will do.

Similarly, most applicants do not think to give any contextual information concerning their careers so far, making it hard for an admissions reader to ascertain whether their planned futures make sense or not.

A BETTER APPROACH

This is a truly critical essay. You will be manifestly unsuccessful in writing the other essays if you have not thought carefully about your future career. It will be extremely helpful to know where you are heading when you try to answer many of the other essay questions. Start with this essay. Do not go on to the other questions until you have completed—at a minimum—a good draft of this essay. (If you cannot answer this question, consider waiting to apply to business school.)

Although not obvious, the place to start is with a quick description of your career evolution so far. Even if the question does not explicitly require this, it is a good idea to offer some information on your past career to set the context for your future objectives and make them sound that much more logical and reasonable, given your background.

After this, you need to ask yourself: What do you want to be, now that you are all grown up? If you do not currently know with any degree of assurance, explore the possibilities by consulting the relevant career literature and discussing the possibilities with family and friends. Only after you have settled on an approximate goal will you be truly ready to apply for an MBA. This does not mean you must be certain of where you are headed, but you should, at a minimum, be able to articulate several possibilities that you intend to explore and that are clearly related to your experiences, strengths and weaknesses, and likes and dislikes. Show that you are being realistic in your planning.

Once you know in general terms where you are headed, how does an MBA fit into your plans? In other words, what is it you need from an MBA program in order to get where you want to go? There are innumerable reasons that would be quite sensible for wanting an MBA. For example, perhaps you want (additional):

- General management perspective
- Understanding of various functional areas
- Knowledge of one specific area (although this might be better served by doing a specialized master's degree rather than the inherently more generalist MBA)
- Exposure to people from different backgrounds (cultural, functional, etc.)
- Understanding of for-profit (rather than nonprofit) firms
- Knowledge of business approaches beyond your own industry
- Understanding of analytical techniques not readily learned on the job
- The benefits that a successful career placement office and strong alumni network can offer

Perhaps you seek to advance in an industry that requires people to eventually jump from a nonbusiness area to the management side of the business. You might be knowledgeable about directing plays, for instance, but want to be able to run a theater; or you wish to jump gracefully from one segment of the business world to another—for instance, from marketing to finance, or from the creative side of a corporation to business management.

The next point is to show that an MBA is right for you *now*, not in several years. The younger you are, the more likely this is to be a critical issue. Standard reasons for wanting an MBA now are:

- You have reached a natural break in your career. For example, you are about to finish a four-year tour of duty in the Navy.

- You cannot progress further in your career without one. In some fields (e.g., management consulting), this might be more an issue of needing to have your "ticket punched" than needing the actual knowledge, but it is a well understood reason nonetheless.

- You could progress without one, but you would do so much more slowly than you would with an MBA.

- You are involved in a family business and need to take over the reins sooner rather than later.

- You are ready to jump into entrepreneurship but need both the management knowledge and credentials of an MBA first.

- Remaining any longer in your field or industry will make your planned transition into a new field or industry more difficult.

Take the approach that you have already had substantial accomplishments but that you could nonetheless go much further, faster, if you had an MBA (and the sooner the better). Above all, do not make it sound as though you know little and have done less.

Be sure you tie this specific school's offerings to your needs (for instance, its top finance program) to show you know and value the fine points of this program. Even if a particular school never asks specifically why you want to attend its program above all others, you must address this question on every application. You cannot afford to let a program think you believe the various schools are interchangeable. If you do, you risk its deciding that you are readily replaced by another candidate who seems to know the program better and value it more highly. Always show that you have "done your homework" on the school and have serious reasons for wanting to attend it over and above other schools.

ADVANTAGES OF THIS APPROACH

Our approach will allow you to show that you know where you are going and that you therefore have a good chance of actually getting there. It will also show you to be sensible concerning what should be a matter of great concern to you—your career. Failure to demonstrate clear thinking about your career will mark you as someone not ready for an MBA. You are likely to miss out on a great deal of the value of an MBA if you do not know what you want out of it, which depends upon where you are headed. Similarly, showing the admissions committee that you have not been serious in thinking about where you are headed suggests that you may not even be serious about business, which is likely to be particularly damaging if you are, say, an arts graduate working in the nonprofit sector at the moment. Addressing the strengths of a particular program rather than simply stating why you need an MBA in general shows that you have done research on the school and have taken the time to tailor your answer to the application. It also suggests to the admissions committee that you are likely to attend the program if admitted, which helps the school boost its "yield on admission" figure that counts in numerous rankings of schools.

QUESTION: WHAT WOULD YOU CONTRIBUTE WHILE AT OUR SCHOOL?

WHY THE QUESTION IS ASKED

Schools want to know what you consider a "contribution." They also want to have certain skills and experiences represented in the student body. This essay gives you a chance to show what you bring to the mix.

THE TYPICAL APPLICANT

The typical applicant mentions a set of boilerplates. First, he claims that he is a very hard worker. Next, he says that he will try to contribute to class discussions, and the fact that he is an accountant will be very valuable in this regard. Last, if he is really thinking hard, he may note that he is a good guy whose company will be enjoyed by one and all.

A BETTER APPROACH

The first step is to show that that you will fit into the school's student body. In other words, you are not hopelessly strange. You have the attributes normally expected of top managers, such as intelligence and determination. In addition, you are accustomed to dealing with others like you and you have typically compared favorably with them. In other words, you will not be intimidated by your classmates.

The second step is to show that you would add something valuable (and unusual) to the workings of the school. These workings are not just in class, but equally important outside of class. Thus, your being able to work well on a team—and in a study group or project team—will be useful here. The usual things that applicants mention are noted below but should not be the focus of your effort if you can find something more interesting to discuss. The "usual" includes:

- Knowledge of industry A, technology B, or function C
- Computing and technology skills
- Leadership in extracurricular activities
- Team player
- A second or third language
- Personal characteristics: sense of humor, likability, determination

Each of these can be worthwhile, but they are best not dwelt upon unless you possess them to an unusual degree. For instance, the candidate (Joerg) whose essays we reprinted in the prior chapter notes that his engineering skills are of a very high order indeed. He can say this because the breadth and depth of his knowledge were extraordinary. (He was finishing a Ph.D. in mechanical engineering from Germany's finest program, had done topflight work in testing the shape stability of fibers, and had significant assignments in North America, Japan, and Africa as well as in various parts of Europe. Comparatively speaking, someone with a bachelor's degree and three years of experience in reverse-engineering widgets might be better served looking for something else to emphasize.)

Unusual items you could emphasize might include:

- *A different perspective.* Are you from an unusual part of the world (at least insofar as where most of this particular school's students come from)? Have you worked with unusual people—for instance, workers with disabilities?

- *Knowledge of an unusual industry, technology, or function.* Consultants, engineers, and accountants are, if anything, overrepresented in MBA programs, but school principals and jazz musicians are not.

- *Unusual work conditions.* Perhaps you are a research associate at a corporate strategy firm, which is a common position for an applicant, but you have done your cost analysis work for a client brewery in Lagos rather than Milwaukee.

- *Personal qualities that are all too rare,* such as a sterling sense of humor. But you will need to back this up with solid evidence.

- *Unusual outside interests.* A person who has published a successful book, been internationally ranked in squash, started a successful part-time business, or whatever has something unusual to talk about. You might not think any of these things are significant, but you are probably better off at least mentioning them than dwelling on the fact that you are yet another junior accountant. For example, you might think that being a top squash player is irrelevant, but remember that one U.S. Supreme Court Justice allegedly chose his clerks largely in light of their skill on the basketball court. Although idiosyncratic, this method of selecting people is by no means atypical. Additionally, you can make the skills and experiences gained from virtually any activity appear relevant in some way to the MBA setting if you are creative.

Remember, too, that a skill that might be considered typical at MIT might be quite rare elsewhere.

The last component of this essay is to show that you are the sort of person who will share knowledge with others in the program. In other words, you are the sort of person who will work well with other people and value their contributions, too.

ADVANTAGES OF THIS APPROACH

Knowledge of what distinguishes you from other applicants is particularly important in answering this question. What you would contribute to a program is best answered by thinking not of the skills many of your peers share but those that seem uniquely yours. Doing so will allow you to appeal to schools hoping to diversify their student bodies on as many dimensions as possible.

QUESTION: WHAT DO YOU HOPE TO GAIN FROM OUR PROGRAM?

WHY THE QUESTION IS ASKED

This question is meant to reveal how you view an MBA program and degree. Are you thinking of it narrowly or broadly? Do you have a clear reason for wanting an MBA?

THE TYPICAL APPLICANT

Too many people mention the amount of money they will make after they have their MBA. Others describe the technical skill or skills they will acquire. And many just mouth the platitudes of how marvelous MBA degrees are, as if trying to convince the admissions staff of this fact.

A BETTER APPROACH

Treat this essay just like the "why do you want an MBA, and why from our school" questions. Start by explaining what you hope to accomplish in your career and what you currently lack in order to do so. Show how an MBA will help you acquire many of the skills and other assets you lack, thus helping you to reach your goals. Then note how this program in particular will be most appropriate for you in addressing these needs. Make it clear that you will gain more from this program than others because it best fits your needs.

Do not stop there, however, because if you do you will make it seem that you are so unworldly as to think that a top-quality MBA program is nothing more than a skill transfer mechanism. In fact, as this book has emphasized, you will gain from the credential itself and the network you can tap into. You can expect to have career opportunities open up to you that someone without a top MBA will never have. You will grow as a result of interacting daily with top-notch students and faculty. And, yes, you can expect to make more money. The problem, however, is to show that you are savvy enough to appreciate the many career benefits offered by a top MBA without looking like a greedy creature intent upon nothing more than maximizing his or her salary. The best way to do this may be to note the ancillary benefits of the school's network without talking about the money or credentials.

ADVANTAGES OF THIS APPROACH

Following this approach will make it clear that you have a well-considered reason for getting an MBA. It fits into your own career scheme and is not something you are pursuing just because it is trendy to do so or because you need your "ticket punched." It will also be clear you have thought through your choice of school.

QUESTION: WHY HAVE YOU APPLIED TO THE OTHER SCHOOLS YOU HAVE?

WHY THE QUESTION IS ASKED

Schools typically ask this question to learn two things. First, they want to learn how much you value their school relative to others you might be considering. Second, they want to understand what is important to you in an MBA program, to see whether it fits with their school.

THE TYPICAL APPLICANT

Most applicants make one of several mistakes. Some applicants tell Boston College they are applying to Harvard and MIT. Boston College is a good school, but it does not realistically expect applicants to choose it over Harvard or MIT. Listing these other Boston-area schools tells BC that the applicant does not really want to attend it, that it is just a backup in case Harvard and MIT both say no. BC is unlikely to get excited about such applicants. By the same token, if an applicant tells Harvard that she is applying to Boston College, Harvard is likely to conclude that she does not really see herself as being of Harvard quality and that she does not have the self-confidence necessary for a top program.

Other applicants reveal they are not certain of what they want from their MBA education by listing very different types of schools. Applying to both Harvard and Darden—two case method schools that educate general managers—

makes sense, but applying to Rotterdam because of its informatics concentration while also applying to ESSEC—the French school devoted to training managers to market luxury brands—suggests the applicant has not yet decided what he is seeking.

A different type of mistake is made when someone states he is applying to school X and no other, for fear of offending school X. If an applicant has good reasons for wanting an MBA, it is highly likely that more than one school will serve his needs quite well. If this is the case, he will be determined enough to want to go to any of a number of schools. Failing to list other schools, therefore, suggests that he is not really serious about getting an MBA.

Another mistake is made when applicants simply state that school X is the best, famous for its (fill in the blank), and is what they have always hoped to attend. This is a mistake insofar as it represents a missed opportunity to market oneself.

A BETTER APPROACH

Start by showing what you need in order to meet your goals. For example, perhaps you are an experienced sales representative who wishes to move into general management. Despite your knowledge of sales, you do not know much about accounting, finance, strategy, organizational development, or the international aspects of business; you may be looking to acquire substantial skills in these areas. Depending upon the kind of company and industry you are aiming for, some of these areas are likely to be much more important than others. Thus, your pitch might be:

My goal: work for my current firm, but in general management

What I am lacking: general management skills, especially in finance, marketing, and strategy

Then show how school X will be right for you. You do this by showing how it meets your requirements. If you want to become a consumer marketer, note that school X has a host of relevant courses. What besides course offerings might be important to you? You might choose on the basis of the languages used at the school, the nature of the student body (age, functional backgrounds, etc.), the reputation of a specific department—and thus the quality and number of companies looking to recruit, say, consumer marketers from the school. Refer to our earlier discussion about how to choose a school.

Apply these factors to the other schools you are considering. Note that each school will be acceptable in terms of meeting the bulk of what you are looking for, but note also that school X is more desirable insofar as it offers more consumer marketing courses or whatever. It is unlikely that any one school will be the most desirable on all counts, which gives you the opportunity to say good things about each school in terms of how it meets your needs. Your conclusion, however, should emphasize the factors that favor school X, thereby putting it at the top of your list.

ADVANTAGES OF THIS APPROACH

This approach will help make it clear that you are serious about getting an MBA. In addition, it shows you have researched this and other schools; it reinforces your seriousness about getting an MBA at the same time that it shows you to be a sensible decision-maker who has gathered data for this important decision. This approach also shows that you value school X, and for substantial reasons—because it better meets your needs than do other schools.

QUESTION: PROVIDE A CANDID EVALUATION OF YOUR OWN ADMISSIONS FILE

WHY THE QUESTION IS ASKED

There are a multitude of reasons for asking a question like this one. It is much like "What are your strengths and weaknesses?"—yet it is broader in scope. Your response will show how much you know about what a top MBA program requires of its students, and what this particular program seeks in its applicants. It will also reveal how honest you are in assessing yourself. Plus it will show how well you know yourself. Although you are expected to be an advocate for yourself, failing to be honest, self-aware, and knowledgeable about the program will suggest that you are not yet ready for it.

THE TYPICAL APPLICANT

One common mistake, seemingly invited by the nature of the question, is to discuss in brief every piece of data in the file. Failing to concentrate on whatever is critical to your application results in a missed opportunity as well as an impression that you cannot prioritize. The other typical mistake results from a candidate failing to appreciate what makes him valuable, generally because he does not understand the nature of the school's applicant pool. For example, he wastes his efforts pitching at length the fact that he has learned a second language (something so commonplace that very few candidates will benefit by belaboring the fact).

A BETTER APPROACH

A better approach requires more than a recitation of the data in your file; you need to be an advocate for yourself. Go beyond the data to show how various pieces of your file are connected; show the implications of the data. Offer something new: if not new information, then at least a new way of looking at previously divulged information.

Start by asking what *critical issues* your candidacy faces. For instance, are you likely to be viewed as not quite up to the analytical mark (due to being in an apparently undemanding job as well as having attended a second-rate university)? If so, marshal whatever evidence suggests that you are a fine analyst. Do not waste space on getting credit for the obvious. If you are the head of a nuclear propulsion laboratory, do not go on about your understanding of physics or mathematics.

This is a perfect opportunity for you to discuss your weaknesses. Do not hope that they will go unnoticed; the chances of this are slim, indeed. Instead, acknowledge them while minimizing the damage by suggesting that you are not really weak in the given area and by putting your weaknesses in the proper career context. For instance, you can note your weak GMAT quantitative score, then suggest that you are stronger at quantitative work than a standardized test score suggests. For one thing, you work on quantitative matters all the time and are readily acknowledged by your boss as superb in this regard. For another thing, you have done well in a variety of quantitative courses. And, to top it all off, your quantitative skills will be the least important attribute to determine your success in running a theater group in the future.

Then *consider what aspects of your candidacy are not yet clear.* Be sure to highlight any results or efforts that will not show up on data sheets or elsewhere. For example, discuss your strength in mentoring others at work if this is a facet of your candidacy that does not provide good stories for inclusion in your essays.

A strong answer is likely to devote the bulk of the available space to no more than several issues; trying to discuss a litany of matters in-depth suggests that you either have too many weaknesses to merit inclusion in this program or lack the judgment necessary to warrant inclusion.

ADVANTAGES OF THIS APPROACH

This approach gives you the chance to color how your candidacy will be viewed. Not only do the leading business schools make admissions decisions on more than raw numbers, but they also want to understand what those numbers *mean*. You can help them see you from the most positive perspective possible. Focusing on the critical issues and marshaling appropriate evidence will show you at your persuasive best. It will also suggest that your knowledge of yourself and the program's requirements are up to snuff.

BUSINESS AND CAREER TOPICS

QUESTION: DESCRIBE YOUR WORK EXPERIENCE

WHY THE QUESTION IS ASKED

This question is, of course, intended to elicit what you have done over the course of your career, and what impact you have had. It is also designed to give you an opportunity to show what you have learned about yourself and your abilities.

THE TYPICAL APPLICANT

Most applicants simply list what they have done in the past without showing what has driven their career choices and changes. The result is a list in which the elements appear nearly unrelated to one another.

A BETTER APPROACH

Look at our discussion of the "job description" essay. Then think in terms of telling stories rather than simply listing events dryly. A good story has conflict; that is, it has obstacles placed in the way of the hero. The hero may be unable to overcome each obstacle, but he tries hard and is unwilling to give up.

One possible approach is to find a theme that unites the elements of your job history. For instance, you show how you responded to challenges that were initially daunting. You tried hard and learned how to do what was required. As you learned better how to do the job, you started to take more initiative. In fact, once you mastered your initial responsibilities, you understood them in a broader context. Having done so, you moved up to the next level of responsibility—or you are now at the point of needing further scope for your talents but cannot move up without an MBA or years of experience on the job.

The telling of your career story should focus upon where you have come from and where you are now headed. If you have changed your direction, explain what happened to change your direction. If you have had your decisions reaffirmed by experience, describe them and how they convinced you that you were on the right track.

This essay is closely related to the "your career and the reasons for getting an MBA" essay.

ADVANTAGES OF THIS APPROACH

Telling stories that focus on obstacles and the attempt to overcome them makes this essay interesting to read. Focusing on your personal development in response to challenges is well aimed for an audience of educators, who are preconditioned to appreciate your developmental capabilities.

This approach also sets up your need for an MBA. You have been overcoming obstacles by learning how to perform new jobs, and you have acquired new skills and knowledge; now you need to take another step up.

QUESTION: DESCRIBE YOUR CURRENT JOB

WHY THE QUESTION IS ASKED

This question may not help schools assess the candidacies of, for example, research associates from McKinsey because the admissions committee already knows what the typical McKinsey RA does. For people in less familiar positions, however, this question enables a much clearer understanding of an applicant's background.

THE TYPICAL APPLICANT

Most applicants simply list a few of the elements of their formal job descriptions or just list their job titles. If you were to say simply that you were a marketing associate for a computer firm, an admissions committee would know almost nothing about your responsibilities. Do you provide field support? Do you do online research only? Do you do competitor analysis? Do you work with the research and development staffs in the development of more user-friendly products? Do you analyze the productivity of different advertising media or promotional campaigns? What do you *do*?

A BETTER APPROACH

There are usually numerous elements to a given job. You must figure out and list the many things you do. Next, you must determine which are the most significant parts of your job and which are most consistent with the position you are attempting to communicate, and then characterize them as favorably as possible. The following should help you with this process.

1. *Is your job important?* Most people would say so only if they are egotists or are making a lot of money and enjoying a very impressive title (Senior Executive Vice President for Marketing and Strategy, perhaps).

Assuming you are not in this situation, does this mean your job is unimportant and you will have to be apologizing for it? No, of course not. A job is of real importance under a number of different circumstances. In particular, work gains significance whenever two things are true about it: (1) the degree of uncertainty is high, and (2) the potential impact upon the firm's success is great. In other words, is there a fair likelihood that an average-quality performer in your job would make a hash of things? If so, would that really affect your firm's performance, or that of one of its components? If the answer to both of these questions is yes, then your job is of real importance.

2. *What is the nature of your work?* There are many different types of work. A market researcher is generally doing analytical work. A brand manager is likely to be doing a combination of analytical work and influence work insofar as she must analyze the factors for the brand's relative success or failure in different market and competitive conditions in her country, and then try to influence the manufacturing, packaging, or whatever department to take the action she wants in order to address these factors. She will typically have no power over these departments and will have to rely on her influence skills (personality, reasoning, expertise, etc.) instead. A restaurant manager will probably be most concerned with managing people, whereas a technical manager may be most concerned with the management of physical processes.

Many other aspects of your work can also be characterized in readily understandable ways. Is your job like being in the police: crushing boredom interspersed with brief moments of sheer terror? Are you expected to perform at a steady pace to a predictable schedule or do you work like a tax accountant, 60 percent of whose work may take place in three months of the year? Are you the steadying hand for a bunch of youngsters? Are you a creative type who will respond flexibly to each new situation rather than simply refer to the corporate manual?

3. *What must you do to perform successfully?* In other words, what challenges do you face? For example, if you are in sales support, one of your biggest headaches might be to get the junior people in marketing—who report directly to the regional marketing manager, and report on only a dotted-line basis to the regional sales manager—to provide the current competitor analysis material to the sales department. This can be characterized as a liaison role. Or, if the relationship is particularly poor, you might describe your role as conflict resolution—particularly in light of the fact that sales and marketing often have an antagonistic relationship.

Perhaps your greatest challenges are satisfying two different bosses with two completely different agendas. If you are in a matrix structure, reporting to the regional manager and an engineering director, you can expect to be unable to please either one. The regional manager is probably concerned with making money today, and wants everyone to work as a team without regard to functional specialties. The engineering boss, on the other hand, wants her people to maintain their specialized skills and the prestige of the engineering department. Working on cross-functional teams without taking time out for updating technical skills may strike the former as standard practice and the latter as anathema. Performing your job well may require balancing these conflicting desires.

A number of other circumstances can lend importance to a job. The more senior the person you report to is, the more important a job will look. Similarly, the fate of prior occupants of your job may be relevant. If the last two occupants of your job were fired, say so. This will make your performance look all the more impressive. If the last occupants were promoted high in the organization, the job will appear to be one given to high-fliers, thereby increasing its significance.

Have your recommenders discuss these points, too.

4. *Do you supervise anyone?* How many people, of what type, are under your supervision? What does this supervision consist of? For example, are you in charge of direct marketing activities, necessitating that you monitor the phone calls of your direct reports and also analyze their performance versus budget and various economic and industry factors?

5. *Do you have control of a budget?* If so, what is the amount you control, and what amount do you influence?

6. *What results have you achieved?* Results can be looked at from many different perspectives. From a strategic perspective, what have you achieved regarding the market, customers, and competitors? From a financial perspective, what have you done regarding costs, revenues, and profits (not to mention assets employed, etc.)? From an operational perspective, what have you done regarding productivity of your unit, of your direct reports, or of yourself; what have you done regarding the percentage of items rejected, bids that fail, and so on? Similarly, from an organizational perspective, have you taken such steps as altering the formal organization or introducing new integration or coordination mechanisms? Provide numbers whenever possible to buttress your claims.

7. *How has your career evolved?* Did you have a career plan in place before graduating from college or university or soon thereafter? If so, did you pursue it wholeheartedly? Did it include a focus on developing your skills and responsibilities? What, if anything, has altered your original plan? What was your reaction to events that altered or affirmed this plan? When dealing with the development of your job with a given employer, be sure to note the employer's *reasons* for promoting, transferring, rewarding, or praising you as well as the fact of these things.

ADVANTAGES OF THIS APPROACH

It is important to take this question very seriously. The answers will provide you with much of the ammunition you will use in responding to other questions. Your current job is of inherent interest to business schools. They will always want to know what you are doing, and with what success, because that suggests a great deal about your talents and interests, the way your employer views your talents and attitude, and why you might want an MBA.

Taking a broad view of the job description enables you to put the best light on your responsibilities and performance. It also allows you to build the basis for later essays, where you will be able to save space by referring to this write-up rather than listing the same things when space is at a premium.

QUESTION: IN WHAT OTHER WAY WILL YOU PURSUE YOUR DEVELOPMENT IF OUR SCHOOL REJECTS YOU?

WHY THE QUESTION IS ASKED

This question helps schools determine two things about you: first, how carefully you have planned for your future, and second, how determined you are to succeed.

THE TYPICAL APPLICANT

The typical applicant notes that he will reapply next year if school X turns him down this year.

A BETTER APPROACH

The starting point is to state what your goals are and what you lack in order to meet them. (For a full discussion of this, refer to the "why have you applied to the other schools you have" analysis.) This will help to demonstrate that you have given serious thought to your future career.

Your needs can probably be met, at least to a reasonable degree, by another MBA program. You should thus almost certainly note that you are applying to other schools.

You should also consider whether some part-time educational programs would meet at least some of your needs. A local school's offering of introductory marketing courses may not suffice to make you into a crack consumer marketer, but will almost certainly be better than nothing.

Another possibility may be training programs that your company offers. Or you could shift jobs (either within your company or by switching companies) in order to learn about a different function or even a different industry. As you will recall from our discussion of why to get an MBA, further job experience is not likely to provide you with the conceptual understanding that is part and parcel of an MBA. Companies seldom feature lectures on quantitative methods for managers or applications of the capital asset pricing model. MBA programs are set up to increase dramatically your intellectual capital, whereas companies are set up to make money, preferably sooner rather than later. A new position or company is not likely to provide you with all that you hope to get from an MBA program, but something is better than nothing.

The last option is self-study. You can always read the interesting popular books in a given field or, better yet, the textbooks used at business schools. This is a difficult way to learn, however, and it is unlikely that you will be able to learn advanced quantitative methods in this fashion.

The conclusion is always that you would prefer to get an MBA, but you will do whatever you can to gain as much knowledge as possible.

ADVANTAGES OF THIS APPROACH

This approach shows that you have considered your future with care. It also shows that you are hungry for improvement in your knowledge and skills, and that you are determined to succeed and action-oriented. If going to school X will not work, you will go to school Y. If you cannot go to a top school, you will continue learning on this or another job. The picture you convey is therefore one of a person striving to reach his or her potential. Remember that you are applying to an educational institution, so showing that you are hungry for knowledge and determined to improve yourself by acquiring it is a "can't miss" proposition.

QUESTION: WHAT ONE CHANGE WOULD YOU MAKE IN YOUR CURRENT JOB (AND HOW WOULD YOU IMPLEMENT THIS CHANGE)?

WHY THE QUESTION IS ASKED

This question is designed to reveal how savvy you are about organizational matters and how analytical you are about your company's operating and strategic needs.

You may be too junior to have run a department or a company, but that should not stop you from thinking about its operations and environment. How much perspective do you have on these things? Can you write a persuasive analytical piece showing that you have been able to step back from your own tasks to take a more senior manager's view? If not—if you can see only your own job's details—you are missing a chance to show that you are, in fact, senior management material.

THE TYPICAL APPLICANT

Most applicants fail to define what this question is really asking. The question itself is open to several interpretations. For example, does it ask you to improve things for you or for your company? How realistic must you be in your suggestion? Must this be an aspect you can indeed change, rather than something that only a very senior manager could affect? All too many applicants end up interpreting the question to mean, "How can *you* make your own job easier to do?" Consequently, they make themselves look self-centered and concerned only about the minutiae of their jobs, since any meaningful change would require someone else's intervention.

Virtually all applicants run into the implied follow-up question: If this proposed change is such a good idea, why haven't you done all you could to implement it? Failing to answer this can make an applicant look hypocritical or ineffectual. If he claims that a change in the pattern of his sales calls will dramatically improve his results, why has he never tried to convince his boss of this? Is it that he does not really care about the company's success or that he cannot imagine persuading his boss to make any change? In either case, the force of the applicant's suggestion is diminished by failing to address the issue.

A BETTER APPROACH

Focus on the benefits for the company rather than personal benefits. In other words, show that the reason the change makes sense is that the company's balance sheet will improve, or some other equally important advantage will accrue—not that your job will become easier.

You may have spotted only one change the company should make. If so, you should certainly discuss it. On the other hand, if you have several possibilities, choose the one that will best do the following:

■ Support your positioning effort, including your current need for an MBA (which can be shown by suggesting that you are outgrowing your current responsibilities).

■ Show that you are thinking about how your job relates to others.

If you do not have any obvious changes in mind, how can you develop some? For one thing, you can look at the examples of this essay included in Part IV. Beyond this, consider the following possibilities:

■ Should the nature of your *reporting relationship* be changed? For example, perhaps you report to a regional manager but would be better off reporting to a functional one. Or perhaps you are matrixed—reporting to two different bosses in different departments—and the matrix structure is preventing decisions being reached in a timely fashion. If so, simplifying the reporting relationship might be appropriate.

■ Should the nature of your *responsibility* be changed? For example, are you currently responsible for revenues but not costs or assets employed? Should you have complete profit and loss (or return on assets employed) responsibility?

■ Should the various *control systems* be harmonized? For example, perhaps the accounting systems are designed to control one thing whereas your bonus is tied to something contradictory.

■ Should any of the company's *major processes or strategies* be changed? For example, perhaps the current market research and advertising budgets are wastefully targeting the wrong market segments.

If you are describing proposed changes in, say, the design of your job or the way in which you are evaluated or controlled, you will want to show that the current standards cause suboptimal performance in a way that your proposed change will not. You may also need to show that the proposed change will not lead to new problems or that any such problems will not be as large as the ones currently faced.

Deal with the implementation issue head-on. In other words, answer the implicit follow-up question as to why, if this change is such a good idea, you have not yet made it happen. Maybe you have just learned of the need for this change, in which case you have not had the time to do anything about it. For example, maybe you just started this job, or you have just received new responsibilities; or perhaps a recent problem first exposed the need for change. Another possibility is that you have been aware of the problem for some time but have been engaged in gathering the necessary data to analyze the situation fully.

The question's phrasing is hypothetical: "What change would you make?" This seems to eliminate the possibility of discussing a change that you have recently made. In fact, business schools would love to have you discuss a change you have actually enacted; the only reason that they phrase the question as they do is because so few applicants have a real example to talk about. If you have actually implemented a substantial, praiseworthy change, by all means discuss it.

ADVANTAGES OF THIS APPROACH

This approach shows that your primary concern is the company's welfare. It also shows that you have analyzed your environment and are aware of the areas of strength and weakness. Using a real example is better than using a hypothetical one insofar as it shows you actually take action and have an impact.

QUESTION: WHAT IS THE MOST IMPORTANT TREND FACING BUSINESS?

WHY THE QUESTION IS ASKED

This question is designed to find out whether you have thought about the "big picture," are aware of the issues currently facing industry, and have the ability to discuss a big topic in a sophisticated fashion.

The typical applicant

Most people discuss the most headline-grabbing item they can think of. In recent years this might have been the moral imperatives of business—with special reference to apartheid in South Africa or oil extraction in Nigeria, or the Asian financial crisis. Their discussion, moreover, tends to resemble the headlines of tabloid newspapers: "Global Disaster Forecast! Major Changes Needed Now!" No research informs the essay. The other, lamentable approach is that of cribbing all too obviously from a recent lead story in *Business Week* or a similar magazine. This tactic makes it appear that you have no original opinions on the matter and can only regurgitate commonplace ideas. Both of these mistaken approaches also tend to reveal little about the applicant because it is unclear why the topic was chosen in the first place.

A better approach

If you have any well-developed views on a subject that relate well to your positioning effort, then by all means discuss them. If you are in the energy business, for example, and firmly believe that global warming will dramatically alter the mix of fuels the developed world will use in the short- to medium-term, then you will probably want to choose this as your topic.

Most applicants do not have such a clear-cut opinion. Instead, they have some not overly well-informed opinions about a handful of topics, any one of which could fit well here. If this is your case, choose the topic that shows you off to best advantage. It should enable you to (1) express sensible but not blindingly obvious views, (2) enhance your positioning, (3) show why you want an MBA, and perhaps (4) show why this school is right for you. This is a rather daunting set of criteria. You may not satisfy each one, but at least it gives you a target. A quick look at one of the many possible topics reveals how to get started.

Globalization is an old favorite response to this question. It is a truism that the increasing globalization of business is continuing to have a substantial impact upon how business is conducted. Is this the right topic for you? It would be highly appropriate for someone applying to a school outside her country, or one that uses a language other than her own for many of its courses. It would also be highly appropriate for someone applying to an internationally focused program, such as the Lauder program at Wharton or one of the European schools whose whole raison d'être is training international managers.

How will you discuss globalization? You might begin with an explanation of how you became aware of this issue in the first place. Have your own company's operations been dramatically affected by foreign competition? Then discuss in what other ways business is being affected by international competition. Next move on to the underlying trends that will cause greater globalization, and finally examine the impact globalization is likely to have upon your industry overall. Your degree of specificity will depend in large part upon the allotted space. This discussion will help you to demonstrate why you want to attend a school that has a serious international focus.

What are some of the other possible topics?

- Deregulation and Privatization
- Service Management (i.e., the change from industrial to service management concerns)
- Changing Demographics of the Workforce (or Managing Diversity)
- Flattening of Organizational Structures (or the Change from Hierarchy to Network)
- The Information Revolution
- The Internet (networked organizations, the death of distance, and so on)
- Consolidation (Mergers and Acquisitions)
- Environmental Limitations
- The Enlargement and Development of the European Union
- Political Turmoil

Is this list exhaustive? By no means; a sensible list might be two or three times this long. Don't assume that your chosen topic is inappropriate simply because it is not listed here.

Does it matter which topic you choose? Yes and no. It matters that you choose something that strikes admissions committees as being quite important—at least after you have explained why it is important. But what is likely to matter more is *how* you discuss the topic you have chosen.

When discussing any of these topics, remember to follow good essay-writing practice. Be specific, referring to events in your own (business) life when possible. For example, if you are discussing globalization, do not wallow in the future demise of the "American-ness" of baseball (or whatever). Instead of looking just at the negative side of change, look, too, at the opportunities and challenges that will come in its wake. You should be able to give a sophisticated treatment to your subject, but this is likely to be the case only after you have done some reading. Has *The Economist* written extensively about this subject? If so, you should know its views, as well as those of other sophisticated journals, and provide relevant quotations to demonstrate your awareness.

Advantages of this approach

This topic should be a godsend, in that it allows you to do so much to further so many of your positioning efforts while ostensibly discussing an abstract concept. You can show, for example, that you have a real need to learn more about organization design and development, thereby necessitating an MBA. At the same time you will show that you have given real thought to a complex issue.

QUESTION: DESCRIBE THE IMPACT OF TECHNOLOGY ON YOUR CHOSEN CAREER OR INDUSTRY

Why the question is asked

Today's MBA programs want candidates who are technologically savvy or, at a minimum, aware of the way in which technology will affect their careers. In addition, they worry about a candidate who, in a period when technology discussions and concerns are part of the general culture, has given little thought to an issue that should be part and parcel of career-planning efforts.

The typical applicant

The typical applicant makes one of three major mistakes. He mentions the most obvious effects of technology ("e-commerce has allowed my company to compete with bigger firms in the industry by reaching a potential market that exceeds our previously limited trading area"), but fails to demonstrate a broader understanding of how current and future technologies will shape his career or industry beyond the next year or two. Another mistake is to assume that technology will have little impact upon his industry because it has not yet done so. Yet another mistaken approach is to focus on the detail of the technology itself rather than the technology's larger impact.

A better approach

Reach beyond the technologies immediately affecting how you do your job. Consider what other technologies are likely to be introduced in the next few years. Ask how each of these will affect some of the basics of your industry:

- Barriers to entry
- Minimum optimal scale and appropriate geographic scope
- Role of intermediaries
- Relative power of producers and consumers
- Range and nature of products
- Will the industry grow or contract? Converge with another industry?

Then consider the impact of these technologies upon careers in your industry. What (new) skills will be rewarded? What sorts of people now in the industry will become redundant?

After doing this analysis, consider which changing demographics, political ideas, and other factors will have a major impact upon the technology-driven changes. Consider also to what degree your forecast changes will be unique to your industry rather than common to all industries.

To develop additional understanding of the relevant factors, look to the most sophisticated journal devoted to your industry; consider also the research reports that Wall Street firms and technology consulting firms publish. For background reading, consult such sources as the *Financial Times*, the *Economist*, *Business Week*, and the *Wall Street Journal*.

ADVANTAGES OF THIS APPROACH

This approach allows you to demonstrate your understanding of the potential impact of a host of factors, technology in particular, upon your industry and upon your likely future career. This big picture synthesis is, of course, the sort of thinking required of senior managers. It contrasts well with the focus on detail that characterizes many applicants' essays.

QUESTION: DESCRIBE A SITUATION IN WHICH YOU PROVIDED A SOLUTION THAT MET WITH RESISTANCE. HOW DID YOU ADDRESS THIS SITUATION?

WHY THE QUESTION IS ASKED

Schools want to identify future leaders among their applicants. The easiest way to do so is to find people who have already acted as leaders, whether or not they had official leadership responsibilities or titles. Insofar as leadership all too often requires pushing others to accept an idea or plan that you have, seeing whether and how you have done so provides loads of information about whether you try to lead and how effective you are.

THE TYPICAL APPLICANT

Some applicants make the mistake of claiming they had a marvelous idea but the fools they work with were so stupid as to reject it. This denigrates their colleagues, of course; it also suggests that the applicants are either foolish to be working with such people or should be able, at the least, to outmaneuver them and get their ideas accepted. Other applicants fail to recognize that the quality of the idea they present needs to be up to scratch. Revealing that they have failed to understand the nature of the problem confronted, or that their proposed solution is likely to be unworkable or cause yet greater problems, sinks their efforts.

There are three primary requirements for a good response to this question. The first is that you have properly analyzed the problem you or your organization face. Second, you need to have designed a solution that makes sense. It needs to be reasonable on its face, or be something you can explain easily in the essay as meeting the requirements of the situation. This includes not exceeding the constraints that the context places upon you. For instance, a company on the brink of bankruptcy probably cannot afford to make a major investment that will not see positive cash flow for five years. (The focus of the question is not on the difficulty of the problem or complexity of the solution you have devised, so do not feel compelled to search for something exotic.)

Third, you need to show the variety of actions you undertook (and perhaps those you considered but decided not to use) to persuade others to accept your idea. There are a host of influence strategies available to you; your choice depends upon numerous factors, including your relative skill at using each and your relationship (boss, coworker, subordinate) to the people you need to persuade.

Here are some concrete examples of how you might have tried to influence your boss:

- You approached her at the right time. The problem was rearing its head, making a possible solution to it all the more attractive, but otherwise things were quiet enough that you could get her attention.

- You showed that other departments or companies have done something similar. Your proposal gains credibility by showing the quality of other organizations that have implemented it, as well as by showing the results they have obtained.

- You obtained endorsements for your idea from people your boss respects. Without going over your boss's head, you can still have others in the company or elsewhere on board to support your idea.

- You made clear that the idea fits her interests. She may be under senior management pressure to fix this problem. By the same token, the problem may take up much of her time.

- You started a small pilot program to show that your idea can work.

- You did a thorough, data-based analysis of your plan, which you shared with her. Perhaps you also built a reasonable timetable for implementation, showing at each point that little has been left to chance.

If you were unable to get your boss's buy-in and decided to bypass her, recognize that you may appear dangerously disloyal. It would probably have been better had you considered alternatives to actually bypassing your boss:

- Volunteering to help your boss with her too-demanding workload by taking over a piece of it. Your willingness to take on additional work would give you something to use in bargaining for freedom to try out your idea.

- If the project seemed too large, you could break it into digestible pieces and get your boss to commit to the first one. After it worked, you could push the second one.

- If someone else in the organization had more credibility for pushing such a project, you might have considered getting him to champion your idea (while getting his agreement to share the credit with you later on). Of course, working through someone else is a viable approach only if you value results more than credit (but this certainly fits what business schools value in applicants).

Keep in mind that most applicants to top business schools are fairly analytical sorts. As a result, they tend to rely on reasoning with people as their sole persuasion strategy. There are actually many types of strategy available. Consider to what extent you have employed bargaining (for instance, trading your effort for someone's support), forming a coalition (using others to influence people on your behalf), getting someone to like you and support you out of friendliness, being assertive (establishing deadlines, making demands, being emotional), or appealing to a higher authority (above your boss's head).

ADVANTAGES OF THIS APPROACH

It is better if you can show yourself as having been able to put your idea into practice (and better yet if it can be seen to have worked out), but even trying and failing can be acceptable if you clearly worked hard and well to succeed. Giving up too easily suggests that you are not determined to have an impact. Following the approach outlined above, however, shows you to be a skillful proponent of your ideas, who is able to employ multiple methods to sell an idea.

MIXED BUSINESS AND PERSONAL TOPICS

QUESTION: WHAT ARE YOUR STRENGTHS AND WEAKNESSES?

WHY THE QUESTIONS IS ASKED

This question is clearly designed to elicit your opinion of yourself. Modest people, and people from cultures less egocentric than that of the United States, have a hard time responding to the first half because it obviously asks you to brag a little. Less self-assured applicants find it hard to be honest and to mention their shortcomings. This question provides a good gauge of how self-confident (or arrogant), accomplished (or boastful), decent (or manipulative), mature, self-aware, and honest you are.

THE TYPICAL APPLICANT

Most applicants list a large number of strengths and one or two weaknesses. Their weakness is generally a strength dressed up as a weakness ("I am too much of a perfectionist"; "I work too hard").

A BETTER APPROACH

Start by choosing two or three primary strengths. Use these to organize your essay by grouping other strengths around them. For example, if you claim that you are very *determined*, you might discuss your *patience* in working hard for a long time in order to achieve something important related to this determination. The problem is not generally finding something good to say about yourself. Usually the problem is limiting yourself to a manageable number of strengths. You want to have few enough that you can discuss them in a persuasive fashion rather than just listing them. Using two or three as central organizing devices (i.e., themes) helps to achieve this goal.

Remember that simply listing strengths is a very weak way of writing. To make your strengths credible and memorable, use illustrations of them. Instead of bragging about being determined, note (with detail) your five-year battle to overcome childhood leukemia.

The bigger problem, however, is finding a weakness to discuss. Simply calling a strength a weakness ("I work too hard") is not sufficient. This tactic is used by countless applicants, and its insincerity is nearly guaranteed to repel those reading your essays. For one thing, you have failed to follow instructions; you were asked to list a weakness and failed to do so. In addition, a failure to recognize your own weaknesses means you are blind to something very important. We all know that even the most accomplished and successful people have weaknesses. It is far better to recognize your weaknesses and thus be in a position to try to overcome them than to pretend they do not exist. If you recognize that a weakness exists, you are in a position to make a constructive change. Being willing to discuss a weakness is thus a sign of maturity and, consequently, a strength in itself.

Do not carry a good thing too far, though, and discuss huge flaws such as your drug addictions. Your choice of a flaw may depend upon exactly how the question is phrased. If you are asked for a weakness, you can certainly discuss the lack of skills or knowledge that currently limit your managerial success and that have occasioned your desire for an MBA. This is an easy version of the question. The hard version asks you about your *personality* strengths and weaknesses. The focus on your personality means you cannot simply respond by discussing what skills you want to acquire. To respond to this you must discuss a true personality flaw. One approach is to look at the dark side of one of your strengths. If you are a very determined person, does that mean your drive is accompanied by a terrible temper? Or perhaps it means you are too willing to trample upon peers' feelings? If you are a strong leader, does that mean you do not always value the inputs of your subordinates? If you have been very successful doing detail-laden work, have you overlooked the big picture? Are you so concerned about quality that you find it overly difficult to delegate or share responsibility? Are you a creative entrepreneur obsessed with your vision who alienates more traditional colleagues?

Be sure to avoid discussing a weakness that will be a major handicap at a given school. For example, if you are applying to a quantitatively oriented program, be leery of talking about your difficulties with numbers.

Be careful to discuss your weakness differently from your strengths. The correct space allocation is probably about three- or four-to-one strengths to weakness. You will note that I say "weakness" because you should discuss only one or two weaknesses. When doing so, do not dwell on your description of it or of the problems it has caused you. Do so briefly, thereby limiting the impact that the specifics will have upon admissions officers. Then note what steps you take, or have taken, to try to overcome it.

You want to describe yourself as having numerous strengths that relate well to your positioning effort without sounding arrogant.

ADVANTAGES OF THIS APPROACH

Grouping your strengths in an organized fashion will give you the chance to cover a lot of ground without taking a scattershot approach. Emphasizing strengths is obviously appropriate. Writing about them in some detail, with appropriate illustrations, will make them memorable. The use of illustrations also makes your claims realistic rather than boastful.

Describing your weakness in a cursory way, and being detailed about the steps you take to overcome the weakness, will gain you points. It shows you to be willing to face up to your flaw without the flaw itself being emphasized. This offers you the best of both worlds.

QUESTION: WHAT ARE YOUR MOST SUBSTANTIAL ACCOMPLISHMENTS?

WHY THE QUESTION IS ASKED

This question obviously gives you a chance to "blow your own horn." You can brag a bit about what you have accomplished in life. Moreover, you have the chance to put your own spin on what you have done. A particular accomplishment is all the more impressive when you explain the obstacles you had to overcome in order to succeed.

The question also allows schools to learn more about you insofar as you must explain why you consider something to have been a substantial accomplishment. Some accomplishments are of obvious significance. Winning the Noble Prize for Physics is obviously significant; you probably do not need to elaborate on the fact of having won it. Other accomplishments are much more personal. For example, if you had stuttered as a youth and finally ended your stuttering in your twenties, this might be an extremely significant accomplishment for you personally. You have probably done things that have had more impact upon the rest of the world, but for you this accomplishment looms larger. You will probably want to talk about it as an example of your determination and desire to improve yourself. This essay gives you the chance to do so.

This question gives you an opportunity to discuss matters that are unlikely to be listed on your data sheets or mentioned by your recommenders. Even if you just discuss accomplishments of a more public nature, including something listed in your data sheet (or discussed by your recommenders), you can personalize it in a way in which just listing it (or having someone else talk about it) does not do.

THE TYPICAL APPLICANT

Most applicants use the whole of their essay to try to demonstrate that their accomplishments are impressive, yet focus on matters that are utterly commonplace (among this applicant group, in particular) and that often took place long ago. Thus, they discuss making the high school basketball team or graduating from college. Another mistaken tendency is to list a string of things rather than to explain one or two in detail, thus essentially duplicating the data sheets.

A BETTER APPROACH

The first step is to determine which accomplishments you will discuss. Your criteria for choosing appropriate accomplishments will be familiar. Which ones will help your positioning effort? Which will be unusual and interesting for admissions committees to read about? Was this accomplishment truly noteworthy and also important to you?

The following criteria are also helpful guides:

- You had to overcome major obstacles, showing real determination in doing so.
- You learned more about yourself.
- You came to understand the need for further skill development and thus, perhaps, an MBA.
- You used real initiative, perhaps by pushing a bureaucracy to respond or bypassing one altogether.
- Your success was unexpected.
- You worked extremely hard toward a clear goal.
- You worked with and through other people.
- Your impact can be clearly seen (i.e., you were not simply tagging along with someone else who did the real work).

If you are trying to show that you have had a lot of relevant business experience despite being only 23, you will probably want one (or preferably more) of these accomplishments to be in the business realm. Not every accomplishment will fulfill all of our criteria, but you should be able to meet most of them in the course of the full essay.

In writing the essay, go into sufficient detail to bring the events to life, but do not stop there. Discuss why you consider this a substantial achievement, why you take pride in it, and what you learned from it. Did you change and grow as a result? Did you find that you approached other matters differently afterwards?

The admissions committee will read this for more than a brief description of the items you list on your data sheet. It will want to learn more about these accomplishments and more about the private you, if you discuss significant accomplishments of a personal nature here. It will want to know what motivates you and what you value. It will also want to see how you have developed as a person and as a professional.

ADVANTAGES OF THIS APPROACH

This question gives you a lot of latitude, as our criteria suggest. Using it to show more of the real you will help you avoid the usual problems people create for themselves in this essay. You do not want to restate the facts you have already listed on your data sheet; you want to show you have been ready to face challenges, determined to overcome obstacles, and able to accomplish things that mattered to you. The essays in Part IV suggest a limitless number of potential topics; the excerpted essays were successful because they revealed their authors' characters while explaining the personal importance of their achievements.

QUESTION: DESCRIBE A CREATIVE SOLUTION YOU'VE DEVISED TO A PROBLEM

WHY THE QUESTION IS ASKED

Because of the rapid change of business practices in the modern economy, MBA programs are naturally concerned about the creativity of their candidates. This is particularly true in an era when many business school students intend to find "the next big thing"—the next great idea for a business—in order to launch their own firms as soon as possible after business school. By asking this question, schools signal that they particularly desire a certain type of applicant. This question is also a means for determining to what extent candidates have performed above and beyond the requirements of their jobs and thus are the stars that schools have always sought.

THE TYPICAL APPLICANT

The typical applicant tells a story about a solution to a problem without showing that the solution was in any way creative. For example, she explains how she tackled an impending deadline by dividing up project tasks among the individuals on a team according to their talents and interests. Although this represents a solution to a problem, it is a stunningly ordinary one. There is nothing creative or even inspired about it.

Still other applicants focus only on the "creative" part of the question, and do not bother to illustrate that this creativity has solved a problem. One applicant, for instance, wrote an essay about his poetry writing.

A BETTER APPROACH

It is obviously necessary to actually answer the question—to show that a creative approach in fact solved a problem. But do not stop there. Describe the nature of the problem; show that it was indeed a difficult one to crack.

Show also that obvious approaches would not have been successful. In so doing, you show that you have tried to turn the problem around and looked at it from every angle, thereby showing good problem-solving skills—and also showing that you did not just get lucky in eventually finding a creative solution. The creative solution will look all the more impressive when set in this context.

After describing the solution you found, be sure to show the impact your solution had. Business schools want to have creative people, it is true, but even more they want creative people who have a major impact upon their environments.

Consider the fellow working for a hair products firm that sells a permanent-wave product that is much less harmful to hair than other permanent waves are, but which faces marketing problems because it is considered to have relatively little holding power. Others in the firm considered trying to convince the market that this product had sufficient holding power by mounting major marketing efforts. This fellow, on the other hand, decided that the most effective way to tackle the problem was to build a machine that measured the shape stability of hair, thereby allowing the firm's product to be compared scientifically against the other products. The result—that it was 80 percent as effective (with dramatically less damage to the hair)—convinced hair salons of its value. This is an extreme example; it is not necessary to have devised a new machine (and received a patent for it) to look like a creative problem-solver. Utilizing a new distribution channel, finding a new way to get the data to resolve an issue, or applying a new analytical technique could all qualify.

ADVANTAGES OF THIS APPROACH

Discussing a truly creative solution demonstrates that you will fit well in the more forward-thinking parts of modern business (and business schools). It also suggests that you challenge yourself to approach problems from a variety of perspectives. Possessing such an open mind makes you a good collaborator on team projects. Showing, too, that you have had a substantial impact via your creative approach marks you as more than a dreamer—it shows you to be someone whose creativity and other attributes are harnessed to being productive.

QUESTION: DESCRIBE A RISK THAT YOU HAVE TAKEN AND ITS OUTCOME

WHY THE QUESTION IS ASKED

As with so many other questions, one function of those about risk-taking is to signal the type of candidate the school wants. In this case, it signals that the school wants people who are not afraid to take a risk. The school recognizes that those who have never taken a risk are very unlikely to do what is necessary to achieve something stunning. For example, the person who runs for president or prime minister risks the embarrassment of being beaten terribly and, perhaps, of losing a safe seat in Congress, Parliament, or Assembly. The person who founds a business risks bankruptcy.

THE TYPICAL APPLICANT

The typical applicant goes to one of two extremes. One extreme is describing a situation that involved virtually no risk to him. For instance, he mentions that he went beyond what his boss wanted done on a project—as if doing extra work placed him in jeopardy. The other extreme is describing a situation in which he had no real chance of success. For instance, he invested all of his savings in a plan to airfreight cement across the continent.

A BETTER APPROACH

Your choice of a topic is critical: You need to strike the right balance. You need to show that you took a not-insignificant risk without looking like a cavalier idiot who would jump out of an airplane without a parachute. If you were successful, you do not need to worry quite so much about what precisely you chose to do and why. (You do need to demonstrate that there was a real risk of failure, though, to avoid giving the impression that you were not taking a risk.)

It is acceptable to have failed; it is unacceptable never to have tried to accomplish something that would entail efforts outside your personal comfort zone. Yet if you failed, you should be careful in your explanations of why you ran this risk, the analysis you did before starting in, and so on. If the risk looks particularly foolish, better that it be something that you undertook long ago. Similarly, you cannot afford to discuss a risk you took if it appears to be part of a pattern of risk-taking from which you learn no lessons. Thus, a senseless answer would involve betting your salary on lottery tickets month after month, as no analysis is likely to make this look like a well-calculated risk, you can hardly demonstrate marvelous data analysis or research skills, the outcome is unfavorable, and your continuing to bet shows that you resist learning anything from the experience.

Whether your story is that of a career, academic, or personal risk, consider highlighting:

- Your analysis of the situation. Especially if your illustration of risk-taking occurred recently, show yourself as someone who gathers appropriate information, examines it from every angle and weighs it judiciously, and then acts appropriately in light of all the circumstances.

- The degree of risk involved, as well as the possible payoff.

- The extent to which you did or did not succeed.

- The impact upon others.

- Your learning—about risk-taking as well as about yourself, your fit with the world (of work, perhaps), and so on.

ADVANTAGES OF THIS APPROACH

Meeting the criteria discussed above will show that you are a savvy risk-taker, neither afraid to take a risk nor willing to plunge ahead without determining whether the risk is worth running. Showing how you determined whether to take the risk and the results of your action gives you the chance to demonstrate a whole range of skills and attributes critical to your positioning.

QUESTION: WHAT HAVE YOU DONE THAT DEMONSTRATES YOUR LEADERSHIP POTENTIAL?

WHY THE QUESTION IS ASKED

Top schools expect to produce top managers—that is, leaders. They are looking for applicants who have already distinguished themselves as leaders, since past performance is the best indicator of what people will be like in the future.

THE TYPICAL APPLICANT

All too often, applicants discuss being part of a group that achieved something noteworthy without making it clear that they themselves were leaders in this effort.

A BETTER APPROACH

This question is deceptively similar to the "substantial accomplishment" essay. The "substantial accomplishment" essay, as I explained above, asks you to describe a real achievement (and what it means to you). The "leadership" essay, on the other hand, is not looking so much for an "achievement" as it is for an understanding of *how you led an effort* to achieve something. In other words, your emphasis should be upon your leadership rather than the achievement itself.

To write this essay, you must understand what leadership is. One obvious example is managing people who report directly to you. Less obvious examples involve pushing or inspiring nonsubordinates to do what you want done. How? Leading by example, using your influence as a perceived expert in a relevant field, influencing through moral suasion, or influencing by personal friendship. You might have led people through direct management or through influence. Describe your method—what strategy and tactics did you employ? And why? You may not have been deliberate or extremely self-aware in your actions, of course, in which case you might wish to discuss what you did and why it was or was not a good choice. What problems did you confront? What did you learn about managing or influencing people? Would another strategy or different tactics/actions have been better choices? Why? Do you now have a developed philosophy of leadership?

You should emphasize that your leadership qualities are the sort that describe a future CEO rather than a high school football hero. In other words, such qualities as maturity, thoughtfulness, empathy, determination, and integrity are highly valuable. So, too, are coaching others to develop their skills, providing emotional support to a team's vulnerable members, protecting the group from an overweening organization, being able to see the best possible outcomes and how to achieve them, valuing other people's input, being able to influence or manage very different types of people, and integrating disparate inputs into a unified perspective.

You are generally better off choosing an example from your business career, but a particularly strong example from your extracurricular or private life could also work.

ADVANTAGES OF THIS APPROACH

Viewing this question as concerning your understanding of leadership, and the ways in which you yourself lead, will result in an essay with the appropriate focus. It is not just your achievement that is at issue here; it is also your method of approaching and resolving leadership issues that concerns the admissions committee. If you show yourself to be aware of the leadership issues inherent in your situation and extract some suitable comments regarding what worked or did not work, and why, you will have the core of a good essay.

QUESTION: DESCRIBE MEANINGFUL CROSS-CULTURAL EXPERIENCES YOU HAVE HAD

WHY THE QUESTION IS ASKED

Schools increasingly recognize that global managers—that is, the leaders of the future—need to be able to understand and interact effectively with a wide range of people, certainly including people from other cultures. This is true not just for people's future careers but also for their participation in the MBA program, where they can expect to deal with a large number of people from other countries. This question is meant to determine whether you have had significant experiences with people unlike you. It is also meant to signal that you can expect such experiences if you attend this program.

THE TYPICAL APPLICANT

The typical applicant discusses being a tourist abroad or having the occasional discussion with a foreigner, reducing foreigners to being exotic and cute rather than real people. Consequently, he never needs to get to grips with what makes them different than him on some fundamental level. Instead, he resorts to celebrating the wonderfulness of diversity as an abstract and empty notion.

A BETTER APPROACH

To show that you have had a meaningful cross-cultural experience requires you to show that you have come to understand how another culture, or a member of it, functions.

One excellent way to show that you have really come to understand another culture is by having lived in and integrated into one. If this is the case, by all means discuss in what ways you are a part of this other culture. Simple, concrete examples tend to work better than grandiose statements about your degree of integration. For instance, if your knowledge of local restaurants is better than that of anyone else in the office, perhaps you are the one entrusted with ordering the late night food that will be delivered to your team.

Having had in-depth arguments with people from another culture is another way to show that you have engaged with it. Conflict regarding big issues such as the role of the family and/or women in society, religious views, the value or appropriateness of your respective political systems, the importance of education, work-life balance, and so on makes for a fine essay.

You can show that you have gotten to grips with another culture in other ways. For example, perhaps you have had to negotiate with people from a different culture over important aspects of a project. Maybe they did not view its on-time completion as critical, or thought the level of resource committed to it excessive (or lacking). Maybe they thought you were intrusive in checking on their performance during the course of the project. Or perhaps they were unwilling to push back against more senior people regarding the composition of the team, the nature of the deadlines or expected performance, or other critical issues. On the other hand, perhaps they were unwilling to push the team to perform up to its maximum level, believing in country-club-style management (keeping everyone happy rather than emphasizing performance). Their ideas about what to expect from superiors, colleagues, and subordinates (within and outside their own culture) are potential grist for your essay-writing mill.

It is not necessary that you have resolved the conflicts you had. A resolution admittedly offers the opportunity to tie up the essay on a positive note, which is often a good thing. An agreement to disagree, however, or even a continuing conflict can work well here, too. You need not seem that you are a Pollyanna who thinks that everything happens for the best, and that reasonable (or even unreasonable) people can all get along well. It is perfectly acceptable that you have understood other people's views but not caved in to them.

ADVANTAGES OF THIS APPROACH

By showing yourself to have engaged seriously with one or more other cultures, you show yourself to have gotten beyond both the tourist ("isn't it fascinating how those people eat dinner at midnight?") and the stereotype ("those Italians certainly have flair") level of dealing with others. This offers you the chance to demonstrate that you have gained substantial perspective on your own culture and, preferably, yourself. This perspective is essential when it comes to communicating and managing across cultural barriers.

QUESTION: DESCRIBE AN EXPERIENCE IN WHICH YOU DID NOT REACH YOUR OBJECTIVES (AND WHAT YOU LEARNED FROM THIS)

WHY THE QUESTION IS ASKED

This question is essentially asking: Are you mature enough to admit that you have made a mistake? Did you learn from it? Can you change and grow? (It is similar to another commonly asked question, "Describe a failure and how you dealt with it.")

THE TYPICAL APPLICANT

Most applicants focus more on the mistake they made, or the failure they suffered, rather than on what they learned from it.

A BETTER APPROACH

You have a great deal of latitude in choosing your failure or mistake. Two factors should govern your response. (1) Try to further your positioning effort. If you are trying to present yourself as a worldly international negotiator, you might wish to show how you flubbed your first negotiations with people from another culture due to your lack of understanding of how they valued different components of a deal. (You can then go on to explain that this started you on the path of investigating the values and beliefs of your negotiating partners and opponents in all future deals, something you believe has underpinned much of your success since then.) (2) Show that you have truly learned from your mistake. One implication of this may be that you will want to choose a failure from your more distant past, not last week. You will not have had much of an opportunity to learn from a recent failure, whereas a failure from two or three years ago may have afforded plenty of opportunity to learn (and to have compiled a set of relevant successes to demonstrate this development). The reason is that you generally need some time to reflect upon matters in order to benefit fully from them. (Similarly, if you choose a distant failure, you are not saying that you are currently making these mistakes. It may be better to admit to having been prone to mistakes long ago, not currently.)

Having chosen your failure, do not belabor your description of it. Remember that it is *what you learned from this failure* that is critical here, not the failure itself. Consider what you learned from the experience concerning yourself, your job, your company, your industry, how to manage people, and so on. One key piece of learning may have been that you came to see your need for much more conceptual knowledge, such as that which you hope to acquire by doing an MBA.

ADVANTAGES OF THIS APPROACH

The emphasis here should be upon your development. We learn more from our mistakes than from our successes. A willingness to admit mistakes and then try to learn from them is one hallmark of a mature adult. It is also the trait of someone who will benefit from more formal education.

QUESTION: DISCUSS AN ETHICAL DILEMMA YOU HAVE FACED

WHY THE QUESTION IS ASKED

The ongoing debate over the proper role of business in society has made ethics an important issue in a manager's training—or so the admissions officers will tell you. The reality may be somewhat different. Business schools periodically feel the need to talk about ethics as a result of recent scandals, although it is clearly a subject of limited interest for most of the professors. The need to appear interested in the subject, at least to critical outsiders, has probably been as important as anything else in generating the use of this question.

For some schools and some admissions officers, this question is a sincere attempt to understand your ethics. For others, the question is not so much about ethics as it is just another chance to see your writing and read another story about you.

THE TYPICAL APPLICANT

Most people have trouble finding something to discuss, so they end up choosing something trivial. In discussing it, they think that a question about ethics must call for a holier-than-thou stance, so they sound like refugees from a sensitivity training session. Another common mistake, which could single-handedly kill your chances of admission, is to describe a situation in which you made an obvious moral transgression and then later "saw the light" and tried to redeem yourself. An example of this error would be to describe how your firm's personnel department accidentally deposited another employee's $10,000 bonus into your account, which you neglected to report until you heard that this other employee had started demanding that the personnel department determine what had become of her payment.

A BETTER APPROACH

The toughest part of this essay is to find a suitable subject. Here are some possible topics:

- *People versus profit.* For example, should you fire the Italian researchers you have working for you now that your firm no longer markets in Italy? They are too old to be hired by someone else. On the one hand, you may feel that you owe it to the shareholders to maximize their returns. On the other hand, you feel concern for the researchers. Is it a clear-cut decision? Maybe, but that is likely to depend upon the circumstances. If the company promised the researchers they would be employed until they reached retirement age, and this was one of the things that helped lure them away from another firm, you will probably feel one way. If the researchers have been working second and third jobs at the same time that they have been officially employed by your firm, you may feel differently.

- *Your career versus someone else's.* When you are in a meeting and your boss takes credit for your idea, what should you do?

- *Taking advantage of someone's lack of knowledge or opportunities.* Should you sell a product to someone who does not know that it will be inappropriate for his needs? By the time he figures this out, you may have moved on to a new division in the company, so you will not face his fury or the long-term consequences of having an angry customer.

The essays in Part IV contain interesting examples of other ethical dilemmas. Note that you can also consider writing about something that happened in your private rather than your business life. In fact, such dilemmas are a part of everyday life, so failing to find one runs the risk of appearing unaware of the moral dimension of life.

This question is asked in one of two different ways. In one version, you are asked simply to describe an ethical dilemma and what you thought of it. In the other version, you must describe an ethical dilemma and what you did in response to it. The second type is obviously more demanding than the first because you must have a situation that you ultimately managed well. Some situations may lend themselves to excellent management, but the nature of a "dilemma" suggests that there may not be a perfect way to handle it.

In writing this essay, you will want to show that there truly was a dilemma, at least on the surface. You will probably want to show that you explored and investigated the nature of the problem, since you were no doubt reluctant to make a snap decision when it appeared that any decision would have substantial adverse consequences. If you are called upon to describe what you did rather than just what you thought, you will want to show that you explored every option and did your best to minimize or mitigate the adverse consequences.

The tone of your essay is another minefield. If you sound like an innocent 7-year-old who believes it is always wrong to lie, you will not fit in a world of tough senior managers who constantly need to make hard decisions with rotten consequences for somebody. On the other hand, if you sound like a Machiavelli, for whom the only calculus depends upon personal advantage, and for whom the potential suffering of other people is irrelevant, you will be rejected as a moral monster. You need to be somewhere in the middle—someone who recognizes that the world and the decisions it requires are seldom perfect, but that it is appropriate to try to minimize adverse consequences as best one can. Only in extreme circumstances would it be appropriate to walk away from the decision (and the job).

ADVANTAGES OF THIS APPROACH

It is critical to find a subject into which you can sink your teeth. Our examples may help you find such a subject, one with layers of detail and dilemma. If you go into depth in exploring it, without sounding like a naïve child or a totally cynical manipulator; turn it about and examine it from different angles; and weigh the various options thoughtfully, you will show yourself to be senior-management material.

PERSONAL TOPICS

QUESTION: DESCRIBE SOMEONE YOU CONSIDER A HERO OR ROLE MODEL. HOW HAS THIS PERSON AFFECTED YOUR DEVELOPMENT?

WHY THE QUESTION IS ASKED

This question is asked in order to understand your personality, your values, and how you interact with others. Admissions committees want to see what traits you appreciate in others. They assume that the qualities you deem especially attractive in others are those you try to develop in yourself. Likewise, they are keen to know that you are capable of sustaining meaningful relationships with others in the program (and beyond) and learning from them.

THE TYPICAL APPLICANT

The typical applicant chooses the first person who comes to mind, often his manager or one of his parents. He then discusses obviously desirable traits—such as generosity, leadership, determination, or loyalty—in vague terms. Others discuss the well-known qualities of a famous figure, such as Martin Luther King Jr., whether or not that person has actually had an impact on their own lives. In both cases, applicants write essays full of praise for the other person, but without ever showing how this person affected them, thereby revealing little about themselves. In essence, these applicants answer only the first of the question's two parts.

A BETTER APPROACH

Do not think of this essay as a "free-for-all." Instead, use it to strengthen your positioning or overcome a potential weakness. Even though you have a lot of leeway in your choice of subject, discussing the right kind of person as your role model can shape your candidacy beneficially. For instance, a younger, inexperienced applicant will be helped by writing a sophisticated essay on a not-too-obvious person. Thus, she should favor a balanced appreciation of a senior manager in her firm or a partially successful politician rather than a hagiographic treatment of her father. A candidate who needs to avoid looking like a total workaholic should avoid discussing a driven entrepreneur and instead opt for someone who can shed light on his personality, values, or noncareer interests.

As a general rule, there is nothing wrong with choosing a common topic, such as one's supervisor, father, or Martin Luther King Jr. But you need to bring the subject matter to life using relevant details and stories that reach beyond the mundane. Admissions officers are not interested in reading for the hundredth time that King was a great leader who forswore violence.

The point should not be that you were impressed by this person. Rather, you need to show in what ways his or her example inspired or impelled your own development. This development need not be career-oriented. In fact, a majority of applicants will be better off focusing on how they developed as people rather than as managers.

When answering any question, even about a relationship with someone else, at least part of the focus must be on you. This is doubly true for this question, but it does require that you show how you have reacted to the other person's example. Here you will use the other person as a foil—he should reflect *your* concerns, *your* values, *your* interests, and *your* attributes. Show how *you* have reacted to his or her example. Remember that you—not your manager or your father—are applying to the program.

ADVANTAGES OF THIS APPROACH

Choosing the right person to discuss can help your candidacy immensely, by cementing your positioning efforts or downplaying a weakness. Choosing a role model with particular personality or leadership traits can help to establish the importance of those traits to you; similarly, the related stories you tell about yourself can establish your claim to those same traits.

Business schools are in the business of educating leaders; showing your self-development efforts can demonstrate that you are likely to get the maximum from any learning environment.

QUESTION: DESCRIBE A DEFINING MOMENT THAT HAS HAD A MAJOR IMPACT ON YOUR LIFE.

WHY THE QUESTION IS ASKED

MBA programs want to know who you are. As has been emphasized throughout this book, you are more than just a set of numbers to your evaluators. This kind of question helps the admissions committee determine who you are, what makes you tick, and what unique life experiences you can bring to an MBA class.

THE TYPICAL APPLICANT

The typical applicant chooses a successful athletic or business effort and then tries to argue that it was truly inspirational and put her on the road to success. Thus, placing third in the low hurdles runoff got her on the varsity track team, an event that caused her to figure out that if she just tried hard enough, she could succeed at anything. Although it is possible to make such an event sound like it was a real milestone in your life, recognize that painfully few applicants succeed in doing so.

The other common approach is to trace the evolution of one's entire life, cataloguing every significant event along the way, even though this represents a failure to answer the question—and forfeits an opportunity to show one's inner self.

A BETTER APPROACH

A good place to start on this question is to examine the *inflection points* in your life, points at which your life changed directions. Such changes tend to show a lot about who you are. Understanding what made you change from a prior course of action allows someone to see how you think, what matters to you, where you are headed, and why. If you have an inflection point or points to consider, ask yourself what event spurred your change of direction. For instance, perhaps the death of your uncle from a hard-to-diagnose disease caused you to dedicate yourself to founding a company to develop a diagnosis for the disease.

If it is hard to come up with an event that spurred a change in you, consider whether another event is a good representative of such a change or, alternatively, shows you overcoming *a major challenge*. For example, you may have suffered from a bad case of stuttering throughout your childhood and adolescence. No single event triggered this, so you cannot discuss one. On the other hand, your fight to overcome the problem may have crystallized when you had to give a presentation at your high school graduation. Of course you agonized for months in advance, practicing and willing yourself to succeed. Your success in getting through the speech might truly have caused you to know that you were finally on the downhill side of the problem and that your life would no longer be ruled by your fear of speaking.

As the last example shows, a seemingly trivial event (giving a speech) can be highly meaningful to you and have a lifelong impact. When discussing something that matters to you but is not clearly a major life event (like the death of a parent), be sure to develop the event's context. In addition, for all events, be sure to discuss the impact they had on you. Even an obviously major event such as being adopted at the relatively advanced age of 8 will benefit from a discussion of your relationship to your adoptive parents, your involvement with adoption organizations, and your own plans for a family.

One type of event tends not to work well here—the sort that is commonplace for the applicants to top schools. Graduating from college or getting your first job are likely to fall flat unless you can invest them with personal significance, as the stutterer discussed above did. In fact, most career situations will not work particularly well. They seldom have had an impact upon your life comparable in scale to the impact of various personal situations. Also, a discussion of career situations fits well in response to other essay questions, so there is seldom a need to make them the focus of this answer.

ADVANTAGES OF THIS APPROACH

This question begs you to tell a life story; doing so can help you greatly in your attempt to separate yourself from those with career experience similar to your own. Showing why you changed your life's course is of inherent interest to those who want to know who you are, not just what you have done. An additional benefit is that a good discussion of changes you have made or challenges you have met shows you to be someone who understands herself well; such self-knowledge is recognized as an important step to becoming a good manager of other people.

QUESTION: WHAT MATTERS MOST TO YOU AND WHY?

WHY THE QUESTION IS ASKED

As with the "defining moment" question, MBA programs want to know who you are and what you value. This question helps the admissions committee determine these things and, as a result, what you are likely to take away from the program. In addition, schools that ask this type of question are usually keen to see to what extent you understand yourself, figuring that those who will make the best managers are those with the greatest degree of self-knowledge.

THE TYPICAL APPLICANT

The typical applicant touches briefly on every (in)significant element of his life: family, friends, career, education, community involvement, pets, reading, travel, spectator and participant sports, and so on. Covering a laundry list of topics is inevitably a poor idea. It leaves little room for real exploration or intelligent insight. It also suggests that you are unable to prioritize. The result is that the committee gets little sense of the core you.

A BETTER APPROACH

If the answer to this question is limited to several hundred words, focusing on one or two elements will be required. In recent years, however, this has been Stanford's pet question, with a suggested answer length of three to seven pages. In this case, the better approach is to utilize an overarching theme that allows you to pull together several related topics without losing focus. In writing page after page, you face a second danger (the first is discussing a laundry list of unrelated topics)—artificially narrowing your discussion to a single topic. Doing so usually causes the applicant to stop writing after just a page or two (bored with his own topic) or, if he writes at length, bores the admissions committee.

The hard part is to choose a theme that advances your desired positioning and allows you to group together the appropriate topics. The applicant who has lived through something traumatic is often able to do so, but others usually need to search harder for an appropriate theme. Thus, the applicant who has endured crushing poverty can use empowerment as his major theme. He can obviously discuss his desire to get a first-class education, gain appropriate career credentials and credibility, and so on. In addition, he can highlight how he has helped others, particularly his siblings, in their quest for success, thereby revealing a more personal side to this topic. Those who have escaped totalitarian regimes, rehabilitated themselves after major automobile accidents, and the like can use big themes such as "freedom" to good effect.

But what about the second category, the person who has no such ready-made organizing devices to hand? A good example is a woman who most values the time she spends with her grandfather. She shows that he has instilled in her a strong work ethic (through his own sixty-year career as a baker), taught her how to cook (one of her favorite pastimes), forged part of her identity (through his sharing of stories about their Danish ancestors), and demonstrated unconditional love (her most valued emotion). This is another example of a theme that permits her to show herself to good advantage, although it was probably not an obvious choice for her when she first confronted the question.

ADVANTAGES OF THIS APPROACH

Writing a lengthy essay that does not lend itself to a chronological approach is difficult. The best way to do so here is to utilize an organizing theme that enables you to pull together several related items. By doing so, you show that you have followed the instructions to discuss one item, not a bunch. Your coherent discussion of related items also gives a clearer, more focused picture of you than is possible with a host of topics.

QUESTION: WHAT DO YOU DO IN YOUR SPARE TIME?

WHY THE QUESTION IS ASKED

Good managers tend to be able to make friends and to socialize easily. This is all the more important in a nonhierarchical, manage-by-influence-rather-than-power world. This question is designed to reveal more about you and to see whether you would fit into the school's social life (and perhaps add to it). This is likely to be much more important for small schools than for large ones, for isolated schools than for urban ones, and perhaps for standalone business schools than for those that are part of a university. The reason is that a smaller, more isolated school will tend to have a very close-knit student body, so someone who does not fit well with the school culture may have a miserable time.

A person with balanced interests, who is not consumed by business to the exclusion of other things, will be able to survive the ups and downs both of business school and of a managerial career. In addition, he is likely to be good company at business school, more interesting to spend time with than a career-obsessive.

THE TYPICAL APPLICANT

Many applicants treat this question too lightly and end up simply listing five or ten things they enjoy doing. This does nothing to help their case.

A BETTER APPROACH

Start by thinking of the things you really enjoy. You probably have a pretty good-sized list. Choose one or two (or three) to talk about. Your selection criteria should include the following:

- The activity matters to you.
- You know a lot about it.
- You can make it interesting to read about.
- It aids your positioning effort.
- The activity's *distinctiveness* (will 90 percent of the applicants write about this?) is apparent.

The appropriate activities to discuss are those that will help your positioning. For example, if you have been a corporate librarian, you may want to reassure schools that you are a very tough and determined person. If you enjoy technical mountain climbing, by all means discuss this activity rather than your Internet chess-playing. The former shows you to be a highly unusual librarian whereas the latter suggests an all-too-stereotypical one who prefers solitary, contemplative pursuits. Some pursuits that are quite worthwhile are actually not ideal choices here because they are far too frequently used. This list includes common sports and physical activities, as well as teaching for Junior Achievement and involvement with Habitat for Humanity. This is not to say you should avoid writing about these, but be sure to exercise as much creativity as possible in discussing them if you do select them. Topics to avoid, almost no matter what, include watching soap operas or situation comedies on television, sleeping, drinking with the lads, hanging out in pool rooms, and so on.

The next step is to write the essay in an appealing fashion. Since your spare time is indeed your own, any activities you pursue should inspire you with real *enthusiasm*, at least if you are a basically enthusiastic sort of person. (Given that business schools want enthusiastic students, you are obligated to sound enthusiastic even if you are not.)

The other key to your essay will be to show that you are *highly knowledgeable and sincere* about the activity. These characteristics are desirable on their own and, equally important, they show that you really do participate in this hobby, sport, or activity. This essay lends itself to "hypercreativity"; make it clear that you are not simply claiming to climb mountains or whatever you discuss.

One way to sound enthusiastic, knowledgeable, and sincere is to go into detail in describing what you do. If you are a mountain climber, you may want to describe one of your best climbs. Why did you choose to tackle this particular mountain? Why this particular route? How did you choose your team?

What criteria did you employ, and why? What were the major challenges that you faced? How did you handle them? What was the aftermath of this climb? Describing these and other matters will also *individualize* you, because even someone choosing the same topic will have had entirely different experiences.

The other quality you should strive to communicate is that you are a very *likable* person. You want to be regarded as interesting and pleasant company. This is especially true for people whose positioning is that they are number-crunching accountants or otherwise relatively isolated.

Should you discuss one or two (or three) activities? This depends upon the number of activities you pursue that meet our criteria and how much space it will take you to describe each one appropriately.

ADVANTAGES OF THIS APPROACH

Choosing only one or two activities to discuss shows that you know how to prioritize and makes your discussion seem focused while giving you the opportunity to interest the admissions committee in what you describe. Discussing unusual activities will also help the committee to remember who you are.

Choosing activities that further your positioning effort has an obvious payoff. Discussing them enthusiastically permits you to build enthusiasm *for you* on the part of the committee.

OTHER TOPICS

QUESTION: TELL US ANYTHING ELSE YOU CARE TO

WHY THE QUESTION IS ASKED

This question is asked for three reasons. First, it gives you a chance to add important information that other essays may not capture. Second, it gives you a chance to explain a weakness or gap in your record, or why your boss did not write a recommendation for you. Third, it will ascertain whether you are able to weigh the value of the additional information you are giving the admissions committee versus the effort required for them to read another essay.

THE TYPICAL APPLICANT

Many people write something, but few benefit thereby. Too many complain about what happened long ago or make excuses for their own failings (or simply substitute an essay from another school). Others add a litany of marginally positive exploits, thereby doing little but diluting the overall impact of their essays.

A BETTER APPROACH

Write this essay only if you can make a substantial, positive addition to your application. Consider first whether you have any substantial weakness in your record that can be explained in a sensible fashion. For example, if you received poor grades during your last two years of college due to the need to work forty hours per week to support your newly unemployed parents, be sure to note this. Explain in a simple, direct way, however, rather than whining or complaining.

Then, ask yourself whether anything important to your positioning has been left out. If there is an important credential or conquered obstacle that you have not been able to discuss, and it will substantially help your positioning effort, then use this essay to bring it to the admissions committee's attention. Resist the natural inclination, however, to gild the lily. Do not tell a third story showing how politically astute you were on the job. If you have explained how well you analyzed a production problem, and a recommender is describing another such effort, do not even think of describing a third one here.

What sorts of things are most likely to qualify for inclusion here? With some schools you will not otherwise have the opportunity to discuss your community activities or other things you have pursued outside your proper job. For example, you might wish to describe your management of the political campaign of a friend who ran for office in your city. Or you might wish to describe what you did in setting up a successful business that you ran on weekends. You may have a specific skill you wish to demonstrate that will not otherwise come across, or you may have rectified a weakness in your record. Perhaps you did poorly at math during your university studies but have since been sufficiently motivated to take a number of continuing education classes in math.

If you have found one item that qualifies as a valuable addition, by all means use it; but what if you think you have six or eight such items? In this case, follow the usual approach and select one, or at most two, of these. This essay is meant to augment the basic application, not substitute for it. You do not want to risk overwhelming admissions officers with too much material, nor do you want to fall into the trap of just listing items.

If you feel that using your material from another school's application will greatly benefit your positioning effort, be sure to explain in your introductory sentence why you are including this information (i.e., what you are trying to achieve with this additional information). Admissions officers are well aware of what questions other schools ask, and will not be impressed if it is obvious you are simply tacking on the answer to another school's question without a clear reason.

ADVANTAGES OF THIS APPROACH

Complaining about one's fate or offering insubstantial excuses for one's failings are likely to annoy admissions committees. Offering real explanations, if available, is better calculated to win their favor. Similarly, lists are seldom of value. It is far better to choose one or two things and then describe and discuss them in sufficient detail as to make their nature and value clear.

QUESTION: WHAT WOULD YOU LIKE THE MBA ADMISSIONS BOARD TO KNOW ABOUT YOUR UNDERGRADUATE ACADEMIC EXPERIENCE?

WHY THE QUESTION IS ASKED

Business schools are aware that the old model of how students undertake their bachelor's degree is becoming less common. Not everyone goes through college taking four courses per term, doing an extracurricular or two, and then working during summer vacations. Now students may jam their course-work into three years, doing little but coursework; stretch it out for five or more years while working half-time or more; put primary emphasis on their internships rather than their courses; and so on. As a result, business schools want to understand the context in which a degree was earned; the grades no longer necessarily "speak for themselves."

THE TYPICAL APPLICANT

The typical applicant whines rather than explains, complaining about unfair professors or pleading that he was sick before critical exams. He fails to take responsibility for his own actions.

A BETTER APPROACH

Focus on presenting the full context of your undergraduate experience. For instance, if the nature and quality of your school are likely to be unknown to the admissions committee, discuss them. Some schools, such as art or music schools, seldom produce candidates for MBA programs.

Foreign schools, unless they are regular feeders to this business school, may well be unknown to the admissions committee, too. The same is true for two-year schools that have recently converted to four-year schools.

What is true about your school may also be true about your department or the curriculum you followed. For instance, if your department attracts the best and brightest students on campus, regularly turning out graduates who win major fellowships and go on to top graduate schools, note this. Similarly, if it is the lowest-grading department on campus, demonstrate this. And, in general, explain the school's grading policies if they are unusual or difficult to understand.

If your activities outside class affected your grades or course selection, explain the causes and the consequences. Athletics, editing the school newspaper, work, caring for a sick relative, or raising a family might well have affected your academic performance. Be sure to point to evidence that you performed substantially better when not spending as much time on nonacademic activities. Also, be careful not to make too much of a fuss about a level of activity that is commonplace among applicants to good business schools. Working eight to ten hours a week might be worth noting, but it should not be posited as the reason for a dreadful GPA.

This essay should not be largely devoted to trying to explain or rationalize your failures. Instead, you should look to demonstrate your successes, particularly if they are not obvious. For example, you may have satisfied the requirements for two majors but not have them both listed on your transcript simply because your school does not officially recognize double majors. Similarly, you may have the highest GPA of anyone in your department but not have gotten departmental honors because they are not given at your school or because, as a transfer student, you didn't qualify for them.

This essay gives you the opportunity to reflect upon your undergraduate experience. Why did you choose the courses and major you did? What did you particularly enjoy and value at the time? What have you come to value more highly in retrospect? What would you do differently given what you now know? Would you, for instance, not simply rest on your laurels for having passed the Calculus BC exam (which eliminated the need to take any quantitative courses at your college) and take some quantitative courses? Perhaps you were trying to maximize something other than your GPA—involvement in political activities, writing for campus and professional journals, earning enough to graduate debt-free, playing varsity sports, or something else. As long as you maintained a reasonable level of academic performance, you can show that the tradeoff was appropriate. Discuss what you learned, how this influenced your choice of career (and outside interests), and what has been most valuable to you in career and life.

No matter what you discuss, be careful about the tone of this essay. Be matter-of-fact rather than whiny. Be pleased with what you learned, academically and otherwise. And if you have a generally strong academic record, resist the temptation to quibble about minor flaws in it. Don't argue that you deserved an A instead of a B+ in some seminar. Instead, just say that the overall record reflects your abilities.

ADVANTAGES OF THIS APPROACH

Looking at your undergraduate career as a whole, instead of focusing just on how best to excuse a low grade or a bad semester, allows you to avoid sounding defensive. Seeing what you gained from your studies and other pursuits also suggests that you are looking to your future rather than remaining mired in a doubtful past. And by fully highlighting your successes, you are able to gain credit for much that might remain hidden in a transcript and for which there may not be an appropriate place elsewhere in the application.

QUESTION: DESCRIBE YOUR ROLE IN A (DIFFICULT) TEAM SITUATION. HOW DID YOU HELP A TEAM REACH ITS OBJECTIVES?

WHY THE QUESTION IS ASKED

This question is asked so that the admissions committee can get an idea of how well you work in group settings. It is also a way for a school to advertise to applicants that it has a team-based approach to learning. Many of the projects you will do at such a school (and beyond) will require strong teamwork and interpersonal skills. Thus, the ability to work well in a team, whether as leader or member, is critical.

THE TYPICAL APPLICANT

The typical applicant focuses on the subject matter of the group effort and forgets to describe group dynamics, the teamwork skills she employed, and what she contributed. For example, she takes great pains to go into detail about the securities laws her investment banking group researched for a particular client rather than demonstrating her skill in helping the team function well under difficult circumstances.

Similarly, many applicants focus on the results of the group effort instead of on the group's functioning and their own contributions.

A BETTER APPROACH

The emphasis in any kind of question about a team effort should always be on group dynamics. The best approach is to focus first and foremost on the team and the interactions between individuals, giving only as much detail about the substantive work as is necessary to make the essay readable and interesting.

Make sure to describe your role on the team, the ways in which you helped move the team forward, and the interpersonal and management skills you employed in so doing. Consider mentioning what difficulties the group encountered; how you influenced people; how you helped manage competing team priorities; how you got others—especially reticent or quiet members of the team—to contribute; how you reduced conflict or dealt with personality clashes; and how your efforts complemented those of others on the team. Consider to what extent it was appropriate to have focused more on the process of working together than on the substantive result.

Although you will naturally prefer to choose examples in which you have led a group, whether as the formal or informal leader, it is also possible to write an impressive essay showing how well you performed as a team member. After all, even a strong leader should know when to follow someone else's lead.

You will also want to discuss your teamwork, managerial, or leadership philosophy, if you have one, to show that you have been an observant student (on the job) of these important subjects. Be sure in this case to link your general views to specific actions you took on the project.

Although a project's results always help to show that it (and thus the team that conducted it) was successful, do not overemphasize them. Do not allow the results to take the focus away from the real issue: your ability to work successfully in a team situation.

ADVANTAGES OF THIS APPROACH

This approach will show that you understand the importance of good team instincts, and that you have a healthy appreciation for how much real teamwork is involved in getting an MBA. It will show that you are the generous, cooperative sort who will get on well with your teammates at school and help those who are not as well versed in team dynamics acclimate.

Choosing an example in which you were the leader of the team can show off your leadership skills as well, whereas choosing an example in which you were not the leader can illustrate your ability to contribute when you are not in charge. This is an important attribute at a top program in which everyone is accustomed to being a star.

TEAM ESSAYS

With schools asking a whole range of questions about applicants' performance on teams, it is useful to keep in mind the traditional model of team development when formulating your response. The four stages of team development are often described as "forming" (selecting members, getting used to one another), "storming" (as serious work gets under way, members battle one another about ideas and plans and how best to work together), "norming" (as members get to know one another's habits and strengths, accepted norms of conduct develop), and "performing" (the team functions at its best, with a consensus about goals and how to function as a true team).

Although this is an optimistic view, which overlooks the fact that team development is seldom so clearly linear (backtracking is frequent), and the "performing" stage is seldom a nirvana of high performance without personality or relationship problems, it does offer a useful checklist. When considering what you had to suffer through, or manage, or what went wrong and why, consult the following list for ideas:

STAGE	COMMON PROBLEMS
Forming	Little trust in each other, especially the leader Limited communication Question purpose of team Brainstorming unfocused Underestimate difficulty and nature of problems to be addressed Refusal to take responsibility for taking action (let alone solving problems) No agreement on ground rules for actions or meetings Team too large or too small, or lacks appropriate skill mix
Storming	Conflicts develop, but are kept submerged Cliques form Recognition of real difficulties faced, but considered too large Overwhelmed by difficulties Attempt to push problems onto others
Norming	Continued development of cliques Anger toward each other nearly out of control Anger toward team leader and more senior managers particularly acute Talk rather than action, as need to resolve conflicts deepens Organization recognizes and rewards individuals, not teams
Performing	Members take on leadership, resisting prior leaders Some members operate independently, risking team dissolution (or backtracking to prior stage) Communication threatens to break down Formerly interesting work now bores members: need for new challenges Team attempts too much or resolves key motivating problems (thereby losing its reason for being)

TEAM LEADERSHIP

When attempting to describe how you led a team, consider what you did to help avoid or mitigate the problems listed above. Then consult the following checklist to refresh your memory as to the various (additional) activities you might have performed as leader:

➤ *Coordinating the Team* (e.g., selecting members, ensuring that members are freed of competing responsibilities, coordinating with other teams working on related issues, making sure meetings take place, running meetings, staying on top of key analyses and actions, keeping team informed of developing issues)

➤ *Obtaining Resources* (e.g., staffing team with appropriate members, freeing members of competing responsibilities, substituting members with different skills as team's needs evolve, obtaining necessary funding)

➤ *Coaching Members* (e.g., providing help in solving specific analytical problems, coaching problem members, assisting members in handling personality conflicts, maintaining sense of urgency, shifting team toward self-management)

➤ *Implementing Solution* (e.g., helping team understand likely implementation difficulties, lining up support of key people outside team, helping team present analyses and plans to rest of firm, ensuring resources necessary for implementation made available)

➤ *Gaining Recognition for the Team* (e.g., initiating formal and informal parties and celebrations as important milestones reached, praising members, making sure people outside team recognize members' (and team's) work, tracking results, ensuring official recognition and rewards for team's results)

A major part of your role is to develop a dynamic, enthusiastic atmosphere in which members are inspired to perform at their best and thereby find fulfillment in helping the firm achieve its goals. This generally requires setting high standards and clear objectives, establishing a sense of the team's value, and using your own actions to create a model of honesty and consistency for the team.

BRIEF NOTES ON ADDITIONAL ESSAYS

QUESTION: WHAT DOES DIVERSITY MEAN TO YOU? HOW WILL YOU CONTRIBUTE TO THE DIVERSITY OF OUR PROGRAM?

■ You can define diversity in terms of nationality, language or culture, job history, age, educational background, political opinions, sex, aptitudes, or any of dozens of other matters. Your choice is likely to reflect your own experiences and, of course, the ways in which you are different from the norm at the program to which you are applying.

■ You should certainly have already asked yourself what this school is looking for and how you can appear valuable to it, so to be asked what diversity you can add should really just be making explicit something you have already had occasion to consider.

■ The second part of this question is largely a repeat of "what would you contribute while at our school?" so refer to the discussion of that question.

QUESTION: WHAT IS THE MOST DIFFICULT FEEDBACK YOU HAVE RECEIVED, AND HOW DID YOU ADDRESS IT?

- Your response to this question will benefit from seeing you have to confront an awkward truth about yourself rather than someone's mistaken impression. By the same token, the feedback should be about something substantial, perhaps calling into question your prospective future, conception of yourself, or core values. Getting a B- in a course hardly qualifies.

- It's fine to admit that you initially reacted badly to the feedback. Being defensive is a normal reaction when confronted with an unpleasant truth, a threat to your status in your organization, or a blow to your ego.

- If it took time to admit to the truth of the feedback, you can usefully show the stages you went through in coming to terms with it. This will add to the credibility of your claim that you did indeed own up to your faults.

- Of course, nothing suggests you came to terms with a difficult truth like a substantial change in your behavior. Show that this is the case. A willingness to accept that you were wrong testifies to your maturity and ability to learn from your mistakes (both of which are important qualities for a would-be senior manager).

- It would help if you can demonstrate that you now encourage in-depth, honest feedback. Similarly, showing that you probe it (unthreateningly), encouraging the person offering feedback to go further in discussing what you could do better (and how), would be all the better. The next steps should presumably be thanking her for the input, mulling it over to understand it fully, and then considering how best to put your new learning into practice.

QUESTION: DISCUSS A PROFESSIONAL PROJECT THAT CHALLENGED YOUR SKILLS

- Start by determining what your professional skills are.

- Look at the most challenging professional project you have faced, preferably one that was successful for you or one that taught you valuable lessons.

- After trying to remember it in real detail, abstract exactly which skills you used (or should have used, but have only come to appreciate since then).

- Remember the attributes your readers are looking for: analytical ability, interpersonal skills, leadership ability, dedication, integrity, and so on.

- Which of these attributes can you illustrate via one of your projects? Which are most important to your positioning effort? Which will be the most interesting to read about? Which can you get someone else to back up in a recommendation?

GENERAL RULES FOR APPROACHING ANY ESSAY QUESTION

It should be apparent after reading the above analyses of essay questions that a thoughtful approach is required when confronting any essay. Remember that a question does not exist in a vacuum. Instead, it is part of the whole application and should be answered in the context of how you wish the whole application package to read.

You will have started by determining what themes you wish to emphasize and how you will maximize your reward/risk ratio. As part of this, you will have chosen the "stories" you want to tell about yourself. This initial effort provides you with the context for an essay. When it is not clear which story to tell, remember these general rules for selection:

- The story is interesting.
- It is unusual.
- It shows you to have senior-management qualities.
- It reveals something not fully revealed elsewhere in the application.
- It is a story *you* should tell, rather than one a recommender should tell.
- It will aid your positioning effort.
- It can be backed up by a recommender.

THE ADMISSIONS DIRECTORS DISCUSS THE ESSAYS

General Advice

➤ The essays are open-ended; different lengths are appropriate for different stories. Our first essay is meant to let us know who you are and what you care about. The second focuses on the usual business school stuff: what do you want to do, and why. We want to see whether you have thought through why you want an MBA—and whether our program is right for you. We want to be sure you know that this is a graduate program, with a very serious, academic, social science underpinning to it. We want to know why you are choosing to pursue such a rigorous, academic program. Sharon Hoffman, Stanford

➤ Too many people try to impress us. Better that you should move us instead. Let us get to know you. We want to know what you've learned, not just what you've accomplished. The bottom line for me is your motivations and passions, not just your accomplishments. Rose Martinelli, Chicago

➤ We want to see how well you understand yourself and whether you are able to communicate this understanding. We want you to shine a mirror onto yourself. We want to know the person behind all those achievements, who you are and what you care about—what motivates you, what you are passionate about. (We're not here to judge what it is specifically, as long as it is not immoral or illegal.) We do care about how well you can communicate this, in writing (surely a lost skill), because communication is an important aspect of management. *Sharon Hoffman, Stanford*

➤ It's compelling to read the application of someone who clearly knows how Haas will help her reach her goals. People who don't know this are likely to be less committed to the academic needs of our program. *Peter Johnson, Haas*

➤ It's important to demonstrate why you want to attend this school. We're trying to assess credentials *and* fit with the school. The more [you] can show there's a good fit, the more confident we can be about it. *Dawna Clarke, Tuck*

➤ We place tremendous emphasis on the essays; they really make a difference to us. We look to find the person behind the achievements. At two o'clock in the morning, when you're taking a break in the midst of a project, you don't want to talk to a résumé who speaks polysyllabic business jargon; you want to talk to someone who's real and compelling. *Sharon Hoffman, Stanford*

➤ Being able to talk about how your past and current professional experience will be useful during your two years here is important. So is a discussion of how the ramping up of one's skill set on the program will help propel you professionally. *Sally Jaeger, Tuck*

➤ Brainstorm with other people, but think about your own strengths and try to give us insight into who you are, not who someone else (such as a consultant) tells you to be. You'll write much better if you talk about yourself rather than someone you aren't familiar with. It's easy to see when people aren't being themselves, and it hurts them. Being made to look like everyone else is not helpful to your chances. *Linda Meehan, Columbia*

➤ Don't give us a list of activities or accomplishments. Think instead about an activity, project, or experience that you can describe to illustrate your strengths. To show leadership in the workplace, for instance, I'd like to see you discuss a project, work group, etc., and use it as an example through which I can see your strengths and skills. This will be more memorable and unique, too. Ask your family and friends what they know about your work. Whatever you've told them about is probably a good essay topic. *Sarah E. Neher, Darden*

➤ Think before you write. Map out your responses before you start. It's great to get advice from people, but in the end you need to write it in your own voice so we can get a good sense of who you are. *Thomas Caleel, Wharton*

➤ The last thing we want is to see you quoting our brochures or our website. I always tell applicants that they're much more interesting than anything I can write because it's their lives, which are compelling and unique. There's some passion burning within you because you want to do something profound, you want to make a profound change in your life—personally, professionally, intellectually. That's why you're applying. So there's some passion there: get it out. Shape it, hone it, but get the story out. It'll be completely unique to who you are. And after looking at thousands of essays, the ones that pop off the page are those that are personal and passionate. *Isser Gallogly, Stern (NYU)*

➤ We read the application essays along with the GMAT AWA essays. We dislike formulaic approaches to essays, whether on the AWA or on the application form. When you're looking at hundreds of essays, those shine through as somewhat superficial. *Dr. Simon Learmount, Judge (Cambridge)*

➤ Applicants are welcome to converse with us about the essays before they apply. They can understand we're not looking for another "I admire Jack Welch" essay. If I have to read one more of those I'll go crazy. Instead, I really want to know who inspires you, who you are as an individual, what makes you unique, what is your true motivation. *Kirt Wood, Rotterdam*

➤ It's a bad idea to write what you think we want to hear. *Peter Johnson, Haas*

➤ We give a limited amount of space for responding to our questions, so differentiating between the essential and blah-blah-blah is critical. *Katty Ooms Suter, IMD (Switzerland)*

➤ Too many essays are the same. See if you can step outside yourself and really look at yourself. The worst thing is trying to tell us what you think we want to hear. I love a funny essay, but I also love essays that show what you think and what makes you tick. *Joelle du Lac, INSEAD*

Should You Submit an Optional Essay?

➤ By all means write an additional essay if something important cannot be addressed elsewhere. A typical example might be someone whose academic career had real peaks and valleys and who consequently needed to discuss the reasons for this. We do not, however, want repetitive information, nor do we want to see essays written for another school (which happens all too often). *Sally Jaeger, Tuck*

➤ It's appropriate to submit an additional essay to discuss an important issue not covered elsewhere. One example would concern explaining a career path prior to business school that does not appear to make any sense. It would be valuable to show why you chose the positions you did and how this relates to getting an MBA. *Peter Johnson, Haas*

➤ It's appropriate to explain a prior mistake, but it's critical to show what is different now. If you got poor grades before, what has changed to suggest that you'll do better now? *Anne Coyle, Yale*

➤ There's no chart laying out the answer to this. It's a matter of judgment. For instance, are you including something that couldn't fit in answer to another question? *THOMAS CALEEL, WHARTON*

➤ You should address something that is missing in your application or that raises questions. If you fail to address it or try to hide it, we'll assume the worst. *KATTY OOMS SUTER, IMD (SWITZERLAND)*

Should You Send Additional Materials?

➤ Don't send additional materials unless they are crucial to understanding who you are, what you do, and what you think. Few people are helped by the additional materials they give us. So think long and hard before sending something in. *SALLY JAEGER, TUCK*

➤ It's OK to submit a newspaper article about you, but almost surely a bad idea to submit a videotape of yourself. *ANN W. RICHARDS, JOHNSON (CORNELL)*

➤ When considering whether to submit additional materials, applicants need to consider what this says about how they'll come across to recruiters later on: whether they'll be seen as able to market themselves well or as annoying. *ANNE COYLE, YALE*

➤ Don't go overboard—no wedding pictures or high school yearbooks. *JOELLE DU LAC, INSEAD*

➤ We discourage people from submitting additional documents; the admissions committee doesn't have time to read them. *ALISON OWEN, SAÏD (OXFORD)*

➤ We tend not to look at extra materials. We want a perfectly level playing field. *DR. SIMON LEARMOUNT, JUDGE (CAMBRIDGE)*

10

How to Write Persuasive Essays

— EXECUTIVE SUMMARY —

◾

Examine your past and present (and goals for the future), and develop the information that you will need to write persuasive essays.
—See Chapter 8 and Appendix VI.

◾

Sift through the material to establish your most effective themes.

◾

Outline, then draft, a complete set of essays before finalizing any one of them.

◾

There is no excuse for basic mistakes: misspellings, grammatical errors, or inserting the wrong school's name into an essay.

◾

Follow this chapter's advice to maximize the impact of your essays.

◾

Allot substantial time to reorganizing and redrafting. Remember, "There is no such thing as good writing, just good rewriting."

*A*s Stanford puts it: "In other parts of the application we learn about your academic and professional accomplishments (i.e., *what* you have done). It is through your essays that we learn more about the person behind the grades, test scores, job titles, and leadership positions (i.e., *who* you are). Our goal is to gain insight into the person behind the résumé. . . . [W]e encourage you to share with us—through your essays—your passions, values, interests, and goals. While there are no 'right' answers here, we have found that the most effective essays emphasize the 'who' as well as the 'what.' Each candidate for admission has a set of unique experiences and perspectives to bring to the GSB community. This is your opportunity to 'talk' to us and to emphasize what you consider to be most important. Tell us your story, and tell it in a natural and honest way."

If you intend to rely on your "numbers" to get you admitted, you will be missing the opportunity to dramatically improve your chances. In fact, the better the school, the more likely it is that the objective data in your application will not determine your fate and that the essays in particular will weigh heavily in the decision.

Admissions officers will judge you on the basis of what your essays reveal about your writing ability (including your ability to persuade, structure and maintain a well-reasoned argument, and communicate in an interesting and professional manner); honesty and maturity; understanding of what the program offers and requires, and how well you would contribute to it; and clear (and believable) ideas about where you are headed. They will want to learn what you have accomplished, who you are as a person, and how well you can communicate. Admissions officers never take the approach of teachers who said, "I'll grade this on the basis of the content, not your writing style."

This chapter is designed to help you actually write your essays. You have learned from prior chapters the types of thing you are likely to want to say, but not how to say it; this chapter addresses that need. In addition to reading this chapter, however, learn about successful essay writing by examining some of the many examples contained in this book.

THE WRITING PROCESS: GETTING STARTED

BEFORE STARTING TO WRITE

Before you start to write, let us review what we know about your audience and its decision criteria.

Your audience is the set of admissions officers who will read your application. Chapter 6 described them as conscientious but nearly overwhelmed by the volume of material they read. They are highly familiar with the determinants of business school and career success. Thus, they will examine your application for convincing evidence of your intellectual ability, managerial and leadership potential, personal characteristics, and career plan. Being in the education business, they want applicants who clearly value learning and education. They will also like evidence that a person makes the most of opportunities, whether they be great or small.

By communicating effectively—showing that you understand what they are looking for, presenting your material in an organized and concise fashion, and not exaggerating or lying—you will gain credibility as a reliable source of information about yourself and as an appropriate candidate. Remember that as important as it is to be sure you are addressing the committee's concerns, your essays should reveal yourself and convey a true sense of who you are as a person. After all, this may be your only chance to do so.

What top business schools are looking for. The four principal criteria mentioned earlier—your intellectual ability, managerial and leadership potential, personal characteristics, and career plan—are common to all of the top schools. (For more detailed information, reread Chapters 7 and 8.)

What does a particular school look for? All schools look for certain traits, such as leadership ability. Yet not every school is looking for exactly the same sort of candidate. Some will concentrate on finding very internationally focused applicants, for example, whereas others want those who are technologically oriented. If you are aware of what a given school is looking for, you can emphasize those aspects of your candidacy that are most suited to their needs. The starting point for learning about a school's specific interests, as discussed in Chapter 3, is to read the material it publishes about itself and speak with its current students and recent graduates.

This chapter focuses on writing individual essays successfully, but bear in mind that each essay is part of a whole application package, consisting of multiple essays, résumé data, recommendations, and interview evaluation. To make sure you keep your eye on the need to provide a well-integrated, consistent application, do not try to finish any one essay until you have done at least a rough draft of all the essays for a given school.

PLANNING

It is important to plan your writing. Planning forces you to think about what you will write before you get tied up in the actual writing. Too many people take the opposite approach, writing random paragraphs, hoping to be able to glue them together later, or trying to write the whole of an essay before thinking about it. The results of these approaches are all too predictable. The material included is a haphazard selection of what might be presented, and the writing is not necessarily organized and coherent. No amount of editing will cure this problem, which is not merely a problem of word choice or transitions. The greatest problem with the write-before-thinking approach is that after expending great efforts, writers are disappointed with the results and must go back to what should have been the starting point—*thinking about what they should say.*

WRITING

1. DEVELOP YOUR MATERIAL

All too many essays sound the same. The poor admissions officer who has to read 5,000 essays, or many more, gains no understanding of an applicant who writes half a dozen essays that could have been written by any of another 500 applicants to the same school. Few applicants take the time to ask what makes them unusual or unique (or valuable). *Your goal is to develop materials that will help you to write stories unique to you, which no one but you could tell.*

Failing to develop your material or examine yourself thoroughly will lead to dull generalities and mark your application with a deathly sense of unsophistication. You will not do yourself any favors by writing "My travels broadened my horizons by exposing me to different cultures" or "The experience taught me that with hard work and determination I can reach my goals." Statements like these do not merit space in your essays if you want to dazzle the admissions committee.

Pulling together the relevant material for your application essays will take substantial effort, especially if you have been working for a number of years at different jobs. The material that might be relevant to the essays could come from virtually any time in your life, and be from any episode or experience.

The best way to start the process of generating material is to fill out the Personal Organizer in the appendix to Chapter 8. As you can see at a glance, there are numerous things to note. Try to fill this out over a period of time, because you will be unlikely to remember everything this calls for in one sitting. Referring to your résumé should be helpful. In fact, you might find it helpful to refer back to earlier versions of your résumé, if you still have them. You may also want to look at your school and university transcripts to refresh your memory.

Consider keeping a notebook (or an electronic file) handy for jotting down ideas, stories, or details about your past or your goals for the future. Reading this book and the many examples in it may also spur your memory. I encourage you to take personal notes in the margins regarding your own experiences.

When you have completed the Personal Organizer, you should have far too much material to use in your essays. This is as it should be. You should feel you have a wealth of material from which you can pick the most appropriate items.

2. ORGANIZE YOUR MATERIAL

Once you have generated your raw material, what will you actually say? If you have already read Chapter 8 and filled out the Personal Organizer, you may have determined what your main themes will be. Now is a good time to recheck that they still make sense in light of the information you have available. Do you have good stories that illustrate your brilliance as an analyst? Do you have the right grades in the most closely related courses to claim this? If not, now is the right time to reconsider your positioning. Think in terms of what would be appropriate organizing themes given the information you do have.

After you have generated your information, you must organize it. There are many methods for doing so. One good way is to try to see what the core of your message is. In other words, what key points are you trying to make? If you can state these, the next step is to group your supporting material according to the appropriate points.

To organize your thinking effectively, it is generally a good idea to outline your essay. This will save you time because the outline will make it clear whether you have too much or too little material, and provides a logical means of organizing your material. It will also allow you to make changes early in the process rather than work on something that does not belong, only to eliminate it after squandering time on it. In other words, the outline is a check on your thinking.

HOW TO MAKE AN OUTLINE

There are several outlining methods commonly used. All follow the same general rule, listing primary organizing ideas against the left-hand margin, with supporting materials indented to indicate their subordination to a larger idea.

I. Primary idea
     A. Subordinate idea
     B. Subordinate idea
          1. Sub-subordinate idea
          2. Sub-subordinate idea
               a. Sub-sub-subordinate idea
          3. Sub-subordinate idea
II. Primary idea
     A. Subordinate idea

It does not particularly matter which outlining method you use. It only matters that it can perform the important functions needed: pulling together related material, showing how idea groups relate to one another, and showing which ideas are primary and in what ways supporting ideas are to be subordinated. You may even find that you start with an informal outline and progress to a more formal one as your ideas become clearer.

3. REVIEW BASIC WRITING RULES

It is usually a good idea, especially for those who are not accustomed to writing anything more than short memos, to review the elements of good writing style. I suggest perusing the latest edition of Strunk & White's *Elements of Style*. It is a good idea to have a book like this on hand as you write and rewrite, in case you need to check up on your grammar or word usage.

4. PREPARE THE ROUGH DRAFT

The fourth step in the writing process is a rough draft. Be sure you are not too demanding of yourself at this point. Even though you want to do a good job, here "the perfect is the enemy of the good." If you are unwilling to write down anything that is less than final-draft quality, you are highly likely to be unable to write anything at all. Rather than take this perfectionist approach, be sure to limit your goal to that of producing a rough draft that incorporates most of the basic points you want to make. Do not be concerned if the order you had planned to follow no longer seems to work well, or if you cannot quite express your exact thought, or if your word choice is awkward. Get something reasonable down on paper as a starting point.

Writers use any number of different strategies when they start writing. No one method is to be recommended above others. This is very much a matter of personal preference. You can use any of the following methods. Choose the one (or invent one of your own) that gets you started on the road to producing a reasonably complete draft.

START WITH THE CONCLUSION

Writers who use this method feel they cannot write the body of the essay until they know what they are leading up to.

START WITH THE INTRODUCTION

When an introduction lays out clearly what will follow, it in effect controls the body of the paper. Some writers like to start with the introduction in order to make sure they have a grip on the body of the paper before trying to write it.

START WITH ANY OF THE PARAGRAPHS OF THE BODY

Some writers like to pick any self-contained part of the body of the paper and write it up, then move on to another part, and then another. These writers like to build the substantive parts of the paper first, and then provide an introduction and conclusion based upon this substance.

WRITE SEVERAL DIFFERENT DRAFTS, STARTING IN DIFFERENT PLACES

This approach involves taking one perspective or starting point for writing a draft, then plowing through the entirety. Then the writer does the same thing from another perspective or starting point. Later, the writer can choose one draft or another, or cut and paste using pieces of each.

A majority of people use the third method—writing paragraphs of the body of the paper. They typically write them individually, then place them together in their predetermined order, and only then develop an introduction and conclusion. They take this approach because they know certain aspects of the subject well and can write about them easily, but require more thought to fill in the remaining pieces, such as the introduction and conclusion.

TWO WAYS TO AVOID WRITER'S BLOCK

Many people find themselves "blocked" when they try to write. They sit and stare at the paper or computer, and it stares back at them. To avoid this, do not put pressure on yourself to do too much at once. When you are in the early part of the writing process, try simply to get the basic elements of your thinking about each subtopic down on paper. Do not worry about the quality of what you are writing until you are editing.

➤ *Technique one.* After you have thought about an essay, try to write down on index cards phrases that convey your various ideas. (Or, of course, use a computer to do the same thing.) Don't plan for too long; just write down the phrases as they occur to you. Then organize the cards into related groups of ideas. Write paragraphs expressing these ideas, perhaps trying to link the related ones together. Then, see if you can place these paragraphs into a reasonably logical order. Next, put this structure into a proper outline, to see if it makes sense. If it does, link the paragraphs with appropriate transitions. If it doesn't, try reordering the paragraphs.

➤ *Technique two.* If it is still too difficult to get rolling with the first method, involve a friend in the process. Explain to your pal what you are trying to convey. Have her take notes on what you are saying. Organize those notes into a logical order, with her help, and then explain yourself to her again, being sure to follow your notes to keep things in order. If you record this and transcribe your recording, you will have a solid rough draft, which you can start to edit.

---

5. EDIT YOUR ROUGH DRAFT

Remember that "the only good writing is rewriting." When you start to edit your rough draft, you are doing your first part of this rewriting.

One of the most important aspects of the editing stage is its timing. Editing without a break between the drafting and the editing stages will limit your insight into the flaws of your draft. You will not see where you skipped a needed transition or explanation because you are too close to the original writing. If you can take a break—at least a night or, better yet, a week—you will be better able to read your draft from the perspective of an outsider.

Make sure you have edited your draft for substance—for what points will remain and what points will be eliminated—before you start editing the language. Otherwise you will devote time and effort to improving the wording of material that should be discarded. (Even worse, you are likely to keep it in your draft if you have gone to the trouble of making it sound good.) This section assumes you will revise your essay three times. In fact, if you are a good writer and have taken the time to think through an essay before doing your first draft, you might well need to edit it only once or, more likely, twice. By the same token, if you are struggling with an essay, it might require more than three revisions to sort out the problems.

One warning: Do not view editing as taking the life out of your essay. In fact, editing's role is to clear out the dead wood, making your points stand out as clearly as possible.

6. REVISE YOUR FIRST DRAFT

The initial revision should focus on the essay as a whole.

Do you accomplish your objective?

Does your essay directly answer the question? Is your main idea clear?

Revise for content

The typical rough draft may have too little and too much material, all at the same time. It will have just touched the surface of some portions of the essay, without providing explanation or convincing detail. At the same time, it may have discussed things that do not contribute significantly to your major points.

A good essay eliminates extraneous material while including all the information necessary to make your point. Your reader needs sufficient evidence to accept what you are saying, so be sure you have adequately developed and supported your main idea. Material that does this belongs, but material that is unrelated to the main idea should be eliminated.

Finally, avoid belaboring the obvious (admissions directors know what an audit is), but do not assume an inappropriate amount of technical knowledge (admissions directors may not know the difficulties in writing a certain type of code).

Revise for organization

A well-organized essay will group similar ideas together and put them in the proper order. To be sure that your draft is in an appropriate order, try to outline it. If it is easy to produce an outline from the draft, and there is a clear logic to the flow of the material, you can be reasonably certain that you have a well ordered essay. Otherwise, reorder your material.

Revise for length

Is your essay approximately the right length? If it is substantially longer than the stated word limit, consider how to reduce the supporting material. If it is shorter than allowed, consider whether to leave it at that length (which is a good thing if the essay successfully communicates what should be your main points) or to expand it by making additional points or providing additional supporting material. If the essay is significantly shorter than the suggested length, you probably need more depth. If you feel you have nothing more to say, you might consider rethinking your choice of topic.

7. REVISE YOUR SECOND DRAFT

Assuming you have successfully revised the first draft of the essay and the content is as you wish it to be, turn your attention to the components of the essay: the paragraphs, sentences, and individual words.

REVISE PARAGRAPHS

A proper paragraph should make only one major point. The easiest way to organize a paragraph is to start with a topic sentence—one that makes the major point of the paragraph—and then to explain or illustrate that point in following sentences. For business writing, starting most or all paragraphs with a topic sentence is often appropriate, particularly for inexperienced writers.

Look next at the length of your paragraphs. Most writers tend to one extreme or the other: Either all their paragraphs are very short or all are very long. A mixture of lengths is a good idea. Having most of your paragraphs between 30 and 150 words is also wise. The occasional paragraph that is substantially shorter or longer is fine, but they should be the exception rather than the rule. The reasons for this are simple: Too many short paragraphs make you look simple-minded—unable to put together a complex idea or group related ideas together—whereas long paragraphs will discourage reading by any but the most conscientious reader. Use short paragraphs for emphasis; use long paragraphs for discussion of complicated points or examples.

The three methods you can use to develop your main idea are to provide *examples*, *explanation*, or *details*. Reading an essay that lacks these three components tends to be unsatisfying and unconvincing. Generalities ("I am a very determined fellow") are unconvincing unless supported with specific examples and explanations.

REVISE FOR FLOW

Even when you have well-written paragraphs placed in the right order, your writing may still be difficult to read because it lacks suitable transitions between ideas or any other means of showing how the ideas relate. For our purposes, the most important method of relating ideas will be using transition words and phrases. Some typical transitions include:

Purpose	*Typical Transitions*
Amplification	furthermore, moreover, in addition
Cause and effect	therefore, consequently, as a result, accordingly
Conclusion	as a result, therefore, thus, in conclusion
Contrast	although, but, despite, however, on the one hand/on the other hand
Example	for example, for instance, specifically
Sequence	first/second, former/latter, first of all/second of all

One other easy way to connect paragraphs is to have the beginning of one paragraph follow directly from the end of the prior paragraph. For example, if you have just said "I needed the chance to show what I could do without over-bearing supervision" at the end of one paragraph, the next one could start out with "My opportunity to prove myself came with the founding of a new office in Toronto." In this example the relationship between the two paragraphs is ensured by having the second grow organically from the end of the first.

Be sure each sentence follows logically from the prior sentence.

CHECK YOUR INTRODUCTION

Make sure it not only introduces your subject but also grabs the audience whenever possible. (If you are writing seven essays for a given school, for example, at least two or three of them should have attention-getting introductions.) A good introduction is interesting as well as successful at conveying your main points. It should appeal to the reader and set the tone for the whole essay. There are many effective openings. You can state an important and interesting fact, refer to something currently in the news, refer to a personal experience, ask a question that you will answer in your essay, or simply state your general point of view. Do not restate the question; it wastes valuable space and is a weak, plodding way to begin.

CHECK YOUR CONCLUSION

A good conclusion does one or more of the following:

- Pulls together different parts of the essay
- Rephrases your main ideas (without repeating anything word for word)
- Shows the importance of the material
- Makes a recommendation

- Makes a forecast
- Points toward the future—showing, for example, how you will make use of something you have learned
- Gives a sense of completion

It should not make a new point that belongs in the body rather than the conclusion, nor should it sound tacked on. The concluding paragraph should develop organically from the material that preceded it.

REVISE SENTENCES AND WORDS

Most essay writers pile on one long sentence after another. Avoid this by breaking up some of the longer sentences to provide variety. Use short sentences to make important points, long sentences to explain complex ideas or develop examples. Also, use a variety of sentence structures to maintain reader interest. Do not, for example, use a "not only . . . but also . . ." structure in every other sentence. Eliminate sentences that sound awkward or choppy when read aloud.

Edit your sentences to eliminate imprecise or wordy language. For example, use "although" instead of "despite the fact that." Add vigor to your writing by eliminating clichés, using fresh and interesting descriptions, and trying to write as much as possible with nouns and verbs, rather than primarily with adjectives (which slow the pace and reduce impact). Similarly, write in the active voice. (Say "I kicked the ball" rather than "the ball was kicked by me.")

REVISE FOR TONE

Your tone can be assertive without being arrogant. Your essays should sound confident, enthusiastic, and friendly. Be sure to avoid pleading ("I'd give anything if you would just let me in.") and whining ("I never do well on those awful standardized tests; it's so unfair that schools even look at the results.").

One way to check the tone of your essay is to read it aloud. Read it first to yourself and then, once it sounds appropriate to you, try reading it to a friend. Get his suggestions regarding what the strong and weak points are, whether there are any mistakes in it, and whether it sounds like you. Does it reflect your personal style? The ideal essay should sound just like your voice, but without repetitious and awkward phrasings and use of such filler as "you know" and "like" (if you speak like that). It should sound relaxed rather than formal, but still flow smoothly.

Some applicants, remembering a high school textbook, try to avoid writing in the first person. In fact, it is not only appropriate to use "I" when writing your essays but essential that you do so. You are being asked to give personal statements, so do not write in the distant and aloof third person.

8. REVISE YOUR THIRD DRAFT

REVISE AGAIN FOR STYLE

See the comments above.

REVISE FOR GRAMMAR, PUNCTUATION, AND SPELLING

The way to spot grammatical mistakes and faulty punctuation is to read your essays over slowly, preferably after having put them aside for some time. Reading them aloud can also help this process. Even if your sense of grammar is keen, however, consider having a friend whose grasp of grammar is extremely good read over each essay. Spell-check the final product; do so yourself, as well as by computer, to catch words that exist but are not what you intended (for example, "manger" instead of "manager").

CHECK THE LENGTH (AGAIN)

One of the key factors affecting most of the essays you will write is that the business schools generally prescribe their maximum length. Failing to observe this constraint raises questions about your willingness to pay attention to the rules that will apply in other situations, so avoid going over the limits. Most schools do not mind your slightly exceeding the limits on one or two essays, but a pattern of exceeding the limits strikes even these schools as unfair. They have established these limits to provide a level playing field for the applicants; someone who exceeds the limits is seen as trying to assert an unfair advantage.

Three revisions is not a magic number, but will be a minimum for most people. There is nothing wrong with putting your work through more revisions.

9. GIVE YOUR ESSAYS TO SOMEONE ELSE TO CRITIQUE

After you have edited the essays to your own satisfaction, or gotten stuck, hand them to several people whose views on writing you respect. They can provide you with an objective view that you may not be able to bring to the essays yourself. Pay attention to their opinions, but do not give up control of what are, after all, your essays, not theirs. Do not let them remove the life from your essays.

10. PROOFREAD

Why proofread your paper if you have been careful in composing the final draft? No matter how careful you have been, errors are still likely to crop up. Taking a last look at the essay is a sensible precaution.

What are you looking for? Basically, the task at this point is no longer to make sure the structure is correct; it is to spot any errors or omissions in your sentences and individual words. Errors tend to show up most often where prior changes were made. Combining two paragraphs into one, for example, may have resulted in the loss of a necessary transition phrase. Grammatical mistakes can also live on.

As with any task that is essentially a matter of editing, your timing is of the essence. Wait until you have already finished what you consider to be your final draft. If you can then put this draft down for a few days, you will be able to give it an effective last look. If not, you risk being unable to see mistakes because you are still too close to the writing. Another useful precaution is to have a friend proofread your essays.

TIPS FOR GOOD WRITING

Do:

- *Give yourself the time to do the essays right.* Start early; it will take time to do the essays. The results will also be better if you take time between steps rather than try to finish an application in a hurry.

- *Answer the question.* Never substitute an essay on another topic, even if it was your best essay for another school. You risk an automatic rejection for failing to do as directed. It is occasionally appropriate to combine your answers to two questions into one if the answers you will give are inevitably linked, but be sure to explain what you are doing and your rationale for doing so.

- *Use humor, but only if it works.* Few people can write humorous prose or recount humorous stories effectively, but if you can manage it, you will definitely distinguish yourself. To check whether you are succeeding, have several people read to make sure it works on paper as well as it would if you were to tell it. Be sure it is not vicious or off-color humor, as this has no place in a business school essay.

- *Keep the focus on you.* For example, do not get carried away in describing the outcome of a project without showing how this relates to you and your efforts.

- *Explain events whenever appropriate.* Many of the things you have done are mainly of interest because of what you learned from them, what you thought about them, and why you did them.

■ *Favor a full description of one event rather than a listing of several.* It is generally better to describe one event or accomplishment at some length rather than to mention a number of them without explaining why you undertook something, what it meant to you, and what you learned from it.

■ *Be specific.* The more specific you make your writing, the more you personalize it and the better the chance that it will be interesting. Generalizations, without specific information and examples, are weak and not necessarily believable. Examples add interest to generalities as well as make generalities clear.

■ *Be reluctant to cast everything in black-and-white terms.* Readers will tend not to trust or believe essays that give only one side of an argument. For example, if you are suggesting making a change in your company's organizational structure, you may be right, but it would be peculiar if absolutely no argument could be advanced to provide some support to the opposing viewpoint.

■ *Use bold and italics to increase readability, but resist overusing them.* Bold print and italics can be helpful in making your meaning clear, but use them sparingly. The essays you are asked to write are much too short, however, to use titles, subheadings, and the like.

■ *Use an appropriate amount of space.* It is generally acceptable to exceed word or line limits slightly, but doing so consistently or without a good reason suggests that you are unable to get to the point or establish appropriate priorities.

■ *Find someone to edit your work.* Explain what you are trying to accomplish and who will be reading your essays, so that your "editor" can both determine whether you are meeting your objectives and correct your grammar. The test of your writing is what the reader understands, not what your intent may have been.

Do Not:

■ *Start to write until you understand what your most important contributions to this program will be.* Reread this school's brochure and the other materials you have gathered and remind yourself of why you are applying to this school (beyond its high ranking or reputation). Review the school's recommendation forms to see specifically what it is looking for in its applicants.

■ *Use your limited space to recite information that is available elsewhere in the application,* such as listing your part-time jobs or mentioning your GMAT results.

■ *Give superficial answers.* Take the application seriously and work accordingly.

- *Pretend to be someone other than yourself.* It will undoubtedly sound phony.

- *Lie or exaggerate.* Doing so causes all of your assertions to be doubted—and many people who have lied have been caught. When this occurs, admissions officers often share the information with their colleagues at other leading schools, thereby eliminating your chance of attending any top school.

- *Think that an essay limit also defines the required minimum amount to write.* No one has failed to get into a business school for failure to write the maximum number of words on an essay. When you have said all that you intend to say, stop.

- *Feel compelled to write the optional essay.* When schools ask if you have anything else to add to an application, far too many people use the opportunity to write another essay that does nothing to enhance their position. Resist the urge unless you can add an important new perspective to your candidacy.

- *Use a minuscule type size to shrink an essay* to a given number of lines, or reduce its borders to nothing. Remember that your readers have to read literally thousands of essays and will not appreciate being forced to squint or use a magnifying glass.

- *Start by saying, "In this essay I will write about . . ."*

- *Use cute or meaningful quotations unless they fit perfectly and do not make people wince when they read them.* Too many people seem to have been taught to start everything they write with a cute epigram, regardless of the fact that it may not fit the subject well or match its desired tone. Shakespeare, Napoleon, and Mark Twain all said a lot of marvelous things, but that does not necessarily mean you should quote them.

- *Use a definition to begin your essay*, absent a very strong justification. This is too often a sophomoric way to begin, so avoid using this crutch.

- *Use only bullet points.* Writing an essay requires that you use full sentences.

- *Complain about the essay topic.* The person reading your essay may be the one who thought up the topic. Besides, you should avoid complaining in general.

- *Discuss your low grades, poor GMAT score, or other weak aspects of your record* unless you have a very good (and plausible) reason for doing so. If, for example, you worked full time and attended school full time, saying so provides the context within which to judge your grades. A simple explanation is appropriate.

- *Use fancy vocabulary for its own sake.* Use the simplest possible language to explain your meaning precisely.

- *Preach.* Provide support for your viewpoint but do not keep repeating your belief.

- *Bore the reader.* A fresh and well-written essay will aid your application effort.

THE ADMISSIONS DIRECTORS DISCUSS HOW TO WRITE THE ESSAYS

Why the Essays Matter So Much

➤ The essays provide a test of succinctness: how well you write them in a short space and still stand out. Business writing is typically short. On the practical side, the essays are meant to be kept short because there is a limit to how much we as an admissions office can get through. *JUDITH GOODMAN, MICHIGAN*

➤ The essays are critical because we need to get to know the person even without meeting him. What I like best is when someone tells the story of his or her life—what influenced and shaped the person, what made him what he is today. I want to learn about his current job, of course, but also about the activities he's passionate about when not in the office. This makes a two-dimensional application more like a three-dimensional person. *ANNE COYLE, YALE*

➤ We have all the data points (where they worked, their GPA, etc.), but ultimately we're admitting an individual. That's why our process is so individualized: we really get to know an individual who will, after all, be a member of the Stern family. You want to express who you are, where you're headed, and why this is important to you—the context behind that data. The essays are where we learn who people really are and what they have to offer. *ISSER GALLOGLY, STERN (NYU)*

➤ If you fail to write your essays seriously, we will assume that you don't care enough about getting into our school to warrant our taking your application seriously. *ANN W. RICHARDS, JOHNSON (CORNELL)*

Should You Ever Exceed the Word Limits?

➤ We don't count the number of words, but what is not appropriate is greatly exceeding the limits. Good writing is concise. Rambling on does not make something important. *SALLY JAEGER, TUCK*

➤ We expect that all applicants will adhere to the word limits provided. *BRIT DEWEY, HARVARD*

➤ No. But it's also not a good idea to turn in 250 words for a thousand-word essay. *THOMAS CALEEL, WHARTON*

➤ No. They're hard coded into the application, but some people hack the program to be able to write more. Unfortunately for them, this definitely does not help their chances. *DR. SIMON LEARMOUNT, JUDGE (CAMBRIDGE)*

➤ We value candidates who can express their message with the amount of space given, which shows a good capacity of synthesis. Should the candidate really think that more space is needed to express other contents, he or she can do so. The school will evaluate if it really was the case or if, instead, it was a mere repetition. *Rossana Camera, Bocconi (Italy)*

➤ One should never exceed essay word limits, nor should one ever submit extra essays. Students who refuse to acknowledge word counts, and who assume that if they give you a long-winded essay, particularly when describing their career, figure this is going to be impressive, but it's actually the biggest turnoff ever. It means they've not read the application form or they're not able to express themselves concisely; if they can't do that, they'll have problems on the program. *Julia Tyler, London*

Advice

➤ Put simply, the person who does thoroughly research his or her MBA options will in most cases write more effective essays. *Linda Baldwin, UCLA*

➤ They have to be readable. People should use a decent size font and language people can understand. *James Millar, Harvard*

➤ A lot of people should review a good book about writing before tackling the essays. *Sally Jaeger, Tuck*

➤ Some are very personal; these are often the ones that hit me. When I read one that whines about undergraduate grades, I can't help but think, "Let's get on with it." *Linda Meehan, Columbia*

➤ Follow the directions. If we say we want essays double-spaced and single-sided, that's what we mean. Similarly, answer the question we ask, not one you might prefer to answer. *Sally Jaeger, Tuck*

➤ The first step in writing your essays is to assess yourself. Next, read and *understand* the questions; then answer them. Determine the themes you want to convey, and sort them by question. Figure out what you want to put where. In other words, scope out your presentation before you even begin. Figure out where you can show your strengths, what weaknesses you need to explain—and where you can do so. Outline the whole set of essays. The biggest mistake applicants make is looking at each piece of an application on its own instead of seeing the whole application as one piece. *Rose Martinelli, Chicago*

Effective Writing

➤ Good writing is focused: It goes to the heart of the question and answers it directly. It is also interesting, using interwoven personal examples to good effect. An element of personality showing through helps makes me want to keep reading. *James Hayes, Michigan*

➤ Effective writing shows who the applicant is and conveys a real spark. Of course, it is also grammatically correct. *Peter Johnson, Haas*

➤ The essays I enjoy most are those offering a good glimpse of who the person is, not just what they've achieved. Some essays are excellent because they're creative, others because of their humor, and still others because of the vivid vignettes that illustrate the applicant's experiences. Let your personality show through essays. People too often try to anticipate what we want to hear. Instead, make sure they sound like you. *Dawna Clarke, Tuck*

Most Common Mistakes

➤ A lot of candidates are hurt by trying to imitate another person's essays, which are inappropriate for them and certainly lack the ring of authenticity. Plus, we're likely to have read the original essays (and perhaps dozens of attempts to imitate them!), which makes the imitation immediately apparent to us. *Michele Rogers, Kellogg*

➤ Applicants routinely do a poor job (or no job) of proofreading. It's remarkable how often we run across spelling mistakes, grammatical errors, and so on. *Sally Jaeger, Tuck*

➤ Far too many write ten times the number of words we ask for, which shows poor judgment. Some people share information that is simply too personal for an essay. One shared the problem his dog was having. He had to help the dog relieve himself several times per day. That applicant was known forever after as "the dog-squeezer." *Anne Coyle, Yale*

➤ Plenty of essays reflect having too many cooks in the kitchen: we get no idea of who the applicant really is. Not answering the question. Trying to be overly elegant and fancy. Being overly creative: we don't need a rhyming couplet. *Thomas Caleel, Wharton*

➤ Each school has questions specific to it that show what the school is about. So you can't just plug the same answers into different essays for different schools. It doesn't work. You may have some core ideas, themes, or content that work across the board, but you can't just take an essay and put it into everybody's application. So be sure you answer the question asked. *Isser Gallogly, Stern (NYU)*

➤ Failure to spell-check and leaving in the name of a different school than the one you're now applying to. Running on and boring the people who are reading the applications. Remember that we read over five thousand applications, so if you keep repeating the same thing, you aren't helping yourself. *Linda Meehan, Columbia*

➤ You'd be surprised how many people cut and paste essays from books. There's nothing worse than that. (Also,) it is crucial to show that they know our program well. If we get the feeling that the application could just as readily be sent to another school, the candidate won't make it past the first stage of our process. *Katty Ooms Suter, IMD (Switzerland)*

➤ The worst essays may be those that fail to answer the question, or those that make statements that can't be supported by the person's history. *Julia Tyler, London*

➤ There are two frequent problems: The essays are far too long or they are filled with charts and graphs, which are inappropriate for essays. *Alison Owen, Saïd (Oxford)*

REUSING YOUR ESSAYS

Business schools want to learn similar things about their applicants, so they tend to ask many of the same (or similar) questions. This is good for you to the extent that you can reuse your essays and cut down on the amount of work you have to devote to additional applications. On the other hand, few things annoy admissions officers more than to receive essays that were obviously written for another school, particularly if the other school's name was left in them.

It is possible to recycle your essays as long as you do so intelligently. The reason for doing so—to save time and effort—is compelling enough that almost everyone will try to use the best essays in more than one application.

There are several situations that require you to make more of a change to a previously used essay than just to switch school names:

■ Your positioning for this school may be different, requiring that you alter your essays sufficiently to reflect your changed positioning.

■ If you applied to one school that required just a few essays, you may have packed brief descriptions of several events into one essay. When writing for a school that has more essay questions, you may spread out these events and use them in several essays. This could also involve lengthening your description of the events. (The reverse process would be appropriate when changing from an application with many questions to one with only a few.)

■ Similarly, the change in essay questions from one school to another may mean that you will no longer answer a question in which you had previously told your most important story. If so, you will probably want to find room for it in one of the essays you are going to submit to the new school.

- Another reason to change your essay is to shorten or lengthen it to conform to a second school's requirements.

  —To lengthen an essay, you may wish to include more examples, elaborate the examples you have already used, or even add additional main points.

  —To shorten an essay, keep your major points but reduce your elaboration of them.

- The hardest part of combining several essays into one is finding a theme that will unite them. If you can do that, it is a simple matter to link them with transition sentences.

FURTHER READING

The Economist Style Guide (The Economist).

Stuart Berg Flexner, ed., *The Random House Dictionary of the English Language* (Random House).

William Strunk Jr. and E. B. White, *The Elements of Style* (Macmillan).

Joseph M. Williams, *Style: Ten Lessons in Clarity and Grace* (Addison-Wesley).

William Zinsser, *On Writing Well* (HarperCollins).

11

RECOMMENDATIONS

— EXECUTIVE SUMMARY —

■

Choosing recommenders correctly is critically important.

■

Approaching potential recommenders must be done carefully.
—Give them a chance to say no.
—Explain why you want an MBA, and why you have chosen the schools you have.
—Explain how important their recommendations will be.
—Brief them fully regarding what they should write.
—Emphasize telling relevant, rich stories.

■

Make their job as easy as possible.

WHY ARE RECOMMENDATIONS REQUIRED?

Applicants complain that recommendations are a waste of time because "all applicants can find someone to say something good about them." These applicants are right to believe that most people *can* find a supporter, but they are wrong about the importance of the recommendation process.

To understand how they can be both right and wrong at the same time, let us compare two applicants, George and Martha. Both George and Martha are 26 and have been working as sales representatives for a sporting goods manufacturer for four years. They both went to a well-known school of Ivy League caliber.

George asks his former basketball coach and his favorite economics professor to write his recommendations. The coach says that George is a popular guy who really loved basketball and was a talented player. His economics professor notes that George loved economics and recollects George's off-stated desire to make a lot of money.

Martha asks her current and prior direct supervisors to write her recommendations. Her first boss quantifies her standing as a sales representative. In her first year she was in the top 50 percent of reps; in her second year she was in the top 10 percent; in her third year she was one of the top five reps out of a total of 180. He explains that she was acutely conscious of having numerous shortcomings when she started but was determined to study the best performers to figure out what she could learn. She also paid careful attention to what her boss said were her shortcomings and what could be done to overcome them. He then illustrated her efforts by recounting how she overcame two specific problems. He concluded by saying that although approximately twenty-five people from the company had applied to top business schools in the last three years, she was unquestionably the best candidate of the lot.

Martha's current supervisor explains, among many other things, that she had risen to be the second-best sales rep in the company, and had been tapped to be the model salesperson newcomers "shadowed" for three days as the culmination of their training. She was chosen because she not only sold effectively but was also able to explain to new reps how to do so—a quality lacking in most reps. In fact, having someone tag along probably cost her a substantial amount of time, but her sales results did not reflect this.

Which one would you prefer as a study-group partner? Martha is clearly the stronger candidate even though George got his recommenders to say good things about him. Martha, however, got a lot more mileage out of her recommendations. She chose the right people to recommend her. She also had them write about important attributes where business school and career success are concerned, and they did so in highly believable ways.

The rest of this chapter is devoted to analyzing how to get your best supporters to do the same.

WHAT DO ADMISSIONS COMMITTEES LEARN FROM YOUR RECOMMENDATIONS?

1. *Your claims are true.* Recommendations are examined first for the extent to which they confirm and support your claims and your positioning. If your essays state that you are a very successful deal-maker for your firm, the admissions officers reading your file will look closely at what your boss has to say to see whether your claim is legitimate.

2. *You have many qualifications.* Recommendations play another important role. They are an opportunity to provide *more information about you,* preferably in the form of stories and illustrations of general points the recommenders wish to make.

3. *Your managerial skills are up to snuff.* You must decide who should write on your behalf, determine what you want your recommenders to say, get them to say what you want said (in the most helpful manner), and get them to send in the recommendations on time. These are typically people over whom you have no authority, so you will have to use influence rather than clout. Thus, the recommendation process is a test of your abilities as a persuader.

4. *You can accurately evaluate others and their perceptions of you.* If you end up choosing someone who writes a mediocre recommendation, your judgment will be questioned at the very least. It may even be assumed that you simply could not find two people who would say something good about you. A mediocre recommendation is death to an application. Bad recommendations are eternal damnation.

One of the telltale signs that an applicant is not strong enough, or has too little experience, is that the recommenders and the applicant himself all tell the same one or two stories. This suggests that the applicant has had few successes.

WHO SHOULD WRITE YOUR RECOMMENDATIONS?

Selecting appropriate recommenders involves sifting many factors. Here we will assume you are to submit two recommendations. (In the next section we will consider what to do if you are asked to submit three.) In general, you will be expected to submit recommendations from people who know you and are well placed to address the key issues concerning your candidacy. As we have already discussed, you will want them to state that you have the appropriate managerial potential, intellectual ability, and personal character. In the past, one recommendation from a current or former boss and one from a professor was the norm. Now, however, getting two recommendations from the workplace is desirable. These can be from your current boss and her boss, from your current boss and your former boss, etc.

Your choice is easier if there are not a lot of obvious candidates. For example, you may have reported to the same person at your company for the last three years, and she likes you and is willing to help you. During that same period, you may have had a "dotted-line" reporting relationship to the engineering manager, who is also happy to help you. In this case, the two obvious choices are likely to be highly appropriate. If this is the case, you are more likely to be concerned about how best to approach and manage these two recommenders than about how to choose among many possibilities.

Most people, however, are not in this position. Some do not dare tell a current boss that they are considering leaving the company. Others work for family companies, and the only boss they have had is Mom or Dad. Here is a starting point for choosing recommenders:

1. Choose people who *know you well*. Do not choose people who are famous (or extremely senior in your company) but will only be able to say that you seem like a nice person and apparently did a superlative job handing out fliers on a local street corner during the last senatorial campaign. Instead, choose people who can make the recommendation *credible* and *powerful* by illustrating the points they make with anecdotes that clearly show you at your best. Need we say it? The people who will be able to do this are those who know you well.

2. Choose people who *genuinely like you*. Why? People who like you will take the time to write you a good recommendation. This is impressive in its own right. A recommendation that looks as though it took only five minutes to write suggests that that's exactly how much time the recommender felt you deserved. In contrast, a recommendation that looks

carefully done and well thought out suggests that the recommender is committed to helping you. One other reason for choosing someone who likes you: She or he will try to put a positive spin on things, choosing examples that show you in a good light and describing them as positively as possible.

3. Choose people who can address one or more of the key subjects: your *business skill*, your *brains*, and your *character*.

Business skill. The ideal person can address the following:

➤ Your maturity: ability to make well-thought-out decisions and retain your self-control under stressful conditions
➤ Your work habits
➤ Your self-confidence and poise
➤ Your creativity
➤ Your thoughtfulness
➤ Your ability to listen
➤ Your ability to work with others
➤ Your ability to motivate others
➤ Your organizational and planning abilities
➤ Your judgment
➤ Your leadership qualities
➤ Your ability to analyze and resolve difficult problems
➤ Your overall managerial potential

Many of the above characteristics are quite personal in nature. For example, self-confidence is a personal quality, yet such characteristics are highly relevant to your business skill and managerial potential.

The person most likely to be able to assess your business ability is your current manager, preferably one who has seen you in operation over a period of time. You may not be able to use your current manager, however. If not, your next best choice might be a prior manager; someone to whom your boss reports (and who has seen your work on a number of occasions, even if at a greater distance than your manager); a manager from another department in your firm; a client; or, if you run your own business, an outside advisor to your firm, such as a banker or consultant. Peers seldom make good recommenders;

their judgment and objectivity are both subject to question. If you do not choose your current boss, or someone else who is an obvious choice, mention the reasons for your choice in an optional essay.

Brains. The ideal person can address the following:

➤ Analytical ability

➤ Quantitative skills

➤ Mental agility

➤ Healthy skepticism

➤ Imagination and creativity

➤ Communication skills (written and oral)

➤ Mastery of other languages

➤ Thoroughness

➤ Research methods

➤ Breadth of scholarly interests

Anyone who has seen you work on difficult intellectual challenges is a possible recommender. The best choice is someone who has seen you tackle such challenges in the workplace. If your work is thoroughly nonintellectual, however, you might be forced to look elsewhere. A former professor or someone who has observed you in a volunteer activity that required managerial skill and intellectual output might be suitable.

Character. The ideal person can address the following:

➤ Your sense of morality

➤ Your integrity

➤ Your dependability

➤ Your motivation and sense of initiative

➤ Your sense of humor

➤ Your involvement with those close to you

➤ Your sense of civic responsibility

➤ How you deal with people below you in business or other organizations

➤ Your social skills

One or both of the people you have chosen to deal with the issues of business skill and brains should be able to address the character issue, too. In other words, you do not need a spiritual or moral leader to address issues of character. The person you select, however, must have seen you in a large number of different circumstances to be able to address these broad issues; his or her knowledge of you may have to be deeper than that required to address your intellectual abilities, for example.

These are the out-and-out rules for choosing recommenders, but the following criteria should also be considered:

1. *Choose someone able to support your positioning.* If you claim to be a marvelous accountant, at least one of your recommenders should be able to discuss just how good an accountant you really are. Failure to choose an accountant who has seen your work over a reasonable period of time would raise a major red flag.

You should also try to take this one step further. Use your recommendations to address any potential weak spot in your application. If you are an accountant worried that the admissions committee will presume you to be humorless, as we discussed earlier in the book, this is your chance to prove what an engaging and funny fellow you really are. Similarly, if you are applying from a nonbusiness background, try to find someone who can address your business skills, or at least the skills that would be most valuable in a business context.

2. *Beware the naysayers!* Certain personal characteristics of recommenders suggest that they will be effective in their support. Someone who is exuberant about life in general will be a good choice, as she is likely to describe an average performer as marvelous, whereas a dour complainer might describe the same performer as terrible. Similarly, an articulate person is likely to write a more impressive recommendation than a poorly spoken one.

3. *Seek out the voice of experience.* Be wary about choosing someone who is not obviously more senior, since it will look strange to have someone junior to you writing on your behalf. (This is potentially acceptable, but be sure to explain it.)

4. *Timeliness counts.* Choose someone who is reliable and therefore likely to complete your recommendation on time.

5. *Where did the recommenders go to school?* People who themselves graduated from your target school are ideal, since they clearly know what is required to succeed in the program. On the other hand, you are probably applying to

numerous schools, so their advantage will not work across the board. By the same token, graduates of comparable quality schools, especially MBA programs, can speak convincingly about your relative abilities.

HOW MANY RECOMMENDERS?

Schools generally ask for recommendations from two people, but some ask for three. As stated earlier, if only two recommendations are required, the general rule is to get two from the workplace. You have more leeway in choosing a third recommender. Consider using someone who has seen you in a significant activity outside the workplace. For instance, if you run a program for a local youth center, the head of the center might be able to give a useful perspective on you in an environment far removed from that of your firm.

If you are a younger or less experienced candidate, and you are asked for three recommendations, the third one may pose a problem. Given your relative lack of bosses or other managers who could write effectively on your behalf, you might want to have a professor (or supervisor of volunteer activities) write the third recommendation. The problem here is that you will reinforce the impression of inexperience. So, at the margin, you should prefer a slightly weaker business colleague's recommendation to that of a professor in order to demonstrate the strength of your business experience.

Another issue arises when you have more potentially excellent recommenders than are called for. This is especially probable for more experienced applicants applying to schools that desire only two recommendations. Should you submit an extra recommendation or not? If the extra recommendation you are considering submitting reiterates points that have been made elsewhere, don't submit it. (Remember the admissions adage: "The thicker the kid, the thicker the folder.") On the other hand, if your recommender can add a truly different and important perspective on your candidacy, I would consider submitting it, but only if it is done in the right way. Approach your extra recommender and explain the circumstances. Then ask that he include with his recommendation a letter that you have written explaining what you are doing. This letter should state clearly that this is the extra recommendation, that the other recommendations are meant to be read first, and that this additional recommendation is to be considered only if the school would consider it appropriate. In other words, you offer this additional recommendation as helpful additional material to be consulted at the discretion of the admissions committee.

APPROACHING A POTENTIAL RECOMMENDER

The typical approach to a potential recommender involves a nervous phone call, in a pleading tone, asking for a big favor. The applicant is desperate to get a letter of reference, so she has to gather up her courage to make her phone call. Once she is on the phone, she hurries through the conversation, with little being done other than some meaningless pleasantries being exchanged and the all-important "Yes, I suppose I can write one for you" being received. This represents at best a completely wasted opportunity. In fact, it may prove to be worse than that.

Ideally, you should start the process about three months before the recommendation deadline. Begin your overture to a potential supporter by scheduling a 30- to 45-minute conference with her. (You will get a better response by having this meeting in person rather than on the telephone.) Run it as a proper business meeting, with a typed agenda and outline of each matter you want to share. Explain briefly where you wish to go in your career and what it will take to get there. Then note the skills and experience you currently lack, and how an MBA will provide many of those missing parts of the puzzle. Then tell her what is required in the application process, being careful to explain how important the applications are, including the recommendations. Tell her you have been considering having one (or two) of several people write on your behalf.

Now comes one of the critical parts of the recommendation process. Make sure each recommender is going to write a very favorable recommendation for you. The way to be sure of this is by giving the person a chance to beg off if she is unable to be highly laudatory. Ask if she believes she would be the right person to write on your behalf. If she is uncomfortable about writing for you because she knows that honesty would require her to be less than highly favorable, she will take this opportunity to suggest that someone else might be more appropriate. If she gives this kind of answer, do not press her. Thank her for her time and move on.

If, on the other hand, she is amenable to being a recommender, give her a further briefing. Tell her how much work will be involved, noting that you will make the process as easy as possible for her, thereby limiting her involvement to something under three hours. (If time is a major issue for her, suggest that you write a first draft, which she can then quickly "adapt." See the discussions below in this regard.) Tell her which schools you are considering and the reasons for each. Explain how you are trying to position yourself in general, and note any differences in positioning for particular schools if necessary. Show her what questions she will need to answer about you, and how these relate to your desired positioning. Suggest "stories" she can tell about you, and how these will fit in with the questions. Provide her with enough detail to refresh her memory about these stories.

MAKING YOUR RECOMMENDER'S JOB EASY

Try to do as much of the work as you can, since your recommender is undoubtedly busy. Give her plenty of time to write the recommendation. Be sure to give her:

➤ The deadline for each application.

➤ Stamped, addressed envelopes.

➤ Several copies of each form, with the objective data already filled in (i.e., with your name, address, etc.).

➤ Copies of your own essays, and a description of your positioning strategy.

➤ If she is writing recommendations for all of your target schools, tell her which main points to discuss to satisfy the requirements for each school in one general letter (although she will still need to fill in the grid ratings for each school). Note that this requires you to know precisely which schools you are applying to.

➤ Samples of the work you did for her.

➤ Copies of evaluations she and others at the firm have given you.

➤ A list of your recent (and past) activities, including why you undertook them, in light of your interest in and suitability for business school.

➤ "Canned" descriptions of the stories you want to tell.

➤ An outline of what you wish her to discuss.

➤ Your résumé (CV).

Be sure your recommender understands what is important and knows how to write convincingly for you—i.e., using appropriate stories with convincing detail.

Suggest that your recommender write a general letter addressing each question asked by the schools to which you are applying. Your outline material should provide her with the basis for writing such a letter, as you should point out to her. (Leave this material with her, of course.) The reason for writing such a general letter is that it will save a great deal of work. This approach also means that she will be indifferent to the number of schools to which you choose to apply. This letter can be made user-friendly by putting in bold print the topics being addressed in each paragraph, so that readers can quickly pick out the points that are of greatest interest to them. Your recommender may suggest that you do a first draft of the recommendations, which she will presumably alter to her taste later on—or she may ask that you write them, and she will simply sign them.

You might need to agree to write the recommendations, following our general guidelines about recommendations in doing so. Be careful, though. Many applicants make mistakes in this situation. (1) Some revert to the simplistic "he is extremely this and extraordinarily that" instead of using appropriate stories to provide credibility. (2) Some fail to make the recommendation sound as though this recommender actually wrote it. Putting yourself in her shoes will help you determine which matters she would emphasize, and how she would discuss them. (In fact, this is a step that you should take before you approach any possible recommender.) (3) Yet another mistake is to overlook the chance to tell stories that would otherwise not be told about you. Remember to bring new information to the table whenever you have the chance.

Whether your recommender writes your recommendations or has you do them, the well-thought-out approach outlined above will prove helpful in a number of ways. First of all, this approach minimizes the chance that you will end up with a lukewarm recommender. Second, your approach will have been highly organized and professional. If you had followed the nervous, pleading approach, why should she tell Harvard that you are a true professional destined for greatness? Third, you know in advance what stories she will tell. This means you will retain control of the admissions process insofar as you have a number of stories you want told about yourself, without undue repetition. Fourth, following this process means you will have a well-written recommendation. If your recommender writes it, she will almost certainly use your outline, just as she will treat the matter seriously, since you have done so. If you write the actual recommendation, you can certainly manage to put together a good statement. Fifth, your professional approach means that your recommender is likely to improve her opinion of you, meaning that she will be a better resource for your future career than she otherwise would have been.

> **TIPS ON HANDLING DIFFICULT ISSUES**
>
> ➤ If you find yourself in the position of writing all your own recommendations, formatting them differently and making them sound as if each recommender was the actual author will help camouflage their authorship. For example, you can format one as a letter and another in the question-and-answer format. Similarly, you can use different typefaces and font sizes.
>
> ➤ If you went to a second-rate or unknown university, or had mediocre grades even at a top school, you should have recommenders take every opportunity to discuss your analytical skills and intellectual leanings.
>
> ➤ Similarly, if you work in the type of job that is assumed not to make many analytical demands (such as selling), have your recommenders discuss your analytical skills and intellectual leanings to whatever extent possible.
>
> ➤ Try to persuade your recommenders to overlook some of your shortcomings and focus on your positive qualities.
>
> ➤ If you are unable to get a recommendation from someone the admissions committee would expect to write on your behalf, be sure to explain why this is so—either in the optional essay question or in a separate note.

WHAT DO YOU WANT SAID ABOUT YOU?
AND HOW CAN YOU INCREASE ITS VALUE?

A good recommendation should show that you are an outstanding individual, one who is an appropriate candidate for a top business school by virtue of having the appropriate management potential. It should also support your individual positioning strategy.

The following all add to the effectiveness of a recommendation:

- It is well written. It is grammatically correct and reflects the thinking of a well-educated person.

- It reflects substantial thought and effort. In other words, the person cares enough about you to spend the time to be as helpful as possible.

- The writer knows you well enough to provide several highly specific examples to illustrate her points. These should not be the same examples you use in your essays or that other recommenders note. As with your essays, the use of illustrative stories and examples will make the recommendation credible and memorable. This will also show that the recommender knows you well, thereby showing you have not "shopped" for one.

- The recommender does not mention things best handled elsewhere in your application, such as your GMAT score.

- It shows you to be a distinctive candidate. The use of examples will aid this considerably.

- The writer discusses your growth and development over time. Your drive to improve yourself, in particular, is worth comment, since your interest in learning and improving is part of what will make you a desirable student.

- Your recommender explicitly compares you with others who have gone to this or another comparable school. Have her quantify her claims whenever possible. For example, instead of "intelligent," have her write "one of the three most intelligent people ever to work for me" (or, even better, "the third most intelligent of over one hundred top grads to work for me").

- The person shows how you meet the requirements, as she sees them, of a top manager or other leader.

The general impression should be that a person of very high caliber wrote a well-thought-out, enthusiastic recommendation for you.

DIFFERENCES BETWEEN THE JOB AND BUSINESS SCHOOL APPLICATION PROCESSES

If you think the emphasis upon recommendations is overplayed, consider the differences between the job application (or recruitment) and business school application processes. Both employers and business schools need to determine the best candidates available. Employers typically recruit relatively few people at a time, often just one. To do so, the prospective supervisors of the new hire will be involved, generally along with some of those who will be co-workers, and, of course, the human resources people. Thus, a substantial number of people will examine the candidates for the vacant post. Business schools, on the other hand, have thousands of candidates to examine and hundreds of vacant seats to fill. Despite this, most of the work will be done by just a dozen admissions professionals.

As the chart on the next page summarizes, employers and business schools get the information they need about candidates in somewhat different ways. Employers rely more on interviews (often putting candidates through a dozen or more) and in-depth discussions with current and prior supervisors of the candidate; business schools emphasize the written recommendations and essays. The processes reflect the time and resources available to firms and schools, and the demands placed upon them. The result is that the business schools lean heavily upon information sources that can most readily be routinized and that provide information in the most efficient time frame.

Thus, if your recommender wants to fob you off with a two-paragraph recommendation letter, modeled on the type of letter she routinely writes to help former employees get jobs, explain to her the differences in the process—and what she needs to do to be helpful.

	JOB APPLICATION/ RECRUITMENT PROCESS	*BUSINESS SCHOOL APPLICATION PROCESS*
Application Economics		
Number of Recruiters	Many	Few
Number to Be Recruited	Few	Massive
Information Sources		
Number and Length of Interviews	Multiple, perhaps lasting many hours	One, lasting perhaps 30 minutes
Nature of Written Recommendations	Short, pro forma letters	Lengthy; responsive to detailed questions
Discussions with Recommenders	Extensive	None
Essays Required	None	Multiple

HOW LONG SHOULD THE RECOMMENDATION LETTER BE?

The recommendation forms may provide limited space for a given response, but your recommender may want to write more. Should you or your recommender treat such space limitations as you do the limitations for essay writing? No. Recommenders are given much more latitude in choosing how best to write a recommendation. In fact, strong recommendations, laced with appropriate stories and appropriate details, tend to be a good two pages long.

AVOID THE WORST RECOMMENDATION PROBLEMS

Two mistakes are shockingly common:

➤ Many recommendations include the name of the wrong school. Be sure to have each recommendation checked to avoid this.

➤ Perhaps one in ten applicants is deliberately sabotaged by a recommender. The jealousy engendered by seeing a subordinate trying to get into one of the world's most famous MBA programs sometimes results in recommendations that excoriate an applicant or, just as deadly, damn with faint praise. This is particularly common when a "good friend" writes the recommendation.

THE ADMISSIONS DIRECTORS TALK ABOUT RECOMMENDATIONS

Whom Should You Choose to Be a Recommender?

➤ A strong recommendation can only come from someone who really knows the candidate. They've worked closely with the candidate and seen him or her in difficult situations and in successful ones. They know the candidate professionally and personally. As a result, they can speak in depth about the candidate's strengths and weaknesses. *Sally Jaeger, Tuck*

➤ A good recommender will know you and care about whether you get in. (Only people who care will take the immense amount of time necessary to do a good recommendation.) He or she will care about you as a person and as a professional—and will have stories and examples to tell about you that will showcase your strengths and make you come alive on paper. *Sharon Hoffman, Stanford*

➤ For those in a family business: Do not use your parents as recommenders. Instead, use a supplier, a customer, or someone else who can be objective about you. *Michele Rogers, Kellogg*

➤ If you are self-employed, consider getting a client or customer to write on your behalf. Do not get a relative to write for you. If necessary, consider your accountant, your lawyer, a person from the local chamber of commerce, or your venture capitalist. *Ann W. Richards, Johnson (Cornell)*

➤ The people you choose should know who you are, what your potential is, and what you can contribute. These are usually your supervisors at work. *Linda Meehan, Columbia*

➤ If you have been at your current employer for less than a year, consider submitting a recommendation from your current supervisor as a third (additional) recommendation, labeling it as such. Get your two primary recommendations from your former employer. *ANN W. RICHARDS, JOHNSON (CORNELL)*

Should You Approach a Colleague, Direct Supervisor, or Someone Higher Up?

➤ Choose someone who has *evaluated you in a workplace or professional context.* Get your direct supervisor, one level above you. Choosing someone at the top of the organization is worthless unless he or she has worked closely with you; in fact, we'll question your judgment for doing so. We want content over flash. *SHARON HOFFMAN, STANFORD*

➤ We ask that one of your recommendations come from your direct supervisor, the person who has worked with you most recently and ideally knows you best on a day-in, day-out basis. That said, there may be specific circumstances when that is not a good idea. For example, if you've only worked for someone for a couple of months, and telling them you want to go to business school will get you fired or cost you your bonus. Or you may work at a family business and your boss is your mother. If that is the case, you may want to have a more objective party, like a client or vendor, do the recommendation. The second one should also be a professional recommendation. It can come from a previous supervisor, a professional colleague, a client, or a supplier: someone who can comment on your business acumen. We want someone who can provide real insight into you as a professional. *ISSER GALLOGLY, STERN (NYU)*

➤ We want the superior who knows you best, which may not be the CEO, the president, or a senator. This isn't a test of whom you can get access to. *THOMAS CALEEL, WHARTON*

➤ We like to see an evaluation from someone with direct knowledge of an applicant's professional strengths and weaknesses. The person should see you on an everyday basis and have responsibility for your work. We do not like recommendations from coworkers, nor do we like recommendations from professors (unless the two of you went into business together). By the same token, we do not want to have the president of your company write niceties about you. *ANN W. RICHARDS, JOHNSON (CORNELL)*

➤ Immediate supervisors are generally a better choice than someone much higher in the company. *DAWNA CLARKE, TUCK*

➤ If the recommender knows the candidate's work very well, she is likely to do a much better job of selling it to us. The recommender's rank is less important than her knowledge of the candidate. The ideal recommender is someone who knows you well and is successful, because someone who has made it to the top has seen a lot of success and can comment knowledgeably on it. *MICHELE ROGERS, KELLOGG*

> ➤ We're not impressed by title. Get your direct supervisor, and/or perhaps the person he or she reports to, to write for you. *Joelle du Lac, INSEAD*

Must Your Boss Be One of Your Recommenders?

> ➤ It's good to use your boss, but if you can't, use a former colleague who has since left the company or a customer or supplier—someone you've worked with. *James Millar, Harvard*

> ➤ Not all jobs are of the "two or three years then on to business school" variety, where a manager expects someone to leave and will provide a recommendation. Having to declare to a company in October that you'll be leaving in August for an MBA means that you'll be working for a long time under difficult circumstances, so we understand applicants having, for example, a former supervisor perhaps at a prior company writing a recommendation for them. *Anne Coyle, Yale*

> ➤ If using your current supervisor would jeopardize your position, choose a past supervisor. We understand how this can be necessary. *Sally Jaeger, Tuck*

Should You Favor Workplace, Academic, or Other Sources?

> ➤ Certainly, if you've been working for three to five years (or more), we prefer professional recommendations to academic ones. *Sally Jaeger, Tuck*

> ➤ We prefer professional recommendations to any other kind. It's a "business school," and "business" comes first. We have a sense of your academic abilities from the transcript, the GMAT, etc., and we have a sense of you from your essays. The recommendations are the only part of the application that comes from an independent third party, so we really want that to be about you as a professional and about your career. *Isser Gallogly, Stern (NYU)*

What Should a Recommender Say?

> ➤ We want to see whether you are able to handle challenges, work under pressure, work in a team, and add value to your department and company. *Ann W. Richards, Johnson (Cornell)*

> ➤ A short recommendation filled with adjectives is too easy to write. It's also boring as well as unmemorable. A strong recommendation supports its points by discussing meaningful examples. It helps the candidate stand out, be three-dimensional rather than two-dimensional. *Anne Coyle, Yale*

> ➤ A recommendation is the only external observation of a candidate, so we look for recommenders to be as honest and insightful as possible. We want to learn whether someone will be a good fit in our community, whether he or she possesses the leadership, teamwork, and ability to work in a multicultural

environment necessary to succeed here. We want to know whether we can help him or her achieve. A recommender should write more, not less, and should give us examples when possible. Remember, we're not looking for perfect people; we'd have nothing to teach them. *ROSE MARTINELLI, CHICAGO*

➤ We are looking for people who have demonstrated that they can follow through on projects and accomplish things, not just get along with people. A great recommendation does this. It has depth, examples which explain how and why this person is in the top 5 percent—it demonstrates what makes the person so outstanding. It should, of course, be well written. *JUDITH GOODMAN, MICHIGAN*

➤ Try to get recommendations of an appropriate length. If they're too short, we don't learn enough about you. If they're too long, they're hard to synthesize. *JOELLE DU LAC, INSEAD*

What Are the Worst Mistakes People Make?

➤ Too many applicants fail to treat recommendations as part of the application process. They don't give people time to complete the process, or they don't give them sufficient information. Manage up. You need to sit down with your recommender to explain matters. Don't accept having to write a recommendation yourself and then giving it to your recommender to sign. *THOMAS CALEEL, WHARTON*

➤ "Coffee-break recommendations" don't work. This is our term for what a recommender produces when he or she did not have or take the time to do a serious job. This is often because a recommender is forced into writing a recommendation without really knowing the candidate. *SALLY JAEGER, TUCK*

➤ Perhaps the worst mistake is to misevaluate your recommender and ask the wrong person to write for you. Doing so tells us a lot about your judgment. *JOELLE DU LAC, INSEAD*

Should You Submit Additional Recommendations?

➤ An additional recommendation is appropriate when someone can contribute an additional, different perspective. For example, perhaps a professor has continued as your mentor. If you've been deeply involved in an outside activity, we like to hear from that organization. *SALLY JAEGER, TUCK*

➤ After you've gotten the two required recommendations, if you think there's somebody who can write about something totally different than those two wrote and that it will give us a better insight into who you are, you might want to include it. But if it's just another one—because you ran into your CEO in an elevator, and you thought that would make a difference to us— don't bother. *LINDA MEEHAN, COLUMBIA*

➤ A lot of things in the application process are a matter of judgment. Consider what the extra recommendation is for, how it's going to be helpful, what additional insight it will provide. Getting a third recommendation about your community involvement because it's incredibly important to who you are as a person and to your career endeavors may be a good idea. Occasionally a third recommendation is a really good idea, but if it's not going to add value, it probably will undermine the strength of your application. *ISSER GALLOGLY, STERN (NYU)*

➤ SDA Bocconi requires two letters of recommendation, possibly one from the academic world and the other from the professional context. . . . We don't encourage candidates to look for additional recommendations. *ROSSANA CAMERA, BOCCONI (ITALY)*

The Value of Letters of Support

➤ I think it's great, particularly at Stern. Fit and community are so important here. When you have a vote of confidence from the Stern community—an administrator, faculty member, alum, or current student—that provides additional assurance that you will probably be a good fit. These people know this community and know what it takes to thrive in this environment. Of course, inundating the admissions committee with a pile of letters that all say the same thing isn't a good idea. At some point it's a bit much. If each one gives additional insight, great—but at a certain point, enough's enough. We get the message that there are people in the Stern community who think you're great. *ISSER GALLOGLY, STERN (NYU)*

Other

➤ As a general rule, we're more concerned with what others say about you than what you say about yourself. We want to see whether you leave a trail of satisfied customers. *SHARON HOFFMAN, STANFORD*

➤ The grid ratings are helpful. It's surprising how many people get very low grid marks. We put the marks into context, of course, since recommenders have all sorts of ways of evaluating people. *THOMAS CALEEL, WHARTON*

➤ Take the time to develop strong relationships with those who are going to be your recommenders. Sometimes that takes a bit more than just working with them. Sometimes it requires building the relationship over the occasional lunch or meeting about your future goals in order to nurture the relationship. Bringing them into the application process early can also help. Seeking their opinion about your choices, talking with them about your goals, and perhaps walking through the recommendation questions with them can help, too. Really take the time to discuss the recommendation in depth with them. *ISSER GALLOGLY, STERN (NYU)*

> ➤ We don't offer an online recommendation. We want to see (and feel and "taste") the letterhead on which a recommendation is written. Similarly, if two recommendations resemble each other too closely, we'll worry about their authenticity. *ANNE COYLE, YALE*
>
> ➤ Recommenders often tip us off to potential personal problems by giving a lesser mark on maturity, for instance, or noting that an area for development is learning to communicate effectively with associates. In such cases, we'd want to interview the candidate. *PETER JOHNSON, HAAS*

MAKE SURE THE RECOMMENDATIONS ARE SUBMITTED ON TIME

The schools can keep you informed as to whether a given recommendation has arrived. If it has not arrived and time is getting short, contact your recommender and ask very politely how her effort is progressing and whether you can be helpful by giving her more information. This will tend to prod her into action without being annoying.

THE FOLLOW-UP

Be sure to send your recommender a thank-you note for her efforts and state that you will keep her informed of your progress. This is simply good manners. If you need extra encouragement to do so, remember that you may need her services again quite soon if schools turn you down this time.

If you manage your recommender well, the chances are that she will submit your recommendations well before they are due. What should you do, however, if you contact your schools and learn that a recommendation is missing? You can certainly call your recommender to encourage her to submit it soon. On the other hand, you can take a subtler approach and send her a follow-up note explaining that you have completed the application process and are currently awaiting schools' decisions. If she has not yet submitted the recommendation, this should spur her into action. If this does not work, contact her again and see whether you can help the process along in some way, such as by writing a draft of what she might say.

Keep her informed as to each school's decision. Also be sure to tell her at the end of the process what you have decided to do, such as attend school X and turn down schools Y and Z, and why. At this time it would be highly appropriate to send her a small thank-you gift, such as a bottle of champagne or flowers. Very few people do this. It is not a terribly expensive gesture, but you can be sure that you will gain greatly in her estimation for having done it.

Do your best to stay in touch with her as you go through business school, even if this means nothing more than dropping a short postcard or e-mail message to her with a few comments about your progress. Staying in contact shows further sincerity in your appreciation of her efforts.

Remember that your recommender is in a position to help your career for years to come and has already shown a distinct willingness to do so. You should do your best to reward her helpfulness. One sound reason for going to a top MBA program is to take advantage of the networking possibilities it offers. It would be silly to throw away a very good contact prior to arriving at business school by failing to treat your recommender appropriately.

SPECIAL NOTES FOR INTERNATIONAL APPLICANTS

If you have a potential recommender who is not able to write well in English (or whatever language is acceptable to the school), your help matters greatly by writing up some stories or even the full draft of a recommendation for her. To the extent that you write well in English, your recommender will be all the more likely to use what you have written rather than struggle with the language on her own. The alternative is to have her write the recommendation in her native language and have it translated into English. In either case, be sure to provide her with an appropriate editor who is a fluent, native speaker of English, and about whose editing and grammar skills you are confident.

RECOMMENDATION EXAMPLE

The following recommendation is superb, albeit double the length (for purposes of this book) that would otherwise be appropriate.

RECOMMENDATION FOR MARGARET

It is my distinct pleasure to recommend Margaret to the Sloan School of Management at MIT, because she is simply one of the most talented people I have ever met, and that includes the CEOs of *Fortune* 500 companies and successful start-ups that I have dealt with professionally over the last few decades.

I am Margaret's manager at MM Harbor. I hired her (from a pool of over 700 preselected talented college graduates from the top colleges and universities in the nation) to become one of her class of 40 investment banking analysts in our New York office. As the Managing Director overseeing the associates and analysts in the high technology division in New York, I have interacted with her on a daily basis for most of the three years she has been with us. Margaret is one of the best people I have ever worked with in my 19 years in investment banking. She easily matches the abilities of my former MBA classmates at Harvard.

An investment banking analyst needs to be skilled at several things: client relations, communications, and complex quantitative assessment and analysis. Those working in the high-tech sector must be skilled in all of those areas *and* be technically knowledgeable about the companies we serve. Margaret has excelled in *all* arenas. She has consistently ranked among the top two analysts in her class of 40 for the three years she has been with us; this is no small feat considering the kind of serious talent we have here and the high expectations we hold for our analysts, who often work 80-hour weeks and are staffed on multiple challenging projects at once.

CLIENT RELATIONS AND COMMUNICATIONS

Margaret is a superb communicator and quickly gains the trust of others she works with, clients and colleagues alike. She is at ease in both informal discussion sessions and the most formal of presentations; her written work demonstrates the highest level of polish and sophistication; she is an astute negotiator; even the quickest e-mail from Margaret is well composed and full of insight!

Margaret is an expert in overseeing our relationships with client companies, even though it is neither expected nor common for those at her level to do so. Though most of our analysts rarely have any contact at all with clients, I recognized Margaret's people skills immediately and have allowed her to take the lead managing several client relationships. Her handling of our recent engagement with Kool Toys, in which they acquired Cat and Mouse Games, allowed Kool Toys to increase market share by 13% and brought us $2.3 million in fees.

Margaret has also managed relationships with existing clients where the client was hostile to us or there was a severe interpersonal problem. A little conflict never ruined a relationship for her. For instance, one of our clients was a well-known systems integration company with whom Margaret had built a good rapport. I essentially let her take the lead on putting together a pitch for them. She asked me to come along for support, even though I knew nothing about the pitch. When we arrived, there were 12 representatives from the company in the room, rather than the expected one or two. This was extremely unnerving. Margaret fielded an hour of rapid-fire, hostile questioning. She remained cool under pressure, and refused to be brought down to their level of unprofessional behavior. She resolutely tackled their questions one by one. She handled herself with extreme maturity and carried her presentation off with confidence despite the circumstances. The client company later accepted our pitch and has worked with us on numerous occasions since that day.

Margaret also has well-honed cross-cultural communication skills. She has asked to be placed on deals with international dimensions, and has excelled in each of them. Fluent in French and with a good grasp of Chinese as well, Margaret has often used her language abilities to get to know overseas clients. She charms them with her knowledge of their language and culture, and demonstrates respect through her willingness to enter their world. She has a wonderful way of recognizing when others feel ill at ease. Margaret is confident around others and keenly understands that the global nature of today's business environment necessitates using different styles of communication depending upon the circumstances.

For example, we had been trying for months to pitch a Taiwan-based software company, as we knew about its forthcoming IPO and wanted to be the lead in the deal. We were to pitch the Chief Information Officer (CIO) for the company, who was heavily involved in all of its financial undertakings. It was an important meeting for MM Harbor, but I invited Margaret as a courtesy. I never really connected with this guy. He was older and Chinese, and I just did not have a lot in common with him. His grasp of English was mediocre, so I was not sure he had a solid understanding of what we had discussed. I felt uncomfortable around him, yet Margaret was completely at ease. She has a confidence that makes her comfortable with everyone—regardless of position or cultural boundaries. That is an important asset when you're dealing with high-level executives and international environments—yet another characteristic of Margaret that sets her apart.

As we were winding up, Margaret asked this man how he liked living in the U.S. after spending the bulk of his life in Taiwan. Such a simple question! The guy opened up to her right away and their conversation slipped between English and Chinese. He talked about how he didn't like NYC itself but enjoyed its cultural offerings. Turns out he's an art lover whose favorite artist is Japanese printmaker Hiroshige, about whom Margaret clearly possesses a wealth of knowledge, even though she formally studied European Renaissance art! Off he and Margaret went on a major printmaking discussion. Margaret is incredibly well versed in many different topics and has a way of using this ability to connect with others, no matter their background. She also intuitively understood—as I had not—that this man had felt uncomfortable diving into a business discussion without getting to know us first or sharing a meal with us, which is how the Chinese initiate professional relationships.

At the end of their conversation, I had gained a relationship with this man and his company, thanks to Margaret and her personal skills. Margaret had gotten him to relax and open up—he was comfortable with her and therefore with me and with MM Harbor. The following year we did over $4 million worth of business with them. MM Harbor is a place where most folks would rather talk about the stock market or baseball than Japanese printmaking. Though Margaret can hold her own in any conversation, she continues to impress me with her breadth of interests and her ability to forge ties with people from all walks of life.

QUANTITATIVE SKILLS AND UNDERSTANDING OF TECHNOLOGY

Margaret surprised me with her capacity for numbers. When she joined the group, my biggest concern about her was the fact that she had a liberal arts background with too much emphasis on the "arts" (as a double English and Art History major) and little experience with numbers. I expected her to possess weak quantitative skills and require a lot of development in this area. I was wrong.

Not only did she learn numbers quickly, she demonstrated an actual *talent* for spreadsheets and analysis—so much so that she became a resource for her peers, and, at times, for me. One time we were in the eleventh hour of closing a major deal with one of the leading software providers. I was homesick. I needed to make a change to some of our projections and get them to the client immediately. I spoke to my boss, the head of the high-tech group nationwide, who made the changes himself and sent them to the client. When Margaret arrived, she took one look at what we had done and found a substantial error in our work. She asked me about it to be sure she was correct, and then very gracefully took care of it with the client. Her understanding of numbers and her ability to analyze things thoroughly and quickly are what saved the day. Had Margaret not been so astute with numbers, we would have severely underestimated the value of the acquisition the software provider was pursuing, hurting them and losing approximately $1.3 million in revenues for MM Harbor.

Now, a few years later, Margaret is widely regarded as the most technically knowledgeable of all the analysts *and associates* in her area. The Managing Director of the high-tech group in Menlo Park even tried to recruit her to his office—a testament to how widespread her reputation has become. The combination of technical understanding and client management abilities' is the single most difficult skill set to find. Most individuals are strong in one area or the other, but not both. Margaret is a star.

Margaret works closely with our Research Analysts and regularly picks their brains to gain knowledge. Last year, Margaret took the initiative to build a matrix of 350 types of technology that our clients generally deal in, listing and comparing their features, benefits, and competitors, so that our entire group had a base of knowledge from which to work when looking at new companies and creating pitches. This became a basic reference manual for our high-tech bankers in six offices worldwide. Our officers gave Margaret a special mention in our MM Harbor newsletter for her initiative and superb work on this project.

When I hire new analysts and associates, I call on Margaret to give presentations to them on the technical details of the companies for whom we work. She has given four presentations thus far for me, and I have found no one else as capable as she to perform these seminars, despite the fact that I need her talent elsewhere as well. Her knowledge of our clients' technologies is simply unmatched.

LEADERSHIP AND TEAM SKILLS

Although Margaret has the qualities of strength and individualism, she has much better team-oriented skills than the majority of people at MM Harbor. Margaret established an informal leadership position in my group as soon as she arrived. She was outspoken enough to represent the whole group of high-tech analysts in New York, and came in with stronger leadership skills than the others. She freely shares her skills and experience with the group, making them look to her even more as a leader. I got used to her being the one to deliver any pushback and knew that when I was dealing with her, I was hearing the voice of the entire group.

Margaret exhibits the courage to make hard decisions and stand by them. Margaret is not intimidated by much, but she also has good judgment. When she has considered the facts of a situation and is certain she is on solid ground, she will not hesitate to take a strong stand. For example, she persuaded the management here to allow analyst-level employees to personally contribute to a certain private equity fund that had originally been reserved for those in Vice President or higher level positions. The analysts and associates looked to her to help consolidate their views and argue them—successfully—in front of management.

Margaret realizes that in any group everything is ultimately about persuasion, negotiation, and compromise. She is such a good leader, looked up to by others, because they know she will accept a decision that does not go her way if she feels she has had a fair hearing. Margaret leads by listening to others and building consensus.

PERSONALITY

Margaret has the highest standards of integrity and never lets anyone down in this manner. I have watched as numerous seemingly "honest" employees allow themselves to stoop to what they see as run-of-the-mill behavior in business settings: for example, milking the company for expenditure allowances by turning in taxi vouchers or meal receipts from social adventures unrelated to work. Margaret is cut from a different cloth entirely—it is a joy to be around her and witness her code of behavior. She is always honest, graceful, and sincere. I in fact respect and trust Margaret so much that my wife and I have begun to hire her as our babysitter during long weekends away—and believe me, we do not leave our nine-, five-, and three-year-olds with just anyone. She has impressed us with her maturity and has passed her responsible and caring ways onto our kids.

Margaret genuinely cares about others and is constantly making sure that her team members are doing well—she can be counted on to take a down-and-out secretary to lunch or to ask after a colleague's ailing mom every day of the week. It is Margaret who remembers all our birthdays and brings in the cake; likewise, it is Margaret who cares enough about our United Way effort to coordinate our volunteer activities and makes sure the Toys for Tots gifts get delivered before Christmas.

WEAKNESSES

Margaret has tremendous strengths in key areas for business success—interpersonal skills, leadership and teamwork skills, maturity, intelligence and technical ability. However, one of Margaret's greatest strengths can also be a liability for her. Margaret has tremendous focus. Her focus allows her to quickly become competent at anything she does. However, when Margaret is absorbed in something, she tends to lose sight of other projects that require her attention. She needs to work at multi-tasking and delegating. Margaret is well aware of her need to develop better multi-tasking skills and has already started to address this weakness. Just last week, in fact, she sat down with me to map out a way for her to meet two deadlines at once, essentially by delegating some of her tasks for one project to a junior analyst.

MARGARET'S PURSUIT OF AN MBA

Margaret has talked about MIT as her school of choice from day one. As an alum of Harvard Business School, I've tried to get her equally excited about the program at the other end of Mass Ave, but she continues to gravitate toward Sloan and its offerings. She gets excited when she talks about MIT's cutting-edge curriculum and its emphasis on the management of technology. She sees your program as unique among the business schools she has investigated. I know that MIT's program is the best fit for her and I sincerely support her in her choice.

Margaret already has a very successful future ahead of her. I will of course spend a lot of energy trying to persuade Margaret to return to my group after she receives her degree. I would be honored and thrilled to work with her again! If she chooses to return to investment banking, she will continue to be a superstar. I would be surprised if she did not become a Vice President and even a Managing Director long before others of her same age and experience. On the other hand, if Margaret chooses to join a technology company in business development or finance, I can similarly predict much success for her. She will be a mover and a shaker no matter what the environment.

I reiterate that Margaret is a most special young woman with extraordinary talents and capabilities. She is a unique individual, and she has a host of rare qualities to contribute to Sloan. Please do not hesitate to call me if I can be of further assistance to you as you evaluate her candidacy.

How This Recommendation Helps Margaret

- Margaret was right in selecting this supervisor to write her recommendation, since he could speak to the breadth of her professional abilities as well as to her personal qualities. She knew that this recommender had a host of interesting stories to tell about her and that he would be sure to write a spectacular, carefully crafted letter of support.

▪ This recommendation is lengthy and well-written, reflecting the time and energy the recommender put into it. He clearly cares about her and wants to show her off as best as possible.

▪ The headlines within this recommendation make it more readable, which is a plus in any piece of this length.

▪ The recommendation not only illustrates that Margaret is successful but also points out the context for her success. It makes it clear that she is successful in an environment full of extremely talented people, where very high expectations are maintained.

▪ The writer of this letter is right to point out that he himself attended a top MBA program, making it clear that he well understands the requirements for success at such a program.

▪ This letter makes it clear that Margaret has true quantitative and analytical talents, which an admissions committee might have doubted upon looking at her college transcript, since she was an English and Art History major. This recommender in fact points out that not only are her quantitative skills and technical understanding far better than those of colleagues with math and computer science backgrounds, but that, furthermore, her depth of knowledge about other fields such as art and literature makes her a fascinating person and skilled communicator.

▪ Margaret's supervisor was also correct to point out the relevance of the candidate's knowledge of technology to MIT's MBA program.

▪ This recommender did well to devote so much space to Margaret's communication and interpersonal skills, as these are critical elements of any MBA candidacy.

▪ Since Margaret has no experience working outside of the United States, she was smart to have her recommender address her international capabilities and cross-cultural awareness, which can be critical in today's increasingly global business world.

▪ This letter makes it clear that Margaret is a real stand-out in many different ways. The fact that this seasoned investment banker working at a highly reputable (and challenging) company thinks the world of Margaret is impressive in itself. The fact that he expresses a desire to work with Margaret again and the level of detail he brings to his stories make his evaluation all the more impressive.

Appendix VII

RECOMMENDATION BRIEFING OUTLINE

(The material below is meant to provide you with an outline for structuring briefing sessions with your recommenders to get them to write the kind of recommendations you need.)

Reason I came to firm X:

My ultimate goals:

How an MBA would help me reach these goals:

Why I should get an MBA now:

Which MBA programs best suit me:

—Why?

—How:

My positioning for these schools:

How recommender can help me:

—Does he/she want to help me?

—Time required:

Show application forms; explain that only "ticking the boxes" and writing a general letter is required.

—Show that the objective information (address, etc.) has been filled in.

Take recommender through outline of an appropriate letter. Include details of stories, copies of evaluations, and so forth.

Discuss style and form of the master letter.

Discuss deadlines.

12

INTERVIEWS

— EXECUTIVE SUMMARY —

Establish your objectives: conveying a good impression, imparting your strengths, demonstrating your knowledge, gaining information.

Prepare yourself by:
—Learning the most likely questions.
—Knowing yourself and your qualifications vis-à-vis those of others.
—Knowing the school.
—Readying your own questions.

Practice via mock interviews, videotaping them if possible.

Familiarize yourself with the do's and don'ts of interviewing.

*I*nterviewing is a critical part of the admissions process at essentially all of the top schools. There are several reasons for this. One is that the greater emphasis upon "soft skills" in MBA programs means that an applicant's personality and social skills are more important than they were in the past. A second reason is that a person's interviewing ability is a very good indicator of how attractive he or she will be to employers at the end of the MBA course. An applicant with good "paper" credentials will be unattractive to a school if he or she is likely to be regarded as a loser by employers later on. A third reason for interviewing is that schools can market themselves better by meeting individually with applicants. This is particularly relevant for the elite schools, which tend to feel they are all chasing the same few thousand absolutely outstanding candidates. These schools welcome the chance to get a jump on their rivals by better assessing candidates and by promoting themselves to their top choices. A fourth reason is that an interview offers a school a unique opportunity to determine whether the applicant is likely to attend the school if admitted. This has become the primary purpose of interviews at more than one school, concerned about the impact of "yields" (the percentage of those accepted who enroll at a school) upon school rankings.

Interviews offer schools the chance to learn much more about applicants. Some things are not readily determinable without a face-to-face meeting. These include your appearance, charm, persuasiveness, maturity, presence, and business mien. Interviews also provide an opportunity to probe areas insufficiently explained in the application.

INTERVIEWING POLICIES

Despite the increased importance of interviews, the interviewing policies of the top schools cover a wide spectrum. For instance, schools vary dramatically in the percentage of their applicants that they interview. Toward one end of the spectrum would be Harvard, which interviews only about 20 percent of applicants; Kellogg would be near the other end of the spectrum, interviewing 90-plus percent of its applicants. The other top schools would be scattered across the spectrum.

The percentage of applicants a school interviews tends to have a major impact upon the nature of the interviews themselves. *Schools that try to interview all of their applicants* face daunting logistical difficulties. They do not have sufficient admissions officers to do all of the interviewing, so they use students and alumni. The use of alums (spread across the world) is necessary not only to handle the substantial volume but also to accommodate applicants unable to get to the school during the interview season. Using students and alums, however, creates certain problems. First, there are serious concerns about confidentiality in such circumstances. Applicants and recommenders alike might be unhappy about having their most private and confidential information and commentary bounced around the globe to people who have only a limited involvement with the admissions process. Second, applicants worry that they will not receive fair treatment if they are interviewed by alums or students. Both alums and students are likely to lack the experience or savvy to know how to formulate a winning position to support an applicant's candidacy. In addition, alums do not generally attend admissions committee meetings to push (in person) for their favorite candidates. Although schools that use alum and student interviewers take their opinions seriously, such concerns are justified: Non-admissions interviewers may not be as effective in their support of you as an admissions officer would be.

Attempting to interview all applicants in a relatively few months also makes it difficult to require interviewers to have full knowledge of candidates before meeting with them. Thus, applicants are often interviewed "blind"—by someone who will not have read their files beforehand. In this case, the interview will be conducted largely on the basis of the applicant's résumé, which will be submitted shortly before the meeting. A policy of interviewing all applicants also constrains the length of the interview; few schools attempting to interview most applicants have a standard interview length that exceeds thirty minutes. In addition, when so many different people are employed to conduct interviews on behalf of a school, a rather standardized approach is taken (in order to simplify the process of briefing the interviewers—and of interpreting the results). Thus, it is common for these interviews to involve the same dozen or so questions being asked of each applicant. (See the box, "Most Likely Questions," later in this chapter for a list of these questions.) Rather than an in-depth probing of what is specific to a given applicant, many of these interviews are relatively shallow chats about the obvious. In sum, interviews with schools that want to meet with all of their applicants tend to be shorter, simpler, and more superficial than those with schools that limit the number of applicants they interview.

Of course, there are enough exceptions to this generality, even at the schools that interview in the highest volumes, that you would be wise to prepare for an in-depth interview. (As the sporting cliché has it, "Practice hard and perform easy.") In any event, being well prepared will allow you to impress your interviewer substantially, whether she has been tossing you the softest of questions or subjecting you to a real grilling.

Near the other end of the spectrum are *schools that try to limit the number of applicants they interview.* Schools such as Harvard, Cornell, and various of the European schools interview only those candidates who are near the top of their applicant pools. In most regards their approach differs markedly from the schools that interview most applicants. These schools tend to use admissions officers rather than alums or students. Their interviews tend to be longer in length and more in depth, with more specific questions. The interviewer tends to know more about his subject from the get-go, because of his having read part or all of the admissions file before the interview.

	SCHOOLS INTERVIEWING FEW APPLICANTS	*SCHOOLS INTERVIEWING MOST APPLICANTS*
Most Likely Interviewer	Admissions officer	Admissions officer, student, or alum
Interview Length	30 minutes or more	30 minutes
Basis of Interview	May include all of admissions file	Résumé or basic data sheet
Type of Questions	May be specific to applicant	Same for all applicants
Difficulty Level	Medium–High	Low

Although the nature of the interview you will face at a given school tends to vary substantially according to where on the spectrum the school is, keep in mind that this position on the spectrum only describes general tendencies. Any one interview (or interviewer) may depart completely from this pattern. Note also that schools change their approach from one year to the next; in recent years several top schools have dramatically increased or decreased the percentage of applicants they interview.

MOST APPLICANTS (WRONGLY) BELIEVE THEY ARE GREAT INTERVIEWEES

Most people feel they interview very well, but the reality is vastly different—only a minority do. To become a good interviewee, you need to prepare well. Although it is generally appropriate to interview, if you are sure to make a poor impression, either improve your interviewing abilities or maneuver to avoid an interview. The people who should try to avoid an interview are those who are pathologically shy, whose language abilities will crack under the strain, or who are so obdurate or contentious that they will inevitably antagonize their interviewers. (Unfortunately, nearly everyone thinks that he or she interviews well. Very few people will eliminate themselves on the basis of poor interviewing abilities.)

BEFORE THE INTERVIEW

ESTABLISHING YOUR OBJECTIVES

The interview is important for all-too-obvious reasons. The fact that the school emphasizes the interview means you have the opportunity to market yourself in a format in which most people do very little good for themselves. Some candidates are afraid of the interview and set themselves hopelessly limited objectives for it. They hope to get through it without embarrassing themselves. Or they hope that the interviewer likes them. You have the chance to make a very positive impression that will further your marketing efforts, so it is up to you to seize it. *Do not simply hope to survive the interview; be determined to achieve positive results.* Use it to reinforce all of your other positioning efforts.

You already have a marketing strategy in place, so go back to it when you are considering what you hope to accomplish in the interview. If you have positioned yourself as a true entrepreneur with great understanding of emerging technologies, for example, this positioning strategy will help you think through the interview and how to prepare for it.

Ask yourself the following questions at the start of your preparations:

1. How do you want the interviewer to think of you? What specific impressions and information do you want her to carry away from the interview?

2. How can you reinforce your strengths and address your key weakness(es)?

3. How can you convey any important pieces of information that may not receive full attention (or any attention) in the written application?

4. How can you show you know a great deal about the school—that you are well prepared for the interview?

5. How can you learn whatever you need to know to decide which school to attend?

PREPARING

Prepare for four aspects of any interview: (1) the likely format of a meeting as well as what to expect of your interviewer, (2) your objectives, (3) what the school offers, and (4) what questions your interviewer is likely to ask.

1. TYPICAL FORMAT

Interview formats differ according to the type of interview to be conducted. Nevertheless, whether of a Kellogg or a Harvard type, they are likely to be structured on the following lines:

- Welcome
- A few easy, "ice-breaker" questions meant to set you at ease, perhaps about how you are, if it was easy to find the location, and so forth
- Predictable questions (if the interview is a Kellogg type) or in-depth questions keyed to your circumstances (if the interview is a Harvard type)
- The chance to ask questions
- Conclusion

The first minutes of an interview may not involve substantive discussion, but they are likely to be important in forming the interviewer's impression of you. Therefore, do your best to appear confident and pleasant even before you get to the heart of the interview.

The typical interview will last thirty minutes, although it may be longer. In fact, alumni tend to differ from other interviewers insofar as they are generally chattier, more interested in selling the school, and less interested in "grilling" applicants than either admissions officers or students are. Admissions officers, in contrast, tend to run a smooth interview and are likely to be extremely focused and to keep interviews very short (typically thirty minutes). Students are typically less smooth, ask very tough questions, and tend to assess applicants in terms of whether they would be assets to the student's study group.

2. YOU AND YOUR OBJECTIVES

One leading American program has long used the interview evaluation form shown here. It lays out very clearly the areas that are of interest to the school and thus the qualities you will want to demonstrate.

A LEADING SCHOOL'S INTERVIEW EVALUATION FORM

HIGHLY DESCRIPTIVE	DESCRIPTIVE	NEUTRAL	DESCRIPTIVE	HIGHLY DESCRIPTIVE

Comments:

Clear Communication Skills   vs.   **Weak Communication Skills**

Conveys thoughts and information
  in a clear organized way

Succinct; to the point

Good, active listener

Appropriate depth in answers

Persuasive; "sells" ideas well

Provides clear explanations

Appropriate expressiveness

Unclear; hard to follow

Goes off on tangents

Rambles, verbose

Too brief; information has to be
  drawn out

Overly factual; monotonous

Makes too many assumptions; not
  sensitive to needs of audience

Shows little or no emotion

Intellectually Curious   vs.   **Lacks Curiosity**

Asks probing questions

Exhibits an eagerness to learn

Open-minded

Seeks out new challenges and opportunities

Looks for unique ways to solve problems

Exhibits a broad interest pattern

Applies self fully; well disciplined

Curious about and understands key
  aspects of our program

Appears apathetic

Tends not to question or probe

Appears to be a "know it all"

Narrow in outlook

Intellectually lazy; may be bright but
  doesn't push self

Too often goes the "tried-and-true" way

Naive about our program or MBA
  programs in general

Strong Social Skills   vs.   **Poor Social Skills**

Personable

Seems friendly and at ease with others

Appropriately assertive; states opinions tactfully

Outgoing; enjoys being with others

Cooperates within a team environment

Strives for leadership positions

Appropriate dominance in group environments

Good sense of humor

Appreciates humor of others

Shows enthusiasm and positive emotions

Sarcastic, biting humor

Overly serious; formal

Loner; overly shy and quiet

Overbearing; domineering

Overly self-oriented

Distant; cold

Lacks tact; blunt

Avoids conflict

Overly critical or negative

Self-Confident   vs.   **Lacks Self-Confidence**

Projects a positive, professional image
  and attitude

Arrogant or cocky

Overly tentative; hesitant

(Continued)

HIGHLY DESCRIPTIVE	DESCRIPTIVE	NEUTRAL	DESCRIPTIVE	HIGHLY DESCRIPTIVE

Speaks with conviction

Handles self well in interpersonal confrontation

Confident of intellectual skills

Looks forward to intellectual challenges and new learning opportunities

Takes pride in accomplishments

Avoids eye contact

Easily threatened or intimidated

Overly concerned about academic challenges

Overly critical or negative

Stays nervous; anxious throughout interview

Committed to Building Relationships   vs.   **Not Relationship-Oriented**

Participates in groups

Seeks out relationships

Active in formal and informal organizations

Concerned about giving back to the organization or group

Takes pride in past affiliations

Approaches new environments with vigor and passion

Gets involved in community service and extracurricular activities

Uninvolved with others

Not a social joiner

Just concerned about what he/she takes out of groups

Waits for others to organize groups and events

Lacks interest in outside activities (high school, undergraduate, work experience)

Hard-Working   vs.   **Lacks Persistence**

Persistent; goes the extra step

Exhibits drive and determination

Willing to sacrifice

Takes initiative; doesn't wait for others' direction

Enjoys and seeks out responsibility

High-quality orientation

Views problems as challenges

High energy level

Goal-oriented

Ambitious

Overly concerned with short-term pleasures

Complacent; coasts along

Takes path of least resistance

Gets overly frustrated with obstacles

Low energy or overly hyper

Drifts; lacks ambition

Does not have well-defined career goals or direction

Independent   vs.   **Dependent**

Enjoys autonomy

Likes to be in control of situations

Self-sufficient

Looks too much to others for direction or guidance

Seeks out structure

HIGHLY DESCRIPTIVE	DESCRIPTIVE	NEUTRAL	DESCRIPTIVE	HIGHLY DESCRIPTIVE
Comfortable working within ambiguous situations			Poorly focused; easily distracted	
Able to develop own goals and focuses well				
Flexible		**vs.**	**Inflexible or Overly Flexible**	
Responsive to changing priorities			Overly concerned about things being a certain way	
Able to juggle several tasks at once				
Deals well with the ups and downs of academic and corporate life			Flusters easily with obstacles	
			Rigid in beliefs	
Takes setbacks in stride			Wishy-washy	

Summary Evaluation

Based on your comments and what you know about our school and its students and graduates, do you:

Feel that this person has well-thought-out reasons for getting an MBA?

Yes   No   Unsure

Agree that this individual has a good understanding of our program?

Yes   No   Unsure

Want this person in your class or organization?

Yes   No   Unsure

Agree that this individual is a good match with our program?

Yes   No   Unsure

Feel that this individual would attend our program if admitted?

Yes   No   Unsure

Vote to admit this person to the program?
Yes   No   Unsure

Overall Comments:

Please document the substance of your conversation with the applicant and your evaluation of the candidate. Please add any additional thoughts, positive or negative, which would assist us in making an informed admission decision.

This evaluation form may not capture everything that could be relevant in a candidate, but it certainly captures enough to show you the way in which a school will assess you. Other schools, of course, have their own approaches, but these, without exception, are similar to the one shown here. The primary differences are that some schools use much briefer evaluation forms, whereas others highlight something particularly important to their own programs. Some of the programs that feature heavy quantitative demands probe applicants' experience and capabilities using various quantitative techniques. Various European (and some American) schools assess candidates' internationalism. Most focus on language skills, understanding of other cultures, experience working in different cultures, and interest in the program's international dimensions.

3. KNOWING THE SCHOOL

Chapter 3, "How to Choose the Right School for *You*," examined many criteria relevant to that decision. It also detailed how to find the information necessary for making a well-informed decision. Let's assume you have read that chapter and followed its advice prior to applying. Now that you are preparing for school interviews, it would be a good idea to review the information you put together on each school with which you plan to interview. In particular, you should be extremely familiar with the information the school publishes about itself. If you tell the interviewer that you plan to major in international business but the school offers no such major, you will look foolish.

If you are going to interview at the school itself, try to spend several hours in advance exploring the school and its environs. Talk with people in the cafeteria or lounge, paying attention to the attitudes they evince. Are they generally pleased with the school? Do they respect most of their professors? Do they think the placement office is doing its job? Are there any particular problems concerning the facility itself, such as crime or lack of late-night restaurants, that might matter to you? It always impresses an interviewer to see that you have taken the time and effort to examine the school up close rather than just reading some materials on it. Knowing what type of housing is available, or which professors students maneuver to take classes from, are the sorts of things that show you to be both determined and resourceful. It also helps you to develop good questions to ask the interviewer without sounding artificial. Even if you are not interviewing on campus, take advantage of any opportunities to visit schools for precisely these reasons. (Interviewers invariably spot the applicants who have done their homework by visiting the school and learning what its program is really like.)

One last point: If you find out which specific person will be interviewing you, ask people you know who interviewed with the same person at the same school about the interview and to see how it was conducted. How formal or informal was it? How rapid-fire? How long? How much was the interviewee expected to initiate, rather than just respond to, questions? How friendly was the interviewer? If you know how this person likes to conduct interviews, you will be able to prepare more specifically.

The advantages of knowing the school thoroughly include:

- You will know that you are prepared, enabling you to relax somewhat during the interview.
- You will be able to ask intelligent questions about the school, thereby impressing the interviewer.

■ You will show yourself as being highly motivated, concerned about your career, and in possession of the right work ethic, which will impress your interviewer.

4. ANTICIPATING THE QUESTIONS

As the beginning of this chapter laid out, school policy regarding how many applicants it interviews affects the kind of questioning you are likely to encounter. At Kellogg-type schools (those interviewing most applicants), there is a substantial chance that you will be asked only the standard questions set forth in the box below.

MOST LIKELY QUESTIONS

➤ For each element (school, job, etc.) of your résumé: Why did you choose this? Was it a good choice? What did you learn? Why did you leave it?

➤ Tell me about yourself.

➤ What do you do for fun?

➤ What are your career goals? How will our program help you achieve your professional goals?

➤ Why do you want an MBA? Why now?

➤ Why do you want to attend this school? How much do you know about the program? To what other schools are you applying?

➤ Why should we accept you?

➤ What would you add to the program?

➤ What are your greatest achievements?

➤ Tell me about a personal or professional failure.

➤ What sort of international experience have you had?

➤ Describe a recent leadership experience.

➤ Describe a recent teamwork experience.

➤ Tell me about a challenge you faced or hard decision you had to make.

➤ What kind of manager are you?

➤ What do you like/dislike about your job?

➤ What is the primary weakness in your application?

➤ What questions do you have?

At Harvard-type schools (those interviewing relatively few applicants), expect questions tailored to your own situation. If you have claimed some marvelous successes, your interviewer may wish to probe to make sure you have not exaggerated the results. Similarly, she may ask for more examples to buttress a claim you've made. Or she may wish to probe for gaps or weaknesses in your career to date. For example, one of the standard things to seek in a résumé is a period of unaccounted-for time. If such a time gap exists in your application, expect to be asked what you were doing then. Your whole application is fair game, so study it closely.

Whichever type of interview you face, the easiest question to prepare for is "Do you have any questions?" You should be ready with two to four questions that reflect your concerns about the school. Keep these in your head rather than on paper, because having to look at your notes will slow the interview down and make it look as though you cannot remember even a few questions.

FURTHER PREPARATION

Whether you expect an easy, Kellogg-type interview, or a probing, Harvard-type interview, prepare as best you can. Start by rereading your answer's to essay questions asked by this school and others. Capitalize on these in-depth marketing efforts you have already undertaken. Then, consult Appendix VIII in this chapter, which lays out a range of possible questions by topic. Consider which ones a savvy interviewer might think to ask you given your profile. Focus particularly on the one or two questions you actually hope the interviewer will not ask.

WHAT DETERMINES THE LIKELIHOOD OF A GIVEN QUESTION BEING ASKED?

In a Kellogg-type interview, you may face a standard set of questions without regard to your own circumstances. Even in an interview for a school that interviews relatively few applicants, your interviewer may ask the same sorts of things of all those she interviews.

However, this will not always be the case. A good interviewer, and often even a bad interviewer, will try to use the interview to learn as much relevant information as possible about you. In interviews that are tailored to you, your profile and background will invite questions quite different from those that would be asked of someone else. If you are in a nonbusiness field that seldom produces MBA candidates, you can expect questions concerning why you want an MBA. If you have a history of career success but just got fired from your job, you can expect questions about what happened. If one of your credentials is relatively weak, you can expect questions about it. If you are an Anglophone trying to get into a bilingual program, you can expect to have your second language probed. An interviewer should also probe for internal inconsistencies ("Why were you paid so little if you were really in charge of the internal audit function?") as well as checking those that sound inherently unlikely ("How is it that you were in charge of conducting an internal control audit of the whole Swedish subsidiary when you had never done anything even vaguely related to such a field?").

The nature of the questioning will depend in part upon the information the interviewer is given. If she is given your entire file, expect her to probe more than if she is given just your résumé. You can thus influence the course of an interview to a great extent by the way you present yourself in your résumé.

The other items an interviewer will probe are things you and she have in common or about which she is simply curious ("What is the cheapest luxury trip down the Nile currently available?"). The more that an interviewer takes this approach, the easier the interview is likely to be. Discussing interests you share is likely to provide an opportunity to share enthusiasms, which is generally easier to handle than responding to probing questions about why you left a good job after just fifteen months. Be sure, however, to keep to your own objectives. You can still make the impression you want by being articulate and well organized even when just discussing trips down the Nile.

PRACTICE

There are two ways you can practice your interviewing skills and responses. The first is by doing mock interviews with others who are applying, or someone else who appreciates what is involved. This is a good first step to understanding what an interview will be like. The quality of the experience will depend in large part upon how prepared your interviewing partner is. If you can find someone who is willing to read your application carefully, and perhaps even read this chapter, then you are ready to get a good interview. The ideal person with whom to team up would be someone who is applying to the same schools, but has a very different background from yours, and who is willing to be tough when necessary in the interview. It can be difficult to find the right person, of course. (It is partly for this reason that I regularly conduct mock interviews with clients, if necessary by phone, to give them a realistic view of what to expect.) It is not only fair but also good for you to switch roles with your partner. If you have to read her essays and data sheets with an eye to seeing what her strengths and weaknesses are, what she will contribute to the program, and the like, you will more readily understand how someone else will do this with you.

Your interview partner can tell you which responses were convincing and which were not (and why). Be persistent and force your interview partner to be specific in noting what worked and what did not. After all, the point is not what you say but *what your interviewer hears* that determines the success of your interview. In fact, simply saying things out loud will often cause *you* to hear what is not right. Speaking out loud often makes it clear that you are wandering instead of staying focused, trying too hard to excuse some prior mistake, sounding too stiff, or pleading rather than convincing. Tape-recording your practice sessions will make this apparent.

If you can videotape your practice interviews, by all means do so. Seeing yourself in action will help you to eliminate bothersome gestures and repetitive phrasings. Particularly annoying is the inappropriate use of "like," "you know," "awesome," "totally," "hey," and so on. Wear your interview outfit to make sure that it, too, passes muster.

The second means of practicing is to be sure you interview first with the schools that matter least to you. If you are applying to three "likely" choices, make sure your first two interviews are with schools in this category rather than the "possibles" or "stretches." This allows you to develop and refine your pitch and get rid of your first interview nerves without too much at stake.

It is a good idea to use both of these approaches if you can. Maximize the potential benefits by debriefing your partner after an interview, reviewing the experience yourself to be sure you understand what worked, what needed more thought, and why. It should go without saying that whatever approach you use, it should be keyed to the type of interview you expect.

PHYSICAL PREPARATIONS

Physical Energy
- Get plenty of sleep the two nights before the interview.
- Eat a solid breakfast or lunch on the day, so that you do not run out of energy.

Appearance
- Arrive at the actual site slightly before the allotted time so that you do not need to rush and get nervous as a result.
- *Men:* Make sure your hair is combed, and your tie is straight and completely covered in back by your shirt collar. Consider carrying an extra tie and perhaps a shirt in case something is spilled at lunch.
- *Women:* Make sure your lipstick is not smudged or on your teeth. Carry extra pantyhose in case of a run.

Location
- Be sure you know where the interview will take place and how to get there (and where to park).

Other

- Take your business cards, several copies of your résumé, and a copy of your application.

- Take a copy of the program's brochure and other relevant information about it to review if you get there early.

- Take the name and telephone number of your interviewer in case your car breaks down or you run into other travel problems and you need to notify her of your delay.

- Consider taking copies of the wonderful brochure you designed for your company, but do not take the two-hundred-pound, greasy widget that you manufacture.

STAYING RELAXED

A modest degree of nervousness is good because it gives you the energy to perform at your best. If you tend to be too nervous, try one of these techniques to keep yourself relaxed:

- ➤ Remind yourself that you have prepared thoroughly (assuming that this is the case) and that this preparation will see you through.

- ➤ Acting positive, by using the appropriate body language, will help you to feel the way you are acting. Positive body language involves keeping your head up, shoulders square, and eyes forward.

- ➤ Breathe slowly and deeply.

- ➤ A great friend of mine, before exams and cross-country races, used to go off by himself and keep repeating, with concentration and intensity, "I am King Kong, I am King Kong."

DURING THE INTERVIEW

A considerable amount of the impact you have in an interview is achieved non-verbally. *Nonverbal signals may constitute over half of the message you deliver.* As a result, it is highly appropriate to consider such factors as dress, physical comportment, and the like in order to maximize the chances of interview success.

DRESS

Business schools are inherently conservative places. The top graduates tend to go off into management consulting and investment banking, the professors consult to top multinational corporations, and the typical applicant is currently working in a corporate environment. This means that the style appropriate for a business school interview is a conservative one.

Rules for Men

- Wear clean, neatly pressed clothes and highly shined, black shoes. Socks should be black or navy blue and over the calf.
- Be sure your clothes fit well. Also be sure your clothes do not look as if you are wearing them for the first time, but they should not be so well worn that this is noticeable.
- Avoid wild colors or styles.
- You will never go wrong wearing a conservative dark blue or gray suit with a white or blue shirt—or moderately striped shirt—and a conservative tie.
- Comb your hair and wear no cologne.
- Be sure your fingernails are clean and well-groomed.
- It should go without saying that your shirt should be 100 percent cotton, long-sleeved, professionally cleaned, and heavily starched. The tie should be pure silk and extend to the middle of your belt buckle.
- If you have a beard or moustache, make sure it is neatly trimmed; if not, be clean shaven.

Rules for Women

- Wear a suit, a pantsuit, or a simple dress, and no more than a modest amount of jewelry, makeup, and perfume. Jewelry should not rattle or otherwise distract.
- Women have more leeway than men in choosing appropriate lengths, colors, and cuts of clothing. Acceptable appearance may alter with changing fashion trends, but do not go wild; be especially wary of skirts that are too short and blouses that are too low-cut or tight.
- In the United States, wear pantyhose (no matter how hot the weather) and eschew bare arms.
- Try not to bring both a briefcase and a purse because it is difficult to be graceful when carrying both.

Rules for Men and Women

- Do not wear such ostentatiously expensive clothes that you might offend your interviewer.

- Your briefcase should be of good leather.

- Be sure you have invested appropriately in mouthwash, deodorant, and other hygienic necessities.

You want to be remembered for what you said, not for what you wore (or failed to wear).

BEHAVIOR

Your goal is to be considered self-confident and relaxed. You can show this by remaining poised and thoughtful throughout the interview.

Physical Behavior

- Greet the interviewer with a smile, an extended hand, and a firm hand-shake (matching the interviewer's pressure).

- Look the interviewer in the eye.

- Do not sit down until invited to do so.

- Do not put anything on the interviewer's desk.

- Do not smoke, drink, or eat anything even if invited to do so—not even if the interviewer herself does. This can distract either you or the inter-viewer, perhaps showing you to be clumsy or worse, without any chance of improving her opinion of you. If the interviewer offers you a cigarette, decline politely but not judgmentally by saying, "No, thank you."

- Do not chew gum.

- Maintain a moderate amount of eye contact throughout the interview, perhaps 40 percent, but do not stare.

- Gesticulate moderately to make points, but do not go overboard.

- Remain physically stationary, without fidgeting. Interviewers often check your response to a tough question to see whether you are exhibiting signs of nervousness (or lying).

- Maintain good rapport with the interviewer by being warm and smiling often. Do not, however, smile idiotically without stopping for the entire in-terview! Doing so will mark you as unbalanced or worse.

- Sit up straight but not rigidly, and lean forward very slightly. This will show that you are interested in what the interviewer has to say, and that you are businesslike.

- Listen carefully, and show that you are listening by nodding or saying "uh-huh," "I see," or "right" occasionally.

- Avoid crossing your arms or folding your arms behind your head.

- Keep your voice well modulated but alive. Speak at a normal speed; do not rush.

Attitude

- *Be upbeat.* Be sure to emphasize your strengths. Do not discuss your weaknesses in any detail unless pushed to do so. Never complain about anything that has befallen you. No complaint about a low GMAT score, sickness during a math exam, or personality conflict with a boss or professor can improve an interviewer's opinion of you.

- *Flatter the interviewer, subtly.* Although a good interviewer will have you do 75 to 80 percent of the talking, that does not mean you will be excused for failing to listen to her. Adopt an attitude similar to the interviewer's. If your interviewer is deadly serious, avoid joking. If your interviewer is lighthearted and jocular, do not sit deadpan. In the first instance, jocularity will make you seem frivolous; whereas in the latter instance, seriousness will make you seem unintelligent. Maintain more formality if your interviewer remains behind her desk throughout the interview, without even coming around to greet you initially.

- *Treat the interviewer respectfully, but not too respectfully.* Treat her as an equal, albeit one who is temporarily allowed to set the direction of the interview. Do not behave submissively. Do not, however, use the interviewer's first name unless and until told to do so.

- *Relax and enjoy yourself.* The relatively few people who enjoy interviews are those who view them as a chance to discuss important matters with an equal who happens to be interested in the same subjects. They view the interview as a time to learn more about the school and as a chance to explain themselves. A little nervousness is to be expected, but exhibiting substantial nervousness works against you insofar as a strong candidate is meant to believe himself well suited to interact at this level.

- *Make sure it is a conversation.* A good interview resembles nothing so much as a conversation. If there is a pause in the conversation, consider whether: (1) You have answered the question fully enough. If you suspect not, ask whether the interviewer would like you to add to the answer. (2) You should follow up with a question of your own related to the same subject. (3) You should simply sit quietly, without tension, with a pleasant smile. Ask the interviewer questions to follow up on what she has said. This helps to build rapport and puts you on a more equal footing with her by getting you out of the role of interviewee answering questions. It is also the way normal conversations work, trading back and forth.

- *Avoid sounding like a robot.* If you follow this book's suggestions and prepare thoroughly for your interviews, you run the risk of sounding preprogrammed rather than spontaneous. It is good to sound as though you have given thought to the relevant issues, but not as though you have memorized answers. How can you avoid this problem? There are three keys: (1) Do not speak in a monotone, or appear to be reaching into your memory for what comes next in your rehearsed response. (2) Focus upon your interviewer. You should be able to remain relaxed, given that you know you are well prepared, and this will allow you to stay focused upon how your interviewer is reacting to you. (3) Occasionally pause before you speak, seeming to get organized before starting.

- *Look interested.* Avoid looking at your watch. Do not stretch in your chair. Do not appear bored, no matter how long the interviewer is speaking.

- *Do not ramble on.* If your answer has gone on too long, cut your losses by briefly restating your main points.

HOW TO READ THE INTERVIEWER

The interviewer's demeanor will help to reveal her reactions to the interview. Smiles and nods clearly suggest that she agrees with what you are saying, in which case you should think about what you are doing right so that you can do more of it. Perhaps your interviewer likes the fact that you are backing up your abstractions with solid examples. Maybe you are keeping your cool when being asked very tough questions.

Looking away from you, frowning, or constantly fiddling with papers or pens may reveal disagreement or a lack of interest. If you sense you are losing the interviewer, try to get back on track by asking the interviewer a relevant question or making comments that are sure to be winners, such as some self-deprecating humor or mention of the incidents that you feel show you in your best light.

It is important to keep in mind whatever the interviewer says in her opening remarks because they may give you good clues as to what she values.

If you are talking too much, your interviewer is likely to start looking away, looking at her watch, or asking such questions as "Could you just summarize this part?"

YOUR QUESTION TIME

A failure to ask questions if invited to do so risks leaving the impression that you either did not do your homework or do not particularly care whether the school admits you. Asking questions gives you the opportunity to show how knowledgeable you are about the process and the program as well as that you are taking a proactive approach to your career future.

If you are asked what questions you have, do not rush into asking them. If you have not yet had the opportunity to make one or two key points, ask if it would be acceptable to go back to the earlier question and then mention what you have just accomplished (or whatever). Even if these points are unrelated to any prior question, feel free to say "I am glad to have the opportunity to ask you a couple of questions, but I hope you will forgive my wanting to mention two things that have come up since I applied. I think they might be relevant to the school's decision making, after which I will continue with my questions." Briefly mention the one or two points. Then go on to your questions.

Try to avoid questions that call for a yes or no response. To understand an area in depth, plan to ask several questions about it. If you think the interviewer harbors major objections to you, try to get her to confess what it is she is concerned about so that you can address her concerns, assuming you have not yet had the opportunity to do so.

Some appropriate questions, in case you are stuck for something to ask, include:

- How do you expect the school to change in the near future?
- Has the character of the school changed in recent years? How? Why?
- What most surprises students about the school? (That is, given their expectations prior to starting, what did they not expect regarding their fellow students, professors, teaching, workload, social life, recruitment process, and so on?)

If one reason for attending the school is that a certain professor teaches there, by all means ask whether the interviewer knows him or her and, if so, what he or she is like as a professor.

Do not try to baffle the interviewer with questions you know she won't be able to answer. If she is an alum of the school, for example, she will not be privy to the school's rationale for its recent decision not to offer tenure to Assistant Professor X. Similarly, do not ask unintelligent questions or ones that can easily be answered with a glance at the school's application materials (such as "What is the usual class size?") just for the sake of asking a question.

Being asked if you have any questions signals that the interview is coming to an end, so do not take too much time.

ENDING THE INTERVIEW

Be sure to smile at the interviewer, shake hands and thank her for seeing you, and leave with an energetic, confident demeanor.

Be careful not to be taken in by an old trick. Once you feel that the interview is over, you may be asked a potentially revealing question as you are being shown out, on the assumption that you may have let down your guard at this point. Or the secretary may be instructed to ask a question such as, "How do you think you did?" in hopes of eliciting a telling comment. Assume that the interview is really over only once you have left the premises.

INTERVIEW WRECKERS

➤ Dressing inappropriately

➤ Being too nervous to look the part of a successful, confident leader

➤ Criticizing your boss or company

➤ Whining about past grades, low GMAT scores, and so on

➤ Blaming others for a weakness in your profile

➤ Appearing blasé about attending the school at hand

➤ Asking no questions—or those readily answered by even a cursory look at the school's website

---

GENERAL RULES FOR INTERVIEWS

The following advice is good no matter what type of interview or interviewer you encounter:

DO NOT CRITICIZE OTHERS

Do not criticize people you worked with or schools you attended; otherwise, you may be viewed as a chronic malcontent. Remain positive. You can still make it clear, for example, that a boss was limited in his ability to develop you, but without sounding critical. Simply state that he was expected to spend most of his time traveling to the regional offices, so he had no time left to worry about the development of his subordinates.

ASSUME THAT INTERVIEWERS (ESPECIALLY ALUMS AND STUDENTS) DO NOT HAVE YOUR FILE MEMORIZED

In fact, most interviewers will not even have seen your file. You can therefore expect to be able to make good use of the same incidents you discussed in your essays.

BE TRUTHFUL

Do not lie in answering questions. Being honest, however, does not mean the same thing as being blunt, so do not volunteer negative information if it can be avoided.

BE YOURSELF

Do not pretend to be someone other than yourself to impress your interviewer. Very few people are able to act well enough to carry it off successfully. Focus instead on presenting the best aspects of your own personality.

NEVER BE LESS THAN HIGHLY COURTEOUS AND FRIENDLY TO THE STAFF

The staff is generally in charge of all of the logistical elements of your candidacy, so do not alienate them. The admissions officers may also ask them to give their impression of you, so make sure it is a positive one.

DO NOT TRY TO TAKE OVER THE INTERVIEW, BUT TAKE ADVANTAGE OF OPPORTUNITIES TO MAKE YOUR POINTS

Interviewers want to feel they are in charge of an interview, since they are likely to make decisions based upon the information they get about you. They need to feel confident that they will be able to get what they consider information relevant to their decision-making, which may happen only if they are able to direct the interview. Taking over the interview may allow you to make the points you want to make, but the risk is far too great that your interviewer will react negatively to this and resent your aggressiveness. Use of polite phrases in a confident tone of voice can keep your interviewer from fearing that you are trying to take over the interview: "Perhaps you wouldn't mind . . ."; "I would find it very helpful if you could . . ."

DO NOT ASK THE INTERVIEWER HOW YOU DID IN THE INTERVIEW

This will put him on the spot and make you sound immature (not to mention lacking confidence). It will not do anything to improve your chances.

STAY RELAXED

A good interviewer takes the following as possible indications that you are lying, being evasive, or hoping that he will not follow up a point:

- Fidgeting (such as twirling your hair, drumming your fingers, bouncing your leg up and down, or picking at a part of your body or clothing. Many people have a tic of which they are completely unaware. Use your mock interview partner or videotape to find yours, and then stop doing it.)

- Speaking much faster or more slowly.

- Pulling your collar away from your neck.

- Avoiding eye contact.

- Giving lengthy, convoluted, or rambling responses.

- Desperately looking for a drink of water.

- Coughing at length before starting a response.

REMAIN CALM EVEN IN THE FACE OF PROVOCATION

An interviewer may be trying to annoy you to see how you respond. A prospective senior manager, it should go without saying, is unlikely to be easily ruffled.

ANSWER QUESTIONS CONCISELY

Do not ramble. Do not take more than two or three minutes for any but the most involved, important question. In fact, two or three sentences is an appropriate length for the majority of answers. You can save time by quantifying whenever possible ("I saved $275,000, which represented 13 percent of recurring costs").

STRUCTURE YOUR RESPONSES

Because you have prepared thoroughly (if you have taken this chapter to heart), you are in a position to respond with structured answers to most questions you will be asked. You do not need to start every response by saying "I did such and such for five reasons. Number one was . . . ," but having coherent and well-organized responses will be impressive.

When you give a general statement, illustrate it with an appropriate example ("I am comfortable in a very international setting. I have been able to work with people of all different backgrounds, such as when I managed a restaurant in New York that had Albanian cooks, Mexican busboys, Portuguese waitresses, a Greek owner, and a yuppie clientele—and I happen to be French, as you know"). Then go on to give an example in which nationality posed a substantial problem and how you solved it.

Summarize any particularly lengthy answers you give.

THE C.A.R. METHOD

One useful framework for structuring your response to a question is what I call the C.A.R. method. When describing something you did, you start with the *C*hallenge you faced, then describe the *A*nalysis and/or *A*ctions you performed, and finally recount the *R*esults you obtained:

➤ *Challenge:* Describe the situation at the beginning of your story, emphasizing what made your task challenging. For instance, perhaps a three-month-long project was mismanaged by someone who knew he was about to quit the firm and thereby squandered the first six weeks, leaving you as a newly promoted project manager to finish the required work in just seven weeks.

➤ *Analysis/Actions:* Describe what analysis you performed—and why—by taking your interviewer through your efforts step-by-step. Make the logic of the process apparent. Discuss what you did as if at each point your interviewer is about to ask, "What did you do next? Why?"

➤ *Results:* Think broadly about the results you achieved. Consider the impact upon the project, your group, the department, and the company. Then consider the impact upon yourself: Did you learn a new skill; demonstrate your abilities to others (and get further responsibilities); or learn something valuable about your abilities, interests, or values?

LISTEN WELL

Be sure you have understood what the interviewer is asking. If uncertain, ask for clarification of the question. Answering the question you thought was being asked, or the one you anticipated being asked, rather than the one she really did ask you will annoy her and suggest that you are either dim or not paying attention. Listening well means more than paying attention to what is being said. It also requires that you encourage the interviewer by appearing interested. In addition, you should be able to sense the feelings behind the comments made.

Sometimes a junior employee will chat with you while you wait for the real interview to start, trying to get you to give your real reactions to the school or your own qualifications, as though a junior person should be on your side rather than the school's. Expect any information you give away to be fed into your file, maybe even given to your real interviewer prior to your upcoming interview.

SPECIAL TYPES OF INTERVIEWS

The first two types of interviews described below are currently used largely at European schools; the last two are found everywhere.

GROUP EXERCISES

In a group exercise, you may be asked to work together with other applicants to solve a hypothetical problem or respond to a case. This is meant to test:

- Whether you can think on your feet and stay cool under pressure
- How creative or innovative you are
- Your verbal communication ability
- Whether you can work as part of a team
- Whether you can lead others
- Your willingness to participate (especially important if you have suspect language skills or cultural background)

These interviews are inevitably tricky because the other "team" members are all trying to get as much airtime as possible, so they are not likely to respond well to attempts to lead them.

How do you determine your own strategy? Start by determining four things: (1) what type of exercise is planned, (2) your skill set and experiences as they relate to the exercise, (3) the skill and experience of other applicants, and (4) your risk profile—how much of a risk you are willing to take to impress the graders of the exercise, given how high you believe your standing is prior to the exercise.

To stand out without looking like a publicity-crazed adolescent, consider prior to the exercise how best to position yourself. Do your homework regarding the exercise, too. Ask the admissions office what to expect in the exercise. Talk with people at the school about their experiences with this or a similar exercise, or see if another exercise is planned for earlier in the same day or the day before, and debrief participants as they exit.

As a general rule, wear your knowledge lightly. Work to impress observers with your openness to others' viewpoints, willingness to explore ideas first proposed by someone else, and overall enjoyment of the process. By all means put forward one or more of your ideas, but try to entice others into exploring them rather than trying to force them to do so. Above all, recognize that your (team-oriented) attitude counts for more than the weightiness of your comments.

PANEL INTERVIEWS

Panel interviews are often conducted with harsh time constraints because they represent a large investment of resources (three or more people's time). This means you should be particularly certain to arrive in advance. Explain that you understand this format places time pressure on the proceedings, so you will strive to give very concise answers to questions, but you welcome requests for additional information.

Start each response by addressing the person who asked the question, then look at other panel members, and then look back to the original questioner as you finish your response.

If you are asked questions by several people simultaneously, look at the most important (a chairperson for the panel) or someone who has not asked a question before and ask her (with a smile) if she could please repeat the question.

FRIENDLY CHATS

One type of interviewer will come on as extremely friendly and casual. She will chat away about recent football results or the interviewee's favorite foods. When she shifts to business matters, she will be completely unthreatening and will agree with anything and everything you say. The danger is that she will lull you into totally dropping your guard so that you end up volunteering information that you would be better off keeping to yourself. You are inclined to consider a person who finds you agreeable, fascinating, and invariably correct to be on your side. Resist this temptation; your interviewer may just be using this technique to get you to open up about yourself.

STRESS INTERVIEWS

Stress interviews are not much in evidence any more, but they still pop up often enough to merit comment. The idea underlying any form of stress interview is that applying enormous stress to an interviewee will cause him to reveal his *true* nature and likely performance under stress in the future. A failure to remain poised will reveal a person's supposed lack of confidence in himself.

What exactly is a stress interview? It can take many forms. You may be put in a position in which bright sunlight will be directly in your eyes, or your responses may be met by long silences. The tendency in this case is to try to fill up the awkward moments by adding to a response, thereby perhaps revealing information you would have been better advised to keep from view.

More likely you will be given too little time to answer questions. As you start to answer a question, your response may be ignored or cut short and taken out of context, and the next question tossed at you as fast as possible. The interviewer may dispute what you are saying and challenge you very aggressively. Your weaknesses can be pointed out at every turn. The interviewer can also be obviously hostile and rude. This will continue for some time, until you react, most probably by becoming angry or resentful that you are not being allowed to get your full answers out.

The key to this situation is to recognize it for what it is. If you know that it is a game, you can respond with suitable bits of gamesmanship. Once you know that you are deliberately being pressured, you have the opportunity to take control of the situation. (This is one of the few circumstances in which it is appropriate for you to take control.) If the sun is shining directly into your eyes, excuse yourself and move your chair to a more comfortable location. If you are being subjected to the silent treatment, respond by smiling at the interviewer and simply waiting for her to ask another question. If, on the other hand, you are being pressured verbally, start by leaning back, smiling, and not saying anything for a few seconds. Then restate the last question, "You have asked me whether this project was really successful." Go on to explain that there are, let's say, four parts to your response. Once you have done this it will be all but impossible for the interviewer to interrupt you until you have finished all four. Be sure to start each portion of your response by saying, "first," "second," and so on.

If you are interrupted again, lean back once more, shake your head and smile again, and say that this approach seems a bit much, and invite the interviewer to engage in a civilized conversation instead.

SPECIAL INTERVIEW SETTINGS: RESTAURANTS

➤ Do not sit until the interviewer invites you to be seated.

➤ Consider the menu when the interviewer invites you to. Pick something midpriced, and do so without lengthy deliberations. Make sure you choose something familiar and easy to eat. Avoid things that splatter or require eating with your fingers.

➤ If the interviewer orders a drink or first course, follow suit by ordering at least some mineral water so that you have something with which to occupy yourself while she is drinking or eating.

➤ Do not order too much, since this suggests a lack of discipline.

➤ Use your discretion regarding alcohol consumption. The safest rule to follow is that you should consume somewhat less alcohol than would be normal for a businessperson in the same circumstances. In Italy it might well be considered rude to refuse wine at dinner, whereas in America it would be considered a sign of incipient alcoholism to have a drink before lunch. Of course, if your interviewer abstains from alcohol, you should too.

➤ In Europe, you should eat with both hands on the table. It is inappropriate both in America and in Europe to place your elbows on the table.

➤ Do not criticize the décor or the food.

➤ Treat the waiters and busboys very politely.

➤ Wait for the interviewer to begin the business end of the discussion. She may prefer to wait until after the drink or first course has been consumed.

WHAT THE ADMISSIONS DIRECTORS SAY ABOUT INTERVIEWS

Why Are Interviews Important?

➤ The paper application informs us about work experience and academic aptitude, but not about emotional intelligence—interpersonal skills, how you get on with others. Our interviews cover the usual basics, such as why you want to go to business school and why Stanford, but they have a behavioral component at their heart. Thus, we might ask: Tell us about a time in your life when you failed; give us an example when you let a team down; give us an example when you managed very well; tell us about a manager who was very good; or, conversely, tell us about a manager who was not. We expect you to reflect on your professional experiences and draw conclusions about yourself as a result. *SHARON HOFFMAN, STANFORD*

➤ Because we weight personal characteristics very heavily in our admission process, interviews are very important. Interpersonal and communication skills are most easily assessed in interviews, not on the basis of a written record. We ask a lot about why they've made various career and professional decisions, to understand their maturity and motivation. Thus, we ask *why* they chose the college they did, the major, the job and company, why they changed jobs, and so on. We ask less about *what* they've done. *Dawna Clarke, Tuck*

➤ We're trying to evaluate people, not pieces of paper. Although you may do a stellar job on paper, the reality is that how you present yourself and communicate with people is also a very important determinant of whether someone will be successful or not. You can't tell this from pieces of paper, so the interview is extremely important. *Linda Meehan, Columbia*

➤ For international applicants, this process is extremely important for us, given this is an English-speaking program. So if you have a difficult time speaking and understanding English, you'll have a difficult time taking advantage of what Columbia has to offer. *Linda Meehan, Columbia*

➤ I can't imagine not interviewing. You learn so much when you ask probing questions while looking candidates in the eye. *Dr. Simon Learmount, Judge (Cambridge)*

➤ First, because students come from such varied backgrounds, this gives us an important common tool for evaluating them. (We interview all our applicants.) Second, we want to have people who can contribute to our case-based program. If you can't articulate who you are in the interview process, you'll probably not be a good contributor in class or study group. Third, we're interested in fit. For example, we want to be sure your goals fit with the strengths of the program. *David Bach, Instituto de Empresa (Spain)*

➤ The interview is a very important step of the selection process. It allows the school to know the aptitudinal profile of the candidate, his or her personality traits, strengths and weaknesses in terms of soft skills. All these are elements that cannot easily be assessed through only, for example, the GMAT. Also, the interview gives the candidate the opportunity to better understand the school, its offer, and peculiar features. *Rossana Camera, Bocconi (Italy)*

➤ We want to see if they are the right fit for the program, but applicants need to do the same, and the interview is a good opportunity to do that. *Julia Tyler, London*

➤ Because we have a very small program, it's important to make sure that an applicant will fit. For example, someone who is really competitive and wants to be ranked in the class—which we don't do—won't fit. *Mary Granger, ESADE (Spain)*

➤ We interview people to see how interested in the program they are. We want to know how enthusiastic they are. It's hard to know this sort of thing from the application alone. GEA TROMP, ROTTERDAM

How Many Applicants Do You Interview?

➤ We're now interviewing on an invitation-only basis. After multiple readings of an application, we'll interview about 50 percent of the pool. We won't admit anyone without an interview. ROSE MARTINELLI, CHICAGO

➤ We aim to interview 40 percent of applicants and then admit about half of those interviewed. ANNE COYLE, YALE

➤ We interview close to 100 percent of applicants. Our interviewers have only the applicant's resume, not the whole file. JAMES HAYES, MICHIGAN

➤ We interview about 50 to 60 percent of applicants. LINDA MEEHAN, COLUMBIA

➤ We interview all of our domestic and most of our international candidates. SARAH E. NEHER, DARDEN

➤ We interview about 45 percent of our applicants. THOMAS CALEEL, WHARTON

➤ It varies a bit from year to year, but it averages about 30 percent. About 60 to 70 percent of those we interview are granted admission. ISSER GALLOGLY, STERN (NYU)

➤ About 35 percent. DR. SIMON LEARMOUNT, JUDGE (CAMBRIDGE)

➤ We interview all applicants, some of them more than once. DAVID BACH, INSTITUTO DE EMPRESA (SPAIN)

➤ We interview almost all of our applicants. The applicants who come from remote parts of the world are interviewed over the phone, if necessary. KIRT WOOD, ROTTERDAM

➤ We interview one-third of applicants and admit about half of those interviewed. Some 89 percent of those receiving offers enroll. KATTY OOMS SUTER, IMD (SWITZERLAND)

Format

➤ On-campus interviews are forty-five minutes; off-campus interviews with admissions officers are thirty minutes, but those with alumni have no specified length (although we recommend they be 45 to 60 minutes). SALLY JAEGER, TUCK

➤ Our interviews are strictly thirty minutes; the first twenty-five minutes are reserved for our questions, the last five for applicants' questions. ANNE COYLE, YALE

➤ They are meant to be between half an hour and an hour. They're usually done in the interviewer's offices, but are sometimes done in restaurants or cafés. They are casual but evaluative, and should be handled as though you're being interviewed for a job. They are not, however, case interviews. *LINDA MEEHAN, COLUMBIA*

➤ We have a thirty-minute blind interview. *THOMAS CALEEL, WHARTON*

➤ We have a set of criteria we apply in evaluating applicants, but we don't have a set interview format. *KIRT WOOD, ROTTERDAM*

➤ The interview is carried out on a one-to-one basis and takes place after the application form has been received and read. *ROSSANA CAMERA, BOCCONI (ITALY)*

➤ There is no standard length or format: Interviews can be formal or over a drink—it varies by culture. We don't want our interviewers to review the applicant's CV or ask questions we've already asked. Instead, we want them to determine whether the applicant is easy to talk to, communicative, personable, and so on. Alumni inevitably ask themselves whether they would have wanted to study with, be in a group with, or be part of the alumni network with this candidate. *JOELLE DU LAC, INSEAD*

What Do You Look for in the Interview?

➤ In reviewing an application, we look for individuals with strong interpersonal skills and the ability to communicate effectively; we also try to enhance our understanding of the candidate's goals, interests, and passions. Is this a person who would be a good "fit?" Would he or she make a positive impression as a corporate recruiter? *PETER JOHNSON, HAAS*

➤ We try to see if the candidate has more to offer than was apparent on paper. We connect a face/person with the application and hope that we can learn more about the individual in the face-to-face interview. *LINDA BALDWIN, UCLA*

➤ It's not meant to be an adversarial process. We want people to be as relaxed as possible. We look for people with strong interpersonal skills. When someone's extremely nervous, they may act out the nervousness in typical ways—stumbling through answers or talking too much or too little. I ask myself how a recruiter would view this person (if this were a job interview). I also consider how the candidate would interact with a team on group project. *PETER JOHNSON, HAAS*

➤ We try to assess whether someone is assertive yet personable, and likely to work well with other people in the program. *JAMES HAYES, MICHIGAN*

➤ The ability to articulate business understanding—for our case method classes. *SARAH E. NEHER, DARDEN*

➤ Fit is very important to us, and interviews play an important part in helping us determine whether an applicant will be a good fit in the Stern community. Also, because our interviewers have read the file in advance, they have the chance to ask about areas of concern—and applicants have the chance to address them and eliminate any doubts in person. *ISSER GALLOGLY, STERN (NYU)*

➤ We use an interview guide, which changes slightly month on month, to ensure consistency. On the basis of the initial screening of the candidate, we'll come up with issues we want to explore. We use this to develop a script for the interview. *DR. SIMON LEARMOUNT, JUDGE (CAMBRIDGE)*

➤ It's important that someone fit well into a learning team. That means they need to be good communicators. It's also helpful if they have appropriate experience. We probe their team experiences. If they say they didn't have any problems in a team, they probably have never been in a team. There are always problems—it's how you handle them that's key. *JOHN MAPES, CRANFIELD (ENGLAND)*

➤ We want to test their ability to engage in an argument and to withstand a challenge. We want to see if they can express their views clearly. We also look at the reasons someone wants to do an MBA, why more specifically at the London Business School. We'll look at his interpersonal skills. A lot of the work we do at London Business School is in a team environment, so we want to know whether someone will be able to cope with that. We want to be sure London Business School represents a good fit for him. And, at the end of the day, we want to know whether someone is going to contribute to the school and then, having done an MBA, go out and sell it for us. *JULIA TYLER, LONDON*

➤ We eliminate about half the applicants on the basis of their written applications. We then look to interview the remaining half. We want to give substance to the paper profile and get beyond the elements that represent good coaching of someone. *JOELLE DU LAC, INSEAD*

Who Does the Interviewing?

➤ Our interviews are conducted exclusively by alums. We try to offer them on a global basis. The goal: All those admitted in the future will have been interviewed. *SHARON HOFFMAN, STANFORD*

➤ Student interviewers do not attend admissions committee meetings. Instead, they give an interview write-up to us. *PETER JOHNSON, HAAS*

➤ They're done primarily by our alumni. Some are also done by a select few well-trained students. The smallest number are done by admissions committee members. *LINDA MEEHAN, COLUMBIA*

➤ Invited applicants can interview on campus with a second-year student, in their own city with an alum, or at a hub city with a member of the admissions committee. There is absolutely no difference among the different options, no advantage to choosing one over another. *THOMAS CALEEL, WHARTON*

➤ Our interviews are conducted almost exclusively by admissions professionals. We think it's important to have trained assessors of talent. *Isser Gallogly, Stern (NYU)*

➤ Our standard approach is to have two faculty members, one from a quantitative subject like finance, one from a qualitative subject, interview a candidate for thirty to forty minutes. *Dr. Simon Learmount, Judge (Cambridge)*

➤ SDA Bocconi interviews all its candidates either on campus by admissions officers or abroad through our alumni interviewers. *Rossana Camera, Bocconi (Italy)*

➤ In contrast to U.S. schools, the admissions officers don't do the interviewing. Alumni and faculty do it. *Julia Tyler, London*

➤ We give selected applicants one or two interviews; each is conducted by an alum. *Joelle du Lac, INSEAD*

What Information Does the Interviewer Have About the Applicant?

➤ Candidates may request an interview at any point in the process. Typically, the interviewer has only the résumé the interviewee brings to the interview. (There are a few exceptions—people who have been unable to interview earlier are reviewed at the end of the process, in which case we will have reviewed their entire file.) We like the interviewer to approach the process without any preconceived notions of the candidate. *Michele Rogers, Kellogg*

➤ Evaluative interviews are conducted by invitation, at the discretion of the Admissions Board, and after applications have been submitted and reviewed. Our interviewers—Admissions Board members and a few HBS alumni—have fully reviewed a candidate's application prior to the interview. *Brit Dewey, Harvard*

➤ Interviewers have your résumé and some notes from the initial review of your file. These notes may suggest specific issues or questions to the interviewer. *Ann W. Richards, Johnson (Cornell)*

➤ When admissions officers interview candidates, they usually have the candidate's file. Student interviewers, however, will have only the résumé. *Peter Johnson, Haas*

➤ Our interviewers have only the applicant's résumé; they haven't read the application. Our interviewer typically goes through the applicant's résumé in chronological order, asking what the person did (and how and why). We usually start at college, asking the reason he chose it. We then ask why he chose his first job—and why he left it. And so on. Applicants often make the mistake of trying not to duplicate what they said in the essays when responding to questions, not understanding that their interviewer is unfamiliar with the essays they wrote. *Anne Coyle, Yale*

➤ They are blind interviews, so the interviewer has just the applicant's name and résumé, not the undergraduate grades and GMAT scores or essays. *Linda Meehan, Columbia*

➤ It's a blind interview; we don't have your information in front of us. Because the interviewer doesn't know a thing about you—and hasn't formed an impression of you—it gives you a chance to drive the interview. *Sarah E. Neher, Darden*

➤ The interviewer has only a résumé. *Thomas Caleel, Wharton*

➤ Our interviews are not blind. So in addition to the readers reviewing the applicant's application, the interviewer gives it a thorough review. So the interview is not just an alumnus/a at Starbucks looking at a résumé for the first time. This is a trained admissions professional who has reviewed the case in its entirety. The applicant has already explained in the application why he wants Stern and why he wants an MBA, so we can have a much deeper, more personal conversation. Applicants have the chance to tell their story in greater depth than they would if we had to take the half hour to cover the basics about their candidacy. We already know the basics. *Isser Gallogly, Stern (NYU)*

➤ The interviewer has the candidate's full file. *David Bach, Instituto de Empresa (Spain)*

➤ The interviewers have the full file available, without the financial aspects (since this is a need-blind process). *Dr. Simon Learmount, Judge (Cambridge)*

➤ Generally our interviewer has the whole application file. *Mary Granger, ESADE (Spain)*

Advice

➤ Be mindful of the time available and the breadth of what you want to cover. If you take twenty minutes to answer the first question, you've undermined yourself. You need to be concise. *Rose Martinelli, Chicago*

➤ Our interviews allow us to get to know candidates better, but they are also designed to let candidates get to know us better, too. To prepare, be sure to research the school well. It's also a good idea to have begun work on your application materials, because this will crystallize many points for you and help you articulate your views. *Michele Rogers, Kellogg*

➤ If you view interviews as information exchanges, you will be more relaxed and sound more sophisticated than if you prepare yourself only for the purpose of responding to questions. *Linda Baldwin, UCLA*

➤ Arrive on time. Dress professionally. Shake the interviewer's hand. Answer the questions. And try to relax. Have a question or two in mind for the end of the interview, but do not ask something easily found in the catalogue—for instance, "Do you have any joint degree programs?" ANN W. RICHARDS, JOHNSON (CORNELL)

➤ Think through how you'd address some questions you can expect. For example, how will our program help you achieve your professional goals? PETER JOHNSON, HAAS

➤ Listen carefully to the question that's asked. Don't try to take over the interview. Provide vignettes to illustrate your points. Rather than simply stating that you're a team player, for example, relate a story showing yourself to be one. (This is good to keep in mind for essay writing, as well.) DAWNA CLARKE, TUCK

➤ Try to inject some personality and demonstrate a sound knowledge of our program. Don't dominate the interview; let the interviewer set the pace. Be respectful of the interviewer's time; don't make it impossible to conclude the interview in thirty minutes by trying to ask a hundred questions. Ask two or three targeted specifically to Michigan.

   If interviewed by telephone, don't read your answers. Written responses are often not quite on point. Not only that—it's obvious to us when you are reading rather than talking. JAMES HAYES, MICHIGAN

➤ Step back and think about what you're trying to accomplish. Reread your application. Be ready to answer typical questions, such as why you want an MBA. Do your homework; know a bit about the school. Be ready to be concise, since our interviews are only thirty minutes long. And don't get your answers off chat boards. Hearing the same answer to a question for the twentieth time isn't positive. Finally, relax a bit. This is primarily a chance to get to know you. We don't do stress interviews or anything like that. THOMAS CALEEL, WHARTON

➤ This is your chance to sell yourself to the admissions committee, so given that you're probably passionate about your story and Stern, it's OK for you to express some excitement. If you're not excited about who you are and what you have to offer, why should we be? ISSER GALLOGLY, STERN (NYU)

➤ Don't try to impress us; be yourself. We want a real dialogue with you. Having already reviewed your file and knowing that you are a viable candidate, we won't have to ask the obvious questions ("Why do you want an MBA?"). Instead, we can learn what you're passionate about—whether it's what's in the news, what the government just did, or something else. We'll see how you synthesize information, which is extremely valuable to us. Make sure that you've written your own essays so that nothing in the conversation will come as a surprise. ROSE MARTINELLI, CHICAGO

➤ Be yourself. Don't approach it believing that we have some ideal applicant in mind, because we don't. We've found over the years that there are many ideal people. KIRT WOOD, ROTTERDAM

➤ Candidates should try to be themselves and "unique," thus allowing the school to truly understand their profile and motivation. Strong coherence between what has been said and expressed in the essays and what is carried out in interviews is essential. It's also important that candidates have well researched the school and program, which helps us to be convinced of the applicants' motivation and choice. *ROSSANA CAMERA, BOCCONI (ITALY)*

➤ Reading the interviewer is critical. For instance, you can tell by the interviewer's body language whether you're providing enough information. *DR. SIMON LEARMOUNT, JUDGE (CAMBRIDGE)*

➤ First, it may be obvious, but really prepare. This is a one-time chance, and you have to shine throughout the day. Second, be yourself. We're not looking for a prototype. *KATTY OOMS SUTER, IMD (SWITZERLAND)*

➤ We are impressed when someone has done his homework and knows about our program—someone who obviously wants to come here. *ANDREW DYSON, MANCHESTER (ENGLAND)*

Unusual Interview Formats

➤ We look for personality, flair, and interesting ideas—and our approach to interviewing reflects these desires. Each interviewee is required to do a ten-minute presentation, preferably on an interesting subject. We'd much rather hear about the escargots de Bourgogne than another engineering project. Some of the excellent topics applicants have chosen include an analysis (by a pilot) of a recent, major airplane crash; how to enjoy scuba diving the first time without being frightened; and a Gaz de France fellow, employed to bribe and coerce people not to report environmentally dangerous or embarrassing things, discussed his job. *PANTÉA DE NOYELLE, HEC (PARIS)*

➤ We invite applicants to participate in a group discussion of a case. We hand out the case in advance. (It's a small case, which we change regularly.) The groups range from six to ten applicants. We observe how they respond to questions and how they work together. The people who will interview them later in the day also observe their performance. This gives the interviewers an additional perspective on them and also provides a useful discussion point for the interview. In addition to the admissions dimension, this case discussion also gives applicants a taste of what it's like to be working in a cross-national group at LBS. *JULIA TYLER, LONDON*

➤ Our interviews take place at IMD in Lausanne and last a full day. We try to get six candidates here at one time. Each one has a one-hour interview with an admissions committee member. Then they have one half hour to prepare a five-minute presentation, often on a consulting-type case. This is done in front of two or three members of the admissions committee. We want to get a feel for their thought processes. Afterwards, they have lunch with a current student. Not only can they ask what they like but this also builds links for future communication. We then bring all six together for a case discussion, based on a case they were given two to three weeks in advance. We see how they interact with one another, work as a team, and analyze the case. We see their interpersonal, team, communication, and perhaps analytical skills. *KATTY OOMS SUTER, IMD (SWITZERLAND)*

➤ Those who can't get to Cranfield are interviewed by telephone. Those interviewed here are interviewed by an academic. The candidate starts off by giving a three-minute presentation (on a topic given to them about two weeks in advance). No visual aids are permitted. A typical topic might be, "It would have been better if the automobile had not been invented. Discuss." It's difficult to get the pros and cons into just three minutes. *JOHN MAPES, CRANFIELD (ENGLAND)*

➤ We have an "observed group" situation as part of our interview day. We're not looking for someone to take over the group, to be aggressive and a leader; we're looking for someone to encourage other people, bring out the best in others, be a good team player. Five or six people would be asked to deal with a problem as a group. They'll be observed by an organizational specialist on the faculty (typically). It lasts for an hour. It's the process more than the result that interests us. *HELEN WARD, MANCHESTER (ENGLAND)*

Biggest Mistakes

➤ Good manners are surprisingly lacking. Some people are late or fail to show up and don't bother to cancel. *SALLY JAEGER, TUCK*

➤ A classic mistake is to ask us, "Why should I come to the Johnson School?" That is not something we can answer for you. *ANN W. RICHARDS, JOHNSON (CORNELL)*

➤ Trying to take control of the interview is a mistake. Let the interviewer ask the questions. Another mistake is to ask the interviewer, at the end of the interview, how you did. It can spoil an otherwise good interview. *PETER JOHNSON, HAAS*

➤ You need to do your research. There's nothing worse than someone coming in, sitting down, and saying, "So, tell me about the Tuck School." *SALLY JAEGER, TUCK*

➤ Rocking and swinging back and forth on chairs is surprisingly common, as is chewing gum during the interview. *ANNE COYLE, YALE*

➤ Some people are so hyped up that they fail to listen to the questions. *ROSE MARTINELLI, CHICAGO*

> ➤ Not being prepared. Being surprised by an obvious question such as "Tell me about yourself," then blathering on for twenty minutes in response. Panicking after the interview and sending endless e-mails apologizing for having messed up. (People often think they've done worse than was actually the case.) *THOMAS CALEEL, WHARTON*

> ➤ By far the biggest is trying to be someone they're not. Next is failing to show specific interest in the school you are talking with. *DAVID BACH, INSTITUTO DE EMPRESA (SPAIN)*

> ➤ Expecting certain questions and then not listening to the questions actually asked. Responding to an expected stock MBA question and not noticing subtle variations on it. Another mistake is to take five to ten minutes to answer a question, thereby frustrating the interviewer. *DR. SIMON LEARMOUNT, JUDGE (CAMBRIDGE)*

> ➤ Many candidates are unprepared for having to analyze and present a case. They think that it's primarily about getting the right answer, whereas it's really about how they deal with information, explore ideas, get a group to explore something with them, and remain open to others' suggestions. *KATTY OOMS SUTER, IMD (SWITZERLAND)*

> ➤ There are three typical mistakes. One is not knowing the program. (If an applicant, having already submitted his written application, is interviewed and during the interview asks, "How long is your program?" he has shown us he has not done his homework and is probably not a serious candidate.) Another is not having any questions to ask. The third is not knowing when the interview is finished—and trying to ask fifteen questions rather than a couple. (Plus, someone trying to ask fifteen questions is invariably asking about things that are readily learned from our website.) *MARY GRANGER, ESADE (SPAIN)*

HOW TO DEAL WITH THE INCOMPETENT INTERVIEWER

What marks an incompetent interviewer? Examples are talking too much, going off on tangents, failing to maintain control of the interview, dwelling on inconsequential matters, and failing to pay attention. Here are some tips for dealing with the most common problems:

SHE TALKS TOO MUCH

The more an interviewer talks, the less information she can get about you. Build rapport with her by providing nonverbal encouragement. You do not want to offend her or be rude, but you still want to get some points across. Do so by appearing to agree with her, following up on one of her comments by immediately saying something like, "In fact, one of the things that first got me interested in school X was . . ." And, of course, take advantage of the break she gives you at the end of the interview when she asks if you have any questions. Phrase your questions as questions, but make sure they are really short advertisements for yourself. For example: "I wonder whether my background—having a master's in mechanical engineering and a lot of practical work experience in several industries—would be a good fit with the program?"

HE GOES OFF ON TANGENTS

If you want to get the discussion back on track, use such phrases as: "Let me be sure that I understand this correctly" (and then repeat the couple of key points briefly); "Could we go back to that first point, such and such"; "In our remaining time, I hope that we will have the chance to touch on the following points, which are particularly important for me: X, Y, Z." Be very friendly and nonconfrontational, showing that you are not trying to take over the interview but are instead trying to take advantage of an opportunity to learn more about the school or sell your own abilities.

SHE CONSTANTLY INTERRUPTS

Make a note of where you are in the conversation when the interruption occurred and recall this for the interviewer's sake when the interview recommences. She will be impressed that you have kept your focus while she was losing hers.

HE FAILS TO PAY ATTENTION

Try to bring him back in, but do not be rude. For example, say something like, "I suspect that I've lost you—I guess that I'm not being clear. Let me try to explain that again, albeit briefly."

AFTER THE INTERVIEW

First, debrief yourself regarding what went well and what went poorly, and why. This will help you with later interviews for other schools; you will be able to anticipate what you might be asked concerning an apparent weakness.

Second, send a *brief thank-you note* to your interviewer. (A handwritten—but legible—note on personal stationery is best, but by no means essential.) Note something that occurred during the interview or something specific she said that enlightened you to make it clear that this is not a form note. You can mention, for example, that you were glad to learn that it will be very easy to get moderately priced housing near the campus. The one absolute requirement of the note is that you get the interviewer's name and title correct, so be sure to get her business card during the interview. If you fail to do so, ask a staff member (or call the office later) to be sure you have the correct spelling and information.

INTERVIEW CHECKLIST

- Clothing: My dress was/was not appropriate and comfortable.

- My entrance, including handshake and greeting, was/was not positive.

- My physical actions (smile, eye contact, body language, avoidance of fidgeting) were/were not appropriate.

- Attitude: I did/did not appear confident, enthusiastic, and friendly.

- Questions I handled well (list each, with what was good about your answer):

- Questions I handled poorly (list each, with what was bad about your answer, and suggestions for improvement):

- General comments:

  —I spoke too much/too little.

  —I did/did not establish rapport quickly and easily.

  —I did/did not stay on a more or less equal footing with the interviewer.

  —I did/did not impress the interviewer without bragging.

  —I did/did not balance sincerity and humor appropriately for this interviewer's style.

- My ending questions were/were not appropriate (and sufficient).

- My exit was/was not smooth and upbeat.

- I was/was not appropriately knowledgeable about the program.

- Interviewer's impression of me:

  —Personal:

  —Professional:

SPECIAL CONCERNS FOR INTERNATIONAL APPLICANTS

Interviewing in a language that is not your own is not easy, especially when you are under substantial performance pressure. This is precisely when your worst verbal tics are likely to show up, including mistakes you have not made since early in your study of the language. Similarly, normal manners of speaking in your own language can be bothersome to others. Highly educated French speakers are accustomed to using a large number of "uh's" and, if anything, seem to gain respect in their own culture for doing so. To English speakers, this same trait when expressed in English can be highly annoying. Check your performance under realistic conditions and go the extra step of asking a native speaker what verbal mannerisms are best eradicated.

Cultural differences manifest themselves at many points in an interview. For example, Americans at all social levels discuss a range of sports and expect others to follow them as well. A CEO would not find it odd to discuss baseball, football, or basketball as well as such sports as golf and tennis, In the U.K., discussing soccer (i.e., football), darts, or other working-class sports would be regarded as bizarre; CEOs would limit themselves to cricket, tennis (i.e., Wimbledon), or the like. Anyone doing business in America should expect sports to serve as a metaphor for business, with constant use of sports terms, whereas little sports terminology would find its way into a British business discussion.

The physical distance people maintain between themselves, amount of eye contact, and many of the behaviors discussed in this chapter are in fact culturally defined norms. Give some consideration to modifying your behavior sufficiently so as to avoid shocking or offending your interviewer. You do not need to disown your natural modes of behavior, but you are unlikely to profit from appearing completely unable to fit into the program for which you are interviewing.

The best way to prepare for a cross-cultural interview is, of course, to speak the appropriate language and spend time in the appropriate setting for as long as possible immediately prior to the interview.

Appendix VIII

INTERVIEW QUESTIONS

The interview evaluation form reprinted in the body of the chapter suggests what business schools want to learn about you—what skills, attitudes, and attributes they value. It does not, however, make clear how they will go about this.

Business school interviewers can take one of two basic approaches. The simplest is to ask you *direct* questions. For instance, an interviewer interested in your desire to have an impact can ask, "How much do you strive for leadership positions?"

A more sophisticated approach is to ask you about this *indirectly*. In this case, the interviewer is likely to focus on various aspects of your past and current experience—in terms of your education, career, and personal life—to see how much supervision and direction you have had in various projects and whether that amount suited you. The questions that generate this information are likely to be more general, along the lines of, "Regarding that cost analysis project, what sort of relationship did you have with your boss? What did you like and dislike about this relationship? What if anything did you try to change? On your next project, what was different?" These more open-ended questions, in which the focus is not made so obvious, are by now standard interviewing procedure. The more experienced the interviewer, and the more time she has available, the more likely she is to use the indirect approach.

(The much-hyped *behavioral interview* is a simple variant of this indirect approach. Behavioral interviewers identify a competence they think important, then try to find an occasion when you were most likely to have demonstrated—or failed to demonstrate—that competence. They look to understand what you will do in the future by understanding what you have done in the most relevant past situations. Thus, they tend to look at your résumé for situations in which you became a leader to understand the extent to which you tried to become the leader [rather than having leadership foisted upon you]. Failing this, they will ask you about situations in which they suspect you could have tried to lead to see whether you indeed made the effort to do so.)

You can prepare for each of these approaches by considering the questions listed on p. 347 (the "most likely questions") and the following list, which together cover the key questions asked about each major topic—education, career, management orientation, goals, interest in business school, and personal life. Of course other questions may be asked, but if you are prepared to respond coherently and consistently to each of these, you will be ready for just about anything else you will encounter as well.

UNIVERSITY EDUCATION (REPEAT AS APPROPRIATE FOR GRADUATE PROGRAMS)

What school did you attend?

Why did you choose that one?

(Regarding a lesser quality school) Don't you worry that you will be overwhelmed by the quality of students attending our program?

What factors most influenced your choice?

What was your major? Why?

In hindsight, are you glad you chose that school? What would you change now if you could? Why?

In hindsight, are you glad you chose that major? What would you choose instead if you could do it over again?

How many hours each week did you study?

In which courses were you most successful? Why?

In which courses were you least successful? Why?

Do your grades reflect your abilities? If not, why did you not do better?

In what ways did your education prepare you, or fail to prepare you, for your career to date?

What did you most enjoy about college?

What did you least enjoy about college?

What extracurricular activities did you participate in? What was your role and contribution in each?

How did you pay for your education?

How would you describe yourself as a college student? Is this still true about you?

General Tips Regarding University Education

- Avoid portraying your university days as a social experience rather than an intellectual one if at all possible.

- If your record is poor, show that you have since gotten serious. If there is any acceptable way to explain a poor record without sounding whiny or childish, be prepared to do so (briefly).

- Show that you were committed to learning, whether for its own sake or for the sake of your career.

- If you have changed your goals or interests several times, show that you have been serious about at least one of them while pursuing it.

- Portray both your academic interests and your extracurricular activities in terms of their contribution to your current (or then current) career interests.

- Discuss your leadership experiences.

- As to changes you might make if given the opportunity to do it all over again, a safe answer is one that would better prepare you for your eventual career, such as by providing further grounding in econometrics or multidimensional scaling if you are currently a market researcher.

- If you are interviewing for admission to a part-time program, do not try to excuse a mediocre undergraduate performance by explaining that you were unable to focus well due to the need to work part-time as well as study. This combination of work and study will be your fate once again in the part-time program, so you will appear unable to handle the responsibilities.

WORK EXPERIENCE (REPEAT AS APPROPRIATE FOR DIFFERENT COMPANIES AND JOBS HELD)

Why did you choose this profession? This firm?

What is your job title? To whom do you report?

What are your key responsibilities?

What resources and people do you manage directly?

Do you manage teams of people? Under what circumstances?

What are the key technical/managerial challenges of your job?

Give an example of a project that required you to do substantial quantitative (or analytical) work. Did it succeed/fail? Why?

What do you do best/worst in your job? Why?

How could you improve your performance? What steps have you taken to make these improvements?

What have your major successes been? What impact have they had?

Did you achieve these on your own? Who else was involved? How?

How do you motivate people?

Tell me about a team situation that worked (didn't work) and why. What did you do about it?

Have you ever worked with a difficult person? What did you do?

Have you worked for a bad manager? In what way was he/she bad? What did you do about it?

Describe a situation when you disagreed with a supervisor (team member). How was this resolved?

Tell me about a situation when people relied on you. Why did they?

How have you demonstrated leadership?

Describe a situation when you initiated change or responded successfully to change.

Describe a failure on the job. What did you learn from it?

Give an example of your international experience. How did it differ from domestic experiences of a similar nature?

What are the biggest challenges your unit faces? What are you doing to meet them?

Where is your industry headed in the next five years? Why?

How does your performance/salary progression compare with that of your peers in the company?

What does your manager most/least like about your performance?

What is your most significant developmental need?

What would you change about your job? What is your dream job? What would you do if you could do anything outside of business?

General Tips Regarding Work Experience

■ Refer to the discussions concerning relevant essays in Chapter 9.

■ When discussing your boss, your description of what was good and bad about him will probably make it clear what you need, and also what you cannot tolerate, in a boss. This also says a lot about your own strengths and weaknesses.

■ Even when describing the characteristics you do not like in your boss, try to be reasonably sympathetic; otherwise, you risk sounding like a malcontent.

■ Any job change should have been motivated by a desire for more challenges, more responsibility, the chance to grow, and so on. In other words, emphasize the positive, forward-looking reasons for making the change. Avoid the negative, backward-looking reasons for the change, such as being unappreciated, underpaid, or disliked by your boss.

■ If you were fired, confess to this fact if necessary, but be sure to note what you learned from the experience.

■ Working fewer than fifty hours per week may suggest that you are insufficiently motivated. A good answer will establish that you work as hard as necessary to achieve your objective.

■ Portray yourself as one who tries to meet or exceed the objective as efficiently as possible. You consider different approaches and look to improve whatever systems are in place if such a change will make it possible to achieve such results more efficiently in the future.

MANAGERIAL ORIENTATION

What is your management philosophy?

What is your managerial style? What aspects of it do you wish to change?

What qualities are essential for a manager to succeed? Which do you possess?

What have you done to develop those under you?

How much do you control those under you? How much freedom do you give them? How do you motivate them?

Who do you regard as a great manager (or leader)? Which of his/her qualities do you wish you had more of?

How do you distinguish between being a good leader and being a good manager?

What do you do best/worst as a manager? As a leader?

Are you a better leader or follower?

What would your subordinates (supervisors) say about you as a manager? Why?

General Tips Regarding Managerial Orientation

■ Refer to the discussions concerning relevant essays in Chapter 9.

▪ Any response that proclaims the unquestionable correctness of one managerial style over another is a mistake. Respond that this is situation-dependent, or that you generally prefer a particular style because of your particular work circumstances.

▪ Explain that when you are the person in a group who is most knowledgeable about a given situation, you take the lead, but you defer to others when appropriate.

▪ Portray yourself as very much output-oriented and not overly fussy about the role you play in a team, although you generally end up taking on a great deal of responsibility, since you seem to welcome it and its challenges more than most do.

GOALS

What do you want to be doing in five years? Ten years? Twenty-five years?

What do you want to accomplish in life?

How have your goals changed in recent years?

Why do you want an MBA? What do you expect to get from it?

Which other schools are you applying to? Why? Why so many/few?

How did you choose these schools?

Which school is your first choice? Why?

What if you are not accepted at a top school?

General Tips Regarding Goals

▪ Refer to the discussions concerning relevant essays in Chapter 9.

▪ You want to show that you are committed to career success.

▪ Showing that you have thought long and hard about your future career demonstrates your seriousness of purpose.

▪ Regarding your long-term goals, do not say that you want to retire as early as possible to lie on a beach somewhere. Saying this would show you to be lazy or overly stressed, hardly ideal attributes for someone trying to get into a challenging MBA program. Discuss instead how you arrived at your chosen goal in light of a consideration of your relative strengths and weaknesses, what you most enjoy, your background and desires, etc.

▪ If you are proposing a substantial career change, be ready to lay out a virtual business plan for it, as if you are asking the interviewer to invest in your future.

BUSINESS SCHOOL

If you have someone on your learning team (case or study team) who fails to complete assigned work in time for a scheduled group presentation, what will you do about it?

What is your biggest concern about attending our school?

What do you think are the biggest advantages (disadvantages) of the case method?

How well will you cope with the international environment (or the fraternity atmosphere) of this program?

Why are you bothering to do a degree rather than just taking a few courses somewhere?

Which courses (professors) here are of greatest interest to you?

What do you hope to get from the program beyond book learning?

What will you contribute here?

General Tips Regarding Business School

■   Please see the in-depth analysis of these issues elsewhere in the book, particularly in Chapter 3, "How to Choose the Right School for *You*"; Appendix II, "Criteria for Assessing MBA Programs"; and Chapter 9, "Understanding the Key Essay Topics."

PERSONAL

Tell me about yourself.

Explain your family background or the circumstances of your childhood.

Who most influenced you when you were growing up? How?

What publications do you regularly read? Why?

What books have you read recently? What impressed you about that one?

What is your favorite book/movie/drama/record and why?

What have you done to keep yourself current, or to develop your skills, in your field?

What have you learned about yourself in the past three months/years?

How would your friends describe you/your personality?

How do you feel about:

—Western reliance on oil?

—African internecine warfare?

—(Anything else on the front pages, especially if it relates to your home region or that of the school?)

How do you spend your time outside of work?

Is your current balance among career, family, friends, and interests the right one for you over the long term?

What activity do you enjoy the most? Why?

What is your greatest passion? How does this relate to your career interests/ leadership strengths?

Who are your heroes? Why?

What decision in your life do you most regret?

What competitive sports have you participated in? Did you enjoy them? Are you competitive by nature?

General Tips Regarding Personal Questions

- Refer to the discussions concerning relevant essays in Chapter 9.

- When describing yourself or what your long-term goals are, be sure a large part (but not all) of your response focuses upon your career. You want to appear career-oriented, but not lacking in personality or other interests.

- Take every opportunity to show that you are highly achievement-oriented and do what you can to develop both personally and professionally.

- At the same time, show yourself to be a sensible and well-balanced person with compelling outside interests, including but not limited to family and friends.

- When talking about your interests, it does not much matter whether you read science fiction, monographs about the Napoleonic wars, or locked-room mysteries, as long as you show that you are knowledgeable and enthusiastic regarding whatever you pursue.

- These questions provide a natural opportunity to subtly strengthen your chosen positioning.

OTHER

Is there anything else you would like us to know about you?

General Tip Regarding Other Questions

- Remember your pre-interview objectives. If you intended to put across several major points, ask yourself whether you have succeeded in doing so. If you have, do not feel compelled to add anything. On the other hand, if you have not, mention briefly but persuasively the points you wished to make along with the supporting examples or illustrations you intended to use.

PREPARING TO DESCRIBE KEY EVENTS

You should be ready to discuss major and minor milestones in your personal, educational, and professional life. Some interviewers prefer to ask very general, open-ended questions to learn how well you can develop an organized, intelligent response. Questions of this nature often revolve around major events interviewers glean from your résumé or application. Prepare yourself by reviewing the relevant aspects of each event you expect to discuss.

In the case of a successful business project, for example, you would want to recall:

- The project's initial objective
- Who originated it
- Who was in charge
- The resources available
- The timetable
- The activities undertaken
- The biggest challenges
- Your role: (1) what you did well and poorly, and why; (2) what skills you used; and (3) what you would do differently in retrospect
- Other people's roles
- The results
- What went right and what did not, and why
- Any conclusions this suggests about the department or company, whether of a strategic, operational, or organizational nature
- What you learned about yourself

It is a useful exercise to write down the half dozen (or dozen) most important incidents you expect to discuss on an index card, using this sort of approach for each. Carry these cards with you for reading when you are waiting in line or have a spare moment. Learn them well enough that you can produce a well-organized, apparently spontaneous summary of each of them at the drop of a hat, but do not memorize the stories by rote. Be prepared to be interrupted by the interviewer, and be ready to carry on with the story smoothly once you have answered his question.

RÉSUMÉS

HOW RÉSUMÉS ARE USED

A few schools require that a résumé be submitted as part of the written application. Résumés are generally used as part of the interviewing process, even at schools that do not require them as part of the application. The typical interview, as discussed in the body of the chapter, is a thirty-minute session conducted by someone (an admissions officer, a student, or an alum) who has not read your file. Thus, her knowledge of you before the interview starts will be limited to the information you present in your résumé. Unsurprisingly, your résumé can greatly influence her view of your candidacy. Follow the rules noted below, and examine the sample résumé, to put together a professional résumé suited to this process.

BASIC PRINCIPLES

There is no one résumé format required. (For example, the résumé given here could have placed the name and address detail in the center of the page, without a horizontal line separating it from the body of the résumé.) Any format that meets the following criteria is likely to be fine:

- Assume that people will spend only fifteen to thirty seconds skimming your résumé prior to an interview. Therefore, keep it to one page—unless, of course, you have already been Secretary of State.

- Unless you have never worked full-time, start with "experience" rather than "education."

- Emphasize important points rather than trying to list everything you have ever done. Less tends to be more for résumé purposes; it shows that you can prioritize and organize.

- Emphasize achievements, providing quantitative or tangible proof of your results whenever possible.

- For jobs you wish to describe in detail, consider separating responsibilities (which you can put in an introductory paragraph form) from your achievements (which you can list as bullet points).

- Use "résumé-speak"—phrases rather than full sentences.

- Make sure your résumé is visually appealing: It should not be so crammed with material that it puts someone off.

- The space devoted to a topic should reflect its importance and, to a lesser extent, its recency.

- If you have sufficient space, include personal information, such as community service commitments or language capabilities, which will round out your profile. Remember that business schools are looking for people who are well-balanced, not just career-driven automatons.

SAMPLE RÉSUMÉ

The following résumé (an amalgam of several people's careers rather than a "real" résumé—so do not try to contact "Paul Simpson") illustrates the basic résumé rules. It is easily scanned: One can quickly determine what Paul has done, when he has done it, and where. Similarly, his employers, responsibilities, and achievements are clear—and the achievements are given weight and credibility by their quantification. He does not try to recount everything he has ever done; rather, he highlights the most important. Substantially more space is given to his professional experience than his education, reflecting the fact that he has been working full-time for seven years (versus four years of college), and the college education concluded seven years ago. Despite the fact that his résumé is packed with interesting information, it retains sufficient white space to remain inviting to the reader.

PAUL SIMPSON

123 Center Ave., Long Beach, CA 91234   (310) 555-0000   ps353.isp.com

Experience

2005–present   **LEVI-STRAUSS**   Los Angeles, CA

Supervisor/Project Engineer—Responsible for manufacturing operations. Manage capital projects for world's third largest blue jeans assembly plant.

Manufacturing

- Supervise 100 employees from three unions; represented Company during union negotiations, which resulted in a four-year contract.
- Reduced inventory levels by 60% through automation of materials management system, with cost savings of $1.6 million per year.
- Partnered with outside vendors to improve cleaning system efficiency by 15%.
- Implemented operator maintenance program that increased production efficiency, resulting in $1.4 million annual revenue increase.

Engineering

- Designed and supervised installation of two production lines, increasing output 17%.
- Implemented strategy that ensured ERP implementation six months ahead of target date.
- Led process improvement team that reduced water usage by 30,000 gallons/day, saving over $130,000 annually.

2001–2005   **U.S. ARMY CORPS OF ENGINEERS**   Bosnia & Los Angeles, CA

Captain—Coordinated range of projects for construction and combat applications. Responsible for deployment readiness of engineering equipment and combat training for 60 soldiers.

United Nations Peacekeepers

- Initiated Civic Assistance program while in Bosnia. Completed 24 projects by working with Bosnian government, humanitarian groups, and military personnel from six countries.
- Directed the construction of a multilane bridge, which enabled UN access to southern Bosnia for delivery of emergency medical and food supplies.
- Supervised construction of living quarters for 1200-member, multinational UN organization.

Combat Operations/Readiness

- Integrated engineering strategy into overall combat operations plans for a 1500-soldier interdisciplinary force.
- Developed and implemented program to monitor equipment readiness and repair status for 415-vehicle fleet, decreasing processing time by 60% and clerical errors by 75%.
- Supervised on-time rail transportation of 600 vehicles during base deployment to Bosnia.

Education

1997–2001   **CORNELL UNIVERSITY**   Ithaca, NY

Bachelor of Science in Civil Engineering

- Captain of ice hockey team (2000-2001); selected to All-Ivy team.
- Ranked in top 10% nationally in ROTC class; supervised training program for 250 cadets.
- Designed and fabricated Formula 1 car as part of independent project team.

Professional Development

- Licensed Professional Engineer in California.
- Additional Coursework (Financial Accounting, Managerial Finance, Negotiations, Leadership, Communication Strategies) at UCLA Extension School.

Personal

- Mediator and Project Coordinator, Orange County Community Mediation Program.
- Led United Way fundraising drive (2007); doubled annual contributions.
- Enjoy furniture restoration, sky diving, golf, and early detective novels.
- Proficient in Spanish.

Part **III**

ON THE ROAD TO BUSINESS SCHOOL

13

Responding to Wait-Listing, Rejections, and Other Disappointments

— EXECUTIVE SUMMARY —

■

To optimize your chance of being accepted from a wait-list,
bring relevant new material to the attention of the admissions office.

■

When reapplying to a school, start by understanding the reasons
for your initial rejection.

—Recognize that you will need to address these deficiencies
to warrant reapplying.

*I*f you have followed our suggested approach, you have applied to six to ten schools. Only a few of them are likely to accept you, and several others are very likely to turn you down. Prepare yourself for rejection by some of your choices. (In fact, if you get into every school, perhaps you haven't aimed high enough!)

Nonacceptance comes in many forms. You may be put on an administrative hold, wait-listed, told to apply again at a later date after you have remedied a specific deficiency, or rejected outright.

Your reaction should depend upon which of these categories applies and which school is in question. If one of your stretch schools says no, for example, you will probably react differently than if one of your likelies says no. Don't overreact to any single school's decision. The vagaries of the admissions process and the differences between schools mean that one school's decision does not have much predictive value in terms of what another school will do. (This is one of the reasons we suggest applying to so many schools.)

RESPONDING TO ADMINISTRATIVE HOLDS

An administrative hold means that the school was unable to make a decision on your candidacy within the normal time period, so your application will be held over until the next decision period. This suggests that your candidacy is strong, but the school will not know if you are quite strong enough until it has seen more of this year's applicants. (It is also possible that an administrative problem is causing the delay, but this is rare.)

Take the opportunity to send a short note reaffirming your interest in the program if the delay is scheduled to extend for more than about a month. If you have strong new information available—such as a promotion or greatly increased responsibilities—by all means, communicate it to the admissions office.

RESPONDING TO WAIT-LISTING

Being wait-listed generally means that you will be admitted to the program only if someone who has been accepted chooses not to come. In fact, schools know that a certain percentage of their admittees will choose other schools or decide to wait a year or two, so they routinely admit more students than they can actually take. The "excess" number admitted, however, is often not sufficient to make up for all those who declined admission. The wait-list is used to manage this situation.

There is an exception to the general rule that a wait-listed candidate will only be admitted if a space in the class opens up. An increasing number of schools wait-list candidates they suspect will choose to go to another school. By so doing, the schools eliminate the likely impact on their "yield" statistics—the percentage of people who, having been accepted, actually enroll at the school. (Managing a school's yield is part of playing the rankings game—controlling the school's admissions statistics to get the highest possible rankings.) The strongest candidates to the school, along with those whose personal ties or academic interests point to another school, are thus likely to receive wait-list treatment.

Do not despair if you happen to fall into this category. For one thing, schools that play this game are delighted to find that they have been overly cautious and that you actually want to attend their school. By communicating to them that you do indeed wish to attend their school, you are likely to be admitted forthwith. For another, by wait-listing you even though your credentials are strong, the school has indicated that it believes you will get into another top school.

The trouble with being wait-listed is that you are not likely to get off the wait-list and into the school until very late in the game, if at all. It is not uncommon for schools to call people on the wait-list only days before the program's start or, indeed, some days after the start. The lower ranked a school is, the more it is at the mercy of the wait-list decisions made at other schools and thus the later it makes its own decisions. Schools atop the list, such as Harvard, Stanford, and Wharton, in effect make the first moves in this game. When they take people off their wait-lists, many of these accepted candidates withdraw from the schools they would otherwise have attended (and at which they had already put down deposits). This second group of schools then goes to their wait-lists, causing the third group of schools to lose some of their accepted candidates. This ripple effect does not conclude until classes are under way.

Your situation may be complicated by the fact that many schools give wait-listed candidates no indication as to where on the wait-list they fall. In fact, most schools do not rank wait-list candidates. This is because admissions officers realize how many variables will not come into play until later in the game. There is no way for them to accurately assess how many—and which types of—wait-list applicants they will need. Depending on the initial yield, the wait-list may not even be tapped at all. In another scenario, business schools may find that they are "short" in one particular category of applicant (say, human resource consultants or commercial bankers) and utilize the wait-list only to fill in such gaps. Another reason wait-lists are not ranked has to do with the priorities of the wait-list candidates themselves. Many will be accepted at other schools and drop completely out of sight. Admissions officers are often uncertain as to how many wait-list candidates are still actively interested.

It is for precisely this reason that you, as a wait-list candidate, must not remain silent (except at those few schools, such as Harvard, that are adamant in not wanting additional communication from those on the wait-list). By making yourself a presence to the admissions committee, you dramatically increase your chances of being one of the lucky few they "tap" in May, June, July, or August. As you are likely to continue to augment your list of responsibilities and accomplishments during this lengthy waiting period, you should communicate them to the admissions office.

The information you will want to impart to the admissions officers might become available at different times. Thus, it is acceptable to send them more than one update to your file, but it is wise to limit your contact to two (or three) instances unless you know for certain that they welcome your constant attention. Find out from the school at which you are wait-listed how it suggests you carry out your contact—whether it wants to receive one or two notices from you or whether it enjoys continuous updates and inquiries from its wait-listed applicants.

What information will be relevant to this process? How should you communicate your new information? Any new information should show you to be even more the dynamic leader, thoughtful and mature decision-maker, and so on that the earlier chapters showed you how to portray. The one thing that makes your task easier at this point is that having gone through all of the applications, you probably have a pretty good idea of where your applications were weakest and thus what sort of new information would be most helpful to your case. Knowing where your applications were initially weak means you can be clever about bolstering these weak points in the months between the initial application and your follow-up communiqués. For example, if you know one weak point is that your responsibilities have remained substantially unchanged for three or four years, there is no time like the present to expand them.

A sound strategy, whether or not you have dramatic new information available, is to send to the admissions committee a short letter that provides any useful additional information you have—and that also restates why you think you would be a valuable contributor to the program, and emphasizes that you still very much wish to attend it. When a business school goes to its wait-list, it wants to be able to make one call per available spot and fill that spot. It does not want to have to contact ten people to find someone still hopeful of attending that school. Neither does it want to have to track down someone, so be sure you remain readily contactable throughout the summer.

THE ADMISSIONS DIRECTORS DISCUSS THE KEY WAIT-LIST ISSUES

Use of the Wait-List

➤ We review applications in rounds. In round one, for example, we admit the strongest people and wait-list some others. We then compare those on the wait-list with round two applicants; we admit some from the wait-list and release some others. *Peter Johnson, Haas*

➤ We use the wait-list to manage numbers, given that we have three distinct rounds of applications. We want to get a sense of the "next" pool before making a decision about some candidates. *Rose Martinelli, Chicago*

➤ We put people on the wait-list for any of a dozen different purposes, including wanting to see how our yields will work or just wanting more time to examine someone's candidacy. *Thomas Caleel, Wharton*

➤ We don't use the wait-list to determine the depth of someone's interest (by seeing whether they'll remain on the list and continue to seek admission). *Peter Johnson, Haas*

➤ We only put people we are happy to admit on the wait-list. Nor do we use the wait-list to balance our class. *Julia Tyler, London*

Additional Materials You Should Submit When Wait-Listed

➤ Read the wait-list letter we send you. If we ask for more information, send it. In any event, send a letter reiterating your interest. It's fine to submit some unsolicited testimonials, including those from people connected with Stanford. *Sharon Hoffman, Stanford*

➤ We're different than most other schools in that we have a "wait-list manager," which gives wait-listed students a chance to talk with somebody from the admissions board. He or she can give applicants a sense of why they were wait-listed. He may also look to get more information from the applicant. Similarly, we might be able to help them to clarify their goals or strengthen an aspect of their application. *Linda Meehan, Columbia*

➤ None. We don't accept additional materials. We send out a very specific set of instructions stating this. Take a deep breath and read the instructions carefully. *Thomas Caleel, Wharton*

➤ We're happy to add material to the file. Sometimes something important has changed that you want to bring to the attention of the admissions committee. You may have gotten a promotion, completed a class, or gotten a new certification. Or you may have retaken the GMAT. If you think there is something you can do to strengthen your application, go for it. An occasional appropriate expression that you are still interested is also OK. Just don't overdo it. *ISSER GALLOGLY, STERN (NYU)*

➤ You shouldn't submit additional materials, but you should keep in regular contact. I'll often give someone a call to follow up on the one or two issues we're concerned about, perhaps asking for an additional recommendation, for example. But we don't want people to submit things unilaterally. *DR. SIMON LEARMOUNT, JUDGE (CAMBRIDGE)*

The Need to Stay in Touch

➤ If you're on our wait-list, let us know you're interested. Call the admissions officer you interviewed with to remind him or her of that fact—and reiterate that it is your first choice. You want to be the first person to leap to mind when we go to the wait-list. In fact, if you were on the wait-list for six months, it would have been appropriate to communicate with us once in the first three months, once in the fourth month, and twice each in the fifth and sixth months. The communication can be simple, just a few lines. *ANN W. RICHARDS, JOHNSON (CORNELL)*

➤ It's a good idea to write an occasional letter—perhaps every six to eight weeks—reiterating your strong interest in the school. You can include any new information that we should know about. It's best to do this in letter form rather than by call because that way it becomes part of your file. *DAWNA CLARKE, TUCK*

➤ Please, do not call all the time. *SHARON HOFFMAN, STANFORD*

➤ The time to contact us is during the spring, when we may be scrambling to put the final touches to a class. This is when we might need people and be open to hearing from applicants who really want to attend MIT. *ROD GARCIA, MIT*

➤ There is a fine line between staying in touch and driving somebody nuts. So using good judgment and knowing appropriate behavior is also instrumental in whether someone gets in or not. *LINDA MEEHAN, COLUMBIA*

➤ Each school lets you know how much contact they'd like. After May 15, candidates on our wait-list are welcome to contact us. In fact, we get to know many of the wait-list candidates much better as a result of our contact with them. *MICHELE ROGERS, KELLOGG*

➤ The most useful thing you can do is hold your nerve and wait until we contact you. *JULIA TYLER, LONDON*

The Importance of Your Desire to Attend Their School

➤ One applicant successfully challenged her waiting-list position by doing so in the nicest possible way—not saying, "I want to go up the waiting list," but, "London Business School is really important to me; let me explain again." So it was reasonable. She was aware of our constraints but able to show that she was self-aware enough to know that she would benefit and contribute to us. She used the system politely. *JULIA TYLER, LONDON*

· *The Wait-List Numbers Game*

➤ There are perhaps eighty to two hundred on the wait-list at any one time. The number of applicants we take from it varies from about ten to twenty-five. We don't rank those on the wait-list. We cherry-pick people as necessary to round out the class. *SHARON HOFFMAN, STANFORD*

➤ Our wait-list may grow to as many as 170 to 200 candidates. It changes over time, of course. Recently we've admitted 35 in one year and 24 in another, but some years we admit no one from the wait-list. We don't rank the wait-list, partly because we're still looking to shape the composition of the class when we take someone from the wait-list (so we don't know in advance who will be most desirable). *SALLY JAEGER, TUCK*

➤ Our wait-list changes as we move through the application review process. As we progress through the rounds, we will release some wait-listed candidates when it becomes clear that they are not strong enough in the wait-list group to potentially receive an offer. Similarly, some candidates who have been wait-listed in early rounds may receive an offer of admission with the round-three or round-four candidates. Since we know that being on the wait-list is awkward and frustrating for applicants, we do our best to communicate frequently about the status of the wait-list. *PETER JOHNSON, HAAS*

➤ On average, we wait-list about twenty to twenty-five applicants; we have taken an average of ten from the wait-list each year. *ALISON OWEN, SAÏD (OXFORD)*

RESPONDING TO REJECTION

The first thing to do when confronting a rejection is to ask yourself how significant it really is. If you have already been accepted by a school you favor, the rejection is truly insignificant. If this is a school you very much wish to attend, however, a different reaction is appropriate.

The next step is to analyze why you were rejected. You may already know the reason, of course, if you were aware of one or two specific aspects of your application that were likely to keep you from being admitted. Even if you are sure you know the reason, though, be sure to contact the school's admissions office to get the committee's views on your candidacy. Not only may you have overlooked a flaw in your candidacy, but schools are also occasionally rather idiosyncratic (or worse) in their judgments. For instance, one candidate to Fuqua was surprised to learn that the admissions committee considered him to have been lacking in community activities. He had been a member of his local school committee for three years and had chaired it for the last two. He was the chair of the subcommittee in charge of the $30-million-dollar building project and also the chair of the budget committee, then instituting a substantial reorganization. He was putting in between a dozen and two dozen hours a week in these capacities (on a purely voluntary basis). He had described all of this in the data sheets of his application and had even devoted much of a lengthy essay to the subject. He assumed that Fuqua must have noticed this. Learning that they had completely overlooked it, he was able to emphasize his involvement even more in his reapplication the following year.

A large number of schools—including Darden, Haas, Kellogg, and Wharton (and many of the European schools)—are willing to tell you why they rejected you. Schools are most receptive to such inquiries during their slow periods, particularly from June to August for programs with September starting dates. They will generally refuse to discuss the matter during their busy periods.

A typical discussion might include an assessment of how you rate in the following areas:

- Academic/intellectual (able to handle the program, based upon your prior coursework, grades, and GMAT results?)

- Career progress

- Career goals (clear, sensible, appropriate for your background, requiring an MBA?)

- Personal qualities (including interpersonal skills, intercultural understanding and experience, leadership and teamwork skills, managerial experience, and extracurricular/community involvement)

A school that is willing to discuss your rejection is doing you a real favor, so be ultra-polite in dealing with its representatives. If you are defensive or hostile—natural reactions to being told that you are less than perfect—you will elicit less useful information from them than you might have if you had been appreciative and welcoming of their input.

Beware, however, of what even these very helpful schools will say. They do not wish to offend you, nor do they wish to have your lawyer get involved. As a result, there are common-sense limits to what they are free to say. Thus, confidential matters, such as what was written about you in recommendations or said about you by your interviewer, may (or may not) remain off limits.

Even if the school you most wish to attend does not offer any feedback, by all means learn what you can from those schools that do (assuming you have applied to some) and apply what you learn to your target school. In addition, check your application against the relevant chapters and examples of this book and ask an appropriate, objective person to do the same. (Or call one of us at www.degreeofdifference.com.)

SHOULD YOU EVER APPEAL A REJECTION?

If you have no truly dramatic new information to bring to the table, do not raise your blood pressure and that of the admissions committee by appealing a rejection. Admissions committees go to great lengths to give applicants a sympathetic reading of their files, by at least two and often three people, so you can count on the school's having considered your application material fairly.

Some schools, on relatively rare occasions, will be willing to reconsider an application based upon presentation of important new information. If you have such information and wish to appeal, contact the admissions office and explain the situation. See if they will entertain an appeal. If so, be sure to present convincing new information, reiterating that you do wish to attend this school and will contribute greatly if admitted. (If you are not absolutely certain that this is your number one choice, do not even consider putting busy admissions people to the trouble an appeal will involve.) Recognize, however, that the odds against being admitted will be very long indeed.

AN ADMISSIONS DIRECTOR COMMENTS ON APPEALS

➤ A student can appeal a rejection, but he or she needs a substantial reason (such as a major change in GMAT score, additional coursework, or a promotion) for us to reevaluate our decision. A belief that we made a mistake, however, is not a reason to appeal. *Sally Jaeger, Tuck*

SHOULD YOU REAPPLY IN THE FUTURE OR SETTLE FOR A LESSER SCHOOL?

The question of whether to reapply is, of course, a complicated one. If you got into one of your top choices, you might wish to attend it this year instead of waiting, hoping that you will get in next year to your first choice. The situation is more difficult if you got into your eighth choice but none of your first seven choices. If you realistically think you will be a stronger candidate in the near future, then it might be a good idea to wait and reapply with your improved credentials.

The important thing here is to analyze in what way you will, or could, be a stronger candidate. As the discussion above recommended, be sure to get feedback from the schools willing to provide it. Be your own critic, too. Look at your application from the perspective of this book, analyzing each component. If it was a glaring weakness, can you do something to improve it? Chapter 7 analyzed in detail what you could do to improve your credentials. If the fault in your application was not the application itself but your credentials, consider what strategy you will employ to improve them. Ask yourself whether a successful effort will significantly change the nature of your candidacy. Also ask yourself whether you are being realistic in thinking that you can make the changes you are contemplating.

Then consider the application itself. Did you write polished, persuasive essays? Do you have reason to doubt that your recommenders wrote assertively and well on your behalf? Did you interview well? If the answer to any of these questions suggests that you have an opportunity to improve your application substantially, what will you do to make the improvements? Are you being realistic in thinking that you will put in the necessary time and effort?

Do not be lazy if you choose to reapply. Rewrite your essays to take advantage of your performance since your initial application, in light of what you have learned was wrong with that application. If a school offers you the chance to submit just one reapplication essay, focusing on what you have done in the last year, do not opt to take the easy route of writing just this one essay if you would be better served by rewriting the whole set of essays instead. Consider using new recommenders, based upon their knowledge of your recent performance. If you use the same recommenders, have them rewrite their recommendations, incorporating new information about you to the extent possible.

WHAT THE ADMISSIONS DIRECTORS ADVISE

Feedback (Regarding Why You Were Rejected)

➤ Reread your application and formulate specific questions for us. It's not a counseling session, but we often lay out possible next steps for people. Record and act on the advice we give. In reapplying, do not just address your weaknesses and what you've done about them. Instead, be sure to show your strengths as well, because we still need to make sense of the whole presentation of you. *ROSE MARTINELLI, CHICAGO*

➤ If I were turned down, I would call and try to make an appointment to discuss the reasons for my rejection. I would not insist on discussing it immediately, because the admissions person on the line will not necessarily have the file handy. Timing is everything; in May, admissions officers will have the time to discuss the case. *ROD GARCIA, MIT*

➤ During a two-month period in the summer, we are happy to provide feedback to potential reapplicants. In fact, one of the original readers of the file usually conducts the session. We think candidates are best served if we try to be as specific as possible in our comments. We don't review the interview and recommendations, which are confidential, but otherwise we provide the actual evaluation. We want to be helpful for those who are trying to determine whether they should go elsewhere for their MBA or try again at Kellogg. *MICHELE ROGERS, KELLOGG*

➤ We offer telephone feedback sessions of fifteen to twenty minutes to those who were denied. We conduct them from June until August. We'll have reread the application for this. Be organized. Reread the application yourself and have a set of questions ready for us. We try to encourage people to reapply if their chances of admission are good, but discourage those without a realistic chance. In that case, we try to discuss appropriate alternatives; it becomes a general counseling session. *SALLY JAEGER, TUCK*

➤ If you schedule a feedback session, be prepared: reread your application. And understand there may be no magic bullet. It's rare we can pinpoint one single thing that needs to be done. It's usually a case of multiple things needing improvement. *THOMAS CALEEL, WHARTON*

➤ We've always given feedback, although it's on a somewhat limited basis because we don't have the resources to give feedback to everyone who is rejected. So we limit it to those intending to reapply to Columbia, not those who are simply curious about the decision. There are some people who get a rejection that encourages them to contact us for feedback. These are applicants we are very interested in and want to have a conversation with. *LINDA MEEHAN, COLUMBIA*

➤ We offer feedback, between June 1 and August 31, to any applicant who was placed on the wait-list but ultimately didn't gain admission. We do so by telephone, in fifteen-minute conversations with an admissions committee member. A discussion of the strengths and weaknesses of your candidacy can be very valuable if you are considering reapplying and want to know what to do to strengthen your reapplication. Be thoughtful about what you wish to get from the session. If you wish to reapply, learn what specific steps to take to improve your chances. If you want to know what taking job X would do to your admissions chances, ask (although I don't suggest structuring your career just to get into business school). *Peter Johnson, Haas*

➤ We don't normally tell people why we rejected them, unless it's someone we want to encourage to reapply. We would tell them verbally. *Andrew Dyson, Manchester (England)*

➤ We are happy to provide feedback if a rejected applicant requests it. We usually do so by e-mail. *Alison Owen, Saïd (Oxford)*

Reapplying

➤ Each year, a number of reapplicants are admitted to HBS. In most instances, their reapplications reflect personal and professional growth achieved through increased opportunities for leadership or improvement in academics. *Brit Dewey, Harvard*

➤ If you reapply one year later, you don't have to resubmit a transcript, and we only ask for one letter of recommendation—from someone different. You need to answer two (different) essays. We encourage people to get feedback from us. They should definitely interview again. The interviewer in that case will review the prior application, so you can discuss what you've done since then. In fact, we keep last year's application in the same file as this year's, so we are very aware of what has or has not changed in the meantime. You need to make changes in your application, of course, because there was something wrong the first time. *Sally Jaeger, Tuck*

➤ Those who were wait-listed and are intending to reapply should have the feedback conversation we offer and then do whatever they can to improve their applications. Applying earlier—whether early decision or just early in the regular pool—is advisable, especially if one of the reasons they were rejected was because of applying too late. *Linda Meehan, Columbia*

➤ One thing a reapplicant needs to address is, why reapply, and why this school? What have they learned from the effort since then? How did it make them more determined to succeed? *Rose Martinelli, Chicago*

➤ Applying to business school is not like rolling the dice, where the more times you roll them the likelier you are to get a given result. Few people should apply here more than once. Reapply only if something substantial has changed in your profile (which is seldom the case for someone who applied in March and is now reapplying in November). For most people,

> my advice is: Give it your best shot, applying to a range of schools. If you get in somewhere, go. Start your schooling there. Get on with your MBA. SHARON HOFFMAN, STANFORD

> ➤ The most successful reapplicants tend to be those who have enhanced a particular area of their candidacy. Some, of course, do absolutely nothing differently. They just reapply—with predictable results. Besides trying to improve my credentials, however, I'd also take another look at my essays. I'd ask myself whether I failed to share the right things, in the right way. MICHELE ROGERS, KELLOGG

> ➤ If you intend to reapply, you should come have a chat with us to see what your chances are and what issues you need to address. ANDREW DYSON, MANCHESTER (ENGLAND)

OTHER OPTIONS

If schools that you want to attend have rejected you (for the moment), do not give up on getting an MBA. If you wanted an MBA for good reasons, there are probably a number of schools that can help you meet your needs. Most people who have investigated schools carefully, including those who produce the school guides and rankings discussed in Part I, sincerely believe there are a hundred-plus quality MBA programs in the world. So even if you applied to an unrealistic set of schools this time around, cast your net a bit more widely or reapply to schools you narrowly missed this time.

One last hint: Many schools have exchange programs that allow you to spend a semester or even two at another school. If you failed to get into London Business School directly, for example, you might still be able to attend it for at least one semester if you go to one of its many "partner" schools. This will give you much of the social and intellectual experience of attending it, as well as letting you tap into its network and list it on your résumé!

14

WHAT TO DO ONCE YOU ARE ACCEPTED

— EXECUTIVE SUMMARY —

■

Take the necessary steps to reserve your place at your chosen school.

■

Upgrade your skills, as necessary, to be able to succeed at business school right from the start. Do the necessary reading, or take the appropriate courses, to achieve reasonable skill levels in the following
(if you have not already done so):

—Spreadsheet, Presentation, and Word-Processing Software
(and the Internet)

—Algebra and Calculus

—Accounting

—Economics

—Statistics

■

If you have additional time, upgrade your knowledge in other areas as well.

ACCEPTING YOUR OFFER

If you are accepted by your top choice, be sure to send in your deposit to reserve your place in a timely manner. If you are accepted by one of your secondary choices before you have heard from your number one school, you may face a dilemma if you are required to send in a deposit immediately. Most schools have become so quick about responding to applications, however, that this quandary is no longer common. If you do encounter it, ask the school that has accepted you whether you can get your deadline extended. Also, ask your first-choice school to speed up its decision making, explaining the situation politely. Mention the school that you will otherwise attend only if it is clearly similar in nature and caliber.

The one time when this is still likely to be a major problem is if you are accepted by a secondary choice and wait-listed by your first choice. You may not get off the wait-list, or be definitively turned down, until the start of school. In this case, you may have to send in a deposit to your second choice, unless you are willing to risk being declined by your first-choice school.

INTERNATIONAL STUDENTS

As soon as you have chosen the school you will attend, begin the student visa process. In the United States, this means getting a Certificate of Eligibility (I-20) form from the school, which verifies that you have the appropriate credentials, language skills, and financial resources to attend the program. This form, along with several others that are security-related and various financial documents, must be submitted to the local U.S. consular office to request the actual visa. This process is all too often delayed by either the school or the consular office, so it is important to begin it as soon as possible.

SHOULD YOU SEEK A DEFERRAL?

You may wish to defer attending business school for a year or more. Recognize, however, that schools' policies regarding deferrals vary dramatically. Some treat young applicants (those applying straight from university or with only months of work experience) differently than other applicants. These schools often admit young applicants on a deferred basis: they are expected to work for a period of two years or so before starting business school.

Regular applicants, however, face a different situation. Some schools offer virtually no deferrals to such applicants. Harvard, for instance, grants deferrals only for those called to military service or facing true medical emergencies. Other schools offer deferrals for additional reasons, such as a unique business opportunity that will not be available in the future.

The fact that a school makes it possible for you to defer does not, of course, mean that you should defer. Sensible reasons to seek to defer (or to be willing to give up an acceptance and reapply in the future) include:

➤ You reasonably believe you can get into a substantially better program in the future.

➤ Your employer has agreed to pay for your MBA if you delay attending business school.

➤ You have a truly marvelous business (or personal) opportunity that will not be on offer again—preferably one that will make you a substantially better candidate if you need to reapply in the future.

THE ADMISSIONS DIRECTORS DISCUSS DEFERRAL POLICIES

➤ We offer deferrals on a case-by-case basis—perhaps ten per year. Personal reasons matter most. For example, a Chinese national had trouble getting a visa; a military man could not get the early release he had expected. *SALLY JAEGER, TUCK*

➤ We only consider offering a deferral in the case of health-related issues facing the applicant or the applicant's immediate family. We don't grant them for professional situations; instead, we ask them to reapply. *PETER JOHNSON, HAAS*

➤ We offer a handful (ten to twenty) of deferrals each year; we decide on a case-by-case basis. In general, we offer them to people facing personal issues beyond their control, such as illness or a difficult job situation (such as when a business will fail if they leave). *ROSE MARTINELLI, CHICAGO*

➤ We almost never offer a deferral, and then only for extraordinarily compelling health reasons. One person needed a year to undergo chemotherapy treatment; another took care of her terminally ill parents for a year. *Sharon Hoffman, Stanford*

➤ We offer very few deferrals—maybe ten to fifteen in a given year. People's plans, goals, and experiences may change in the meantime, so we suggest they apply when they're ready to attend. *Michele Rogers, Kellogg*

➤ We offer deferrals only for medical reasons. *Ann W. Richards, Johnson (Cornell)*

➤ We understand life happens. Applicants wishing to defer need to contact me directly. Under some circumstances we will defer for up to a year. A visa issue or family emergency might well qualify, but having a new opportunity at work or being unable to make up your mind whether to attend now or in the future will not. *Thomas Caleel, Wharton*

➤ Our policy is not to defer, although occasionally there are extenuating circumstances for which we will defer someone. *Linda Meehan, Columbia*

➤ Deferrals are not granted. So we have a reapplication policy rather than a deferral policy. Given that people's circumstances change dramatically in the course of a year, we want to see where you are after a year. Have your career goals changed? Has anything changed radically in your career? Essentially, are you the same highly qualified applicant? We don't think filling out an abbreviated application is too much of a burden, and it's in the Stern community's interest to maintain the highest standards. *Isser Gallogly, Stern (NYU)*

➤ There are some people who request a deferral to use it as a backup, intending to apply to other schools next year. If someone is absolutely sure he wants to attend, he can pay his reservation fee now and be assured of a place. If someone is not absolutely sure, we'd encourage him or her to reapply. *Dr. Simon Learmount, Judge (Cambridge)*

➤ Our admissions decision is valid for two years, so people can choose to attend now or later (which many people do). *David Bach, Instituto de Empresa (Spain)*

➤ We offer deferred admission to people who have the chance to do something particularly important in their careers. To keep people who have not thought through their futures from stringing us along, we require that they pay us their tuition now. They can go off for a year on their project, but if they do not attend London Business School next year, we'll simply keep their money. It's amazing how this clarifies people's thinking. *Julia Tyler, London*

➤ We do not offer deferrals unless a personal problem makes it necessary. Otherwise, we have someone withdraw and reapply when they are ready to attend. (If someone does get a deferral, there is no requirement that he or she forgo applying elsewhere in the meantime.) To reserve a place, a deferred person must deposit 1,500 euros (which is in addition to the initial deposit), an amount that is likely to be increased soon. *JOELLE DU LAC, INSEAD*

➤ The primary reasons for granting deferrals are candidates' work commitments (such as being stuck on a continuing, vital project) and funding issues (such as their proposed funding falling through). *ALISON OWEN, SAÏD (OXFORD)*

LEAVING YOUR JOB

Leaving your current job may fill you with joy, sadness, or a mixture of the two. No matter which, it is important to resign in a highly professional manner. Even one misstep can harm your future prospects.

Once you have decided to leave, step carefully. Do not pop into your boss's office and wax ecstatic over your newfound freedom. Instead, think about how much notice you should give. You will obviously give at least as much as is called for in your employment contract. Whether you should give more depends upon a balance of several factors:

- Are you likely to be regarded as a traitor or spy or bad influence? If so, you may not be welcome in the office; you may be ordered to clean out your desk immediately.

- How hard and time-consuming will it be to transfer your knowledge and responsibilities to a replacement? Must you be the one to train your replacement?

- How has the company treated others at your level who have resigned, especially those who are not going to work for competitors?

- What is your relationship with your boss? If your boss is truly reliable, perhaps you can tell her in advance of an official announcement in order to give her time to make appropriate adjustments without jeopardizing your paycheck.

- Does your company know that you have applied to schools? If so, you should tell them sooner rather than later.

- How much do you want to continue working? If you would just as soon have more time off before starting school, you do not need to worry about being dismissed too quickly.

RESIGNING

Schedule a meeting with your boss on a Friday afternoon, so that she will have the weekend to reconcile herself to your decision. Explain what you have gotten from your job and from her. Think in terms of what you have learned about your industry, analytical aspects of your job, people management skills, how to present material (oral and written), and so forth. Then explain why you are going off for an MBA. (If your boss wrote a recommendation for you, all of this can be done briefly, of course, because she already knows much of this.) Note that you are doing it as a smart career move rather than to get away from the work environment.

Give a short, simple letter of resignation. Then tell your closest colleagues of your decision. Once again, explain why you are leaving and how much you benefited from working with them. Not everyone will be happy about your news. Some will be sorry you are leaving, whereas others will be envious. Just "grin and bear" any hostility you encounter.

To leave the best possible impression, be sure to:

- Complete any pending projects.

- Turn over all of your files, with detailed explanations regarding how you would suggest your replacement proceed.

- Train your replacement yourself, if possible.

- Ask for a concluding review of your own performance, assuming that your boss is not angry about your leaving.

- Consider mentioning what aspects of your position vis-à-vis the company could be improved, but only if you think your boss would be pleased to get this input.

- Consider scheduling a telephone call with your replacement one week after she starts work to help her out (and volunteer to call a second time at her discretion).

- Make every effort to stay on good terms with your former colleagues and boss.

PREPARING FOR BUSINESS SCHOOL

RATIONALE FOR STARTING THE PROGRAM WELL PREPARED

If you are ambitious enough to seek a top MBA degree, you are probably also eager to do well in the program.

The easiest way to accomplish this is by starting the program well prepared. The student who is poorly prepared will find it difficult to succeed. The poorly prepared student is highly likely to struggle in the first term and barely get through the first set of courses. As a result, he will be perceived by his professors and fellow students as someone who has little to offer. The redemption process is not likely to start, if ever, until after the core courses have been completed. Only then will he be able to compete on somewhat equal ground with other students. At that point, it is likely to be too late to retrieve the situation entirely.

This will be reflected in the initial job offers to students because most of them finalize their job situations long before they graduate. In fact, many students at two-year programs who take summer jobs at the leading consulting firms and investment banks will have accepted offers from their summer employers before the halfway point of the second year. This means that they will have capitalized on their first-year grades and reputations. Their second-year performance will be essentially irrelevant to their post-MBA starting job.

WHO KNOWS WHAT FROM THE OUTSET

How do the strong performers do it? Do they enter business school already knowing all that an MBA has to teach them, thereby negating the purpose of the program? There *will* be some students who have already gained a bachelor's degree in business, then worked for a consulting firm for several years, learning a great deal about business analysis and performance. These individuals are comparatively rare, however. Most students will have certain assets in terms of their prior coursework and experience, but they will tend to have very limited knowledge of half of the core courses. Finally, some students will have no appreciable business experience or understanding.

There are thus three groups of entering students: know-it-alls, know-somethings, and know-nothings. The first group should do their best to maintain their enthusiasm for the whole of the program, since they tend to suffer from a very high rate of boredom and burnout. (This is understandable, given that they are often getting an MBA more to have the credential than to really learn something.) The second and third groups, however, can help themselves greatly by taking the time to prepare before the start of the MBA program.

THE ELEMENTS OF GOOD PREPARATION

Let's take a look at the core courses of a typical MBA program. Most programs require students to take a standard course (or two) in each of the following areas:

Accounting	Operations Management
Economics	Organizational Development/
Finance	Human Resources
Information Systems	Quantitative Methods/Statistics
Marketing	Strategy/Business Policy

Several skills are not necessarily taught separately, but they tend to underpin success in the core courses:

Computer (spreadsheet, presentation, and word-processing) and Internet skills

Use of a financial calculator

Calculus (and algebra)

Case analysis

Presentation skills, both oral and written

Peter Robinson, in his fine book *Snapshots from Hell: The Making of an MBA* (Warner, 1994), shows what it is like to be underprepared for the start of business school. Robinson was a presidential speechwriter who entered Stanford Business School without any perceptible quantitative skills or understanding. His resulting struggle makes painful, if often funny, reading. To avoid the nightmarish scenario of Robinson and other innumerates, take the following suggestions to heart.

SKILLS: THE BARE MINIMUM

COMPUTER

Before you take another step, ensure that your computer skills (*Internet, word-processing, presentation*, and *spreadsheet*) are adequate. If you have not regularly used a computer for such tasks, plan to put in several dozen hours, making sure you can do the following without difficulty:

- *Internet:* E-mail; attach a file to a message; manage information, and exchange information between documents; find useful resources and information of any type anywhere on the web; and create a simple web page.

- *Word Processor:* Enter and format text; add headers, footers, and page numbers; change fonts and type size; copy, move, and save blocks of text; manage files; use standard tools such as "find" and "replace," spell-check, and center; work with tables; combine spreadsheet-generated tables and graphs with text; and print a document.

- *Presentation:* Create, save, and open a basic presentation; duplicate, move, and delete slides; change slide layout; add clip art, charts, headers, and footers; insert tables, worksheets, and graphs; and print a presentation.

- *Spreadsheet:* Enter text and numbers; add titles and labels; enter formulas; use functions (such as sum and product) in formulas; copy and move data; create charts; and print. You should be able to build a simple income statement and balance sheet, using formulas to change data into usable information. You should also be able to link spreadsheets to provide summary data. In addition, you should be able to do standard statistical analysis with your spreadsheet package. (See the discussion below regarding how to prepare for the quantitative methods/statistics course.)

It is too late to start to learn such things once you are at business school.

Find out which programs your school uses. (Most schools, by the way, use Microsoft Office for Windows [including *Word, PowerPoint,* and *Excel*] and PCs rather than Macs.) Any introductory paperback that explains the basics of these programs is suitable for this task.

It is important to be able to use these tools quickly and easily. Thus, you need to be able to put together a spreadsheet showing that you expect unit sales to increase at the rate of GDP increase plus 2 percent annually, energy consumption to remain proportional to volume, inventory to grow at the square root of the increase in unit volume, and so on, without being overwhelmed by the task. To use *Excel* comfortably, for instance, you must practice setting up a dozen or so spreadsheets. Many books provide appropriate examples. Simply get one that is keyed to your software package, titled something like "Financial Analysis with Excel." **(For up-to-date suggestions of appropriate readings, consult my website, www.degreeofdifference.com, which lists and describes readings at various levels of detail and difficulty. It also makes purchasing them easy.)**

FINANCIAL CALCULATOR

The fluent use of a financial calculator is taken for granted by most students in business programs. The standard calculator in recent years has been the Hewlett Packard 17bII+. If you are not comfortable using a reasonably full-featured calculator, I suggest you learn how to use this one before getting to business school. *The Owner's Handbook and Problem-Solving Guide* provides a good guide to using the calculator. Do not feel compelled to work your way through the whole booklet, but do read the initial chapters, which show how to get started and how to use the percentage and calendar functions, as well as the basic financial and statistics functions. Glance at the later chapter on such things as investment analysis, bonds, and leasing. These features may not be meaningful yet, but they will prove immensely useful soon, so know what is available. Also, be sure to learn about the automatic memory stack to understand how to make use of the calculator's memory capabilities.

Calculus

Many programs require that incoming students be comfortable using calculus. Most have introductory math "boot camps" to get the innumerate up to speed. Anyone attending such a school should take as much calculus as possible before school starts, and not depend upon the boot camp alone. An appropriate course would give an overview of differential and integral calculus and, perhaps, introduce mathematical modeling. If no courses are available, it should be a simple matter to hire a tutor to guide you through an appropriate text. The math used in business programs is definitely not as rigorous as that used in engineering programs, for example, and certain elements of calculus (and statistics, for that matter) are far more important than others. Texts for scientists or engineers will thus be more difficult than is necessary and will highlight techniques that will be of little use at business school. Larry J. Goldstein et al.'s 736-page book *Calculus and Its Applications*, 11th ed. (Prentice Hall, 2006) is a reasonable choice. Those seeking a more outline-like treatment are advised to try Edward T. Dowling's *Mathematical Methods for Business and Economics* (McGraw-Hill, 1993), a 384-page book in the Schaum Outline Series. This covers equations and graphs, functions, systems of equations, linear algebra, linear programming, differential and integral calculus, and the calculus of multivariable functions. It is in outline format, though, and quite terse, so it is perhaps best used with the aid of a tutor. It does provide an immense number of examples and problems, however.

Those who have forgotten even basic math are advised to prepare with Peter H. Selby and Steve Slavin's *Quick Algebra Review: A Self-Teaching Guide*, 2nd ed. (John Wiley & Sons, 1993), a 240-page book that provides a thorough review and is quite suitable for self-study, or Joanne Lockwood et al.'s *Introductory Algebra: An Applied Approach*, 7th ed. (Houghton Mifflin, 2005), a 565-page book that offers a more thorough treatment, starting from ground zero.

Presentation and Communication Skills

You can expect to do a lot of presenting both at business school and in your future career. In fact, the more senior you are, the more presenting you are likely to do. This is therefore one of the key skills to develop during business school. Mary Munter's fine book, *Guide to Managerial Communication*, 7th ed. (Prentice Hall, 2005, 208 pages), gives a good overview of how to approach both oral and written presentations (as well as other types of writing). The advice is concise and clear.

PREPARING FOR THE CORE COURSES

So much for the preliminaries; now let's look at the substantive courses. The key here is to avoid shouldering a full slate of courses for which you are not adequately prepared. If you have no idea of the basics of accounting or finance and you are going to take courses in both at the same time, along with several other courses in which you are comparatively weak, you will be in for a tough time. Limit yourself to only one quantitative or heavily conceptual course per term in which your background is a distinct liability. Notice that I emphasize the quantitative courses. Most students, whatever their backgrounds, feel that the non-quantitative courses, such as Marketing and Organizational Behavior, are the easiest to survive without any relevant background. The tough ones to survive are the quantitative courses and the heavily conceptual courses.

THE DIFFICULT COURSES

The most quantitative (and thus difficult) courses are Accounting, Quantitative Methods/Statistics, and to a lesser extent Information Systems. Economics, Finance, and perhaps to a lesser extent Operations Management are a cross between quantitative and conceptual.

THE NINE CORE DISCIPLINES—GETTING A JUMP START

There is no need to panic at the sight of the (lengthy) lists below. Many of the suggested readings can be handled in fairly short order—and most successful applicants need prepare for only two or three courses.

ACCOUNTING

Taking the introductory accounting course at a top-flight business school is often a demanding proposition. The course is taught at a high level and unfolds very quickly. The inclination of the professor to speed is likely to be reinforced by the substantial number of accountants and financial analysts in the class. Do not try to get up to their level before class begins, but at a minimum you should familiarize yourself with double-entry bookkeeping, the accrual concept, and the basics of the balance sheet and income statement. Ideally, you should also have a nodding acquaintance with the concepts and principles underlying external financial statements—including the accounting cycle (from recording financial transactions to the preparation and analysis of financial statements)—as well as how managers use internal accounting information in their decision-making.

A traditional means of preparing for financial accounting is Robert N. Anthony and Leslie K. Breitner's classic 304-page self-teaching text *Essentials of Accounting*, 9th ed. (Prentice Hall, 2006). This book takes you by the hand through a series of exercises that will teach you the basic vocabulary and methods of accounting. A good alternative is Joseph Peter Simini's 162-page *Accounting Made Simple*, 2nd ed. (Doubleday, 1988). Better yet, take an introductory accounting course at a local school. I suggest that you take the financial accounting course rather than the managerial one, or a class that combines the two fields.

Consider reading a book that shows some of the uses of financial accounting information. A particularly good possibility is Bob Vause's 288-page *Guide to Analysing Companies*, 4th ed. (Profile Books, 2005), which does a thorough job of explaining how a company's economic health can be analyzed, covering many important accounting and finance issues in the process. Reasonable alternatives to Vause are provided by James Bandler's 142-page *How to Use Financial Statements: A Guide to Understanding the Numbers* (Irwin, 1994) and Chuck Kremer et al.'s 198-page *Managing by the Numbers* (Basic Books, 2000). Any of these would make a good companion to Anthony and Breitner or Simini.

The readings discussed above focus on financial accounting, which is geared toward the preparation of information for external users of the data, primarily investors and the government (especially the tax authorities). Managers, however, generally look at different data to help them manage the company's operations. This data is the focus of *managerial accounting*. A very readable, albeit lengthy, treatment of the subject is offered by Michael W. Maher et al.'s *Managerial Accounting: An Introduction to Concepts, Methods, and Uses*, 9th ed. (Southwestern, 2005, 608 pages). If you lack the time to prepare fully for this subject, consider reading the book's first three chapters, which offer a good overview.

The accounting knowledge you acquire will be of value in many of the other courses you take, so do not worry that you are overinvesting effort in learning accounting before business school.

ECONOMICS

Some schools teach just one economics course, perhaps calling it Managerial Economics. Others teach both microeconomics and macroeconomics. The important thing is to be used to the way in which economists think. Microeconomic concepts such as supply and demand analysis, price and income elasticity, complementary and substitute products, opportunity costs, game theory, and externalities should be part of your tool kit before you arrive at business school. Useful preparation would be taking an intermediate microeconomics course at a local school. Better yet, take a managerial economics course if one is offered. At the macroeconomic level, concepts concerning the problems of unemployment and inflation, monetary and fiscal policy, and the like should be familiar to you, although it is more important to be comfortable with micro- than macroeconomic thinking.

This is one field that will be difficult to teach yourself. If you are unable to take an appropriate course, consider hiring a tutor to guide you through a suitable book. N. Gregory Mankiw has written a whole host of introductory texts, any one of which would be a good choice. His *Brief Principles of Microeconomics*, 2nd ed. (Harcourt College, 2001, 427 pages) is an elegant treatment of microeconomics. Other of his books cover macroeconomics or both micro- and macroeconomics. A strong alternative is Paul Heyne et al.'s *The Economic Way of Thinking*, 11th ed. (Pearson, 2005, 557 pages). It covers both micro- and macroeconomics, although it is much stronger on micro.

John Duffy's *Cliff's Quick Review: Economics* (Cliff's, 1993, 156 pages) gives a very good, but very brief, review of the relevant micro- and macro-issues. As such, it would be a good review for someone who has taken the relevant courses, but would probably be much too terse to be readable for an economics novice.

If you feel up to the challenge of more difficult (but more useful) material, consider Ivan Png's *Managerial Economics*, 2nd ed. (Blackwell, 2001, 592 pages), which provides extremely interesting examples. Another alternative is *Fundamentals of Managerial Economics*, 8th ed. (Southwestern, 2005, 688 pages) by Mark Hirschey, which includes very good discussions of linear programming and finance topics such as capital budgeting.

FINANCE

The introductory financial management course will examine investment and financing decisions: sources and costs of capital, tax strategies, capital budgeting, optimal capital structure, valuation and portfolio analysis, and appropriate dividend policies. If you have the basics of related areas such as accounting and microeconomics under your belt, finance will not be a complete mystery. Nevertheless, several books offer good treatments of finance that will stand you in good stead.

Burton G. Malkiel's *A Random Walk Down Wall Street*, 9th ed. (W.W. Norton, 2007, 480 pages) discusses modern financial theory and its relevance to personal investing. Although it focuses on investment decisions rather than financial management, its explanation of risk and return, basic concepts of valuation, the capital asset pricing model, and other foundation stones of modern financial theory makes it a good introduction to finance as well. It is highly readable despite being written at a high conceptual level. Robert C. Higgins's *Analysis for Financial Management*, 8th ed. (McGraw Hill, 2005, 412 pages) covers the usual financial management topics in a readable fashion.

The same is true of John A. Tracy's *The Fast Forward MBA in Finance*, 2nd ed. (John Wiley, 2002, 336 pages). (These last two suggestions are best read after preparing for accounting, whereas the first one can be read without having any accounting knowledge.)

INFORMATION SYSTEMS

The introductory information systems course typically focuses on the managerial issues presented by information systems development, deployment, and use. It is likely to cover strategic information systems, the impact of different information systems on organizations, outsourcing, current and emerging technologies, and the systems development life cycle. It is not devoted to teaching you how to program or to use software tools. (It is assumed that you are comfortable using such tools already.) A simple guide for CEOs to know how to talk to (and manage) their chief information officers—or is it the other way round?—is presented in Mark D. Lutchen's *Managing IT as a Business: A Survival Guide for CEOs* (John Wiley, 2004, 242 pages). It focuses on how to link IT and corporate strategies as well as how to define technology needs and risks. A more in-depth overview of these issues is presented in Lynda M. Applegate et al.'s *Corporate Information Strategy and Management*, 7th ed. (McGraw Hill, 2005, 672 pages). The *Economist* magazine's periodically revised *Pocket Information Technology*, *Pocket Internet*, and *Pocket Telecommunications* books provide useful overviews and glossaries of their respective fields.

This field is uniquely subject to obsolescence, so the above publications should not be favored if something much more up-to-date is available.

MARKETING

The introductory marketing course looks at how to define markets, plan product lines, promote the products, establish and manage distribution channels, and establish prices. It will analyze buyer behavior, target-market development, segmentation of buyers, and so on. It is not necessary to have a lot of marketing background prior to getting to business school, partly because the concepts are more intuitively obvious than those in other areas. If you would like to increase your comfort margin, however, you could read the excellent Roger J. Best book, *Market-Based Management*, 4th ed. (Pearson Education, 2004, 506 pages). It provides a realistic view of key marketing problems. A fine alternative, although widely available only in the U.K., is Cranfield School of Management's *Marketing Management: A Relationship Marketing Perspective* (MacMillan, 2000, 316 pages). Another reasonable choice, albeit at a slightly lower level than the first two, is Alexander Hiam's *Marketing for Dummies*, 2nd ed. (John Wiley, 2004, 384 pages).

OPERATIONS MANAGEMENT

Operations management courses look at the planning and control of operations in manufacturing and service firms. Topics covered generally include forecasting, capacity planning, material requirements planning, just-in-time manufacturing, scheduling, facility layout, facility location, and quality management concepts. I do not suggest that you plow through a production and operations management textbook to prepare for this field. Instead, it would be helpful if you read one book to become familiar in a general way with the main issues. An interesting view of American, German, and Japanese practices, traditions, and strengths and weaknesses is presented in *Lean Thinking* by James P. Womack and Daniel T. Jones, 2nd ed. (Simon & Schuster, 2003, 396 pages). This provides a good overview of the three systems and along the way illustrates many important issues in manufacturing (and nonmanufacturing) management, with in-depth examples drawn from half-a-dozen industries. The book is quite good in discussing the relevant evidence in a readable fashion, and is of particular value in introducing new MBA students to methodological matters in a painless manner. Those wishing a more traditional introduction can try Jack R. Meredith and Scott M. Shafer's *Operations Management for MBAs*, 3rd ed. (John Wiley, 2006, 445 pages). It covers the full range of issues seen in a first operations course, including quality management, mass customization, benchmarking, enterprise resource planning, and business process design. It is particularly good at showing how an understanding of operations matters for those planning careers in finance, marketing, and other fields.

ORGANIZATIONAL DEVELOPMENT/HUMAN RESOURCES

This course can be taught from any of a number of different viewpoints. A modern perspective is offered by looking at how organizations develop. A traditional one focuses on organizational behavior—how individuals and groups act within organizations, and how best to manage people in organizational settings. Another focuses on how to design the structure of organizations. Yet another looks at human resource issues, such as how to recruit, select, train, develop, appraise, reward, and dismiss employees. A combination of these views offers what may now be the most common means of teaching the course. The appropriate reading for this course will therefore depend upon the perspective the course adopts.

Rather than trying to read a book in each field, you might prefer an abbreviated view of all four in Stephen P. Robbins's *Essentials of Organizational Behavior*, 8th ed. (Prentice Hall, 2004, 330 pages). A good alternative, albeit minus the human resources perspective, is Andrew J. DuBrin's *Fundamentals of Organizational Behavior*, 4th ed. (Southwestern, 2006, 383 pages).

One major caution: Do not do any of this reading until you are comfortable in the other areas discussed here. This subject is the one most people find easiest to pass, and success in it is not generally rated as very impressive by other students. Thus, reading to prepare for this field, if it displaced other preparation, would represent an overinvestment—and poor use—of time.

QUANTITATIVE METHODS/STATISTICS

Quantitative methods for managers generally include decision trees, sensitivity analysis, scheduling and queuing theory, linear algebra and programming, and various statistical methods. The statistical techniques ordinarily covered include descriptive statistics, random variables, probability distributions, sampling techniques, statistical estimation, hypothesis testing, contingency tables, analysis of variance, regression (simple and multiple) and correlation analysis, and time series forecasting. (This course is almost sure to make extensive use of microcomputer statistical software, including spreadsheets.) It is not vital that you be up on all of these, but you should have a basic understanding of the standard statistical tools. An introductory statistics course is a valuable investment; otherwise, use a tutor to guide you through the basics. The book you use could be a standard statistical text, such as Dennis J. Sweeney et al.'s *Essentials of Statistics for Business and Economics*, 4th ed. (Southwestern, 2005, 672 pages).

If you will be reviewing largely on your own, there are very few books that you can realistically expect to get through. A marvelous exception, however, is Jessica M. Utts's *Seeing Through Statistics*, 3rd ed. (Thomson Learning, 2005, 560 pages), which provides a thorough treatment of the conceptual issues in a highly intuitive manner, complete with excellent examples. Another notable exception is David S. Moore and William I. Notz's *Statistics: Concepts and Controversies*, 6th ed. (Worth, 2005, 480 pages). It covers basic materials (up to but not beyond regression analysis) in a highly readable fashion, with a good selection of questions and examples. A much less sophisticated but eminently readable approach is found in Peter Garrity's *The Fast Forward MBA in Business Math* (John Wiley, 2000, 342 pages).

Another approach is to learn statistics via a text (and CD-ROM) that is matched to a statistics or spreadsheet program, with canned data files provided as the basis for set exercises employing a range of different statistical techniques. A good choice would be Kenneth N. Berk and Patrick Carey's *Data Analysis with Microsoft Excel* (Thomson Learning, 2003, 591 pages), which provides an extremely sophisticated introduction to the field.

There are many good texts on corporate strategy now available. Michael Porter's *Competitive Strategy: Techniques for Analyzing Industries and Competitors* (Simon & Schuster, 1998, 396 pages) was arguably the first modern book on corporate strategy; it is still the most widely read. A very sophisticated second reading would be Sharon M. Oster's *Modern Competitive Analysis*, 3rd ed. (Oxford University Press, 1999, 434 pages).

ADDITIONAL PREPARATION

For those who are generally ready for the core courses—and gluttons for punishment—several other subjects might be worth considering:

GAME THEORY

Game theory underlies much of the recent thinking on microeconomics and strategy. A highly readable introduction is provided by Avinash K. Dixit and Susan Skeath's *Games of Strategy*, 2d ed. (W.W. Norton, 2004, 665 pages). It is nontechnical but thorough, with a rich set of interesting examples. A less expansive introduction is provided in Avinash K. Dixit and Barry J. Nalebuff's *Thinking Strategically* (W.W. Norton, 1993, 393 pages).

INFORMATION ECONOMICS

A microeconomic view of the modern information economy is given in Carl Shapiro and Hal R. Varian's *Information Rules: A Strategic Guide to the Network Economy* (Harvard Business School Press, 1999, 368 pages). Although by no means new, it remains the best guide to the field.

LINEAR ALGEBRA

The foundation for much mathematical modeling, linear algebra is a suitable subject for precourse study. A relatively simple text is Bernard Kolman's *Elementary Linear Algebra*, 8th ed. (Prentice Hall, 2003, 656 pages). A more sophisticated text is David C. Lay and Eric Stade's *Linear Algebra and Its Applications*, 3d ed. (Addison Wesley, 2005, 576 pages).

MANAGEMENT SCIENCE

If your math (especially calculus) is already up to snuff, and you want to start applying it to business problems, consider Bernard W. Taylor's *Introduction to Management Science*, 9th ed. (Pearson, 2006, 800 pages), which provides a reasonable overview of key topics, including linear, integer, and nonlinear programming; decision analysis; queuing theory; simulation; network flow models;

transportation and transshipment analysis; inventory management; forecasting; project management; and multicriteria decision making.

ORGANIZATIONAL DESIGN

An underlying issue in many courses, but one that is seldom addressed in sufficient depth, concerns how best to coordinate activities. This is analyzed in a very straightforward, readable fashion in Jay R. Galbraith's *Designing Organizations: An Executive Guide to Strategy, Structure, and Process*, 2nd ed. (Jossey-Bass, 2002, 197 pages), which discusses possible organizational structures (functional, product, market, geographical, process, and hybrids), including the advantages and disadvantages of each, and the circumstances calling for the use of one rather than another.

THE LIBERAL ARTS GRADUATE'S SURVIVAL LIST

An entering student does not need to be at home in all of the areas mentioned in this chapter, but the more he knows the better. A reasonable minimum familiarity would include:

➤ Internet searching and e-mailing

➤ Microsoft Word, PowerPoint, and Excel

➤ Robert N. Anthony and Leslie K. Breitner's *Essentials of Accounting* and Bob Vause's *Guide to Analysing Companies*

➤ N. Gregory Mankiw's *Brief Principles of Microeconomics*

➤ Jessica M. Utts's *Seeing Through Statistics*

➤ Single variable calculus (especially derivatives) and, of course, algebra

➤ HP-17bII+ calculator use

Remember that anything you find difficult to grasp two months before the program starts will get much more difficult when you have to learn it along with all the other concepts and techniques that are being piled on you each day.

WHAT THE ADMISSIONS DIRECTORS ADVISE

How to Prepare

➤ If they haven't taken them already, we recommend that incoming students take live or online classes in calculus, microeconomics, and financial accounting. *ROD GARCIA, MIT*

➤ For success at Darden, move to Charlottesville with enough time to get fully settled before class starts. Also, sign up for the prematriculation courses we offer, which are not just a good review of statistics and such, but are also an introduction to the case method. *SARAH E. NEHER, DARDEN*

➤ Don't work up until the minute you need to leave for school. You're about to make a huge investment in yourself that's more important than another month of salary. Get caught up on your sleep. Get centered. Then enjoy the (educational) process. *THOMAS CALEEL, WHARTON*

➤ One of the most important things in the application process is "know thyself." The second is "know thy program." You need to understand the level the program is at and the level you are at. If you think when you walk in the door of the program you'll have a deficit, you should definitely address it beforehand. *ISSER GALLOGLY, STERN (NYU)*

For Career-Switchers

➤ Do a bit of pre-diligence. Learn about the industry that interests you and reach out to it. Have coffee with the hiring people at top firms to learn about their business. Or post something on our e-board: new admits from that industry will be happy to talk with you about what it's like. *THOMAS CALEEL, WHARTON*

➤ An arts graduate who wants to switch careers after getting an MBA needs to take full advantage of the opportunities in and out of class. She needs to get a start on her new career while she is at business school, some relevant experiences that will help her appeal to an employer in the field. If she were interested in consulting, for example, she could do some small business consulting on a part-time basis, whether she gets paid or not. This won't be possible, though, if she has to spend twenty hours of time preparing for her accounting or economics class. Many students who are economics majors don't waive the basic economics course, so competing with them when graded on a curve is tough if you have never seen economics before. *LINDA BALDWIN, UCLA*

For International Students

➤ For international students, we suggest a class in which they have to participate—in English—to get them used to that. This is a problem many of our international students face. *ROD GARCIA, MIT*

➤ Americans are very used to class participation in some form, whereas most other nationalities are not. As a result, I'd suggest international students consider taking the university's ESL summer course, which includes use of the case method. *SARAH E. NEHER, DARDEN*

15

HOW TO GET THE MOST OUT OF BUSINESS SCHOOL

— EXECUTIVE SUMMARY —

Get your life organized before the first day of class.

Understand how best to manage your time.
—As Chapter 14 noted, adequate preprogram preparation is vital.
—Capitalize on the skills of others by structuring a strong study group.

Recognize that business school is about more than class work.

Keep stress under control.

Take advantage of the social (and networking) opportunities.

HIT THE GROUND RUNNING

To get the most out of business school, you must be ready to start working hard from the beginning of the first class. There are two keys to this. The first is to be organized and in control of your new life before classes start. Find and move into your new apartment and get it stocked and organized before classes begin. Take care of all other life-in-a-new-location business before the start of classes as well: Have your telephone hooked up, open a new bank account, and familiarize yourself with your new campus and its facilities. Don't be living out of a suitcase in a hotel and looking for an apartment and some furniture during the evenings when you should be doing your class assignments.

The second key, discussed at length in Chapter 14, is to be up to speed on the basics before you start classes. This means knowing how to use a spreadsheet and word-processing package as well as a financial calculator; being comfortable with some amount of calculus and statistics; being familiar with accounting and economics fundamentals; and, of course, being ready to participate fully in case discussions in English (or the relevant language).

TIME MANAGEMENT MATTERS

Business schools deliberately give you more work to do than any human could possibly manage to complete. They want to force you to do two things. First, they want to make you seek out help from other students, generally through study groups. This sort of team formation is exactly what businesses expect of their better employees, so it is appropriate for business schools to try to generate it as well. Second, you are expected to learn how to prioritize your assignments. Some readings are critical, and you should do them thoroughly and well. Others are overly long and should just be skimmed for their main points. Still others are essentially for fanatics only and should (I hope) be ignored. Just as in any executive position, the potential work facing you greatly exceeds your time available to do it. You must learn what is most important for each course and focus on precisely that, doing additional work only as time allows.

Falling behind is the biggest trap you face. If you fail to keep up, you will face ever increasing problems. Falling behind results in a downward cycle: You have trouble following today's lecture because you hadn't prepared for it, so you must do extra work to make up for your lack of understanding of the lecture, meaning that you will never have time to get ready for tomorrow's lecture, underpreparation for which will mean that even more work is required to be able to make up for your lack of understanding of it, and so on.

Time management extends to your whole business school experience, not just your classes. This chapter recommends that you get involved in student clubs and sports, and get to know your fellow students and professors. You must learn how to do your classwork efficiently, as the following two sections discuss, and also decide in advance how you will spend your free time. Arrange your schedule to make time for the key activities you value most highly, and limit your involvement with other matters. You might have time to participate actively in two clubs, a sport, and a volunteer group, along with attending various career services workshops and special lectures that interest you, but you are unlikely to be able to participate in six or eight clubs and play as many sports, too.

CHOOSE YOUR STUDY GROUP WISELY

Study groups are an important part of business school for almost everyone. Many schools choose your first-term or first-year study group members for you, but if you are allowed to choose your own study group, do so carefully; its makeup can be a major influence on your whole business school experience. You will rely on your study group in your first term. You will be able to use it as a sounding board before you present ideas in class, which will keep you from making some silly comments and encourage you to share genuine insights. You will also use it extensively to prepare assignments when you do not yet know how to reduce your work to manageable proportions by doing only the essentials and skipping the rest. It will be very helpful in getting ready for your first sets of exams, helping you master concepts that are difficult for you but easy for someone else in the group.

Even after your first term or first year, a good study group will live on in importance. You may meet for major assignments and exam preparation in later semesters. If you picked the right group, you will have become close friends with some of its members. You will be able to help each other for years to come. In fact, this will be the core of your own contact network.

An ideal study group is invariably made up of individuals who are strong in very different aspects of business, yet who are personally compatible. Obviously, every group will contain a variety of personalities, but an optimal group would include neither any control freaks, who cannot trust others with responsibility, nor any lazy bums, who will not do their fair share of the work.

ATTENDING THE PRETERM (SUMMER) SESSION

In recent years, schools have developed more and more extensive preterms— sessions that start one or several weeks before the start of the formal courses. These sessions typically include calculus and statistics refreshers; they may also include instruction in standard software packages, economics, use of the Internet, accounting, and so on. Their increased length is due in part to the desire to get everyone up to a comparable level in business basics before school officially begins, and in part to the need to extend the school year because the expanded teaching of soft skills during the year has squeezed out some of the time necessary to develop basic skills.

Preterms were once attended largely by the minority of students who desperately needed remedial help in mathematics. At many schools, however, these are now attended by a majority of the incoming students. Anyone not attending consequently risks being an outsider when the regular term begins. Therefore, even if you do not need the instruction on offer during the preterm, consider attending if only to get your networking and study group formation underway.

CUT TO THE CHASE

There are too many assignments in business school, and they are too long to do all of them completely. You have two key ways to keep from being overwhelmed. One of them, described above, is to form an appropriate study group. The other, and arguably more important one, is to learn how to do the essential work first and the inessential later (or not at all).

One group of students comes to business school trained in these techniques, so try to follow their example. Students who have worked in corporate strategy consulting firms like Bain & Co. and McKinsey have spent several years learning exactly this. What you will see them do is ignore extraneous detail and side issues and home in on one or two critical issues of a case. They will generate impressive analysis of those one or two issues rather than scatter their efforts and do unimpressive analysis of two dozen issues. They will be well prepared to discuss cases (or readings) on this basis, but they will not have had to expend prodigious amounts of work and late nights to do so. To work effectively, you must learn to see the forest rather than the trees, the big picture rather than only the details. You will do detailed analyses, but only as they relate to the critical issues.

DEVELOP SKILLS AND KNOWLEDGE THAT ARE VITAL TO YOUR CAREER (AND DIFFICULT TO DEVELOP OUTSIDE OF BUSINESS SCHOOL)

A number of skills beyond those taught in the core courses will be vital to your career progress. The softer skills include negotiation ability, oral and written communication prowess, and the ability to influence different types of people in a range of situations. Harder skills include the ability to price money, analyze currency risk, put together worldwide cash-flow models for large corporations, or build econometric models of factors influencing demand for complementary products across various markets.

The time to build your intellectual tool kit is during the program. Take courses that will build strong skills rather than just give you the sort of knowledge you could readily acquire on your own. If a certain industrial marketing course involves learning little more than you could get by reading a standard text on the subject, take something like the marketing research course that develops advanced statistical modeling techniques instead. Select courses for the chance to develop the softer skills, too. Many graduates who have been out for five years or more say that the most valuable course they took, or the one they wish they had taken, was a negotiation course, because so much of what they do in every aspect of their jobs involves negotiating.

In addition, look for opportunities to build your skills in extracurricular settings. In particular, look for chances to give stand-up presentations whenever you can, because this sort of skill will be critical to your advancement throughout your career, and it is something few people are ever truly good at.

**WHAT THE ADMISSIONS AND CAREER SERVICES DIRECTORS
SAY ABOUT GETTING THE MOST OUT OF BUSINESS SCHOOL**

General

➤ Although academics are a substantial part of your MBA experiences, there is more to the experience. Learning how to structure teams, motivate people, manage differences with people, and lead are all parts of the MBA experience. The foundation for important relationships, both business and friendship, evolve not only during the two years of school but over one's lifetime. A portion of the time is spent in dialogues with professors and business executives that extend beyond the classroom presentation to meaningful exchanges of ideas, opportunities, and so on. This is a time in life to get the maximum out of your two-year investment. Learning a language, exploring areas of interest that have clamored for attention, and even traveling to new markets through exchange programs or DOJs (days on the job) are some of the benefits. Why make academic skill the only return on your investment? *LINDA BALDWIN, UCLA (ADMISSIONS)*

➤ Write down personal goals as to what you hope to achieve during your two years, and then break them down into quarterly goals—even to monthly and weekly goals. One of the things that is difficult about business school is that there are so many ways to spend your time. If you don't consider up front why you're going to business school and how you're going to get the most out of it, you're likely to find that time will get away from you. To the extent business school is an investment in yourself, being organized and disciplined about it can be very useful. *ANDY CHAN, STANFORD*

➤ You get out of business school—especially a case method school—what you put into it. It's a great time to experiment and develop, which you cannot do passively. So my advice is: be active—active in the classroom, active in the student clubs. Experiment with different leadership roles; experiment with different industries or functions that you're not familiar with. Take classes in areas you know little about. Broaden your knowledge base. Business school is the time to do that, and the only way to do so is to be active. *EVERETTE FORTNER, DARDEN*

➤ The type of person who goes grade hunting, who even takes courses he's already familiar with in order to boost his grades, doesn't get as much as he could out of business school. *ANDREW DYSON, MANCHESTER (ENGLAND) (ADMISSIONS)*

Career-Switchers

➤ In a remotely challenging economy, changing careers can be difficult if you don't plan ahead. Think carefully about what you really want to do, what applicable skills and other assets you have, and the job search that will be necessary. Not only do you want to be realistic, you also want to come across to potential future employers as both realistic and knowledgeable. *John Worth, Darden*

➤ The more thoroughly you can think about how to connect what you've done in the past with what you think your future will be, the better. You have to be self-promoting. You'll have lots of opportunities to explain to other students, alums, professors, and employers how (and why) you're going from career A to career B. As you discuss your career shift, learn how to build your story so that it's more and more compelling. Don't just rely on your MBA to be your ticket to your new career. Develop your story. *Glenn Sykes, Chicago*

➤ Career changers need to be flexible and patient. Simply coming to Wharton (or whatever school) isn't an automatic ticket to a new job. Students looking to make a complete change need to think about ways to take that half- or quarter-step toward the new career during the summer internship or first job out of business school. Students coming from the Peace Corps and wanting to enter investment banking may have to be ready to take a job in a firm's treasury function, for instance, and gain an understanding of the capital markets, before making a further move toward the sort of job they ultimately want. Similarly, they should be flexible by being prepared to take a great job in a small firm in a small city rather than believing that only working for a big-name firm in New York will suffice. *Peter J. Degnan, Wharton*

➤ We'll often tell students that if they have a free summer before they come to go do some projects with organizations that interest them—to begin building their résumés to start "making the change." Conducting informational interviews with friends and acquaintances who have interesting jobs is also very beneficial. People love helping students, so take advantage of this "limited-time opportunity." *Andy Chan, Stanford*

➤ We call career development the "broken cookie" model, where the cookie has to fit together. One-half of the cookie is understanding yourself, doing personal career assessment in terms of what you want to be doing and what skills you have to bring to the party. The other half is understanding industries, functions, and companies so that you can assess where, culturally, you'll have the best fit. You need to take advantage of the wide variety of things that happen outside of the classroom, including career and company events. Most leading business schools bring phenomenal speakers and companies to campus and have poor turnouts by students because of their workload. Students can get so caught up in their studies that they overlook the tremendous events going on around them that they should take advantage of. *Everette Fortner, Darden*

➤ Before they even begin the program, they should start networking with their current contacts—whether that be people at their current employer, alumni of their undergraduate school, or other peers. They should learn as much as they can about the industry and function they're interested in. *PAMELA MITTMAN, STERN (NYU)*

➤ We encourage them to make use of all of our facilities to explore the realities of different jobs. For example, does the working style and culture of the industry (and firm) match their own? Use the time early on to learn about alternatives. Explore one through the first-year shadowing project (following a business leader through a week of activity), another through the group consulting project. *CHRIS BRISTOW, LONDON*

➤ By the time people arrive at business school, they should have at least started the process of figuring out where they are headed, but a two-year program does give students the opportunity to explore different career options. *CHRIS BRISTOW, LONDON*

➤ Don't depend just on doing an MBA as the means to make the change. Be sure to identify the skills you already have that you can transfer to the new career. *KATTY OOMS SUTER, IMD*

Nontraditional Students

➤ Determine where you are headed as soon as possible. Develop a strong rationale for it that you can present to others. Networking will be crucial here, not just in learning what jobs are out there but also in helping you to develop an in-depth knowledge of the field. Bridge the chasm between the old field and the desired one: Demonstrate academic excellence in it and get a part-time job or internship that makes you more desirable. A summer job between years of business school is crucial for a career-changer. Have both a plan A and a plan B. You may have to take a job initially that isn't your dream job but will position you to get what you really want down the road a little. *REGINA RESNICK, COLUMBIA*

➤ Take advantage of as much as possible and establish your career focus quickly. Develop your support systems early on, too—including the student affairs office, career management, and faculty, both as mentors and supporters. Avoid the herd mentality; know yourself and what *you* need. *ROXANNE HORI, KELLOGG*

➤ Nontraditional applicants will want to develop individualized job-search strategies with career services. It starts with self-assessment: why you chose business school, your goals, and the environment that fits you best (including balancing life and work). You need to be realistic. *REGINA RESNICK, COLUMBIA*

➤ Business school and a lot of MBA careers require you to be comfortable doing quantitative analysis. To the extent people are willing to do some work on the quantitative side—Excel and statistical analysis, for example—before school starts, they will have helped themselves greatly. So give yourself time to get ready before you go. *ANDY CHAN, STANFORD*

Establishing Career Direction

➤ It is very helpful to know where you're headed before you get to business school. Even though you may change your mind and get turned on to a new field during business school, knowing what you value and what your interests are will prove helpful. For one thing, you will not get seduced by whatever is hot at the moment. REGINA RESNICK, COLUMBIA

➤ The clearer you are about where you think you want to head, the easier it is to make choices about how you spend your time at school, whether it be classes, clubs, or extracurricular activities, or which companies you're going to get to know and visit. To the extent it can be done, it's of incredible value. It can make the job search–career management process a lot clearer and smoother. ANDY CHAN, STANFORD

➤ Companies come to campus within weeks of your arrival first-year. They start networking with you and want to hear a good, solid story of why you're back at business school, why you're interested in their company and industry. So you have to strike a balance. You can't come to business school, anymore, completely ignorant of what you intend to do. You need to have thought through some of the possibilities for your career. Business school is then a great opportunity for you to explore multiple paths and figure out where the best path is going to be. EVERETTE FORTNER, DARDEN

THINK ABOUT YOUR CAREER DEVELOPMENT

Presumably, one of your primary reasons for being at business school is to propel your career forward. If you do nothing other than work hard for your classes, however, you will miss a large part of what business school offers in terms of career advancement. Several nonacademic parts of the business school experience are ideal for career enhancement, as are specific courses. Discuss with potential future employers and the career services office which skills you should master and which experiences you should gain during the program. Some suggestions:

■ Take advantage of the opportunity to get to know your *classmates*. You will learn a lot from their experiences and will profit from their friendships in the future, including in career terms. Staying in touch with them will provide you with important career advice and information.

■ Get to know *faculty* members, especially in your chosen field. You will learn a lot more about a field if you spend time with the faculty members who are doing research in it. They will also be able to put you in touch with good industry sources to discuss the field and potential employers or specific job prospects. You do need to avoid the appearance of trying to cozy up to them simply to improve your grades or to benefit from their largesse without giving back as well. A sincere interest in learning about the field, on the other hand, will meet with a positive response.

■ Join *student organizations* that are relevant to your likely future career. For example, if you are interested in management consulting, join the management consulting club. You will have a chance to get to know the other members who are themselves interested in consulting. They will be valuable contacts in the future for information about the industry, job opportunities, and the like.

■ *Practice your skills* in club settings and elsewhere. Businesses hire people who are leaders, communicators, skilled analysts—in other words, doers. You have a chance to demonstrate and refine these skills in various settings during business school, including by helping to run a student club, by working for a volunteer organization, or by working part-time for a business in a field related to the one in which you intend to work upon graduation.

■ Take advantage of the professional services offered by the *career services office*. Take their résumé preparation and interviewing workshops; have them tape one of your presentations and several mock interviews; and, most important, consult them about your career plans. Take the career assessment tests they give; have them analyze your personal and professional goals; ask for their perspectives on where you are most likely to derive both satisfaction and frustration in your chosen field. These experts are a source of knowledge you would have to pay a great deal to consult outside of business school, so be sure you do not waste an opportunity to get their input free of charge.

■ Join the local or national *industry association(s)* relevant to your field. For instance, if you are an automotive person, joining a relevant automotive association will give you access to people throughout the industry. You can join a relevant committee or help out in some other way. Note, too, that it is particularly easy to get published in most relevant industry periodicals. If you are clever, you can develop relationships with those who will be your future employers or clients.

Consider how to *combine activities to maximum effect*. For example, the automotive person discussed above, faced with the need to write a paper for a marketing course, could choose a paper topic based upon his discussion with the editor of a major industry association's journal of what would constitute an interesting piece that the journal would like to publish. Then the student could research the topic, making sure to discuss it with relevant industry executives, visiting in person those at companies he would most like to work for in the future. Executives are generally quite willing to help a student, especially one at a prestigious school. This easy access makes it possible to do a very good article for publication; the associated course paper will look all the more interesting for the real-world input it incorporates. The student should update the executives he interviewed, thanking them for their input and sending them copies of the finished paper and article. Doing so is a simple courtesy; it is also a way to keep in front of them. Whether or not they look to hire him, these executives will be a useful part of his network, as will the people at the industry association. After having written one such article, it is even easier to get published in the future. Given that headhunters scour such industry publications when trying to find appropriate candidates for their assignments, publishing this article could pay yet more benefits. (The same benefits would accrue for someone giving a presentation at an industry gathering.) The extra effort involved in writing for publication rather than just for a class is minimal relative to the potential benefits on offer.

KNOW WHERE YOU ARE HEADED

Potential employers will compare you with other members of your class and those at comparable business schools. Before committing yourself to an all-consuming effort to get top grades—which will generally come only at the expense of most of the other benefits and pleasures business school can offer—figure out where you want to go and what it will take to get there. Talk with the career services professionals to determine what GPA, course selection, extracurricular pursuits, and so on will make you an attractive candidate for your chosen (type of) employer. If you intend to work for a bulge-bracket investment bank, for example, you will need to get better grades than if you intend to open a chain of restaurants (where your GPA will be next to irrelevant). But even the most grade-conscious employers do not look just at grades, so make sure you understand how the rest of the package you offer will work for or against you.

The optimal mix of courses, grades, extracurricular pursuits, prior work experience, part-time work experience during business school, and other skills will vary by field and employer. The better you understand in advance of attending business school what you hope to do afterwards, the better able you will be to chart your business school path effectively.

NETWORKING

One of the most valuable assets you will have upon graduation is your network of contacts from your MBA program. This network can help you to get jobs and even, through knowing whom to call for information and assistance, help you in your current job. The key to building an appropriate network is, of course, to make friends, avoid making enemies, and impress as many people as possible. The impression you should make is of being clever, hardworking, a great team player, dependable, sensible, and comfortable working under pressure. In other words, your performance at business school will have a major bearing upon the network—as well as the skill base—you develop. Do not go to extremes in trying to network, however, because people trying to curry favor rather than develop relationships will always run the risk of annoying people.

The networking opportunities MBA students are most likely to overlook, however, are not those within the business school but those outside: alums, engineering and law students who will work in the same industry, local businesspeople, and so on.

KEEP STRESS UNDER CONTROL

The first months of business school are loaded with stress. You will probably be in an unfamiliar environment, surrounded by people you don't know, and be expected to produce more work faster than you ever have before. In addition, you may be competing with people of a higher quality than you have ever encountered before. This, combined with your high expectations for your own performance, can generate tremendous pressure.

Such pressure can be good or bad. Pressure can motivate you to work hard in a focused fashion. On the other hand, too much pressure can paralyze you and leave you unable to work or concentrate.

To avoid being overwhelmed by stress, *be aware of the signs.* If you feel panicked about not meeting your goals, or enraged about what is being asked of you, or if you are feeling the physical symptoms of stress (such as stomach or digestive problems; compulsive consumption of food, alcohol, or cigarettes; or severe tightness in your neck and shoulders), you may well be suffering from excessive stress.

Then *recognize what is causing your stress.* This is likely to be a combination of two things. First, you are demanding too much of yourself. You are expecting to complete every assignment down to the smallest detail, without using your study group for appropriate help, and you are probably expecting to get through the whole program without falling flat on your face a few times. Be realistic; disappointments and mistakes are a normal part of the learning experience. Second, you are failing to appreciate that business school programs deliberately give you more work than anyone could do in the time available.

This can be a rotten combination. You need to learn, as noted above, that you should expect only to complete the most important parts of your assignments, not all of them. You must carefully and firmly prioritize what you will do and what you will skip.

In addition, keep your everyday life under suitable control:

- Get regular exercise. Pick a sport or activity you enjoy and devote half an hour or an hour to it at least five days each week. This will provide you with a suitable outlet for your anxiety, anger, and frustration. If you like to exercise with others, you can kill two birds with one stone. This source of social interaction may be especially important if you are concerned about devoting enough time to friends and family outside of the MBA environment.

- Eat properly. Too many late-night pizzas, or burgers wolfed down minutes before class, will eventually sap your energy and health.

- Get a reasonable amount of sleep, and make sure that once a week you get an extra couple of hours to help make up for your overly demanding schedule.

- Do not eliminate all sources of relaxation and pleasure to make room for your new responsibilities. Giving up your favorite activities will only make you feel your stress and make you less motivated to complete the more painful aspects of your program.

- Last, do not let yourself be bothered by trivial annoyances. Learn to kid around with someone about the sillier aspects of your existence, including those that rile you despite their not being worth your annoyance, let alone anger. For example, if you are cut off by a driver on the way to school, it is not worth screaming and yelling at him just because you are not suitably relaxed. The more such occurrences bother you, the greater the cumulative level of stress you will feel.

DON'T FORGET THE SOCIAL EXPERIENCE

Get involved in school life. Join several clubs, participate in a sport or two, and get to know your classmates and your professors. If you are married, involve your spouse in as many activities as possible, because it will enrich your experience to be able to share it with someone who truly understands what is involved, and he or she will enjoy the time rather than resenting your new and all-consuming lifestyle.

16

FINANCING YOUR MBA

— EXECUTIVE SUMMARY —

■

Calculate the full cost of an MBA.

■

Consider your options in terms of programs and financing alternatives.
—Schools' aid policies differ dramatically, giving you opportunities
to save a lot of money.
—There are many financing strategies available, but few are realistic unless
you start working on them early in the process.

■

But do not leap to attend a program just because it will save you money
in the short run.
—Business school should be considered a long-term investment:
Look for the best value, not the cheapest option.

*G*oing to business school can be a very expensive proposition. Those attending the leading private schools without grant aid can expect to spend well over $100,000 for their two years. Even those attending an American public school—and paying resident tuition—may spend over $60,000. These figures represent the *direct costs* of the program, but the indirect costs are also important. The *opportunity cost*—or money forgone—is the amount of money you could have earned had you continued working (or begun to work) rather than going to business school. Similarly, if your spouse has to take a lower-paying job or change careers, this also represents a potentially substantial opportunity cost.

Despite the size of these sums, the financial consequences of attending a *well-chosen* top school suggest that it is a very good investment. The question of how you will finance your MBA is nonetheless of critical importance. Whereas the minutiae of filling out financial aid forms are beyond the scope of this book, this chapter will examine the major financing strategies you can employ consistent with your career choices.

CALCULATING THE COST OF BUSINESS SCHOOL

FULL-TIME PROGRAMS

The *direct cost* of attending a given school will depend upon its tuition rate, living expenses in the area, and the duration of the program. Schools are quite good about providing applicants with information about the cost of attendance (based upon the experiences of their current students) in application materials. For instance, Chicago's budget for the 2006–2007 academic year was:

Tuition (10 courses)	$41,600
Activity fee	129
Health service fee	483
Health insurance	1,824
Administrative service fee (first year only)	850
Lifetime credentials fee	35

Books	2,100
Rent/utilities	13,500
Food	5,400
Personal	2,550
Transportation	1,350
Computer (first year only)	3,000
Total	$72,821

To this should be added the expense of moving to the school, and traveling to and from "home" during holidays and so on, if it is far from your current residence.

This estimate will not necessarily be a totally accurate one for you, of course, depending upon such things as how luxuriously you intend to live during business school, how many times you intend to visit home (and how much it will cost for each visit), and so on, so be sure to alter the bottom-line figure to reflect your personal circumstances.

In general, the direct cost of attending a school will depend mainly on its tuition rate, the living expenses in the area, and your chosen lifestyle. Annual tuition and fees can range from about $14,000 to more than $45,000, with the top private schools all charging at the high end of that range. (European one-year programs, which may last ten to twelve months, can be even pricier.) Other costs (housing, food, books, transportation, personal expenses, etc.) for a single student can range from $13,000 to more than $30,000, as estimated by the schools themselves.

PART-TIME AND EXECUTIVE PROGRAMS

Part-time programs tend to have similar fee structures, but the economic burden is generally lower. First, the payments will be spread over the longer period it takes to complete the program. Second, participants usually continue to work—and thus earn money—during the program. Third, many employers will subsidize the effort. (But, largely as a result, little financial aid is available for part-time programs. In particular, virtually no grants [scholarships] are offered for part-time study.)

Executive MBA programs have traditionally been paid for by employers rather than by the participants themselves. Largely as a result, tuition for EMBA programs is generally more expensive than for either full-time or part-time programs. Tuition currently ranges from $60,000 to $125,000 for an EMBA program. (This is the total tuition, not the annual amount.) Financial aid is seldom available for EMBA programs.

FINANCING SOURCES

Frankly, the largest source of funds for most MBA students is likely to be their own savings—another reason to work for several years before applying. The second largest is loans, with scholarships and other sources making up the remainder.

HOW DO PEOPLE TYPICALLY PAY FOR THEIR MBAS?

Full-Time Programs	*Part-Time Programs*	*Executive Programs*
Savings	Salaries	Employers
Loans	Savings	Salaries
Grants	Employers	Loans
Part-time jobs		
Employers		

GRANTS

THE SCHOOL ITSELF

The first place to look for financial aid is the school itself. Schools have a variety of means of helping students, including scholarships and assistantships. These funds may be limited according to the student's nationality, residence, ethnic background, gender, financial need, or relative quality (i.e., an applicant in the top 10 percent of an entering class in terms of prior scholastic achievement, GMAT scores, and estimated managerial potential may be offered scholarship money when an applicant at the "bottom" of the entering class might not be). Schools can allocate funds on the basis of need, merit, or a combination of need and merit, or as a means of attracting certain types of students. (Check with each school you are considering to ascertain what types of institutional aid are available and what application forms are required.) American schools generally give merit-based aid to 15–40 percent of their students; European schools, to 5–20 percent.

OUTSIDE GRANTS

Scholarships are available from sources other than the business schools. They are most often given on the basis of residence, membership of a specific ethnic group, military service, relationship to a relative who served in the armed forces or is a member of a particular civic organization, or interest in a particular area of business.

To look for grants in the United States, consult the following websites for free scholarship searches:

www.finaid.org   www.fastweb.com
www.salliemae.com   www.scholarships.com

Or, consult the following:

- Phillip C. McKee, Cynthia Ruiz McKee, *Cash for Graduate School: The Ultimate Guide to Grad School Scholarships*
- Laurie Blum, *Free Money for Graduate School*

(Do not, however, pay anyone to conduct such a search for you. This field is notoriously loaded with charlatans.)

To maximize your chances of getting a grant, do your homework before applying:

- Learn the mission of the scholarship organization.
- Analyze the selection process. It is probable that it will overlap in key regards with the business school selection process. Therefore, start your analysis by looking at the relevant sections of this book.
- Consider how you can position yourself for maximum appeal, given your possible fields of study and career path after business school.
- Discuss the process with prior winners of the award.
- If an interview is part of the selection process, find out who does the interviewing and what their interests are likely to be.

European students, especially Scandinavians, may qualify for aid from their respective governments for attending a top-quality school no matter where it is located. Similarly, there are numerous grants available for nationals of a European Union nation who will attend a school in another EU member country.

LOANS

Only a minority of students at the top schools receive merit grants; a substantial majority of students take on a very substantial debt load to pay for business school. The average debt level upon graduation is now in excess of $50,000. For those with good credit histories (see the box on page 445), it is generally easy to borrow such amounts. Whether you should do so, of course, is another question. After all, borrowing influences not just your financial future but also your career future. If you graduate with a massive debt load, you will be under pressure to take the most lucrative job possible.

GOVERNMENT

Many governments offer subsidized loans for graduate education. In the United States, for example, there are three government-funded types of loans generally on offer for business school education: Federal Perkins, Federal Subsidized Stafford, and Federal Unsubsidized Stafford. American citizens or permanent residents are eligible for the various federal loan programs.

PRIVATE LOANS

Private loans are on offer from well-established educational lenders. In the United States, these include Citibank, Nellie Mae (a largely private loan agency), Sallie Mae, Key Education Resources, TERI, and the Access Group. (See "Additional Information Sources" at the end of the chapter.) Note that all of these involve credit checks and require a satisfactory credit history. One easy way to determine whether you are likely to be approved for a private educational loan is to contact a lender, such as the Access Group, which offers a preapproval process. Once you have provided your information, the lender will conduct a credit check and notify you of its decision. If you qualify, you can complete the loan application process, or simply rest assured that you will be able to qualify for a loan when the time comes.

CHOOSING LOANS

When comparing loans, consider both the fees charged for origination or guarantee and the interest rates. Origination or guarantee fees can be charged upon disbursement of your money or when you go into repayment. In either case, consider these fees in your calculations. Interest rates in private loan programs are seldom flat rates. Instead, they are based upon the Treasury Bill, LIBOR (London interbank offer rate), or prime rates, with an additional several percentage points tacked on. This means that the actual interest rate will fluctuate with these market interest rates. It is, of course, easy to determine the cheapest rate if the loans you are examining all use the ninety-day T-Bill rate or all use the prime rate as the basis of their calculations. It is a bit trickier to compare rates if one lender uses the T-Bill and another the prime rate. To determine what will be cheapest, calculate the current rate in effect by looking up the relevant T-Bill and prime rates and then adding the relevant percent figures.

Try to keep any loans you take out with the same lender as any prior educational loans you have. This will make your record keeping and repayment simple.

THE IMPLICATIONS OF YOUR CREDIT HISTORY

Note that all student loans—government and private—depend upon your credit history. If you have loans in default, have made late credit card payments, and so on, your ability to borrow may be limited. To make sure you have a clean credit history, or to start the process of cleaning up your record, obtain a copy of your credit report by contacting one of the relevant credit reporting agencies. In the United States, three agencies dominate the business:

➤ Equifax: www.equifax.com or (800) 685-1111

➤ Experian (formerly TRW): www.experian.com or (888) 397-3742

➤ Trans Union: www.transunion.com or (800) 888-4213

Free credit reports, plus tips on how to manage your credit history, are also available from www.myfico.com and www.freecreditreport.com.

LOAN REPAYMENTS

- *Grace Periods*. Most private loans, as well as some government loans, have a six-month period after graduation during which no payments are required.

- *Loan Repayment Assistance Plans*. A number of leading American schools have programs to ease the financial burden for those who enter nonprofit or government work. Full or partial loan repayments are made on behalf of those working for qualifying employers.

REPAYMENT AMOUNTS

The following chart provides amortization data to help you determine the amount of monthly payments you will make for any given loan. To utilize it, first determine the amount of principal for each loan. (Note that unsubsidized loans will accrue interest during your period of study, meaning that the total amount to be repaid will have increased.) Once you have the principal amount, check the chart for the duration of the loan and its interest rate. The associated figure in the chart shows how much you will repay monthly *for each one thousand dollars of principal*. For example, if you borrowed $20,000 for twenty years at 10.0 percent, you will need to repay $9.65 per thousand. Thus, you will need to repay $193 per month (i.e., 20 x $9.65). If you borrowed the same amount, at the same interest rate, but for ten years rather than twenty, you would need to repay $264.40 per month.

| | | | INTEREST RATE | | | |
NUMBER OF YEARS	5.0%	8.0%	9.0%	10.0%	11.0%	12.0%
5	10.61	20.28	20.76	21.25	21.75	22.25
10		12.14	12.67	13.22	13.78	14.35
15		9.56	10.15	10.75	11.37	12.01
20		8.37	9.00	9.65	10.33	11.02
25		7.72	8.40	9.09	9.81	10.54
30		7.34	8.05	8.78	9.53	10.29

To calculate the exact loan payments facing you, consult one of the following loan calculators:

> www.finaid.org/calculators/loanpayments.phtml
> www.accessgroup.org/calculators/loan_repay.htm
> www.scholarships.com/loanpayment.asp

HOW MUCH DEBT IS TOO MUCH?

The general rule is that the better the school you attend, the more you are likely to earn, both in your first job out of school and throughout your career. Attending a better school thus makes a high level of debt more affordable than would be the case if you attended a lesser school.

Nevertheless, the question of how much debt is appropriate for you depends upon your individual circumstances. If you intend to take a relatively low-paying public sector job upon graduation, you may view a $75,000 debt as inconceivable. If you take a job at a leading investment bank, on the other hand, with total first-year pay of $140,000 or more, the same $75,000 would probably look manageable. This fact could well alter your choice of jobs, which might or might not be a problem. If you have to focus on the salary and bonus of your first year in order to facilitate debt repayment to the exclusion of all else, you may take a job that is not appealing in terms of the actual work, the specific firm, the city, or your future prospects. This would be an unfortunate consequence of your debt situation.

Let's put the question of borrowing into perspective. In terms of the amounts you will have to repay, someone who borrows $75,000 for ten years at 8–10 percent interest will face a monthly, post-tax payment of approximately $900–$1,000. This would ordinarily require an annual income in excess of $65,000. This is well below the starting salaries of most people graduating from top schools, except those students who take low-paying public sector or public interest jobs. These figures suggest that the size of a loan necessary to fund an average student will not be large relative to his or her post-MBA earning capacity.

YOUR EMPLOYER

Your *current employer* may be willing to help you pay for your MBA. Employer assistance depends primarily upon the type of program you attend and how much the firm values you. Employers have traditionally paid tuition and fees for executive MBA programs. For part-time programs, employers often pay all or part of tuition and fees. For full-time programs, however, it is rare for employers to pay. (See Chapter 2 for further discussion of employer funding of MBAs.)

A firm's valuation of you depends not just upon your performance but also upon its ability to replace you with an appropriate substitute. Thus, in a tight labor market, a firm is likely to value you more highly than in a slack one. Even if you are hard to replace, however, the firm must forecast its need for you several years into the future, which is often difficult to do.

Check to see what arrangements your firm has previously made for other employees who have gone to business school. If your firm has not sponsored someone before, you may need to work hard to convince it of the value of doing so. (The bigger the firm is, the more likely it is to have a program in place to offer assistance.) Some of the points you might make include agreeing to remain with the firm for a specified number of years after completing the degree (with your improved skills), and trying to do any large projects that the school requires in conjunction with the firm, so that the firm gets the "free" advice of a group of talented business students and perhaps that of a professor as well. Be sure to ask your chosen school about how best to present "sponsorship" to your employer. Schools tend to be well informed about how other similar employers have benefited from sponsoring someone, and will know how other students have successfully pitched the idea to their own firms. Weigh the value of getting assistance from your employer versus the commitments you may need to make to remain with the firm after you graduate. If your primary reason for going to business school is to switch careers, note that the older you get, the harder it is to make a change.

Another possibility is to get an educational loan from your employer. Many firms that do not pay for employees' education will at least provide very low-cost loans to facilitate such education. This is particularly true of financial institutions.

When the labor market is particularly tight, *new employers* may pay part or all of a new recruit's tuition retroactively. This is most often seen with the traditional employers of MBAs: strategy consulting firms and investment banks.

THE TAX DEDUCTIBILITY OF BUSINESS SCHOOL

In many countries, the cost of higher education meant to enhance your professional skills is automatically tax deductible. The higher the marginal tax rates, the more valuable such a deduction will prove. (The same is true regarding the opportunity to carry a tax loss forward or backward.) Policies vary dramatically from one country to the next, however, so be sure to investigate this subject with care.

The United States is a particularly complicated case. Every American taxpayer can, at a minimum, claim a Lifelong Earning Credit of $2,000 for graduate education. Some, however, will be better off claiming a different deduction instead. (The Lifelong Earning Credit and the Deduction for Higher Education Expenses are mutually exclusive. For a discussion of these two possibilities, as well as the impact of employer education assistance upon your own taxable income, see two IRS publications: IRS 970, Tax Benefits for Education; and IRS 520, Scholarships and Fellowships.)

In order to deduct more of the full cost of business school (which includes the expense incurred getting into business school) rather than just claiming the $2,000 Lifelong Earning Credit, there are two basic requirements. You need to maintain or enhance skills required by your employer, without qualifying for a new trade or business. Thus, if you were a market researcher for a high-tech company and return to this work (and perhaps the same employer), doing very similar work albeit at a higher level, you may well qualify for a deduction. Note that students on part-time and executive MBA programs generally find it easier to qualify than do those on full-time programs because they (the part-timers) tend to continue to work in similar fields for the same employer throughout and immediately after their MBA programs.

Be sure you discuss these matters with your accountant or tax lawyer. The rules are very complicated and the case law messy, so you may not get a definitive answer even then. In that case, your risk profile may be the determining factor as to whether or not you claim a deduction.

OTHER SOURCES

You may qualify for special assistance programs if you are a military veteran. If you are married, you can always beg your spouse to support you through the program. Lastly, consider reacquainting yourself with your parents. Their financial aid may involve fewer restrictions and qualifications than other likely sources of financing, not to mention the fact that they may be your only realistic choice for assistance.

EVALUATING FINANCIAL PACKAGES—AND TRYING FOR MORE

EVALUATING AND COMPARING AWARD PACKAGES

Be ready to evaluate, compare, and perhaps negotiate financial aid packages at different schools. When evaluating an aid package, or comparing various aid packages that you have received from schools to determine which is best, consider these factors:

■ *The length of the award:* The most obvious consideration (for two-year programs) is whether the award is for one year or two.

■ *The portions of scholarship versus loan funding:* Two schools can offer to fill your financial need in radically different ways. One business school might give you 60 percent of your $60,000 total need in scholarship aid whereas another might offer only 15 percent in scholarship, forcing you to take on substantial debt.

■ *The terms of the loan repayments:* Not all loans are created equal. Subsidized loans, for example, for which the government or institutional lender will pay interest while you are still in school, are better than unsubsidized ones. Loans without origination fees are preferable to those with fees.

BARGAINING

Prior to the mid-1990s, applicants to the top schools could not successfully haggle with schools about their financial aid offers. If Michigan offered you a $2,000 grant and $14,000 in loan, you took it or went elsewhere. That is no longer entirely true.

In the last few years, some schools have started to bargain—rather surreptitiously—with the applicants they most wish to catch. This started with schools well below the top level, but has now reached well up the ladder. Even though the bulk of truly top schools looks to be resisting out-and-out bargaining, it is safe to say that of the top 20 schools (however defined), at least a substantial minority now engage in some degree of bargaining.

The financial aid game differs according to whether a school offers need or merit aid. A school offering *need-based aid* will be unlikely to try to match another school's aid offer. Instead, you need to show that your financial need is greater than the school appreciated. For example, perhaps you will need to make more trips home than budgeted or your living expenses will be higher due to recent rent increases in the area.

When considering improving your offer at a school offering you *merit aid*, keep the following notions in mind. Do not expect all schools to be equally interested in you. The higher up the list of admitted students you find yourself, the greater your potential bargaining leverage. Even if a school definitely wants you, a higher-ranked school is unlikely to try to match the offers of lesser-ranked schools, believing that you will probably attend it anyway.

Of course, the clearest rule of all is that failure to try for a better offer results inevitably in failure. If a set of comparable schools admits you, take the best offer you have from one and show it to the others to see whether any of them will improve their offer to you. Some of them may try to convince you that you will actually do better, financially and otherwise, with the offer they have already made you. By all means pay attention to this perspective; it may well be right. But by the same token, see whether you can get more money out of the school (regardless of whether you believe the argument they have made).

The more schools of similar repute that have admitted you, the greater your leverage with any one of these schools. (As a result, you should apply to many schools that are similar to one another.) This principle can, however, be taken too far. Do not expect Fuqua (Duke) to pursue you avidly if you look like a great fit at another school but a poor one at Duke, because the effort to pursue you would not be worth the time of Duke's financial aid people. If you have strong ties to Darden (University of Virginia), for example, and no compelling interest in a program done particularly well at Duke, expect Duke's financial aid people to focus on other people rather than on you. The obvious lesson here is to show how you would be a perfect fit for the program, and vice versa, without foreclosing the reasonable possibility of your going elsewhere.

BARGAINING APPROACHES

➤ When the school gives no merit grants whatsoever, emphasize your poverty. Note that your expenses (rent, child care, auto repairs, and so on) will run higher—and perhaps your (and your significant other's) earnings will run lower—than the school anticipated in its aid award.

➤ When the school gives merit grants, remember that it is most likely to be willing to match another school's grant the better the other school's reputation/rankings, and the more the two are rivals due to geography or similarity of programs.

The discussion above may suggest that bargaining is a fixture at nearly all schools. That is not (yet) the case. Bargaining is just now becoming important in the business school financial aid game, but it will certainly increase as more and more schools try to buy talent. The leading schools (and their would-be rivals) are increasingly competitive. Given the advent of bargaining throughout the American undergraduate (college) world, more and more of those applying to business school will expect to haggle over business school financial offers; this will propel the competition for business student talent even further into the world of bargaining.

One last note to the wise: When trying to determine which schools are most likely to put toe (and whole leg) into these waters, note that new deans of business schools are most likely to try to improve the student profile at their schools by changing the basis for awarding aid.

STRATEGIES FOR FINANCING YOUR BUSINESS SCHOOL EDUCATION

KEEP YOUR SPENDING UNDER CONTROL

BEFORE BUSINESS SCHOOL

Business schools will consider your income, not just your savings, when calculating how much money you should be able to contribute. Harvard, for instance, expects you to save 10 percent of your income each year working before business school. Therefore, wasting money on frivolous purchases in the years before business school can have unintended consequences. Take a look, well in advance of applying to business school, at how schools calculate your expected contribution to make sure your current spending plans will not come back to haunt you.

Be careful, also, not to run up too much credit card or other consumer debt. Not only is it an expensive way to finance your spending, but failure to meet your payments will also make it difficult or impossible to gain government or private business school loans. Make sure, too, you manage carefully your existing educational debt (taken on for college and, perhaps, graduate school). Defaulting on this, or even being late with payments, can also limit or eliminate your ability to get new loans for business school.

DURING BUSINESS SCHOOL

Live as inexpensive a lifestyle as you can manage. It will allow you to live better upon graduation, when your loan repayments will be lower than they would be if you had lived at all extravagantly during business school. In addition, the less debt you have, the more career flexibility you will retain. If your debt is $125,000, you will feel pressured to work in the highest paying corporate environment possible.

CONVERTING TO RESIDENT STATUS

Many American state schools charge somewhat less for nonresidents than private schools do, and much less for state residents. Many states also provide scholarship aid for residents attending school in that state. Residence is therefore an important concept as far as state schools are concerned. Most states require you to have lived in the state for at least one year (without being a full-time student) to be considered a resident. (You may also need to be an American national to be considered a resident.) Documentary evidence that they may take into account includes local bank accounts, drivers' licenses, voter registration, rent receipts, and telephone bills.

At the California schools it is very easy to enter as a nonresident student in the first year, yet be converted to resident status for the second year. In other states, this is very difficult to do. In fact, it often requires marrying a state resident to accomplish this conversion. As a result, getting the advantage of Michigan's, North Carolina's, Virginia's, or Texas's resident tuition probably requires becoming a resident prior to business school.

	RESIDENT *(IN-STATE)*	*OTHERS*
Haas (UC Berkeley)	$23,984	$35,159
Ross (Michigan)	$14,272	$28,690
MIT	N/A	$42,634

WORKING DURING BUSINESS SCHOOL

THE LOCATION TRADE-OFF

It is possible to work during the second year of a two-year program. (At one-year programs, however, the pace is generally too intense to permit much work during the program.) At some programs, as many as one-quarter of the students work part-time. Some work at the school as graduate (course) assistants and the like; others work for local firms.

In general, the schools that offer the lowest cost of living are in locations where it will be hard to earn a great deal of money working part-time during the school year. Charlottesville, for example, is a less expensive place to live than is New York City. By the same token, part-time jobs at local firms pay much better in New York than in Charlottesville. If you intend not to work during business school, you may find the University of Virginia a bargain relative to NYU or Columbia. On the other hand, if you *do* intend to work during your second year, Charlottesville may represent a false economy insofar as you could more than make up for a higher cost of living through your earnings elsewhere. This is, of course, yet another example of the fact that your choice of business school is heavily conditioned by the extent to which you already know what you will do during business school.

IS THE FINANCIAL AID DECISION INDEPENDENT OF THE ADMISSIONS DECISION?

Few top schools take account of your need for financial aid in making their admissions decisions, unless you are an international and must qualify for a visa. Numerous schools that wish to have foreign students but lack the funds to sponsor them do give preference to foreign students able to pay their own way.

THE ADMISSIONS AND FINANCIAL AID DIRECTORS DISCUSS THE ADMISSIONS IMPACT OF NEEDING FINANCIAL AID

➤ The applicant's need (or lack of need) for financial aid is irrelevant. *SALLY JAEGER, TUCK*

➤ We have no information about someone's financial need when making admissions decisions. *DAWNA CLARKE, TUCK*

➤ The admissions committee doesn't have any idea whether an applicant has any need for aid; that's handled totally separately by the financial aid office. The same is true for international and wait-listed applicants: the need for financial aid does not affect the admissions decision. *ANNE COYLE, YALE*

➤ An applicant's need for financial aid, or lack of need, has absolutely no impact on the admissions decision. *MARY GRANGER, ESADE*

➤ We have fifteen scholarships (for a class of ninety) and substantial loan aid available for students. We have never turned someone down due to financial need. *KATTY OOMS SUTER, IMD (SWITZERLAND)*

➤ Applicants should take responsibility for their own funding. We consider an applicant's financial need, but it's not the first thing we look at—and it rarely affects a decision. *ALISON OWEN, SAÏD (OXFORD)*

SUMMARY: THE BASIC STRATEGIES

By starting the process early, you make it possible to play the financial aid game well. Keep in mind the following strategies, based upon the previous discussion:

1. Save money before going to school.

2. Work until a week or two before school starts. Although it is a good idea to start school relaxed and rested, you should not need a two-month holiday to achieve this.

3. Shift income away from the base year used to calculate need-based financial aid awards. Do what you can to get a Christmas bonus the year before—or New Year's bonus the year after—the critical base year, or get paid in options rather than salary. Avoid realizing any capital gains, which are treated like income.

4. Consider shuffling your assets by transferring funds, for example, to your parents or siblings. If your grandparents or rich uncle intend to help out with your education, suggest that they wait until you graduate, at which time they can repay your outstanding loans.

5. Nail down any outside grants you can.

6. Consider reacquainting yourself with your parents. Their financial aid may involve fewer restrictions and qualifications than other likely sources of financing.

7. Become a resident in a state (or country) that offers reduced tuition to residents at a business school you wish to attend.

8. Consider delaying your marriage if your prospective spouse will add to your joint assets and earnings. (You could even consider divorcing such a person, but I am loath to advise such a thing.)

9. Live cheaply during business school. You can save several thousand dollars a year by living frugally.

10. Get a grant based upon performance in business school. Many schools make awards for "best performance in Financial Accounting" or "highest grades by a first-year student."

11. Work for as many weeks as possible during the summer between years of business school (assuming that you attend a two-year program).

12. Consider logging as many hours as practicable in the last half of business school at the best-paying (local) firms. Note that salaries differ dramatically

from one location to another, so if you intend to work part-time, take this into account when choosing a school.

13. Attend a one-year program rather than a two-year program.

14. Attend a part-time or executive program, with employer support.

15. Upon completion of your degree, ask your new employer to reimburse your tuition or to pay off your loans.

PRIMARILY FOR AMERICANS

16. Accelerate necessary expenses (such as buying a car or computer) to reduce cash on hand, which is used to calculate loan and grant eligibility. Various assets, including cars, computers, books, clothing, furniture, appliances, and school supplies, do not count as assets for these calculations.

17. American analysis of financial need does not consider retirement funds, so using withdrawals from such funds to finance your education should be a last resort.

18. If you will enter the governmental or nonprofit sector upon graduation, attend a school with a Loan Repayment Assistance Program.

19. Attend an American public school (such as Anderson or Haas) that permits students to pay resident tuition in the second year of the program.

20. Enter a field that makes your business school expenses tax deductible, assuming that you will return to it upon graduation.

Despite all of the above advice, do not believe that attending a lesser business school for a reduced price is generally a better idea than paying full tuition at a demonstrably better school. You are making a long-term investment, so think in terms of value rather than just in terms of price.

SHOULD YOU TRADE DOWN IN SCHOOL QUALITY TO SAVE MONEY?

When should you take a merit scholarship at a lesser school instead of paying full tuition at a better school? When should you go to a public business school with lower tuition than a somewhat better private school (with higher tuition)? A lower-priced Canadian school than a higher-priced American school? There are numerous factors to consider:

➤ How large is the quality (and reputation) difference between the two schools?

➤ To what extent do the two schools offer the courses you want and other elements (such as location and atmosphere) you most value? (See Chapter 3,

"How to Choose the Right School for *You*," for a full discussion of these elements.) What are the earnings possibilities during summers and term-time at the two schools?

➤ What amount of scholarship is on offer?

➤ What field do you intend to enter? How certain are you of this? If you are likely to enter the public sector, huge debts may prove a major constraint upon your ability to enter such a field (although your attractiveness to such employers may well depend upon the quality of the school you attend). The same is true if you hope to start a business.

➤ The more likely you are to enter a high-paying field, the less importance you should attach to the debt you may carry upon graduation.

➤ Note that performance pressure may be much less at the better school, oddly enough, because your rank in class may not matter much to your employment chances. At Stanford, it may be sufficient simply to graduate to get the type of job you want, whereas you may need to be in the top 5 or 10 percent at a lesser school to get such a job. Check with your desired employers about what it takes from each school.

MAKE SURE YOUR FINANCING STRATEGY IS CONSISTENT WITH YOUR CAREER GOALS

When considering how to finance a business school education, be sure to think through the implications of your financing strategy. Make sure your financing approach is consistent with how you intend to do business school. Do not expect to work twenty-five hours a week for a local firm while also trying to graduate as the top student in your class. Do not expect your earnings from a summer job between your first and second years to be massive if you intend to pile up public interest credentials. (Public interest positions, especially during summer internships, pay modestly.) Similarly, make sure your financing approach is consistent with your post-MBA goals. Thus, do not pile on $125,000 of debt if you intend to take five years off to start a family.

To plan your financing effectively, you therefore need to have a good understanding of where you are headed: how you intend to spend your time in business school and what type of career you intend to have (and when). Do not leave your financing strategy to chance. Instead, start the process of determining how best you can finance your business school education early in the application process.

ADDITIONAL INFORMATION SOURCES

UNITED STATES

- A good place to start your research is at www.finaid.org, which is the most comprehensive financial aid site and also provides links to numerous other resources.

- FAFSA (Free Application for Federal Student Aid) may be obtained at www.fafsa.ed.gov, (800) 433-3243, or (319) 337-5665

- Private loan programs
  Access Group: www.accessgroup.org; (800) 282-1550
  Citi Assist: www.studentloan.com; (800) 967-2400
  TERI Loan: www.teri.org; (800) 255-TERI
  Key Education Resources: www.keybank.com/education; (800) 539-5363
  Sallie Mae: www.salliemae.com/mbaloans; (888) 272-5543
  Nellie Mae: www.nelliemae.com; (800) 367-8848
  North Star Total Higher Education: www.northstar.org; (888) 843-3095
  My Rich Uncle: www.myrichuncle.com; (888) 697-4248

- Scholarships and loans for minorities
  The Consortium for Graduate Study in Management: www.cgsm.org; (314) 877-5500
  For those who intend to work in financial services, contact the Robert A. Toigo Foundation: www.toigofoundation.org; (510) 763-5771
  National Black MBA Association: www.nbmbaa.org; (312) 236-2622
  National Society of Hispanic MBAs: www.nshmba.org; (877) 467-4622

- Veterans
  Department of Veterans Affairs: www.gibill.va.gov; (888) 442-4551

UNITED KINGDOM

- The Association of MBAs (AMBA) offers an extensive loan program in conjunction with NatWest Bank: www.mbaworld.com; +44 (0) 20 7246 2686

- *The Grants Register: The Complete Guide to Postgraduate Funding Worldwide* (Macmillan)

INTERNATIONAL STUDENTS GENERALLY

- Contact the embassy or consulate of the country where you intend to study to see what scholarships they know about, and what information sources they can recommend for foreign nationals.

- Check financing sources in your own country to see which, if any, will allow you to use financial awards outside the country.
- Check with one or two leading local business schools (and one or two business schools in your target country, as applicable) to see what information and financial sources are available.

Part IV

APPLICATION ESSAY EXAMPLES

ESSAYS

*T*his book contains 111 successful essays written by 24 different applicants to leading MBA programs. Nearly all of them appear here in Part IV, although five essays by Joerg appear in Chapter 8.

Thus, in front of you, you have a full menu of essay types—written in response to a large variety of questions asked by the top schools in the United States and Europe. The essays reflect the many interests and experiences of the applicants writing them, and a diverse lot they are. There are sixteen men and eight women. Among them are applicants of many different racial and ethnic heritages, including Latin, Chinese, Middle Eastern, and Indian. A substantial number were born and raised outside the United States, in places such as Colombia, the Netherlands, Haiti, Denmark, and France. Some of the applicants have special issues they needed to address, such as a physical or learning disability, or a poor college record. The applicants' backgrounds range from two to fifteen years of full-time work experience, in fields as varied as journalism, investment banking, law, technology, government, manufacturing, entrepreneurship, and the military.

These essays have been selected in order to give you a wide range of materials from which to benefit. The vast majority of essays are part of complete essay "sets," meaning that all of the candidate's essays written for a school are included. These give you the opportunity to get a full picture of the applicant (sometimes topped up with an additional essay or two written to another school). Following each applicant's essays are brief comments that will help you to understand why they were successful. The essay examples printed here are all winners, although—where appropriate—I have noted what an applicant might have done differently to improve an essay. (Many of these candidates were my clients, but that is by no means uniformly true.)

Note that actual names have been used when desired by the applicants and have been changed for those who desired anonymity. In some cases, applicants even wanted their identities lightly disguised by changing the names of their companies or bosses. Thus, there is no uniform policy followed here, except that of honoring the wishes of each applicant. All essays have been reprinted as they appeared to admissions officers; no grammatical or other changes have been made to them here.

Essay numbers do not correspond with the programs' own numbering system and are used only so that the essays can be easily referenced in the comments that follow each set. (Note that some schools change their essay questions from year to year. Some of the essays reprinted here are from previous applications, thus giving you some idea of the full range of questions asked in the past—and likely to be recycled in the future.)

You will not want to read this lengthy section page by page. The charts on the following pages are meant to facilitate your picking and choosing whatever is of greatest interest to you. For example, if you are coming from a traditional "feeder" firm or industry, such as management consulting or investment banking, and want to see how others like you distinguished themselves, you can benefit from the essays of candidates like Mark, Uri, or Victor. If, on the other hand, you have had a career in the creative arts or journalism, take a look at the essays by Terry or Doreen. Whatever your circumstances, you are likely to find one or more applicants who were similarly situated.

To get the most out of this section, do three things:

1. Read the best examples—those of Ingrid, Uri, Harold, Marne, Madeline, and Paul—to see how professionally someone can market him- or herself. These are textbook examples of winning essays.

2. Refer to the discussion in Chapter 8 of overall marketing principles and the Chapter 9 analysis of specific essay topics you will need to address.

3. Look at the efforts of the people who most resemble you in terms of their backgrounds, critical issues, target schools, and so on.

Of course, you should never copy what these applicants have done. These examples will, however, give you an idea of the kinds of approaches successful applicants have taken. Adopt the attitude of an admissions director when reading them and ask yourself just what worked and what failed for each applicant, and then ask what lessons there are for you.

OVERVIEW OF THE APPLICANTS AND THEIR ESSAYS

APPLICANT	NATIONALITY (OR ETHNICITY)	CAREER BACKGROUND	SPECIAL ISSUES TO ADDRESS	ESSAYS INCLUDED
Joerg	German	Engineering doctoral degree candidate	Lack of full-time work experience	Kellogg (in Chapter 8)
Steve	American	Navy pilot	Switch from military to private sector	Anderson (UCLA) Stern (NYU)
Mark	American	Strategy consultant	Learning disability	Kellogg
Ingrid	Haitian	Investment analyst at international development organization	———	Harvard Wharton
Uri	Israeli American	Investment banking analyst	How to distinguish himself from others	Haas (Berkeley) INSEAD
Dave	American	Manufacturing manager	Nontraditional route: blue-collar career before entering college	Michigan
C.L.	Chinese American	Marketing and business development roles at various Internet start-ups	Lack of solid training as result of Internet career	Johnson (Cornell)
Harold	Dutch	Business and technical manager of scientific instrument manufacturer	Learning disability	Stanford Sloan (MIT)
Iehab	Egyptian American	Accountant; Business development analyst for beverage company	———	Harvard
Terry	American	Commercial photographer	Weak quantitative abilities; mediocre college grades	Rotterdam
Jon	Danish	Shipping executive	Lack of proper bachelor's degree	London
Marne	American	U.S. Treasury deputy assistant secretary	Switch from public to private sector	Harvard
Steven	African American	Municipal finance analyst	———	Columbia

APPLICANT	NATIONALITY (OR ETHNICITY)	CAREER BACKGROUND	SPECIAL ISSUES TO ADDRESS	ESSAYS INCLUDED
Greg	American	Company manager; Sales rep. and manager (computer and consulting firms)	Reapplication; Lack of career focus	Kellogg
Victor	Chinese American	Investment banking analyst; Operations manager of Internet start-up	How to distinguish himself from others	Tuck (Dartmouth)
Cynthia	American	Concert musician; Software sales associate, IT consultant	Older; College degree in music; Problematic college transcript	Sloan (MIT)
Carl	American	Lawyer; Counsel at Internet start-up	Switch from law to business	Wharton Executive MBA Program
Joseph	Colombian	Manufacturing and operations manager	———	Tuck (Dartmouth)
Madeline	American	Management consultant	Physical disability	Fuqua (Duke) Stern (NYU)
Paul	Iranian American	Accountant; Founder of consulting firm	Dismal college grades	Michigan Yale
Sameer	Indian	Engineer; IT executive	Reapplication	Chicago Tuck (Dartmouth)
Doreen	American	Journalist	Weak quantitative abilities	Columbia
Anne	French	Airport manager	———	INSEAD
Roxane	American	Chemical engineer	How to distinguish herself from others	Stanford Darden (Virginia)

THE APPLICANTS AND THEIR ESSAYS, TOPIC BY TOPIC

Essay Topic	Joerg	Steve	Mark	Ingrid	Uri	Dave	C.L.	Harold	Iehab	Terry	Jon
Career progression, future goals, why an MBA	X	X	X	X	X	X	X	X	X	X	X
Leadership experience		X		X					X		
Failure or difficulty				X		X				X	X
Beliefs challenged or ethical dilemma				X							
Accomplishments	X	X		X	X	X			X		
Personal and family background		X									
Outside of work I enjoy	X		X							X	
Team situation				X							
Community or extracurricular activity											
What matters most to you								X			
Decision that has influenced you					X						
Culture shock					X						
Idea for a product or business						X					
Evaluate two quotations		X					X				
People would be surprised . . .			X								
In what way can you uniquely contribute	X										
Focus on innovation								X			
Introduced or managed change								X			
Hero or mentor									X		
Defining moment									X		
Invest $25 million in community											

MARNE	STEVEN	GREG	VICTOR	CYNTHIA	CARL	JOSEPH	MADELINE	PAUL	SAMEER	DOREEN	ANNE	ROXANE
X	X	X	X	X	X	X	X	X	X	X	X	X
X				X								X
							X			X	X	
								X				X
X								X		X	X	
							X					
				X		X						
	X									X		
		X								X	X	X
				X								
X												
X												
		X										

Essay Topic	Joerg	Steve	Mark	Ingrid	Uri	Dave	C.L.	Harold	Iehab	Terry	Jon
Management of technological change											
Write your own job performance review											
Character in a book											
Describe yourself											X	X
Creative solution to problem											
Value of diversity											
Trends in your industry											X
Three people to dinner											X
Effect one change at work											
Alternatives to MBA											X
Influenced by people, events, situations											
Relive one day											
Value and respect in others											
Review your autobiography	X										
Additional information		X		X		X		X			

STEVE
UCLA/ANDERSON

1. Please provide us with a summary of your personal and family background. Include information about your parents and siblings, where you grew up, and perhaps a highlight or special memory of your youth.

I grew up in Pomona, New York, a suburb of New York City. It was an idyllic setting to grow up in; there were rolling hills, deep forests, and cozy houses with huge lawns. My neighborhood was full of families with kids close to my age, so I always had friends nearby. I have plenty of great memories of pickup basketball games, playing kickball in the street, and just cruising around the neighborhood on my bike with my buddies as the summer sun went down.

MARNE	STEVEN	GREG	VICTOR	CYNTHIA	CARL	JOSEPH	MADELINE	PAUL	SAMEER	DOREEN	ANNE	ROXANE
				X								
											X	
									X			
							X		X		X	
								X				
								X				
											X	
											X	
												X
												X
								X				
			X	X				X				

My parents were also products of the suburbs: they had both grown up in New Jersey and had met at a Rutgers University dance. My father was a dentist; my mother had earned her bachelor's degree in education, but had only taught typing for a few years before she left in order to raise a family. They lived briefly in South Carolina, where I was born, while my dad served in the Navy's Dental Corps. After he left the service, they moved back north, where two years later my younger brother Gary was born.

Gary and I are close as adults, but we were very different as children. I was the straight arrow growing up, very interested in school and an academic overachiever. Gary, on the other hand, was more of an "in-crowd" socializer, especially as a teenager. Although he was as bright as I was, he didn't apply himself academically. He was more artistically inclined—he wrote some intriguing short stories—and was interested in classic counterculture works like Kerouac's "On the Road" and the music of the Grateful Dead. Despite our differences, though, we couldn't help but influence each other. I may have been the role model as the older brother and the star student, but I owe Gary for making me more open to new ideas and ways of thinking.

My mother had grown up in a strict Orthodox Jewish home. My father's parents had also been fairly observant Jews. Although as adults they were more secular, they still took great pains to make sure that Gary and I were well exposed to our religious heritage. It was something that I didn't appreciate then, but do now, especially as a religious minority in the Navy. We both went to Hebrew school from kindergarten through age 13. In Hebrew school, I participated in an advanced study group called Torah Corps, where we learned not to simply read Hebrew, but to chant it directly from the Bible, a skill usually only found among rabbis or cantors (Jewish song leaders). All the extra studying paid off when I was able to chant from the Torah at my Bar Mitzvah, a great honor.

The Jewish upbringing that my parents gave me led to one of my favorite childhood experiences: the summer I spent in Israel before my senior year of high school. I spent six weeks with a Zionist youth tour visiting every inch of that country. I prayed at the Western Wall, wandered through the back alleys of Old Jerusalem, and climbed up to the mountaintop fortress of Masada at dawn. I visited Yad Veshem, the solemn Holocaust Memorial Museum. I finally was able to make a tangible connection to my heritage and to understand why my parents had raised me the way they did. At the end of the sixth week, our group played a huge game of capture-the-flag on a wide expanse of sand dunes on the shores of the Mediterranean Sea. I'll never forget that mixture of adventure, freedom, and pride I felt as I ran around on the land where my ancestors had once tread. Those are feelings that I will always cherish.

2. Discuss a situation, preferably work-related, where you have taken a significant leadership role. How does this even demonstrate your managerial potential?

I had a great chance to lead people when I represented the Navy at the United States Marine Corps Weapons and Tactics Instructor (WTI) Course, one of the most fabled schools in Marine Aviation. I attended to learn how we could use our aircraft, the E-2, to support Marine troops fighting on the ground. While there, I was assigned to the Command, Control and Communication (C3) planning group, consisting of about fifty students. We were responsible for planning how the Air Force, Navy and Marine elements would operate together during a series of exercises. We planned and executed a series of successful missions over a four-week period. Finally, the time came to conduct the final exercise, which built on the lessons we had learned up to that point. The WTI instructors chose me to lead the C3 group in planning the exercise and to present the plan to all the participants. The brief and the exercise, both huge successes, demonstrated that our armed services could work together to help the Marines win a ground war.

My success in leading the group shows that I am capable of leading a diverse team. Our group consisted of people from a wide variety of military backgrounds, from

Navy fliers like myself to Marine infantrymen. We all had different ways of trying to solve the problems facing us, and I was the one who had to develop, for example, a tactical communication plan that we could all live with. The experience also shows that I can delegate effectively. In order to successfully develop this sophisticated plan, I divided the C3 group into smaller working groups, led by subordinates whom I picked because they knew far more than I did about certain aspects of command and control. This experience helped me to develop greatly as a leader.

3. Describe your most significant personal accomplishment to date, explaining why you view it as such.

I consider earning the legendary "wings of gold" worn by a US Naval Flight Officer the greatest accomplishment of my life. The Navy's flight training program tested my physical and mental stamina to the utmost. Although I exercised rigorously in preparation for flight school, the obstacle course and the forced runs in soft sand were still extremely challenging. Yet once I mastered the physical training, I still had to cope with the truly difficult part: flying. The ability to perform day after day under tremendous pressure defines a Naval Aviator. For most of us, this is a skill we acquire over time with a great deal of effort. Studying my in-flight procedures beforehand was much harder. Like most new aviators, when I sat down in the cockpit and the scorching Pensacola summer sun beat down on me as the aircraft's canopy snapped shut, the temperature would rise and the stress would build.

Still, I persevered, and eventually I even thrived under pressure. In order to succeed, I learned to stop dreading my upcoming flights and instead to look forward to them as challenges. This attitude of overcoming challenges has been key to my success ever since, and that is why I consider earning my wings such an important milestone.

4. Discuss your career goals and why you want an MBA, particularly at this point in your career. Why, specifically, are you applying to The Anderson School?

I want to design a career that combines my long-term interest in finance with the experience in telecommunications that I acquired in the Navy. As an intern at the Securities and Exchange Commission during college, I became fascinated with securities and corporate finance. Later, as a Naval Flight Officer in the E-2 Hawkeye, I learned a great deal about digital data links, systems very similar to wireless phone networks that the military uses to transfer information between ships, aircraft, and ground stations. I believe that in the next few years, the internet will expand from PCs to wireless phones, personal data assistants, and other handheld devices. The telecom giants like AT&T and MCI Worldcom will be vying to do business with or acquire growing companies that provide goods and services over the internet. I want to finance these high-growth, high-risk companies. My short-term goal is to join the corporate finance division of an investment bank in order to acquire experience financing telecommunications deals and to make contacts. My long-term goal, after about 5 years at an investment bank, is to join a venture capital firm which invests in early-stage wireless internet companies.

To successfully make this career transition, I cannot rely on my Navy experience alone. Although I have been a successful leader, I need to learn the language of business. I need to gain the general management perspective of someone who will finance, staff, and lead small companies. I need to learn, in a structured academic setting, to work with people to solve business problems. In short, I need an MBA.

Anderson is the ideal place for me to learn what I need to know to begin my new career. The school's entrepreneurial focus perfectly complements my goals. I plan to be, first and foremost, a financier. Anderson's strength in finance gives me confidence that I will be well-prepared to become an investment banker first. However, as my career shifts from simply financing businesses to building them, I will need to see new business opportunities like an entrepreneur does. I believe that the entrepreneurship classes taught by the undisputed leaders in the field, like Cockrum, Geis, and Yost, will help give me the perspective I will require a few years down the road, when I am trying to show a hard-charging young entrepreneur how to grow her company as fast as possible without burning through all of her—or someone else's—cash. I also look forward to participating in the Venture Fellows Program, which will give me the opportunity to learn firsthand what it is actually like to finance startup companies.

What equally attracts me to Anderson, though, is the value it places on teamwork. As I mentioned in Essay 2, I have had the chance to lead diverse teams in a military setting. My experiences have taught me that teamwork is an absolutely indispensable quality for success in that environment, because no single person has the skills, knowledge or judgment required to solve every problem. I believe that the same is true in the business world. I look forward to the challenge of overcoming obstacles and meeting goals in a group where, unlike the highly structured Navy, there is no clear leader and each of us comes from a vastly different background and brings a different perspective to the table. Learning how to succeed in business as part of such a team may be the best thing I take away with me when I graduate from the Anderson MBA program.

5. Is there any other information that you believe would be helpful to the Admissions Committee in considering your application?

When I left my squadron for my next assignment in 1997, I knew that I wanted to leave the Navy to pursue a career in business. However, I had only begun to truly investigate my career options and I did not have clearly defined, long-term goals. I was interested in both business and law. Although I never planned to practice law, I thought that law school would give me a broad base of analytical training to which I could add an MBA and then enter the business world. Since I was still serving in the Navy in San Diego, I decided to enroll at the University of San Diego School of Law's part-time program. I intended to ultimately complete the JD-MBA program at that university.

My decision to enter USD Law School was the wrong one for me for two reasons. First, I had not thought hard enough about what I wanted to do with the rest of my life. Although I loved the intellectual rigor of law school and learning by analyzing cases, I found myself drawn more and more to a career that involved financing growing companies. I rediscovered what I had known when I was working at the SEC, but had forgotten after many years in the Navy: finance, not law, was my passion. This fact was reinforced by a moment of clarity during my Contracts class, when our professor discussed the Black–Scholes theory of options to help illustrate a point. The subject captivated me and I knew then that I was in the wrong program.

Second, I realized that I was selling myself short. I knew that I was capable of excelling in a full-time MBA program at a top school. I felt that I was someone who could add value to a class full of high achievers. I wanted to be part of a group of people from diverse backgrounds, who would offer the widest variety of perspectives on the cases that we would study in business school. Although USD was a good local school, I knew that even by transferring from its law school to its business school, I would not gain the rigorous education and diverse student body that I sought. Once I realized that I had made a wrong turn in my career planning, I took a year's leave of absence from law school, just to do some more self-evaluation and to confirm my decision. After a year, I was convinced I was right and I withdrew from law school.

Although I regret enrolling in law school, I am glad that the experience helped me to clarify my goals. It also confirmed that I enjoy the challenge of, and can succeed in, a graduate-level curriculum. Now that I have a much better idea of where I want to go in my career, I will be better able to contribute to the Anderson MBA program and to take advantage of the opportunities that it offers.

I believe the following information serves to clarify my character and will help the admissions committee to further understand my candidacy.

I grew up in a predominantly Jewish New York suburb. My parents took me to temple fairly often. It was very difficult for me to maintain my beliefs once I joined the Navy. It was a vastly different culture, one that was Christian by default. This was especially apparent to me aboard the aircraft carrier. The prayers that were played over the ship's loudspeaker at night, although supposedly nondenominatinal, implicitly reflected Christian teachings that were unfamiliar to me. While the ship would not schedule flight operations on Easter or Christmas, which were official days off, I would have to fight not to fly on Rosh Hashanah or Yom Kippur so I could observe those holidays.

I have gradually become more interested in practicing my religion as a means of preserving my identity. I have tried to observe the holidays as best I could by attending services aboard ship or overseas. I have also sought out opportunities to meet with other Jews in the Navy to pray together, although there are very few of us, and these opportunities have been limited. For example, I am currently on a temporary assignment at a US military base in Riyadh, Saudi Arabia. During Yom Kippur, the holiest day in Judaism, I wanted to attend services. I found out that there was only one other Jew on the base. Although technically we could not hold a service with only two of us (Jewish law requires ten people), we made up an informal service anyway. We continued to meet on Friday nights and publicized our meeting in case anyone else wanted to join us. Although it has been a challenge to maintain my Jewish identity in the military, I am glad that I have not lost touch with my heritage.

NYU/STERN (Selected)

1. **Think about the decisions you have made in your life. Describe the following:**

    Past: What choices have you made that led you to your current position?

    Present: Why is a Stern MBA necessary at this point in your life?

    Future: What is your desired position upon graduation from the Stern School?

I grew up in a comfortable middle-class neighborhood where it seemed that everyone wanted to be either a doctor or lawyer. I joined the Navy because I wanted to try something that seemed different and more exciting than those more predictable careers. I also wanted to travel the world and work as part of a team to achieve a greater goal than simply enriching myself. I chose to become a Naval Flight Officer because the idea of taking off and landing on an aircraft carrier thrilled me. It was an experience I'll never forget! I also chose the aviation field because I knew it would give me a great opportunity to lead people. After flight training, I joined VAW-116, a squadron which flew the E-2 Hawkeye radar aircraft. I eventually became a mission commander, leading a five-man crew on missions patrolling the Iraqi-Saudi border during Operation Southern Watch. My responsibility was huge; my crew directed the actions of up to 80 US fighter jets patrolling an airspace the size of North Dakota. A wrong decision on my part could mean the difference between shooting down an Iraqi jet and an innocent airliner. Fortunately, all of our missions went well.

After three years in VAW-116, it was time to transfer to a shore position. I reasoned that getting a senior-level perspective on how the decisions that affected the fleet were made would help me become a better manager. So, I chose to become the Assistant Air operations Officer for the staff of a three-star admiral who was responsible for all of the aircraft carriers and squadrons in the US Pacific Fleet. While there, I directed 30 people in scheduling over 200 training flights, 4 times a year. I gained an appreciation for how hard it is for the Navy to accomplish all its training requirements. I continually had to balance the need to prepare our aircraft carriers for their Persian Gulf deployments against the continual lack of people, aircraft or parts necessary to train the carriers and their flight crews on how to deal with the dangers they would encounter over there.

After almost 9 years in the Navy, I decided it was time to leave. I wanted to combine several of my interests and pursue a career in finance. In the meantime, I have chosen to use the period between the end of my service commitment and the beginning of business school at an Internet start-up. This job gives me the chance to develop entrepreneurial skills that complement my Navy leadership skills. It has been a completely different experience, and a refreshing one!

To successfully transition to a career in finance, I cannot rely on my Navy and limited start-up experience alone. Now, I need to learn the language of business. In particular, I need to understand finance at the theoretical level. At the same time, I need to build a strong network on Wall Street with the true movers and shakers of the financial world. Stern provides me these opportunities like no other school does. I am especially interested in taking the Corporate Finance and investment Banking courses to help me develop the quantitative skills I will need. Of course, Stern's proximity to Wall Street means that I will get the chance, through the Chief Executive lecture services, to see guest speakers from all the top investment banks. Perhaps most importantly, at Stern I will be a short walk away from Wall Street. I will be able to visit these firms, meet their people, and experience their corporate cultures in a way that would be impossible if I were attending a school in any other city. No other MBA program offers me all these advantages.

I want to design a career that combines my long-term interest in finance with the experience in telecommunications that I acquired in the Navy. As an intern at the Securities and Exchange Commission during college, I became fascinated with securities and corporate finance. Later, as a Naval Flight Officer in the E-2 Hawkeye, I learned a great deal about digital data links, systems very similar to wireless phone networks that the military uses to transfer information between ships, aircraft, and ground stations. I believe that in the next few years, the internet will expand from PCs to wireless phones, personal data assistants, and other handheld devices. The telecom giants like AT&T and MCI Worldcom will be vying to do business with or acquire growing companies that provide goods and services over the internet. I want to finance these high-growth, high-risk companies. My goal after completing the Stern MBA is to join the corporate finance division of an investment bank and specialize in raising capital for telecom deals. After a few years in investment banking, I would like to sue my skills and my network of contacts to switch to the venture capital industry, where I can help to guide these telecom startups to success from their earliest stages.

Transitioning from a naval career to a financial one will be my greatest challenge yet. To be successful, I need to attend an MBA program where I will have the best education, the best access to the financial world, and the best location in the world to study business. Clearly, Stern is that program. I look forward to a chance to attend.

2. **Please agree or disagree with two of the following quotes. Give relevant reasons and/or examples to support your answer.**

"The truth is always the strongest argument."—Sophocles

I agree. My experiences in the Navy have taught me that in resolving conflicts or trying to achieve a favorable outcome in a crisis, telling the truth is the best course of action. One example that comes to mind occurred when I was the Legal Officer for my

E-2 squadron. My primary task was to help the Commanding Officer enforce the Uniform Code of Military Justice, the laws that regulate our behavior in the Armed Forces. I accomplished this task by investigating alleged violations of the UCMJ by members of our squadron, gathering evidence, and, if necessary, bringing charges against those individuals. I also assisted the CO in conducting Captain's Mast, an informal court where the CO was both judge and jury and could punish the offender.

Airman Malone, a young sailor in our squadron, had a serious disciplinary problem. He had twice before been found guilty of failing to perform his duties and treating his superiors disrespectfully. At his third Captain's Mast, the Co decided to kick Malone out of the Navy. Technically, he couldn't simply force Malone to leave; Malone was entitled to a review board where he could defend himself. But most young sailors didn't know that, and the CO made it clear to me that he didn't care if Malone was ever fully appraised of his rights.

I sympathized with the CO. Malone was a bad influence on the squadron and didn't fit well in the authoritarian Navy culture. Still, I argued that we should be truthful and inform Malone of his rights. I knew that the risk that Malone would find out we had not been forthright with him, appeal the discharge, and bring our wrongful action to light outweighed any possible gain that we would get from discharging him quickly. More importantly, what kind of precedent would that set? By not allowing an accused person to exercise his rights, we might achieve the result we wanted, but only by compromising the values of the military justice system we were supposed to be upholding. The CO reluctantly agreed and let Malone know that he could contest his discharge. Luckily for the squadron, Malone waived his rights and left the Navy voluntarily. By telling Malone the truth, we not only achieved the optimal result for the squadron and the Navy, but also handled the situation ethically.

"Change in all things is sweet."—ARISTOTLE

I disagree. Although change may at times bring positive effects, it can also have negative counter-effects. For example, it cannot be denied that the end of the Cold War has had a great positive impact on the world economy, spread freedom throughout the world, and lessened society's fears of global annihilation. At the same time, however, the resulting cuts in US defense spending have taken a terrible toll on the quality of our national defense. I have seen this effect clearly throughout my nearly nine years in the Navy. The Navy of today is far less capable than the one I joined in 1991. While we once had nearly 600 capable ships, now we struggle to maintain less half that number. We have a severe shortage of parts of our ships and aircraft, so much so that squadrons returning from deployment have to give up all their airplanes to other squadrons that are departing because there simply are not enough to go around. This puts the first squadron at a serious disadvantage when it has to start training for its next deployment, since it may not have a full set of aircraft for several months. Our military personnel deploy overseas more often than they did ten years ago. Recent crises in North

Korea, the Middle East, and the Balkans demonstrate that there are still threats to US interests and world peace, which justify our military presence.

I dealt with these problems firsthand in my Air Operations job at COMNAVAIR-PAC. The changes of the last ten years have been great for our economy and have made many of us feel that the world is a safer place in which to live, but the changing times have not been so sweet for the US Navy. Although today the lack of a major threat to the United States from abroad may allow us to focus more on economic and social concerns, we may not have that luxury a few years down the road. In the future, when the specter of a major war looms over us, the defense cuts of the past few years may have disastrous consequences for our society.

Comments

- Admissions officers evaluating a Navy pilot's application are likely to have several automatic concerns. They will worry that he may be too macho, too isolated from the civilian world (to be a good contributor at business school), and clueless about the direction of his future career. Steve addresses each of these potential problems in his essays.

- Steve does a great job of showing that he has all the positive leadership and teamwork traits of a Navy pilot, but also has a softer side as well. His discussions of his strong Jewish faith, his admiration of his family members, and his desire to uphold the Naval honor code in defense of a problematic recruit all testify to his emotional maturity.

- Steve demonstrates that he is in touch with the business world and has a reasonable idea of where he is headed, despite having little experience working outside the military. His discussions show that he has not remained isolated in the Navy, unaware of what a corporate life might hold for him. He also illustrates an intelligent awareness of current events—defending the military, yet not with arrogance or unawareness of the opposite view—in the second half of Stern essay number two.

- Steve at times could have done better filling in the details concerning his accomplishments, giving readers a better idea of just how impressive a fellow he is. In discussing his Wings of Gold, for example, he could have used more detail to show just how rare the achievement is. In the WTI example, likewise, he could have better illustrated his successes with a detailed discussion of the results.

- Steve is wise to include a discussion of his brief, failed attempt to attend law school. He makes an intelligent argument for his initial interest in law school while still putting to rest any concerns the admissions committee might have about his indecision regarding law versus business.

MARK

KELLOGG (Selected)

1. **Briefly assess your career progress to date. Elaborate on your future career plans and your motivation for pursuing a graduate degree at Kellogg.**

Spending a great deal of my younger life in the outdoors, I developed a keen interest in geology and the natural environment. In college I chose a Geology major with the intent of one day owning my own geomorphology consulting firm. But the summer before my senior year, a friend and I started a painting company; in four months we expanded from 2 to 8 employees due to good marketing. Building this company sparked my interest in the strategy of developing businesses. Thus, after college I chose to go into consulting, selecting an unusual firm, Markowitz & McNaughton, Inc. (MMI). Traditional consulting firms primarily utilize secondary information, but MMI uses competitive analysis to build strategic models. On a typical 60 day MMI engagement, the first four days are spent studying the client's internal assumptions and secondary information. The remaining time is spent speaking directly to the people shaping the market and influencing the client's business (customers, competitors, and market experts). My father, a CEO and President, taught me that you can't make accurate decisions unless you have good intelligence that is transformed through analysis into actionable implications. MMI, as a small firm, also gives new analysts immediate opportunities to work directly with clients. Additionally, roughly one third of MMI's business is international, which allowed me insight into various business cultures.

I was immediately given the opportunity to prove myself on the "firing line," presenting my work directly to clients, performing extensive primary research, and using competitive analysis techniques (Porter Analysis, SWOT, etc.) to develop actionable business strategy. My first engagement thrust me into the thick of a market entry assessment of the DVD adhesive market. Responsible for using primary research to map out a virtually non-existent market in four weeks, I pounded the phone, calling industry experts and attempting to make sense of the contacts' often-conflicting opinions. To make matters more difficult, the primary competitors were private subsidiaries of larger companies and didn't have to disclose any information. 80 telephone conversations later, I had a detailed understanding of the top competitors' R&D programs and I had identified which customers would present the best account opportunities. I developed a 360-degree understanding of DVDs and one of MMI's largest accounts.

I was promoted to Senior Associate in a record ten months. I was stretched in several directions, responsible for training and managing analysts, directing smaller client engagements, and participating in pitching MMI's services. Training two analysts, each four years older than I and with prior work experience, taught me a tremendous amount about managing peers and senior individuals. Both analysts have been rapidly promoted into management, yet they still seek my counsel when dealing with problems. I was appointed to Training Manager, specifically tasked with coordinating new analysts' merger and acquisition training. I worked with both senior executives and new analysts to revise the training manual and played a key role assisting MMI in redefining its training program. New analysts' initial training now takes place in a concise two weeks instead of four.

After only 18 months at MMI, I was promoted to Project Manager (PM). I am now responsible for creating client strategy, managing client relationships, developing client accounts, and pitching new business, as well as managing my team. Directing the competitive analysis program for a leading manufacturer of ATM machines has provided me with unprecedented experience developing a current client and incorporating MMI's approach to strategy into the client's corporate strategy. The client's international sales were declining and its internal self-assessments were not yielding a solution. I convinced the client that MMI should talk directly with its competitors and customers in the client's key countries. My solution refocused the client's misdirected marketing efforts onto key accounts and showed specifically how it could dramatically improve aftermarket service. My new strategy has yielded the client several new accounts, in turn, the client has engaged MMI to assess the remainder of its global sales & marketing operations.

Managing employees and clients in over 35 engagements has provided a solid foundation and understanding of how to lead and motivate teams of varying ages and backgrounds, affirming my interest in eventually becoming a CEO. My short-term career goal is to switch from consulting to managing corporate strategic marketing in an emerging growth business unit or company. This will allow me to further hone my management skills while playing a principal role in a growing organization; more importantly, it will help prepare me for my long-term goal of becoming CEO of an emerging growth technology company. An MBA would accelerate my career by providing an environment where I could immerse myself in a diverse group of individuals who are also seeking to expand their intellectual and practical business knowledge.

Although I have taken extension courses in accounting and finance and learned a considerable amount, I need a firmer grounding in the rudiments of business to reach my goals. Kellogg's nine core course during the first two quarters will allow me to expand my understanding of business and build a solid foundation in general management. The remaining flexible four quarters will allow me to pick courses that will enhance and develop my skills in Marketing, Management & Strategy, and Technology & E-Commerce. Courses such as Management of Technology with Professor Greenstein and Strategic Management of Technology & Innovation with Professor Gellman are among the many key courses that will help me develop my practical understanding of how to lead an emerging growth company. Participating in Kellogg's "high octane" student-initiated clubs such as the High-Tech Club and the Marketing Club will allow me to work with my peers to create opportunities for everyone to continue learning beyond the classroom. Kellogg's experiential learning opportunities (Global Initiatives in Management and student-initiated LEAP) will allow me to integrate the academic theory into "real world" practice. It will also give me an opportunity to get a head start in an emerging growth industry before I graduate from Kellogg.

Kellogg's commitment to building leaders that understand how to simultaneously lead and participate in numerous teams and multiple organizations will prepare me to be a successful collaborator in emerging growth technologies. Kellogg's commitment to teaching students how to realistically manage such technologies as they rapidly converge with established companies is crucial to my development. The unique team learning environment at Kellogg fundamentally centered on enhancing each team member's learning, will create the type of environment I enjoy and thrive in. At its core, Kellogg will provide me with a framework and way of thinking that will build on my management experience and understanding of competitive strategy to help me become a poised leader.

2. **Outside of work I enjoy . . .**

It was June, 1978. I was four years old and my dad was taking me on my first backpacking trip. He woke me on Saturday at 4:00 a.m. and I grudgingly fell out of bed. I was unhappy, because I wanted to spend the weekend playing with my friends. As the Oldsmobile diesel station wagon trudged eastward towards the Cascades, I fell asleep. As we started our hike, the damp, cold cloak of morning twilight hung over Mt. Hood. I looked up at the pasty, gray clouds and scuffed my boots in the dirt, not understanding why we were walking into what seemed like oblivion, but as the sun rose as we crested a hill, my eyes fell upon the uncensored beauty of the white, rugged, and sharp, snow-capped ridges of Mt. Hood. I was awestruck and fascinated with this pile of volcanic rock. During that weekend, I found a raw and unblemished beauty in the mountains that could not be replicated anywhere else. The waxing and waning of the alpine glow at sunrise and sunset could not be captured in a photograph. There was an indescribable beauty in the brief moment when the sun's fingertips touched the mountain's snow and rock turning them a blazing red.

Outside of work, I love to climb mountains. There is an unparalleled mental calmness that gives me a chance to reflect on where I am in life and focus on where I am going. Although I enjoy the physical exhilaration of climbing, there is an uncommon bond which forms within my climbing team, even when we are gathered from all over the world: the US, France, Switzerland, Chile, and Ecuador. Our lives are literally in each other's hands. I find very few places in my life where I am utterly dependent on someone else' decision and judgment. The mountains have taught me many lessons about dealing with others and myself. Probably one of the most important is humility; failure to admit that I have made a mistake or that I need help can have dire consequences. At a deeper level, climbing is really about judgment; a good judgment cannot be made unless all of the environmental (e.g., route and weather), team, and individual factors are carefully weighed and considered. Many things are out of my control in the mountains, one must react to situations as they are presented. When I was climbing Mt. Constance (Olympic Mountains, Washington), the weather was perfect, sun shining, not a cloud in the sky. As my climbing partner and I crossed onto an east facing ridge the snow was already slushy from the morning sun. Although the snow would be safe to cross on the way to the summit, by the time we descended, the sun would have sufficiently melted the snow, making it prone to an avalanche. We chose to turn around, satisfied with a day in the mountains, and headed home knowing this summit would be here for another day.

For me the ultimate pleasure in climbing is not the summit, it is the process of climbing, the focus, reliance, trust and camaraderie among climbing partners or a rope team and the humbleness I experience around these stone sentinels called mountains.

3. Many people may be surprised to learn that . . .

Many people may be surprised to learn that I am dyslexic and have struggled with a learning disability my whole life. People are most often surprised because I attended a "top" college (Williams), have published an article, and have been promoted rapidly at work. In addition, I am orally articulate, I clearly convey my thoughts and ideas. My co-workers are very surprised, because every project we work on results in a clear, well-written document. What few people realize is that I have struggled my whole life to learn how to deal with my disability, which primarily manifests itself as errors in spelling and grammar, as well as occasional slips in visual processing and organization of written information.

Since I was diagnosed in first grade, I have worked with tutors to develop learning methods that would allow me to succeed with dyslexia. In first grade, I failed every spelling test and read well below my grade level. Every Tuesday afternoon, while the rest of the class played games, I was tutored on visualization skills and memory concepts designed to help me with spelling, writing, and reading. By fifth grade, I aced 90 percent of my spelling tests and read at a sixth grade level. In high school, I had a rude awakening. During a meeting with all of my teachers, my faculty advisor/history teacher suggested I find another school to accommodate my dyslexia, insinuating I shouldn't be enrolled at Lakeside, one of the Pacific Northwest's most prestigious high schools. My teacher's words could have demoralized me, but instead I used his criticism as a motivator. In addition to continuing tutoring, I developed a highly organized writing program in which I systematically applied the tools learned and lessons from past mistakes to improve. I learned to confidently approach teachers and professors, not to ask for assistance, but to clarify assignments, thus ensuring I covered every aspect. In college, I co-founded Students with Disabilities Support Network. Our efforts significantly contributed to the assignment of a dean dedicated to students with disabilities, insuring support for others like us.

Fortunately, dyslexia has had a limited impact on my life beyond the fundamentals of reading and writing. I have excelled at math and science, demonstrating that a strong ability to draw together disjointed pieces of information into one cohesive thought. I became a successful writer for my high school newspaper and was published in "Northeastern Geology" for my research in college. Today, dyslexia still presents minor challenges to me, but I've learned to acknowledge these challenges, develop a plan to improve them, and utilize past lessons to deal with future obstacles.

I can say without a doubt, my struggle with dyslexia has engrained in me the fundamental understanding that to overcome any challenge it takes dogged persistence and dedication.

Comments

- Mark differentiated himself from the many consultants in the applicant pool by explaining in detail the "competitive analysis" model upon which his firm was founded, making his experience distinct from that of the typical strategy consultant. In addition, he demonstrated his growth at the firm in many different directions, emphasizing his managerial responsibilities, which also differentiate him from the bulk of young consultants.

- Mark tells a nice story in the second essay, providing a more compelling piece of writing than one that begins with, "I enjoy hiking and mountain climbing." As with many successful essays, the simplicity of the message and the commonness of the experience are made compelling through detail and a memorable story.

- Mark was right to deal with his learning disability directly rather than trying to cover it up. He demonstrates conclusively that he has been proactive in getting help—and has been successful despite the challenges his dyslexia has imposed.

INGRID

HARVARD

1. **Please describe three different leadership experiences that have been significant for you. Feel free to draw on work, personal, or extracurricular activities. What did you learn as a result of these experiences?**

As a junior at the University of Miami, I led the Society of Women Engineers through a period of change which saw the society increase membership threefold. As elected president, I initiated a yearlong program of charity work, scholastic involvement, and membership growth. The society became a positive force on campus, organizing two major fund-raising events (US$10,000 raised) to help victims of Hurricane Andrew and encouraging academic achievement within the membership. I also established the SWE Tutoring Program, which helped more than 150 first year students in core engineering classes. I felt tremendous satisfaction when students thanked me in the halls and shared the good news of receiving an "A" in their exams.

Six months after joining the International Finance Corporation (part of the World Bank), I worked on a Brazilian project where the client needed to refinance some US$90 million of short-term debt. In December 1998, the IFC called off the project following rumors of an imminent Real devaluation. I believed that the company had greater export capacity and would benefit from the devaluation. After the Real devaluated in January 1999, my convictions were confirmed by the company's tremendous growth in exports. I presented my findings to senior management, who then asked me to take the lead in reviving the project. Over the next six months, I flew several times to Sao Paulo to met with creditors and discuss various debt rescheduling structures. I was able to convince (through detailed credit risk analyses) three banks to refinance more than R$60 million; as a result, we were able to disburse the loan. Today, our clients are generating strong cash flows and proving that our decision was a sound one.

Following my performance on the above-mentioned project, I was recently given the lead on a university project in Argentina, a responsibility rarely given to investment analysts. I coordinate work among the legal, technical and environmental departments within the IFC and work directly with the top executives of the university. During the appraisal process, I became aware of the university's difficulties in collecting tuition fees and the need for a formal student loan and collection program. I have subsequently arranged meetings between the university, local banks in Argentina specializing in consumer lending, and the IFC education specialist to study ways of implementing such a program. My client will lead the way in this endeavor in Argentina and the IFC-supported student loan program could pave the way for similar agreements throughout South America.

These experiences have taught me that while I am comfortable in leadership positions, I also value teamwork. In all three situations, I was required to supervise and coordinate teams with diverse backgrounds and manage entire processes. The first experience at UM taught me how to delegate authority and manage my academic and extracurricular time. It also enabled me to overcome my fear of public speaking. In the second experience, even though I had only been with the IFC for a few months, I was able to convince management of my convictions and implement my ideas. My third leadership experience taught me the importance of admitting one's limitations and seeking advice from senior colleagues. Through all three experiences, I acquired the ability to quickly prioritize tasks, handle pressure and make spontaneous decisions. These experiences have also taught me the importance of listening to others; I am referring to "active" listening—not only hearing and understanding what is said, but showing that you are listening. I learned the value of a simple thank you and a smile in expressing appreciation to colleagues. Finally, I have learned that as a leader, there is a time to lead and a time to follow, a time to succeed and a time to fail, a time to be confident and a time to be humble.

2. Recognizing that successful leaders are able to learn from failure, describe a situation in which you failed. Why did you fail?

Shortly after joining the IFC, I became part of a team of four analysts working on a large Brazilian project. We were each given specific tasks and held regular meetings to follow up on our progress and discuss what we each had left to finish. As time went by, I felt that two of my teammates were not performing their tasks very well. Finally, after one memorable meeting, I blew up. I criticized them for their lack of effort and professionalism. I reminded them that this was a team effort and they were letting the team down. I wanted to show management that their decision to hire me a good one; if the first team I worked on failed, it would be a poor reflection on me.

An argument ensued and criticisms were thrown recklessly around the room. After an hour of bickering, we angrily left the meeting. This episode eventually made its way to the senior investment officer on the project and I was called into her office soon after. My mistakes were discussed candidly and I realized that instead of showing management that I was worthy of the position, I had done the opposite. I had let my emotions get the better of me and as a result, created negative feelings amongst the team members. I had failed to be patient and discuss concerns in a constructive manner. I neglected to assess the capabilities of my peers and discuss openly our strengths and weaknesses before attacking the problem. I was selfish and placed personal goals in front of the team's success. My father once told me that, "Failures are really rehearsals for success." Now, I apply what I have learned from this rehearsal to my current leadership roles and enjoy the success of being able to effectively communicate with the project team.

3. **Describe a situation when your values and/or beliefs were challenged. What did you do, and why?**

My faith in God was greatly challenged when I was diagnosed with breast cancer while pursuing my graduate studies at Stanford University. I had always been a spiritual person and though I was aware of the many injustices on earth, I never doubted the justice of God. That is, until the day I had personal reason to doubt His fairness. "If He, God, exists at all, how could He, of Whom it is said is loving and just, allow this to happen to me?"

I stopped attending church and no longer prayed. My emotional pain was far greater than my physical pain. Losing my faith, not my hair, was heart-wrenching. The Bible teaches us that faith keeps hope alive. But what about when we are certain that we have come to the end of the line and feel that God has failed us? I felt anger, disappointment, discouragement, confusion, emptiness, fear and pain. One day, I received in the mail a beautiful and inspiring card that read: "If God had meant for Today to be perfect, why would He have invented Tomorrow?" I pondered the positive message of this card and understood that carrying negative feelings could only be detrimental to my recovery.

I made a conscious effort to spend time in spiritual reflection and read several books on the subject of prayer and healing. I turned to inspirational writings, people, and Bible verses. I joined a religious support group. It is hard to remain discouraged when we surround ourselves with hope. I started attending mass once again. Worship keeps us from falling into the pit of self-pity that is always beckoning when sickness has its black grip on us. I have come to realize that while God does indeed permit trials in our lives, He reveals His power and love through them. As Apostle Paul instructs, "Faith is the substance of things hoped for, the evidence of things not seen."

4. **Describe your three most substantial accomplishments and explain why you view them as such.**

Obtaining my Master's degree at Stanford University while fighting breast cancer is easily my most substantial accomplishment. Four months after joining Stanford, I was diagnosed with breast cancer, I had just turned twenty-four. Because cancer tends to spread easily in young people, my doctors decided that we would treat the tumor very aggressively. I underwent five months of heavy chemotherapy, then six weeks of radiation while pursuing my graduate studies. I can still recall those dreadful chemo sessions: most of the patients would sleep while receiving chemo through an IV, and I would be studying for a mid-term or reading a case study to be discussed the next day in class. I never lost sight of my goal: obtaining my Master's degree. I put forth every iota of strength that I possessed—physical, mental, spiritual—toward this accomplishment. I stumbled many times along the way, but with the help of God, family, friends and sheer will, I found the inspiration to carry my cross. I value this achievement as it demonstrates my motivation, determination, and capacity to overcome an extraordinarily high level of both physical and mental suffering.

My second greatest accomplishment would have to be my undergraduate honors thesis. I had always been interested in issues relating to the greenhouse effect, global warming, acid rains and pollution. These environmental catastrophes stem from the fact that we obtain our energy by burning carbon fuels such as oil, natural gas, and coal. One way to reverse this trend is to produce carbon-free fuels. I decided to write my thesis on a renewable solar-hydrogen energy system and work under the guidance of Dr. T. Nejat Veziroglu, Director of the Clean Energy Research Institute at the University of Miami. Dr. Veziroglu organized the first international conference on hydrogen energy in 1974, and co-founded the International Association for Hydrogen Energy in 1975. I wanted the opportunity to work under the guidance of such a legend. However, Dr. Veziroglu generally only supervised research conducted by PhD students. During my junior year, I had taken a graduate class taught by Dr. Veziroglu. Though my pertinent questions in class had left a good impression on my professor, it was my determination and passion for learning that ultimately convinced him that I could carry through with such a complex analytical project. I spent extra hours in the library researching, participated in an international conference on hydrogen energy, and sought advice from PhD students specializing in solar-hydrogen energy systems. I successfully defended my thesis and earned an award for most outstanding engineering student of the year.

Gaining employment at the World Bank as an investment analyst is my third most significant accomplishment to date. As a general rule, the World Bank is extremely selective in hiring investment analysts. Interested candidates must possess intellectual ability, communication skills, maturity, and potential for career advancement. Minimum credentials for employment generally include an MBA degree from a first-rate program, industry knowledge, and/or knowledge of at least three languages. As an investment analyst in the Latin American department, I am one of the youngest of fifteen analysts and only one of four without an MBA. Moreover, prior to joining the Bank, I had only a year and a half of full-time work experience. After less than two years at the IFC, I was offered a promotion to an investment officer position at the IFC's field offices in Mexico, Buenos Aires, or Sao Paulo. I turned down the offer as it involved a three-year commitment in the field. This would conflict with my current goal of pursuing an MBA.

5. What are your career aspirations and why? How will you get there?

My experiences at the IFC have been precious, but they have left me with one humbling self-assessment. I do not yet possess the tools necessary to achieve my short and long term professional goals. I require the "MBA experience" to help complete the personal package that will ultimately lead to the attainment of these goals.

My short term professional goal is to work for an investment bank in one of its Latin American departments. I have acquired some expertise in the region through the World Bank and believe that the Latin American market is still very much untapped. My experience at an investment bank will be crucial to my long-term career goals as it will provide a solid base in the areas of corporate finance and capital market funding.

In the course of a few years, I hope to accumulate enough experience (and capital) to create my own business: a financial advisory firm for small to medium-sized companies located in Latin America. The focus of this enterprise would be to assist smaller firms with their investment decisions and the due diligence required for obtaining funding. I have seen many companies turned down by the IFC because they lacked a proper, well-defined investment and financial plan.

Harvard will assist me in attaining my goals in many ways. Firstly, I would love to participate in Dr. Michael Porter's Initiative for a Competitive Inner City (ICIC) field study program. America's inner cities have similar characteristics to those in Latin American such as limited access to funding, poverty, and lack of education. Learning how to leverage an inner city company's competitive advantage will allow me to apply the same principles to my Latin American venture. Secondly, I am applying to Harvard to surround myself with both students and faculty of the highest caliber. Finally, the unparalleled devotion of Harvard alumni to their alma mater and their willingness to assist and counsel current students are strong indications that Harvard is indeed a very special place.

6. Is there any other information that you believe would be helpful to the Board in understanding you better?

I would like to take this opportunity to tell the Board more about my background and how I believe my distinctiveness could enrich my learning experiences as well as those of my classmates at Harvard.

I was brought up in a family that was internationally oriented, and intellectually and culturally diverse. My mother is French-German. My father is Lebanese-Haitian. The blending of these four diverse cultures has had a unique impact on my character and my perspective on life. I grew up between Haiti and France. Living in France gave me an appreciation for a democratic society, a modern economy, and the arts, and allowed me to travel extensively throughout Europe. In Haiti, I spent a lot of time with my Lebanese grandmother, who taught me a great deal about the Middle Easterner civilization and culture.

My parents openly challenged the Duvalier dictatorship, which ravaged Haiti from 1957 to 1986 and their conviction instilled in me the desire to remain faithful to my own beliefs. Their fight also taught me the dangers and injustices of an anarchic and dictatorial government (we often had to live in hiding) and the disastrous impacts it can have on a country. Haiti, once known as the "Pearl of the Caribbean," is today one of the poorest countries in the Western Hemisphere.

Since leaving France, my wings have taken me to amazing faraway places from Latin America, to the east and west coasts of the US. My job at the IFC involves extensive traveling and has taken me to more than seven countries in Latin America. Many of our client companies are located in the interiors of countries, so I have had the fortune to experience life outside of the capital cities, from staying at a bed and breakfast in Chiapas, Mexico, to spending a day with the Guarani Indians in Brazil.

In business school, my impact will penetrate discussion inside and outside the classrooms. I believe I can add value by sharing various skill sets and traits with my classmates: a background in project finance in emerging countries, a solid grounding in mathematical applications achieved through my engineering degrees, a comfort level with three foreign languages and, most importantly, my perceptivity and sensitivity attained through my upbringing in seemingly incompatible cultures. I have won the friendship and trust of truly talented and genuine people wherever I have lived or traveled. I look forward to forging lasting friendships at Harvard as well.

Finally, from my perspective, if you are willing to admit me and to put your faith in my abilities, then it will be my responsibility to contribute as much as I can to the school and to the program. I will take the initiative to be active in any clubs, organizations, or events in which my skills and efforts can help to improve Harvard and/or provide some service to the community. The business world can be harsh and I want to bring some humanity to it. I appreciate your taking the time in considering my application and I hope that the provided information demonstrates that I am worthy of being included in next year's class.

WHARTON (Selected)

1. Please discuss the factors, both professional and personal, influencing the career decisions you have made that, in turn, have led you to your current position. What are your career goals for the future, and why is now the appropriate time to pursue an MBA at the Wharton School? How will you avail yourself of the resources at the Wharton School to achieve these goals?

After graduating from Stanford University with a Masters in Engineering Management, I returned to Haiti to work in the family-run printing and publishing firm, Le Natal, SA. My father lamented that he no longer had the energy he possessed when he opened Le Natal in the 1970's and felt that his daughters needed to bring some young blood to his company. My older sister could not handle both the administrative and operational arms of the business by herself. I welcomed the opportunity to learn about the business that had sustained us and could hardly wait to apply my engineering skills in a practical way.

As production manager, I was in charge of all the production processes on the printing floor from the management of work flow and order fulfillment processes to inventory control and equipment acquisition procedures. During the year and a half I spent at Le Natal, I learned how a large publishing and printing company operates and acquired a deep knowledge of its technology, production, marketing, distribution, and financial aspects. My engineering experience taught me to identify the root causes of problems and develop permanent solutions for them. I was able to design and implement changes in our inventory and human resource management methods which were highly beneficial to Le Natal. I set up and led a workforce to develop an inventory control and machine scheduling systems, which reduced order backlog by 60% and curtailed setup labor by 40%. I redesigned our produce costing and pricing systems, which on average increased gross margin by 12%. Additionally, I focused on further developing my interpersonal skills by establishing monthly staff meetings, which improved communication between workers and managers. I also actively participated in the development of a comprehensive customer service management program, organizing seminars for our clients on successful print-based marketing campaigns. The seminars covered newsletters, seasonal direct mail campaigns, and creation of a business identity and updated company logo. My work experience in Haiti also gave me a better understanding of the problems facing private companies in developing countries: lack of funding, lack of education, and lack of training for employees. As a result, I am more sensitive to the issues faced by my clients in my present role as investment analyst at the International Finance Corporation (IFC), the private arm of the World Bank.

I had always cherished the desire to work for an international organization dedicated to the development of third world countries. Having lived in both France and Haiti, I witnessed at a very young age the disparities between developed and underdeveloped nations. When my younger sister decided to return to Haiti to work at Le Natal, I seized the opportunity to apply for a position at World Bank. Since joining IFC almost two years ago, I have achieved significant strides in my professional development. As an investment analyst, I have had intensive on-the-job experience in project finance. I have been involved in a variety of deals (ranging from US$20 million to US$200 million), which have included acquisitions, financial restructuring, and company expansion. I have had the opportunity to work on various industries including the retail, food and beverage, pulp and paper, ceramic, and automotive industries. The spectrum of clients I have worked with have been very enriching—SMEs with less than US$1 million in sales annually to companies posting annual revenues of US$.5–.8 billion. I have learned to appraise investment projects, design financial packages, negotiate with sponsors, and supervise project implementation. I have had extensive client contact and have been given an incredible amount of responsibility. I have had the opportunity to work with and learn from teams with diverse backgrounds. While my experiences at the IFC have been precious, they have left me with one humbling self-assessment: I do not yet possess the tools necessary to achieve my short- and long-term goals.

When I observe senior managers and directors at the IFC, I marvel at their exceptional ability to lead their people and manage their businesses. It is their superior business skills and uncanny ability to lead—for the most part acquired through business school—that have been most instrumental in their professional advancement. While it might be feasible to attain these two critical success factors without business school, I do not want to delay a personal growth imperative. Just as companies know to benchmark externally to truly understand their potential, I know I will grow immensely by working, playing, learning and competing with classmates who share a commitment to growth and a desire for achievement.

Wharton will assist me in attaining my goals in many ways. Wharton's integrated curriculum will help hone my skills in various academic subjects and business disciplines. What particularly excites me about Wharton is the profound sense of purpose and community, as evidenced by the Students for Responsible Business (SRB) Program. Additionally, through activities like the Annual Wharton Business Plan Competition and resources such as the Wharton's Sol C. Snider Entrepreneurial Center and the Small Business Development Center, Wharton demonstrates its commitment to entrepreneurship. It is crucial that I master this discipline, since it plays an integral role in my future plans. Wharton's emphasis on ethics and the honor code is important to me. Achievements gained at the expense of honesty are tarnished and I have always strived to achieve my personal and professional goals with integrity. I am applying to Wharton to also surround myself with both students and faculty of the highest caliber. Finally, the unparalleled devotion of Wharton alumni to their alma mater and their willingness to assist and counsel current students are strong indications that Wharton is indeed a very special place.

My short-term professional goal is to work for an investment bank in one of its Latin American departments. I have acquired some expertise in the region through the World Bank and believe that the Latin American market is still very much untapped. I am convinced that a position with an investment bank will not only expose me to a large number of companies and industries, but will also provide the opportunity to learn about the structuring of sophisticated financial transactions, from mergers and acquisitions to private debt and equity placement. Contacts made at the investment bank will also prove invaluable for my long-term professional goal.

In the course of a few years, I hope to accumulate enough experience (and capital) to create my own business: a financial advisory firm for small to medium-sized companies located in Latin America. My Latin American venture will assist middle-market companies in finding the capital necessary to operate and grow their businesses. It will be particularly sensitive to investment decisions concerning family and other closely-held corporations (common in Latin America), advising on maximizing corporate and shareholder value, capital structure planning, strategic partnership, and corporate restructuring. This requires both judgments acquired from experience as well as a strong knowledge of the financial markets and the underlying industry markets. I will acquire these skills at Wharton and during my years at an investment bank.

2. **At Wharton, the Learning Team, which consists of approximately five first-year students, is often assigned group projects and class presentations. Imagine that, one year from now, your Learning Team has a marketing class assignment due at 9:00 a.m. on Monday morning. It is now 10:00 p.m. on Sunday night; time is short, tension builds, and your team has reached an impasse. What role would you take in such a situation? How would you enable the team to meet your deadline? (Note: The specific nature of the assignment is not as important here as the team dynamic.) Feel free to draw on previous experience, if applicable, in order to illustrate your approach.**

In my previous graduate group assignments at Stanford University, I always ended up as the leader of the various teams I worked with. I must confess, however, that I have never been in an impasse so close to the deadline. However, an adamant group member or extraordinary circumstances (sickness, death of a loved one, family problems) could easily lead my colleagues and me to the situation presented above. I suspect that I would, as in my previous experiences, lead my Learning Team at Wharton towards preparing the best and most innovative marketing assignment possible, even under the circumstances.

I am reminded of one particular assignment for my technology entrepreneurship class during my graduate studies at Stanford. I was part of a group of five students preparing a business plan for a high-tech start-up. The business plan would be presented at the end of the quarter to a group of venture capitalists at Silicon Valley. The assignment involved coming up with an innovative and feasible business concept and conducting detailed market forecasting, scenario analysis, determination of the company's core competencies, financial projections and contingencies. With two and a half months left, it was necessary to come up quickly with a viable business concept. I took immediate action and organized several brainstorming sessions. During our brainstorming meetings, I made it clear to my teammates that wild ideas were permitted, even encouraged, and that none of us should fear feeling foolish in expressing his/her thoughts. Indeed, I recorded all ideas on a large piece of newsprint to reinforce the "no-criticism" rule and give the group a tangible sense of collective achievement. My team was very diverse and included two Americans, one Indian, and one Peruvian. Additionally, my colleagues had worked in different industries, including the software industry, IT consulting, and movie industry. While I thought that my colleagues were more experienced, and thus better suited to lead the team, I was designated as the leader. I believe my teammates trusted my judgment from the pertinent questions I asked in class and my willingness to help others. Additionally, they felt that I was not interested in personal gain, but that I was someone who would operate on behalf of the group. After several avid discussions, we finally agreed on "creating" a start-up providing on-line translation solutions for multilingual internet and intranet communications. As team leader, I began by formulating the different tasks that needed to be completed, and asking the team members' opinions on what areas they would each like to focus on. Before undertaking our assigned tasks, I reinforced how crucial our analyses were for completing the project. The success of our group would depend on the sum total of our individual performances. Towards the end of the quarter with the deadline approaching and pressure rising, I suggested that we go hiking in Yosemite during the Memorial Day Weekend. This would allow us to step back for a minute, enjoy each other's company outside of school, and hopefully return refreshed for the final sprint. We not only reached the highest peak in Yosemite, but we also ended up winning the business plan competition that year at Stanford.

I have learned a lot about group psychology in my various group assignments at Stanford and at the IFC. The team leader is present to give direction and motivate his colleagues, but ultimately, everyone needs to feel that he/she is equally contributing to the task at hand. Indeed, the team leader must ultimately assign leadership on specific sub-projects to individuals on the team. At Stanford, our "venture" called on expertise across various disciplines to create a successful strategy. I have also observed that people have different working styles. Some like to think for hours before writing something on paper; others like to jot down ideas immediately. Some enjoy working with the music on; others need complete silence to focus. Some enjoy taking regular short breaks; others prefer to work long hours and take longer breaks. One of the many roles of the group leader is to effectively manage the differences and bring out the team's creativity and humor.

I am convinced that the same will hold in the case of my Learning Team at Wharton. The numerous Wharton alums that I have met at the IFC come from all walks of life—they are a reflection of the possible composition of a typical Learning Team. As leader of my Learning Team, I would likely apply the same principles and methods used in my previous team assignments at Stanford and at the IFC, as well as incorporate any lessons learned. Going hiking in Yosemite might not be feasible for this particular assignment, but my Wharton teammates and I could take a short drive to the Pocono Mountains (not at 10:00 pm though!) or stroll by the Schuylkill

River to refresh our minds and discuss ideas candidly. I will likely run into the situation where some members are very adamant about a particular view with which the rest of the group does not necessarily agree. Whether at Stanford or at the IFC, I have learned that in this particular situation, it is crucial that we be flexible, put ourselves in each other's shoes and "try on" others' views. Many times, a better understanding of another's thinking can lead us to revise our own views and/or find logical arguments to better explain the nature of our disagreement. Often the failure to acknowledge the other side's perception can lead to emotional outbursts that can only be detrimental to the group's effort. In my business plan team at Stanford, we had decided that whenever we felt anger, frustration, discouragement, or any other negative feelings, we would write them down on a piece of paper and place them in what we had nicknamed the "garbage basket." Additionally, we were fortunate to have among us a Tai Chi devotee, who with his relaxation and breathing techniques helped us tremendously in times of pressure and frustration. I still do some of these exercises and would be happy to share them with my Learning Team at Wharton.

At Wharton, I know that I will be in teams with diverse individuals. I know that we will encounter differences in opinions, which will invariably lead to delays. My experiences at the IFC and at Stanford have taught me that an efficient working relationship involves good communication, trust, respect, acknowledgement of emotions, and active listening. These are some of the skills I will bring with me to Wharton. Moreover, I am sure that I will learn many team-building skills from my classmates. With this in mind, I have no doubt that we will be able to meet our deadlines in a well-organized and timely fashion.

Comments

- Ingrid shows herself to be someone who likes to "take the bull by the horns." Throughout her applications, she continuously showcases the ideas she has generated and the initiative she has taken in order to produce spectacular results, even in the face of daunting odds: reviving the Brazilian project after the devaluation of the Real, realizing the need to create an Argentine student loan collection program, obtaining her Master's degree while undergoing chemotherapy.

- In the second Harvard essay, Ingrid might have created an even more powerful piece had she illustrated that she eventually remedied the ruined relationship with her teammates, and then provided an example of how she used better skills to get past a team frustration after that initial failure. Concluding the failure essay in this manner would have put to rest any fears that the admissions committee might have had about her potential to act in such a negative manner again during a frustrating team exercise.

- Ingrid cloaks the most basic of facts with interesting contextual stories to create essays that work in her favor. Though it is generally not advisable to use the receipt of a university degree, for example, as an illustration of one's greatest accomplishments (doing so wastes a perfectly good opportunity to tell a story that the admissions committee cannot see from a glance at one's transcripts and résumé), Ingrid takes the fact of having earned a master's degree and turns it into a story worth relishing. In fact, she peppers all of her essays with relevant details that cannot be gained elsewhere.

- One note worth mentioning: In her essay set for Wharton, Ingrid rounded out her experience at the World Bank with information about the year and a half after college when she returned to Haiti to manage production at her father's paper plant. An essay on this topic for Harvard would have nicely contributed to that set of essays as well, though they stand up perfectly well on their own.

- Ingrid's second Wharton essay is right on target insofar as she focused on team dynamics rather on the substance of the marketing assignment and drew upon her past team experiences to illustrate how she would approach the Learning Team situation. On the other hand, the essay contains a bit too much fluffery. Concise writing is a virtue in a business environment.

URI

BERKELEY/HAAS

1. "The unexamined life is not worth living."—*Socrates, The Apology* by PLATO

    In light of the above quotation, please discuss a decision you have made that, in retrospect, has had a profound influence on your present circumstances. In hindsight, would you have made a different decision? Please explain.

Since a young age, my Israeli heritage and Jewish background have strongly influenced the choices I make. My family history has largely defined who I am and what I value. I felt strongly about joining the Israeli army during my high school years. As a Tzabar (a person born in Israel), I felt it was my duty to my country. I was born into a family with a strong national identity and, like many of today's American Jewish youth, I am also a grandson of Holocaust survivors. Joining the army mattered to me because I believe that the presence of Israel is the single most important hope for preventing another such atrocity.

When I announced my intentions of joining the Israeli army to my parents, they opposed my idea. I learned for the first time that my father was a Prisoner of War in Egypt during the 1973 Yom Kippur War. This led him to leave Israel to seek a kinder, easier life for his children. If I chose to enlist, I would be going against my father's values and dishonoring him. I grappled with the decision of either joining to fulfill my national duties, or not enlisting to keep my father from being unhappy.

In addition to my father's wishes, I pondered the other pros and cons associated with the decision. If I joined, I would benefit from the first-class training that Israeli soldiers receive. Potential employers would value the experience. On the other hand, joining would mean I would be delaying my college education by more than three years while potentially missing out on what most Americans consider some of the best years of their lives.

I decided to find a compromise by participating in activities that helped educate Americans about the tragedy that befell European Jews during the Second World War. Contributing to a closely associated cause served as a substitute to military duty that satisfied both my parents and me. In hindsight, this decision has had a profound effect on my present circumstances because it motivated me to better understand my heritage and background. Joining the Israeli army would have helped me learn more about my background, but perhaps only from one perspective, making me somewhat closed minded. I have since developed a strong understanding of Middle East cultural and financial affairs and the Holocaust, making me an expert on my heritage. Understanding my heritage and background has been significant to me. The pursuit of this knowledge has helped me learn more about myself and the world I live in.

Shortly after I made the decision not to enlist in the Israeli army, I participated in "the March of the Living," a two-week college credit program to educate international students about the Holocaust, in 1992. 52 members of my family were murdered in death camps so this experience had additional value to me, over and above its educational aspect. For me, the March of the Living was an opportunity for mourning and understanding the terrible atrocities my family underwent during the Holocaust.

In addition to helping me learn about my family's history, the March of the Living mattered to me because it allowed me to put the different talents I have accumulated over my lifetime to work. As I was Hebrew conversant, I was able to lead student groups in a number of different experiences on this trip to Poland and Israel. Participants looked up to me because of my "savvy" with the country, people, and language. My knowledge of the Bible allowed me to lead religious ceremonies, often dealing with the Holocaust tragedy; writing skills proved helpful when I had to create a speech for the final ceremony; my understanding and sensitivity allowed me to console participants through periods of mourning. The leaders of the program chose me to represent the entire US delegation (more than 3000 students) by speaking at our final ceremony at Auschwitz in Poland. If I had joined the Israeli army, I would have missed out on this experience because I would have been required to enlist before the March began.

My contribution to Israel eventually became an active campaign for Holocaust education. I became a recognized speaker on the subject, leading discussions at synagogues, churches, city community centers, and schools. I was even invited to speak at a number of fund-raising events around the country. I valued this because it allowed me to spread my message about the importance of Holocaust education. It gave me the opportunity to explain how important awareness is. Indeed, even in our modern time, atrocities resembling the Holocaust still occur. I was recently honored with the invitation to lead and mentor a group of students on the 2000 March of the Living trip.

Because I did not enlist with the Israeli army, I felt obligated to pursue knowledge about my Israeli heritage, which often gave me direction when making career decisions. Six months after I began working at Barclays, I was offered the opportunity to service clients located across the Middle East. I was eager to accept the position because it gave me a chance to better understand my family's background.

The task of competing in the emerging market sector, an arena where US bulge bracket firms have dozens of committed people, was challenging. I was one of only two Debt Origination officers at Barclays Capital assigned to cover more than 100 borrowers in 26 countries, including most of the Middle East and Eastern Europe. Barclays Capital had no ratings advisory team, no offices in these countries, and no transaction credentials in the sector. Our competition possessed all of the above. In hindsight, I might not have chosen such a challenging endeavor if my heritage was not so important to me. I benefited greatly from this experience because it was an opportunity to build a business from scratch and understand the perseverance necessary for such a task.

Initially, I made contacts with central banks, financial institutions, and corporate borrowers. Eventually, my work required my colleague and I to fly to the Middle East to present Barclays Capital's credentials to government officials in the region. Although our firm had no Middle Eastern emerging market track-record, we positioned well for these bond offerings by discussing the transactions we had done for Western European sovereign borrowers. Over the phone, I spoke with the Republic of Lebanon's funding officers at least twice a week, teaching them basics of bond underwriting. Our conversations became more open and the funding officers came to trust me.

When crunch time came and the Republic was deciding which investment bank to include in the syndicate of its next Eurobond, I was informed by Lebanon's funding officials that Barclays would not be included. Senior officials in Lebanon's funding office felt obligated to use French banks and US bulge bracket firms because of historical relationships. Although I was disappointed to hear that the decision was being made based on "relationships" instead of merit, I did not give up. I remembered that Maysoun Al-Hariri, the daughter of Prime Minister Rafiq Al-Hariri, was a graduate of the University of Michigan, my alma mater.

I used the alumni office to contact Maysoun personally to explain my dilemma. She was happy to influence her father, the Prime Minister of Lebanon, to pressure the funding officers into giving Barclays Capital a role in the syndicate. Had I joined the Israeli army, I might have developed a closed minded attitude that might have prevented me from pursuing such help.

Minutes before the bond was launched, we were officially informed of our role in this prestigious benchmark transaction. This was the first Middle Eastern emerging market deal in which Barclays participated, an important milestone that my colleague and I initiated. After two years, my team has successfully positioned Barclays Capital as managers in 17 emerging market transactions. My responsibility for Barclays Capital's Middle Eastern clients in Israel, Jordan, and Lebanon was significant to me because it allowed me to develop a good understanding of business culture in the region, a perspective that I would have not gained had I joined the Israeli army.

Learning about my heritage has been important to me because it has laid the foundation for my values. The morals and ethics I adhere to are largely based on the Jewish faith and Israeli culture. Family and community are therefore important to me. The idea of bettering oneself through education and scholarship is a concept to which I hold fast. Values such as self-determination and equal rights for all men and women are central to my beliefs. I first learned about the connection between these values and my faith from my parents as a child and from my Rabbi during preparation for my Bar-Mitzvah, but I extended this knowledge only after I made the decision not to enlist with the Israeli army. I improved my knowledge of religion with University courses. This helped me confirm the connection between my values and my faith.

Being able to incorporate my interests and values into my daily life has made me more passionate about my heritage and its meaning. Today, I continue to develop my knowledge of the Middle East by participating in an Arab-Israeli discussion group in New York that my roommate (a Sudanese) and I co-founded. I might not have gained this open-minded perspective if I had chosen to join the Israeli army.

As a grandson of Holocaust survivors and a son of a prisoner of war, what continues to motivate me to give 100% effort in everything I do is the fact that I am the first generation of my family to grow up without being subject to the horrors of war. I am eager to see my potential, given the wonderful opportunities my parents and the United States have offered me. My heritage is therefore important to me because it has given me the opportunity to realize how lucky I am.

In hindsight, I believe the decision not to enlist in the Israeli army was a good one for me. In addition to having a profound effect on my character and knowledge, this decision has helped to give me a better understanding of the world I live in. Growing up in a nationalistic Israeli family, during my youth, I was often bombarded by anti-Arab rhetoric and misguided beliefs about the Islamic religion. Having worked in the Middle East while at Barclays Capital has opened my eyes to the wonderful culture of the Arabic world. The pinnacle of my newfound appreciation and tolerance of other cultures is my friendship with a Sudanese national, who is my roommate in New York. The decision not to enlist and instead pursue expertise on my own heritage and Middle East affairs has made me a better, more open person.

2. Please discuss your intermediate and long-term professional goals and why you want an MBA at this point in your career. In what ways do you think an MBA degree will help you achieve these goals? What do you want from an MBA program and why have you chosen the Haas School?

My short-term aspiration is to continue developing my management skills while working in a stimulating environment, perhaps with a venture capital or private equity business. My next term goal is to eventually build and manage my own corporation. With my Israeli background, my long-term career aspiration is to contribute to the Middle East peace process by creating and working on business ventures that involve cross-national cooperation in the Middle East.

My experience at Barclays has laid the foundation for my future goals. The training program, which I completed with distinction, encompassed a broad array of relevant skills, from government bond trading and derivatives to managing time and presentation skills.

Working in the debt capital markets, I further developed my strengths. Most of our team's business pitches in the Supranational Group revolved around carefully tailored pitch books that required gathering information from dozens of people and numerous research sources. I helped our team achieve a number of benchmark transactions including the first ever Global Yen offering managed by a European bank and the first and largest ever Global Sterling transaction. In addition, I helped Barclays become a member of the prestigious Selling Groups of Freddie Mac, the World Bank, and Fannie Mae, a title bestowed on only the best service providers in the business.

With a good understanding of the debt capital markets business, my second posting was to help build the Emerging Markets Group, a new business for Barclays Capital. This experience allowed me to develop my organizational skills while I enjoyed more freedom to be entrepreneurial and more direct responsibility, with the management of 3 analysts. The task of competing in the Emerging Market sector, an arena where US bulge bracket firms have dozens of committed people, was demanding. My team successfully positioned Barclays Capital as a manager in 17 emerging market debt offerings, which allowed me to develop the right contacts with corporate, bank, and government officials in Lebanon, Jordan, Egypt, and Israel, where I will eventually open my own company.

After two years of working in Europe I was given the opportunity to help build Barclays new primary bond business in the US. This opportunity gave me exposure to yet a third market, the US corporate bond market. My team increased Barclays presence in the US primary market by managing the roles in more than 60 debt offerings by the middle of 1999. Barclays averaged one primary management position each month before I joined the firm.

My experiences at Barclays have given me the opportunity to develop an understanding of businesses across different products and clients, knowledge that will prove useful in the pursuit of an MBA. Despite my wealth of experiences, I do not yet possess all the tools necessary to achieve my goals. My reasons for pursuing an MBA at Haas are to increase my business knowledge and management skill set, gain credentials and credibility to run my own business, and be introduced to a network of potential business partners.

The academic experience at Haas will increase my problem solving skills. My learning will be structured by top professors who have real world business experience. I plan to concentrate in Entrepreneurial Studies and am especially attracted to classes which will allow me to analyze and consider my own ideas for new businesses.

The Haas MBA provides a graduate with a tremendous amount of credibility. Firstly, the fact that Haas's professors are such highly respected educators is well recognized among the business community. The Haas MBA allows one to master the basic theories of business practice (Finance, Accounting, Marketing, etc.) while concentrating on a particular field of interest. The Haas MBA program requires rigorous study. A Haas MBA on one's resume is considered an indication of an ability to handle complex challenges. Gaining the credibility or credential that a Haas MBA provides will be very useful when I pursue investors to finance my own business.

The diversity of experiences that Haas Business School students bring with them to the classroom is second to none. The challenge of studying at the pace and caliber that Haas demands requires serious commitment. These individuals form a network of professionals that will provide me with a source of information and support. Given my long-term goal of contributing to the Middle East peace process by promoting cross-national business projects in the region, an MBA from Haas would prove especially useful as the study body at Haas features a diverse set of nationalities, some of which are Middle Eastern. The Haas MBA is the logical next step in my career path and I look forward to the opportunity.

INSEAD (Selected)

1. **Describe what you believe to be your two most substantial accomplishments to date (at least one must be professional), explaining why you view them as such.**

I once received a box of chocolate. How I attained it is a story worth relishing.

In the summer of 1994 I came to London, having accepted a summer internship with an investment boutique. Once I arrived (having already committed to an apartment) I learned that the boutique had gone belly up. There I was in London, 20 years old and jobless, with a non-exchangeable plane ticket to return home in several months.

I walked the city of London with my resume in hand, Few firms agreed to meet with me on such an informal basis. In fact, the Bank of England asked 3 security guards to escort me from the building when I revealed I had no "official" appointment.

With enough persistence, I managed to find a rewarding internship with Barclays Global Security Services. That internship eventually opened the door for post-graduation interviews with Barclays Capital (where I spent the last three years). Within four months of beginning my job, I became the first "Graduate" promoted to "Analyst." I earned an unusually large amount of responsibility, including that of pricing bonds for a number of prestigious borrowers, including the Bank of England.

Invited last year by the Bank of England's funding officers to their offices, I lit up as I walked through the same doors I had been escorted from three years earlier. As I was leaving, I was presented with a box of chocolate in thanks for my exemplary service. That gift represented what I had accomplished in my career so far.

When I arrived in New York City more than a year ago, I decided that I wanted to commit more time to two things: charity work and music (I play the trombone and euphonium). I looked for a way to accomplish both of these goals at once by co-founding a swing bank that performs for charitable causes.

My first task was finding the musicians and a place to rehearse. By our fourth rehearsal we had grown into a swing-band of almost 20 musicians; a local music studio near my office offered a practice room at a cheap price. We registered the band as a not-for-profit organization. Band rooms, jazz clubs, restaurants and bars are eager to hire us because their entertainment expenses become tax deductible. The money from our performances contributed to an organization of the manager's choice.

Our first performance took place at the Orange Bear Bar in Manhattan. Since that debut, we have scheduled performances at five different ventures. I expect our band will average playing one venue each month over the coming year, raising more than $40,000 for charitable causes including the American Cancer Society, New York Cares, and Amnesty International.

2. Have you ever experienced culture shock? What did it mean to you?

During college I was offered the opportunity to study abroad at the University of Vienna Business School. I was eager to accept the position because it gave me a chance to better understand my family's background; one set of my grandparents is from Vienna.

When I arrived in Vienna, I was quickly adopted by the University's student population through a "Buddy System." I enjoyed everything from Wiener Schnitzel to the Viennese Opera, and even learned how to dance the Viennese Waltz. I benefited from the Austrian educational system that required me to learn business in the German language. During this initial transition, I experience no culture shock at all.

I established friends with a group of five Austrians and was comfortable doing most everything with them: studying, bar-hopping, dining, etc. One evening, a month into our friendship, we discussed religion. I never imagined I'd hear the reactions I received from two of those students when I told them I was Jewish.

One of the students had a grandfather who served in Adolf Hitler's SS and worked at a concentration camp in Poland. He believed his grandfather had done a good thing because "at the time it was necessary to eliminate Jews for the war effort." I was shocked at his comments. What confused me further was that another student agreed with him. This one told me that although he liked me and believed I was an exception, he believed that generally, Jews are bad people. Driven with emotion, I left the table, More than 50 members of my family died at the hands of the Nazis. After that dinner those two students never called me or asked me to join them, but I remained friends with the other two, who later revealed their differing opinions.

Although I was very familiar with popular sentiment about Jews in Austria during World War II, I had naively believed that for the most part, this sentiment had faded. Having grown up in a politically correct environment in South Florida, I never imagined that people would openly admit to me that they hated Jews. This realization constituted culture shock.

Comments

- Uri presents a superb set of essays with several strong themes that help to make him an extremely memorable candidate: persistence in all endeavors; commitment to his heritage; open-mindedness; a wealth of knowledge about the Middle East, debt capital markets, and emerging markets.

- Uri's first essay explores an unusual topic that quickly grabs the reader's attention and sets the stage, showing him to be exceptionally loyal and committed to his cultural upbringing, as well as risk-taking, though not cavalierly so. The essay is ideal in that it discusses a real "decision," not an event in which the conclusion was so obvious that it did not require much weighing of pros and cons. Throughout the essay, Uri continues to consider the benefits of his original decision, which is effective. He ties the whole essay together well, even though it ventures off into many different directions. He deftly incorporates many different aspects of his candidacy to Haas, without losing his primary focus.

- Uri constantly demonstrates the tangible results he has accomplished in all his endeavors—representing a delegation of three thousand at the March of the Living's final ceremony, successfully managing sixty debt offerings to build Barclays' new primary bond business, and so on.

- Like his Haas essays, Uri's INSEAD essays tell wonderful stories that help to bring the details of his candidacy to life. His second accomplishment in essay one packages two aspects of his candidacy—his community service and his musical talent—into one example, allowing him to kill two birds with one stone. The second INSEAD essay on his travel to Austria—again reminding the reader of the candidate's open-mindedness, as he is, after all, an Israeli whose family members were Holocaust victims—is a wonderful way to express many of his main themes within an intriguing tale.

DAVE

MICHIGAN

1. What has been your most significant professional accomplishment? What has been your toughest professional challenge and how did you address it?

My most significant professional accomplishment was also my toughest professional challenge: establishing the A Domani Coffee Co. Never before had I been faced with so many different difficulties and challenges, and yet I met them all with the attitude that I could find a way to solve any problem.

Before we could open for business, I had to get all of the permits for operation, explaining to the city officials what type of business I would be running and what type of facility and equipment I would be using. I went before an Allentown Review Board to seek permission to display signs. In addition, I remodeled the facility for our business, first requiring that I had to have plans drawn up and reviewed by more city offices. Once the city approved the plans and permits, I hired contractors to remodel the facility. Many times I worked along side some of the contractors to help speed things along. For example, when the plumber worked to finish the hook-ups for the water lines in the basement, I worked under the counter running the water lines to the espresso machine and sinks. I had the business up and running in about two months.

After I opened up for business, I was responsible for day-to-day operations. I managed two shifts of operations with a total of 10 employees. Hiring, managing, and, in some cases, firing a couple of employees was not only challenging, but also taught me a great deal about people management. Some of the challenges I faced with the employees were sexual harassment, stealing, and people not showing up to work as scheduled. I also had many positive experiences with the employees as well. For instance, I implemented team meetings, during which I would share information with the employees about how we were doing, and seek their suggestions as to how we could improve in certain areas or set and meet goals. Through these meetings, the employees and I were able to both improve our service and increase our sales by using the suggestions and ideas brought up at these meetings. I was also responsible for ongoing marketing and customer relations. On average, I worked 14 hours a day, 6 days a week.

In establishing A Domani Coffee I was able to realize a life long dream, and gain experience that will benefit me for a lifetime. I have known many people who regret that they never took chances in life, and many of these people wished for a second chance to embrace an opportunity presented to them. I earned the trust of others who had risked their money with me, hoping to profit from a good business idea and lots of hard work. A Domani Coffee is still in operation today; I laid the foundation for a successful enterprise through careful planning, hard work, and my natural ability to manage people and challenging situations.

2. **What are your post-graduation career plans? How will your education, experience, and development to date support those plans? How will an MBA from the University of Michigan Business School help you attain your goals? For Tauber Manufacturing Institute Applicants: Please answer the above question as it relates to your career interests in manufacturing and how you see the TMI program helping you attain your goals.**

My post-graduation career goal is to pursue a position as a director level manager within a manufacturing company. Then, I want climb to a position of senior management, directing all aspects of manufacturing from product design to marketing and sales within a manufacturing company.

My career in manufacturing began when I enrolled in Cascade High School's Production Plastics program. I learned many of the manufacturing techniques involved in plastic product production. This led to my first job in manufacturing at Chemical Proof, a manufacturer of fiberglass holding tanks and pipes. Later, I was recruited by Designer Marble, a manufacturer of cultured marble bathtubs, sinks, and countertops. At both companies I improved production processes by tapping my education and developing experience in manufacturing techniques.

I accepted a job at Boeing as an aircraft mechanic. I was involved in all phases of the manufacture of the 747, 767, and, to a smaller extent, the 777 airplanes. I manufactured and installed parts ranging from structural to electrical components, and I worked closely with engineering design teams to implement product design changes. I also worked with foreign and domestic airline customer representatives during the final delivery of aircraft. Eventually I was assigned as a lead overseeing 10-20 union employees. I was able to develop many of my leadership skills as a result of this challenging assignment.

After I was laid-off from Boeing, I went into the coffee business with a friend. This opportunity provided me with the ability to make decisions regarding all aspects of the business. From our personal funds and the investment of others we raised an initial $100,000. I was responsible for the initial set up of the entire operation. This included obtaining all permits for operation, overseeing the remodel and operations of our facility with a budget of $60,000, purchasing all equipment and supplies with a budget of $30,000, and conducting the marketing with a budget of $10,000. During operation I was responsible for the daily accounting, continued marketing, hiring employees, and managing two daily shifts of operation.

My decision to return to Boeing was influenced by my desire to learn more about advanced manufacturing techniques. I was recognized for my experience in all the aspects of manufacturing and business, and was offered a position as a change analyst. I was responsible for scheduling engineering changes to these airplanes. My main task was to lead resolution teams composed of engineers, suppliers, and planners resolving conflicts to the manufacturing schedule presented by the engineering changes.

My career progress has been based on my natural tendency to lead and a commitment to hard work. The Michigan MBA Program would enable me to formalize my business experience by gaining knowledge of business principles and practices that my experience has not provided. Gaining an understanding of the many aspects of product development and what is required to bring a product from idea, through design, and to eventual production is the key to meeting my career goals. The TMI Program will greatly enhance the value of my many years of experience in manufacturing. The combination of my experience and a world class education provided by the Michigan MBA Program will ensure the fulfillment of my career goal to direct the manufacturing of a world class firm.

3. **Describe a failure or setback in your life. How did you overcome the setback? What, if anything, would you do differently if confronted with this situation again?**

When I survey my life, searching for a failure or setback, I'm unable to find one. This doesn't mean there haven't been any, as some would define them, but rather it is a reflection of my attitude toward such events. I believe that facing challenges with an attitude that redefines setbacks and failures as opportunities is the reason for my inability to see any real failures or setbacks in my life. To highlight my attitude toward such, I will provide an example of when I was faced with a lay-off from The Boeing Co.

In 1989 while I was still in high school, I started working for The Boeing Co. I worked 12 hours a day, 7 days a week for 5-week rotations, receiving two days off every 5th week. I was comfortably supporting my wife and 2 children, averaging $50,000 a year with all of the overtime. In the process, my wife and I had made plans to purchase our first house with 5 acres of property. I was also beginning to see the opportunity for my career advancement, and started filling in as a lead, first for weekend duty, and then for longer periods of time. My manager had even hinted at the idea that I could soon be considered for an entry level management position. I felt that my life was going in the right direction. I was a young man with a great job and excellent prospects for the future. This lasted until the spring of 1992 when production slowed, and the company started laying-off employees.

During the time that Boeing was laying-off employees, I was witness to emotional breakdowns by many people I worked with, even to the point of seeing crying at work. This was a traumatic time period in many of my co-workers' lives. People were mired in negativity surrounded me, yet I never shared the same feelings of fear and concern. I had become comfortable with the lifestyle provided by the income, enjoyed my job, and was sure, given the opportunity, I would have made a great manager. But at the same time, I knew this situation was going to provide an opportunity for a new positive direction in my life.

A good friend of mine suggested that we go into the specialty coffee business. I saw this as the opportunity that the situation at Boeing had provided, and I wholeheartedly committed myself to this new direction. My attitude toward losing my job at Boeing, which many viewed not only as a setback but also as a traumatic loss, gave me the chance for an experience of a lifetime. Instead of letting circumstance dictate a setback or failure in my life, I started and operated a small business that is still running to this day. I expect to face many more challenges in life, and I will face them with the same attitude that I have always faced challenges with, not allowing them to become setbacks or failures.

4. **Describe an idea you've had for a new business or product or a new service line of an existing entity.**

While I was operating the Domani Coffee Co., I had the idea for a new service: providing delivery of our products to the local businesses and office buildings near our location. Since our product and service was new to the area, I had already completed several marketing schemes to bring attention to our grand opening. I wasn't satisfied with the amount of foot traffic that we had on a daily basis, and wanted a better way to reach our revenue goals.

I knew that there was at least one major factor in Allentown that was different from the Seattle area: the weather. In Seattle the weather is mild. When it rains, it is actually more of a mist than the torrential down pours that I found on the East Coast. Also, during the winter the temperature rarely falls below 40 degrees. Since I had started operations in late February, I soon realized that I wasn't thrilled to travel outside in the extreme cold. This difference in climates between Seattle and Allentown led me to my idea. I noticed that those patrons who were brave enough to leave the warmth of the office to brave the cold for our irresistible coffee would often times take as many as six beverages back with them. I started informally surveying the customers to find out more about their office settings and their coffee drinking colleagues. My intuition was confirmed. The weather was contributing to the lack of foot traffic. But I also discovered another reason for the lack of envisioned customer enthusiasm.

Many of the customers had expressed to me time constraints prevented them from leaving the office for the required period of time to get coffee from us. It immediately dawned on me. We were the only business of our nature in the downtown core, and I had expected some of the customers to walk up to six blocks for our coffee. Although many of the customers would have walked twice that distance for our coffee, their employers wouldn't let them. In Seattle there is literally a coffeehouse on every street corner, and many times two or three in between. I decided to take the coffee to our Allentown customers. This, at least to my knowledge, had not been done in Seattle.

I hired an employee who would be dedicated to deliveries. I wrote up a menu, and had my delivery employee take these to all of the businesses and offices where we would deliver. Before the employee made it back to the shop from delivering the menus, we were already receiving orders. Within two weeks this new service proved so successful, I had to hire another employee to help with deliveries. And after two months of offering this delivery service, it made up about one third of our business between the hours of 9am to 3pm. We delivered everything from our whole bean coffee, providing coffee and pastry packages for meetings, to daily office coffee setups. This idea proved to be quite successful, and led to the expansion of our customer base.

5. If there is any other information that you believe is important to our assessment of your candidacy, feel free to add it to your application.

I would like to share a couple of the activities that I enjoy participating in outside of work and school. These activities are an important part of my life, and will give you a better understanding of my personal side.

I enjoy spending time and playing with my children. This has led to my enjoyable experiences coaching and helping out with some of their sports teams. When I volunteered to umpire for the Mill Creek Little League baseball games, my main objective was to try to make it fun for all of the kids and parents. I learned a lot about how to keep competitiveness from getting carried away, as it can with parents and coaches. Because of my involvement in the Little League, I was asked to help coach the Little League all-star team of nine and ten-year-olds, made up of twelve kids selected by the team manager. Because of my involvement in the league, I was asked to become the Treasurer for the league. My effort to involve myself in my children's activities also included coaching their football team. One of the most memorable experiences of coaching the football team was when we played before a Husky football game at Husky Stadium at the University of Washington. Our team had been the top fundraiser for Richmond Junior Football, which earned us the reward to play in Husky stadium. All of the kids and the coaches loved the experience. The local news station filmed our game, and the highlights were aired along with the highlights of the Husky game.

Another activity I enjoy is working on Northwest Coast Indian Art. I was able to learn from two internationally recognized Northwest Coast artists. Jay Haavik, my first teacher, taught me the fundamentals of the artwork, such as the form and different tribal styles. After my skills advanced, he invited me to work on a commissioned project for a hospital that was being built for the Puyallup Indian Tribe. Jay designed a traditional cedar house screen with a traditional story design on it, common on the front of the long houses in the past, that was twelve feet high and twenty feet long. In the center of the screen was a totem pole that was fifteen feet high and three feet wide. I was responsible for the painting of the design on the screen, and spent about a month on the project. I also learned how to carve masks from Israel Shotridge, a world-renowned Tlinget artist. I spent about two weeks with him in Ketchikan, Alaska and learned about the traditional forehead masks of the Tlinget Indian. After I returned home I carved a mask and donated it to the Everett Community College Foundation auction. It sold for four hundred and fifty dollars, which went to a scholarship fund for Native Americans. Although I don't have as much time as I would like to work on art, it is still a passion I enjoy when I have the opportunity.

Comments

- Dave is clearly a unique candidate. He worked in several manufacturing capacities after high school before completing a college degree in his thirties. To be a plausible candidate, Dave needed to show that he belonged at a top program. He did so, in part, by emphasizing the variety and depth of his experiences. (His well-written essays and strong college grades also helped show him to be an atypical blue-collar worker.)

- Dave shows a breadth of experience in manufacturing, having worked at Boeing for many years as a union employee, team leader, and change analyst. Above and beyond his obvious familiarity with manufacturing, he also demonstrates a creative, entrepreneurial dimension through his stories about A Domani Coffee. His discussion of that venture is especially useful because it lays out in detail the diverse skill sets needed to start and run such an operation, from obtaining business permits, to remodeling a site, to purchasing supplies, to hiring and training employees, to creating innovative marketing techniques.

- The fifth essay provides necessary balance to Dave's otherwise career-focused discussions. He highlights two interests: spending time with his children through coaching and umpiring kids' sports activities, and creating artwork inspired by the Northwest Coast Indian style.

C.L.
CORNELL/JOHNSON (Selected)

1. **Why are you seeking an MBA from the Johnson School? What do you hope to experience and contribute here and what are your plans/goals after you receive the degree? What factors have influenced your career decisions to date?**

It was during the spring of 1993 that I saw the future and grabbed it. I was in the middle of my second year in college studying communications, working hard to do my best to graduate to a career that would be safe, stable, and a comfort to my family. Yet all that changed the moment I saw the internet. Despite the volatility of my first job at a start-up and the numerous voices telling me to find a safe career, the inspiration that I drew from working in this exciting industry, determination to succeed, and my ability to adapt to change have led me to where I am now.

I am applying to the Johnson School because my background in production and marketing has not prepared me adequately to deal with the broad strategic questions faced by executives in the internet industry. It is difficult to gain new skill sets in areas such as finance and operations in a start-up environment where one works 60 hour weeks and the focus is on rapid-fire, weekly launch schedules. Only with a business education will I be exposed to the broadest cross-section of highly trained professionals and have the opportunity to learn new skills.

My strong interest in applying to the Johnson School stems from my research findings that Cornell is in the forefront of business education. The program's strong analytical foundation was a factor in my decision to apply. The core program would be beneficial to my growth as an executive by giving me a strong base of knowledge to work from. The Johnson School's reputation as a top school for entrepreneurship was a major factor in my decision to apply. The program's dedication to modules like venture capital and valuation of businesses will help me achieve my goals.

I can make a significant contribution to the Johnson program, assisting students who are interested in working in the internet industry by sharing my knowledge and experience, gained at companies such as Wired, CNET: The Computer Network, Beyond.com, and Clip2.com.

The skills I have acquired through non-work related activities will enable me to contribute to building an academically supportive community. My experiences leading San Francisco Women on the Web (SFWoW), a 2,000-plus member professional women's organization as Point Woman (executive director) have prepared me to help build, mentoring and professional programs and professional growth workshops to enhance the experiences of my peers at the Johnson School.

After my MBA, I want to become the founder and CEO of an internet company that makes technology easy and fun for people to use.

2. **Please agree or disagree with the following quotes. Give relevant reasons and/or examples to support your answer.**

> *"Tell me to what you pay attention and I will tell you who you are."*
> —JOSE ORTEGA Y GASSET

I agree with Jose Ortega y Gasset, who said, "Tell me to what you pay attention and I will tell you who you are." What people deem important, what they pay attention to, reveals a great deal about their perception of the world and their action within it. I believe myself to be a prime example of this.

I pay a great deal of attention to technology-related issues. As a child, I was always fascinated by new technology innovations and ideas. Growing up, I was an avid consumer of new technology; I was one of the first in my school to try out new technology, from CD players to Atari. As an adult, that fascination with technology translated into a career in the high technology industry. In 1993, I saw the first Mosaic browser, which transformed the way I thought about the global economy, communications, law and culture. What started as a hobby and study in school became a full fledged love affair with the Internet and a career that has led me to where I am today.

Since childhood, I have always been concerned about women's rights. I started out as a mini-activist, fighting for girls' rights to play flag football with the boys in elementary school, then progressed to seeking out women's scholarships in high school. In college, my attention to women's rights issues deepened even further, leading me to become a founder of a new sorority on campus and to join an Asian Women's cooperative at UC San Diego. It seemed only natural after college that I would join a women's professional organization such as San Francisco Women on the Web (SF WoW), a 2,000-plus member organization. I felt it was important to join and support women's professional organizations such as SF WoW because, despite the gains that women have made in the professional world, they still have few resources to turn to for information, support, problem solving and leadership in the high tech industry. My passion for women's rights led me to become a member of the Steering Committee for the organization, allowing me to fight for women's rights in the business world. By seeing what I've always paid attention to, women's rights, most people were not surprised when I was elected Point Woman (executive director) of SFWoW in March, 2000.

Finally, after my parents' devastating bankruptcy, I became acutely aware of the plight of low-income families and their struggle to survive. My concerns were especially acute, in part because I live in the San Francisco Bay area, where high tech millionaires share the street with homeless families. It was to no one's surprise that my concerns about low-income families and homelessness led me to volunteer for Habitat for Humanity when I moved to San Francisco in 1996.

What I have paid attention to has shaped who I am today. I can't help but agree with Jose Ortega y Gasset.

"The truth is always the strongest argument."—Sophocles

I was organizing a career for San Francisco Women on the Web (SF WoW) at the same time that the organization was recruiting sponsors for its annual Top 25 Women on the Web Awards. This job fair was a highly anticipated event that recruiters in the high tech and internet industries were interested in attending because of the low cost of attendance, the high caliber of women job seekers, and the shortage of qualified employees in the industry. Due to the size of the donated venue space, as well as the intimate and casual atmosphere the organization wanted to achieve, there was a limited number of tickets available to recruiters.

One well-known company had recently approached SF WoW to become a sponsor of the Top 25 Awards. This same company was late with its RSVP to the career fair; by then, the event was closed to recruiters. The official representing the company stated that if their recruiter were unable to attend the event, the company would not donate sponsorship money for the Top 25 Awards. In order to avoid conflict, we could have lied and told the organization that their RSVP was made in time, or we could have lied to other waitlisted recruiters, allowing the organization's employers to jump to the front of the waiting list.

However, I agree with Sophocles' quote, "The truth is always the strongest argument." I believed strongly that SF WoW, as a non-profit, must not let corporations dictate its policies because it would be damaging to how the organization was run in the future, setting a precedent that could repeatedly encourage the organization to bow to corporate pressure. I made the decision that we could not alter our career fair policy. We told the company the truth, that their representative RSVPed too late to attend the event. Further, I convinced my fellow Steering Crew members and the sponsorship team to stop negotiations with the organization concerning sponsorship possibilities after receiving the thinly veiled threat made by the representative of the company. When asked by members why this company had not sent a representative to the job fair, I told SFWoW members the truth.

Though we risked damaging our relationship with this company, I spoke to the official representing the organization and stated very truthfully that we were faced with trying to run a nonprofit organization that was dependent on the good will of the business community for its survival. I spoke plainly to the fact that for the long-term health of the organization, we could not change our policies based on the demands and threats of large companies. I felt that we could risk setting a precedent as a non-profit organization whose goals and ethics could be manipulated by corporate sponsors.

Though the official was initially angered that the company would not be represented at the event and chose not to help us obtain sponsorship this year, she later recontacted us and has begun speaking to us about possible upcoming partnerships. Because we spoke truthfully to her concerning the situation, she has acquired a grudging respect for the leadership of the organization and we still have the opportunity to build a partnership with that organization in the future.

Comments

- C.L. realized that she could not risk resting her entire candidacy on a career spent bouncing among various Internet start-ups. Since the professional Internet job-hopper is common stock in the pool of applicants to top business schools, anyone with such a profile needs, like other candidates coming from common pre-MBA backgrounds, to illustrate how he or she differs from the rest. C.L. sets out some other themes on which her candidacy can rest: her devotion to women's issues; her (brave) leap into the Internet industry at its very infancy, back in 1993; her aid to her family in the face of bankruptcy.

HAROLD
STANFORD

1. What matters most to you, and why?

The Netherlands is a very small country. To drive from north to south or from east to west will generally take less than three hours. Despite its size, Holland has historically always been an important trading nation. In the sixteenth and seventeenth century, the Dutch merchant marine was second to none and even today, the harbor in Rotterdam remains the largest seaport in the world. In 1999, the Dutch were also the second largest foreign investor in the United States. In school, the Dutch are told that Holland got its status as an international trading nation because of the open-mindedness of their forefathers. In the sixteenth century, when it was quite common for governments to actively suppress other opinions, the Dutch tolerance attracted many different-thinking foreign entrepreneurs. These businessmen helped build the social atmosphere Holland is now known for. This traditional Dutch value of "open-mindedness," i.e., being open to new ideas, without prejudice, is also what matters to me most.

To understand why being open minded is so important to me, we have to look at my background. When I was eight years old I was diagnosed with dyslexia and even today I can still very vividly remember the frustration of not being able to keep up with the other children in reading and writing. Everyone else in my class was already able to read out loud, when I still had to spell every single word. Luckily my physical education teacher, who had noticed that my coordination was also underdeveloped, was aware of scientific research that suggested there was a link between physical coordination and language skills. He advised my parents to try therapy in this direction. This suggestion back then was no less controversial than it is today, and in retrospect demonstrated a tremendous amount of open-mindedness on the side of my teacher and my parents. As only an eight-year-old, I, however, did not yet have the capacity to comprehend this and I despised the exercises.

I certainly wanted to find a solution for my language problems, but I was convinced that "jumping rope" and "dribbling balls" wouldn't help me with reading or writing— a notion that made maintaining the rigorous schedule of two, 45-minutes sessions a day even harder. It was no fun to be bad in reading and writing, but it was worse to see my classmates playing outside while I was trying to complete a seemingly pointless exercise of "bounce a tennis ball off the wall and catch it for ten consecutive times" for the seventh time. Although I did the exercises every single day for more than four years, the ones that I specifically remember are those that I practiced during the first summer vacation I was in therapy. I think they stuck with me since they seemed particularly useless during a period that school was the last thing on my mind and my reading and writing hadn't noticeably improved yet.

The four years of daily exercises did, however, make a tremendous difference in the end. Slowly but steadily I climbed from the absolute bottom of my class in language skills to the top half. When I was first diagnosed with dyslexia, most of my teachers doubted I would ever be able to attend "preparatory scientific education" (the most advanced level of high school education available in the Netherlands and a prerequisite for admission to university) and many of them still were skeptical when I had to choose a high school at age twelve. On my own and without pressure from my parents, I decided that I wanted to try "preparatory scientific education." The next six years were by no means easy. The curriculum required training in six languages (including at least one year of Latin and Greek) and I was still by no means a language "star." In 1993, however, I graduated with honors, and I went on to have a very successful academic career afterwards (see transcript).

Suffering from dyslexia as a child definitely taught me to work hard, stay focused, and believe in myself. These are all values that proved to be very important in my later career, but also values that I think I would have picked up if I hadn't suffered from dyslexia. The one thing, however, that I think I would have never learned in quite the same way is the importance of an open-minded approach, and that solutions to problems every now and then come from very unsuspected directions.

My conviction that there are always other ways to solve a problem certainly enhanced my academic career in Applied Physics. However, I think that the value I had learned to put on "open-mindedness" led me to make a particularly important decision during my internship at the Innovation and Technology Center (ITC) of Philips Display Components in Eindhoven, the Netherlands. As part of the Physics curriculum, Delft University offers a "Business & Technology" specialization for students who want to pursue a management career in the high-tech industry and the work I did at the ITC was part of this specialization.

Philips Display Components is among the world's largest producers of television tubes and at a scientific conference I had attended a presentation about the technical problems associated with the commercial production of these products. In listening to the talk, I began wondering if, as the speaker suggested, the production problems were indeed related to the technical limitation of the computer software used to design the systems. No matter how sophisticated the software, the final results will after all only be as reliable as the data one starts with. I speculated that the designers initially had to make a lot of assumptions, since not much was yet known about the system, and that the production problems were partially related to an unawareness of how many "guesses" the designers had made. I asked the lecturer for his information and approached him a few weeks later with a proposal. I suggested to investigate if the number of design assumptions could be gradually reduced, and if it was perhaps possible to close in on the production specifications little by little (the open-minded thinker in me tried to find an alternative approach once again).

I worked at the ITC for five months and it was an experience I will never forget. I got the opportunity to meet with numerous people throughout the entire organization, from the person operating the machine on the factory floor to the manager of the entire business unit. The people were very helpful and more than 50 of them attended the defense of my graduation thesis in front of the university's graduation committee. I later learned that a number of my most important recommendations were implemented as part of an ISO 9000-related reorganization. The most important thing I came to realize during this period was that large organizations, like Philips Display Components, have a distinct disadvantage in profiting from new ideas.

Almost all of the people I had spoken with told me about the inertia that had to be overcome to change things, and how many people had to be involved in this process. It became clear to me that although the people were clearly open to new ideas, large organizations are simply less able to take advantage of different approaches due to their shear size. This realization made me wonder if a large technical organization was really as likely an employer for me as I had always assumed.

In my mind, I made a comparison to sailing, my favorite hobby. I had navigated everything from single person dinghies, to 90-foot clippers with two masts, and I had enjoyed sailing all of them. I understood, however, the aspects that made sailing the dinghy fun were completely different from those that made sailing the clippers fun. The 90-foot ships were fun since it was an incredible experience to stand on the helm of 120 tons of wood and steel and carefully anticipate what was coming up, while the dinghies were fun because of the possibility to take advantage of every shift in wind and every change in water current. Neither boat (or technique) was better in my mind than the other one. They were just distinctly different. On the clippers, it was important to not forget the effects the shifts in wind and current would eventually have on the ship since it was by no means immune to these forces, but emphasis of the experience was on planning far ahead. A ship this big could, after all, not react that quickly. Similarly in the dinghies, it was important to plan ahead, since weather conditions could severely affect the outcome, but the emphasis of that experience was on taking advantage of the small changes in the conditions. I felt that it was the same way in business. Both large and small companies were interesting and fun to work for, but I had come to realize that the emphasis in a large company did not lie with taking advantage of many new ideas and approaches.

At the same time, I had also come to realize that my urge to work in an "open-minded" environment, an environment where the pursuit of new ideas was not merely encouraged, but a part of the way business was done, was so strong that it was worth leaving my country and moving away from friends and family for. I talked to numerous small companies in all parts of the world and eventually found what I was looking for at ScienceTech Inc. in Pleasanton, California. ScienceTech Inc. was interested in the work I had done for my "Electron Optics" specialization and encouraged me to pursue my ideas for a product at their company. The company was furthermore located close to Silicon Valley and California had an excellent entrepreneurial climate. San Francisco, with its reputation for tolerance and "open mindedness" was less than 45 minutes away. I bought a one-way ticket to Oakland (it was cheaper than San Francisco), packed two suitcases and moved.

ScienceTech Inc., with its employees from more than 15 different countries, turned out to be every bit as open-minded as I had hoped for. It was a very different company than I was used to. ScienceTech is active in the scientific instrumentation business and I quickly found out that this sector has its own dynamics and is still primarily controlled by scientists and academics. In this field, a scientific paper in an influential journal, or a presentation by a leading scientist, can mean the difference between failure and success of a product. This was also a sector where companies were willing to make large investments based upon a single two-hour demo. I learned that for someone with an open-minded approach who was willing to combine scientific and business methods, there were many unexplored opportunities in this industry. An excellent example is a project that one of the four people who report to me led. In this project, we were able to generate over $1 million in sales before even starting the development of the product. We combined the traditional marketing approach used in the scientific instrumentation sector (scientific presentations, publishing results from experiments), with the concept of "product positioning." Although the concept of product positioning is well known and widely used elsewhere, this is a concept that is not often used in the scientific instrumentation business.

I really enjoyed the stimulating environment at ScienceTech and I constantly felt that people were interested in finding ways to help realize my ideas. By being open to new ideas and other methods, I was often able to be a better colleague and a more effective manager. For example, an Asian scientist I was working with once explained to me that in his culture it was common to discuss a problem by first heavily simplifying it, and then slowly making it more and more difficult. By adapting to his approach, I was able to achieve more with him in a day than weeks of my own traditional tactics would have yielded. By not judging anyone on his appearance, background, or education, I was able to pick up important skills from the most unlikely people. I learned from my Cameroonian roommate how to do business with a French University, and from a Chinese refugee with no formal education how to negotiate my salary in the United States. My languages training also helped in this respect. By being able to say a few words in the native language of colleagues, or by understanding an expression he or she was unable to translate in to English, I was often able to "break the ice" and get different ideas on the table.

I think that my "open mindedness" to a very large extent also has contributed to my team-building skills. My work certainly required me to form very diverse teams. A lot of the products ScienceTech designs are so complicated that it is often necessary to consult extensively with experts in different countries. For instance, a team I recently assembled to resolve a problem for a customer in Japan consisted of a professor from Austria, a consultant from Germany (living in the French Caribbean Island of Guadeloupe), an engineer from Slovakia (living in Japan) and an American machinist (who worked in our production facility more than 3,000 miles from my office). With its members so far apart and all in different time zones, this might not appear to be a very effective team at first sight. The approach I took, however, was to look for a positive side to everyone's different geographical location. The different working hours of all my team members meant that I was able to discuss the adjustments to the instrument with the machinist who made the parts during the day, have the Slovakian engineer collect new data in the evening, have the data analyzed by the expert in Austria during the night, and discuss the results of the analysis the next morning with the consultant in Guadeloupe who helped design the system. Working in this fashion, we were able to resolve the problem in only two weeks instead of the two months it would have taken us if I had followed a more conventional approach.

Although I usually try to live up to my conviction to be "open minded" in the fashion I described, it also has to be said that every now and then, this is not as easy or "automatic" as I would like it to be. Especially now, for I have four people reporting to me and it is sometimes difficult to have patience enough to see someone try an approach I do not fully believe in, or acknowledge that there might be a better way than the method I am used to. Reminding myself of how far I have come by being open minded, since I learned the importance of "not dismissing an idea because it seems unconventional" as a teenager, usually helps me come to terms with these situations.

I have been in California now for more than five years and since September 2000, I even have a US greencard (which I received based on my work for ScienceTech and after the recommendation by eight prominent scientists and business leaders under the so-called "Aliens with Extraordinary Abilities" provision of the US immigration regulations). I furthermore managed to build up a new life, with many new friends (in additional to my old friends, who I luckily managed to keep as well) and I met a nice German girl who I now share a life together with in San Francisco. Miriam is a doctor at the University of California in San Francisco and last year started her specialization to become a radiologist. She is probably that what matters to me second most.

2. **Why do you wish to earn an MBA degree, particularly at the Stanford Business School? How will this experience help you achieve your short-term and long-term goals?**

In 1989, I decided to study Applied Physics because I felt it would provide me with thorough scientific training and a broad enough perspective to get started in the high tech business. Now, eleven years later, I want to go to Stanford Business School because I believe it will offer me the general management training I need to further advance the career I started after I graduated from Delft University in the Netherlands.

Given that Applied Physics is widely regarded as one of the most challenging programs at Delft University of Technology, choosing Physics might not have appeared to be the shortest route to a career in industry. I, however, felt that Delft was an ideal fit, because it offered a "Business & Technology" specialization, which would not only satisfy my love for science, but also address my interests in business. Five-and-a-half years later, and approximately one year quicker than the average student, I graduated with not only the "Business & Technology" specialization I had envisioned from the start, but also with an "Electron Optics" specialization (only one single specialization is required, see transcript). While in Delft, I had become interested in a technology which uses electrons instead of light to form very high magnification images of materials. I did extensive research on these "electron microscopes" and it was this second specialization that brought me to the United States.

I started at ScienceTech Inc., a $32 million scientific instrumentation company, as a Project Manager. With a small team, I developed a product based on my university research that is still one of the cornerstones of ScienceTech's Analytical Product line. With a list price of more than $350,000, and currently over $8 million in annual revenues, the product quickly caught the attention of Senior Management and within two years I was promoted to Program Manager responsible for all Analytical Product development.

I really enjoyed this new position. It was exactly the job I had envisioned when I decided to study Applied Physics. The technology was very interesting and I considered the management aspects to be a real challenge. One of the accomplishments during this period that I am most proud of is that I inspired a change in the corporate culture of my company. When I came to ScienceTech, there was not much enthusiasm for working in teams and feedback had originally ranged from "I am too busy to go to meetings" to "my project is too complicated to explain to everyone." I, however, felt that it would not be possible to develop the products I envisioned without being able to draw upon the experience of my colleagues in different disciplines. The familiarity of ScienceTech's team with the scientific instrumentation business had, after all, been one of my reasons in coming to California. I also felt that many of the project delays were actually caused by a lack of teamwork.

I set up a widespread program to change this attitude, a project that allowed me to both demonstrate my leadership skills and enhance them further. I structured ScienceTech's informal development process and established clear goals for each phase to improve cross-functional communication. I systematically started collecting input from sales, marketing, manufacturing, and others. I organized team meetings and gave presentations. I tracked progress and provided feedback on how we were doing against schedules. I introduced "post-mortem" meetings after projects to analyze what we could do to improve further, and took many other initiatives that nobody had taken before.

Slowly but steadily all these measures help to change the attitude and the formation of multifunctional project teams is currently the standard rather than the exception at ScienceTech. Although the full advantages of this approach will only be known in a few years from now, the benefits to the Analytical Product line are already clear. Sales of every single product that was designed by a team in this fashion exceeded its target by at least 20% (and in some cases 100%), and none of the projects have been late.

Last year, I was promoted to Program Director and became responsible for the entire Analytical Product line. In this new position I was able to get an even broader perspective of our business, working on formulating strategic development goals and a repositioning of our products. ScienceTech's historic focus on the academic world had left the larger high tech industrial market largely unexplored. By working together with the VP of Sales and the VP of Marketing, I was able to compile a long-term development plan and started guiding our research in this new direction. This decision was initially questioned but, while we have by no means completed the process and some of the skepticism still exists, we are already starting to see the benefits. Sales forecasts are currently up more than 40% compared to when I became responsible for the product line.

It is clear that my career has progressed very well over the last five years, even though my approach was sometimes unconventional. Over the last year I have, however, also come to realize that if I want to keep growing my product line, I will need to acquire additional general and strategic management skills. The "Business & Technology" training I received in Delft combined with my "Electron Optics" specialization gave my career a great start, but over the last five years the playing field has steadily been raised and I have now reached a level where my current business training is no longer sufficient.

Proper strategic management is essential to grow the business, especially in small companies. Money and resources are usually very scarce while ideas are plentiful. Without very careful consideration on how to run the business, which products to develop, and how to position the products, it is very easy to over stretch these growing organizations. Because companies like ScienceTech rely so much on revenues of current products in order to expand their business, over stretching the organization will quickly halt growth and prevent the company from reaching its full potential. Due to ScienceTech's size (only 140 people) and nature (a large percentage of employees with scientific backgrounds), it is difficult to acquire the experience I need on the job. The lack of managers with a formal training in general and strategic management is felt so strongly that ScienceTech's Senior Management team recently offered to contribute to my MBA tuition.

Although ScienceTech did not ask me to make a commitment towards returning after my MBA, and although I realize that there will be a wealth of other opportunities after completing a top MBA program, I consider returning to my former employer as part of the Senior Management team an attractive option. In the longer term, I would like to focus my career on the management of smaller high tech companies and help them position their businesses and products for optimal growth. I envision myself initially in the position of R&D director or vice-president (depending on the size of the company) and later in the position as CEO or maybe even owner of my own high tech company.

Given my high tech career focus, Stanford is, of course, an ideal fit with its proximity to Silicon Valley and its emphasis on the technology sector. Courses like "Marketing High Technology" and initiatives like those of the "High Tech" club are directly relevant to my career goals. My preference for Stanford, however, goes far beyond just these aspects. Especially small scientific instrumentation companies have many entrepreneurial aspects to them in the sense that once their instrumentation becomes accepted in the scientific world, there is an enormous potential for marketing the same technology to the much larger industrial market. Stanford's Center for Entrepreneurial Studies is therefore of particular interest to me, and initiatives like the "Stanford Project on Emerging Companies," that documents various business aspects of Bay-area startups, immediately attracted my attention. After a careful evaluation of all top business schools, I have come to the conclusion that Stanford has the strongest and most relevant entrepreneurial program. Another important aspect in my preference for Stanford is the quality and diversity of the student body. Not only do I believe that the feedback from fellow students will add depth to discussions, but I also think that the quality of the class will in many respects set the standards for the professors to teach up to.

Unique Stanford aspects, like the ability to shape the program by designing my own research project during the second year and the ability to select the courses that fit me without having to declare a specialization, add to the business school experience. Part of my objective for pursuing an MBA, after all, is to broaden my perspective and to become familiar with business practices from outside my own industry. I am convinced that there are many more common business techniques, next to product positioning, that can be used in the scientific instrumentation sector.

The most important reason for choosing Stanford, however, is my belief that many of the products in the high tech sector are getting so complicated, that it is impossible for one person to be an expert on all parts of these systems. These products can only be designed, built, and sold by teams of the best and the brightest people working together. I think that schools that ignore this reality will fail to educate managers that can be leaders in the high tech field. It is the cooperative team aspect of the program that sets Stanford apart.

MIT/SLOAN

1. **Prepare a one- to two-page cover letter seeking a place in the Sloan School of Management MBA Program. It should point out the features of your résumé**

that you believe to be of interest to the Admissions Committee, both in your education and in your work history. Further, please comment on your career goals and those factors which influenced you to pursue an MBA education at Sloan. Additionally, discuss which management track appeals to you and how it fits your professional aspirations. We are also interested in what you believe you can contribute to the Sloan School and your fellow students, and we encourage you to describe your most substantial accomplishment.

In response to your request, I am writing to inform you about my objectives and qualifications for admission to the Sloan MBA program, and to provide you with my résumé.

I would like to draw your attention to the educational and professional sections of my curriculum vitae. I believe that my extensive scientific training at Delft University in the Netherlands, one of Europe's finest academic institutions, provides me with the analytical background that is required for the quantitative aspects of the Sloan program. My graduation among the very top of my class, and my decision to pursue both an "Electron Optics" and a "Business & Technology" specialization, while only a single specialization was required, demonstrate that I will be able to handle the notoriously heavy workload of Sloan's first semester. As an Applied Physicist, I am furthermore used to relating abstract principles to real-world problems, a skill that will be useful at the MIT Sloan School of Management.

In 1995, I moved to the United States and joined ScienceTech Inc., the world's leading manufacturer of scientific instrumentation for Transmission Electron Microscopes. After several promotions, I eventually became responsible for the company's entire line of Analytical Products which comprises over 40% of the company's $32 million business. One of my professional accomplishments I am most proud of is my ability to build strong and effective teams. I personally introduced cross-functional teams to ScienceTech and ensured their effectiveness by organizing weekly team meetings, by formalizing the development process in ScienceTech's first project manual, and by many other initiatives. My cross-functional team approach has not only resulted in a $3.5 million sales increase in my own products, but is also credited for a 15% sales increase in the product lines that copied my style. My team building skills will be an important contribution I can make to my class at MIT.

Next to broad professional experience, my extensive career in the scientific instrumentation field has also given me unique insight to an industry that has its own dynamics. In this field, a scientific paper in an influential journal, or a presentation by a leading scientist, can mean the difference between failure and success of a product. This is also a sector where companies are willing to make large investments based upon a single two-hour demo. My in depth knowledge of this special industry will help to diversify discussions and perspectives at Sloan.

For someone willing to combine scientific and business methods, there are furthermore many unexplored opportunities in the instrumentation trade. An excellent example is a project that one of the four people who report to me is leading. We combined the traditional marketing approaches used in my sector (publishing results from experiments, etc.), with the concept of "product positioning," and generated over $ 1 million in sales. Although the concept of product positioning is widely used elsewhere, it is not often used in the scientific instrumentation business. Opportunities like this will be interesting to other students of the Sloan School of Management.

Although I have increased the sales forecast for the Analytical Product line by almost 45%, my current position as Program Director has helped me realize that I need additional financial, marketing, and strategic management skills to further grow my product group. Especially for small companies, proper strategic management is essential to grow the business. Money and resources are usually very scarce while ideas are plentiful. Without very careful consideration on how to run the business and how to position the products, it is very easy to overstretch these growing organizations. ScienceTech's small size (only 140 employees) and its nature (large percentage of employees with scientific backgrounds) make it difficult to acquire the management skills I need, on the job. This has motivated me to pursue more formal business training.

In investigating my options, I found that MIT's program was the best fit for my background and objectives. Sloan's "New Product and Venture Development" track offers exactly what I am looking for. I very much share the track's vision that the skills required of Executive Managers in the high-tech sector are similar to the skills needed by entrepreneurs. NPVD courses like "Management of Technological Innovation," and "Marketing Strategy" will introduce me to many of the state-of-the-art design and marketing methodologies pioneered by MIT faculty, and will help me understand the "bigger picture." Courses like "Planning and Managing Change" will further advance my leadership skills, and help me reach my goals in the always-changing high-tech field.

ScienceTech will partially sponsor my MBA and returning to them as part of the Senior Management team is an attractive option (although not required). In the longer term, a degree from MIT Sloan's School of Management will help me pursue my dream to become CEO or owner of my own high-tech company.

2. **The goal of the Sloan MBA Program is to prepare graduates to be effective and innovative leaders in the global economy. As technology, innovation, globalization, and entrepreneurial opportunity become more important, managers need to understand how to develop new management models and methods and to make them work. Explain how the MIT Sloan MBA Program's focus on innovation will help you achieve your career goals.**

Innovation and technology have played important roles throughout my career. I decided to study Physics because I felt it would provide me with thorough technical training, and a broad enough perspective to remain relevant in the high-tech industry. Delft University in the Netherlands was a particularly good fit because it offered a "Business & Technology" specialization which would not only satisfy my love for science, but also address my interests in business. In 1995 and approximately one year earlier than the average student, I graduated with not only this Business & Technology specialization, but also with one in "Electron Optics."

Based on my electron optics research, I developed a new product at ScienceTech that is still one of the company's cornerstones. With over $8 million in annual revenues, management quickly noted it and within two years, I was promoted to Program Manager, responsible for all Analytical Product development. I really enjoyed this new function. The technology was very interesting, and the position allowed me to introduce innovation in our business practices, too. For instance, when I came to ScienceTech there was not much enthusiasm for working in teams. I, however, felt that it would not be possible to develop the products I envisioned without the help of my colleagues. I also felt that the lack of teamwork was causing project delays. By systematically putting people from different disciplines (sales, marketing, manufacturing, etc.) together, I was able to change people's teamwork attitude. The benefits of these teams and my other creative improvements in our business practices (like using customers to help with product development) are clear; we designed more than ten brand new products, and sales of each of these products exceeded its target, sometimes by more than 100%. None of my projects has furthermore been late.

Last year, I was promoted to Program Director and became responsible for the entire Analytical Product line. In this new position, I was able to get an even broader perspective of our business by working on repositioning my products.

Especially these last two positions have made clear to me that disciplines in the high-tech sector are quickly merging, and that managers will be required to further innovate business practices as a result. In my current position, I not only need to be familiar with the high-tech aspects of my company's products, but I also need to be comfortable with issues involving accounting, operations, and marketing. My last project had a $950,000 development budget, and required extensive cost accounting. Currently I am working on the installation of an assembly line for this new instrument, which requires significant insight in operations management, while my work on the brochures for the same instrument requires a good grasp of marketing. In the future, work will certainly become even less rigidly constrained to functions like R&D, accounting, operations, or marketing. Tomorrow's high-tech leaders will therefore need to be able to develop new management methods to make these flatter organizations work. It is exactly this realization that convinced me to pursue business school and attracted me to MIT.

Globalization has also had a profound effect on my sector. The incredible complexity of the newest high-tech products and the ultra-fast development cycles force companies to look for experts on a global level. A recent team I assembled consisted of a professor from Austria, a consultant from Germany (living in Guadeloupe), an engineer from Slovakia (living in Japan), and an American machinist (working in Pennsylvania). By making use of the time difference between the locations of the members, this team allowed us to work around-the-clock and the diverse skills of the team members gave us the competitive advantage we needed. The advancing communication methods (internet, video-conferencing, etc.) will make this type of international team standard practice. Executive Managers that want to grow their businesses will therefore need to find ways to make these new global structures function. Sloan's focus on innovation will give me the skills to accomplish this.

The entrepreneurial emphasis of the Sloan program in combination with the program's inventive focus is a particularly good fit for my industry. Many of the markets and business methods in my sector are new and unexplored. Leaders in my field need to be generalists who are able to recognize new opportunities, and quickly move between business areas. As I pursue my goal of becoming CEO of a high-tech company, I need to be able to find solutions to an extremely wide variety of issues. Familiarity with established management practices and case studies alone is not sufficient to deal with the unique nature of the problems of innovative companies like ScienceTech. The MIT Sloan MBA program's focus on entrepreneurship and innovation will allow me to develop new management solutions to meet the challenges that come with exploring uncharted territory.

3. **Describe a situation where you introduced and/or managed change in an organization. Tell us how you influenced others in an organization (business, school, extracurricular activity) and comment on the professional and/or personal attributes you used to do that and how these attributes (and others) might be important to the attainment of your career goals. How do you expect the Sloan School to further the development of these attributes?**

After I was promoted to Program Director, I made an analysis of ScienceTech's markets and development plans. The academic market had always been our most important market, but on occasion we also sold to industrial customers. Semiconductor manufacturers, for instance, had analyzed components in their chips with our detectors. This market was relatively small, since our specimen preparation requirements were very time consuming. Although the resolution of our electron-based detectors is much better than the resolution of conventional light-based detectors, the advantage was not important enough to justify the extra time.

Two recent developments in the semi-conductor sector are changing this situation. A new manufacturing technology using ultraviolet light is shrinking components to dimensions beyond the resolution of the detectors currently employed. At the same time, Focused Ion Beam (FIB) technology is reducing the time to prepare samples for our analysis technique. The impact of FIBs has come as a surprise. These instruments—originally designed for modifying semi-conductor devices—can often reduce our specimen preparation time from several hours to less than 30 minutes.

When I came to realize the incredible impact the combination of FIBs and ultraviolet-light-based production technologies could have on my company, I gradually found myself in charge of managing "change" more than technology.

ScienceTech had not anticipated these developments, and our entire sales, marketing, and development strategy had to be modified to take advantage of this tremendous opportunity. My decision to change the focus of my product line—and 40% of ScienceTech's business—so drastically was initially questioned. I used a combination of my most important personal and professional qualities to convince my colleagues about the validity of my plans, and to persuade them to support my efforts.

My network of contacts, and my familiarity with a wide variety of national and international customers, proved to be one of my most important assets in managing this change. My knowledge about the production practices at companies like Intel helps strengthen my presentations, and my personal relationship with developers at advanced research labs like Lucent Technologies helps me to collect information about the technologies ahead.

Another quality that was important in bringing about our change in market-focus was my personal background. The Dutch are well known for their open mindedness and pragmatism. I adapted these values at a young age. An unconventional physical therapy approach helped me overcome childhood dyslexia, teaching me the importance of being open to different ideas, while my family's down-to-earth attitude taught me to be practical. By being open to diverse methods, I am often a more effective leader and better able to facilitate change. For example, an Asian scientist we were working with explained to me that in his culture it was common to discuss a problem by first heavily simplifying it, and then slowly making it more difficult. By encouraging my team to adapt to his approach, I was able to help ScienceTech develop an improved method for measuring gate-oxides (a critical chip parameter), in only a few days. By not judging anyone on his appearance, background, or education, I am able to pick up ideas from the most unlikely people. A German service engineer—who never finished his university degree—first told me about FIBs, and helped me set off ScienceTech's change in market focus. My pragmatism allows me to look beyond complicated models and dense data, and helps me to get the attention of our industrial customers.

The third way in which I was able to influence my colleagues is by my ability to work together with people from many different backgrounds and by being a strong team player. My strong communication skills, first shaped by teaching sailing as a 15-year-old to adults, are extremely important in coordinating any team efforts.

Although we by no means have completed the process of redirecting our efforts to the industrial market—and some skepticism still exists—ScienceTech is already starting to see the benefits. Sales forecasts for next year are up by almost 25%. I am confident that the same attributes that helped me effect these changes will also be important in reaching my future goals. Experience with a wide variety of public and private sector organizations, plus characteristics like open-mindedness, team skills and pragmatism are important for any leader. The MIT MBA program will help me develop these attributes by further broadening my perspectives through the interactions with the international and diverse student-body Sloan is so famous for. My open-mindedness in combination with the innovative character of the program, the faculty members who bring the research to their classrooms, and the extraordinarily flexible curriculum will help me develop new ideas and methods. Sloan's recently enhanced training in "leadership," and the outside-the-classroom initiatives like the Sloan Leadership Forum will prepare me for the role of Executive Manager. The program's quantitative strengths united with my pragmatism will go together as embodied in MIT's "mind and hand" motto.

Comments

- Here are two winning sets of essays, complete with distinctive themes, compelling stories, and much evidence to show that Harold is a special breed.

- The first Stanford essay presents a key organizational difficulty to candidates: what theme will provide coherence while allowing an applicant to show multiple facets of his candidacy. Here, Harold manages to highlight nearly every single one of the important aspects of his candidacy—his Dutch nationality, his strong scientific education and training, his commitment to teamwork, his love of international settings, his fight to overcome an early diagnosis of dyslexia, even his passion for sailing—under the umbrella of a single "open-mindedness" theme. He further pushes the idea of his open-mindedness and use of unconventional approaches in his second essay, making his candidacy even more memorable. By establishing the nature of his career to date, he paved the way for a sophisticated discussion of his desire to attend the program and his future goals.

- In his MIT application, Harold again sets himself apart by highlighting unique experiences. For example, he describes the distinctiveness of the scientific instrumentation industry, his technical expertise in the field of electron optics, his success at fostering a cooperative workplace environment, his Dutch upbringing, and the exceptional international quality of the teams he has assembled.

IEHAB
HARVARD

1. **Choose a recent experience in which you acted as a leader. Briefly outline the situation, then describe your leadership role, how you were effective and what you learned.**

   Acacia, our largest real estate client in the Phoenix office, was an audit job consisting of eight separate audits. In the prior year, our audit team came in significantly over budget and failed to complete the job by the required deadline, which delayed the client's investors from filing their tax returns on time. The client was very upset and threatened to change auditors if things didn't improve the following year. It was in this context that I took over as project manager for Acacia, managing a staff of four people. I had two objectives—to complete the audits on time and under budget. To facilitate both of these objectives, I rescheduled most of the work from the first three calendar months of the year, when everyone is busiest, to August, when people have more available time, are not as rushed, and are also billed out at a lower rate. I also used the worksheets from the prior year's audits as templates for the client, so they understood exactly what information they needed to provide to our audit team, thus making it easier for them to cooperate with us. In addition, we agreed to maintain constant communication with the client, which kept them apprised of our job status and helped to ensure their prompt assistance in order to complete the audits as quickly as possible. As a result, we finished up all of the audits with several weeks to spare, while at the same time converting our largest real estate client from an unprofitable project with a negative, double-digit profit margin to one with a significant profit margin (nearly 30%). In the process, I realized that our objectives could more easily be attained through mutual cooperation, timely communication and proper planning on both sides.

2. **Identify someone you regard as a hero, a leader or role model whom you admire. Describe how this person has influenced your development.**

I admire Michael Jordan's ostensible qualities, primarily in the game of basketball, which has inspired me to use his attitude toward the game in my approach towards life. First, he always developed new skills to stay at the top of his game. Similarly, I am constantly learning new aspects of business that enhance my skill base, such as accounting, finance, management and business development. Second, he was multi-dimensional, playing defense and offense well. For my part, I am analytical, sociable and active, getting involved in various activities while staying on top of my studies or getting my job done.

As a leader, Michael Jordan pushed his teammates to be better, but was always able to carry them if necessary. I always made sure that my team's objectives are achieved, whether it is forming a rock climbing club or getting audit jobs completed by the required deadlines. Jordan also does a lot of public service. I heard numerous stories of how he encouraged personal development and spent time with the less fortunate. In school, I developed a program to prepare business students for the workforce. While working in the US, I built houses as a Habitat for Humanity volunteer, and taught LSAT students for Kaplan. In Egypt, I participated in a human resource development program similar to the one I established in school.

Finally, Jordan loved his job. His passion for the game was reflected in his determination and performance. That same type of enthusiasm carries me through any opportunity I encounter, whether it is trying to open a restaurant, going into public accounting, or re-establishing my roots in Egypt. These are the traits that I admire and have applied in my own life to enhance my personal and professional development.

3. **We all experience "defining moments," significant events that can have major impact on our lives. Briefly describe such an event and how it affected you.**

My parents came to the US from Egypt in 1970. Twenty-seven years later, while I was employed with Ernst and Young, I went to visit my father in New Mexico for Thanksgiving. When my father called his sister in Egypt, I tried to speak with her and her children, but found I could barely say anything but hello to them. Frustrated about the possibility of never really knowing my family, I decided that I needed to go to Egypt and re-establish my family connection, learn about my heritage, and acquire my parents' native tongue. Subsequently, I found a position working for Al Ahram Beverages Company (ABC) and came to Egypt.

While in Egypt, I have developed my knowledge of the Arabic language so that I can now communicate easily with my aunts, uncles, and cousins. During this time, I have witnessed some of my relatives graduate from high school and college, and others get engaged, married and even have children. I have observed how these significant events are traditionally commemorated in Egypt, whether it was a sabooah, a ritual my cousin celebrated for his son's first birthday a week after he was born, or a fattha, a customary ceremony held for another relative's engagement. Having been a part of these and other special occasions, I am encouraged by how people here in Egypt enjoy life despite all the difficulties and shortcomings associated with being in a third-world country.

Most importantly, I am now more aware of the significance of family in my life. I have become extremely close with my family here in Egypt, while developing an increased understanding of their language and culture, which has also allowed me to be closer to my parents in the US.

4. **Describe your three most substantial accomplishments and explain why you view them as such.**

As an avid rock climber in college, I realized that if I formed a University-sponsored club, it would provide me and my fellow climbers with the visibility to attract potential members, while also obtaining University funds to subsidize our climbing trips. Intrigued by this idea, I drafted a charter and provided all the required information to the University's recreation department, and in 1995, the University of Arizona Rock Climbers (ARC) was founded. I served as the club's first president, organizing climbing trips and contracting with Rocks 'N Ropes, an Indoor climbing facility, to sponsor our club as well as provide a meeting and training place for our members. Through word of mouth and advertising in the University paper, our membership increased to nearly 20 members in the first year.

My second substantial accomplishment was jumpstarting ABC's joint venture with Unilever to produce and distribute Lipton Ice Tea in Egypt, which had come to a standstill as both sides were in disagreement as to the structure of the arrangement.

Although both parties had agreed to an equitable partnership, Unilever's proposed business model served only to ensure Unilever would earn handsome profits on its product concentrate, while ABC would barely cover its marginal costs for providing the venture's manufacturing and distribution services, resulting in a 2 to 1 profit split in Unilever's favor. In addition, Unilever wanted ownership control, which would allow them to consolidate the joint venture's activity.

However, ABC also wanted to recognize the JV's revenues for financial statement purposes on a consolidated basis. With disagreement over these and other issues, both parties threatened to terminate negotiations.

Shortly after joining ABC, I developed a proposal for the JV incenting both sides to participate in the venture, while at the same time ensuring that the deal itself was equitable to both parties.

To resolve the issue of consolidation, I proposed that the JV sell the product to ABC's distribution company, who would then resell the product at a price that included a markup equal to the distribution fee. That way, Unilever could consolidate the JV's sales, yet both entities would be able to recognize substantial revenues from the partnership.

To address the equitable distribution of profits, I suggested two alternatives. The first was to increase ABC's aggregate service fee markup to equal the corresponding markup of Unilever's fees on its concentrate. The second alternative was to substitute ABC's equity stake in the venture with a preferred return calculated on any excess profits earned by the venture.

After submitting this proposal to Unilever, the process moved rapidly, and we were able to come to an agreement on both issues. As a result, we consummated our joint venture with Unilever, only the third such business arrangement formed with Unilever worldwide. And no less important, we were able to obtain an additional $1.5 million and $34 million over five years in projected ABC net profit and revenues, respectively, above what Unilever originally proposed. Thus, I was able to come in and make an immediate impact working for ABC.

My third accomplishment was also in business development. As project manager, I was instrumental in the $75 million acquisition of Gouna Beverages, ABC's only local alcoholic beverage competitor. I was responsible for execution of the deal while leading the financial, legal and technical due diligence teams. In addition, I drafted the bid proposal, made revisions to the business plan, and developed financial projections for the resulting acquisition, which consolidated our position as Egypt's monopoly producer of alcoholic beverages and gave us control over the remaining fifteen and forty percent market shares of beer and wine, respectively.

5. How would a Harvard Business School education help you to reach your professional goals?

Based on my experiences working in business development for ABC in Egypt, I am becoming increasingly familiar with the Egyptian marketplace just as it is shifting from a bureaucratic, public sector environment into a free market economy. In the near future, Egypt will require more people with sophisticated business acumen to effectively aid in the country's development, as there is currently a severe gap between the supply and demand of such talent. My immediate goal is to return here and join ABC's executive management team as a senior business development manager and aid in capitalizing on its numerous growth opportunities both locally and within the Middle East and North African region. In the longer term, my goal is to lead ABC or one of many other public sector companies into a productive, private enterprise as Egypt slowly becomes part of the global economy over the next decade.

Now that I have had meaningful and substantial real world experiences, I know what I need to learn and what areas I need to strengthen. I have developed a solid foundation in accounting, finance, management and business development, and I am now seeking more exposure to the general management core foundation and an understanding of the latest management methods, along with an emphasis in corporate strategy, areas where Harvard is revered. Harvard's incredible resources also cannot be overlooked, whether it is the Baker Library or Harvard's worldwide alumni network. Moreover, as a person who has lived abroad and worked on complex issues, I am excited by Harvard's global initiative to continually develop its international perspective for managing in a global economy, in addition to its emphasis on business simulation, leadership, values and decision-making within the context of the HBS learning model.

6. **Is there any other information that you believe would be helpful to the Admissions Board in understanding you better? Please be concise.**

ENTREPRENEURSHIP AND THE PHAT CAT

I have always wanted to operate my own business. This entrepreneurial spirit led me to pursue a degree in entrepreneurship and attempt to open a restaurant. While enrolled in the entrepreneurship program at the University of Arizona, I developed a business and marketing plan for a college sports theme restaurant called the Phat Cat, which meshed well with our sports teams, known as the "Wildcats." To aid in my research, I even took a job at Applebee's restaurant, which had the casual dining type atmosphere I was looking to replicate while incorporating a sporting theme in a location close to the University.

Although most of the projects in the program were mainly hypothetical in order to understand the types of issues that entrepreneurs face, I was intent on carrying my project to fruition. Outside of developing the business plan and modeling the financial analysis, I negotiated with potential suppliers, looked at various locations, met with architects, contractors, realtors, attorneys, and city officials to obtain necessary building and safety permits. I even recruited a manager from Applebee's, who worked with me to obtain a loan from the Small Business Administration. I also arranged for licensing of University sporting materials, and secured a location across the street from the University that had previously been a generic sports bar.

In the end though, the equity financing I was seeking from a private investor fell through at the last minute, as the investor began having second thoughts and refused to put forth the funds until we had tied up all the remaining loose ends. Without these funds I was unable to secure the small business loan, and subsequently could not commit to a lease or the anticipated expenditures necessary to start the business.

I was initially disappointed—first, for not realizing my goal, and second for devoting all that time to a project which never materialized. However, I later realized I needed more real-life business exposure to develop the knowledge and gain the experience necessary to make my own venture successful, as well as develop the contacts to obtain the necessary funds for the project to materialize.

FIVE YEARS IN COLLEGE

The reason I spent five years in college is that I initially majored in engineering before switching to business, and took on a double major in finance and entrepreneurship. In addition, I was involved in a number of extracurricular activities, while also working during the school year to finance my school and living expenses. Despite these pursuits, I managed to maintain my GPA above 3.5 throughout my college career, which allowed me to keep my four-year Arizona Regents' tuition scholarship and also resulted in numerous accolades, including six semesters on the Dean's List, induction into the Beta Gamma Sigma Honor Society, and even an Entrepreneur Minority Scholarship. However, I did not take summer courses, as the tuition scholarship that I earned did not cover summer school. Instead, I worked during the summers in order to earn additional money for college.

PURSUIT OF A CPA

Before I graduated in May 1996, the companies with positions for which I was applying, such as banking, were telling me that I needed more of an accounting background. Consequently after graduation, I began preparing for the certified public accountant (CPA) exam scheduled for the following November, while still employed at Applebee's restaurant. I interviewed with several companies on campus in the fall of 1996, and after taking the exam in November, I accepted a position with Shell Oil Company starting in January 1997. In February 1997, I was notified that I had passed the November exam, despite the fact that I had not majored in accounting. Six months later, I went into public accounting as an auditor for Ernst and Young, where I eventually obtained my CPA certification.

Comments

- Iehab shows in this set of essays that despite his solid training as an accountant, he also possesses a creative and entrepreneurial spirit. He thereby becomes an ideal candidate for business schools, who are attracted to students with a firm foundation in business fundamentals yet who also show some more flair than the typical "gray suit."

- Iehab's second essay on Michael Jordan is particularly well done because it continuously makes a connection between the basketball player's qualities and the candidate's own, without sounding like a silly, adolescent hero-worshiper.

- The third essay presents a compelling story that also illustrates how and why the candidate's career path took the direction it did. In addition, the essay shows that Iehab is the type of person who pays attention to issues of character and is earnest about working on his weaknesses.

- Overall, Iehab wisely chooses to use a breadth of topics—from successes at Ernst and Young and ABC, to his move to Egypt, to his rock climbing experiences—to demonstrate the full measure of his candidacy.

TERRY

ROTTERDAM SCHOOL OF MANAGEMENT

1. **What are your career objectives? In what specific ways would attendance at the RSM help you to fulfill these intentions? (Explain how your study plan fits in with your previous training and your career objectives.)**

I trained as a photographer and have, since graduating six years ago from the Art Center (Pasadena), run my own commercial photography business in Munich. In this time I have learned a great deal about the advertising industry specifically and about business more generally. But I feel that I have reached the limit of what can be done here. I have surpassed my initial goals and, in fact, outgrown them. Having run a small business, I now want to learn how to manage a larger business, either my own or someone else's. This is why I want to earn an MBA: it is the most efficient way to learn all the components of how to run a business on a larger scale.

I understand a great deal about certain aspects of marketing and marketing imagery. I have gained much experience in analyzing customers and in intuitively understanding their needs and wishes. I have also dramatically improved my knowledge of selling in the past six years. Yet I want to study all the other principal aspects of running a business in much greater depth as well. And whereas I may know about these things for a small company in my particular industry, I would like to explore them on a larger scale and independent of my own particular business sector (advertising).

After completing an MBA I see myself working in marketing, either in a corporate structure or as a marketing consultant. Business to business marketing would be my area of choice, as opposed to consumer marketing, but I believe it would be a mistake to limit my future possibilities too soon. That would go against the reason why I want an MBA, which is to broaden my knowledge of business and my horizons, not to narrow them.

Although marketing is my natural field, I want to be able to perform well in other areas of business too. Even if I do in the end spend the bulk of my career in marketing, I believe a solid knowledge of all aspects of business is indispensable for success at the highest levels in marketing. Just as a modern manager must be able to communicate with people of diverse cultural backgrounds, in order to effectively operate in the worldwide market, in the same sense he must also be able to communicate effectively with the various members of other departments of the company. For example, I suspect that a major hindrance to managing change effectively is the inability of many people within a company to see problems and changes from the other person's (and department's) point of view.

I want to get a high-quality MBA, with a marketing emphasis, from a very international school, preferably one located in Europe. RSM, with its strong core curriculum and attractive marketing electives, not to mention its outstanding reputation, fits my needs perfectly. I believe that RSM would provide an excellent "bridge" between my previous work experience running my own business and my future career marketing goals.

2. **Please give an account of your personality (your strengths and the traits that you would like to improve).**

I would describe myself as CREATIVE, INQUISITIVE, RESOURCEFUL, SELF-CONFIDENT, and ORGANIZED. *Creativity* is the one trait without which I could not imagine myself. Whatever I am doing, be it private or business, active or passive, I think about how I could do it differently, in a way perhaps no one has before. My *inquisitiveness* as a child was so well known that my friends often called me by the nickname "Questions." Fortunately this natural curiosity of a child has never left me. I was drawn to commercial photography through this curiosity, along with my desire to use my creativity and *resourcefulness* professionally. I was also attracted by the opportunity to work with so many different types of people and businesses, as is possible in advertising.

Self-confidence can be both a strength and a weakness. It has helped me a great deal in many aspects of my life, for example in starting up my own business in a foreign country. But it can have a negative side, for example when I become overconfident and neglect to analyze a given situation carefully enough.

One of the first things clients tell me they notice about me is my passion for *organiz-ation*. A large part of my clients being German, a nation notorious for its organiz-ational zeal, makes this praise all the more remarkable. This strength also leads to my greatest weakness: my habit of getting too involved in the details, even on occa-sions when it would be better to concentrate on the general picture. Being aware of this tendency helps me in my effort to improve it.

3. Discuss your interests outside of your job.

At the risk of it sounding like a cliché, I must admit that my greatest interest in life is my family. As the father of a four year old daughter and two year old son, I am daily confronted with such endless curiosity, energy, enthusiasm, and other sources of joy and fascination that I would hardly require any other interests. Nevertheless I do have many other areas of interest, which I pursue whenever possible. The first one began early in my life—internationalism. My parents raised me in a very in-ternational atmosphere. From my fifth year on we spent every other summer trav-eling outside the United States, principally in Europe, but also through many other parts of the world. The alternate summers we traveled throughout America. These travels imbued me with an insatiable interest in the world, in all of its many cultures and nations, not just in their present state, but throughout history. They also were critical in forming my own view of myself. I do not see myself as an American living and working in Europe. I see myself as an international person with a European cultural base. This strong international aspect of my childhood's family life has, not so coincidentally, also been carried over into my adult family life: my wife is half Italian and half German. Our children are consequently citi-zens of three different countries. At home we speak English, German, and Italian.

I am also very interested in history and *literature*. I was torn between the two when it came time to choose my major for my first undergraduate degree. I wanted a ma-jor which would allow me to pursue a strong liberal arts education, and both were well suited. In the end I chose German Literature over history because of its added benefit of giving me the opportunity to learn a second language at the same time. Nevertheless, history remains one of my greatest interests, particularly ancient his-tory. When I can find the time, I especially enjoy reading original texts from an-cient authors.

Another strong interest of mine is *astronomy*. Although I was only able to take one general course on astronomy while at university, it is a subject which never ceases to fascinate me. The infinite vastness of the subject, and the endless possibilities involved in theorizing about the nature—past, present, and future—of our uni-verse, is indescribable. One aspect of astronomy which I find especially interesting is its nature as a science where one can spend an eternity studying it purely from the perspective of physical laws and mathematical equations, or equally well studying it strictly from a philosophical point of view as the ultimate subject of metaphysics.

I also enthusiastically enjoy *sports*. Tennis is my favorite sport, and the one I have participated in on a competitive basis as well as recreationally. Aside from tennis, I also enjoy skiing, squash, and golf.

4. **Describe a situation when your objectives were not met and what you learnt from it.**

Aside from working for companies through their advertising agencies, I also work with many companies directly, usually with their marketing departments. In one such case I was given the job of producing an image for the cover of the annual report of a large German bank. This single image was of immense importance to the bank. They wanted it to incorporate many different symbols of their diverse business activities. I set myself the objective of producing an image which would satisfy all of their needs.

This developed into an extremely complicated production. Logistically it was necessary to plan, organize and then construct a complex set in the studio. Creatively it was a challenge to develop an image which could communicate so much without departing from the bank's established corporate imagery. I was successful in designing and building the studio set and in developing what I regarded as an appropriate image. This "success" was for naught, however, because I failed to maneuver successfully the complex hierarchy of decision makers inside the bank's marketing department. At the first level of authority, the person I dealt with initially had no real authority to make decisions on her own. Hence she could give me information as to the client's wishes, but she could not make commitments as to how these should be visually realized. At the second level, her boss, who could, was only sporadically available for consultation, even though the project was being done under great time pressure. At the third level, the person ultimately responsible for the annual report was essentially unavailable. This structure of building walls between each level of authority made it impossible for me, within the given time constraints, to determine what the client really wanted to communicate and how.

I had failed to establish at the outset of the project exactly what they wanted from me, and to make clear the degree of communication I would require of them in order to complete the project on schedule. Because of this failure they did not use my photographs. This experience showed me the great importance of determining the goals and structures of cooperation—how two partners intend to work together—at the outset of a collaboration.

Comments

- Terry is very successful in addressing each possible issue raised by his candidacy. His quantitative abilities are addressed in part by his GMAT score and his noting in his interview that he had already enrolled in a Managerial Economics class and had begun receiving individual tutoring in calculus. He addresses the issue of his analytical abilities indirectly by presenting his essays in a very persuasive way and by discussing hobbies that have an intellectual component (such as astronomy). He addresses the business interest and knowledge issue by demonstrating that he has long been in business insofar as his photography operation is first and foremost a business.

- Note how he gets right into a discussion of his business background and success at the beginning of the first essay. He knows that one of the concerns he needs to address is the extent to which he has a business background, appropriate goals for an MBA program, knowledge of what an MBA program entails, and so on. He goes a long way to answering these concerns in the first half of this essay. Similarly, his comments about his goals for future employment sound sensible. He shows that industrial marketing would not be too much of a stretch from what he has already done. Lastly, his discussion of managing change and communicating within companies sounds like a young corporate executive's views rather than those of a photographer, further emphasizing his solid business background. The message: He is a businessman, who happens to be in the commercial photography business, rather than an artistic spirit unaware of business.

- Terry's discussion of his outside interests in essay three suggests that he has strong intellectual interests, in history and astronomy, to lend depth to his self-portrait. In terms of the critical issues he faced, this helps deal with possible concerns about his analytical capability. His discussion of his sporting interests is meant to show that he will fit in with the young executive crowd at business school, rather than to impress anyone with his great skill or unusual interests. (As a photographer, the questions for him concern whether he can fit in with the business school environment, not whether he can stand out in terms of bringing something unusual.) The essay's initial focus on fatherhood marks him as mature. The rest of the essay shows him to be thoughtful and interested in the world. He would probably be an interesting and engaging conversational partner.

- His last essay shows him as a photographer, which is nearly absent from the other essays and is thus important here. It also shows that he has had extensive involvement with corporate organizations and issues, which is relevant to the concern about his business background and understanding.

- Terry had his recommenders address his analytical capabilities (in addition to all their other comments), which was a sensible move given his mediocre undergraduate results. (It should be mentioned, however, that he did extremely well in his second bachelor's degree.)

Jon
LONDON

1. Our students participate in the MBA programme for many valid reasons, for example: to change from a specialist to a broader career; to move upwards within an organisation; to change organisations or industries; to change job function or to work in a different country. Please explain why you wish to earn an MBA qualification. There is no "right" answer, so please be as frank as you can.

I wish to earn an MBA qualification as it will significantly assist me in achieving my career goals.

Since I was 19 years old I have known the type of career I wanted. Working for seven years in a highly international environment, with a two year stay in the Far East, has only confirmed my decision.

I want a management position working for a multinational concern in a foreign country. Experience has shown me that I possess the personal qualifications needed to become a successful manager, and I feel that I can reach the very summit of a multinational concern significantly faster if equipped with the management tools taught at London Business School.

All of my experience has been in shipping, with just one company. As valuable and enjoyable as it has been, I recognize that I would be best served by exposure to new concepts and experiences. I want to get to the top of a large multinational, but to do so (even in shipping) will require that I develop knowledge and skills beyond those I now have. For example, as I note in the next essay, I want to gain a more profound understanding of finance and corporate strategy.

I also want to understand the nature and operations of other industries, since it is clear that no one industry such as shipping contains the best example of how to approach the full range of problems that I will encounter in my career. This exposure both to intellectual concepts and practical knowledge is most easily found, I suspect, at a highly reputed business school. I suppose that I could learn some part of what I seek by working for another firm in a different industry, but I certainly doubt that I will learn as much in a short time. After all, an MBA is meant to be a highly organized intensive learning experience.

An MBA will allow me to work without boundaries. It will assist me in becoming a truly "global executive," a career path which is the logical consequence of my upbringing and education, as I have always considered it one of the largest intellectual challenges in life to work and function in a culture different from my own.

My conclusion is that the education I am looking for is best achieved by earning an MBA qualification from London Business School. Its international environment will train me for future work in foreign cultures with foreign languages and, last but not least, significantly different ways of doing business.

I already have substantial management experience and I want further management education, but not the one-size-fits-all type education. I want to be able to pursue certain key areas in real depth. As I mentioned above, I intend to focus on finance and corporate strategy. These are the factors which have led me to London Business School.

2. **Please explain what your experience at work tells you about your likely strengths and weaknesses as a manager and how you hope to see your career progress over the 5 years following the MBA programme. Please include an assessment of the effect of *not* obtaining a place on the MBA programme.**

The key word to describe my career progress and personal development over the next five years following the MBA programme will be: international. I determined many years ago that I want to pursue an international education and career and that focus remains unchanged. I am ready to work in any country in the world, as long as the job is challenging and rewarding.

In five years I anticipate working in a management position for a multinational company in a foreign country. I know one of my responsibilities will be to explore new business opportunities, both outside and within the borders of the country in which I am working. This responsibility will preferably lead to extensive deal-making and possible joint ventures, during which I will make full use of the finance and corporate strategy skills I have obtained at London Business School. All through my career I have been involved in new business projects of that kind and I have found it to be extremely challenging and stimulating.

No matter where in the world I work, I will continue expanding my knowledge of foreign cultures and languages. My interest in these issues has always been substantial and I expect my education in that field to continue for the rest of my life.

The internationalization of business has created a pool of expatriates who are working for foreign companies in foreign countries. These global executives speak several languages and know an industry or a foreign country very well. This group of people will inevitably grow over the next five years following the growing globalization of the business world, and I want to continue being a part of it.

If I do not obtain a place at the MBA programme I will still continue to pursue my career plans. I will, however, be forced to seek the necessary managerial tools elsewhere. This solution will obviously be more time consuming.

As described earlier, I am presently pursuing the second half of the Danish management education, H.D. This is not, however, on the same level as London Business School. I will continue with the H.D. if I am not accepted at London Business School, but I would be sorry to lose the opportunities which London Business School offers.

3. Please describe what you believe to be the major trends in your industry.

I believe that there are three major trends in the fuel oil industry:

—Decreasing availability of fuel oil

—Deteriorating quality of fuel oil

—Implementation of drastic measures to prevent oil spills

DECREASING AVAILABILITY OF FUEL OIL

Fuel oil is a by-product of the refining process when refining crude oil. It is primarily used for utilities and as fuel for larger vessels (when used in the maritime industry fuel oil is referred to as "bunkers").

Up until now fuel oil has been readily available. In older refineries the fuel oil output amounts to 30–40% of the crude oil volume processed. However, by means of advanced technology, this share is being significantly reduced. Newer refineries install so-called "cat-crackers" and "hydro-crackers" to break the molecular compounds in the crude oil. These refineries yield a larger amount of distillates, leaving only 10–15% of fuel oil.

Refineries can also choose to install so-called "cokers" (at a cost of approximately US$1 billion per refinery unit). These refineries are so efficient in the refinery process that they leave no fuel oil at all.

DETERIORATING FUEL OIL QUALITY

Not only does the improved technology in the refining industry lead to lower fuel oil output but the quality of the fuel oil is also deteriorating. When refiners become better at extracting the best products such as gasoline and gas oil from the crude oil, the by-product, the fuel oil, is of a lower quality.

The increasingly poor quality is forcing the major shipping lines to take measures to protect themselves against fuel oil that is not within the international ISO specifications.

A.P. Moller has, as a direct consequence of the deteriorating fuel oil quality, introduced the concept of "pre-delivery testing" when bunkering around the world. The introduction of such a concept is necessary to protect the shipping companies against fuel oil which does not live up to the ISO specifications. A pre-delivery test is carried out by an independent surveyor 24 hours prior to the bunker delivery. The fuel is analyzed and compared to the ISO standards.

This way of avoiding expensive and time consuming off-loadings of non-standard fuel from the vessels is slowly spreading in the market. The major shipping lines are beginning to copy the principle of never accepting a bunker delivery without a pre-delivery test. In the case of A.P. Moller, the concept has dramatically decreased the number of debunkerings.

OIL SPILLS AND OPA-90

As a consequence of the "Exxon Valdez" disaster in Alaska in 1990 the US implemented the "Oil Pollution Act of 1990" (called OPA-90). The law makes it impossible for carriers of crude oil to limit their financial liabilities in case of an oil spill. As an example of the amounts involved, the US Coast Guard is requiring that all vessels taking bunkers in US territory must present a bank account with a minimum deposit of US$50 million to cover the first part of the cleaning job after a possible oil spill. Possible environmental damage is notoriously difficult to quantify, which leaves open the possibility that a company could be held responsible for highly speculative damages.

The introduction of such drastic measures has been a hard blow to my industry. It is presently very difficult to buy fuel oil in US ports. The majority of well-established oil companies have totally withdrawn from the US bunker market—companies such as Texaco, Shell, and Mobil. The oil majors have withdrawn from the US bunker market as they cannot afford to pay the insurance needed to meet a claim from the government in case of an oil spill.

THE BUNKER INDUSTRY IN FIVE YEARS

I could easily foresee that in five years time no vessels would take bunkers in US ports since the consequences of an oil spill in US waters are fatal for almost any company with the present US legislation. Several US suppliers have already seriously considered supplying bunkers in international waters.

Due to tighter and tighter availability and a deteriorating fuel oil quality the marine industry could very well be forced to change from fuel oil to gas oil. Gas oil is a better product which is extracted at an early stage of the refining process. The availability is more or less unlimited and the quality superb.

However, due to the heavy investments required to take full loads of gas oil, the change from fuel oil to gas oil might not happen within the next five years, but rather within the next ten. The possible change from fuel oil to gas oil would significantly change the competitive situation in my industry. Japanese shipping lines are already using gas oil on board some of their vessels and the engines on board these vessels are built for that purpose.

That means that if the change occurs the Japanese will have a major competitive edge by being one or two years ahead of their competitors with regard to investments in new engines, etc.

4. Please describe a situation, either work or personal, where you faced particular frustration or difficulty. What was the outcome and what did you learn from the experience?

I have chosen to describe the situation when I was repatriated to Denmark after having stayed in the Far East for only a little over two years. I had expected to be there for perhaps a decade or more. I found my unexpected repatriation frustrating and difficult to handle.

My contract in Thailand was open-ended. When I had stayed in the Far East for only a few months I was approached by the Far East Manager himself. He told me that I, and a few others in similar situations in countries in the Far East, should consider ourselves "life-time expatriates." He now believed he had gathered the strongest team possible in the Far East and had thus decided that all future job rotations should be among ourselves. He saw no reason to waste valuable experience by sending people to other parts of the world.

From that day on I started planning my life according. I traveled intensively in the Far East, not only in my capacity as Quality Coordinator but also during weekends and holidays. I made an effort to understand the various cultures in the Far East, to get to know the distinctions between the countries, and to familiarize myself with the A.P. Moller offices throughout the region.

After having stayed for two years in Thailand I was approached by the Personnel Department in Denmark and told, much to my surprise, that I was to take up a position in the Oil Purchasing Department in Copenhagen. I was to become the right hand man for the manager of the department. My specific responsibilities were to be Far Eastern purchases, with a total budget of US$ 90 million. One of the A.P. Moller vice presidents, whom I had worked for before I was sent to Thailand, had made a strong case to get me for the position. The manager of the department had for some time needed someone with the ability to analyze potential cost savings and evaluate the existing working procedures.

The frustrating thing was, however, that I felt that this transfer was definitely not the best use of the company's resources. It had taken me two years to build a good network of national and foreign business people operating in Thailand. I spoke the language better than any Maersk expatriate before me and was in the unusual position of having the locals behind me in every project I initiated.

I would have liked to see the results of the projects which I had worked hard for: the establishment of a well-functioning marketing section, the foundation of the Danish Chamber of Commerce, my recommendation for our company to enter into business in Laos, the implementation of a Total Quality Management system, and lastly the strong relationship to our multinational customers that I had built during my stay.

Also on the personal level I felt frustrated. For two years I had done everything to assimilate myself to the life in a foreign country—the life that I had always wanted—and now I was going home. It was difficult not to feel that this was a step backwards.

The ironic thing was that when I came home I got the most interesting job I have every had, and being responsible for the Far East I could utilize a lot of the experience I had gained by living there. I still traveled in that part of the world, mostly in Singapore and Hong Kong, and in the Copenhagen office I soon obtained a position as a bit of a Far Eastern expert.

It was, however, in my position as a right man for the manager that I realized the true potential of my new assignment. Working in Copenhagen I was much closer to the actual decision makers on the strategic level than I could ever be working for an agency such as Maersk Thailand.

I soon obtained a position as deputy for the manager of the department and by January 1, 1995 I was officially made Assistant Manager. I have for two years now been involved in a number of projects, some which were initiated by Mr. Maersk McKinney Moller himself, and have had the rare opportunity to present my recommendations directly to the top management of the company. I would never have had the opportunity to participate in meetings with Mr. Moller, at the age of 26, had I stayed in the Far East.

My initial frustration at not being able to see the long-term results of my efforts in Thailand proved to be without reason.

5. **If we asked three of your closest associates to describe you, what would they say? Which adjectives would they use and why? What would they say are your strengths and weaknesses?**

Very early in my career in the Oil Purchasing Department I was exposed to the higher levels of the A.P. Moller hierarchy. The Vice President of the Group showed me the confidence allowing me to participate in meetings concerning the long-term strategy for the Group's oil purchasing activities because I was perceived to be *responsible*.

I have a *strong sense of focus* and managed to pass my exams without losing focus at work (please refer to "Higher Education"). The same year as I passed the exams I was promoted to Assistant Manager (deputy) of the Oil Purchasing Department. (An equivalent managerial level has as of today only been obtained by four people from the class that graduated in 1990. This places me among the top 10% of my year.)

People who work for me would say that I possess *strong leadership abilities* and that I am a *motivator.* The daily price negotiations within my department follow a certain routine and it takes approximately two months to become familiar with a new area like, for example, the Arabian Gulf. Therefore I have introduced a rota system that makes sure that every employee becomes familiar with all areas of the world and that everyone is facing new challenges every day instead of routine work.

My immediate superior in Thailand would mention the word *empathy*; the ability to understand signals and interpret the feelings of other people. He would also mean the ability to adjust, to create confidence, and to get a decision through without the use of force.

My sense of empathy was put to a test when I first arrived in Thailand. My superiors had very high expectations for some of the projects that I was responsible for and I was determined to make these projects a success. At the same time I had to realize that I was a very young manager, only 22 years old, working in a culture in which age automatically means respect and authority and in which you under no circumstances can make anyone "lose face," especially not people older than yourself.

I have a *restless nature*. Fortunately, with my present job I never have to look far to find new challenges as the interests of my company cover the whole world. Once a procedure has proven cost efficient in one part of the world, I take the experiences gained and implement them in ports similar in character around the world in order for A.P. Moller to stay one step ahead of competition.

I can be *intolerant* at times. That is if I feel that some of the players on my team are not totally committed. To achieve goals and stay ahead of competition, commitment is essential and when met with a lack of same, I find it very difficult not to voice my dissatisfaction. I am also rather *impatient*. If it has been decided what course of action to take I find it very hard to wait. I prefer action over waiting any day.

I hope my closest associates would describe me as *a good friend*. I try to help the people I care about and it is extremely important to me to have a good relationship with my family and friends.

6. **If you could choose any 3 people who have ever lived to join you for dinner, whom would you invite and why?**

If able to choose freely among people who have ever lived, I would invite the Norwegian writer and member of the resistance movement, Nordahl Grieg, the Danish philosopher, Soeren Kierkegaard, and the Danish businessman and shipowner, Maersk McKinney Moller. These three people have all in their own way contributed to the way I think and the way I want my future to be.

The topic of the dinner should be: "Commitment to your own life and commitment to changing things for the better."

Nordahl Grieg was a Norwegian poet and writer who died in 1943, shot down over German territory while serving as a pilot in the Royal Air Force.

When the Nazis invaded Norway in 1940 he was entrusted with the Norwegian gold reserves by the king. He flew the gold reserves to England and joined the RAF. There he started working as a news speaker in the broadcasts to the Norwegian resistance movement and until the day his plane was shot down he gave the Norwegian people the same faith in victory as Winston Churchill was able to give the rest of the free world.

What makes Nordahl Grieg outstanding in my eyes was his determination to fight for what he believed in. Even though he was a poet and a writer he still had the vision to see that ideas alone are not enough. Idealists will always be defeated by aggressors if they are not able to be equally disciplined. He had the will and determination to do what had to be done.

Soeren Kierkegaard was a philosopher who in the 19th century was able to make his small country known around the world. His works concentrated on the subjects which have interested people throughout time: how should life be lived, and, what is the meaning of life.

Kierkegaard was for a short while engaged, but soon had to realize that he was totally unable to commit himself to marriage or any other close contact with his fellow human beings.

What fascinates me about him is that even though he was unable to live a so-called "normal life," he was still able to write brilliant books about subjects such as "the meaning of life."

In his book "Either-Or" Kierkegaard describes the relationship between aesthetics and ethics. Being a philosopher he is trying to establish whether life should be lived in an aesthetic or in an ethical way. His conclusion was that the correct road to travel was somewhere in between, and without ethical values and commitment life is not worth living.

My third guest for dinner would agree with that statement. *Maersk McKinney Moller* is the owner of the A.P. Moller Group. His father, the late A.P. Moller, founded the company, and under Maersk McKinney Moller the company has grown to be the largest shipping company in the world. Moller has earned respect all over the world. He is the only non-American who has ever been on the Board of Directors of IBM and he has received more distinctions than any Danish businessman before him.

It is, however, not the distinctions but rather his business ethics which have made him respected all over the world. He has a motto that Nordahl Grieg would also agree with: "He who has the ability also has the duty," and he has lived by it all his life. He, and his employees with him, has had the ability to build a large concern without losing focus on the ethical values necessary to survive in the business world in the long run.

Another of Moller's mottoes sounds like a cliché, but has proven highly workable as a company motto. Through this motto one gets a good understanding of his perception of how life should be lived: "everything that is worth doing is worth doing well."

Working for Maersk McKinney Moller has taught me that he is a man with a strong determination to do the best he can. He has managed to imbue the whole A.P. Moller group with that same way of thinking and has through his own life shown how far one can get with determination and personal commitment.

I believe that the participants in my dinner party, including myself, would agree that the will to do your best is a very important qualification if you want to succeed in the business world. Success will then follow, like an unintentional side effect of your personal commitment to a cause larger than yourself.

Comments

- Jon had an interesting combination of a weak educational background and an extremely successful career to date. He needed, therefore, to emphasize the latter and either camouflage the former or show that it did not matter because his inherent abilities were sufficient that a lack of formal education should not be of concern. In fact, he did all of these things. He made sure that he capitalized on his successful, varied career by telling a wide range of stories from his business life. He camouflaged his lack of traditional education by referring to classes he was taking, by discussing everything in a very logical and well-thought-out fashion, and by explaining work he had done that had a very analytical component. These approaches, taken together, made it clear that he has plenty of intellectual horsepower. (For more about his strategies, see the following points.)

- In the first essay Jon shows that he knows two strengths of the London Business School program and is a very appropriate candidate for it insofar as a strong grounding in finance and corporate strategy are exactly what he wants. He also states a clear rationale for getting an MBA.

- Essay two features perhaps the weakest part of Jon's effort: his wooly description of his future goals as "working in a management position for a multinational company." He should have been much clearer about what he wanted to do in the future.

- In essay three, he demonstrated a strong overall strategic understanding of his industry, showing that he has not just remained in a cubicle, but has instead considered the context in which he is operating. Indeed, his analytical discussions, plus good prose, belie his lack of formal education.

- Note his emphasis in essay six upon a writer and a philosopher, part of the effort to overcome his modest academic credentials. He also chose to emphasize his Danish-ness by choosing two Danes and one Norwegian, only one of whom is known to the outside world. This is a useful counterbalance to his internationalism, which is evident throughout his discussion of his Asian experiences and his desire to operate internationally. The Danish-ness suggests that he is not stateless and will indeed bring a Scandinavian as well as global perspective to bear during the program.

- Note how positive he is throughout these essays about his career to date and his prospects. At no point is he complaining or depressed. Similarly, he is very positive about his company. He notes that it is a top company, suggesting that he must be a top-quality manager to be working for it. His very positive approach, which includes being a veritable booster for his company, suggests that he will probably be a booster for the business school he eventually attends, something that cannot fail to have value for a school.

MARNE

HARVARD

1. **Choose a recent experience in which you acted as a leader. Briefly outline the situation, then describe your leadership role, how you were effective and what you learned.**

In 1998, the near collapse of Long Term Capital Management demonstrated how problems at one institution could threaten the stability of the entire financial system. Market participants, the press, and Congress demanded strong action from the Department of Treasury, where I was the Deputy Assistant Secretary for Banking and Finance.

The key challenge was to resolve differences between Treasury staff, who believed the markets would correct themselves, and Members of Congress, who wanted an immediate and forceful response. To break this impasse, I proposed that we conduct a study that would provide Congress with recommendations on how to prevent such incidents in the future. This would satisfy the calls for action while demonstrating that Treasury officials and other financial regulators were responsibly managing the issue. The proposal would also provide Congress with an opportunity to support a tempered and well-reasoned response that would not unsettle the markets.

Initially, I was the lone advocate for this course of action, and I knew that it was going to be difficult to persuade key decision-makers to adopt my approach. First, I convinced Treasury staff that the political environment required tangible, public action of this sort. Then, I argued my case with the Secretary of the Treasury, and, once he agreed, I assisted him in eliciting the support of other financial regulators. Once we achieved consensus, I met with Members of Congress to explain that we were addressing the issues fully and that quick legislative action was unnecessary. We eventually released our report to public praise and subsequently have been working with Congress to enact the legislative recommendations that stemmed from our study.

Through this experience, I learned that leadership is not immediate—it can be a process of developing ideas that bridge differences in views, building consensus, and taking the necessary actions to achieve the final goal.

2. Identify someone you regard as a hero, a leader or role model whom you admire. Describe how this person has influenced your development.

During my tenure at the Treasury Department, I had the privilege and opportunity to work with and learn from a remarkable leader, former Secretary of the Treasury Robert Rubin. By word and example, Secretary Rubin taught me the importance of managing an effective decision-making process and valuing each individual's contributions.

Secretary Rubin's formula for successful decision-making is based on three principles: the only certainty is that there is no certainty; every decision should be made by weighing probabilities; and decisions should be judged not just on their results, but also on how they are made. He understands that a manager's success depends upon his ability to draw on the various strengths of his colleagues. Therefore, he gives his subordinates substantial authority and recognition and listens to those around him regardless of where they fall on an organizational chart. Some managers fail to recognize colleagues' accomplishments for fear of being overshadowed. Secretary Rubin did the opposite, resulting in a stronger team and greater success.

As a manager and decision-maker, I have tried to follow Secretary Rubin's example by seeking the views of my staff before making decisions. As a result, they feel more involved in the process and I make more informed decisions. I also attempt to resolve problems by applying Secretary Rubin's three principles. For example, when we were trying to get Congress to enact Treasury's amendments to the Commodities Exchange Act, we were often faced with difficult and tense situations. In order to get through those moments, I employed a structured process for evaluating the potential outcomes of each possible course of action. I worked to make sure that each member of the team was empowered by the process. This methodical and inclusive approach helped my team avoid making mistakes that could have jeopardized our goal.

3. We all experience "defining moments," significant events that can have a major impact on our lives. Briefly describe such an event and how it affected you.

I have long been passionate about our country's democratic system, but I developed a greater and more personal appreciation for its meaning and value when I taught English in 1990 to a group of students in Czechoslovakia through the nonprofit Education for Democracy. When we put down the books, and shared the stories of our lives, I gained insight into how our system of government affects its citizens' attitudes and aspirations.

I will never forget when my youngest student, Thomas, who seldom spoke in class, came to visit me. I asked him questions to learn about how he was adjusting to the changes his country was undergoing during its transition to a democracy. Thomas described his love of math and, with some embarrassment, confessed his dream of becoming Finance Minister of Czechoslovakia. I told him that with hard work and determination, he could do it. He seemed stunned that I had taken his dream seriously. Perhaps this was the first time Thomas was exposed to such optimism and support. I understood, as an intellectual matter, the notion that it matters to live in a democracy. However, this conversation made me conscious that I took basic democratic principles for granted and perhaps, should not. Thomas' thoughts helped me see the extent to which a democracy fosters individualism and the belief in the upward mobility of people.

That summer experience provided me with a renewed understanding about why our system of government is important and helped crystallize my post-collegiate career goals. From a young age, I was interested in government and its role in helping people. My experience in Czechoslovakia sparked an interest in me to engage in the national affairs of my country and participate directly in the democratic process. It inspired me to go to Washington and try to make a contribution to a system of government that allows us to take for granted opportunities of which others can only dream.

4. Describe your three most substantial accomplishments and explain why you view them as such.

Like other recent college graduates in Washington, my first job at the Treasury Department was a mid-level, non-policy position. I soon desired a more substantive job and preferably one in Legislative Affairs, the office that helps develop the Department's policy positions and then advocates them before Congress.

When I approached the head of the office about hiring me, she offered to provide me with an opportunity but was frank about the challenges I faced in making such a rare transition. The major obstacle was overcoming preconceived ideas others had about my ability to handle the policy job, given my age and the less substantive job I held at the time. Instead of being discouraged, I studied the issues and learned everything I could about the legislative process. I rose quickly to become the Treasury Department's youngest Deputy Assistant Secretary, replacing someone who had been a partner in a major law firm. I knew I had successfully accomplished this transition when Secretary Summers remarked to me, "When we first met, who would have guessed that I would be sitting here making these decisions as Secretary and that you would be one of a handful of core advisors advising me on my next move."

For decades, there had been broad agreement among the business community, consumer groups, and government officials on the value of repealing the 1930s Glass-Steagall Act and modernizing the nation's financial laws, but they disagreed about how to write the legislation. In 1999, my role was to lead the Treasury team through the legislative thicket and build a strong coalition that would insure that an acceptable bill survived the legislative process.

One of the many potential deal breakers for the Administration was the requirement that banks invest in under-served communities. To get what we wanted on this issue, I knew it was important not to appear too eager for the bill or to allow members of our coalition to make a deal prematurely. However, we eventually reached a point when I realized that unless we showed some flexibility on this issue, we would never complete the bill. Some of my colleagues resisted but I explained that the momentum was going our way and that we needed to act. With little time to deliberate, I gently steered them back into the room to resume negotiations with the Members of Congress. That was the night we successfully closed the deal on the financial modernization bill that earned overwhelming bipartisan support in the House and the Senate.

In October 1999, when President Clinton signed this sweeping legislation into law, he proclaimed it as one of his most substantial accomplishments. While I am certainly proud of the end product, the real accomplishment for me personally, was my ability to stay focused, think strategically and learn the art of deal making, when to make compromises and when to stay and fight.

It is easy when working in the federal government to feel disconnected from the very people you are trying to help. Moving people off welfare and into jobs is arguably more difficult than getting the controversial 1996 welfare reform legislation passed. I wanted to do my part to help some individuals make that transition successfully. To this end, in 1994, I began volunteering with Sunshine Inc., an organization that provides women with children a home and assistance while transitioning from welfare to work.

Accomplishment in this context meant something different from accomplishment in my career. It meant mostly doing the little things right: finding surplus furniture to create a pleasant and conducive living environment and persuading organizations to donate clothes, books and toys for the children. I also worked directly with one mother, teaching her how to plan financially. I felt a tremendous sense of accomplishment in helping these women improve their lives and develop new skills and confidence.

5. **How would a Harvard Business School education help you to reach your professional goals?**

I am pursuing a Harvard Business School education in order to transform my experience in the public sector into a career in the private sector. At Treasury, I have worked to bring change to the financial services industry from the public sector. Going forward, I would like to work towards becoming a leader in this crucial and dynamic industry. I believe Harvard Business School is the logical next step in beginning this transition.

With the guidance of HBS professors and my classmates, I can strengthen my communication, management and analytical skills and learn to apply them to the private sector. HBS can provide me with training in core business areas, including finance, accounting, economics and general management, that I need to excel in the business world. The classroom experience modeled on a real business environment will give me exposure to different kinds of problems and the analytical tools needed to solve them. The case method would introduce me to a broad range of real company problems; I would contribute a different perspective based on my experience in the public sector.

One particular aspect I found rewarding about the public sector was the opportunity to work with a diverse collection of some of the brightest and most committed people I have ever met. My mentors at the Treasury Department brought perspective, judgment, knowledge and contacts that they gained from their experience in the private sector. I learned from top-level economists, finance experts, and management consultants, and I want to continue to learn and grow with the best. That is why I want to go to Harvard. Moreover, it is a long-term goal of mine to return to the public sector at a very senior level. I believe that Harvard MBA training and private sector experience would yield benefits that would ultimately make me a better public servant.

Comments

- As a high government official, Marne did not need to worry about distinguishing herself from many other applicants with similar backgrounds—there are few, if any. Her key task was to show that she would fit in at business school. By illustrating her serious grasp of issues relating to finance (through her work at the Treasury Department), Marne put to rest any concerns the admissions committee might have about her aptitude for business classes or her interest in finance and management.

- Marne demonstrates an enormous sense of ambition and perseverance, having climbed the ladder at the Treasury Department to become the youngest person ever to have attained her position, which had been held by a partner in a major law firm before her arrival. These details help demonstrate the seriousness of the role she attained, which might not otherwise be apparent to admissions readers whose knowledge of politics and the ways of Washington is likely to be minimal.

- The third essay further supports Marne's profile as someone who is passionate about the role of government while also adding an international dimension to a candidate whose résumé shows no work experience outside of the United States.

STEVEN

COLUMBIA (Selected)

1. What are your career goals? How will an MBA help you achieve these goals? Why are you applying to Columbia Business School?

My career goal is to create the nation's premier municipal management consulting firm. While I plan to work for a leading management consulting firm upon initial completion of my MBA, I seek the entrepreneurial challenge to one day create my own advisory firm to serve municipalities. Furthermore, once my advisory firm is established, I hope to pursue senior level challenges and opportunities within public sector entities as they arise. A desire to enhance the services available for urban residents, thus improving the livability of American cities, drives my career goals. Providing municipal advisory services will enable me to determine the future of American cities and thereby positively impact the lives of its citizens.

My interest in assisting municipalities is a result of a dedication to community service, academic study of public sector entities, and my professional background in municipal finance. I have volunteered with community service organizations in various capacities for the past fifteen years in an effort to help people help themselves. The majority of my volunteer work has been in primary and secondary education, with particular emphasis on improving the educational readiness of minority children so they may compete in our global economy. Through my volunteer efforts, I realize the value and necessity of community and public service.

The last two years have been pivotal in focusing my professional goals toward a career intent upon improving public sector entities. In 1995, I enrolled in New York University's Robert F. Wagner Graduate School of Public Service as a Master's in Public Administration (MPA) candidate, where I received a Public Service Scholarship to study financial management of public sector entities. In 1996, after several years of commercial and corporate banking, I made a successful transition to the area of municipal finance.

My professional career has been devoted to providing solutions, both financial and non-financial, to middle-market and Fortune 500 clients. After graduation from college, I went to work for the Advisory Board Company, a consulting firm that assists 300 banking institutions worldwide. As a research analyst, I uncovered and wrote about the best practices in the financial services industry for our clients. My research was broad, covering topics varying from executive compensation to the improvement of customer service standards. After a year of consulting, I pursued an opportunity in a commercial lending training program at Commerce Bank, a previous client. This training program entailed a full year in the commercial credit department, where I analyzed financial statements, wrote credit reports summarizing the structure of proposed transactions, and provided recommendations to senior management.

After making a difficult decision to leave Commerce Bank to be closer to family in New York I joined NatWest markets as a corporate credit analyst. I wrote credit submissions to support the needs of the investment banking unit for twenty-five Fortune 500 corporations. While helping to provide financing for some of the world's largest corporations proved challenging, and exciting, my true interests and career direction were to be found in municipal finance. As I wished to continue my employment with NatWest Markets, I successfully pursued an internal transfer to the Bank's Public Finance Unit last year.

My move to municipal finance enabled me on a professional level to structure transactions that provide public sector entities with needed financial services such as credit enhancement, liquidity support, and capital market products. When I was initially hired, my role was exclusively to monitor an existing portfolio. As I have excelled in learning municipal finance, I have assumed an expanded role in finding, structuring, and winning new business.

In supporting a vice president, I uncover new business opportunities with issuers, financial advisors, and other municipal bankers. We attempt to market proposals that meet the needs of the client but also make good business sense for the Bank. Once our proposal is accepted, it is my job to ensure that the deal is approved internally by formally submitting a credit package detailing the proposed structure, the issuer, and the underlying security supporting the transaction. Once approved internally, the Bank can make a firm commitment to our client, and proceed to document and close the transaction. While we employ legal counsel to assist in documenting our transaction, we ourselves take an active role in the documentation process to ensure the Bank's interests are protected. After a transaction has closed, it is my responsibility to report annually on the financial condition of the client to the Bank's credit committee.

The most profitable, time-consuming and intriguing account for which I am responsible is that of the city of Washington, DC. The challenges facing Washington are numerous, and require me to monitor both its complex relationship with the federal government, as well as its internal difficulties in reversing years of economic and demographic decline. Unfortunately, financial mismanagement, cronyism, and excessive waste have brought our nation's capital to the brink of financial ruin. As a provider of financial resources to Washington, and as an interested student of politics, the dismal state of affairs in the District of Columbia has shaped and strengthened my belief that leadership, integrity, and management ability, as well as financial skill and expertise, are crucial to turning around poorly run municipalities.

While my career goal is to provide advisory services for municipalities, I need to gain the necessary skills to successfully implement my vision. Majoring in financial management and public finance at NYU has taught me the basic tenets of municipal finance. However, this focus is intended as an overview for students pursuing careers outside finance. I seek to obtain a thorough finance education, as well as a solid understanding of private sector concepts and entrepreneurial skills that will allow me the opportunity to implement my ideas. The time is right for me to earn my MBA because my professional goals are clearly focused, and I will be completing my MPA in May of 1998. The MPA has directed my professional goals toward advising municipalities, and has prepared me to pursue an MBA, which will round out the educational gaps needed to successfully implement my vision.

I find Columbia Business School attractive for many reasons. First, Columbia has identified the importance of the public sector through its concentration in public and non-profit management. Second, Columbia will allow me to gather the necessary skills including a strong finance and management background, as well as an entrepreneurial focus, needed to run my own municipal advisory firm. Third, Columbia's location in New York is attractive. Having lived in the area for three years, I believe that New York's vast resources and prominence in both the business community and government sector make it the most appropriate location in which to develop the contacts and skills needed to become a successful entrepreneur, consultant, and manager.

My commitment to improving urban centers has led me to the goal of creating an advisory firm dedicated to serving municipalities. The skill set I will develop at Columbia will enable me to reverse years of urban neglect and decline and help to improve the livability of American cities for their residents.

2. **Discuss your involvement in a community or extracurricular organization. Include an explanation of how you became involved in the organization, and how you help(ed) the organization meet its goals.**

Much of my involvement with community service organizations has centered on improving the educational skills of minority children. I have placed special emphasis on educational preparedness because of its importance in our increasingly competitive global economy. Having educators as parents has particularly influenced this interest in minority education. While I have assisted educational organizations such as Junior Achievement, Inroads, and the Youth Education Initiative in the past, my current work with Sponsors for Educational Opportunity (SEO) has proven to be the not inspirational and challenging.

SEO attempts to improve the academic standards of minority children in New York City. The program offers after-school tutoring, educational field trips, and a mentoring program in order to develop well-rounded students. I became involved with SEO through the mentoring program, in which I serve as a role model to an eleventh grade student from Brooklyn. The relationship involves weekly telephone calls, and two to three activities monthly, I structure activities to be educational, culturally challenging, and fun. Whether the activity is spending an afternoon at a museum or attending a cultural event, my principal goal is to expose this student to new environments and concepts.

I attribute much of my own success in life to childhood involvement in programs like SEO. Thus, my volunteer efforts with SEO have a special meaning because I appreciate sharing my experiences with others. I am an ardent supporter of the mission and purpose of SEO and through mentoring I am able to contribute to both the organization's goals and the educational development of a young adult.

Comments

- Steve did not have to do much to set himself apart from other applicants—he naturally distinguishes himself through his discussions of his community service record, extensive background in commercial lending and municipal finance, and his interest in public administration, complemented by an MPA from NYU. Unlike most applicants who profess a dedication to community service, his dedication shines through as a result of his lengthy involvement in urban renewal and municipal restructuring, both as a volunteer and in his career.

GREG

KELLOGG (Selected)

1. Briefly assess your career progress to date. Elaborate on your future plans and your motivation for pursuing a graduate degree at Kellogg.

My ten-year career (seven post-graduate) has included owning two businesses and rapid advancement into leadership roles in three companies. I have enjoyed the challenges of increasing levels of organizational responsibility and numerous opportunities to develop the talents of my peers and direct reports (further explained in essay 2). As the Business Manager of a $2.7M division, I led College Pro's "team-management restructuring project." To attain our profit goal, it was necessary for me to learn budgeting and forecasting, while the restructuring project improved my performance management and problem-solving abilities. As the National Director of Recruiting and Training, I focused on projects designed to affect corporate growth and profitability. For example, I performed the strategic and operational analysis of SIDEA Corporation (a software training company), which was subsequently acquired by College Pro, giving it entrance into the rapidly growing technology industry.

A critical turning point in my career occurred in February 1997, when I failed to gain admission to Kellogg's MBA program. Although this was certainly disappointing, it served as the catalyst for my career change into the "new economy." Upon joining Forrester, I focused on the development of my sales skills and the study of technology's impact on business strategy. Indeed, my ability to assimilate this information enabled me to grow my territory as an Account Executive by 310% in 1998 and win clients such as Novell, America West Airlines, Janus Funds, Verio, and Level3. My time at Mainspring has seen this organization transition from research and advisory services to true strategy consulting and become a publicly traded company. We now compete directly with companies such as McKinsey, BCG, and Sapient, and are subject to the whims and demands of the capital markets. In preparation for these changes, I significantly elevated the caliber of our sales professionals, designed a sales methodology that fosters collaboration with our consulting partners, and restructured performance management and compensation systems (further explained in Essay 4A).

Upon completion of my MBA degree, my immediate professional objective is to obtain an executive management position with a small telecommunications company to further prepare me for corporate leadership. Ultimately, I aspire to become the CEO of a large telecommunications/Internet infrastructure company. My experiences at Forrester and Mainspring have piqued my interest in this industry and provided me with direct exposure to its unique challenges and benefits. Rather than join the management ranks of Cisco or Qualcomm, for example, my objective is to lead an organization from the early stages of its development as a private company through to its emergence as a market leader. Achieving this goal will require dedication and mastery of a wide range of skills. To date, my career has been focused in areas such as leadership, business development, and strategic planning. To lead my organization effectively, I will need a comprehensive understanding of additional business skills such as finance, operations, and global management. It is vital to supplement my current work experience and liberal arts degree with a formal business education. I am particularly interested in pursuing my MBA at Kellogg. In today's increasingly competitive business environment, effective leaders must be champions of change and adaptability. Having had such positive experiences in team management at College Pro and Mainspring, it is important to me to participate in a collaborative learning environment that offers case study, simulations, and team-oriented learning styles.

As a future business leader, I will be required to manage sophisticated business units as well as make strategic decisions in a complex environment. I will thus need to develop greater aptitude with business analytical tools and expand my knowledge of business practice in a wide range of functions and industries. Kellogg's innovative curriculum will provide me with proficiency in critical core areas such as finance, global management, and operations, while simultaneously allowing me to pursue my interests in technology and entrepreneurship. Perhaps most crucial to me, however, have been my interactions with Kellogg's current students and alumni. In addition to their obvious business talent, I was impressed by their enthusiasm and admiration for their ongoing Kellogg experience. My involvement in the Notre Dame community has given me a deep appreciation for this type of educational environment, and Kellogg's reputation in this area is truly exceptional.

2. **Each of our applicants is unique. Describe how your background, values, and non work-related activities will enhance the experiences of other Kellogg students.**

My most rewarding experiences have involved helping others who are less fortunate or struggling to achieve their true potential. This has proven to be the case in my personal and professional life, where I have had the privilege of contributing to several people's pursuit of self-actualization.

As a Notre Dame student, I was very active in athletics, student government, theatre and my entrepreneurial ventures. Although I found these experiences stimulating and enriching, my exposure to community service forced me to grow on a more pronounced level. Through my participation in various service activities, such as the Christmas in April Project (inner-city housing renovation), I learned how others could benefit from my time and energy. My work as a volunteer basketball coach further enhanced the value I placed on service to others. Perhaps my greatest contribution to the Notre Dame community was my role as the Renovation Coordinator of The South Bend Homeless Shelter. My leadership and project management abilities, which I had developed at College Pro, enabled our team to complete the renovation in a cost-effective and timely manner. I found this distinctly gratifying because I used my business skills on giving back to my community rather than just on generating profits.

Since graduating from Notre Dame, I have continued to stay active with local charities in greater Boston. I raised over $6,000 for various charities through my participation in athletic leagues and events such as the Boston Marathon and the Boston New York AIDS Ride. In addition, with some of my investment proceeds, I founded a small charitable foundation focused on helping disadvantaged children. I recently became a member of the Junior Board of the Nativity Preparatory School (a small, inner-city, Catholic school for "at risk" boys) and am allocating some of my foundation's funds to sponsor one of the students.

In my professional career, I have held numerous leadership positions that have given me the opportunity to utilize my business skills to benefit others. In my first year as a General Manager at College Pro, for example, I met with an underperforming franchisee named Tom. According to my predecessor, Tom lacked the skills to succeed as evidenced by his production of only $45k during his first year (franchisees average $55k). During my initial meeting with Tom, I learned about the extraordinary challenges he had faced as a franchisee and about his future career plans. Tom grew up in a disadvantaged neighborhood in Providence, where family circumstances forced him to move out on his own at age sixteen. He had completed high school and was pursuing a degree at the local community college while financially supporting himself as a janitor. He told me that his first year with College Pro was not representative of his abilities and that he would excel if given a second opportunity. Because I had heard this many times from franchisees whose initial performance was mediocre, I was skeptical about Tom's chances for significant improvement. Through subsequent conversations, Tom demonstrated a great deal of maturity and introspection regarding his franchisee experience. It also became clear that he possessed the fire that is essential for success in the business world. I agreed to give Tom a franchise for a second year, and we established mutually agreed-upon and attainable goals. To maximize his chances for success, I worked very closely with Tom to identify his deficiencies and help him overcome them. This involved creating a tailored training program targeted at improving his skills in hiring and production management. I also focused on elevating his confidence and pushed him to achieve to his full potential. By providing Tom with training, coaching, and motivation, I contributed to his accomplishments. In the summer of 1994, Tom produced $123k—a 173% increase in sales—and was the highest producing second-year franchisee in New England. He earned over $30k in profit, and I awarded him "Manager of the Year" in recognition of his achievements. Tom was subsequently hired as a General Manager and has since risen to become a Vice President in the New England division. Because of these experiences, I believe in a broad definition of leadership that measures success across a spectrum of both business results and individual impact. As a Kellogg student, I will be actively involved in the learning that takes place outside the classroom. In addition, my professional and personal experiences will enable me to get my fellow classmates excited about the broader applicability of their positions and influence.

Comments

- Greg is a solid business school candidate, but he needed to find a way to weave together a career built from several different jobs and make sense of it for the admissions committee. He does just that in his first Kellogg essay, while demonstrating the results of his leadership and impact in each of his three careers: as a business manager of a house-painting company, as a salesperson at Forrester, and as a consultant at Mainspring. The first essay also showcases his ability to react well to disappointments through the candid discussion of how he funneled his one-time denial from Kellogg into a positive career change.

- The personal story about his relationship with and belief in an employee helps to round out Greg as a humanitarian with strong people and communication skills.

VICTOR

DARTMOUTH / TUCK (Selected)

1. **Discuss your career progression to date. Elaborating on your short-term and long-term goals, how do you see your career progressing after you receive an MBA? Why do you want an MBA from Tuck?**

When I first joined Dain Rauscher Wessels, my career goals were well defined. My Wharton finance education and the pending two-year Analyst program propelled me toward a successful career in investment banking. My success in the Analyst program confirmed my ambitions. In less than eighteen months, I competed in 10 equity offerings and 4 merger transactions and was promoted to senior analyst. As senior analyst, I directed the work flow of new projects and supervised the work of junior analysts.

While I quickly mastered the quantitative analysis and problem solving skills required to be a successful analyst, my exposure to client companies was limited to that with senior management and then only to financial matters. As I participated in the never-ending stream of initial public offerings that became the internet frenzy of 1999, I became increasingly interested in the operations of the companies that I helped bring public. As I sat across from these seasoned managers during meetings, I was often amazed at their ability to keep abreast of developments in marketing, product development and even personnel attrition. Soon, I wanted to experience first hand what my clients often talked about.

My opportunity came ten months ago when Alex Bond, CEO of Reel.com, offered me a job one night as we were discussing Reel's initial public offering. My role would be to analyze Reel's operations and make Reel operate more efficiently. It was an amazing opportunity to explore and learn about every functional department of an online retailer, but I had my reservations. My early promotion to Associate at Dain Rauscher Wessels was imminent, and I was less than thrilled about Reel's loss leader business model. In the end, my desire for operational exposure and my long suppressed sense of adventure prevailed.

My contributions at Reel.com significantly impacted its bottom line; at the same time my experiences there had significant impact on my career outlook. Based on my analysis of Reel's customer base, I, advocated the elimination of costly marketing initiatives, such as free shipping, that had significantly impaired Reel's gross margin. These suggestions were against prevailing wisdom within Reel that online customers are extremely price sensitive and reduction in marketing promotions would reduce Reel's revenues, the benchmark which the investment community uses to judge performance. Believing that higher pricing would become a critical issue for Reel, I appealed to Alex. I explained my analysis of the customer data in terms of Reel's bottom line and showed him a recent research report conducted by Boston Consulting Group, which concluded that many online retailers were slowly increasing prices and slashing discounts. After winning his support, I presented my analysis in a PowerPoint presentation at the next management meeting and proposed a compromise: a two-week trial period during which prices would be increased and no promotions would be offered. Reel's revenues remained steady during those two weeks and everyone's attitude toward promotions and discounts thereafter changed. Within one quarter Reel's gross margin increased from—16% to 4% while revenues increased slightly. In addition, I instituted other cost-saving changes at Reel, such as the outsourcing of Reel's customer service functions and the elimination of under-performing online marketing agreements. These efforts reduced Reel's monthly cash burn rate by $1 million to $4 million.

Unfortunately, these efforts did not reduce Reel's cash burn enough and further funding was unavailable after the decline of capital markets last spring. The failure of Reel did not surprise me. Being its former banker, I had no illusions about the viability of its business model. What did surprise me, however, was the excitement I felt at Reel making decisions and seeing their impact. Even in Reel's final days, negotiating a fair selling price of Reel's assets to Buy.com, a competitor, from a position of extreme weakness was pure adrenaline rush. I have caught the start-up

fever and crave the excitement that comes with taking risks and shouldering responsibility. While I initially planned on going back to investment banking after
acquiring some operational and managerial experience, my plan has evolved
through my experience at Reel toward an entrepreneurial path. In the near term,
I want to focus on becoming a better manager and broadening my skill set.

Consequently, I joined Unexplored, another start-up focused on providing online
travel software to the adventure travel industry. The eleven-month old company had
just acquired two small technology companies in the US and was completing another
acquisition in London. The senior management has concentrated on acquisitions and
fund-raising, and no one had yet thought about how Unexplored would be managed
internally. My mandate from the board was to utilize my experience at Reel.com to
create Unexplored's first overall operating budget. Within two months of my arrival
at Unexplored, I completed an operating budget that provided some order and focus
to Unexplored. I also imposed financial control by redesigning Unexplored's accounting system to track departmental expenditures and adding the review of actual
and budgeted operating results to the agenda at monthly board meetings.

While my accomplishments at Reel.com and Unexplored brought me closer to my
long-term goal of being an effective senior executive, there are many more steps
ahead. An MBA experience at Tuck will help me make the next giant leap by providing an academic framework under which to further develop my managerial
skills. An effective manager communicates a compelling business vision to lead and
motivate his team. The fundamental business concepts I learn at Tuck will provide
me with the necessary tools to think strategically and anticipate new trends. An effective manager also understands group dynamic and proper use of incentives to
motivate the team. The general management curriculum at Tuck as well as the team
oriented academic environment will enable me to further develop my leadership
potential and improve my ability to work within a team.

Lastly, I am excited about Tucks' diverse student body. Interaction with so many
different perspectives, whether from a different industry or a different culture, will
be an invaluable experience that will have a tremendous impact on my professional
development. In short, I believe that attending Tuck School of Business will be an
enriching and crucial step in preparing me to be an effective manager and will provide an experience that will greatly influence all aspects of my life.

2. **Your company's IPO has been successful and your share of the IPO has given
   you financial independence. The company's founder strongly believes that
   success must be shared and has mandated that each member of the firm must
   reinvest a substantial portion of the gains into the business or civic community. Beyond this directive, there are no other guidelines. For the sake of the
   argument, assume that the amount of capital you have to reinvest is roughly
   $25 million. What path will you take and why? Is this in the best interest of
   the stockholders?**

I lived in Palo Alto for ten months during 1999. One of the epicenters of Silicon Valley, the town was buzzing with entrepreneurial activity and wealth creation. What is most memorable about Palo Alto, however, is not Stanford University or the various internet ventures scattered about University Avenue, but a bridge over highway 101. This is no ordinary bridge. Physically, it connects Palo Alto with East Palo Alto. In terms of socioeconomic levels, it bridges far greater distance than its 100 feet width; it connects the model town of the internet economy with the only true ghetto in the Bay area. While most dot-comers in Palo Alto that I have talked to deplore the quality of life in East Palo Alto, few believe that the situation concerns them or matters to the process of wealth creation that is taking place in the rest of Silicon Valley.

What many have overlooked, however, is that East Palo Alto may present a solution to one of Silicon Valley's most serious problems, the shortage of skilled labor. Having worked at two internet startups in the last year, I witnessed first hand the difficulties firms face as they attempt to attract and retain qualified employees. Often, the largest impediment to growth, the mantra of the new economy, is the slow pace of hiring and filling mission critical positions. Therefore, I see a tremendous opportunity for a venture to invest in increasing computer literacy amount high school students in East Palo Alto, provide a potential pool of skilled labor to the high tech industry and possible reverse the vicious spiral of low tax base, lack of educational funding, under performing students and lack of career opportunities. If I had $25 million to invest from a Silicon Valley startup, I would try to build another bridge over highway 101. This time it would soar over the digital divide and distribute some of Palo Alto's wealth to its impoverished neighbor and help East Palo Alto reap some of the rewards of the information age.

Specifically, I would establish an organization called High Tech Careers with a mission to increase computer literacy among high school students in East Palo Alto and generate interest in high tech careers among these students. High Tech Careers will have two focuses, teaching East Palo Alto students basic computer skills and working with leading high tech companies in Silicon Valley to create internship programs for those students who have successfully improved their computer skills.

High Tech Careers will first negotiate with East Palo Alto school board to lease one classroom in every high school. These classrooms will be designated as computer-learning centers and High Tech Careers will invest part of the initial $25 million in computers, network infrastructure, and qualified instructors to staff these computer-learning centers. These centers will offer up-to-date computer classes, both during and after school hours, on common office applications, programming languages, and networking fundamentals. These classes will not replace but rather supplement the existing curriculum. Students will be encouraged and enticed to attend these extra classes with possibilities of internships with leading high tech companies in the area such as Cisco and Hewlett-Packard. I optimistically believe that with ample coaxing, these students, who have been bystanders in the wealth creation that is taking place around them, will take advantage of these classes to improve their career prospects. In addition, the going rate for a high tech intern in Silicon Valley is nearly $20 an hour while non-skilled positions for high school students pay less than half that amount. I hope that discrepancy will be a powerful incentive for these students to take advantage of High Tech Careers' computer classes.

High Tech Careers will also actively recruit leading high tech companies to join its network. It will work with the client companies who have joined its network to create onsite internship programs. Internships would enable East Palo Alto students to gain real world work experience, apply what they had learned in the computer-learning center, and assume responsibility associated with the workplace. Internships will also significantly benefit High Tech Careers' clients, who will gain much-needed temporary employees to alleviate the chronic labor shortage in Silicon Valley. The internship program will also serve as a screening program for High Tech Careers' clients to identify and nurture talented individuals who may become full time employees in the future. High Tech Careers will generate revenues from fees received from its client companies in exchange for services such as successful placement of candidates in internship programs, successful placement of internship participants in full time positions, and the administration of internship programs. As the organization's operations grow and its revenues scale, it is projected that the venture will eventually reach profitability. High Tech Careers will seek equity investments beyond the initial $25 million from its client companies. These equity investments will further fund High Tech Careers' operations and further realign the interest of the company with its clients.

High Tech Careers will be established as a not-for-profit and tax-exempt corporation. Any profit derived from fees paid by its high tech clients will be reinvested in the company to extend its program, first in East Palo Alto and later in other impoverished communities. Initially, the success of the venture and its mission to increase computer literacy among high school students in East Palo Alto will satisfy my interests as the sole shareholder of High Tech Careers. As High Tech Careers' client companies invest in the venture, I believe their interest of increasing the supply of skilled labor in Silicon Valley will be closely aligned with the mission of High Tech Careers. Aside from the shareholders, the other two stakeholders, the high school students of East Palo Alto and the community of East Palo Alto will all benefit from the success of High Tech Careers. The students will benefit from increased knowledge of computers and the internet, exposure to the excitement and responsibilities of the workplace and improved career prospects. The East Palo Alto community will benefit in the future as more of its young members become technology professionals and join the middle class. These professionals will enlarge the community's tax base and provide role models to the next generation of technology executives.

3. The admissions committee welcomes any additional comments you may wish to provide in support of your application.

I am very fortunate to have lived in three different cultures. My experiences gave me a unique perspective on politics, outlooks on life, and cultural diversity that I believe will stimulate intellectual discussion and add to the cultural diversity at Tuck.

I was born in Shanghai in 1976, a year in which Mao Tse-Dong died and the Cultural Revolution ended, which led to the return of my father to Shanghai after ten years of forced resettlement in the countryside a thousand miles away. Of course, I was not aware of any of these changes. I grew up in a world where everyone lived contented lives in equal poverty and absorbed the communist ideology that was taught in school. That life changed as I followed my parents to New York where my father pursued a graduate degree in Biology. Suddenly, my new teacher in social studies no longer considered communist a good thing; and while people seemed to possess all the things that no one I knew had in Shanghai, I also saw panhandlers who had almost nothing for the first time in my life. What was even stranger was that almost everyone believed in a divine being, which I knew did not exist because I had always been told so. At ten, I was faced with two opposing moral systems and was not sure which one was correct.

I eventually decided that both are valuable and accepted them equally. I liked the fact that my Chinese background, especially my early communist education, left a lasting impression on me. That background made sure my political views are slightly left of my friends at Wharton or my colleagues at Dain Rauscher Wessels. The lack of background in organization religion also enables me to appreciate the stories of the Bible and the Koran equally. The compromise between what I knew in Shanghai and what I later learned in the US prompted a more objective view of cultural values and opened my mind to the myriad perspectives that are out there. I look forward to contributing my own mix of Chinese and American values to the discourse at Tuck and exploring new perspectives among the diverse student body.

While American culture did not replace my Chinese upbringing, I became fascinated with its different values and the origin of these values. My father turned me into a history buff when I was six by buying me comic book versions of Chinese epics such as the Tale of Three Kingdoms. I soon followed up with other books published by the communist press that left me with a Sinocentric view of the world. To counter that perspective and to better understand the new society that I found myself in, I became interested in Roman history and Latin. I took up Latin in junior high school while simultaneously learning English. At Penn, I added Attic Greek and Middle Egyptian to Latin and decided to pursue a degree in Classics alongside my degree in Finance. In the course of four years, I completed 47 credits of coursework instead of the normal 32 required for graduation. The extra work I put in at Penn was well worth the effort and continues to enrich my personal life. It is still a pleasure to pick up a new biography on Justinian, my subject of my senior year thesis, at the local bookstore or to attend an occasional Classics lecture at UC Berkeley. My background and interest in ancient history and classical languages will contribute to the variety of student interests at Tuck and extend the intellectual discourse beyond the scope of business and management.

My parents were surprised at my interest in Classics and the fact that I earned a degree in the subject. What has surprised my parents even more is the strange turn that my personal life took as a result of my studies. At Penn, in order to understand more recent European scholarship on Roman history, I followed my professors' advice and began learning Italian. My slow progress in the subject forced me to seek more drastic measures, and I went to Milan for one semester of total immersion learning. Besides improving my Italian, I met my wife in Milan, who was studying at the same university. Meeting Francesca has introduced me to a host of new experiences. I have since learned to cook pasta the correct way—al dente—become familiar with the various wine denominations of Italy and their particular flavors, and appreciated the passion and the subtleties of European soccer. I plan to introduce my new-found Italian flair to the Tuck community.

Comments

- Victor gets a lot of mileage out of his interesting, well-balanced background and interests. He shows that he has a solid investment banking analyst background as well as (financial and) operations experience in a start-up environment. His discussions of his dual career are spiced with interesting stories and evidence of positive results.

- Furthermore, he shows a remarkably positive attitude about life, demonstrated, for example, through his clearly satisfied feelings about his career shift, even after Reel.com failed.

- The second Tuck question failed to elicit clear responses from most candidates because many did not understand the intentions of the last part of the question. Victor came up with a logical, creative answer that demonstrates the observations he made while working in Silicon Valley concerning the inequities among residents of northern California. Ultimately, however, he should have shown how the plan to create High Tech Careers would benefit the stockholders of the original start-up company, though he was not alone among Tuck applicants in thinking that as the sole owner of the $25 million, he was the "shareholder" to which they were referring. (Ideally, he might also have answered a natural question that his idea raises: Do start-ups in Silicon Valley indeed have a need for high school students, whose contributions would be largely unspecialized and part-time?)

- His well-written third essay, giving his personal history, dispels any possible interpretation of him as a narrow, only-money-matters investment banker. His dual cultural background, combined with his newer love of Italian culture (and the classics), marks him as a citizen of the world.

CYNTHIA
MIT / SLOAN

1. **Prepare a one- to two-page cover letter seeking a place in the Sloan School of Management MBA program. It should point out the features of your résumé that you believe to be of interest to the Admissions Committee, both in your education and in your work history. Further, please comment on your career goals and those factors which influenced you to pursue an MBA education at Sloan. Additionally, discuss which management track appeals to you and how it fits with your professional aspirations. We are also interested in what you believe you can contribute to the Sloan School and your fellow students, and we encourage you to describe your most substantial accomplishment.**

To the Sloan School of Management Admissions Committee:

I write to submit my application for the Sloan School class of 2000. I have enclosed my resume, the application materials, and all relevant credentials. I have a highly unusual background, which includes some difficult personal challenges I have overcome to arrive at my current position. As a result, my supplemental information is fairly extensive, and I hope you will have the time to evaluate it thoroughly as it will provide much insight into me as an applicant.

My undergraduate degree is in music performance, a rare major among your applicants. My first career was as a classical musician, playing viola. I made some notable achievements in that field. My unusual background means I have unique contributions to make to a Sloan class. My musical background has trained me in disciplined creativity. I tend to find unexpected ways to solve problems and am not limited by obvious answers. This is a characteristic that directly maps onto my career in technology. Technology and the business environments it supports are constantly changing. My creativity assists me in keeping pace with the highly dynamic nature of technology.

In addition to discipline and creativity, music requires working well with others. No performance is effective unless all the members are in agreement about how to deliver it. The group process in music closely parallels my experiences in team settings at work. I have spent the last few years working as an Account Manager. As such, much of my focus has been interpersonal in nature, so I have gained an unusual level of experience and outstanding abilities in working with others, When I was charged with leading one of the multi-million dollar deals I delivered at Computer Associates, I used the same consensus building and team building skills I had been using since childhood in my musical training. I can contribute my experience in team environments, both musical and professional, to my Sloan classmates.

Although I achieved a lot in my early music career, it is the act of completing my undergraduate degree that stands as my greatest accomplishment to date. The biggest challenges I have faced in life surrounded my college education (see Section III, #4 for details). My father was an active alcoholic for the first half of my college career. I had to leave school twice, once for a period of three years, because my parents could not afford it after he lost his job. In my final semester, my mother became terminally ill and died. I spent as much time at home with her as possible, but it meant I could not finish all my coursework. I had won an internship in New York and could not stay in Ann Arbor to finish my degree at the end of that semester. I was so overwhelmed and exhausted by my experiences that a long time passed before I could face up to this omission and rectify it.

There are no words to express the joy I felt the day I donned my cap and gown. I had overcome every obstacle in my path, and triumphed over challenges that would have stopped others less determined. Overcoming the obstacles I did, I forged an internal strength and confidence that remains with me today. In finishing my degree, I received more than just the piece of paper; I received many of the character traits that make me who I am today.

After leaving school, I knew I would not pursue music as a profession. Although I worked full time for four years before discovering my love for technology, that work was not as relevant to my current career as my experience since 1990. My resume reflects 10-plus years of full time experience, but my experience in my technology career totals only 7 years, a figure that is more consistent with other candidates for your class.

My early business career started with a temporary assignment at a small telecommunications company. That is where I received my first exposure to computers. Computers excited me in many of the same ways music had. For the first time since I had left school 4 years earlier, I knew the career path I wanted to pursue. I found technology so compelling that I eventually found a position with a company that focused on one of the emerging technologies at the time—CD-ROM. I learned about hardware, software, marketing, and selling. As the Convention Manager, I went to the biggest industry trade shows (Comdex, MacWorld, etc.), managing our exhibits and our people (both permanent and part time) and selling the technology. I worked directly with our major vendors such as NEC, Hitachi, Denon, and Pioneer.

One of my vendors suggested I would do well in sales. That suggestion put me on my current career path. After selling technology consulting services to the Wall Street community for several years, I was totally hooked. I had seen how the information technology departments in banks and financial service firms designed and built applications to run their businesses. I learned about the technologies that corporate America depends on—databases, on-line transaction processors, networking infrastructures, mainframe computers, and client server architectures.

While I enjoyed selling services, I wanted to increase my technical expertise. I decided to go to a major software company. At over $4 billion in annual revenues, Computer Associates (CA) is one of the largest software companies in the world. CA focuses on the software that runs businesses—the databases that track transactions on Wall Street, the security software that protects banking systems from hacking, the manufacturing and inventory systems that run production lines, and the enterprise-class object technology that heralds the future of business processing. Working with Fortune 100 and government clients in Manhattan, I got a firsthand understanding of how the mission-critical information technology is deployed and managed in the service of strategic business goals at some of the largest corporate and government sites in the U.S.

My time at CA gave me everything I wished for in my technology career. I gained exposure to technology law (including intellectual property issues) and contracts. I had some of the largest clients in the world—Time Warner and Home Box Office (HBO), M&M Mars, the City of New York, Merrill Lynch, the Federal Reserve Bank, and the NYPD. I became proficient in the technological details of software. I structured long-term financial agreements that were calculation intensive and exposed me to elements of finance and accounting. However, CA does not offer other career opportunities to its sales professionals. In the last year of my time at CA, I knew that I would seek a graduate business degree—another pursuit CA does not support. I found myself in a Catch-22 situation. Although CA provided full tuition reimbursement, if I revealed my intentions to attend graduate school, my management would have considered it as a statement that I was not committed to my job. Also, CA does not provide competitive base compensation. I needed to have a larger flow of guaranteed income in order to save for school. After a thorough search, I chose to move to Magna in November of this year.

I could not be happier at Magna. I doubled my salary and received an equity position. I have been empowered to help develop the organization (see Section II, #2). I indicated to Magna at the beginning that I intended to pursue graduate school. My boss and our Chairman are flexible enough to have committed to making whatever arrangements are necessary—tuition support, a summer position, etc.—for me to realize that goal. Talented people in all areas of the software industry are in high demand. Magna has demonstrated that, having landed me, they are willing to do what is necessary to retain me.

In my recent positions, I have seen a profound disconnection between business goals and technology management. I have a lot of ideas about how to become a part of the solution, as a consultant or CIO, by centralizing technology in an organization and aligning technology more closely with business objectives. However, I currently lack the skills to implement my ideas. While I have had some experience in marketing and selling technology, I have yet to study organizational development or technology strategy and planning. I was delighted when I discovered the ITBT track at Sloan. The ITBT curriculum is nothing short of revolutionary, and it is directly in line with my past experience and my future objectives. The ITBT track at Sloan is the only program I have seen at a major business school that provides integration of all the cross-functional courses a manager needs to be truly successful in managing technology into the future. ITBT is not just a technology concentration that makes a polite nod toward management science. Since the ITBT track requires participants to train in most major areas of business activity, the track manages to wed technology to business in a relevant way.

Although I have a number of characteristics that distinguish me from the rest of your applicant pool, I also have the skills necessary to succeed in and benefit from the Sloan program. My 700 GMAT score demonstrates I have a better aptitude for business school programs than 97% of the other aspiring MBAs who took the test. In preparation for applying to Sloan, I undertook outside coursework to develop the quantitative skills necessary to be admitted. After not having taken a math class since high school, I completed two years of college math last year, achieving straight As in every class through Calculus II. I have done equally well in statistics and accounting. I am currently enrolled in economics (see attached current school schedule), and I expect similar results. While my quantitative skills help me to fit in with the pool of other aspiring Sloan students, the same skills set me apart as well. People who are capable in the areas of creativity and interpersonal skills, as I am, are not usually as adept in quantitative pursuits. My strong abilities on both sides of the equation distinguish me from the bulk of other applicants.

Thank you for considering my application. I look forward to having the opportunity to attend the Sloan School.

2. **The goal of the Sloan program is to educate business leaders to operate in a world where technological sophistication and the international environment necessitate increasing organizational change. With this in mind, discuss your views regarding the management of technological change as a vital skill for future managers, what impact technological change has had on your chosen field, and how MIT will prepare you to face these challenges.**

Managing technological change will be the single most vital skill for managers in the 21st century, particularly senior managers. Technology management will even take an even higher priority than globalization, because globalization, in large measure, depends on technology. The businesses that can manage technology best will reap the greatest competitive advantages globally.

Technological change has not just impacted my chosen field—it is my chosen field. As a representative for a software vendor, it has been my job to know my clients' information technology (IT) environments and demonstrate solutions that will assist them in making changes. Working with my clients at Computer Associates ("CA"— a $4 billion software company) put me right in the middle of IT in both the public and private sectors. After negotiating a $7 million global contract, my colleagues and I received a rare private tour of an M&M candy plant. I thus saw firsthand how M&M Mars uses technology for manufacturing. I designed a long-term contract for New Jersey Transit (the state bus and rail transportation agency) that changed how they managed their technology costs by reallocating funds from the operating budget to the capital budget when the Governor mandated operating cost reductions. I helped multiple agencies throughout the City of New York update their IT environments for the new millennium by including $1 million of year 2000 solutions as part of a $9 million long term agreement. Some of HBO's (Home Box Office) most important corporate information consists of digital assets (i.e., original films and programs). We investigated HBO's possible use of CA's object database as a new way to manage those assets and gain greater efficiency in their use. These projects demonstrated to me the vital role technology management plays in business strategy and operations in every industry.

The role of IT in business has shifted dramatically over the last decade. It used to be that IT was nothing more than a tool, a cost center for a business. Now, IT is the business, promoting competitive advantages, operational efficiencies, better customer service and even new products. Despite the critical role IT now plays, many organizations still treat IT as separate from business functions. Business people and IT experts often do not communicate effectively, so technology implementation occurs without anyone ever answering the question, "What is the value to our business?"

The degree to which IT remains isolated from strategic business priorities reflects the degree to which the business loses. If IT is not in touch with the users it supports, failure results because technologists develop products for technology's sake rather than for a concrete business result. A website can be loaded with java applets, VRML, and flashy graphics, but if it does not provide a tangible business benefit (better market intelligence, increased revenue or market share, reduced operating costs, higher customer satisfaction) and if the information from that website cannot be captured and integrated into the corporate information assets in a useful fashion, how well invested was the time and money to produce that site? On the other hand, business users lose opportunities because they are either unaware of what IT is capable of delivering or cannot leverage the existing IT resources. Many users currently have access to applications that are stable, feature/function rich, and efficient. But they are arcane—ugly to look at, difficult to learn, and inflexible. Users have the power to get the information they need, but they may not know how. These same systems, while state-of-the-art when built, do not have the adaptability required by a fast-paced, global business environment.

Businesses already have in place vast numbers of IT assets that are not being efficiently utilized. The problem will only be compounded as new technologies continue to emerge. Businesses will need people dedicated to evaluating and, where it makes sense, integrating emerging technologies. The availability of new technologies is outpacing the supply of technology literate business people who can assist in making adoption decisions.

To close the communications gap, gain efficiency from existing resources, and effectively take advantage of new technologies, companies will need two things: technically knowledgeable business managers and ongoing organizational changes to allow better strategic utilization of IT. [This is where I come in and why a Sloan MBA is best credential for my career aspirations. I have a business-based technology background.] I need to leverage my existing background and develop the additional skills in, for example, strategic planning and managing organizational change that will allow me to bring my vision of efficient IT organizations to fruition.

In addition to enhancing my existing background, study at MIT will provide me with the rigorous grounding in quantitative skills that has not been available to me in my previous studies and is provided by precious few MBA programs. The team-focused nature of Sloan's program will allow me to gain from the diverse experiences of my colleagues and assist me in continuing to develop the skills necessary to work in a team environment—which will be critical to future technology managers as they reach out across diverse areas of the business. I also want the opportunity to write a thesis. I have not seen much published research on the changing role of technology in business and how best to manage it. I think I can develop and deliver a powerful paper on the subject, and MIT will give me the opportunity and the resources to produce work of this nature.

I am passionate about technology. MIT provides a unique environment that is, in large part, dedicated to the study of business technology. In the words of Professor Thurow in your brochure, I see MIT as "the best place in the world where technology and management intersect." I look forward to having the opportunity to take advantage of this environment.

3. **Describe a situation where you introduced and/or managed change in an organization. Tell us how you influenced others in an organization (business, school, extracurricular activity) and comment on the professional and/or personal attributes you used to do that and how these attributes (and others) might be important to the attainment of your career goals. How do you expect the Sloan School to further the development of these attributes?**

My boss at my new job encourages me to take action wherever I feel I can contribute to the organization. It is a large part of the reason I made the move to Magna Software. Because of his support and because Magna is a small organization right now, I have the luxury of rapidly initiating and implementing new ideas and changes. Being able to do so is one of the things I like best about my new job, and I am taking full advantage of the opportunity.

Magna needs to generate revenues as quickly as possible in order to secure further venture funding. There are several obstacles to overcome in order to deliver quick sales. As a small company, Magna suffers from lack of name recognition. Also, our market space, "Application Development Tools," is crowded and is a difficult category in which to differentiate a product. A marketing study indicated we could benefit technically from integration with a systems management platform. CA's Unicenter product is the industry leading systems management platform, and it has a large installed base in the Wall Street financial community, which is Magna's target market. I saw that partnering with CA would solve two problems for Magna: product differentiation (since our product would be one of a very few development tools that was integrated with Unicenter) and name recognition (through association with

CA's established branding). Additionally, Magna would gain access to CA's substantial installed base in our target market. I arranged and attended the initial meeting, and Magna is moving forward with the partnership. I am now responsible for managing the CA relationship and the integration of our product with Unicenter.

Since much of the application development in Magna's target market is conducted as part of Big Six consulting firm engagements, I also suggested to my boss that we aggressively pursue relationships with those firms. If Magna, as an Application Development Tool vendor, was to ignore the Big Six, we would be overlooking an important dynamic in how application development occurs on Wall Street. If Wall Street needs development expertise, it is likely to turn to a full-service solution provider (like a Big Six firm) that has financial market expertise as well as systems development capabilities. Wall Street will not trust a small, unknown software firm (like Magna) alone for mission-critical systems development. However, if Magna is the tool brought in by the Big Six, we gain instant credibility and penetration.

Magna, having had an engineering focus for many years, has shunned liaisons with consultants, feeling that the Magna technology was a product that could stand on its own and be directly marketed to any client. I had to perform a delicate, difficult internal sell to change that attitude. However, I was finally able to alter the internal perception of the value of relationships with consultants, and I have recently begun to bring Magna to the Big Six.

In both instances there were many skills I used to bring about change: analysis, planning, teamwork, patience, maturity, communication, listening, negotiation, compromise and persistence. The first step was to do a thorough analysis and develop a plan of action. I analyzed where the Magna's benefits would be, and ensured I had considered any pitfalls that might exist. I enlisted support for my ideas from several colleagues and took their input before talking to my boss. In the process of doing so, I found a strong ally—Tom, our VP of Development. He had come from a Big Six background and knew the value of partnering with them. Tom had tried unsuccessfully to enroll my boss and our Chairman in the value of the idea, and was willing to try again. Tom's support, perspective, and information about his experiences helped me in formulating my approach.

I did not approach my boss until I was sure of the value the partnerships could bring to our sales efforts, and could articulate a plan for how to reach out to CA and the Big Six. Next, I made sure I allowed my boss to react to my ideas, without challenging him or arguing. When I had listened enough to understand his concerns, I addressed them, incorporating examples of some of the CA Unicenter clients we would be able to reach and some of the Big Six application development engagements I had encountered at our target clients. I again highlighted the ways the partnerships would assist Magna in achieving our sales goals. Since he was not ready to decide immediately, I gave him some time to think it over. After a week or two, I broached the subject again. By this time, Tom had also taken up the discussion with my boss independently. It took some time, but he finally gave me the go-ahead.

While the skills listed above are important to success in all areas of life, they are particularly important to a successful career in technology management. As so beautifully illustrated by the ITBT track curriculum, successful technology management in the future will require more than computer expertise. The sweeping impact of technology across all industries and all areas of business operations will require managers who are as adept at "soft skills" as they are at understanding hardware and software. Because technology affects business processes, the undertaking of technology management is the undertaking of effecting continual organizational change—working with people and processes in diverse teams that may include technologists, strategists, financial experts, and functional experts.

The ITBT track at Sloan is the only major MBA program that provides an integrated foundation of general management disciplines presented from within a technology management perspective. The Proseminar program grounds the ITBT track in the ever changing reality of technology practices in actual businesses. I am confident that the Sloan School is the best place for me to develop both the hard and soft skills I will need to be an effective technology manager in the future.

4. Please elaborate on your leadership activities.

Prior to the recent leadership experiences I have detailed in Section II, #2, my most significant leadership experience occurred at Computer Associates (CA). I was put in charge of building a long-term financial deal with M&M Mars, a multi-billion dollar food manufacturer, for all CA software at over 30 sites globally. I was designated the single point of contact for all CA activities related to the deal. There were several different groups I needed to manage: the business applications sales group, the information management sales group, the systems management sales group, the CA technical support group, CA corporate management, and the management from over 30 client sites. Different groups within CA had different agendas. It was my job to establish the direction of the deal and unify everyone's efforts consistent with that direction.

First, I had to develop a vision of where the deal was going and a strategy to get there. Then I had to communicate this information in a way that would gain people's support. To build the kind of rapport with people I needed meant being flexible enough to recognize and accommodate a wide variety of personal styles.

Although I had responsibility for the deal, I was not vested with any formal authority. In the absence of this, it took a tremendous amount of drive and persistence to keep things moving in the right direction. It required a lot of energy to maintain my own focus and that of the group in the face of the inevitable obstacles and changes inherent in such a large project.

While I needed cooperation, I also had to have the strength to stand up to challenges. One manager at another location deliberately pulled rank to try to intimidate me into making a concession to his group. I did not lose my cool, but neither did I back down. The manager ultimately went to my Divisional VP, who unequivocally supported me. The other manager was not pleased with the outcome, but I gained his respect.

Due to the work I did on this deal, I was promoted two levels. The deal was successfully closed shortly after I was promoted. My experience taught me effective leadership requires a balance between consensus and assertiveness, as well as a wide range of interpersonal and communication skills.

I have also served in several leadership capacities outside of work. In my 12 years (1980–1992) of work with Al-Anon, an all-volunteer, community service group for people with alcoholic friends or family members, I was elected as group leader and acted as a personal sponsor to several people. As group leader, I was responsible for preparing and leading the meetings. As a sponsor, I was the primary support contact for several individuals, and was responsible for assisting them in resolving issues outside of the meetings.

At Landmark Education, between 1984 and 1988, I served as the leader of several teams. In Ann Arbor, I led logistics teams that produced seminar events. In New York, I was the Computer Team Leader, responsible for the team that performed the corporate data processing for all seminar enrollments in the region.

5. **Please elaborate on your hobbies and interests.**

One of my lifelong interests has been playing viola. The focus of my early education was music. The training required to become a musician in a major professional orchestra is grueling by any standards, and I trained at the top of the classical music field from an early age. Before I graduated high school, I had traveled and performed throughout the U.S. and Europe. My youth symphony was chosen as the one international orchestra to participate in the Schools Proms Concerts, a celebrated international festival at Royal Albert Hall in London. The local PBS station, KTCA, sent camera crews with us to England and made a documentary about it. I was selected as the "hostess" of the show and had the honor of acting as the spokesperson for the group.

I spent two summers at Tanglewood, studying with the Boston Symphony—earning college credit and early admission to Boston University. Money was always tight for our family, so I graduated high school early and worked full time in order to pay for my second summer at Tanglewood. During college, after competing in national auditions, I was selected to attend the Los Angeles Philharmonic summer program, under the direction of Michael Tilson-Thomas. Once there, I was selected as the principal violist. The position involved leading the section and playing several solo passages in concert. We performed with the LA Philharmonic and gave concerts at the Hollywood Bowl. While in the program, I took and won an audition for a professional orchestra position with the Sacramento Symphony before I had even graduated from college.

It was a rude awakening at 25, when I discovered I would not be able to earn the kind of living I desired in music. However, after working in business and earning a much better living than I could as a musician, I made the decision not to pursue music as a career. I found I enjoyed my music even more without the pressure of relying on it to provide me with a living. Business, particularly technology, was providing me with new stimulation and satisfaction, and I was excited about it as a career choice. I also knew that I would have a more comfortable lifestyle and the money to spend on music (i.e., for lessons, classes, equipment, and tickets to NYC performances) by staying with business. Ironically enough, it was after having made the decision to leave music as a full time career that I finally played at Lincoln Center and, at long last, Carnegie Hall. Music remains an integral part of my life. I will always be a musician, and I am confident that I have made the right decision about what role music will play in my life.

I have an unquenchable thirst for learning, so I am always trying new hobbies. I have enjoyed cooking since childhood, when I used to bake with my mother. I still make dozens of Christmas cookies every year. Several years ago, I took up gardening. I particularly like herbs and vegetables because I can share them with others as gifts and use them myself for cooking.

I have always enjoyed fitness activities such as step aerobics and biking. Recently I took up rollerblading, and I have found there is nothing that compares to skating outdoors on a beautiful spring or fall day. I have also found there is nothing to get my adrenaline pumping like a rousing game of rollerhockey every now and then!

I have also enjoyed my volunteer work with the Drumthwacket Foundation since moving to Princeton. Drumthwacket is an historic estate that serves as the official residence for the Governor of New Jersey. Although recently the bulk of my time has been devoted to preparing for graduate school, I have served there as a docent whenever possible. My duties have been to learn the details of the estate's history, to lead tours through the mansion, and to be available to talk to guests when the Governor is entertaining. (I even had the opportunity to meet Governor Whitman last year.) The mansion features art and antiques that relate to the history of New Jersey or the local area—Princeton or Trenton (the state capital). For example, the Tiffany silver from the retired Battleship New Jersey is prominently displayed in the dining room, with figurines of Liberty and Prosperity (the symbols on the New Jersey state flag) adorning the punch bowl. I enjoy educating others about the house, its furnishings, and the state and local history associated with the estate. You can see people's interest grow as they come to understand that each of the items is not just a beautiful piece, but also part of their heritage as state residents.

Recently, I suggested to the director of the foundation that I build a website for Drumthwacket that would allow it to maximize the revenues from its gift shop. I expect to complete the project this spring. It is satisfying for me to put my modern technology skills into service for an organization dedicated to preserving history.

6. Please elaborate on any special academic circumstances you wish to explain.

I faced several unique challenges in my undergraduate career. First, a music school curriculum is generally undervalued from a credit standpoint. For example, a two-credit orchestra class required six hours of in-class rehearsal, two hours per day of practice dedicated to that class, and evening concerts. My orchestra class demanded 18 hours of work per week for two credit hours. Chamber music and lessons (my most important class) required similarly disproportionate time commitments to credit hours. More importantly, however, I faced personal challenges over the course of my undergraduate career that significantly disrupted the pursuit of my degree.

I graduated from high school in 1979. My father was an active alcoholic at that point, and his drinking was at its pinnacle that year as I began college. In February of my freshman year, I found out my parents had not paid any of my Boston University bills when I was denied my monthly meal ticket and directed to speak to the administration. The family stress took its toll on me and negatively impacted my work. My academic performance was also affected and my grades slid. I knew that if I wanted to stay in school, I would have to transfer to somewhere less expensive and closer to home beginning in the fall of 1980. I chose University of Michigan because of its excellent music program and because I had friends, who provided a support system, in Ann Arbor.

In August of 1980, the summer after my freshman year of college, my father was placed in a treatment program mandated by his employer. Although he successfully completed the program, he lost his job and was unemployed for most of my first year at University of Michigan (1980–81). At the end of that spring semester, my parents could not pay for school, and I had to drop out of Michigan. I was determined that my family circumstances would not prevent me from completing my education. I talked to banks, but I could not secure any loans (since I was still a minor). Finally, I discovered that since University of Michigan is a state school, it would insure that any resident who qualified for admission received enough financial aid to attend.

I investigated the residency requirements and learned that establishing residency would require me to live full-time in Michigan for three years on my own, since my parents were not state residents. At the end of that time I would have to submit tax returns and other documentation to show that I had earned enough money to be fully self supporting without any aid from my family. In the fall of 1981, at the age of 19, I became the head of my household. During the three years I was out of school, I juggled making a living with continuing my musical studies. I held two to three jobs concurrently, waitressing and playing in local orchestras in order to pay for my viola lessons. Despite being out of school and having to support myself, I continued with my studies.

In the fall of 1984, I successfully completed my residency application, secured a bank loan (since I was now over 21) for the balance my parents had not been able to pay, and returned to school. Even though I still had to work several jobs to support myself, I was able to bring my grades up and make significant progress in my viola studies. In the summer of 1985, I attended the L.A. Philharmonic summer program (see Essay #3). While in Los Angeles, I also auditioned for and won a professional position in the Sacramento Symphony. I met a conducting student to whom I became engaged.

In the fall of 1985 I began my final year of college with the knowledge that I had secured a position in my chosen (and highly competitive) field. Very few musicians graduate music school having already won a professional audition. I felt I had finally put all the struggles of the last several years behind me and was again moving in a positive direction.

In January of 1986 my mother was diagnosed as being terminally ill and given 12 weeks to live. The semester had already begun when we received the diagnosis. I was faced with the option of dropping out of school again if I wanted to spend time with my mother. I agonized over the decision. I had faced such a long delay already that I did not want to postpone my degree any further. I decided to complete as much coursework as I could while traveling between Minneapolis and Michigan. I made arrangements with my professors and was able to spend most of the semester at home. I prepared and performed my recital (without which I could not graduate), but there were several elective credits and one music theory course that I had not completed earlier that remained to be finished before I could receive my degree. Meanwhile, the Sacramento Symphony had gone on strike, so I had to look for other post-graduation options on top of helping to care for my mother.

During the semester, I auditioned for and was accepted to an internship program at Carnegie Hall and my fiancé was accepted to Juilliard for graduate studies. My mother died in April of 1986. We moved to New York City in June, despite my incomplete degree. I was emotionally and mentally exhausted. I needed to spend some time away from school since all it did was remind me of a long series of painful events.

Just after I found an apartment and signed a lease in New York, I received notice from the Carnegie Hall Program that it had lost funding and canceled its program for the year. A few weeks later the Sacramento Symphony called. The strike had ended. Could I come to California to accept the orchestra position?

I was now committed to a lease and to my fiancé—who was attending grad school at Juilliard. My opportunity in New York had just evaporated at a time when I could not replace it with something comparable. My new commitments required me to stay in New York rather than accept the Sacramento Symphony position or go back to finish school.

I was struggling personally to integrate the events of the last several years. I could not even pick up my viola, let alone function well enough to take auditions. The next year or so was just about going through the motions every day and beginning to recover. My fiancé and I ended our engagement. In the first year, our relationship had been through his move from California, my mother's death, and our move to New York, as well as new career adjustments. It proved to be too much for us to handle.

I had no focus whatsoever on my career, nor did I finish the credits left on my degree for some time after this. I needed to work since I had acquired a significant amount of debt going between Michigan and Minnesota when my mother was sick. This is the point at which I began working full time. I gradually worked on the outstanding credits for my degree via University of Michigan independent study, and finished the highly specialized music theory requirements at The Juilliard School.

I have only one regret in my life—not finishing my undergraduate degree sooner. My delay in completing this task was in no way a reflection of the value I place on my degree or on education in general. Because of my earlier experiences, finishing my degree became an emotionally charged situation. I procrastinated due to the painful memories associated with school. If I had it to do over again, I would have finished immediately. My regret has been exacerbated by the process of applying to MBA programs, because I am reminded of it every day. I was haunted by this element of my life as long as it was unresolved. For years I had a recurring nightmare that I was a senior in high school and suddenly realized in June that I had cut an entire semester of a required class, thereby preventing my graduation. I would wake up with a racing heart. Since I have completed it, my degree has ceased to occupy my nightmares and has instead come to symbolize a dream come true. Now I dream at night about getting my MBA, and my dreams are filled with positive expectations. I have forgiven myself this oversight and moved forward. I hope you will forgive it, too.

I believe the following situation is the result of a simple administrative error. However, to be on the safe side I want to explain two "E" grades on my University of Michigan transcripts.

In my Junior year at Michigan, I missed a final in Music Theory 451—Analysis of Tonal Music, I had an A in the class until that point. Since I missed the final and did not make up the exam in a timely fashion, I received a grade of "Incomplete." I had until I graduated to make up the work. I got an A in the next course in the series, Music History 452—Analysis of 20th Century Music, for which MT451 was a prerequisite. I planned to complete the coursework in my last term. At that point, I had to leave school for most of the semester due to my mother's illness and death. It took me a long time to find a comparable class that was available at an institution that would satisfy Michigan's requirements and was scheduled at a convenient time. When I finally did make up the course, I did so at the Juilliard School. I received As in the classes. However, for reasons unknown to me, Michigan did not remove the "Lapsed Incomplete—E" from my transcript.

Also in my Junior year, there is an unofficial drop grade for a freshman-level Music History/Musicology class—MH 140. My coursework prior to coming to Michigan allowed me to be waived out of the course.

These situations came as an unpleasant surprise to me. I was not aware of the "E" grades until I had to calculate my GPA for MBA applications. I thought both grades had been resolved prior to the conferral of my degree. I will be contacting the University of Michigan to see whether I can have corrections made.

7. Is there any additional information you wish to share?

Although my application has presented many facts about my circumstances, it has not presented some of the intangible qualities that I have acquired as a result of these circumstances. I would like to leave you with some impressions of who I am in addition to what I have done. Also, because my second career of technology is such a departure from my musical background, I wanted to explain the road I have taken to get here.

One of the things that is a fundamental part of "who I am" is the rampant alcoholism found on both sides of my family. For instance, in November my uncle died of liver failure. Quite frankly, he drank himself to death. Like my uncle, the members of my mother's family have never recovered from this devastating disease, and their lives serve as an ever present reminder about the dangers I, too, could face.

On the other hand, my father, his brother, and his sister (all alcoholics) have been sober for 15 years or more. Their lives serve as an ever present reminder of what courage and commitment can accomplish. They inspire me. Each of them has faced and overcome an unbelievably daunting challenge—made a choice that literally meant life or death. One time when I was irritated with my dad about something and complained to my brother, he brought my dad's situation into laser-sharp focus for me. He said, "Can you imagine waking up one day at 44 and realizing you've failed professionally and financially, your marriage is on the rocks and you've mistreated your wife and children for the last two decades?" My brother's distillation of my dad's experience created in my mind's eye a view of an enormously high wall, a wall that looked insurmountable. In that moment I realized my father had made it over the wall, and I was humbled by the courage and the faith the task had demanded of him.

The respect I have for that side of my family and the lessons I have learned from my experiences during my dad's recovery motivate me to always strive for the best, to always push the edge of the envelope. I have learned that with commitment and dedication anything is possible. Their successful efforts at sobriety have taught me never to say "Never." Seeing my family accomplish a recovery they never imagined possible has given me the courage to take risks (like leaving a successful career and going back to school at age 36) because I have absolute faith that I am capable of achieving much more tomorrow than I can possibly imagine today.

Making the choice to be sober does not just magically fix everything. At best, the recovery process is a long, hard road back. The process requires resources (from both you and those closest to you) that are unimaginable at the time of commitment. I believe that if everyone knew in advance how hard the road is, very few would actually brave it. I am profoundly grateful that my family did.

I also learned a great deal from my experiences with my mother. I learned from her death that life can be over at any second—with no warning, no sense of fair play, no rules. So while I am in it, I better play at the top of my game at every moment—not procrastinate, not wait until another day. My mother's death taught me I can never know for sure which sunrise will be my last.

I came to realize that life was not all about me and my problems. I now know that everyone else's difficulties are just as real to them as mine are to me. While my challenge now is applying to MIT, my classmates at the Community College I am attending face much different challenges. Most will never have the abilities or opportunity to attend a top ten business school. However, they feel as strongly about reaching their goals as I feel about getting into MIT. The pain of going through my mother's death gave me more respect for other people's struggles, regardless of whether or not they would be struggles for me.

I also appreciate the gifts I have been given and recognize them as just that—gifts. Every day I open my eyes is a gift—one that was denied my mother at a young age. My good health, sound mind and sound body are all gifts. My intelligence and musical talents are gifts. The work I have done and the discipline I have exercised to develop those gifts have been my doing, but the raw material was given to me at birth. Not everyone has the same good fortune. That is another lesson that has been reinforced by my colleagues at the Community College.

Going through my mother's illness and death taught me to appreciate all that is good in my life. When I arrive at Penn Station in New York City during my morning commute, sometimes I look at the long line for the escalators and think, "Oh, man! I do not want to have to walk up the stairs!" For me the thought that immediately follows is, "Thank goodness I am well and healthy enough to be able to walk up the stairs."

When I was about 8 and living in Detroit with my family, I was reading a newspaper article about a young, drug-addicted prostitute who was badly abused by her boyfriend. I went to my mother and said, "She got what she deserved. I would never do what she did." My mother told me not to judge others because we never know what has brought them to their current situations. I could not believe she was defending this woman's choices! Then she said something to me that took me years to understand. She said, "Cynthia, there, but for the grace of God, go I." Those words still echo profoundly throughout my life. Whenever I catch myself wanting to judge someone harshly, I remind myself that given the alcoholism and difficult experiences I endured growing up, things could have turned out very differently for me. I could have been the alcoholic (like my father) or the woman who married young and never completed her education (like my mother).

I will never take another day in my life for granted. I will never neglect my health and well being. I will never again have a hard heart. I will always have tremendous compassion for those less fortunate, for those who suffer. I love my work, and I will always approach it with energy and passion. However, despite being the major priority in my life, it will never be the only priority.

While my application has focused on my recent professional life, my earlier musical life was also a substantial influence on who I am. In the beginning, I did not understand what people saw in classical music, but I will never forget my first Beethoven symphony. It was then that I began to develop my passion for music. I found I could spend hours working on a single movement or a single set of passages because I ached to make my fingers and my heart become the source of Beethoven's magic. The experience held power for me unmatched by anything I have experienced since. It was an epiphany. The more I learned, the more I hungered to learn. I spent three to four hours a day practicing and rehearsing after school. In a family full of "addicts," I had found my drug of choice, only it was a life-giving addiction, something that grew in a positive direction. Music brought me fulfillment, not misery, and led me on an upward spiral of growth and expansion, rather than the downward spiral that surrounded me, pulled at my life daily.

In the end, the work was a small, small price to pay for the passport I earned. Music transported me. When I was playing, my world was limitless. I became an explorer in a vast new universe. I became able to travel to places some can only dream of, places unimaginable to others. I discovered an inner landscape that I never before knew existed, one that reached outward and brought immeasurable joy to my day to day reality.

I was completely absorbed in my music. I needed the strength and stability I drew from that absorption. As my inner world began to soar, my outer world continued to crumble. I am convinced that without the unerring, powerful inner compass my musical life provided I would not have survived, let alone thrived. By every leading indicator, I was a youth at tremendous risk, and it can be said that my music saved my life.

I have seen others who have faced similar difficulties in their lives become embittered and cynical. Perhaps one of the greatest miracles of my life is that, despite my experiences, I remain an optimistic, positive person. I enjoy even the simplest pleasures in my life, like watching the daffodils I planted come up every spring. I am endlessly curious and always seeking to learn new things and meet new people. I sincerely enjoy getting to know people and learning from them, a fact that has been a source of my success in a sales career. I also have a great sense of humor. Short of going into a stand-up comedy routine on paper, however, that is a difficult quality to convey in a business school application.

I choose to see the benefits of my life experiences, rather than the detriments. The challenges I have faced have given me the strength and self-confidence that are two of the strongest parts of my character. I have also developed tremendous focus and the capacity to accomplish anything I set my mind to. My determination and persistence are as much a part of me as my creativity and compassion. I have prepared myself for an MBA as well as I know how to. I have spent in excess of $6,000 in the last year and a half for tuition, test fees, application fees, GMAT prep courses, books, software, and travel expenses incurred in visiting schools. With the exception of semester breaks, I have not had a free Saturday since October of 1996 because I have been in one class or another. I have spent in excess of 30 hours a week outside of work studying, researching and writing for the last year. I changed jobs to earn more money for school. I have sought out and maximized every opportunity I could find in order to develop myself into the kind of candidate who will learn from and contribute to the Sloan School Class of 2000. The results so far have been satisfying. In the last year, I have developed quantitative abilities (calculus, accounting, statistics) I never thought I would, and found I enjoyed doing so. I have kept myself on an upward track in terms of professional development. I have disposed of any personal issues that would prevent me from taking full advantage of an MBA program.

I began my higher education in Boston a long time ago. It was the beginning of many difficult years for me. I have covered so much ground and come so far in the intervening time. It would be very meaningful for me personally to go back to Boston to finish what I started there. I truly love technology, and I have already become a valuable technology business professional. I want to take my technology career to the next level through a Sloan MBA. I have worked hard to become qualified for the opportunity to attend MIT, and I know I could contribute my maturity, my creativity, and my professional perspective to the Sloan community.

Comments

- This is an exceptionally long set of essays; nearly every one would be better off writing less than half this amount. Cynthia, however, had a large number of things to explain. She needed to show, for instance, the connections between her musical and high-tech careers and elucidate how her passion for music metamorphosed into a very different kind of career. She similarly needed to discuss (rather than ignore) her age (she is a good deal older than the typical MBA applicant) and length of time in the workforce. She does a fabulous job laying out the details of the various unusual (and sometimes unfortunate) circumstances of her life, making sure always to demonstrate why the information is relevant to her candidacy to MIT. An understanding of her harrowing journey from college to the present is important for admissions officers in their evaluation of her candidacy, since her transcript contains several false starts in obtaining her undergraduate degree, several grades of "incomplete," and other irregularities common to "nontraditional" candidates.

- It is difficult for those who work in IT or other capacities intimately related to high-tech to answer questions about how technology has affected their careers, since technology is the career. While not skirting the question, Cynthia uses the second essay to showcase her excellent grasp of overall industry issues, further hitting home (as she does in all her essays) that despite an early career in music, she possesses the technical knowledge, quantitative skills, and raw intellectual talent necessary to succeed at Sloan and beyond.

CARL

WHARTON EXECUTIVE MBA PROGRAM (Selected)

1. What are your ultimate career objectives? How will the WEMBA program contribute to your attainment of these objectives?

For years my friends would tell me I was the happiest lawyer they knew. How things have changed!

For nine years I worked as a litigator at a plaintiff class action firm, prosecuting a caseload of complex class actions alleging securities and financial fraud. My experience in securities and financial fraud litigation gave me an education in business disasters and how managers dealt with them, from failed new products to financial fraud committed to create the appearance of fabulous success (or to conceal the effects of an overall business downturn). With the more egregious frauds, I found myself focusing on what went wrong with the company leadership and when—what the chief executives did wrong and what circumstances and pressures led them to the point at which they took the wrong path.

I also gained experience with the business of running an entrepreneurial class action firm. Securities class actions typically last for years and cost hundreds of thousands to over a million dollars to prosecute. The attorneys generally pay the costs of litigation up front for everything from copying charges to private investigators' and experts' fees, and recover only if they succeed in winning a judgment or reaching an agreement to settle the case. My effective use of resources in advancing the ball was key: I had to make appropriate strategic and tactical choices every day.

These cases are usually run with a group of lead counsel firms, each designating its own team of lawyers to work together on the case—despite often-conflicting desires for control and power. I usually dealt with (especially early in my career) more experienced lawyers who were geographically dispersed, and my strategy for leading these teams was ordinarily accomplished through influence—using preparation, creativity, perseverance and often humor—rather than imposed through use of aggression or a dominating personality. While I was capable of such behavior, I personally value reasonableness and fairness in dealing with others, and persuasion was always my first strategic choice. This enabled me to build relationships of trust with my colleagues and co-counsel despite our different agendas. These values were not always rewarded in the litigation context, where, at least in the environment in which I practiced, aggression and confrontation were often paramount. But my way was ultimately effective, both within the firm and in running my caseload—I was made a partner in my first year of eligibility and was jointly responsible for recovering over $160 million on behalf of our clients in the course of my career.

My reasons for leaving litigation were professional and personal. While I enjoyed the intellectual challenge and the excitement of litigation, after nine years I felt that I was spending my career criticizing others' decisions rather than making my own decisions and creating something myself. Ultimately I felt that I was spending too much of my professional energy focusing on assigning blame, and I wanted to be part of a team that was creating something other than a lawsuit. On a personal level, I felt that my personal values of reasonableness and fairness were not a great fit with the work I was doing every day, and that I needed to change my career to more accurately reflect who I was and who I wanted to become.

I left litigation as a partner in the firm and joined an Internet based integrated media company with about 65 employees, focused on the teen boy demographic. I joined the company because I had great faith in the CEO's leadership talent and was interested in exploring a management role in an intense yet collaborative work environment. This company offered me that opportunity.

I had a dual role: General Counsel and Director of the Relationships Channel. As General Counsel, I worked closely with the CEO, outside counsel and key players in the Company to create an overall legal strategy, balancing budgetary and logistical realities. I moved quickly up the learning curve on IP issues and worked to establish a copyright policy and trademark strategy for our limited launch in February, 2000. While I worked hard to get up the learning curve on the specifics of IP and other issues, my litigation experience with business disasters served me well—managing risk proactively based on the resources at hand was a natural fit for me. I felt very capable of evaluating the various risks and costs and, with the help of outside counsel, came up with a solid, comprehensive and proactive legal plan that protected us without blowing our legal budget.

As General Counsel I worked with managers in many functional areas of the business, including engineers (IP issues, privacy policy, security), sales and public relations. I reviewed all content before it was posted on the site and was involved in editing decisions, including attribution of quotes. I was part of the senior management team, attending meetings of the board of directors and weekly management meetings with the CEO and her other direct reports. As Director of the Relationships Channel, I met with focus groups and high school boys to find out what issues they faced, what resources they had, the amount of time they spent online and whether they would seek online advice. My responses to boys' questions about their parents, friends and crushes were then published on the Relationships Channel of our website.

My ultimate career goal is to move to a management role at a publicly held company and eventually attain the CEO position. The WEMBA program will help me gain expertise in finance, marketing and financial reporting and more broadly in organizational management, and will give me a credential that my peers will recognize and respect. As a litigator, while I learned a substantial amount about leading and managing groups, financial accounting, negotiation, strategy and tactics, my perspective on business was primarily that of an advocate and was limited to legal and ethical issues of fiduciary duty, legality and liability. Yet, in a sense, I also used the "case method" to study business disasters in great depth during these years and learned much about leadership as a result. At the internet company, my experience was very broad; I interacted with and influenced decisions in most functional areas at the company. The WEMBA program will help me continue to broaden my perspective and learn more, from professors and classmates, about leadership and the various functions in business. I believe that my legal training and business experience at the Internet start-up, combined with a powerful business degree from Wharton, will give me a rare and valuable perspective on leadership and management issues.

Comments

- Lawyers often make weak MBA applicants. They too readily believe that a good GMAT score and undergraduate GPA make them attractive candidates, thereby missing the fact that business schools crave candidates whose professional experience will allow them to contribute to the classroom and project experience of their classmates. Furthermore, they generally look to be running away from law rather than toward business.

- Carl shows that he had legitimate reasons (both professional and personal) for wanting to leave law, despite the fact that he was a very successful litigator. It was important that he demonstrate he had the intellectual energy and ambition to be successful in law, but that his values and interests eventually led him into business. Likewise, it is important that he had worked in a business capacity for a time before applying to the executive program, which allowed him to justify his interest in business and prove himself able in this new environment.

- The older an applicant, the more important it is that his career direction be clear. This is particularly likely to be problematic for a self-sponsored executive MBA applicant, let alone for someone intending to get out of law. Carl is able to show that he has a clear direction set for his future career, and that his goals are in fact achievable.

JOSEPH
DARTMOUTH/TUCK (Selected)

1. Discuss your career progression to date. Elaborating on your short- and long-term goals, how do you see your career progressing after you receive an MBA? Why do you want an MBA from Tuck?

In May, 1993, as the airplane's wheels touched down on Barranquillan soil in Colombia, South America while the tropical sun set, Robert Frost's "The Road Not Taken" flashed through my mind. Back on the other side of the Caribbean sea were opportunities that were perhaps gone for good: entrances to engineering grad schools such as UC Berkeley and an acceptance to GE's two year Manufacturing Management Program. But my decision to return to Colombia—a country where I wanted to make a difference by helping out in any way that I could, especially using my recently acquired engineering background—was made. Ahead instead was the unknown. Feeling despondent and scared, I thought to myself, "What on earth have you done?" The prospect of returning, against my family's and friends' advice, to the country that I had left when I was twelve, a country about to enter civil war, did not seem reassuring.

Seven years later, I can confirm that by moving to Colombia I made the right decision personally and professionally, though it has entailed marching to the beat of a different drummer.

Personally, I have learned to regularly meditate and do yoga. I am a certified hypnosis therapist, and I can cook a paella, a Spanish rice with everything in it from squid to alcaparras, and most dishes in between. Athletically, after three years of sweat and commitment, I was able to get my black belt degree with only one black eye in the process. I am a member of a rare breed, kaizen-inspired managers who can dance salsa and merengue and delicately juggle a soccer ball at the same time. But perhaps I am most proud of having seen an Andean condor at 12,000 feet and of having survived the hepatitis A virus in the same year, a humbling experience indeed. A now true-believer in God, I am undergoing the third year of a theology program organized by the Roman Catholic church, though I am not baptized yet, since I do not like to swallow anything whole.

Professionally, two major events have influenced my thinking and shaped my development since moving to Colombia.

The first event has been starting a company, JCD Fastener Distributions, in Barranquilla, Colombia. A few years back, I saw a need in Colombia for a fastener that was not currently offered in the market, the drywall screw. I knew that it would be better if the country's economy—in the worst recession in 70 years—would show signs of recovery before trying to fill this customer need, but took the plunge anyhow. I found an excellent supplier, brought in a half-container of drywall screws from Taiwan, and managed to sell in the first month of operations four times the amount I had anticipated!

The company is into its third year, and I am widening its product lines to include other products, such as hardened steel nails and steel lock washers. JCD Fastener Distributions now has 25 employees, annual sales of $1.5 million, and over 200 customers. The satisfaction of having built something from nothing is a difficult feeling to describe, perhaps similar to what a painter feels as he creates a work. Having done this under the most trying economic conditions with very little startup capital forced me to be very creative and careful.

The second event has been saving a company, the Industrial Rivets Group (where I started out as a reengineering specialist and have worked my way to general manager), in a developing country, my most substantial accomplishment to date. When I arrived in Colombia, South America, in 1993, I was in for a complete surprise. The company that had recently hired me, though in business for over forty years and considered large by Colombian terms, had just got hit by the effects of the opening of the Colombian economy, the apertura, and began to hemorrhage. I stuck by my guns, and began to work, even to pray! I had never seen a company fall behind two weeks on the payroll and be mostly out of raw materials, with 335 worried faces to confirm my fears daily.

I knew I had to act, and act rapidly! As a reengineering specialist, I led technological changes in the company that ranged from designing and operating realtime company-wide computerized one-lot kanban systems of production to implementing jidoka (or autonomation machines with the autonomous capability to use judgment) and electronic andon projects (trouble lights and sounds that signal machine down time). As also a marketing manager, I reduced the company's total finished products from over 10,000 references to below 500 references, eliminated non-profitable lines (and developed new, more profitable ones), slashed work-in-process and finished goods inventories to a third of what they were, and eliminated the previous sales representative dominated distribution system, replacing it with company-owned warehouses in Colombia's main cities. As chief operating manager, I traveled throughout North, Central and South America, opening markets and clients. This international experience taught me to develop sensitivity to other cultures and to other ways of doing business. And as a general manager, I reduced debt from 50% of assets to 40% of assets, and converted more than three million dollars of short-term debt to medium-term debt at much more favorable rates of interest, with a two-year grace period on the capital, and consolidated the company as the leading manufacturer of fasteners in northern South America.

Seven years later, the company has only 150 direct employees who produce twice the output of the previous 335 employees. As difficult as these human resource changes were, they were done in the most humane way possible, mostly through severance pay and early retirement packages (which basically do not exist in Colombia—I developed a hybrid form of early retirement in which the worker is assured his full pension at retirement age and a monthly stipend until that time), and, in some cases, the possibility of returning. The company now operates under modern flow manufacturing and JIT engineering concepts, under a total kanban system, exports heavily, and competes head-to-head with Taiwan and mainland China.

My greatest satisfaction comes from the mutual respect and team-building with the company's employees, due to the bonding and trust that resulted from the survival of such a critical and anguishing situation.

This experience of introducing and managing change and influencing others in an organization left a definite mark on my way of thinking and behaving. First, I learned that introducing and managing change is about people and teams, more than just numbers. Though it was necessary to read and thoroughly understand the Industrial Rivets Group's financial numbers to change and save the company, it was just as important to be a good cultural reader of the organization and its people. Ultimately, the success or failure of virtually all of the many projects which we implemented, whether of a technical nature, such as developing a new product, or of a "softer" nature, such as recruiting and starting up a sales organization in a new city, came down to the team that was in charge of it. Even a promising or "sure" concept sometimes failed the first time we tried it because the team members behind its implementation could not work together. In these cases, by having the team work out its differences or in a few extreme cases by changing some of its members, we were finally able to implement the change. Team dynamics were therefore focal in developing a critical mass to effect company-wide change to break down the walls of inertia (which were sometimes large) and to set the wheels in motion as our process of kaizen began.

Second, I learned that most organizations, unlike what most people think, fail not necessarily because of a lack of money but because of a lack of entrepreneurial spirit, ideas, and action, and an unwillingness to take calculated risks. Since the Industrial Rivets Group was in serious financial trouble when I began to work there, we had to focus on innovative ideas, minimize their risks, and rapidly implement these ideas, the more the better, which in turn helped our cash flow position. But if we had not changed our business strategy towards massive kaizen, reengineering and innovation, in an environment where creative ideas were the order of the day and valued, surely even a large amount of cash would not have been enough for us to survive and recover.

Finally, my work at Industrial Rivets taught me to think globally in order to understand growth. Prior to this, the company focus was mainly on the internal market and on the neighboring countries, but our recovery gave me the confidence to assume larger risks on a more global scale. Today, we export to virtually every major country in North, Central, and South America.

These two events of starting a company from scratch and of saving another have given me a beginning direct working knowledge of grass roots entrepreneurship, financial and innovative management in a technological environment flavored with strategy decisions, product development (for example, I developed hardened steel zinc-plated nails in Colombia) and project management, fundamental elements of Tuck's MBA program. Though my hard work experiences have been very formative, I must humbly recognize that I have been forced to improvise at times, even as the general manager of the Industrial Rivets Group, because my academic and professional education is not complete.

With a Tuck MBA, I hope to round off the personal package that will ultimately lead to the fulfillment of my academic and professional goals. I am drawn to Tuck because of its deep tradition of entrepreneurship, globalization, and financial and technology management (areas that are empirically familiar to me), within the perspective of the general manager. Additionally, Tuck's strong sense of community and purpose evidenced by its alumni's venerable ties to the school and to its students, by its small size, which further fosters this collective spirit, and by the respect of the business community for the school, is proof of Tuck's uniqueness and is strongly appealing. If fortunate enough to be admitted to Tuck, with my unusual international background in entrepreneurship, technology management, and change implementation, I could contribute to the school and to my fellow students through class participation, team-building (such as through the Effective Teamwork course) and the Field Study in International Business, and community service activities such as those of Tuck Volunteers.

At Dartmouth, I hope to continue developing team-building and change management expertise, be it through study groups, classes, or extra-curricular activities (such as those of the Technology Club), in an environment where different cultures and ways of thinking (and approaching problems or situations) are valued. In particular, courses such as Leading Organizations; Management of Organizational Change; and Countries and Companies in the International Economy interest me very much, because the Amos Tuck School Program, even from the start, as evidenced by the Tuck General Management Forum, begins to cover these leadership, change and team-building aspects as it looks at how to manage and design the global organization of the future. Dartmouth is the ideal place to continue developing as a global team-playing entrepreneur and leader; the first-year study group approach is further proof that the Tuck School as an institution regards innovative team-oriented leadership as central.

My short-term post-MBA goals are to continue growing as a manager and entrepreneur and to continue making a positive contribution to Colombia, a country that is in dire need of responsible and ethical business leaders. My long-term post-MBA goals are to be the general manager of a larger company, and more importantly, to start a foundation which will improve the quality of life of the community where I live and work. In my opinion, Tuck's entrepreneurial but collaborative and intellectually rich environment offers this opportunity of a lifetime by the ethics-based leadership skills, technical know-how, lasting friendships and international networking possibilities it provides.

2. What are your interests outside of your job?

In the study of universal death bed literature, one finds two leitmotifs: relationships and contributions. Simon Bolivar, the great independence leader and writer of Colombia, Venezuela, Ecuador, Peru and Bolivia, near the very end of his life wrote his final letters to Manuelita Saenz, his lifelong collaborator and herself a dynamic activist very much ahead of her times. In these letters he reminisced about his professional and personal relationship with her, and on the sacrifices and contributions that had been necessary to obtain independence from the Spanish crown. As people look back on their lives in this critical moment, these two dominant themes stand out. People in their last wakeful days focus on the lives of others they touched and changed and on the contributions they made to society and to others.

Both within and outside of my job, this is what I have most tried to do: to touch and to contribute to others, wherever they may be, in significant ways that stand the test of time. Early in my career, I thought I could do this by moving to and working in

Colombia, South America, a troubled country where I felt that I could make a difference.

As I now look back on the seven years that I have been here, perhaps the richest part of my experience in this country has come from the relationships I have formed and nourished, including those relationships stemming from my interests outside my job. In particular, my relationships with two very different people, Dr. Bruno Mazzilli and Dada Divyapremananda, stand out as relationships I will look back on for a long time to come. They have influenced me tremendously and have made a difference in their communities by their contributions to others; meanwhile, I have touched them as well.

I first met Bruno Mazzilli through my interest in hypnosis. After months of training, the critical moment came. I felt a nervous glow on my face as Bruno, a master hypnotist and communicator and director of the Clinic for Hypnosis Therapy in Barranquilla, Colombia, called my name in front of a group of students of hypnosis. "Senor Jose," he called out in his soft voice, "Will you please lead the class in our exercise for this afternoon?" I stood up, smiled, and began the process of walking the group through a mental journey involving the five senses.

Despite being over sixty years of age, Bruno often works over seventy hours a week, fueled by an intense drive to positively influence and heal others. He is a far cry from the theatrical displays of hypnosis seen on television. He does not make a high income, but lives modestly and contentedly doing what he loves. I have seen incredible things happen in his clinic, such as the time when a poor 17-year-old high school dropout suffering from marked stuttering and a learning disability, through an extended treatment which I helped lead, was rid of his stuttering and academic insufficiency. He is now a first semester engineering student.

I have been impacted by Bruno in three ways. First, I have learned that the goal in whatever you do should be to help others, for that is where true reward lies, even though it may mean foregoing material gratification. Second, Bruno, by having published various books, and by his research in the field of clinical and experimental hypnosis, has taught me the importance of "writing it down" in a country where documentation often gets neglected. Third, Bruno has shown me that it is okay to follow your heart and internal beat. In allowing me, as a therapist in his clinic, to work with and help his patients, I have gained an appreciation for and understanding of my fellow human beings that would not have been possible otherwise. Through the research I have helped Bruno with, I feel I have also been able to contribute and give back to him for all the time he has spent instructing me and sharing his work and knowledge with me.

With his colorful orange turban and tunic, Dada Divyapremananda appears to be just the opposite of Bruno. But, in fact, he is also fueled by the same intense drive to help and heal others. As the founder and director in Colombia of the Ananda Marga Yoga and Meditation Organization, which has its headquarters in India, he offers meditation and yoga classes to the community for free, as well as talks on ayurvedic medicine and lifestyle. Additionally, nearly twenty years ago, Dada founded a school that charges no tuition and offers classes from the kindergarten to the high school level in one of the most marginalized communities of the city, a community that most city dwellers are afraid to even enter.

But perhaps what most drew me toward Dada was his background as an Italian physicist that contrasts with his profound knowledge of the ayurvedic (Hindu spiritual) tradition. In his talks and interaction, Dada uses concrete examples from chemistry and physics, such as Planck's constant and its applicability to quantum mechanics and apparently random events in our lives, that contrast with the mysticism often associated with meditation and asceticism. I talk lengthily with Dada on a weekly basis, help out at the school, and participate fully in the activities of Ananda Marga. But what has most marked me about Dada is his sincere conviction that we are here to help others. Though meditation is fundamental, he insists, it is only through community projects such as the school he founded and runs for free that tangible change can be seen, felt, and utilized by the community, and credibility maintained. As such, meditation and frugal living is the means, but contribution to others is the end objective.

The second main reason I came to Colombia was to grow in the area of contribution-building. A particular project stands out in my mind: though small in comparison to the other projects I have led in my work, it matters most to me because of the difference it has made in the quality of health (and life) of others, and because it is an entirely personal initiative that is done with very few resources but which affects many people.

In 1999, after having survived and recovered from the hepatitis A virus, I was faced with an appalling fact that more than 2% of all Colombians will be forced to undergo a similar fate. However, no one was doing anything to stop this, despite the fact that this disease and one of its variances, hepatitis B, are completely preventable through vaccination. I felt I must do something, since the Colombian government health program very rarely provides vaccinations, and only does so in the case of newborn infants.

Armed with this sad truth, in the middle of that year I launched an initiative, Vaccines for Cienaga, with our company and one of our main clients as sponsors, that targeted a very high-risk community. The community was Cienaga, which is the geographical equivalent of Macondo, Gabriel Garcia Marquez's land of magical realism in his Nobel-winning novel "One Hundred Years of Solitude." The truth is a far cry from the literary paradise of Macondo, with violence, poverty, and very poor sanitary conditions reigning in this forgotten community of fishermen.

The first weekend, with a nurse on-hand, and one volunteer, we posted shop at the local centro de salud, or government health center. We were able to vaccinate 100 children, between the ages of 2 and 12, though most of the mothers were skeptical at best. We returned for the second dose 30 days later, with some attrition from the first round. The third round, 5 months later, had a larger turnout. Though this program is only in its second year, more than 250 children have been vaccinated so far. This may not seem like a large number, but to me it represents 250 people that do not have to experience what I needlessly went through. Furthermore, in a country with so many problems like Colombia, the important principle is to act positively and consistently.

This principle of taking significant action positively and consistently is what most motivates me to continue forward in these two areas of relationships and contributions. With the examples of Bruno Mazzilli and Dada Divyapremananda, both persons who have made a lasting change in their communities and in people's lives, and the Vaccines for Cienaga Program, I have come to realize that, despite the tremendous odds, if more of us act, and develop a critical mass in so doing, we may be able to create lasting change.

Comments

- Right off the bat, readers know that they are dealing with someone unusual. First of all, Joseph has nerve. He moved back to his native Colombia, where civil unrest and economic uncertainty lay ahead; he saw a customer need and started, during an economic downturn, a company to meet it. Second, he discusses at length his involvement in hypnosis and spirituality, issues that are difficult to pull off without sounding unsuited for the hard-core nature of business school and the students it attracts.

- In both of his essays, Joseph expresses the importance of community, his sense of humanity, and his concern for others, whether fellow employees facing layoffs or Colombian children facing health dangers. This theme works particularly well when applying to Tuck, a school very much concerned with maintaining a strong sense of community.

- The introduction of Joseph's second essay is rather roundabout; he might have been more effective in getting to the point (what he likes to do in his spare time) quicker, eliminating the first paragraph and some of the more extravagant details about his two spiritual mentors.

MADELINE
DUKE/FUQUA

1. Please discuss your previous professional experience, your long-term career goals, and the role the MBA will play in those plans. Why are you interested in the Fuqua School of Business?

Three simple words excite and inspire me. They make my mind race, my heart flutter, and my adrenaline soar. All it takes are these three simple words: better, faster, cheaper.

As a process improvement consultant, I am on a mission to change and no process is safe from my grip. I want to re-engineer the system at the Baltimore Orioles' will-call ticket window, reorganize the process flow at my local bagel shop, and redefine the mission and short-term goals of the Human Resources Department in my consulting firm. Most important, I want to apply these three words to myself. Equipped with an MBA, I will be a sharper, savvier, smarter businesswoman.

The foundation skills and capabilities I developed through my work for PricewaterhouseCoopers (PwC) have laid the groundwork for my business education. I have developed and honed my quantitative analysis skills by performing complex financial reviews for the Federal Emergency Management Agency. During my tenure at the Department of Housing and Urban Development, I learned how to model Federal economic development programs after successful international community financing institutions and market the initiatives to local community leaders. Consulting to a nonprofit established by the Federal Communication Commission, I provided technical assistance to rural health care providers seeking funding for telemedicine and tele-health programs, innovative vehicles for administering health care. This experience sparked an interest in technological innovation and the ways technology can reinvent a traditional industry.

Seeking to fuse my interests in nonprofit organizations and technology, I pursued a project management opportunity in PwC's new e-Philanthropy Group, which provides Internet-solutions to nonprofit organizations. E-Philanthropy is an industry in its infancy and this type of work only recently emerged within PwC. I learned much of the industry knowledge on my own and consulted with clients using the limited available resources in an environment that can only be characterized as entrepreneurial—new industry, new ideas, and new skills. This was a tremendous prospect for me to cultivate leadership and management skills while leaving a mark on an emerging group. After joining e-Philanthropy, I balanced my client and project management responsibilities with marketing the e-Philanthropy Group internally within PwC, pursuing business leads outside of PwC, and building a multi-disciplinary e-Philanthropy team that blended a mix of skills and personalities. While I have helped to build a business—a nonprofit-technology consulting business—within PwC, I know that an MBA would have helped me do this better, faster, and cheaper.

Upon earning my MBA, I plan to pursue management and strategy in a for-profit capacity that serves the nonprofit sector. I enjoy my current line of work—empowering nonprofit organizations with technology-related tools. In the short term, I want to serve as a strategy consultant, focusing on management and technology, to mid-size nonprofit organizations. Eventually, I plan to start my own consulting firm that specializes in solutions for nonprofit organizations.

I recognize that a Fuqua MBA would provide me with critical tools to help me achieve my career goals. I plan to add the foundation of a business education—accounting, finance, operations—and build on my current skills to develop an expertise in certain areas—management, entrepreneurship, and technology. Considering my career goal to start my own consulting firm, I am attracted to Duke's Management major and the Entrepreneurship and New Technology activities. Classes such as *Entrepreneurship*, *Managing Technical Transitions*, and the *Strategic Planning Practicum* are closely aligned with my interests, reinforcing my belief that Duke is the ideal place for me to pursue an MBA.

In addition to Fuqua's academic excellence and flexible, four-term structure, I am drawn to the Association of Women in Business (AWIB), which is similar to the Women's Information Network (WIN), an organization in Washington, DC to which I have committed time and energy. I am a strong advocate of women's issues, mentoring programs, and networking opportunities. Recently, I was honored with WIN's "Young Women of Achievement" Award in recognition of my dedication to this organization. AWIB will allow me to continue my commitment to women's issues and will provide a forum by which to exercise and further develop my leadership ability.

What stands out most in my mind about Duke is its "spirit of collaboration." The concept of "Team Fuqua," though initially intangible, crystallized in my mind after visiting Duke, speaking to my colleagues and friends who are Duke alumni, and learning about current students' experiences. Their stories have brought clarity to the viewbook description and distinguished Fuqua from other leading business schools as an institution that places extraordinary value on camaraderie.

I know that Fuqua takes its commitment to community seriously. My commitment to improving my community is a constant in my life. I plan to work as hard for the Duke community as I have for every other environment in which I have lived. As evidenced by my work experience and community service commitments, I will make an excellent addition to this cooperative and community-oriented environment.

Only a few words excite me more than 'better, faster, cheaper:' The Fuqua School of Business!

2. **Tell us about your personal history and family background and how they have influenced your intellectual and personal development. What unique personal qualities or life experiences might distinguish you from other applicants? How will your background, values, and non-work-related activities enhance the experiences of other FSB students and add to the diverse culture we strive to attain at Fuqua?**

My father's older brother, David, is dying of renal cell carcinoma, a rare, hereditary form of kidney cancer. I say "my father's brother" because David and my father have been estranged for my entire life. Pained by this alienation, my dad has tried to reconcile but to no avail. Recently, David's wife called to ask that my dad be tested as a stem cell donor match since a transplant was David's only chance for survival. As a perfect match, my dad has undergone thrice daily injections of a painful serum that stimulates stem cell growth but causes convulsions, seizures, and the risk of heart attack. David has returned home from the hospital, armed with my father's immune system in his body. He is successfully fighting the cancer that only weeks ago, was certain to kill him.

Of course, who wouldn't do such a thing for one's brother? What touched me about my father's action was not the fact of it, but rather that he never blinked, never considered his anger or hurt, or even *reconsidered* during his weeks of resulting pain and illness. The solar system of my dad's life revolves around family, spirituality, and a fierce ethic of giving back to the world around him. "Tikkun olam"—in Hebrew—"repair the world." This ethic of service operates as a keystone in the structure of my parents' lives. As such, it has become equally important in mine. It is not enough, they have taught me, to strive for personal happiness and achievement; rather, one must make better the world in which one lives.

In 1996, my family founded the House of Hope, a non-profit residential facility for Jewish men recovering from alcohol and drug addictions. My dad had recognized the lack of transitional housing for Jewish men upon their release from prison due to drug-related crimes. It soon became apparent that the House, in order to continue operating, required a business strategy and marketing plan to attract residents and donors. Jerry, one of the House residents, and I volunteered our time to meet this need. Jerry is a young man with spina bifida, recovering from an addiction to alcohol and marijuana. Though he has been clean for over two years, he struggles daily to maintain his sobriety. Together, we designed a website and created its content, obtained local press coverage for the House, presented grant requests to funders, and developed a long-term public relations plan. Throughout the process, I learned about Jerry's shame of losing his family's trust, his struggle to regain it, and his gratitude to the House for enabling the healing process to occur. Jerry wrote in his journal, which is published on our website, "I believe that the House not only saved my life but enabled me to get a life." Likewise, the Friday nights I spend interacting with residents like Jerry, and their families, have enriched my life by demonstrating the human potential for truth, frailty, and forgiveness.

Tikkun olam, according to my parents, is not an easy pursuit and often presents unforeseen challenges. For example, when I began my career, I approached a woman I admired about creating an informal network within my firm for women to mentor one another. She advised me to assimilate and not distinguish myself as a woman. I was shocked by her response. Searching elsewhere to meet this need, I found the Business Women's Network (BWN) and quickly assumed a leadership role by becoming the BWN chairperson. I focus my energy on offering monthly events and workshops for women to empower themselves in their organizations so they don't need to hear—or believe—that the only way to succeed in business is to "assimilate and not distinguish one's self as a woman." An area where the world still needs repair is in the under-representation of women in both business school and in the upper echelons of the corporate world.

The funny thing about tikkun olam—repair the world—is that it focuses on one's environment and community, rather than the individual who resides in it. As part of my dedication to tikkun olam, I've come to terms with a part of me that is broken as I've learned how to repair it. I've been hearing impaired since I was six years old. When you are young, successful and reasonably attractive, people often assume that all of your parts work. They assume that things inside your head will remain intact. They never expect that a serious of sudden movements while dancing, kickboxing, or just laughing hard with friends, will cause a hearing aid to whip out the side of my head like a small cruise missile. When I finish crawling around on the floor in search of the prize and hold it gingerly between two fingers, people seem astonished when I just pop it right back in. As people age, they become more comfortable with broken parts and bodily failings as they accept their own physical weaknesses. I'm just 26 years old, and I've spent the last 20 years watching people avert their eyes, pretending they don't see as I stick my ears back into my head.

I'm in a staff meeting, focused on my colleagues, but there's no mistaking that familiar sound, "putt-putt-putt." I shake my head from side to side and then give my ears a few gentle taps. It's still there, "putt-putt-putt," The hum of my hearing aid battery sputtering as it fades like a car out of gas on the side of the road. Even as I adjust to the sounds I won't be hearing for the next few hours and the duration of the meeting, I feel things around me fall into focus. Equilibrium takes hold as my eyes tune to the lips and gestures of those sitting around me. Sometimes I think I hear more when I actually can't. It's harder to lie to me when the batteries are dead. An uncomfortable seat squirm, a skeptical arched eyebrow, or a defensive slouch shout out their messages.

For years, as a child, I wore my hair down every day to hide my hearing aids. No ponytails or braids or baseball caps because kids don't walk around advertising an Achilles heel. As I grew older, I learned, as many do, to accept this part of me. Now, I often forget how surprised others may be when they learn that I wear hearing aids. When I'm nearly deaf to the world around me, running across the room after my rogue projectile, or trying to shake the "putt-putt-putt" away, I sense their disconcert most keenly. I can't help but wonder how my future classmates will respond to my hearing impairment.

I'm excited about the possibility of becoming a Fuqua student. Fuqua strikes me as a place that appreciates diversity, supports ambition, tolerates frailty, and inspires community, Tikkun olam begins by repairing oneself and one's community, whether a religious community, a gender-based community, or a health-related community. In business school, I plan to affiliate with a new set of communities—at Fuqua, in Durham, and in North Carolina—and step forward as a leader and a supporter of my classmates' philanthropic and volunteer endeavors.

3. **Discuss a personal failure that had an impact on your professional practices or management style. Why do you consider the situation a failure? Did it change your professional outlook? If so, how?**

In late 1996, when I was twenty-one years old and new to the consulting world, a government agency hired my firm to assess a Federal grant administration program. My task was to research 72 cities that received Federal grants to assess their success in implementing economic development initiatives. Five of the 72 cities I reviewed did not meet the performance requirements.

The night before a scheduled press conference in which the Agency's Secretary would present the study's results, I met with top Department officials to review my research. They instructed me to alter my findings. The "low-performers" I had identified were to be changed to "high-performers" and in their place, five other cities were to be designated "low-performers," thus at risk of losing their Federal funding. The officials' instructions, motivated by their poor relationships with the political leadership of the five newly identified "low-performers," contradicted my research.

Our meeting took place well after midnight and my project managers were unavailable to provide assistance. In the past, my project managers had instructed me to do whatever was necessary to satisfy the client. Perceiving that the contract and my job were at risk if I did not comply with the client's instructions, I altered the reports.

Immediately after the experience, I felt guilty and disillusioned. I tried to rationalize my actions and convince myself that the decision-makers were privy to certain information that supported their determinations, but I knew that it was not true. I had experienced an astonishing attack on my moral code and I had failed to act with integrity.

I have reflected on this troubling incident at various stages in my career to reassess how I would handle the situation. I would like to believe that as a more seasoned consultant I have learned to assess the propriety of requests and effectively disagree with clients. My colleagues respect me and I believe they would support my decision to disagree with the client. I am confident that with my skills and abilities, I would easily find work elsewhere. I hope that is faced with such a moral dilemma today, the right choice, the clear choice, would be the choice I make. Simultaneously, I am faced with the reality of doubt. It is easy to sit at one's computer and write of future infallibility and choices made with brave distinction. But life is never so simple, I realize the freedom I have as a young, single woman in a strong economy. I have the freedom of choice—to leave a job, to live off my savings if fired, to have confidence that my skills are easily marketable elsewhere. I have the freedom to claim that I would never again make the "wrong" choice. Even as I write these words I wonder: what will happen when I have a family dependent on my income, a mortgage payment to meet, or the scare of a recessed economy to consider? Or, what will happen if the moral choice I am forced to make is not as plain as altering a report? What if future choices prove insidious, unexpected, and almost intangible?

This failure and its reflective aftermath armed me with a heightened awareness of the frailty of morality. If confronted with an ambiguous decision in the future, I hope to recognize the dilemma it presents so that I may respond calmly and with confidence, guided by my moral code, to make the right choice.

NYU/STERN (Selected)

1. Creatively describe yourself to your MBA classmates.

"8-13-86, Wed.: Today we had pineapple, cornflakes, bread, milk, and water. All I had was a spoonful of cereal, 1 piece of bread & a glass of water. Then, after breakfast, we went to an African supermarket Everything is so cheap! We went to a museum and saw all sorts of mammals and birds. For lunch, Joseph gave us leftovers—chicken with no bones, brown rice, and salad with gooey tomatoes—yuck. Afterwards, we hung out and the cousins played dodge ball and the grown-ups just watched. For dinner, get ready for this—we had pizza! It was so-so. After dinner we roasted marshmallows on the fireplace. It was a good day. Bye!"

A good day? A day marked, measured, and evaluated by the food I consumed? That constitutes a good day? Would *you* have known that this is an entry from my 1986 journal, documenting a journey to Kenya?!

Recently, I uncovered that old travel journal in the back of a desk drawer. Surprised by what I read, I laughed, once again seeing through my eleven year-old eyes, filtering out the museums, the exotic safari, arid rich history of Africa, and instead, focusing on a month-long, gastronomical extravaganza. Of course, this shouldn't have surprised me. I live through my stomach. Both significant life events and ordinary everyday occurrences are catalogued in my memory by what I consumed at those moments.

When I smell oranges, I still think about my high school basketball games. I was an atrocious basketball player. Though I offered my team five feet and nine inches of solid height, I lumbered awkwardly down the court, missed simple passes, and unknowingly committed countless fouls. My coach and teammates patiently assisted me with endless drills and exercises to improve my foul shots, rebounding, and speed. I never improved. Though towered over the opposition, I could not react fast enough to a fake pass or lay-up. At the end of the season, when the coach recognized each team member's contributions with a special award, I received the 'Best Fan Award,' because my dad attended every game of the season and brought orange slices for my teammates during halftime.

The smell of certain foods immediately transports me back to my parents' kitchen in Baltimore. The aroma of chicken soup reminds me of warm family gatherings when we celebrated the Jewish holidays. I can picture my grandfather, working diligently, chopping walnuts and apples to make charoset, a traditional food eaten during the Passover holiday. He sings while he works, and even now, the sound travels through my mind with the smell of this memory.

During our summer family reunions, the Stein family consumes bushels of crabs steamed in Old Bay, a spicy seasoning that stings one's lips and tongue. Only a cold beer can alleviate the painful sensation. Younger members of the family have their crabs "washed" to remove the spices and avoid the pepper's sting. When I first ate my crabs "unwashed," in proper Stein tradition, my relatives acknowledged this milestone by presenting me with ice cubes to numb my aching lips from the effects of the Old Bay.

After finding that old journal, I shared it with friends. And while they laughed as I had, they were not surprised. They reminded me that I have not changed much in the years since my journey to Kenya. As we gathered around my coffee table, sharing a spread of pate, roasted red peppers, camembert, and wine biscuits, they challenged me to read to them from a more recent travel journal, written during our 1996 trip to Europe:

"Saturday, 7-20-96: My 30-pound backpack was starting to wear on my neck and back as we debated our next destination. Amidst the discussion, we noticed passerby with the most succulent nectarines and peaches. Distracted from our aching bodies, we searched for the source of the fruit and quickly discovered an outdoor market. After bargaining in French with the vendors, we amassed an abundance of delectable treats—ripe strawberries, fresh hearts of palms, marinated mushrooms, creamy brie, and a crusty baguette . . ."

I expect that in another ten years, the smell of a doughy, New York bagel will evoke memories of early morning group work with my Stern classmates on the Integrative Strategy Exercise. A cup of steaming, rich coffee will remind me of a quick break between mid-morning classes at NYU. And, the food I eat when I celebrate my acceptance to Stern will evoke feelings of success for years to come.

Comments

- Madeline's introduction to the first Duke essay is catchy; the way in which she concludes the essay—using the same theme, but expressing her excitement about the Fuqua program—is even more appealing. Madeline demonstrates that she brings with her to business school a seriousness of purpose regarding "process improvement," highlighted not only by her career as a consultant but also by her personal passion for improving things and making life better for others, in the spirit of "tikkun olam."

- Madeline's devotion to service takes on added depth through her showing that her family has a strong service tradition. Her story about her father's heroics could come across as a plea for sympathy (and better treatment) from the admissions committee, something highly likely to backfire, except that she uses it as a mere backdrop to her own story.

- Madeline discusses her hearing disability in a humorous and matter-of-fact manner, showing herself to be unusual and also able. In so doing, she avoids the trap of showing self-pity by overdramatizing her story.

- In the third Duke essay, Madeline discusses a serious mistake she once made, making it clear that the error occurred out of youthful earnestness to do the right thing. She convincingly demonstrates the strength of the impact that this failure had on her and her psyche, thereby reassuring the committee that she would not falter in such a way again.

PAUL

MICHIGAN

1. What has been your most significant professional achievement? What has been your toughest professional challenge and how did you address it?

My most significant professional achievement is my transformation of the Arthur Andersen approach to auditing hedge and venture funds. Continuously seeking innovative ways to make contributions to the overall practice as well as my clients, I developed a standard hedge and venture fund audit package that our audit teams could use to better control the quality of each job and reduce its completion time by 40%. This new approach was implemented on all 25 of our hedge and venture fund audits and added value to these engagements by eliminating duplicate efforts among audit teams and leveraging collective industry expertise within the office. I also distributed the new package to our New York and Chicago offices to enable them to enjoy similar benefits. This accomplishment was a key factor in my early promotion to Manager, as it helped develop my ability to manage and make an impact on our entire firm, rather than just my clients.

My toughest professional challenge was my first management of an Initial Public Offering (IPO) while at Arthur Andersen. The client was ResourcePhoenix.com, a provider of web-enabled transaction processing services. The three-month project began in August 1999 and culminated with the procurement of $35 million of capital. In between these two points, however, the challenges that presented themselves and my resolution of them significantly helped define my capabilities.

This engagement was paramount to my career development for several reasons. First, this project was my first assignment as a newly promoted Manager. As if the management of an IPO for a first-year manager wasn't enough of a challenge, I was presented with several additional hurdles. Aside from a tight deadline and countless sleepless nights, these included: the lack of an experienced client accounting function, the absence of IPO experience on my team, and a whole assortment of complex technical accounting issues. In fact, these issues were so technically complex, that I was forced by firm policy to contact the Worldwide Professional Standards Group for concurrence with all of my interpretations.

To tackle these issues, I developed a comprehensive training seminar to educate the client team on this process. I spent two full weekends outlining the critical steps of an IPO with the CFO, controller, and accounting team, and communicated exactly what would be expected of them in the months to follow. I stressed that once a company is public, the level of scrutiny it undergoes with respect to its performance and administrative prowess skyrockets; no room for mistakes.

Orchestrating a harmonious team effort, I engineered a plan of attack to work with the client, the attorneys, and the underwriters to resolve all pending issues and take the client out to market successfully. This engagement and all of its difficulties stands as a testament to the value of collaboration and effective management, and further allows me to appreciate the benefits of a Michigan MBA.

2. **Describe your post-graduation career plans. How will your education, experience, and development to date support those plans? How will an MBA from the University of Michigan Business School help you attain those goals?**

Through my experience at Arthur Andersen, I used the audit as a lens to obtain insight on how businesses function, and to develop my analytical and managerial skills. I have also juxtaposed my corporate experience with the founding of my own strategy consulting company, specializing in high technology, which has broadened my outlook.

In the course of performing my consulting work, I had the opportunity to serve as interim CFO of DotVantage, an application service provider that helps companies implement online marketing campaigns. I became fascinated by this infantile industry, which attempts to solve the pervasive problem of bringing together vendors and customers in a technology-driven environment. Following my passion, I recently wrote two research papers on the state of the industry. The first, "Beyond Broadcast Marketing," is published in the December 2000 edition of Marketing Today, and the second, "Spiral Marketing," is in revision with Professor Caroline Henderson at Dartmouth's Tuck School of Business. I also recently conducted a presentation on my technology marketing theories to a UCLA Extension E-Marketing class and have been invited to lecture next month to an audience of 2000 members of the Orange County Multimedia Association, and to a marketing class at Dartmouth College.

My attraction to high technology has driven me to actively lead and define its future, with the short-term goal of launching a high technology company and the long-term goal of fostering its growth and development. Specifically, I would like to build a software application that makes practical use of the concepts I have postulated in my e-marketing research. While I am at Michigan, I would like to collaborate with others who may be interested in pursuing this venture and assemble a diverse management team, comprising individuals with differing backgrounds and perspectives. After developing a bulletproof business plan and an alpha version of the software, we would utilize the vast network afforded by the Zell-Lurie Institute to pursue sources of funding. Upon graduation, I would collaborate with my team to commence operations and grow the company. In the long run, I would like to work as our CEO, using my vision and experience, together with my Michigan MBA, to oversee our operations and develop cutting-edge strategies and products to empower companies to better utilize technology to establish beneficial customer relationships.

There is no better place for me to gain the skills that will enable me to attain my goals than Michigan, with its preeminent reputation for developing first-rate entrepreneurial and e-business skills. Specifically, I have taken a keen interest in many of the elective courses in the Entrepreneurship and e-Business tracks (*Leveraging Human Capital for Entrepreneurship and Growth, Data Base Management Systems, Data Mining and Applied Multivariate Analysis*). I would like to immerse myself in the entrepreneurial community at Michigan and use my own start-up experiences as a foundation for my studies. Also, I truly appreciate the school's collaborative emphasis; I have proven through my experiences in collegiate athletics and start-up consulting that I thrive and can contribute much in this type of environment. It is these strengths I see in Michigan that, when combined with my goals and experiences, make it the ideal place for me to pursue an MBA.

3. Describe a failure or setback in your life. How did you overcome this setback? What, if anything, would you do differently if confronted with this situation again?

My uphill battle in the sport of rowing has had a profound impact on my life. I entered college as a chubby kid who had never participated in athletics, yet soon after I began my freshman year, I joined the men's lightweight crew. Because I was about 30 pounds over the 160-pound lightweight limit, and, at 5 feet 10 inches, too short to row heavyweight, I would have to ease off on the cupcakes. I would also have to learn how to actually row. It was soon obvious to me, and to everyone else, how difficult it would be to make the boat given my lack of talent and experience. Fortunately, in rowing, there are no cuts; the rigorous 36 hours per week regimen, which includes 5 am practices six mornings a week, takes care of this on its own.

My first two years, I went nowhere. Ignoring common sense, I wouldn't quit. I sat with the coach in his motor boat during most of our practices, usually filming the rowers and carrying the coach's toolbox. I spent so much time filming instead of rowing that the team named me "Scorsese." The summers served as my catch-up time. I joined a local rowing club in my hometown and spent countless hours training. One summer, I competed in two marathons, and rode my bike from Los Angeles to Canada—1100 miles, in 10 days.

The following spring, I beat out six other men for the final, undecided seat in the varsity eight. My off-season work had paid off. We won the Pacific Coast Championship that year, and I was awarded "Most Improved Oarsman."

That summer, I was one of twenty men in the U.S. invited to the National Team Development Camp to train for the Olympic Festival and World Trials. After the first month of camp, and two weeks prior to these events, I suffered a devastating injury, slipping two disks in my back and putting an abrupt end to my rowing career. This was a crushing blow to me, as I still had a year of eligibility remaining and desperately wanted to test my abilities at the national level.

I redirected my love of the sport into coaching. I secured the Freshman Men's coaching position at UCSB, becoming the first student in the history of the University to coach the rowing team. Using my personal, colorful stories to motivate a bunch of lazy freshmen, I led my crew to an undefeated season and Pacific Coast Championship during my first year. The freshman team performed so well that I was promoted to Varsity Men's Coach mid-season, supplanting the struggling incumbent, an Olympic gold medalist. I coached the otherwise struggling varsity team to a win at the Newport Regatta and a silver medal in the Pacific Coast Championships. For my contributions, I received the lifetime "Excellence in Coaching Award" from the University. The following year, I led the varsity to a 4th place finish at the national championships.

The setbacks I overcame in my journey from out-of-shape "Scorsese" to Olympic hopeful taught me the value of perseverance and hard work. Those I overcame in my injury and transition to Head Coach taught me how to coach my peers, and how to use my own experiences to lead, motivate, and develop people.

4. **What's the most creative solution to a problem or situation you've ever developed?**

In 1999, I left Arthur Andersen to move to Southern California with the goal of launching my own strategy consulting firm. Fresh out of public accounting, I lacked marketing skills, capital, and the breadth of skills and network to build a practice on my own. I needed access to a wide range of skill-sets and competencies. My challenge was to build this infrastructure with my limited budget and cold calling skills. Recognizing that there were many other small service providers facing the same challenges, I decided to develop a network of 12 companies, with various skills, that would cross-refer work. I approached law firms, information technology consultants, business appraisers, and web developers.

One of my first cross-referrals, sourced through a relationship I built with a principal in the emerging growth practice of the law firm of Riordan and McKinzie, was a large project for Beatscape.com, an online source for music licensing. I developed Beatscape's business plan and financial forecasts, and presented its innovative concept to a prominent overseas venture fund to complete a private placement of $1.5 million. In exchange, I referred to her firm a newly formed hedge fund in need of $30,000 of legal work.

Next, I created a short-term business plan to cover a clothing company's next year of operations and generate positive cash flows. After my negotiation of a lucrative licensing deal with a German clothing distributor and my development of an online sales strategy, the company turned a profit for the first time in a decade.

More recently, through another referral, I secured a high-visibility consulting project for KnightRidder.com, the online subsidiary of the second largest newspaper publisher in America. Working closely with the Director and Assistant to the President, I engineered a complex financial model that analyzed both the economic and accounting impacts of two different methods of spinning off this $600 million subsidiary from its parent. The company's management team is currently evaluating these two alternatives using my findings as the basis for discussion. The visibility I have gained from my performance of this work will undoubtedly result in additional future projects for my consulting firm.

By uniting several businesses behind the common goal of boosting market share, I was able to generate a successful bartering network that made up for limited capital and human resources. I learned to identify a common need, organize people and entities, and create incentives for all parties to take action, in the process helping both my own business and others, and establishing a first year client base of sixteen and revenues of nearly $200,000.

5. **Describe an experience or experiences you've had that highlights the value of diversity in a business setting.**

Through acting, whereby I study the psychology and behavior of people in preparation for my roles, I have developed a keen understanding of human dynamics. For example, I recently played the part of Ricky Roma, the lead salesman in David Mamet's Pulitzer Prize winning play, Glengarry Glen Ross. To play the character of Roma required that I study not only the cutthroat real estate sales industry, but also the inner motivations of a selfish, Machiavellian businessman. As part of my character development, I took a couple of salesmen out to lunch, and convinced them to allow me to observe their daily activities and to assist them on a few sales calls. I visited several small real estate outfits and studied the actions of the various salesmen. From one salesman, I picked up a habit of selfishly asking questions without really listening for an answer. From another, I learned how to turn friends and business partners against each other to make a sale. Analyzing the personalities and actions of these men taught me to appreciate psychology, sociology, and many other disciplines with which I would otherwise have limited contact.

My understanding of human dynamics has helped me better develop people at work. At Arthur Andersen, I often led training seminars to new-hires at our training facility in St. Charles, Illinois. Fresh out of college, these new-hires were faced with the challenge of integrating their traditional "textbook" education with real world client situations. Aside from teaching them accounting and auditing skills, I placed great emphasis on the development of interpersonal skills. By observing and speaking with my students and understanding their fears prior to working on their first client engagements, I noticed a common thread of insufficient training in relationship building and interactive skills. I set up several mock client situations and used my acting skills to role-play several challenging, stressful scenarios. I taught my students to interpret body language and speech tonality, and how to use physical and verbal cues to create an environment of mutual trust. My students soon developed a sufficient comfort level that would enable them to better succeed when they returned to their respective home offices. To this day, a year after having left Andersen, I still frequently receive e-mails mentioning the extent to which the lifelong skills I taught them in St. Charles help them. One staffperson in particular recently notified me that her interactive skills had developed so noticeably that she was leaving accounting to pursue a sales career.

My unique experiences in acting allowed me to reach my business trainees in a way no one else was able to, giving them a valuable set of skills that they would have otherwise gained only from several years of trial-and-error, if at all.

6. **If there is any other information that you believe is important to our assessment of your candidacy, feel free to add it to your application.**

I acknowledge that my poor undergraduate record calls into question my ability to perform in a challenging academic setting. I have actively taken steps to improve my candidacy and demonstrate that these grades are not reflective of my academic abilities. My poor grades are in part attributable to my complete focus on collegiate crew; I often devoted over 36 hours per week to this endeavor as an athlete, and 60 hours per week as a coach. Because I attribute much of my current success to the skills that I developed through rowing, I have few regrets.

Nonetheless, I have established an "alternative transcript" to demonstrate my ability to thrive in a demanding academic setting. Over the past two years I have taken a handful of post-baccalaureate courses at the U.C. Berkeley and UCLA Extension Programs, and have earned "A's" in all of them. I have published articles in respectable journals of three different fields—finance, accounting, and marketing—and I am currently working on another with Professor Caroline Henderson at the Tuck School. Further, I have been a guest professor at UCLA, have scheduled a marketing lecture at Dartmouth College, and have developed a course entitled "Strategic Planning and Development," which I hope to soon teach at UCLA Extension School of Business and Management.

I have done all that is within my power to strengthen my candidacy; there is little else I could possibly do to address my scholastic performance of the early 90's. Perhaps the best measure of my transformation is that I could now literally teach the classes I struggled with as an undergraduate. I ask that the Admissions Committee take note of my commitment, desire, and ability to succeed at Michigan Business School.

YALE (Selected)

1. **The Yale MBA program is small, and the range of perspectives diverse. With this in mind, tell us what qualities you most value and respect in others, and describe one quality that your Yale classmates will value and respect most about you. Give an example.**

I believe that a person is no better than his ability to inspire others to do well and be happy. As such, I place a high value on benevolence and sense of contribution. To showcase this quality, I need not look any further than a member of my own family—my "Uncle" John Ghaznavi, who at the age of seventeen came to the

United States from Iran with only a suitcase and letter of admission to West Virginia University.

With his dramatic turnaround of Glenshaw Glass, he became runner-up for the 1996 Ernst & Young Turnaround Entrepreneur of the Year and then led the $500 million leveraged buyout and merger of Anchor Glass Company with Consumers Packaging. Despite his very "American" success, John has maintained a commitment to his heritage. As a Board member of the American-Iranian council, he established the Second-Generation Iranians Project to bring together young Iranian-Americans with young Iranians, fostering cooperation between two groups residing in nations at conflict. John also adopted an abandoned infant that he found at a mosque in a northern Iranian village; Shirin Ghaznavi is now a healthy, happy first-grader.

John understands his responsibility to give back to the community that nurtured his own growth, and he demonstrates that capitalism does not run counter to humanitarianism. I look to John as an example of how to manage my own success and give back to my own community. Inspired by John, I have developed a similar sense of contribution. Specifically, I enjoy helping Iranian-Americans to build a presence in the local business community. Through my recent guest appearance on The Ali Maybodi Show, an Iranian radio program based in Los Angeles, I held a question and answer session in Farsi and discussed business issues to help young Iranian-Americans succeed in the local business community. Meanwhile, I met a young Iranian entrepreneur whom I subsequently assisted in launching an Internet business.

I also place a high value on integrity and selflessness. I was recently reminded of their importance while preparing for my portrayal of Ricky Roma, the lead salesman in David Mamet's Pulitzer Prize winning play, Glengarry Glen Ross. To prepare, I had to study the inner motivations of the kind of person I lack respect for: a selfish, Machiavellian businessman. I took a couple of salesmen out to lunch, and convinced them to allow me to observe their daily activities and to assist them on a few sales calls. From one salesman, I picked up a habit of selfishly asking questions without really listening for an answer. From another, I learned how to turn friends and business partners against each other to make a sale. A successful actor must be a keen observer of human dynamics and behavior. Analyzing the behavior of these men reinforced the value I place on integrity and character, especially under the lures of notoriety and material wealth.

I believe that my fellow Yale classmates will appreciate my unique ability to coach my own peers, a quality I first developed in college after overcoming a major athletic setback. After my third year in college, I was invited to the U.S. Rowing National Team Development Camp to train for the Olympic Festival and World Trials. There, two weeks prior to these two events, I suffered a devastating injury, slipping two disks in my back and putting an abrupt end to my rowing career. This was a crushing blow to me, as I still had a year of eligibility remaining and had been determined to test my abilities at the national level.

Rather than drowning in the sorrows of my injury, I redirected my love of the sport into coaching. I secured the Freshman Men's coaching position at U.C. Santa Barbara, becoming the first student in the history of the University to coach the rowing team. Using my personal, colorful come-from-behind stories to motivate a bunch of lazy freshmen, I led my crew to an undefeated season and Pacific Coast Championship during my first year of coaching. In fact, the freshman team performed so well that the men's varsity approached me in the middle of the racing season to coach them as well. Politically, this was a difficult maneuver, as the varsity men were effectively firing their own coach: a newcomer to the program, but an Olympic gold medallist and rowing legend. This situation created mutiny in the program and marked the climax of our season. After heated debates among the athletes, the coaching staff, and the University's administration, I was appointed interim Head Coach for the remainder of the season, supplanting the incumbent. I led the otherwise struggling varsity team to a win at the Newport Regatta and a silver medal in the Pacific Coast Championships, and received the lifetime "Excellence in Coaching" award from the University for my contributions to the program. The following year, I was promoted to full-time Head Coach of the Men's Varsity, and led my team to a 4th place finish at the Intercollegiate Rowing Association National Championships.

My injury and transition from rower to coach marked a transformation in my life. Coming off of a winning season as an athlete, I was committed to leading the team to another championship—it had never occurred to me that I would accomplish this feat as coach of my own peers. This presented me with a multitude of challenges. One challenge was to earn their respect by being seen as someone from whom they could learn. I achieved this through allowing the team to take note of my achievements in the sport, and then by using colorful stories to demonstrate my points. For example, to teach the virtues of tenacity, I would allude to my previous three-year journey from obese McDonald's faithful to lean Olympic hopeful. This process made me an exceptional motivator and speaker. At the beginning of each season, I would engineer our mental and physical training regimen based upon a collaborative agreement. By holding frequent meetings, listening to my team and asking the right questions, I was able to identify common goals and structure a viable plan to attain them. Further, I became very adept at communicating to each person as a unique individual. Some athletes respond positively to certain coaching techniques, while others require more innovative methods. Whereas one athlete will voluntarily hold his wrist straight during the stroke upon my critique, another will require me to devise a more creative way to make myself clear—perhaps to duct tape a steel wrench or a fork along the length of his wrist so that it remains immobilized.

My experience coaching my peers will enable me to better relate to others, and to more effectively share my knowledge and experiences in a collaborative, non-evasive manner.

Comments

- Paul had been successful in two different fields at the time he applied. He had begun as an auditor at Andersen, then founded his own consulting firm. It is not particularly difficult to demonstrate success at a large firm that, like Andersen, has a well-established grading system in place. An entrepreneur, however, faces a substantial problem in this regard. Paul addressed this in part by demonstrating his impressive understanding of spiral marketing, evidenced by his two published articles and his invitation to teach MBA-level classes on the subject.

- Paul has an enviable ability to tell a good story using effective language, evidenced especially in Michigan essay number three. Although athletic endeavors rarely make good essay material because of their ordinary outcomes and trite themes, Paul creates a real winner with this tale of ups and downs during his career as rower and coach.

- Paul's fifth Michigan essay is unusual; most candidates limit themselves to a discussion of ethnic or racial diversity rather than realizing that diversity can mean many things. This essay helps to show yet another interesting side to Paul by highlighting his acting career and how it has benefited him in the workplace.

- Paul's final Michigan essay is an ideal example of how a candidate can utilize the extra essay question to his benefit. Paul framed his candidacy in such a way that forces admissions officers to realize that he has indeed made up for his less weak collegiate academic record through his more recent academic and professional endeavors.

SAMEER

CHICAGO REAPPLICATION (Selected)

1. **What have you done to strengthen your application since you last applied? Has anything about why you are seeking an M.B.A or an I.M.B.A., what you hope to experience, or your plans and goals changed since you last applied? If yes, how so?**

I was accepted to several top MBA programs last year, but Chicago remains my top choice business school, so I decided to wait out another year. Since being waitlisted by Chicago I have made considerable strides in my professional, academic, and civic life.

On the professional front, I joined Broadband Communication, a broadband wireless Internet startup, as the Director of Engineering. I worked with the core management team and the McKinsey consultants to develop the business plan, immersing myself in business analysis. As the Director of Engineering, I was responsible for demonstrating the technology to several investment banks and venture capitalist firms such as Menlo Ventures, Credit Suisse First Boston, and Goldman Sachs. The grueling sessions with the potential investors made it very clear that broadband wireless provided significant opportunity for value creation.

We were successful in raising the first round of capital and keeping the product development at full cycle. We were so thrilled with the success that we expanded the west-coast research and development staff to 55 people. All this came to a shattering crash when the investors backed out from investing the several million dollars needed to deploy a test market. The VCs were awed by the concept but there were no takers for a lead position in the venture; the risks associated with putting out such large capital made our company unattractive. Finally, we decided that the company had to abandon the broadband wireless-internet service side and evolve as a products company.

The cost containment and reduction in my role at the company made going to Business School undeniably attractive. Even though I had gained substantial practical knowledge, I was still lacking sound business fundamentals. While I had caught-up on learning the fancy terms such as EBITDA and ARPU, the fundamental approaches to arriving at these numbers was still missing. Furthermore, the thought of joining a business school other than Chicago kept me away for another year. I decided to join Wireless Communication as the Executive Director of Network for Region B.

As an Executive Director, I am a part of Wireless Communication's Leadership team, tasked with undertaking one of the most aggressive growth plans in the wireless industry. In a short period, I restructured my organization to enable this aggressive expansion of Wireless Communication's service in Region B. In addition, I prepared a roadmap for launching wireless data services. As an Executive Director, I am responsible for managing the company's regional assets of over $250 million. My experiences with the startup and other companies have helped me identify disconnects and effectively address issues that will enable Wireless Communication to become a market leader.

On the academic front, I have been able to formally complete my MS in Electrical Engineering by resolving the issue surrounding the transfer of courses and gaining full credit for the scholarly paper (see last year's application.)

At Wireless Communication, I have been actively involved in procuring funds and other resources for programs such as Christmas in October. I helped set up two volunteer teams that painted and repaired several homes in Region B. My mother's bout with Pancreatic Cancer and her subsequent fall to the disease has kept me involved in several community activities that help increase cancer awareness. I volunteered as a floor host at the M.D. Anderson Cancer Center in Houston and subsequently have been involved with CaP CURE's initiatives in increasing Prostrate Cancer awareness. I played an active role in lobbying support from the local political leaders to declare September as the month of Prostrate Cancer Awareness Month. Even though the effort did not yet bear fruitful results, I believe the gratification of being a part of such an effort was very fulfilling.

Creating life long friendships with highly energetic, extremely talented peers and learning from professors who are the leading thinkers in Entrepreneurship and Finance remains the centerpiece of my desire to be a part of the GSB community. I hope that the admissions committee looks at my experiences and sees in me a candidate fit to be a part of the esteemed Chicago GSB community.

2. If you were a character in a book, who would it be and why? What do you admire the most about this character, and how does it relate to you personally and/or professionally?

If I were a character in a book, it would be Alex Rogo in Eliyahu M. Goldratt's and Jeff Cox's "The Goal." Rogo has just been promoted as UnoCal's Burnside Plant Manager. He is quite thrilled at the opportunity of returning back to his home town after 15 years, but the grim reality hits when he finds that he has been given 3 months to get the money-losing plant in order.

I feel as though I have been in Rogo's shoes in my last three jobs—helping reorganize a large company, working diligently to save a startup, and now turning around a wireless operation for a large carrier. Just like the main character Rogo, I believe in learning from others and holding firmly to my core values. Rogo is willing to involve his team and with their help dissect the problems faced by his plant. This reminds me of my efforts of identifying the problems at Cellular Communications, by engaging the employees. Just like Rogo, I believe that the role of a change agent is to challenge conventional wisdom and build the business around sound fundamentals rather than on fancy terms and measurements, introduced without keeping "The Goal" of the company in mind.

In Rogo I see a man who has risen through the ranks, has seen the ups and downs of family life. I see a man passionate about his employees and his peers. I see someone who stands up for his employees and gives his very best to preserve their jobs. What impresses me most about Rogo is his belief in himself and his persistence in following his beliefs. I can certainly relate to him in my quest to give Chicago GSB my second shot.

TUCK REAPPLICATION (Selected)

1. What aspects of your candidacy do you want the admissions committee to recognize as the strongest, and perhaps the most distinctive, feature of your application to Tuck?

Every year there are numerous students who apply to Tuck with profiles that are quite similar to my own—a Master's degree in Electrical Engineering with average grades, a 3.4 GPA and a fair GMAT score of 700. I urge the admissions committee to look past these bare credentials and evaluate my application in light of the leadership and entrepreneurial skills that I have demonstrated throughout my professional and social life. Most importantly, I urge the admissions committee to recognize my desire to be a part of the Tuck program.

In the last seven years of my professional development I have had opportunities to play a significant role in opening a consulting office for the world's largest wireless consulting company, help restructure a Joint Venture, play a significant role in raising capital for a startup, and be a part of the leadership team of the world's largest wireless carrier.

I started my career as an engineering consultant for a wireless consulting company, Global Consultants. As a consultant I worked with several clients and developed a passion for resolving challenging problems. The consulting job taught me to formulate complex engineering problems and work with people from diverse backgrounds. The ability to manage people and produce results helped me in procuring lead positions in helping with the disaster recovery efforts during the Northridge earthquake and launching the first digital wireless system in California. My willingness to take chances and venture out to seek new business opportunities helped me in opening a consulting office that produced a significant portion of the company's business in Latin America. I not only learned how to manage in a new culture but also created significant business and personal relationships with clients all over world. The opportunity of working at Spectrum's Headquarters exposed me to the issues and challenges faced by a large telecom carrier. This opportunity opened doors to Cellular Communications, where I was selected as one of 20 members of a committee to orchestrate a reorganization of over 1000 people. I am most proud of being an effective change agent, who broke ranks and solicited employee feedback to eliminate disconnects throughout the reorganization effort at Cellular Communications.

I consider myself most fortunate to have been selected by John Doe, a widely respected CEO, to help out with the Broadband Wireless Internet startup. John had successfully taken a large company public and currently serves as the Chairman of another technology company. John knew me from my earlier job at Global Consultants. I was extremely excited when he asked me to be a part of his core team, which had just started the business planning and broadband wireless internet services office in Northern Virginia. The East-Coast office focused on developing the business plan, procuring the capital, and planning the product rollout. At Broadband Communication I worked diligently conducting technology demonstrations and putting together the business plans for the "last mile solution." Even though the venture did not mature as we had planned, I learned from our failure and hope to bring in valuable experience to many other companies, who might one day face the same challenges that we were exposed to with the startup. If I look back into my life, I would have never imagined having the tremendous luck of being an Executive Director of Network for Wireless Communications.

Early in my childhood, my parents taught me that the road to success is paved with good deeds and hard work. I have followed this advice and always strive to give my best in performing activities and contributing in school or at other volunteer programs. My mother's bout with Pancreatic Cancer and her subsequent fall to the disease has kept me involved in several community activities that help increase cancer awareness. I served as a floor host at the M.D. Anderson Cancer Center in Houston. I have been actively involved with CaP CURE's drive to increase community awareness of Prostrate Cancer. As a volunteer I strive to be a knowledge ambassador and a strong patient advocate. It is this passion that has helped me in convincing several friends and acquaintances to share their time and to volunteer to help terminally ill. I have always paid particular attention to creating the team chemistry and promoting collaborative attitude. It is this drive that has made me successful in engaging people and elevating the awareness of promoting civic causes.

I hope that my desire to join Tuck and give up a lucrative and a prestigious career bears testimony of my drive to make more out of my life than head out a division of a large company. I hope that these attributes of my application make me competitive, demonstrate my holistic development, and provide the edge that is representative of the Tuck student body.

Comments

- Sameer's essays are reapplication efforts. In his former applications to Chicago and Tuck, he had already discussed most of the significant facts and figures regarding his career, which allowed him to focus on the bigger picture in these new sets of essays.

- Sameer shows that he is more than just an ordinary engineer with technical talent. He proves that he possesses (and is recognized for his) breadth of understanding about the telecom industry. In addition, he demonstrates that he has managed budgets, collaborated in creating business plans, and participated in raising capital from investors—functions not ordinarily associated with technical employees.

- In the Tuck reapplication essay, Sameer helps readers to regard him as a unique individual rather than as a stereotypical "Indian engineer"—an increasingly common sort of applicant. By the same token, he is totally woolly when describing, in the fourth paragraph, what he learned from the failure of his company. He never gets beyond platitudes that essentially anyone in a failed start-up could have written.

DOREEN

(*Note:* She was applying for a special program at Columbia. Journalists who specialize in business and economics are eligible for a one-year non-degree program [the Knight-Bagehot Fellowship] that the Columbia Graduate School of Journalism offers, which includes classes at the Business School. Those who complete this program can apply for a second-year fellowship [the Wiegers Fellowship] through the Business School to complete their MBAs. Thus, she was in her first year of study, applying to complete a second year and thereby finish her MBA.)

COLUMBIA

1. What are your career goals? How will an MBA help you achieve these goals? Why are you applying to Columbia Business School?

Journalism is not a career for me; it is a calling. There are deadline pressures. The low pay is frustrating. Politicians I cover are disrespectful. Yet I can think of no other work that is as challenging, stimulating and rewarding.

For the past 14 years, I have been based in Peru, Venezuela, and Puerto Rico, reporting and writing on business and politics for American, Latin American, and Caribbean media. Reporting has taken me far—to banks in Lima, electronics assembly plants in Haiti, coffee farms in Jamaica, corporate headquarters in Japan, and insurance offices in London, to name just a few places.

As a journalist, I have the chance to channel my curiosity, ask questions, learn and give back to the community. I get to meet people, travel, research and stay on top of current events. I get an opportunity to foster greater awareness and understanding. I get a chance to make a difference.

I became a journalist without even knowing it. The siren call sounded when I was transplanted from my native New York to the U.S. Virgin Islands. I wrote friends in New York about living without winter and with limited water supplies. I told them about high prices for food and low prices for liquor, about being a white minority and about life on a small Caribbean island. Even before entering college, I had my first job in media at the V.I. Post newspaper in St. Thomas.

To learn more about the region I call home, I pursued Latin American and Caribbean studies at Wesleyan University. There I embraced the idea that content should take precedence over form in journalism. I believe that editors and avid reading can improve one's writing style, but knowing a topic in-depth gives added value to readers and distinguishes a journalist from the pack. I specialized in business and economic journalism in Latin America and the Caribbean.

Throughout the years, I have realized the need for continuing specialization. Today, I am focusing on finance through a Knight-Bagehot Fellowship in Business and Economic Journalism. My interest grew in the wake of the Latin American debt crisis and the North American Free Trade Agreement. I recognize that equity financing, short-term capital flows and direct foreign investment have increasingly important roles to play in Caribbean and Latin American development. At Columbia, I've also learned that financial systems require solid information flows to efficiently allocate capital. Specialized financial reporting therefore proves essential in hemispheric development.

After Columbia, I plan to return to journalism to work in international business news, especially on Latin America and the Caribbean. There's a gap to fill, because business news on the hemisphere remains under-reported in U.S. media. Washington rightly worries about immigration, drug-trafficking and money-laundering, and hemispheric free trade nowadays. Yet U.S. media still dedicates little space to the root causes of those problems in the economies of developing nations in the Americas.

Particularly disturbing for me is the scant attention given to the Caribbean Basin. The diverse, multi-lingual and fragmented Caribbean runs the risk of marginalization in today's global economy, where even large nations feel compelled to form trading blocs to compete. The Caribbean's future has important implications for the United States and beyond. Clearly, international executives and policy-makers could use more specialized economic coverage on Cuba, Haiti, Grenada and Panama—to name just several nations that have surfaced as prime U.S. security concerns in recent years.

To continue bringing these issues to public attention, I plan to return initially to The San Juan Star newspaper in Puerto Rico, which has granted me a leave of absence during my Columbia studies. There, I plan to expand my freelance coverage, which already has included articles for Bloomberg Business News, the Caribbean News Agency, The Denver Post and other media. Later, I hope to work at a large media outlet—likely in the United States. I believe that experience at a larger organization can provide greater access to editing and research resources, a more competitive environment to hone my skills and a larger readership base for my work.

I also hope to use the knowledge gained through reporting at Columbia to help develop business and economic skills in other journalists in the Caribbean and Latin America. For starters, I am already planning several seminars at The San Juan Star on accounting and finance topics learned at Columbia Business School.

My ongoing year at Columbia has not changed my calling, but it has opened up new avenues to pursue my interests and expand my contribution through economic journalism.

2. In reviewing the last five years, describe the one or two accomplishments of which you are most proud.

In 1993, Puerto Rico's economic life was on the line. The Clinton administration wanted to slash tax breaks for U.S. manufacturers on the island—endangering 40 percent of the Puerto Rican economy and more than 150,000 jobs. But Puerto Rico's business community and its pro-statehood government could not agree on how to counter the attack.

At The San Juan Star, Puerto Rico's only English-language daily newspaper, I covered manufacturing and international trade. I knew that tax breaks were Puerto Rico's economic lifeblood. I jumped on the story. For seven months, I covered as many angles as I could find. I went to factories and interviewed everyone from hourly workers to CEOs. I interviewed top Puerto Rico executives, Washington officials, U.S. multinational lobbyists, Wall Street analysts and Caribbean Basin leaders. Stories filled the business section front pages—and the hard work paid off.

The Star's in-depth coverage helped stimulate debate and action. It played a role in getting Puerto Rico business and government to adopt a more concerted approach to the issue. My articles were regularly faxed from San Juan offices to Washington and served as an important information source stateside, especially to U.S. government and business executives who could not read Puerto Rico's Spanish-language media.

After months of vigorous debate, Washington and Puerto Rico reached a compromise: the tax incentives were cut, but far less than initially proposed. I felt proud to have used my bilingual skills, business specialization and networks to serve as a communications link of this vital issue. That year, the Puerto Rico Manufacturers Association named me Journalist of the Year, the island's top business reporting award. But more importantly, I felt I had contributed to the community at a critical time.

"Would you accept a Knight-Bagehot Fellowship?" the caller asked.

"Yes, Yes, Yes," I yelped. "I want it. I want it."

Years of work in the Caribbean and Latin America had brought me regional recognition, but the Bagehot was a sign that my efforts commanded respect outside the area as well. I was proud to have been chosen to study at Columbia and in New York.

Then came a roller coaster ride.

First was math camp. My confidence plummeted. I hadn't studied math since high school in 1973 and never studied even pre-calculus, let alone calculus. I cried over my problem sets—despite Prof. Peter Garrity's good humor. Then, I patiently started from scratch, reviewing addition, re-learning algebra, seeking out help from teaching assistants and classmates, studying hard—and—I passed, barely.

Next came classes in accounting and finance, with a language that sounded strikingly similar to Chinese. I thought I would never understand. Yet, as the semester wore on, it started to make sense. I worked with colleagues and professors, hit the books and prayed for the best. By January, I was happily surprised when the call-in grading system electronically informed me of straight As at CBS.

I am very proud to have the opportunity to study at a university again and to have learned that hard work does pay off. I am energized by the challenge of grasping new concepts and hope to take on more. I enjoy the stimulation of tackling the new and meeting performance goals.

3. **Discuss a non-academic failure. In what way were you disappointed in yourself? What did you learn from the experience?**

I should have completed my bachelor's degree years ago, but it has taken a return to academia at Columbia University to get me to do it. Not having the degree has been a personal failure. I have felt that I'd let my parents down, when they had worked so hard to put me through college. I also felt inhibited to seek full-time work in the U.S. media, fearing disqualification without a degree.

Still, for years I did not complete the senior essay needed to fulfill requirements for a Latin American studies degree from Wesleyan University. Working in small, understaffed newspapers in nations with huge development hurdles and with fascinating stories to cover, I had always been so absorbed by my work in journalism that I had never set aside the months to research and write the paper.

College had not been easy for me. I started at age 16, a time when I was moved more by hormones than homework. An impressionable teenager, I was confused by intellectually aggressive campus culture after years at a small high school in the Caribbean, where community meant more than competition. I took a semester off, but then missed the intellectual challenge, returning to Wesleyan only to seek exchange programs to try other environments for learning. I studied for separate semesters in Spain, at the University of Texas at Austin, and finally completed my required course-work for Wesleyan's Latin American studies program at Catholic University in Peru. Then, I decided to stay in Lima, lured by Peru's rich history, politics and culture. I aimed to complete my senior essay there, hoping to write a case study on U.S. food aid in Lima's slums, an outgrowth of an urban anthropology course there. I never finished. In Lima in the early 1980s I could not find the documentation on U.S. policy that I needed, and, out of school, I lacked a professor to advise me on the project. I became engrossed in journalism and put the paper on hold—until now.

My current academic year at Columbia at age 36 has given me the time and tools to undertake the project, with the goal both to complete my Wesleyan requirements and to continue studies at Columbia to obtain an MBA. I am currently working with Chazen Institute professor Ronald Schramm on an independent study on multinational business location decisions, focusing on tax incentive programs in Puerto Rico and Ireland. At Wesleyan, the Latin American Studies program director, Anne Wightman, also is working with me to ensure the paper fulfills requirements as a non-credit senior essay to allow Wesleyan to award me a bachelor's degree.

I am relieved to be redressing this failure and happy to re-embrace academia at Columbia. I have learned over the years to better appreciate the dynamism, debate and stimulation a university environment offers. Columbia provides an especially rich environment by incorporating the resources available only in a global city like New York.

4. Discuss your involvement in a community or extracurricular organization. Include an explanation of how you became involved in the organization, and how you helped the organization meet its goals.

Fellow reporters active in the Puerto Rico Journalists Association had heard my pitch repeatedly: Why did we stand up for press freedoms in Puerto Rico and not speak out for press rights in neighboring countries? Why did we look at issues narrowly, in a local context, and not comparatively at how other places dealt with crime, privatization, and other issues?

My international perspective came from years reporting in South America and elsewhere in the Caribbean. Most Puerto Rico journalists had not reported off the island.

In late 1991, colleagues approached me to run for a position on the association's board of directors and, specifically, to focus on expanding international awareness among members. During my one-year term, I proposed and helped organize a conference on the press in Haiti.

The seminar came amid escalating repression and violence in that military-ruled country, including censorship and closure of radio stations and newspapers, as well as torture and even killings of Haitian reporters. About 75 people attended the event, mainly journalists. Speakers included, among others, two international news agency correspondents and a prominent Haitian-born University of Puerto Rico economics professor, who spoke on the role of radio news for Haiti's mostly illiterate population. I moderated and provided an overview of violations against the Haitian media, citing reports from Amnesty International and other human rights groups.

It was the association's first seminar on Haiti. The event helped meet the group's goals of defending press freedom and expanding international focus. A colleague also wrote an article for a U.S. media magazine, bringing the subject to the attention of U.S. colleagues as well.

5. Columbia Business School is a diverse environment. How will your experiences contribute to this?

As a business journalist specialized in Latin America and the Caribbean, I believe I help enrich Columbia's diverse environment in many ways.

First, as a reporter, I am unafraid to ask questions in public. In journalism, questions are a sign of inquisitiveness and strength. Colleagues in the entering MBA class have told me they're glad that I unabashedly ask professors to clarify concepts or explain complex graphs and equations in plain English. They say that my questions reflect their own concerns, but they are too shy to speak out. Many come from competitive corporate environments where questions tend to be seen as signs of weakness.

Second, my experience in the Caribbean and Latin America enlivens discussions on economic policy and globalization. In class, I ask questions about options for small, open economies and bring up examples from countries I've covered. Outside the classroom, I am working with a group of fellow students interested in the Caribbean and Latin America to organize events related to the region, including a panel on investment trends in Cuba and another on Caribbean stock exchanges.

Comments

- Doreen has an interesting tale to tell—returning to school in her mid-thirties to improve her knowledge of business and economics, not to get a job on Wall Street but to improve her coverage as a journalist. And, not surprisingly, given that she writes for a living, she tells her tale well. She makes it clear exactly why she wants to do an MBA. (Unlike most other applicants, she does not need to worry that she will sound like everyone else in the applicant pool.) She also does a good job of humanizing and individualizing herself with her discussion of her college experiences and how she failed to complete her bachelor's degree on schedule. Another strong point is her discussion of what she can contribute, based upon her experiences in first-year MBA classes. She is in the unique position of having already taken her first-year classes and is thus able to capitalize on what she has learned and contribute in unique ways.

ANNE

INSEAD

1. Please give an account of your work experience so far and describe your current job.

I started working for AirInter in 1987, just after completing my original studies. I worked for six months as an attaché direction (assistant) for the Strasbourg-based regional manager. When I returned to the company after doing my degrees at the Faculté de Droit, Aix en Provence, I was the assistant manager to the Lyon station (i.e., airport) manager. I very much liked being at the point of contact with the customers, ground staff, and flight crews.

I therefore applied to be a station manager myself, eventually getting the job in Mulhouse which I have held up until my recent pregnancy leave. One could divide the job into four components.

The first is the management of 150 people, with an operating budget of 45–50 million francs and a capital budget of approximately 10 million francs. The management responsibility is nearly total. The station manager decides how many people to hire, who to hire, and how to train them; the manager also manages the facilities and finance functions, deciding, for example, when and how much to invest in replacing equipment, in addition to running the ongoing operations of the facility.

The second component involves seeking out "handling agent" business for other airlines. This means that one performs all the ground functions to enable KLM, for example, to make daily stops at the airport. In other parts of the AirInter system this is a simpler task because the company generally has a monopoly at each airport. Because this is not true at Mulhouse, the marketing and bidding processes are trickier. This part of the business, by the way, currently generates revenues of approximately 15 million francs, a substantial increase over the last several years.

Thirdly, the manager must be "on call" at all times. The airport runs nearly twenty four hours a day, and it is on an international border, so there are constantly major decisions to be made. For example, the recent Airbus 320 crash at Mont St. Odile took place near Mulhouse, necessitating that I head to Strasbourg, the airport nearest the crash, to help the overwhelmed manager there.

Fourthly, I represent the company's interests in front of the airport authorities. This is particularly important in Mulhouse for two reasons. The first is that we do not have our customary monopoly position there, having to share the airport with Swissair. The second is that we are the world's only bi-national airport, with both Swiss and French authorities having power. In commercial, immigration, and security matters things are much more complex in Mulhouse than elsewhere because of the multiplicity of interested parties, making good representation of the company all the more important.

Further descriptions of the challenges involved and my relative success in handling them are to be found in the essays.

2. **Give a candid description of yourself, stressing the personal characteristics you feel to be your assets and liabilities.**

My assets can be divided into three general categories. The first is that I have *strong interpersonal skills*. I work well with a wide range of people, whether young or old, French or German, graduate or laborer. For example, I was regarded as a strong team player when I worked on the AirInter corporate staff with other young graduates. Later I managed a group of 150 ground employees and commercial staff—essentially none of whom had a university background—as station manager at Mulhouse airport and developed such a good working relationship that we were virtually unique in having no work stoppages during my tenure. [The personal characteristics underlying this probably include the fact that I am very much bien dans ma peau (comfortable with who I am) and not overly emotional on the job. This calm under fire is particularly valuable as a station manager in the airline business, being respected by all, and making it very comfortable for people to work with me.]

The second is that I am a *good analyst*. While station manager at Mulhouse, for example, I was unable to learn from our controle de gestion (accounting) people whether we made money as handling agents for other airlines. So, before bidding on such work, I did an analysis of this business which revealed its underlying costs, thereby enabling me to know how and when to bid for it. The costs of this work are highly complex because of the large number of different groups involved in performing it, without keeping proper activity-based cost data, and, because the complexity added to the system due to the need to handle additional types of aircraft, is inherently difficult to quantify.

The third is that I am very *hard-working and determined*, something I may have acquired from my immigrant parents.

My weaknesses are also quite clear. I am not a really creative person, being more of a practical nature. I dislike personal confrontations and go too far out of my way to avoid them. For example, I sometimes prefer to redo something a subordinate has done poorly rather than confront him with his mistakes. By the same token, I may be too demanding of my subordinates and colleagues and be inappropriately disappointed when they appear not to be as committed to the business as I am.

3. Describe what you believe to be your most substantial achievement to date, explaining why you view it as such.

My most substantial accomplishment was making a real success of my first operational job, that of station manager of Mulhouse Airport. I faced several barriers that made my ultimate success all the more pleasing. I was the only person ever to be given such a post without many years (typically twenty-plus) of experience in a station. In fact, I had only 18 months' experience, and none managing people, at the time. In addition, the airport I was given is one of the most complicated in the Air-Inter system. (Mulhouse is the world's only bi-national airport, being operated jointly with Switzerland.) Perhaps of significance as well is the fact that I was the first woman to be made station manager.

My success in this position can be measured on several dimensions. The first is that we turned this airport into the model for the whole AirInter system in terms of early adoption of new techniques. If, for example, other station managers want to learn about computerized check-in of international passengers, formerly done manually, they are told to see how Mulhouse does it. Secondly, we managed to operate throughout this period without any strikes or work slowdowns, even in the face of a mechanics' walkout throughout much of the rest of the system. This was due to our willingness to listen carefully to what each of our work groups felt, and to what they knew about how best to run the business. We also managed to integrate the Air France and AirInter operations when the two firms merged without serious disruptions. I personally felt pleased that I was able to manage supervisors who had an average of 25 more years of experience and three fewer degrees than I did.

4. **Describe a situation taken from school, business, civil or military life where you did not meet your personal objectives, and discuss what you learned from this experience.**

I was made assistant manager in Lyon approximately four years ago. I started with high expectations but left after just one year with none of these expectations realized.

Despite getting on well personally with my manager, I never found a way to work well with him. He gave me virtually nothing to do and thwarted my efforts at carving out areas in which I could work. The basic problem was that he was new at his job and was unwilling to delegate because he did not yet understand what his own job entailed.

This was a bad situation which I initially hoped would improve of its own accord. Nothing happened, however, until I pushed to get another assignment.

What I learned was quite simple. The inability to work in a positive manner was devastating to me. I was not able to report to work and just read memos all day or stare out the window. I also learned that personal compatibility is not sufficient to guarantee professional compatibility as well. In addition, I reaffirmed my basic notion that the world is not waiting to give me the job; I have to manage my own career just like I have to manage any other task I care about.

5. **Comment on the main factors which you believe account for your academic and professional development to date. Explain your career aspirations and why you chose to apply to INSEAD now.**

The characteristics I mentioned in Essay Number One—having good interpersonal skills, being a good analyst, and being very determined—have contributed significantly to both my academic and my professional development. The additional factors to note are two. My academic progress resulted in part from my great curiosity about my studies; I greatly enjoyed being a student. (And thus, perhaps, my graduating from the Faculty of Law with high honors.) My professional development undoubtedly owes a great deal to my enthusiasm about the airline industry.

I hope to remain in the airline industry, preferably on the operational side, albeit in higher positions. I very much enjoy the general management nature of dealing with customers on the one hand, and all of the airline's staff (such as flight crews, commercial agents, ground crews, and the corporate staff) on the other.

My reasons for wanting an MBA are set forth in Essay Number Six. My reason for wanting to attend INSEAD are also described there. The reason that I wish to attend INSEAD now are quite simple. With the birth of my baby I have reached a natural break point. Also, I have now gained enough practical experience to benefit from additional education.

6. **If you were given the opportunity to effect one change in your work environment, what would that be? How would you implement this change?**

I would change the compensation and promotion system. Right now AirInter operates just like a government bureaucracy. Promotion and pay are determined by a combination of seniority and exam results. As a station manager I cannot reward more than three or four of my 150 employees, and that only with a 3000 franc bonus. Not only am I basically unable to reward good performance, I am unable to penalize poor behavior. This is clearly inappropriate in a company which should be attuned to the coming global competition in the airline industry, a competition which will require far better performance than we now manage.

Changing the system will be a major task. At my level in the company I currently try to work around the problem by seeking to allow one employee to take a promotion exam a few months ahead of schedule, or whatever. The real task, however, is system wide. To convince the more conservative, not to say lower-performing, part of management that this is necessary will not be easy but it will be simple compared to changing union attitudes.

I am not able currently to commission a consultant to compare our performance levels with those of leading American carriers, or to lay out a disaster scenario of how fast we will go bankrupt in the event of unfettered competition in the future. In any event I am not sure that such major change can be made absent a crisis, although the British Airways change is certainly worth studying. As a personal matter I intend to pay close attention to questions of organizational change at business school, particularly as they can be applied to this sort of service industry. If possible I hope to study exactly this case so as to help to push AirInter's management and unions at least a bit in the right direction.

7. What means of ensuring your personal and professional development are you seriously considering as an alternative to INSEAD?

I have concluded that an MBA is the right step in my professional development at this time. I want to get more of a senior management perspective than I saw as a veritable kid at Ecole Des Affaires de Paris (EAP) years ago. Now that I know how a company functions, and what is particularly relevant to the industry that I have chosen, I am anxious to get started on a top program.

The two programs that I have looked at seriously are those of INSEAD and IMD. I want top programs devoted to development of senior, general managers. I also want a one year program because I think that two years represents a greater time commitment than is appropriate given my current level of knowledge and operating experience. Lastly, I want a very international perspective given the increasingly global nature of the airline business, making these two schools the natural choices in Europe.

If I am not admitted I shall consider other career options. It will be difficult to gain the perspective I am seeking at AirInter because several of its attitudes run directly counter to those appropriate for the future. It is, for example, run by engineers with little marketing-and no customer-orientation. Consequently, if unable to pursue an appropriate MBA, I shall try to get a job with a non-French company with a real devotion to marketing and customer service. This will probably mean an American carrier.

8. What do you feel you would contribute during your time at INSEAD?

My background in the airline industry gives me several things to share with my classmates. I have learned a great deal about the airline industry for one. Also, I have had several years of running a 150 person operation, working not just for a French company but with several large international carriers as clients as well (in our handling agent capacity), all within the unique bi-national structure of Mulhouse Airport which requires constant cooperation and negotiation with my Swiss counterparts. In addition I have managed groups of people very different than myself, insofar as they are true "blue-collar," unionized employees.

These experiences have contrasted with the work I initially did as a corporate staff employee at corporate headquarters, so I know that this perspective will be a bit different than what the typical management consultant or banker will bring. Because I enjoy working on teams with very different sorts of people, due to what I can learn as well as my own opportunity to contribute to their learning, I look forward to participating in such groups at INSEAD.

Comments

- Overall this is an exceptionally successful effort that highlights Anne's numerous strengths and takes full advantage of her being a relatively senior person, with an unusual job, when compared with other applicants. Note, too, that this is a very lean application: There is no excess to her essays.

- In her job description, she does an admirable job of quantifying her responsibilities as well as explaining what they are. The latter is important for a job that is not likely to be well known to admissions officers.

- Her second essay is very effective. She presents a convincing case for her several strengths, focusing on a limited number of them rather than simply listing a large number. She handles her weaknesses in the right way by listing several that are believable, but not disabling, without dwelling upon them.

- In the last line of her third essay she shows that she may be "overeducated," but is still very practical at heart, thereby addressing one potential issue.

- One small flaw: In the fourth it is not clear that she has extracted all potential learning from her failure. She makes it sound like it was all her boss's fault, but is that necessarily true? On the other hand, she has gleaned important personal career management information from this experience, recognizing that rather than indulge in recriminations she should simply move on.

- In essay five she does something few applicants do: She relates her successes to her personal and professional strengths. In other words, she ties together essays two and five. By showing how her strengths have contributed to various professional successes and her professional development, she makes those strengths clearer and more believable than they otherwise would be.

- In essay six she shows two positive things about her: She bears heavy responsibilities (150 people work under her) and she is aware of the international aspects of her business (which she makes clear by discussing American and British operations).

- In the seventh essay she makes clear why she needs a second business degree: Her first one was done when she was still a youngster, and she needs the sort of senior management perspective that is not part of a BBA education and would, in any event, be nearly irrelevant to nineteen-year-olds.

- Throughout the application she shows how international she is. Whether she is discussing the organizational change efforts at British Airways or discussing what is involved in running a binational airport, she makes it clear that a truly international program like INSEAD's is her natural home.

ROXANE
STANFORD

1. Each of us has been influenced by the people, events, and situations of our lives. How have these influences shaped who you are today?

Growing up in a single parent family has shaped who I am more than any other factor. My parents separated when I was ten years old. My mother, who had never worked outside the home, suddenly had to support my sister and me. Shortly after starting her first job as a secretary, she injured her back and had to have surgery. This kept her out of work for six months. During this time, she received only seventy five percent of her already meager salary. To make things worse, my parents' divorce was not yet final so my father was not paying child support.

These were especially difficult times for our family. We nearly lost our home and could not afford to heat it. My mother applied for food stamps but did not qualify because she owned a car and was unwilling to give it up. She could not give up the car because she would have no way to get to work when she had recovered from her injury (there was no public transportation in Reno at the time). Somehow we managed to survive these difficult times through sacrifice and help from friends and family.

I learned many important lessons about life during this period of my childhood. This experience brought our family closer together and showed us that with sacrifice and hard work, we would always be able to get through the hard times. It has also given me a greater appreciation for the things that I now have. While I am happy to have a well paying job and look forward to even more success in the future, I am very aware of how fortunate I am. Because I began working when I was fourteen years old, I was able to learn the value of hard work at an early age. I developed a strong sense of determination and the belief that I could have all the money and success I wanted as long as I was willing to work for it. The difficult times I endured during my childhood are largely responsible for the work ethic that has resulted in my success to date.

When I was sixteen, my mother remarried and we moved to a small town east of Reno. This experience also had a major impact on my life. Life in a small town was very difficult for me. While my sister and I acquired instant popularity after moving there, it was still difficult to truly break into such a close-knit society. Having come from a larger city, I found many of the people in this town to be rather close-minded. I often found myself as the sole defender of outsiders, minorities and others who did not fit the small town mold. I also spoke up and challenged conventional ways of doing things if they did not make sense. This outspokenness often caused me problems and kept me out of organizations such as Honor Society. However, I believed that it was more important to stand up for what I believed in than to yield to peer pressure. This conviction has remained with me through the years. I continue to fight for what I believe in rather than conform to the status quo in order to keep from making waves. While this is often the more difficult route, I believe it is the right one.

I left home a week after graduating from high school and moved back to Reno. I found a job and enrolled at the University that summer. I was able to finance my entire education through scholarships and work. While it required a tremendous amount of effort and focus to work part time and graduate at the top of my chemical engineering class, I was still able to devote much of my spare time to dance. I had always wanted to become a dancer when I was growing up but we could never afford the lessons. However, when I entered college I was able to obtain a dance scholarship at an off-campus dance company. To attain success with so many demands on my time required me to learn to manage my time effectively. This period of my life was a lot of work but was also the most rewarding. When I finally graduated and was offered a job at Chevron I had no one to thank but myself. To this day, when I am feeling down or running low on self-confidence, I think back to this accomplishment.

In recent years, traveling has been the major influence in my life. Now that I am working full time, I am able to travel every year. Traveling outside the country has allowed me to meet people with many different viewpoints and priorities in life. This has forced me to examine my own beliefs and challenge my assumptions of the kind of life I want to lead. While I will always want a successful career, I now know that there is more to life than just work. I spend my spare time reading literature and history and studying French because I believe that it is important to have a well rounded education to get along with people of all types.

All of these events have shaped who I am today. I have a very high work ethic and am determined to achieve the goals I set for myself. I work hard and expect to be compensated for my efforts, but because of my modest beginnings I am always aware and appreciative of how far I have come. I believe this makes more sensitive to the positions of those less fortunate than I am. Finally, my travels have forced me to remove my own small town blinders and have opened my eyes to all that our diverse world has to offer.

2. How do you see your career developing? How will an MBA further that development? Why are you applying to Stanford?

I am applying to the Stanford MBA program at this time because after five years of engineering and planning experience at an operating company, I have come to a crossroads in my career. As I have gained experience and received increased exposure to the business side of the oil industry, I have become aware that my engineering training has not prepared me adequately to deal with the broad strategic questions faced by senior level managers. I am seeking an MBA to supplement my work experience and gain high intensity exposure to the other business functions which are important to running a successful business. In addition, a general management education will increase my career flexibility. Without a formal business education, it would be very difficult for me to change business functions or move into a senior level management position outside the chemical process industries.

My future career goal is to advance to a senior level management position dealing with strategy and international management for a multinational corporation. I am interested in strategy because I feel my strongest skills are in identifying the root causes of problems and developing and implementing lasting solutions to them. I am especially interested in international corporate strategy, because during my tenure at the Richmond Refinery, products sold into the export market have become increasingly important to our refinery's profitability. Chevron's planners and oil traders typically come from the engineering ranks and therefore lack the business skills necessary to analyze the refinery's competitive position in new markets. At times it is even difficult to identify the refinery's competition in these markets. As a result, the export market is viewed not as a viable market worthy of cultivation, but as a dumping ground for products which allows the refinery to operate at capacity.

Stanford's emphasis on a general management education fits well with my future career goals. I am not pursuing an MBA degree with an emphasis on operations expressly because my experience is in this area. I am more interested in gaining a broad understanding of each of the functional areas of business so I will be able to deal effectively with issues which impact the entire organization. In my current position as a Planning Analyst, I recommend changes in operation designed to increase refinery profitability. Historically, Planning Analysts at Chevron only considered refinery operation when making these recommendations. However, as the business becomes more complex and competitive, additional aspects such as payment terms and inventory carrying costs should also be incorporated to ensure profit maximization. Because I have had very little exposure to the other functional areas, it has been very difficult to incorporate these operating costs into my economic analyses.

Finally, an MBA will give me the skills necessary to be an effective change agent. While "fighting fires" often leads to a successful career at Chevron, this is not an effective form of management. Many of these problems occur as a result of poor planning. I believe that problems should be anticipated and avoided. By adopting a broader perspective and a strategic viewpoint, change can be managed and the road into the future can be made smoother. While I have incorporated these ideas into my career to date, I believe a general business education will allow me to apply these strengths more effectively and at a much higher level in the organization.

3. The issue of diversity increasingly is recognized as a critical element of successful workplaces. What specific changes would you implement in your current company to address inequities and/or enhance diversity?

As the workforce becomes smaller and more poorly educated, it is becoming increasingly important for companies to not only accept but nurture diversity in their organizations. To be competitive, companies must hire the most qualified candidates available. They can no longer discriminate on the basis of gender or ethnic background if they expect to hire the most productive workforce available. Economic necessity will ultimately break down the barriers that women and minorities currently encounter in the workplace.

I personally have seen this phenomenon at my own company. Oil refineries typically do not have particularly good track records in terms of diversity. As a result, my company is currently facing a crisis with respect to encouraging diversity in the workplace. Because we do not have women and minorities in highly visible positions, we are finding it increasingly difficult to attract young women and minorities to our company. As a result, we have not been able to hire the most qualified college graduates.

A top-down approach is required to facilitate cultural change in a large organization. If diversity is to be valued at the bottom levels of an organization, it must be very clear that it is valued at the top. First, management must be educated as to what constitutes diversity and how discrimination occurs. While blatant discrimination still exists, subtle unconscious discrimination is far more common. Unless people are aware of what constitutes discrimination, they will continue to discriminate unknowingly.

As part of the educational process, the benefits of diversity should be stressed. Diversity is becoming increasingly valuable in the workplace because it introduces concepts from a wide range of viewpoints and ultimately results in more innovative solutions. While the workforce in the refinery is becoming technically more diverse, those people who conform to traditional role models continue to be the most successful. As a result, the organization suffers. I have seen countless cases where the most qualified person was passed over for a promotion because he or she did not "fit the mold." This is particularly devastating because the "mold" does not exclude people only on the basis of gender or race, but also on the basis of educational background, age and personality. By employing narrow definitions, the organization ultimately suffers.

To break down these paradigms, management must focus on work products and results rather than work processes when making promotional decisions. For example, our management has been reluctant to place women in line management positions because it was feared that women would not be tough enough to handle the job. However, many women are more effective than men in dealing with the blue collar workers because they are able to develop good working relationships with them. What is important is not how tough women are, but whether or not they will get the job done. Because management is focusing on work processes rather than results, women are being place in "nice" staff jobs rather than the highly visible line supervisor positions.

A final topic is minority outreach programs. While these can be effective they can also create animosity among other workers who fear reverse discrimination. However, the dismal record of our company for hiring minorities requires that we implement special programs to develop minorities for our future workforce. If these programs are to be successful, they absolutely must be based on performance. Hiring minorities to meet quotas only encourages labeling and ultimately hurts those people it is designed to help. By developing and hiring only candidates who can perform at the same level as their peers, we will break down the stereotypes which currently pervade our workplace.

4. Describe a day in your life you would like to relive.

The day I would most like to relive is not just a day but an entire era of my life. That era begins the day I entered college. While my college career continues to be one of my most substantial accomplishments, with the experience I now have, I would have done some things differently. For example, I would have worked hard at my engineering studies but I would have taken more liberal arts courses. My last semester I took a literature course which ended up being the most enjoyable class I had in college. While I continue to read widely in my spare time, I miss the classroom environment where I could discuss my impressions with others. Since leaving college, I have not found anyone who is interested in discussing literature. This class made me realize that there are many things I am interested in besides engineering and business and I would have liked to have had more exposure to them while I was still in the university environment.

I would also have taken the opportunity to live abroad. I never seriously considered doing a semester overseas because I was worried about the expense and I was afraid it would force me to add an additional year to my studies. While both of these concerns were legitimate, I now know the benefits would have far outweighed the costs. Having had the opportunity to travel since graduating from college, I realize how much my life is enriched every time I leave the country. This aspect of my life has become one of the most important to me and I intend to work overseas at some time during my career. I want to experience a foreign country from the perspective of a resident rather than just a tourist. I em especially fond of France and have recently resumed my French studies.

I also would have spent more time deciding where I wanted to attend college. I did not apply to any schools other than the University of Nevada-Reno because of the expense. I now know that I would have been able to finance my education one way or another and that cost should not have been the only factor. In addition to thinking about where I wanted to go, I would have challenged my ideas of what I wanted to do. I decided to be an engineer my junior year in high school. After that time, I spent all my effort on achieving that goal. Since women are still rare in engineering, I had many people tell me that I would not succeed in accomplishing this goal. This provided me with even more drive and focus to get the job done. However, once I finished college, I found myself asking if this was the right career move. Ultimately I decided that it was, but I found it disturbing that I might have spent the previous four years working toward a goal I really did not want. I vowed never to jump so blindly again.

Fortunately for me, this is an era that I can "relive." Now that I have examined my professional goals and decided that graduate business school is the next career step I really want to take, I am once again faced with the chance to do the things I did not do the first time around. Now that I am more mature and have a better idea of what is really important to me, I will be sure to take full advantage of all that this opportunity has to offer. I will take an active role in organizing study tours to foreign countries, take a wide range of elective courses, and join student organizations that will allow me to meet people with similar interests.

VIRGINIA/DARDEN

1. **Specifically address your post-MBA short- and long-term professional goals. How will Darden assist you in attaining these goals?**

(See her essentially identical answer to Stanford essay number 2.)

2. **The Darden School seeks a diverse and unique entering class of future managers. How will your distinctiveness enrich our learning environment and enhance your prospects for success as a manager?**

My broad manufacturing experience will enable me to bring a unique perspective to the learning environment at Darden. During my employment at a large oil refinery, I have worked in various aspects of manufacturing including the design and operation of the equipment used to produce a wide variety of petroleum products.

In my current position, I plan the operation of the refinery as a whole to maximize profit in a dynamic, market-driven environment. I believe that my experience in manufacturing will provide a much needed perspective on how things are really accomplished in the field. For those students who are not familiar with the tremendous inertia working against change inherent in a large manufacturing facility, my experience will provide insight and, at times, a reality check.

My experience will provide yet another unique insight into the diversity issue. I have spent my career working in an environment in which traditionally very few women have worked. I have had to learn to deal with people who doubted my abilities based on my gender alone. I have been able to build a very good professional reputation in an environment where women are often labeled as weak and unable to survive in the difficult refinery atmosphere. The perspective I bring with respect to the diversity issue is unique and will enhance any discussions which take place on this subject.

I am willing to speak my mind which is critical in a classroom in which the case study method is utilized. In addition, I work well with people of varied backgrounds and am able to utilize the specific strengths of others to develop workable solutions to problems. In a team environment, one is required both to give and take. I have had the chance to develop these skills in my present position. Because teamwork is essential to the success of the case study method, these skills will be invaluable to me at Darden.

Finally, I spend all of my vacation time traveling and devote much of my free time to reading and studying French. Traveling has forced me to remove my small town blinders and open my mind to other ways of doing things. Traveling has increased my awareness of the fact that the American way of doing things is not the only way and that flexibility and sensitivity are absolutely necessary to get along with others. I have found that this applies not only to people of different nationalities but also to fellow Americans whose views may be different from my own.

These experiences have benefited me both in my personal life and on the job and I believe that they will be assets for me at Darden.

3. **Describe a significant leadership experience, decision-making challenge, or managerial accomplishment. How did this affect your professional/personal development?**

My biggest leadership success took place last year when I was the process engineer assigned to two heavy oil processing units. One of these units provided feed pretreatment for the other. I was approached by Operations Coordination and was asked if Widuri resid, a low value fuel oil stream, could be fed to the upstream of the two units. This would allow a portion of the resid stream to be upgraded to gasoil, a high value intermediate product. I agreed to address the technical aspects of the problem and asked Operations Coordination to deal with the logistics.

When we reconvened to finalize the plan, it became apparent that the logistical constraints would render the project uneconomical. Having gathered the physical property data, I realized that the Widuri resid could be fed directly to the downstream unit. I suggested we bypass the feed pretreatment step entirely. This would allow us to upgrade the entire steam rather than only a small portion of it as the original plan would have required. In addition, it would avoid some of the operating costs.

Operations Coordination was enthusiastic, but I knew it would be difficult to sell the idea to Operations. A resid stream had never been fed directly to the downstream unit and I knew Operations would be concerned about damaging the catalyst in that unit. This was a major operational change, but I was confident it would work. I gathered the necessary data and developed a plan which included a good monitoring program and contingency plan. This would allow us to identify and respond to any unexpected problems if necessary. Two weeks later I organized a meeting for all the interested parties and presented my plan which anticipated and addressed management's concerns. The following day the resid was being fed to the downstream unit. This project resulted in profits to the refinery of $8 million over a five month period.

This project marked a change in my career in terms of maturity and initiative. Prior to this, my efforts were focused primarily on my own sphere of operation. The success of this project gave me the self-confidence to assert my leadership skills. I began to approach problems from a refinery-wide perspective. In addition, I began to challenge traditional approaches and offer more innovative solutions.

4. **What is the most difficult ethical dilemma you have faced in your professional life? Upon present reflection, would you have resolved this dilemma in a different manner?**

My junior year in college, I was offered a summer internship working in a metallurgical laboratory for Gold Fields of South Africa Limited. The opportunity to work overseas while gaining valuable work experience prior to graduation was very appealing. I accepted the job and immediately completed the paperwork required to obtain a South African work visa. In addition, I began planning the details of a trip I would make to Europe on my return. I wanted this experience so badly that I turned down an excellent opportunity to work at the Argonne National Laboratory outside of Chicago that same summer.

I was offered this position in the Fall of 1985. Early in 1986, the political situation in South Africa began to deteriorate rapidly and a State of Emergency was declared by the South African government. Several friends working for Gold Fields assured me that I would not be in danger if I were to go to South Africa. However, my conscience began to get the better of me. I attempted to justify accepting the job offer on the basis that I should see the situation first hand in order to judge it. In addition, I was well aware of the importance of South Africa to our nation's supply of strategic minerals. I believed that American involvement in South Africa was necessary to ensure change in that country's racial policy while assuring that America's strategic interests were tended to.

As the situation worsened, however, I found my decision to go to South Africa increasingly difficult to justify. I could no longer ignore the pleas of the African National Congress to remove outside support of a racist government. I knew that I was offered the serious position because South Africa was experiencing a serious "brain drain." By agreeing to work in South Africa, I personally was supporting the racist policies of the Afrikaaner government. As much as I hated to do it, I had to cancel my plans.

In retrospect, it is still a difficult problem. It is impossible to judge a problem as complex as Apartheid from the thirty-second news briefs provided by the media. Had I gone to South Africa, I would have gained valuable insight into this problem that I could never hope to get from the outside. This experience would have given me a different perspective about racial tensions in our own country. However, I still cannot justify the personal growth I would have realized when there was much more at stake for the people of that country.

Comments

- There is a lot to like in Roxane's essays. She does a very good job of distinguishing herself in several ways. First, she successfully positions herself as a woman who has had to work hard for the success she has enjoyed. She is from a relatively poor family from a very small town, so her career success owes a great deal to her determination and cleverness rather than her family's situation. Second, she shows that she is a very talented engineer by emphasizing her highly profitable successes. This is all the more impressive for the fact that there are very few women to be found in her sort of industry. Third, she demonstrates that her talents are not limited to engineering. Her essays are very well-written, suggesting that her communication skills are much better than might be anticipated. In addition, her 730 GMAT score had her in the top 2 percent in both verbal and quantitative, again demonstrating her intellectual balance. Fourth, she shows that she has already had substantial managerial success and yet would still benefit substantially from an MBA. One of the factors in her managerial success is the fact that she understands how to work with and through other people. Her political savvy appears well developed. Her teamwork and political skills are valuable items at a time when business schools emphasize these "softer" skills. Lastly, she makes it clear that she will bring a lot to her classmates in terms of her relatively unusual skills, experiences, and attitudes.

- The net result is that she appears to be an engineer who is very skilled at her job, but brings much more to a school than just engineering knowledge. Given the great number of engineers applying to leading business schools, it is useful for her to be able to position herself both as a top-quality engineer and as more than just an engineer (the "have your cake and eat it too" approach).

INDEX

School names are in **bold**; page numbers in *italic* indicate tables.